Evolutionary Economics

The International Library of Critical Writings in Economics

Series Editor: Mark Blaug

Professor Emeritus, University of London
Consultant Professor, University of Buckingham
Visiting Professor, University of Exeter

This series is an essential reference source for students, researchers and lecturers in economics. It presents by theme an authoritative selection of the most important articles across the entire spectrum of economics. Each volume has been prepared by a leading specialist who has written an authoritative introduction to the literature included.

A full list of published and future titles in this series is printed at the end of this volume.

Evolutionary Economics

Edited by

Ulrich Witt

Professor of Economics
University of Freiburg

An Elgar Reference Collection

Published by
Edward Elgar Publishing Limited
Gower House
Croft Road
Aldershot
Hants GU11 3HR
England

Edward Elgar Publishing Company
Old Post Road
Brookfield
Vermont 05036
USA

A CIP catalogue record for this book is available from the British Library

Library of Congress Cataloging-in-Publication Data
Evolutionary economics/edited by Ulrich Witt.
    p. cm. — (The international library of critical writings in economics)
  1. Evolutionary economics. I. Witt, Ulrich. II. Series.
HB97.3.E95 1993
330.1—dc20
                                                            92-38915
                                                                CIP

ISBN 1 85278 593 4

Printed in Great Britain at the University Press, Cambridge

Contents

Acknowledgements

The editor and publishers wish to thank the following who have kindly given permission for the use of copyright material.

American Economic Association for articles: Paul A. David (1985), 'Clio and the Economics of QWERTY', *American Economic Review*, **75** (2), 332–7; Robert Sugden (1989), 'Spontaneous Order', *Journal of Economic Perspectives*, **3** (4), 85–97.

Association for Social Economics for article: John M. Gowdy (1985), 'Evolutionary Theory and Economic Theory: Some Methodological Issues', *Review of Social Economy*, **XLIII** (3), 316–24.

Basil Blackwell Ltd. for article: Joseph Schumpeter (1928), 'The Instability of Capitalism', *Economic Journal*, **XXXVIII** (151), 361–86.

Cambridge University Press for articles and excerpt: Joseph A. Schumpeter (1947), 'The Creative Response in Economic History', *Journal of Economic History*, **VII** (2), 149–59; Viktor Vanberg (1986), 'Spontaneous Market Order and Social Rules: A Critical Examination of F.A. Hayek's Theory of Cultural Evolution', *Economics and Philosophy*, **2** (1), 75–100; John M. Gowdy (1985), 'Evolutionary Theory and Economic Theory: Some Methodological Issues', *Review of Social Economy*, **XLIII** (3), 316–24; Richard H. Day and Jean-Luc Walter (1989), 'Economic Growth in the Very Long Run: On the Multiple-Phase Interaction of Population, Technology and Social Infrastructure', W.A. Barnett, J. Geweke and Karl Shell (eds), *Economic Complexity, Chaos, Sunspots, Bubbles and Nonlinearity*, 253–89.

Elsevier Science Publishers BV for articles: Robert Boyd and Peter J. Richerson (1980), 'Sociobiology, Culture, and Economic Theory', *Journal of Economic Behavior and Organization*, **1** (2), 97–121; Katsuhito Iwai (1984), 'Schumpeterian Dynamics – An Evolutionary Model of Innovation and Imitation', *Journal of Economic Behavior and Organization*, **5** (2), 159–90; W. Brian Arthur, Yu M. Ermoliev and Yu M. Kaniovski (1987), 'Path-dependent Processes and the Emergence of Macro-Structure', *European Journal of Operational Research*, **30** (3), 294–303.

Elsevier Science Publishing Company, Inc. for article: Cesare Marchetti (1980), 'Society as a Learning System: Discovery, Invention, and Innovation Cycles Revisited', *Technological Forecasting and Social Change*, **18**, 267–82.

JAI Press for article: Jack Hirshleifer (1982), 'Evolutionary Models in Economics and Law: Cooperation Versus Conflict Strategies', *Research in Law and Economics*, **4**, 1–60.

Every effort has been made to trace all the copyright holders but if any have been inadvertently overlooked the publishers will be pleased to make the necessary arrangement at the first opportunity.

In addition the publishers wish to thank the library of the London School of Economics and Political Science and The Alfred Marshall Library, Cambridge University for their assistance in obtaining these articles.

Introduction

What Evolutionary Economics Is All About

As if he foresaw what evolutionary economics is all about, Alfred Marshall once postulated that 'the main concern of economics is . . . with human beings who are impelled, for good and evil, to change and progress' (Marshall 1961, p. xv). In his own writings, in particular the *Principles*, Marshall did little to develop a theoretical underpinning for the concern he had identified (Mirowski, 1988, ch. 1; Hodgson, 1992, ch. 7). To the contrary, he effectively contributed to the dissemination of neoclassical core concepts like market equilibrium, optimally adapted economic agents, and the representative individual or firm which form a remarkable contrast to what would seem suitable tools for explaining change. Given the impact which Spencerism and Social Darwinism had on most sciences towards the end of the 19th century (see Bowler, 1989, ch. 10) Marshall's idea of an 'economic biology' was thus probably not more than a fashionable aphorism. All the more outstanding appears therefore the young Schumpeter's *Theory of Economic Development* of 1912 (first, and henceforth cited English edition 1934) which presented for the first time a consistent evolutionary argumentation to explain change and progress in the economy without even any inspiration by or recourse to Darwinism.

From the beginning of his career Schumpeter was an original thinker determined to follow his own bent. In his habilitation thesis (second dissertation) at the University of Vienna he chose to elaborate on contemporary theoretical problems (Schumpeter, 1908). In the gist of his argument he relied on the neoclassical school as represented by Pareto, obviously separating himself from the common Austrian approach which then dominated among economists in Vienna. In discussing the neoclassical theory, in particular how the economy is supposed to reattain equilibrium after it has been disturbed (Schumpeter, 1908, part IV), he must have noticed that something was missing. There was no explanation for what disrupts the conjectured equilibrium and drives economic change – and thus for the most significant feature of the historical development. Schumpeter tried to fill the gap. He developed a theory which portrays economic development as a perennial gale of restructuring and expansion. The vehicle is the innovative recombination of the resources carried out by pioneering entrepreneurs. Although, in the original exposition, the theory is coined to explain the cyclical patterns of 'prosperity and depression' (Schumpeter, 1910), the major argument is that economic change is systematically produced 'from within the economy' (Schumpeter, 1912/34). Indeed, it is this endogenously caused change, the innovation driven self-transformation process addressed in Schumpeter's theory, that makes up the evolutionary element in his approach.

Evolutionary economics may thus be characterized by its interest in economic change and in its causes, in the motives and the understanding of the involved agents, in the processes in which change materializes, and in the consequences. In fact, although the contributions to evolutionary economics have a rather heterodox lineage they all seem to agree in this broadly stated interest (Witt, 1991). As endogenously caused change appears on many different levels, research has been done

- on the changes of aggregate economic activity under the influence of an incessant, yet possibly discontinuous, flow of innovations (*Schumpeter 1928* and *Schumpeter 1947*; *Haag, Weidlich, and Mensch 1987*; Kleinknecht 1987; Silverberg 1987; *Freeman 1990*);

- on the performance of industries and firms in the competitive innovative struggle and the relevance of Darwinian concepts to understanding this problem (*Alchian 1950*, *Winter 1971*, *Nelson and Winter 1980*, *Iwai 1984*, *Matthews 1984*, *Gowdy 1985*);

- on the functioning of markets as perceived in an evolutionary perspective (*Hayek 1978*, *Witt 1985*, *Metcalfe 1989*) and on the 'path-dependency' of historical economic developments (*David 1985*, *Arthur, Ermoliev, and Kaniovski 1987*, *Kuran 1989*, Lesourne 1991);

- on the emergence and variation of societal rules and institutions that form the changing framework of economic interactions (*Hayek 1967*, *Boyd and Richerson 1980*, *Hirshleifer 1982*, *Vanberg 1986*, *Sugden 1989*);

- on the change of production technologies and the impact on the growth of human population and its welfare in the very long run (*Marchetti 1980*, *Boulding 1981*, *Day and Walter 1989*, Faber and Proops, 1990);

- and on what, at the level of individual behaviour, is at the bottom of all striving for change (*Loasby 1983*, Dopfer 1986, Witt 1989a).

However – an indication of a rather early stage of this research programme – a general analytical framework and a coherent organization of the many problems and phenomena of change have not yet been achieved.

In order to make progress and to give the reader a basic orientation, this introduction tries to outline how the various aspects may be thought to relate to each other. Section II starts with the ideas developed in the Schumpeterian tradition. Section III discusses the influence of this tradition in the domain of industrial organization research where attempts have been made to blend it with the metaphor of natural selection. The core problem of economic theory, the coordination of individual economic activities through markets, is reconsidered in Section IV from the point of view of evolutionary economics. Section V turns to the phenomenon of path-dependency that plays a crucial role for certain features of the market process as well as for institutional change. The formal notions in the background give an opportunity to briefly review the more general understanding of socioeconomic evolution. More concrete implications that may be derived with respect to economic growth are addressed in Section VI. Section VII offers some conclusions.

The Schumpeterian Tradition

As already mentioned, Schumpeter (1934) was the first writer to provide a consistent evolutionary interpretation of economic change. However, the special aim of his pioneering work is to explain the aggregate economic unsteadiness as it manifests itself in the business cycle. He develops a theory of entrepreneurship and submits that the aggregate fluctuations can be derived from the particular time patterns of entrepreneurial activities. Being an entrepreneur is, according to Schumpeter, not an occupation or a profession, but rather a

---

References given in italics refer to articles reprinted in this volume.

unique, and rarely found, capacity of carrying out new combinations of resources, i.e. innovations. Entrepreneurial activities are thus innovative by definition, and they are held to give rise to an incessant competitive restructuring of the economy and to economic growth. Hence, the mainspring of endogenous economic change is to be found in the peculiar personality and motivation (discussed in detail in Schumpeter 1934, pp. 74–94) of a particular class of economic agents, the entrepreneurs. Schumpeter relies here on hypotheses about the entrepreneur's psychology, her/his motivation, and the social background which have later on been supported by McClelland's achievement motivation theory in psychology (McClelland and Winter, 1969). It is important to note that, for Schumpeter, the information on the underlying inventions and discoveries is readily available. It is not the creation of novel ideas as such but their carrying out, their translation into concrete innovative ventures, that is interpreted as what entrepreneurs achieve.

Since Schumpeter identifies the business cycle with cyclical patterns in entrepreneurial innovative activities, the question arises as to how the latter come about. As there is no reason to assume a cyclical pattern in the provision of new ideas and inventions the suggested cycles in innovative activities must be explained by the special circumstances under which the entrepreneurs operate. Schumpeter offers a rather complicated explanation. Entrepreneurial talents vary, he claims, as do the difficulties to be met at different stages of an innovation's diffusion. Only the most gifted entrepreneurs are assumed to be the pioneers capable of overcoming the hurdles facing an entirely new venture and, according to Schumpeter, there are only few of such entrepreneurs. Once the initial hurdles have been taken, however, less entrepreneurial talent is required. There are more people able to do the same – which increasingly becomes a matter of imitation – and, at the same time, a multiplier effect boosts aggregate economic activity so that everything becomes easier (Schumpeter, 1934, pp. 223–30). It is argued that, to provide the pioneering entrepreneurs with a basis to calculate their daring innovative ventures, a reliably assessable state of economic affairs must prevail, which is attained only in a stationary state ('circular flow') after earlier innovation cycles have faded out (Schumpeter, 1934, p. 243).

The rather complex set of hypotheses implies a 'swarm-like' appearance of entrepreneurs, a new swarm entering the scene each time the innovative boost brought to the economy by the previous swarm has ebbed away. The hypotheses are supposed to explain cyclical growth patterns. Opinions as to how convincing the suggested explanation is may be divided. Be it as it may, neo-Schumpeterian research has later abandoned these assumptions and, initiated by Schumpeter (1935) himself, also expanded the cyclical growth patterns into the long waves of Kontratieff cycles. In this literature several competing, but in any case more compelling, explanations for the long-term variation in innovations and aggregate economic activity have been suggested (Mensch, 1979; *Haag, Weidlich, and Mensch 1987*; Kleinknecht, 1987); Silverberg, 1987; cf. *Freeman 1990* for an introduction). More fundamental doubts may be raised as to whether the exclusive reliance on the figure of the entrepreneur in Schumpeter's early approach is overdoing the personalization sometimes to a point where it resembles an elite theory. A theory of entrepreneurship alone, important as it may be, indeed seems too narrow a basis for evolutionary economics, and it implies some biases which are difficult to accept.

Given his predilection, it is no wonder that Schumpeter (1934) tends to overemphasize the role of spectacular innovations and, by the same token, underrates small-scale innovative activities. Borrowing concepts from biology, this is sometimes put in terms of a controversy between punctualism vs. gradualism. It is often argued that major innovations and small-scale innovative improvements of technologies and products systematically alternate (Sahal, 1981; Nelson and Winter, 1982, ch. 11; Dosi, 1982). Moreover, the exclusive focus on the entrepreneurial role tends to bias attention to the supply side and the institution of the market as such, ignoring all other forms of innovative activities and institutions in which they are economically significant. When Schumpeter stresses entrepreneurial will and the capacity required to turn into reality that which he assumes readily available – new knowledge – he obviously plays down the role of novelty and its creation. This does not fit well with the emphasis on the endogenous causation of economic change since, in effect, an explanation for the ultimate source of change is thus circumvented. How and why the new knowledge is generated, how the relationships between search, discovery, experimentation and adoption look like, all this is left open.

Some of these biases have been later corrected; some however, have not. Schumpeter himself changed his assessment of the role of the entrepreneur. He argued explicitly that the pioneering promoter loses out against the teams and trained specialists of the large corporations and trusts and becomes increasingly obsolete. Instead of being an heroic leader's achievement, innovative activities become the form of bureau and committee work (Schumpeter, 1942, pp. 132–3). However, Schumpeter remained reluctant to address the problem of how novelty emerges in the economy. After abandoning the psychologically backed theory of the entrepreneur his approach had therefore arrived at a point where it was open to invasion by neoclassical reinterpretations. Indeed, this was what happened in the last two decades. Neoclassical writers were attracted by Schumpeter's provocative reappraisal of the concept of competition. His vision of an incessant, routine-like, industrial innovativeness which revolutionizes production processes, supply of goods, and the organization of the economy embraced monopolistic practices as a necessary concomitant (Schumpeter, 1942, ch. 8) and thus grossly deviated from the assessment derived from the static model of perfect competition.

Presumably the latter implication is responsible for the fact that nothing in Schumpeter's work has been given more attention than this rather isolated conjecture about the relationships between market structure and innovativeness, today discussed in innumerable contributions under the heading of 'Schumpeterian competition'. However, much of that work, empirical as well as theoretical, is totally unrelated to evolutionary economics. In fact, there have been major efforts to recast the notion in terms of optimal innovation race strategies and equilibrium investments into innovative activities, the neoclassical core concepts (see Kamien and Schwartz, 1982 and Baldwin and Scott, 1987 for surveys). In a sense, Schumpeter's reluctance mentioned above to take the problem of how novelty emerges in the economy seriously invites such reinterpretations. When Schumpeter (1942) abandoned the figure of the entrepreneur together with the respective psychological hypotheses (which are irreconcilable with a plain neoclassical model) this paved the way for eliminating the last traces to what was originally created out of a concern with the inadequacies of the neoclassical tools for explaining change and progress.

Natural Selection and Innovativeness on Industry Level

The fact that Schumpeter (1942) offered little theoretical underpinnings for the conjectured systematical relationship between market structure and innovative achievements in industries hampered the empirical work on 'Schumpeterian competition'. The results that could be obtained on such a basis are rather insignificant (Kamien and Schwartz, 1982, p. 92). Problems reach from finding suitable statistical measures for key variables, such as market structure and the number and economic relevance of innovations, to the derivation of independent, perhaps more readily testable, implications. Attempts at improving the theoretical basis of the Schumpeter hypothesis are therefore straightforward. However, notions like optimal innovation decisions and innovation races suggested in the neoclassical theoretical elaborations have a serious defect. They have to start from the assumption that the properties of the innovations are already known to the decision makers so that they can optimally respond to them. Indeed, all competitors are viewed to search for the same 'innovation' – which must be something that hardly deserves that label. What in reality is a highly opaque search and a groping that reflects the slow formation of problem understanding and knowledge, appears in this literature as a perfectly understood problem of investing into competitive R&D activities with probabilistic returns. No wonder thus, that several scholars in evolutionary economics have felt challenged to do better. An originally unrelated theoretical dispute turned out to be helpful in preparing the ground: the debate about the economic analogue to the natural selection argument.

The 'economic natural selection' argument refers to biological analogies in the theory of the firm that were discussed in the beginning of the 1950s (*Alchian, 1950*; Penrose, 1952). It is obviously inspired by Darwinian thought which, as has been explained, had never been appreciated by Schumpeter. The question raised was to what extent diversity in the firms' goals and performances would be eliminated by competition which may be supposed to drive all those forms out of the market that are not able to operate sufficiently profitably. In the more bold formulation by Friedman (1953) this was turned into the question: does optimizing behaviour have a selection or survival advantage over other forms of firm behaviour and is it thus possible to vindicate the neoclassical optimization approach? As was carefully explained by Winter (1964) and *Winter (1971)*, but was also already pointed out in the early debate in the 1950s, the latter formulation tacitly presupposes much more than Friedman seems to have been aware of. In order to judge to what extent all the preconditions on which the argument depends are fulfilled, various possible behavioural patterns must be carefully explored under diverse possible environmental conditions. This is, of course, exactly what the argument hoped to avoid. In such an exploration it turns out, moreover, that Friedman's claim is far from being generally valid. A weaker version of the argument (suggested earlier by *Alchian, 1950*) claims sufficient profitability, however the firm achieves it, as the sole criterion for survival. This may well be true, yet the criterion does not, as such, say very much (Witt, 1986).

The work by Winter has been one of the foundations for a series of papers by Nelson and Winter and for their influential book (Nelson and Winter, 1982). The characteristic of their approach is a synthesis of ideas from organizational and behavioural theories of the firm, in particular as suggested by the Carnegie school (Simon, 1955; March and Simon, 1958; Cyert and March, 1963) on the one hand and a loose analogy to the model of natural selection on the other (see *Nelson and Winter, 1980*). It is precisely in this synthesis that the loose ends of the line of thought are taken up again which Schumpeter (1942) left with his assessment that the role of the entrepreneur as an innovator was taken over by teams and departments in corporate organizations. Where Schumpeter had no detailed conceptions as to how those corporate divisions operate, Nelson and Winter try to provide a theoretical basis. Following the notions of bounded rationality as developed by the Carnegie school they argue that organizations are based in their internal interactions on behavioral routines, rules of thumb, and regular interaction patterns. Production planning, calculation, price setting, and even the allocation of R&D funds thus follow rule-bound behaviour.

Since Winter (1975) had convincingly argued that there is little in the realm of the theory of firm that corresponds to the structure of reproductive processes in biology, Nelson and Winter interpret routines in only loose analogy to the theory of natural selection as 'genotypes'. The firm's specific decisions thus derived, the 'phenotypes' may be more or less favourable for the firm's overall performance as measured in terms of profitable growth. Assuming that routines which successfully contribute to growth will not be changed, the actual expansion can be understood as an increase in relative frequency of those 'genes', while routines affecting deteriorations in the firm's performance are unlikely to expand. Indeed, drawing on the satisficing hypothesis (March and Simon, 1958, pp. 47–52), it can be argued that those deteriorations trigger a search for improved routines – a kind of intentionally produced mutation.

Among the results which Nelson and Winter obtain from extensive simulation experiments conducted on this basis is the conclusion that their approach supports the inverse rather than the original Schumpeter hypothesis concerning the relationship between market structure and innovativeness. According to the inverse hypothesis, the degree of concentration within an industry, pointing to a potential for monopolistic practices, is a consequence of, rather than a prerequisite for, a high rate of innovativeness in the industry. This result may not be surprising given the special assumptions underlying the simulations. What Nelson and Winter did demonstrate, however, is that their organizational, routine-based, evolutionary approach provides a foundation so that innovative activities in the markets become theoretically accessible. Other authors took up, varied, and extended the approach. *Iwai (1984)*, for example, was able to provide a simple analytical model using a logistic function to describe the sequential diffusion of ever more cost saving technologies in an industry – a useful first approximation of what, more precisely, Schumpeter's 'perennial gale of creative destruction' may mean to an industry.

More recently, the analogy to Darwinian concepts has been taken up once more. In part this happened in response to new developments in biology, such as the controversy already mentioned about gradualism vs. punctualism and, in so far, seems to have confirmed the rather loose character of possible analogies (*Gowdy 1985*). In part, the discussions may be seen as responding to subjectivist queries and to the insight that bounded rationality usually means that theoretical predictions become inherently dependent on initial conditions. If, because of limited cognitive capacities and an only subjectively rational use of information, general predictions about individual behaviour can no longer be derived, competitive selection may be the only systematic influence which still produces regularities. Evolutionary economics would then have to rely heavily on a thoroughly elaborated theory of competitive selection (*Matthews, 1984*; *Metcalfe, 1989*).

Market Process in Individualistic and Population Perspective

An evolutionary approach to explaining what happens in markets may take different stances and focus on different aspects. One may feel a need (i) to develop a deeper, psychologically backed understanding of how knowledge is acquired and used individually, and to derive implications on this basis about the market process and market institutions (*Loasby, 1983*). A different attitude would be (ii) to trace the role of competitive selection, as a population-bound mechanism transcending the level of the individual, in search for regularities in the market process (*Metcalfe, 1989*). Or (iii) focus may be put on the power and efficiency of a system of markets not only as a decentralized information processing device but also as a novelty generating and testing institution (*Hayek, 1978*). Finally, one may (iv) address the interplay of coordinating tendencies arising from competitive adaptations in the markets and de-coordinating tendencies caused by the introduction of novelty, i.e. by innovation competition (*Witt, 1985*). In any case the insights gained about the diverse facets of the market process should merge into a consistent picture.

It would be an overstatement to say that such a grand view is already feasible. However, various bits and pieces do already show considerable coherence and complement each other. If, to start on the individualistic level, imperfect knowledge and uncertainty are the conditions under which economic agents act, then the question emerges as to how this state changes under the human capacity to learn (a problem already identified, but not further pursued by Hayek, 1937). More precisely, it seems crucial to ask of what nature learning is. Consider Bayesian learning which is assumed to start from a nucleus of truth (the prior knowledge of the true probability distribution) and implies a convergence of subjective beliefs to the true conditions. Given such a kind of learning one might be inclined to accept the view that eventually – abstracting from the possibility of social dilemmata or rationality traps – all agents in the economy will have learned to coordinate their activities. They thus end up in a state of general (market) equilibrium in which all their knowledge based expectations are confirmed. This is, of course, the neoclassical, general equilibrium version of the coordination story. Its disadvantage is that further change cannot be explained by this theory. After all adaptations have been made further change cannot come but from outside.

Since evolutionary economics interprets change, at least to a significant extent, as being generated by the agents themselves, i.e. as endogenously created, learning must be assumed to be of a different quality. It must include creation of novel ideas and insights, discovery, and expansion of knowledge. Indeed, this seems to be a core problem of any individualistic foundation of evolutionary economics (Dopfer, 1986; Witt, 1989a). *Loasby (1983)* rightly points to the close relationship to positions held by the Austrian school of thought and by other subjectivists such as Shackle. For instance, Shackle (1958, ch. 1) clearly objected to the usually not much reflected assumption that the alternatives (more technically the state space) which decision makers face is always already given, and that the decision makers only 'learn' in an adaptive way about its properties (e.g. associated probabilities). Contrary to this convenient notion, it is one of the most remarkable capacities of human decision makers that they can create and extend what, in the subjective imagination, are the (future) alternatives to choose from. How is the creative task, which is so important to understand the ultimate source of change, achieved? On an individualistic level this question suggests enquiring, as Loasby indeed starts to do, into what insights psychology might have to offer.

However, even though a deeper understanding in this respect seems essential to develop an individualistic foundation for evolutionary economics in general, and an understanding of the market process in particular, one problem remains. Whenever the sphere of the creative mind is entered, the subjectivity of newly created ideas has to be acknowledged (Witt, 1989a). Subjectivity is likely to mean diversity of individual purposes and desires out of which novel ideas emerge. The subjective particularities of each individual case are difficult to reconstruct and objectify. This obviously delimits the scope of individualistic explanations, but not necessarily that of evolutionary theorizing. What appears necessary is to extend analysis to the population level. In their interactions the agents, intentionally as well as unintentionally, impose mutually binding constraints on each other. As in a selection process, these constraints determine which actions will turn out to be tolerated or even rewarded and which will not. The constraints and their effects may often by reconstructible without knowledge of the particularities of the subjective motives and views of the involved agents.

As emphasized by *Hayek (1978)*, an especially powerful (but certainly not the only) form of interactions that reveal the difference between rewarded and non-rewarded undertakings are those in the market place. The competitive market process operates like a selection device discriminating between innovative individual activities whatever the subjective state of the innovator is. Often, the diversity of behaviour exposed to the logic of this selection device may even be denoted in terms of observable attributes like cost differentials, quality features, market penetration measures, etc. Then the effect of selection can be expressed by a diminishing variance of these attributes in the population (see *Metcalfe 1989*). This amounts to a perspective similar to what is called population thinking in biology which is obviously at odds with the notion of the representative individual.

Whether an individualistic approach is chosen or one that relies on the revelation and selection capacity of the markets, the emergence of novelty and its diffusion through the markets always has allocative consequences and calls for a reconceptualization of a core element of economics – the theory of coordination. Coordination has come to be identified today almost exclusively with the concept of general equilibrium which focusses on a state where the optimal, individual plans happen to be mutually compatible (a notable exception being the Austrian interpretation suggested by Kirzner, 1973; Lachmann, 1986; O'Driscoll and Rizzo, 1985). Building on admittedly strong assumptions general equilibrium theory is content to demonstrate the existence of such a state in a logical exercise. Originally outlined as an entirely static notion attempts to invent a dynamic story around it had a limited success (Fisher, 1983). There is no idea, *a fortiori*, as to why there should be any motivation to come up with novelty once every one is, in the equilibrium, in an optimum. In this version of coordination theory there is obviously only room for activities such as arbitrage, adaptive learning, and parameter adjustments by which the coordination of individual plans in the economy is increased. Innovative activities which, in the first place, de-coordinate and disrupt may occur, but they are 'exogenous' events, i.e. events outside of what the theory wants to explain.

In an evolutionary perspective, by contrast, coordinating and de-coordinating activities are usually simultaneously present and jointly form the observable market processes (see *Witt, 1985*). Accordingly, market processes usually perpetuate 'disequilibrium states' as neoclassical theory labels them without offering an explanation for the regularities governing these states. Learning and adjusting on the one hand and the search for, and trying out of, innovations on the other coexist. The consequences of other agents' improved knowledge and adjustment may well be imagined to induce dissatisfaction with those who profited from having an edge in information or a possibility of arbitraging. The dissatisfaction may trigger the search for new possibilities of action and, as a consequence, may cause a state 'far from equilibrium' to persist.

Path-Dependency, Institutional and Societal Evolution

One peculiarity that may occur in the coordination of individual economic activities in the markets has gained considerable attention in the last years. It is the observation of apparently irreversible self-reinforcing tendencies resulting from 'network-externalities', 'learning-by-using' and other instances that give rise to increasing returns to the adoption and application of one solution or standard out of several competing ones. The increasing returns may then 'lock-in' (*David, 1985*) the development in such a way that further adoption/application decisions are bound to favour the same solution or standard even if it turns out not to be the most effective one. The background of the phenomenon thus is a multiplicity of possible (technological) solutions, and the increasing returns to adoption/application are thought to induce interdependencies between the agents' decisions. This means that instead of a unique coordination equilibrium which was supposed to exist under neoclassical assumptions the technology here implies a multiplicity of mutually exclusive equilibria or, to denote the dynamic nature of the problem, attractors.

The phenomenon is rather typical for a class of problems arising from non-linear dynamics. It implies 'path-dependency' (*Arthur, Ermoliev, and Kaniovsky, 1987*), a significant feature of evolution, which can be characterized as follows. Assume a multiplicity of only locally stable attractors as it regularly seems appropriate where evolution takes place. The future time path describing the historical development of a system then depends on which of the alternative basins of attraction has already been, or will be, entered. In a more imaginative metaphor one may speak of a (multidimensional) 'adaptive landscape' on which evolution proceeds, with a multiplicity of basins of attraction. The topography is defined distinctly, and its shape is explained differently, in the different disciplines in which evolution plays a role. Yet formally the shape seems to depend in many cases on similar factors. These are environment conditions (such as natural constraints and the features of competing technologies designed to loosen those constraints) and frequency-dependency effects (such as those produced by increasing returns to adoption or, to give another example, by differential growth rates as caused by selection processes). Accordingly, an 'adaptive landscape' can be imagined to change its shape through modifications of the environment conditions which may destabilize and relocate local attractors and the boundaries between their basins of attraction. With the same effect a reshaping may occur through the emergence of novelty (Witt, 1991).

These are very abstract notions of evolution. Theoretical development in evolutionary economics is still far from a detailed understanding of what constitutes the 'adaptive landscape' and what determines its shape, not to speak of concrete models of a corresponding generality. In first attempts bifurcations and other phenomena of non-linear dynamics have been analysed within the limited context of technological development (e.g. *David, 1985* and *Arthur, Ermoliev, and Kaniovsky, 1987*; see also Silverberg, 1988) or aggregate economic activity (*Haag, Weidlich, and Mensch, 1987*). A prerequisite for more global notions would seem to be a comprehensive theory of socioeconomic evolution. Unfortunately, this is also lacking with the exception, perhaps, of the 'grand view' proposed by Hayek (1971, 1979 epilogue,

1988) which, of course, is far from providing any detailed explanation or precise specification of the conjectured processes and their relationships.

Hayek assumes three levels of evolution. The first one is that of genetic evolution in which primitive forms of social behaviour, of preferences, and attitudes effectuating an order in social interactions have been fixed genetically during man's phylogeny. Second, there is the evolution of the products of human intelligence and knowledge. Freed from the finite existence of each individual brain by efficient forms of coding, storing, and transmitting information, human knowledge has expanded enormously so that today it allows the mastery of nature to an impressive extent. Third, and this is what Hayek considers the core of his approach, there is another level of evolution: cultural evolution as it operates 'between instinct and reason' (Hayek, 1988, ch. 1). Culture, in Hayek's interpretation, is neither genetically conditioned nor rationally designed. It is a tradition of learnt 'rules of conduct' (*Hayek, 1967*) whose role is often not even understood by those who follow the rules. They are passed on through cultural transmission – a 'blind' process, in the sense that it is not consciously planned or controlled.

Quite obviously, these ideas come close to the theory of cultural transmission recently developed in sociobiology (see *Boyd and Richerson, 1980*; Hayek himself draws on older sources in sociobiology in which cultural transmission does not yet play a role). How rules come into being, and which ones, is a question of historical accident, not so, according to Hayek, the question of which ones survive. The latter is determined by the selection process that underlies cultural evolution, a selection process operating on groups of humans sharing the same rules of conduct. Those groups succeeding in developing and passing on rules better suited to govern their social interactions are supposed to grow and feed a larger number of people. Their relative superiority may enable them to conquer and/or absorb less well equipped, competing groups and thus, unintentionally, propagate the superior sets of rules. A growing population requires increasing specialization and division of labour which, in turn, presuppose the spontaneous order to increasingly extend. The rules become ever more differentiated, abstract, and difficult to understand.

Over thousands of years Hayek thus sees an 'extended order' spontaneously emerging which enabled modern societies to achieve a historically unique level of civilization and productivity. This order, the most important achievement of which, Hayek (1988, ch. 3) submits, is trade and the emergence of a system of markets, embodies an impersonal intelligence as it has been accumulated during the selection processes in the form of surviving impersonal rules of conduct. Hayek's theory thus underlies the 'twin ideas of spontaneous order and evolution'. The backbone of the former is a system of impersonal rules of conduct, the backbone of the latter a 'group selection' hypothesis (see *Vanberg, 1986*). Both taken together suggest that natural selection does not only 'choose' between competing species; it also chooses between the competing groups of humans as the unit to which acquired cultural norms and rules are fixed which are more or less suited to efficiently coordinate social interactions. The gist of the argument is, of course, to give the theory of spontaneous order a new foundation.

The theory was first conceived of by the Scottish moral philosophers David Hume, Adam Smith, Adam Ferguson, and their forerunner, Bernhard Mandeville (who, with their theory, apparently inspired Darwin in a kind of reverse transfer, cf. Schweber, 1977; Bowler, 1989, pp. 151–86). They clearly recognized the division of labour and the system of anonymous markets as a spontaneous order, and they understood the meaning of private property rights, freedom of contract, and the rule of law as prerequisites of such an order. (Indeed, Hayek (1967b) rightly refers to the fact that the very idea of evolution, i.e. of the development of increasingly complex structures, is older than Darwin's theory. It can be found already in a line of thought in the arts, social sciences, and law beginning in Germany in the 18th century, and linked to names such as Herder, Savigny, and Wilhelm von Humboldt (see also Bowler, 1989, pp. 104–108).

The hypothesis that regularities in social interactions may be constituted by the individual choices of all participants without anybody having intended or even understood this effect is also a cornerstone of Austrian economic theory on which Hayek heavily draws. It has, presumably independently of Scottish moral philosophy, been derived by Menger (1963, first German edition 1883) on the basis of such concrete examples as language, custom, moral, manners, and common law. For Menger all individual actions taken together spontaneously establish a mutually coordinated behaviour which helps all, and which everybody, by forming a habit, takes for granted and expects as a prevailing regularity or order. It is perhaps only today that, with the tools of game theory, the logic of the conjectured processes can be fully understood. Indeed recent research on the evolution of economic institutions, informed by game theory, proceeds along these lines (*Hirschleifer, 1982*; *Sugden, 1989*; Witt, 1989b; Wärneryd, 1990). It is not a fully blown theory of societal evolution as it has been alluded to above, but makes an important contribution to such a theory and helps to clarify several issues which Hayek's grand view has left open. Moreover, the models developed in this context confirm in a striking way the importance of path-dependency. The multiplicity of attractors comes here in the configuration of multiple equilibria of the underlying games. Institutional evolution is accordingly characterized by more or less frequent transitions between different attractors governed once again by a frequency-dependency effect which may even take such dramatic forms as revolutions (see *Kuran, 1989*).

Development and Growth in the Long Run

The abstract notions discussed in the previous section may be suggestive for identifying general features which characterize economic evolution as such, as well as for directing the search for appropriate analytical conceptions. On a more concrete level it seems straightforward to ask which new theoretical interpretations of economic growth and development in the long run may thus be derived. An answer to this question has been given in the evolutionary approach which shows a considerable shift in emphasis.

If man's genetic inheritance from the times of fierce selection pressure in human phylogeny is considered, it is only natural to assume a strong human preference for the satisfaction of physical needs which increase the chance of survival and of the preservation of the species. Although there may be significant individual variance in this respect, and in spite of the fact that in industrialized economies the volume of production has long exceeded what is necessary for immediate physical survival, economic evolution in the long run seems to have been influenced by this preference in a very elementary way. The poorer the economy, the more desperately people have been striving to satisfy their caloric needs. The most serious natural constraint in the production of food is accessible energy. It may therefore be conjectured that much of economic growth and development in the long run depends on the feasible technological and institutional devices which determine the amount of energy at man's disposal. Innovative activities in these devices have shifted the constraint. Indeed, improved utilization of existing energy sources and the opening up of new resources have not only helped to feed an ever increasing number of people, but also to relieve modern man from much of the strenuous manual labour which extended production and mobility would otherwise require.

If this conjecture has something to it, it may be worthwhile reconsidering the basics of growth theory in terms other than those of the usual factors of production, namely by recourse to the two factors knowledge and energy (*Boulding, 1981*, Weissmahr, 1992). These two factors crucially interact in human history. There is a strong incentive to search for new knowledge that allows an increase in energy consumption, and an even stronger one when resources threaten to be depleted. Discovery, invention, and innovation seem to conform to strikingly regular patterns in this respect (see *Marchetti, 1980*). As a consequence, economic development and growth are likely to follow a path of technological and institutional changes which is intimately related to the increases in energy utilization (Hesse, 1992).

Even though historical evidence for the correlation between extending knowledge and increasing human energy consumption is impressive, the global conjecture gives little information as to how the process of growth and institutional and technological change may take place. The conjecture focusses on long-term shifts in the ultimate constraints of human economic action (constraints clearly described already by Georgescu-Roegen, 1971). It does not imply hypotheses about other constraints, many of which may be considered man-made and may qualify as being path-dependent in the above defined sense. However, a more detailed understanding of the interaction of the various constraints and their respective dynamics as suggested, for instance, by *Day and Walter (1989)* seems necessary to integrate into the long-term perspective all the other insights provided by evolutionary economics. Work in that direction, although urgently needed, not least in view of its obvious relevance for ecological problems that have recently gained a mounting interest, has barely begun.

Conclusions

In this introduction an attempt has been made to draw together the various traditions contributing to evolutionary economics, to briefly outline what they are concerned with, and to make the contours of a research paradigm visible that contrasts with the prevailing interpretation patterns of neoclassical economics. Indeed, many of the diverse contributions seem to be motivated by the conviction that the basic analytical tools of the predominant neoclassical approach – optimal adaptation, unique equilibria in which all individual plans are compatible, and the typological method of representative behaviour – are unsuitable to explain economic change and its regularities. There may be aspects of modern economies where the influence of endogenously generated change is negligible. If so it is possible to abstract from this kind of change without losing much explanatory power (and to the extent to which this is true the two research programmes may turn out to be non-rivalling). Yet this cannot be said of the overwhelming economic development that has been, and still is, transforming the appearance of all sectors of the economy for about three centuries. In order to understand the dynamics that come to the fore here, a whole series of new notions and analytical tools have to be substituted for the established ones. As the ideas developed in the subsequently reprinted contributions should show, evolutionary economics may be able to provide the necessary new orientations and tools.

References

Alchian, A.A. (1950), 'Uncertainty, Evolution, and Economic Theory', *Journal of Political Economy*, **58**, 211–21.

Arthur, W.B., Ermoliev, Y.M., and Kaniovsky, Y.M. (1987), 'Path-dependent Processes and the Emergence of Macro-structure', *European Journal of Operational Research*, **30**, 294–303.

Baldwin, W.L. and Scott, J.T. (1987), *Market Structure and Technological Change*, Chur: Harwood Academic Publishers.

Boulding, K.E. (1981), *Evolutionary Economics*, Beverly Hills: Sage Publications.

Bowler, P.J. (1989), *Evolution – the History of an Idea*, Berkeley: University of California Press, rev. ed.

Boyd, R. and Richerson, P.J. (1980), 'Sociobiology, Culture and Economic Theory', *Journal of Economic Behavior and Organization*, **1**, 97–121.

Cyert, R.M. and March, J.G. (1963), *A Behavioral Theory of the Firm*, Englewood Cliffs: Prentice Hall.

David, P.A. (1985), 'Clio and the Economics of QWERTY', *American Economic Review*, **75**, Papers and Proceedings, 322–7.

Day, R.H. and Walter, J.-L. (1989), 'Economic Growth in the Very Long Run, on the Multiple-Phase Interaction of Population, Technology, and Social Infrastructure', in W.A. Barnett, J. Geweke and K. Shell (eds), *Chaos, Sunspots, Bubbles, and Nonlinearity*, Cambridge: Cambridge University Press, 253–89.

Dopfer, K. (1986), 'Causality and Consciousness in Economics: Concepts of Change in Orthodox and Heterodox Economics', *Journal of Economic Issues*, **20**, 509–23.

Dosi, G. (1982), 'Technological Paradigms and Technological Trajectories: A Suggested Interpretation of the Determinants and Directions of Technical Change', *Research Policy*, **11**, 147–62.

Faber, M. and Proops, J.L.R. (1990), *Evolution, Time, Production and the Environment*, Berlin: Springer.

Fisher, F.M. (1983), *Disequilibrium Foundations of Equilibrium Economics*, Cambridge: Cambridge University Press.

Freeman, C. (1990), 'Schumpeter's Business Cycle Revisited', in Heertje, A. and Perlman, M. (eds), *Evolving Technology and Market Structure – Studies in Schumpeterian Economics*, Ann Arbor: Michigan University Press, 17–38.

Friedman, M. (1953), 'The Methodology of Positive Economics', in Friedman, M., *Essays in Positive Economics*, Chicago: University of Chicago Press.

Georgescu-Roegen, N. (1971), *The Entropy Law and the Economic Process*, Cambridge, Mass.: Harvard University Press.

Gowdy, J.M. (1985), 'Evolutionary Theory and Economic Theory: Some Methodological Issues', *Review of Social Economy*, **43**, 316–24.

Haag, G., Weidlich, W., and Mensch, G. (1987), 'The Schumpeter Clock', in D. Batten, J. Casti and B. Johansson (eds), *Economic Evolution and Structural Adjustment*, Berlin: Springer, 187–226.

Hayek, F.A. (1937), 'Economics and Knowledge', *Economica*, **4**, 33–54.

Hayek, F.A. (1967a), 'Notes on the Evolution of Systems of Rules of Conduct', in F.A. Hayek, *Studies in Philosophy and Economics*, London: Routledge and Kegan Paul, 66–81.

Hayek, F.A. (1967b), 'Dr. Bernhard Mandeville', *Proceedings of the British Academy*, **12**, London: Oxford University Press.

Hayek, F.A. (1971), 'Nature vs. Nurture Once Again', *Encounter*, **36**, 81–3.

Hayek, F.A. (1978), 'Competition as a Discovery Procedure', in *New Studies in Philosophy, Politics, Economics, and the History of Ideas*, Chicago: Chicago University Press, 179–90.

Hayek, F.A. (1979), 'The Three Sources of Human Values', Epilogue to *Law, Legislation, and Liberty*, London: Routledge.

Hayek, F.A. (1988), *The Fatal Conceit*, London, Routledge.

Hesse, G. (1992), 'A New Theory of "Modern Economic Growth"', in U. Witt (ed.), *Explaining Process and Change – Approaches to Evolutionary Economics*, Ann Arbor: Michigan University Press, 81–103.

Hirshleifer, J. (1982), 'Evolutionary Models in Economics and Law', *Research in Law and Economics*, **4**, 1–60.

Hodgson, G.M. (1992), *Economics and Evolution: Bringing Back Life into Economics*, typescript.

Iwai, K. (1984), 'Schumpeterian Dynamics, Part I and II', *Journal of Economic Behavior and Organization*, **5**, 159–90 and 321–51.

Kamien, M.I. and Schwartz, N.L. (1982), *Market Structure and Innovation*, Cambridge: Cambridge University Press.

Kirzner, I.M. (1973), *Competition and Entrepreneurship*, Chicago: Chicago University Press.

Kleinknecht, A. (1987), *Innovation Patterns in Crisis and Prosperity*, London: Macmillan.

Kuran, T. (1989), 'Sparks and Prairie Fires: A Theory of Unanticipated Political Revolution', *Public Choice*, **61**, 41–74.

Lachmann, L.M. (1986), *The Market as an Economic Process*, New York: Basil Blackwell.

Lesourne, J. (1991), *Économie de l'order et du désordre*, Paris: Economica.

Loasby, B.J. (1983), 'Knowledge, Learning, and Enterprise', in J. Wiseman (ed.), *Beyond Positive Economics?*, London: Macmillan, 104–21.

March, J.G. and Simon, H.A. (1958), *Organizations*, New York: Wiley.

Marchetti, C. (1980), 'Society as a Learning System: Discovery, Invention, and Innovation Cycles Revisited', *Technological Forecasting and Social Change*, **18**, 267–82.

Marshall, A. (1961), *Principles of Economis*, 9th edition, London: Macmillan, (first edition published in 1898).

Matthews, R.C.O. (1984), 'Darwinism and Economic Change', in Collard, D.A., Helm, D.R., Scott, M.F.G. and Sen, A.K. (eds), *Economic Theory and Hicksian Themes*, Oxford: Clarendon Press, 91–117.

McClelland, D.C. and Winter, D.G. (1969), *Motivating Economic Achievement*, New York: Free Press.

Menger, C. (1883), *Problems of Economics and Sociology*, Urbana: University of Illinois Press (first German edition 1886).

Mensch, G. (1979), *Stalemate in Technology*, Cambridge, Mass.: Ballinger.

Metcalfe, S. (1989), 'Evolution and Economic Change', in Silberston (ed.), *Technology and Economic Progress*, London: Macmillan, 54–85.

Mirowski, P. (1988), *Against Mechanism – Protecting Economics From Science*, Totowa, N.J.: Rowman & Littlefield.

Nelson, R.R. and Winter, S.G. (1980), 'Firm and Industry Response to Changed Market Conditions: An Evolutionary Approach', *Economic Inquiry*, **28**, 179–202.

Nelson, R.R. and Winter, S.G. (1982), *An Evolutionary Theory of Economic Change*, Cambridge, Mass.: Harvard University Press.

O'Driscoll, G.P. and Rizzo, M.J. (1985), *The Economics of Time and Ignorance*, Oxford: Basil Blackwell.

Penrose, E.T. (1952), 'Biological Analogies in the Theory of the Firm', *American Economic Review*, **42**, 804–19.

Sahal, D. (1981), *Patterns of Technological Innovation*, New York: Addison-Wesley.

Schumpeter, J.A. (1908), *Das Wesen und der Hauptinhalt der theoretischen Nationalökonomie*, Leipzig: Duncker & Humblot.

Schumpeter, J.A. (1910), 'Über das Wesen der Wirtschaftskrisen', *Zeitschrift für Volkswirtschaft, Sozialpolitik und Verwaltung*, **19**, 271–325.

Schumpeter, J.A. (1928), 'The Instability of Capitalism', *Economic Journal*, **38**, 361–86.

Schumpeter, J.A. (1934), *The Theory of Economic Development*, Cambridge, Mass.: Harvard University Press (first German edition 1912).

Schumpeter, J.A. (1935), 'The Analysis of Economic Change', *Review of Economics and Statistics*, **17**, 2–10.

Schumpeter, J.A. (1942), *Capitalism, Socialism, and Democracy*, New York: Harper.

Schumpeter, J.A. (1947), 'The Creative Response in Economic History', *Journal of Economic History*, **7**, 149–59.

Schweber, S.S. (1977), 'The Origin of the *Origin* Revisited', *Journal of History of Biology*, **10**, 229–316.

Shackle, G.L.S. (1958), *Times in Economics*, Amsterdam: North Holland.

Silverberg, G. (1987), 'Technical Progress, Capital Accumulation, and Effective Demand: A Self-Organization Model', in Batten, D., Casti, J., and Johansson, B., (eds) (1987), *Economic Evolution and Structual Adjustment*, Berlin: Springer.

Silverberg, G. (1988), 'Modelling Economic Dynamics and Technical Change: Mathematical Approaches to Self-organization and Evolution', in Dosi, G., Freeman, C., Nelson, R., Silverberg, G., and Soete, L. (eds), *Technical Change and Economic Theory*, London: Pinter, 531–59.

Simon, H.A. (1955), 'A Behavioral Model of Rational Choice', *Quarterly Journal of Economics*, **69**, 99–118.

Wärneryd, K. (1990), *Economic Institutions – Essays in Institutional Evolution*, Stockholm: Gotab.

Weissmahr, J.A. (1992), 'The Factors of Production of Evolutionary Economics', in U. Witt (ed.), *Explaining Process and Change – Approaches to Evolutionary Economics*, Ann Arbor: University of Michigan Press, 67–79.

Winter, S.G. (1964), 'Economic "Natural Selection" and the Theory of the Firm', *Yale Economic Essays*, **4**, 225–72.

Winter, S.G. (1971), 'Satisficing, Selection, and the Innovating Remnant', *Quarterly Journal of Economics*, **85**, 237–61.

Winter, S.G. (1975), 'Optimization and Evolution in the Theory of the Firm', in R. Day and T. Groves (eds), *Adaptive Economic Models*, New York: Academic Press, 73–118.

Witt, U. (1985), 'Coordination of Individual Economic Activities as an Evolving Process of Self-Organization', *Economie Appliquee*, **37**, 569–95.

Witt, U. (1986), 'Firms' Behavior Under Imperfect Information and Economic Natural Selection', *Journal of Economic Behavior and Organization*, **7**, 265–90.

Witt, U. (1989a), 'Subjectivism in Economics – A Suggested Reorientation', in K.G. Grunert and F. Ölander (eds), *Understanding Economic Behavior*, Boston: Kluwer, 409–31.

Witt, U. (1989b), 'The Evolution of Economic Institutions as a Propagation Process', *Public Choice*, **62**, 155–72.

Witt, U. (1991), 'Reflections on the Present State of Evolutionary Economic Theory', in G.M. Hodgson and E. Screpanti (eds), *Rethinking Economics*, Aldershot: Edward Elgar, 83–102.

Part I
Schumpeterian Themes

THE JOURNAL OF ECONOMIC HISTORY

VOL. VII NOVEMBER 1947 NO. 2

The Creative Response in Economic History

I

ECONOMIC historians and economic theorists can make an interesting and socially valuable journey together, if they will. It would be an investigation into the sadly neglected area of economic change.

As anyone familiar with the history of economic thought will immediately recognize, practically all the economists of the nineteenth century and many of the twentieth have believed uncritically that all that is needed to explain a given historical development is to indicate conditioning or causal factors, such as an increase in population or the supply of capital. But this is sufficient only in the rarest of cases. As a rule, no factor acts in a uniquely determined way and, whenever it does not, the necessity arises of going into the details of its *modus operandi,* into the mechanisms through which it acts. Examples will illustrate this. Sometimes an increase in population actually has no other effect than that predicated by classical theory—a fall in per capita real income;[1] but, at other times, it may have an energizing effect that induces new developments with the result that per capita real income rises. Or a protective duty may have no other effect than to increase the price of the protected commodity and, in consequence, its output; but it may also induce a complete reorganization of the protected industry which eventually results in an increase in output so great as to reduce the price below its initial level.

What has not been adequately appreciated among theorists is the

---

[1] Even within the assumptions of classical theory this is not necessarily true; but we need not go into this.

Joseph A. Schumpeter

distinction between different kinds of reaction to changes in "condition." Whenever an economy or a sector of an economy adapts itself to a change in its data in the way that traditional theory describes, whenever, that is, an economy reacts to an increase in population by simply adding the new brains and hands to the working force in the existing employments, or an industry reacts to a protective duty by expansion within its existing practice, we may speak of the development as *adaptive response*. And whenever the economy or an industry or some firms in an industry do something else, something that is outside of the range of existing practice, we may speak of *creative response*.

Creative response has at least three essential characteristics. First, from the standpoint of the observer who is in full possession of all relevant facts, it can always be understood *ex post*; but it can practically never be understood *ex ante*; that is to say, it cannot be predicted by applying the ordinary rules of inference from the pre-existing facts. This is why the "how" in what has been called above the "mechanisms" must be investigated in each case. Secondly, creative response shapes the whole course of subsequent events and their "long-run" outcome. It is not true that both types of responses dominate only what the economist loves to call "transitions," leaving the ultimate outcome to be determined by the initial data. Creative response changes social and economic situations for good, or, to put it differently, it creates situations from which there is no bridge to those situations that might have emerged in its absence. This is why creative response is an essential element in the historical process; no deterministic credo avails against this. Thirdly, creative response—the frequency of its occurrence in a group, its intensity and success or failure—has obviously something, be that much or little, to do (a) with quality of the personnel available in a society, (b) with relative quality of personnel, that is, with quality available to a particular field of activity relative to quality available, at the same time, to others, and (c) with individual decisions, actions, and patterns of behavior. Accordingly, a study of creative response in business becomes coterminous with a study of entrepreneurship. The mechanisms of economic change in capitalist society pivot on entrepreneurial activity.[2] Whether we emphasize opportunity or conditions, the responses of individuals or of groups, it is patently true that in capitalist society objective opportunities or conditions act through

---

[2] The function itself is not absent from other forms of society; but capitalist entrepreneurship is a sufficiently distinct phenomenon to be singled out.

The Creative Response in Economic History   151

entrepreneurial activity, analysis of which is at the very least a highly important avenue to the investigation of economic changes in the capitalist epoch.[3] This is compatible with widely different views about its importance as an "ultimate cause."

Seen in this light, the entrepreneur and his function are not difficult to conceptualize: the defining characteristic is simply the doing of new things or the doing of things that are already being done in a new way (innovation).[4] It is but natural, and in fact it is an advantage, that such a definition does not draw any sharp line between what is and what is not "enterprise." For actual life itself knows no such sharp division, though it shows up the type well enough. It should be observed at once that the "new thing" need not be spectacular or of historic importance. It need not be Bessemer steel or the explosion motor. It can be the Deerfoot sausage. To see the phenomenon even in the humblest levels of the business world is quite essential though it may be difficult to find the humble entrepreneurs historically.

Distinction from other functions with which enterpreneurship is frequently but not necessarily associated—just as "farmership" is frequently but not necessarily associated with the ownership of land and with the activity of a farm hand—does not present conceptual difficulties either. One necessary distinction is that between enterprise and management: evidently it is one thing to set up a concern embodying a new idea and another thing to head the administration of a going concern, however much the two may shade off into each other. Again, it is essential to note that the entrepreneurial function, though facilitated by the ownership of means, is not identical with that of the capitalist.[5] New light is urgently needed on the relation between the

---

[3] Arthur H. Cole has opened new vistas in this area in his presidential address before the Economic History Association, "An Approach to the Study of Entrepreneurship," The Tasks of Economic History (Supplemental Issue of The Journal of Economic History), VI (1946), 1–15.

[4] An exact definition can be provided by means of the concept of production functions. On this, see Oscar Lange, "A Note on Innovations," *Review of Economic Statistics*, XXV (1943), 19–25.

[5] It is sometimes held that entrepreneurship, although it did not require antecedent ownership of capital (or very little of it) in the early days of capitalism, tends to become dependent upon it as time goes on, especially in the epoch of giant corporations. Nothing could be further from the truth. In the course of the nineteenth century, it became increasingly easier to obtain other people's money by methods other than the partnership, and in our own time promotion within the shell of existing corporations offers a much more convenient access to the entrepreneurial functions than existed in the world of owner-managed firms. Many a would-be entrepreneur of today does not found a firm, not because he could not do so, but simply because he prefers the other method.

two, especially because of the cant phrases that are current on this topic. In the third place, it is particularly important to distinguish the entrepreneur from the "inventor." Many inventors have become entrepreneurs and the relative frequency of this case is no doubt an interesting subject to investigate, but there is no necessary connection between the two functions. The inventor produces ideas, the entrepreneur "gets things done," which may but need not embody anything that is scientifically new. Moreover, an idea or scientific principle is not, by itself, of any importance for economic practice: the fact that Greek science had probably produced all that is necessary in order to construct a steam engine did not help the Greeks or Romans to build a steam engine; the fact that Leibnitz suggested the idea of the Suez Canal exerted no influence whatever on economic history for two hundred years. And as different as the functions are the two sociological and psychological types.[6] Finally, "getting new things done" is not only a distinct process but it is a process which produces consequences that are an essential part of capitalist reality. The whole economic history of capitalism would be different from what it is if new ideas had been currently and smoothly adopted, as a matter of course, by all firms to whose business they were relevant. But they were not. It is in most cases only one man or a few men who see the new possibility and are able to cope with the resistances and difficulties which action always meets with outside of the ruts of established practice. This accounts for the large gains that success often entails, as well as for the losses and vicissitudes of failure. These things are important. If, in every individual case, the difficulties may indeed be called transitional, they are transitional difficulties which are never absent in the economy as a whole and which dominate the atmosphere of capitalist life permanently. Hence it seems appropriate to keep "invention" distinct from "innovation."

The definition that equates enterprise to innovation is a very abstract one. Some classifications that are richer in content may be noticed because of their possible use in drawing up plans for specific pieces of research. There is the obvious classification—historical and systematic—of the phenomena of enterprise according to institutional forms, such as the medieval trading company, the later "chartered companies," the partnership, the modern "corporation," and the like, on all of which

---

[6] The relation between the two has attracted interest before. See, e.g., F. W. Taussig, *Inventors and Money-Makers* (New York: The Macmillan Company, 1915).

The Creative Response in Economic History 153

there exists a vast amount of historical work.[7] The interaction of institutional forms and entrepreneurial activity, the "shaping" influence of the former and the "bursting" influence of the latter, is, as has already been intimated, a major topic for further inquiry. Closely connected with this classification is the old one according to fields of activity—commerce, industry, finance [8]—which has been refined by the following distinctions: enterprise that introduces "new" commodities; enterprise that introduces technological novelties into the production of "old" commodities; enterprise that introduces new commercial combinations such as the opening up of new markets for products or new sources of supply of materials; enterprise that consists in reorganizing an industry, for instance, by making a monopoly out of it.[9]

But there are other classifications that may prove helpful. We may classify entrepreneurs according to origins and sociological types: feudal lords and aristocratic landowners, civil servants—particularly important, for instance, in Germany after the Thirty Years' War, especially in mining—farmers, workmen, artisans, members of the learned professions, all embarked upon enterprise as has often been noticed, and it is highly interesting from several points of view to clear up this matter. Or we may try to classify entrepreneurial performances according to the precise nature of the "function" filled and the aptitudes (some may even add motivation) involved. Since all this presumably changed significantly in the course of the capitalist epoch, economic historians are particularly qualified for work on this line.

Though the phrase "getting a new thing done" may be adequately comprehensive, it covers a great many different activities which, as the observer stresses one more than another or as his material displays one

---

[7] Gustav von Schmoller introduced the subject into his general treatise (*Grundriss*) of 1904. But the novelty consisted only in the systematic use he made of the result of historical research. Less systematically, the subject had entered general treatises before.

[8] Financial institutions and practices enter our circle of problems in three ways: they are "auxiliary and conditioning"; banking may be the object of entrepreneurial activity, that is to say, the introduction of new banking practices may constitute enterprise; and bankers (or other "financiers") may use the means at their command in order to embark upon commercial and industrial enterprise themselves (for example, John Law). See the recent book by Fritz Redlich, *The Molding of American Banking—Men and Ideas* (New York: Hafner Publishing Company, 1947).

[9] This case emphasizes the desirability, present also in others, of divesting our idea of entrepreneurial performance of any preconceived value judgment. Whether a given entrepreneurial success benefits or injures society or a particular group within society is a question that must be decided on the merits of each case. Enterprise that results in a monopoly position, even if undertaken for the sole purpose of securing monopoly gains, is not necessarily antisocial in its total effect although it often is.

more than another, may, locally, temporarily, or generally, lend different colors to entrepreneurship. In some cases, or to some observers, it may be the activity of "setting up" or "organizing" that stands out from the others; in other cases, or for other observers, it may be the breaking down of the resistances of the environment; in still other cases, or for still other observers, simply leadership or, again, salesmanship. Thus, it seems to me, there was a type of entrepreneur in early capitalist industry that is best described as a "fixer." Modern history furnishes many instances of entrepreneurship vested in a company promotor.[10] The typical industrial entrepreneur of the nineteenth century was perhaps the man who put into practice a novel method of production by embodying it in a new firm and who then settled down into a position of owner-manager of a company, if he was successful, or of stockholding president of a company, getting old and conservative in the process. In the large-scale corporation of today, the question that is never quite absent arises with a vengeance, namely, who should be considered as the entrepreneur. In a well-known book, R. A. Gordon has presented much interesting material bearing upon this question.[11]

II

The economic nature, amount, and distribution of the returns to entrepreneurial activity constitute another set of problems on which investigation may be expected to shed much-needed light. Conceptual difficulties confront us here even before we come up against the still more formidable difficulties of fact finding. For the "profit" of the English classics, which was analyzed by J. S. Mill into wages of management, premiums for risk, and interest on owned capital, was a return to normal business activity and something quite different from, though influenced by, the gain of successful enterprise in our sense of the term. What the latter is can best be explained by considering a special case. Suppose that a man, realizing the possibility of producing acceptable caviar from sawdust, sets up the Excelsior Caviar concern and makes it a success. If this concern is too small to influence the prices of either the product or the factors of production, he will sell the

---

[10] In a sense, the promotor who does nothing but "set up" new business concerns might be considered as the purest type of entrepreneur. Actually, he is mostly not more than a financial agent who has little, if any, title to entrepreneurship—no more than the lawyer who does the legal work involved. But there are important exceptions to this.

[11] Robert A. Gordon, *Business Leadership in the Large Corporation* (Washington, D.C.: The Brookings Institution, 1945).

The Creative Response in Economic History 155

former and buy the latter at current prices. If, however, he turns out the unit of caviar more cheaply than his competitors, owing to his use of a much cheaper raw material, he will for a time, that is, until other firms copy his method, make (essentially temporary) surplus gains. These gains are attributable to personal exertion. Hence they might be called wages. They may with equal justice be attributed to the fact that, for a time, his method is exclusively his own. Hence they might also be called monopoly gains. But whether we elect to call them wages or monopoly gains, we must add immediately that they are a special kind of wages or monopoly gains that differ in important respects from what we usually mean to denote by these terms. And so we had better call them simply entrepreneurial gains or profit. However, it should be observed that if this venture means a "fortune," this fortune does not typically arise from the actual net receipts being saved up and invested in the same or some other business. Essentially, it emerges as a *capital* gain, that is, as the discounted value of the stream of prospective excess returns.

In this simple case, which, however, does constitute a type, the investigator is not confronted with difficulties other than those involved in fact finding. Also, it is clear what happens with that surplus gain: in this case the entrepreneurial gain goes to the entrepreneur,[12] and we can also see, if we have the facts, how, to use a current phrase, the "fruits of the progress involved are handed to consumers and workmen." The speed of this process of "handing on" varies widely, but it would always work, in isolated cases like the one under discussion, through a fall in the price of the product to the new level of costs, which is bound to occur whenever competition steps up to the successful concern. But even here we meet the practice of innovators striving to keep their returns alive by means of patents and in other ways. The gains described above shade off into gains from purposive restriction of competition and create difficulties of diagnosis that are sometimes insurmountable.[13] Cumulation of carefully analyzed historical cases is

---

[12] It should be obvious that this does not mean that the whole social gain resulting from the enterprise goes to the entrepreneur. But the question of appraisal of social gains from entrepreneurship, absolute and relative to the entrepreneurial shares in them, and of the social costs involved in a system that relies on business interests to carry out its innovations, is so complex and perhaps even hopeless that I beg to excuse myself from entering into it.

[13] Still more difficult is, of course, responsible appraisal, that is to say, appraisal that is not content with popular slogans. Measures to keep surplus gains alive no doubt slow up the process of "handing on the fruits of progress." But the knowledge that such measures are available may be necessary in order to induce anyone to embark upon certain ventures. There

the best means of shedding light on these things, of supplying the theorist with strategic assumptions, and banishing slogans.

If innovations are neither individually small nor isolated events, complications crowd upon us. Entrepreneurial activity then affects wage and interest rates from the outset and becomes a factor—the fundamental factor in my opinion—in booms and depressions. This is one reason, but not the only one, why entrepreneurial gains are not net returns (1) to the whole set of people who attempt entrepreneurial ventures, (2) to the industrial sector in which innovation occurs, (3) to the capitalist interests that finance entrepreneurial activity and to the capitalist class as a whole.

Concerning the first point, I might have made my special case more realistic by assuming that several or many people try their hands at producing that caviar but that all but one fail to produce a salable product before the success of this one presents an example to copy. The gains of the successful entrepreneur and of the capitalists who finance him—for whenever capital finances enterprise the interest is paid out of the entrepreneurial gains, a fact that is very important for our grasp of the interest phenomenon—should be related not to his effort and their loan but to the effort and the loans of all the entrepreneurs and capitalists who made attempts and lost. The presence of gains to enterprise so great as to impress us as spectacular and, from the standpoint of society, irrational is then seen to be compatible with a negative return to entrepreneurs and financing capitalists as a group.[14]

It is similarly clear that entrepreneurial gain is not a net accretion to the returns of the industrial sector in which it occurs. The impact of the new product or method spells losses to the "old" firms. The competition of the man with a significantly lower cost curve is, in fact, the really effective competition that in the end revolutionizes the industry. Detailed investigation of this process which may take many forms might teach us much about the actual working of capitalism that we are but dimly perceiving as yet.

---

also may be other compensating advantages to such measures, particularly where rapid introduction into general use of new methods would involve severe dislocations of labor, and where entrepreneurial gains are important sources of venture capital.

[14] Whether this actually is so in any particular case is, of course, extremely difficult to establish. The successes stand out, statistically and otherwise; the failures are apt to escape notice. This is one of the reasons why economists seem so much impressed by peak successes. Another reason for faulty appraisal is neglect of the fact that spectacular gains may stimulate more effectively than would the same sum if more equally distributed. This is a question that no speculation can decide. Only collection of facts can tell us how we are to frame our theory.

The Creative Response in Economic History   157

Concerning the third point, while we have a fair amount of information about how the working class fares in the process of economic change, in respect to both real wages and employment, we know much less about that elusive entity, capital, that is being incessantly destroyed and re-created. That the theorist's teaching, according to which capital "migrates" from declining to rising industries, is unrealistic is obvious: the capital "invested" in railroads does not migrate into trucking and air transportation but will perish in and with the railroads. Investigation into the histories of industries, concerns, and firms, including surveys of sectors in order to point out how long a typical firm stays in business and how and why it drops out, might dispel many a preconceived notion on this subject.

III

Finally, I should like to touch one more set of problems on which we may expect light from historical analysis, namely, the problems that come within the range of the question: does the importance of the entrepreneurial function decline as time goes on? There are serious reasons for believing that it does. The entrepreneurial performance involves, on the one hand, the ability to perceive new opportunities that cannot be proved at the moment at which action has to be taken, and, on the other hand, will power adequate to break down the resistance that the social environment offers to change. But the range of the provable expands, and action upon flashes or hunches is increasingly replaced by action that is based upon "figuring out." And modern milieus may offer less resistance to new methods and new goods than used to be the case. So far as this is so, the element of personal intuition and force would be less essential than it was: it could be expected to yield its place to the teamwork of specialists; in other words, improvement could be expected to become more and more automatic. Our impression to this effect is reinforced by parallel phenomena in other fields of activity. For instance, a modern commander no doubt means less in the outcome of a war than commanders meant of old, and for the same reasons; campaigns have become more calculable than they used to be and there is less scope for personal leadership.

But this is at present only an impression. It is for the historian to establish or to refute it. If, however, it should stand up under research, this would be a result of the utmost importance. We should be led to expect that the whole mechanism of economic development will change significantly. Among other things, the economy would progressively bureaucratize itself. There are, in fact, many symptoms of this. And consequences would extend far beyond the field of economic phenomena. Just as warrior classes have declined in importance ever since warfare—and especially the management of armies in the field—began to be increasingly "mechanized," so the business class may decline in importance, as its most vital figure, the entrepreneur, progressively loses his most essential function. This would mean a different social structure.

Therefore, the sociology of enterprise reaches much further than is implied in questions concerning the conditions that produce and shape, favor or inhibit entrepreneurial activity. It extends to the structure and the very foundations of, at least, capitalist society or the capitalist sector of any given society. The quickest way of showing this starts from recognition of the facts that, just as the rise of the bourgeois class as a whole is associated with success in commercial, industrial, and financial enterprise, so the rise of an individual family to "capitalist" status within that class is typically [15] associated with entrepreneurial success; and that the elimination of a family from the "capitalist" class is typically associated with the loss of those attitudes and aptitudes of industrial leadership or alertness that enter our picture of the entrepreneurial type of businessman.

Now these facts, if they are facts, might teach us a lot about such fundamental problems as the nature of the class structure of capitalist society; the sort of class civilization which it develops and which differs so characteristically from the class civilization of feudal society; its schema of values; its politics, especially its attitudes to state and church and war; its performance and failures; its degree of durability. But a great deal of work needs to be done in order to arrive at scientifically defensible opinions about all these and cognate things. First of all, these "facts" must be established. How far is it really true, for instance, that entrepreneurs, while not forming a social class themselves but originating in almost all existing strata, do "feed" or renew the capitalist stratum? To put it differently, does the latter recruit itself through entrepreneurial successes? Or, to put it still differently,

---

[15] That is to say, successful entrepreneurship is that method of rising in the social scale that is characteristic of the capitalist blueprint. It is, of course, not the only method. First, there are other possibilities within the economic sphere, such as possession of an appreciating natural agent (for example, urban land) or mere speculation or even, occasionally, success in mere administration that need not partake of the specifically entrepreneurial element. Secondly, there are possibilities outside the business sphere, for business success is no more the only method of rising in capitalist society than knightly service was in feudal society.

The Creative Response in Economic History 159

does the "typical" history of industrial families lead back to entrepreneurial performances that "created" a concern which then, for a time, yielded capitalistic surpluses by being merely "administrated" with more or less efficiency? How much statistical truth is there in the slogan: "Three generations from overalls to overalls"? Secondly, what is, as measured by observable results, the economic and cultural, also political, importance of the further fact that, though the entrepreneurial function cannot be transmitted by inheritance, except, possibly, by biological inheritance, the financial or industrial position that has been created can? How much truth is there in the contention that the industrial family interest is, in capitalist society, the guardian of the nation's economic future?

These questions, which could be readily multiplied, have often attracted attention. Every textbook of economic history contains some material about the origins of entrepreneurs of historical standing, and a number of studies have been inspired by full awareness of the importance of the answers for our understanding of capitalist society and of the ways in which it works.[16] But these studies are few and that attention has been desultory. We do not know enough in order to form valid generalizations or even enough to be sure whether there are any generalizations to form. As it is, most of us as economists have some opinions on these matters. But these opinions have more to do with our preconceived ideas or ideals than with solid fact, and our habit of illustrating them by stray instances that have come under our notice is obviously but a poor substitute for serious research. Veblen's—or, for that matter, Bucharin's—*Theory of the Leisure Class* exemplifies well what I mean. It is brilliant and suggestive. But it is an impressionistic essay that does not come to grips with the real problems involved. Yet there is plenty of material. A great and profitable task awaits those who undertake it.

Harvard University   Joseph A. Schumpeter

---

[16] An example is the study by F. J. Marquis and S. J. Chapman on the managerial stratum of the Lancashire cotton industry in the *Journal of the Royal Statistical Society*, LXXV, Pt. III (1912), 293–306.

[2]

THE ECONOMIC JOURNAL

SEPTEMBER, 1928

THE INSTABILITY OF CAPITALISM

I. *Economic Stability under Static Conditions*

§ 1. THE many "instabilities" created by the War and by post-war vicissitudes, whilst very properly engaging the attention of economists in all countries both as to diagnosis and as to remedial policy, do not, in themselves, present to science any new or startling problems. There is nothing strange in the fact that events such as the breakdown of Russia or, generally, disturbances arising from without the sphere of economic life, should affect its structure, its data and its working. In this paper I shall disregard them entirely, and deal merely with the question whether or not the capitalistic system is stable in itself—that is to say, whether or not it would, in the absence of such disturbances, show any tendency towards self-destruction from inherent economic causes, or towards out-growing its own frame. The interest of such an investigation is primarily scientific; still, an answer to that question is not without some diagnostic value, and, therefore, not without some, if remote, bearing upon policy; especially as there is, it seems to me, a marked tendency to reason upon post-war figures and about post-war problems, exactly as if they reflected something like the normal working of our economic system, and to proceed, on this basis, to conclusions about the system as such.

By way of clearing the ground, it may be well, first, to distinguish the kind of stability or instability we propose to discuss, from other phenomena covered by the same terms. Looking, for instance, at France, with her stationary population and enterprise and her vast colonial empire, and at the opposite state of things in Italy, the observer may well have an impression of instability—let us call it, "political" instability—which, however, has nothing to do with economic instability in our sense; for in the economic systems of these countries there might still be perfect stability. Or if we assume a state of things in which the whole of the industry of a country is monopolised by one single firm, we should probably agree in calling such a system unstable in a very obvious sense—let us label the case as one of "social instability"—whilst it could be highly stable economically. Instability in still another sense would obtain in a system, for which equilibrium wages were at a point below what workers will put up with—although there need not be any tendency in the economic conditions themselves to produce any change at all *by the mere working of the system*. Finally, special cases of instability may arise from particular influences from without, which cannot properly be charged to the economic system at all. England's return to the gold standard is a case in point. "Stabilising" the pound at what was, viewed from the standpoint of existing conditions, an artificial value, naturally meant dislocating business, putting a premium on imports and a tax on exports, intensifying losses and unemployment, thereby creating a situation eminently unstable. But this instability is evidently due to the act of politicians, and not to the working of the system which, on the contrary, would have evolved a value of the pound exactly fitting the circumstances. In short, the economic stability we mean, although it *contributes* to stability in other senses, is not *synonymous* with them, nor does it *imply* them. This view must, of course, seem highly superficial to anyone who assumes the existence of as close a relation between the economic and other spheres of social life as, for instance, Marx did. As, however, it would be waste of time to prove to English readers the necessity of separating these several spheres, I may confine myself to these remarks.

Secondly, we have to define what we mean by " our economic system " : We mean an economic system characterised by private property (private initiative), by production for a market and by the phenomenon of credit, this phenomenon being the *differentia specifica* distinguishing the " capitalist " system from other species, historical or possible, of the larger genus defined by the two first characteristics. Although few things seem to me to be more firmly established by historical research than the fact that economic history cannot be divided into epochs corresponding to different systems, it is still permissible to date the *prevalence* of capitalistic methods from about the middle of the eighteenth century (for England), and to call the nineteenth century κατ' ἐξοχήν the time of *competitive*, and what has so far followed, the time of increasingly " *trustified*," or otherwise " organised," " regulated," or " managed," capitalism.

Thirdly, capitalism may be stable or not, simply in the sense that it may be expected to last or not. Its history might be full of the most violent fluctuations or even catastrophes—as it undoubtedly has been so far—and these fluctuations or catastrophes might even be inherent in its working—which precisely is what we want to form an opinion about—and we might still, in a real sense, have to call it " stable " if we have reason to expect it to last. Whenever we mean no more than this—that is to say, when we merely mean to speak of the question of what may be termed the institutional survival of capitalism, we will henceforth speak of the capitalist *order* instead of the capitalist *system*. When speaking of the stability or instability of the capitalist *system*, we shall mean something akin to what business men call stability or instability of business conditions. Of course, mere instability of the " system " would, if severe enough, threaten the stability of the " order," or the " system " may have an inherent tendency to destroy the " order " by undermining the social positions on which the " order " rests.

§ 2. The business man's meaning of stability we have now to translate into the language of theory. It will shorten matters and facilitate exposition if I state at the outset that, barring differences on a number of particular points, the following remarks run entirely on Marshallian lines. But I could equally well call them Walrasian lines. For within serious economic theory there are no such things as " schools " or differences of principle, and the only fundamental cleavage in modern economics is between good work and bad. The basic lines are the same in all lands and in all hands : there are differences in exposition, in the manner—and mannerism—of putting things, for example, according to the relative importance different authors attach, respectively, to rigour and generality or to vicinity to " real life." Then there are differences in technique, the very greatness of Menger, Böhm-Bawerk and Wieser, for example, consisting in their having achieved so much with such shockingly clumsy and primitive tools, the use of which was an insurmountable bar to correctness. There are, furthermore, differences in individual pieces of the analytic machine—as, for example, between the Walrasian and the Marshallian demand curves, or between the rôle assigned to coefficients of production respectively by Marshall and Walras—Pareto—Barone. Finally, there are differences as to particular problems, the most important of which are the theories of interest and of the business cycle. But this is all. There is no difference in fundamentals—Clark's productivity or Walras' equilibrium or the Austrian imputation or Marshall's substitution or Wicksell's compound of Walras and Boehm-Bawerk being all of them in the last analysis the same thing, and all, in spite of appearances to the contrary, equally far removed from, and at the same time and in the same sense descendants of, Ricardo's patchwork.

The economic system in the sense of conditions and processes reduces itself for the purposes of Theory to a system in the scientific sense of the word—a system, that is, of interdependent quantities—variables and parameters—consisting of quantities of commodities, rates of commodities and prices, mutually determining each other. This system has been found to be stable, and its stability to be amenable to rational proof, under static conditions. Not as stable, it is true, as economists would have held sixty years ago, when most of them—nearly all, in fact, except the Marxists—would have most confidently asserted absolute stability both of the capitalist *order* and the capitalist *system :* stability has fared very much as the theory of maximum satisfaction did. Just as newer methods, whilst yielding correct proof of what they left of the competitive maximum, have considerably taken away from its importance, so similarly, whilst showing that we have, generally, as many equations as we have "unknown" quantities, and therefore a determined state of equilibrium corresponding to a given set of certain data which turns out to be stable under appropriate conditions, they have also shown that the exceptions to this general "determinateness" are considerable. Even apart from cases such as the possibility of the offer curve of labour [1] curling back or such as the case of the value of money in a system of bimetallism without legal ratio,[2] we have many instances where equilibrium cannot be said to be determinate. The case where both supply and demand are inelastic, is an example.[3] It may be said, for example, that the

[1] This, of course, does not make equilibrium entirely indeterminate, but only makes the system have several, mostly two, different solutions.

[2] It is worth while emphasising, however, that there is no indeterminateness when two or more commodities circulate as money and every transaction is concluded specifically in one of them. The instability only arises if contracts are in terms of "money" generally, so that payment can be made in any of those commodities.

[3] Another has been pointed out by Wicksell, *Geldwert und Güterpreise :* If coefficients of production be constant and if there be no alternative use for the factors of production—their quantity being, moreover, fixed—then there would be indeterminateness of their shares in the product. Still others have been discussed by Marshall, Edgeworth, Taussig ("Is Market Price Determinate ? " *Quarterly Journal of Economics,* 1921, and Divisia (*Economique rationnelle,* 1928, p. 410: This case of indeterminateness arises only from the absence of any true marginal utility of money. It has been pointed out before by Prof. Cassel, and is, of course, easily remedied.)

home demand for wheat in the United States is highly inelastic within a considerable interval of price. Supply, again, though very variable, is equally inelastic—if it be permitted to apply this term to supply for shortness sake—within intervals of time too short to allow for extension or contraction of acreage; and this may, perhaps, partially explain the instability of American farming.

But although illustrations of this and other cases abound, the determinateness of static equilibrium under competitive conditions is yet a broad basic fact, and this equilibrium is stable, provided that supply price [1]—the price of "willingness to sell"—is an increasing function of quantity of product. This condition rests on the fundamental fact that the extending of production by any given industry means withdrawing quantities of factors of production from increasingly "important" other uses, which, of course, does not show within single firms—any more than the influence on demand price of increasing output shows within the field of action of single firms in a state of pure competition— but is yet the force the balancing of which against decreasing marginal utilities of product determines the distribution of resources between industries. There is, it is true, an interval for practically every industry in which this condition is not satisfied, owing to the tendency which it embodies being over-compensated by fixed costs distributing themselves over an increasing number of units of product. As long as this is the case, there cannot be a point of stable equilibrium.[2] But the

---

[1] The supply price schedule meant here is the series of supply prices at which, given the methods of production actually in use and embodied in given plants and under given general conditions and trade practices, the respective quantities of product would be forthcoming. The schedule, therefore, refers, in an obvious sense, to a point of time. It does not, however, take account of chance occurrences, such as momentary market situations on the one hand; and it does not, on the other hand, take account of any but marginal adjustments, *capable of being decomposed into infinitesimal steps :* so it might be called a short period, normal. But the objections to this would be the implication of the existence of some long-period normal and, besides, the emphasis which this manner of expression lays on the element of time, whilst the important thing is not the lapse of time as such, but what happens during it.

[2] Not even if, in the familiar illustration, the demand curve cut the supply curve negatively. For even then it must be to the interest of every single producer, who *ex hypothesi* neglects the influence of his own action on price, to go on producing in this case. Whilst this lasts, there is *movement* towards equilibrium (and this distinguishes *this* case of "increasing returns" fundamentally from others), but not equilibrium itself. Whilst other cases of the compound called "increasing returns" *vires acquirunt eundo*, and thereby may lead up to a monopoly, this one can hardly do so. It may offer, however, instances of increasing cost for an industry as a whole in the face of the presence of decreasing unit cost in every single firm.

effect of this spends itself necessarily and, therefore, stable equilibrium will nevertheless eventually emerge, although there may, and often will, be a prior instability—instability of the kind which is one of the sources of what is called "overproduction."

Any other cause of "increasing cost" is excluded by the static hypothesis, the justification for accepting such an arrangement being that it separates clearly different sets of phenomena, which stand in need of different treatment. Innovations in productive and commercial methods, in the widest sense of the term—including specialisation and the introduction of production on a scale different from the one which ruled before—obviously alter the *data* of the static system and constitute, whether or not they have to do with "invention," another body of facts and problems. And so does that part of "external economies," which is represented by such instances as the trade journal, the bureau of standards, the "pooling" of reserve stocks of materials incident to the presence of a large market in them and so on. The reader is asked to stay judgment about the exclusion of these things until later. Here it is only necessary to point out that we should have to emphasize the heterogeneous nature of all these phenomena the very moment we included them. In any case we should have to recognise that there is no "law of decreasing cost" of the same kind as, and symmetrical to, the law of increasing cost.[1] The relation of the two can, perhaps, be best seen by means of the analogy with the "demand side"

[1] By law of increasing cost we may mean four things entirely independent of one another : first, we may, as above, mean what is of the very essence of the economic process and, indeed, only another way of stating the law of satiable wants, that the significance of successive doses of means of production must always increase as they are drawn into any one industry for the reason that they are actually or virtually taken away from others. Secondly, we may, as pointed out before, mean that successive doses of any one factor of production applied to a constant quantity of the others yield a decreasing physical increment of product, everything, especially method, remaining the same. The most "practical" way of making use of this proposition is to consider a given plant, embodying both a given method of production and an inelastic set of supplementary costs, and to vary elements of prime cost one at a time. This is perhaps the best tool we have to deal with the routine work of the management of a single firm. It has, however, nothing whatever to do, thirdly, with a community being driven in the process of expansion of production to exploit less and less fertile productive opportunities. This has been well stated in Prof. Sraffa's acute study, "Relazioni fra costo e quantita prodotta," *Annali di Economia*, 1925, epitomised in an article in this Journal, December 1926, and commented on by Prof. Pigou in the issue for June 1927. And, fourthly, there is the prophecy to which Ricardo owes the epithet of pessimist, that improvements (in agriculture) of productive methods will in the long run fail to counterbalance increasing costs in the second and third sense, in case population should keep on increasing.

of the problem. Empirically we evidently could arrive in very many cases at demand curves which would slope upwards instead of down (cp., for example, Prof. Moore's demand-curve for pig iron). And there are, of course, very many similar cases, the special point of interest about the pig-iron curve being the fact that its periodicity is indicative of the business cycle. Nobody, however, thinks less on that account of what is universally considered to be the "true" slope of the theoretic demand curve. Everybody, on the contrary, recognises that what happens in such cases is a shifting—by which term we mean to cover inexactly not only displacement but also distortion—of the theoretic curves, every one of which retains its fundamental characteristic in obedience to the "law" it has been constructed to represent, and that any curve displaying a positive slope is merely a statistical [1] or historical curve fitted through a family of successive theoretic ones. The same applies to—if I be permitted to waive for the sake of shortness the objections to speaking of so doubtful a thing—supply curves. There is only one theoretic supply curve; and it slopes upwards in all cases. Changes of data do not make it slope down, but shift it, or, more correctly, break it off [2] and start a new one. And through these changing positions—in all of which these curves retain their slope and meaning—we may, if we so choose, fit historical curves, which will certainly often slope down. They will, in fact, display

---

[1] The theoretic curve can, of course, be determined statistically without ceasing to be a theoretic curve, the above distinction not turning on the fact, or possibility, of statistical determination, but on whether or not the curve expresses or illustrates a *theorem*, thereby acquiring logical unity as distinguished from what could be termed "descriptional" unity. Now I am far from overrating the importance of this distinction : On the one hand, theory itself is only a way of describing facts; on the other hand, any descriptional unity may, by some progress of analysis, turn into a logical unity any moment—in fact, the frontier between the two continually shifts in the progress of science. But this is no reason for simply ignoring it and for co-ordinating things, which do not stand on the same plane.

[2] This links up with another distinction, the importance of which is best seen by means of an example : Von Böhm-Bawerk's theory of interest stresses the importance of the "roundabout" process of production. But it is not the *running* of production of a given degree of roundaboutness which matters, but *the act of introducing* greater "roundaboutness." There is a drop—in its nature discontinuous, irregular, "unpredictable" and "historically" unique—in costs the moment production starts on the new plan (on *any* successful new plan, no matter whether it involves roundaboutness or not), but there is no further and continuous saving of costs per unit of product in the running of it. Generalising : Changes of *data* may be represented by lines connecting the displaced and distorted theoretic curves. If they are small and frequent, these lines may themselves *look* like our curves. But they never *are* theoretic curves and have not, in this sense, any theoretic meaning.

no regularity at all. It may not even be quite easy, in some cases, to guard against the supreme misfortune of total cost being actually smaller for a greater output than for a lesser one, for changes of *data*, once admitted, would sometimes produce this result, which could not, in competitive circumstances, be handled by assuming that the larger quantity would be produced but partially destroyed.[1]

There is nothing new or startling in thus limiting the scope of this part of our analytic engine. In fact, we are doing no more than to sum up what has been an unmistakable doctrinal tendency ever since it came to be recognised, first, that increasing cost in the sense of decreasing physical response to productive effort applied to a constant quantity of one of the factors is no peculiarity of agriculture, but a general phenomenon—a phenomenon which, given the same conditions, applies to all kinds of production and, given other conditions, does not apply even to agriculture; secondly, that there is a more fundamental tendency at work to make the second derivative of total cost with respect to output positive, and one which has nothing to do with the physical " law of decreasing returns," whence the difficulty of filling certain empty boxes. We are merely clinching, on the one hand, what seems to us to be the true real-cost-phenomenon, and, on the other hand, what seems to us to be both the meaning of economic " statics " and the nature of static equilibrium. That this is perfectly in keeping with the fundamental drift of Marshallian analysis, I will try to show in a footnote.[2]

---

[1] Cf. H. Schultz, "'Theoretical Considerations Relating to Supply," *Journal of Political Economy* for August 29, p. 441. Therefore the assumption $\frac{dy}{dx} > 0$ remains arbitrary, unless reinforced by Cunynghame's criterion $\frac{dy}{dx} > \frac{y}{x}$.

[2] Marshall, indeed, repeatedly protests against the limitations of the static apparatus (cf. especially a letter of his to Prof. John B. Clark). Now if it were true that reasoning by means of it is " too far removed from life to be useful," then the greater part of the analysis of the *Principles* would be useless—as would be the greater part of any exact science : For Marshallian analysis rests just as much on static assumptions as Prof. Clark's structure. But it is not true. There is nothing unduly abstract in considering the phenomena incident to the running of economic life under given conditions taken by themselves. On the contrary, it means giving this class of problems the treatment they require. And Marshall himself has contributed substantially to the perfection of this treatment by forging such invaluable tools as his consumer's surplus and his quasi-rent. He has, furthermore, made use of static assumptions both in his theory of distribution and in the fundamentals of his catallactics; in fact, in one decisive point, when dealing with refinements calling for rigour of analysis, he has confined his argument to increasing cost. And he has, finally, himself insisted on the irreversibility of, and on the difficulties peculiar to, a declining supply curve, and come, in doing so, very near to saying much the same as what has been said above. Loyalty to

§ 3. There seem to be, however, two other sources of instability due to indeterminateness within the precincts of the "static" system. By universal consent, single monopoly yields determined and stable equilibrium, but dual and multiple monopoly, or, generally, the case in which firms can and do take account of their own influence on price, is held, by very high authorities, to fail to do so. Cournot's treatment and the objections raised against it, first by Bertrand and then by Edgeworth, are well known. As this case is not only more important practically than either of the cases of "free, pure or simple" competition on the one hand, and of single monopoly on the other, but also the more general one in a theoretic sense—for the competitive hypothesis is, after all, an additional condition and very much in the nature of a crutch—the breach in our wall seemed a rather serious one. To clear up the matter has been one of the last of the many services Knut Wicksell has rendered to science.[1]

---

tradition, aversion to appearing too "theoretical"—which carried so much weight with him—and that tendency of his, to which we owe so much in other respects, to take short cuts to the problems of practical life, may account for his not taking the final step and for what I cannot but agree with Mr. Keynes in considering the least satisfactory part of his analysis, successfully assailed by Prof. Sraffa. This entailed a string of consequences, but fundamentally what we have said is but a development of a trend overlaid indeed by other things, but yet present in the *Principles*.

We may add the weight of Prof. Pigou's authority. For in the article quoted in a previous note, he excludes, for the sake of "logical coherence" of the cost function, the bulk of those phenomena, which we ourselves propose to exclude for the same reason. He, indeed, even rules out what we have called the fundamental law of cost ($\phi''(x) > 0$). But this he does merely on the technical ground that it is "impossible to construct a cost function" in the event of changes in the relative values of factors of production being liable to occur in consequence of changes in the scale of production of an industry. On the other hand, he does not entirely rule out external economies. But what he retains of them are merely "variations in aggregate costs associated with, and due to, variations in the scale of output" (*l.c.* p. 189); and if we insert, as we must, the word "automatically" in this sentence, very few, if any, cases will be found to answer the criterion, as has been pointed out by Prof. Young (*Quarterly Journal of Economics*, August 1913, p. 678). Of course, expansion and improvement are closely allied in real life. But, as we shall try to explain in the text, the main causation is the one from improvement to expansion and cannot adequately be dealt with by static analysis at all. If this be correct, Prof. Pigou's position will be seen to approach closely the one taken up in the text, if the reader take hold of the fact, that economies, before becoming "external," must generally be internal ones in some firm or firms of the same *or some other* industry.

I do not mean, furthermore, to raise by what I have said objections to the attempts to determine cost functions statistically. On the contrary, I am a humble admirer of the pioneer work done by Prof. H. L. Moore and his followers, even though I beg leave to point out that to speak of "moving equilibria" may prove misleading, in the face of the fact that what really happens is *destruction* of equilibria in the received meaning of this term.

[1] It is with reluctance that I contradict the great shade of Edgeworth. But there seems to be no warrant to assume indeterminateness in the case of what

The simplest form of the second case of what I call "correspective prices" is presented by exchange between two monopolists. It is again Prof. Edgeworth's authority which accounts for well-nigh universal acceptance of the view—first expressed by him in his *Mathematical Psychics*—that there is indeterminateness of price within an interval (on the contract curve) which must in general be considerable. He even went so far as to describe the state of things in a trustified economic world as a "chaos." Here, therefore, is a rich source of instability opened up. Naturally, any theorist might well be tempted to link up what instabilities he sees with this possible explanation of them. Nor can we reply by pointing to the fact that prices fixed

---

Prof. Pigou calls Monopolistic Competition. Taking into consideration the limiting instance only, that of Duopoly, which can be easily generalised, and assuming both competitors to be in exactly the same position, we are, first, faced by the fact that they cannot very well fail to realise their situation. But then it follows that they will hit upon, and adhere to, the price which maximises monopoly revenue for both taken together (as, whatever the price is, they would, in the absence of any preference of consumers for either of them, have to share equally what monopoly revenue there is). The case will not differ from the case of conscious combination—in principle—and be just as determinate. The only other alternative which presents itself in the absence of any hope of driving the competitor out of the market, is best "visualised" by starting from one monopolist controlling the market and then introducing a second one (Cournot's procedure). It is perhaps more "realistic" to assume that the first monopolist will not, as would be to his ultimate advantage, readily surrender half of his market to the newcomer, but that the latter will have to force his way in. And this case is equally determinate, as has been shown by Wicksell in his review article on Prof. Bowley's "Groundwork" (*Ekonomisk Tidskrift*, 1925, and *Archiv für Sozialwissenschaft*, 1927). Taking, as the unit of the price p, that price at which the output would be zero, and, similarly, as the unit of the quantity sold x, that quantity which could be disposed of at the price zero (Edgeworth), we have $p = 1 - x$. A single monopolist would, if there are no costs, maximise px and charge a price of $\frac{1}{2}$, selling $\frac{1}{2}$. The second man, having to face this situation, will obviously maximise *his* output, x, multiplied by price—that is, $x_2 p = x_2 (\frac{1}{2} - x_2)$, and, therefore, sell $\frac{1}{4}$. Whereupon the first will have to readjust *his* output, x_1, and to offer $\frac{3}{8}$ and so on. This finally leads to a limit at the price of $\frac{1}{3}$, when each of the two sell $\frac{1}{3}$, the price being higher and the quantity sold smaller than under competition. There is nothing absurd in this. It cannot be objected that neither of the two competitors is justified in assuming, in deciding on how to adjust his output, that the other will stick to *his*. For no such assumption is really involved, the above argument aiming only at describing the process of *tâtonnement*, out of which the equilibrium price is finally bound to emerge, and things would remain substantially the same if some of the steps were to drop out—just as the equilibrium of perfect competition does not necessarily come about by every one of the theoretical steps of bidding actually taking place in practice. Nor can it be said that the two monopolists would, on reaching what we have called the equilibrium price, try to retrace their steps. For neither of them could do so singly without losing his customers. They could do so only together—the case would become one of single monopoly. The same result has been independently arrived at by Dr. Chamberlin in his *Monopolistic Competition*, as yet unpublished.

by trusts display in many and important instances much less fluctuation than could be expected under competitive conditions; for non-economic forces, pressure of public opinion or fear of government action, for instance, might account for that. And the authority of Prof. Edgeworth has been reinforced by the not less weighty authority of Prof. Pigou.

Now it is perfectly true that there is, in this case, just as in the case of one-sided monopoly, much less *guarantee* of a tendency towards equilibrium prices actually asserting itself. We have much less reason to expect that monopolists will, in either case, charge an equilibrium price, than we have in the case of perfect competition; for competing producers *must* charge it as a rule under penalty of economic death, whilst monopolists, although having a *motive* to charge the monopolistic equilibrium price, are not forced to do so, but may be prevented from doing so by other motives. Furthermore, it is quite true also, that such things as bluffing, the use of non-economic force, a will to force the other party to their knees, have much more scope in the case of two-sided monopoly—just as cut-throat methods have in the case of limited competition—than in a state of perfect competition.

But there is yet more than academic interest in stating that our theory does not break down at this point. Equilibrium is determinate even in this case—even if we take so extreme an instance as a trade union comprising all the workmen of a country, quite sure of the allegiance of its members, capable of preventing immigration from abroad or from other strata of society, and an employers' union similarly constructed. If we assume that each party has a definite monopoly-demand-curve and knows the curve of the other; that each party wants to get the best terms it can—the workmen's union offering varying amounts of labour and providing for those of its members who may have to be kept unemployed—without attempting to attain victories or to inflict defeats; and that the contract is to cover the whole period of account (the "*uno actu*" condition), then the barter point between the parties is perfectly determined, and *not* only the range within which there will be barter. It could be indeterminate only for reasons which would make the case indeterminate also in competition. Nor can it be held that the assumptions alluded to are so very far from reality. They are, if anything, nearer to reality than the assumptions implied in the idea of theoretically perfect competition: It is, for instance, much more common than observers believe whose attention is naturally focussed on abnormal cases, for employers and workmen to meet in precisely the frame of mind assumed, and to view with misgivings all the economic, political and social risks of holding out or of a struggle, which may turn out bad business even in the case of success. By proceeding by way of Walras' *prix crié par hazard* or simply by inspecting the two schedules plotted against one another, our statement will too readily be found to hold good to make it necessary to give formal proof.[1]

§ 4. So there is rather more of stability [2] about the economic system than we should expect on most of the authoritative statements. But how much this amounts to, depends entirely on the nature of that other restriction, which we have introduced alongside of the competitive assumption just discarded : the " static state," which we define both by a distinguishable set of facts and by an analytic apparatus or theoretical point of view. The set of facts consists in the sum of operations which form the essence of the ever-recurring circular process of production and consumption and which make up a self-contained whole. It is no valid objection to say that this process cannot be thought of independently of growth or, generally, change. For it can.

---

[1] The well-known Edgeworthian apparatus commonly used to prove the contrary merely shows that the *elements described by it* do not suffice to determine more than a range. Prof. Bowley in his " Groundwork " reaches, in dealing with the case of one employer and one workman, the result of incompatibility of the respective maxima only by implying that the workman could produce the product by himself. The " Groundwork " contains, however, two most suggestive approaches to the problem of universal monopoly, the one embodied in a note carrying that title, the other leading to the theorem that there is determinateness in the case of *either* the products *or* the factors—but not both of them—being monopolised. Arguments analogous to those of our text seem to show that at least the same sort of determinateness obtains in these cases too.

[2] This stability is of the same nature, and its exact proof of the same value, as the stability of any other exact system. Of course, it is compatible with a large amount of instability in the actual phenomenon. Part of this instability is unimportant, both for theoretical and for practical purposes; another part, whilst practically important, is yet uninteresting in a discussion of principles; still another, however, has, as we shall see, both practical and theoretical importance. None of these groups of cases affects the fundamental importance of exact proof of stability in the sense meant, as would be obvious everywhere except in economics, where the sterility incident to the prevalence of interest in the " practical problem " has yet to be overcome and where scientific refinement is still an opprobrium. But it must be borne in mind that our arrangement excludes all important cases of determined but unstable equilibrium. For the above argument, therefore, and within our meaning of terms, determinateness spells economic stability under static conditions, although, of course, these two things do not coincide logically and always require separate proof. The shortest way to satisfy oneself on this point is by verifying the statement, that of all cases of equilibrium known to Marshallian analysis, only the stable ones remain—apart from chance equilibria which occur during the process of Walrasian *tâtonnement* —for a static theory as above defined. Correct proof of this stability has not been given so far, but does not seem to meet with any great difficulty.

Just as a child's blood circulation, although going on concurrently with its growth or, say, pathological change in its organs, is yet capable of being singled out and dealt with as a distinct real phenomenon, so that fundamental circular process can be singled out and dealt with as a distinct real phenomenon, and *every analyst* [1] *and every business man does so deal with it*—the latter realising that it is one thing to figure out the outlay on, and the income from, a building in given circumstances and another thing to form an idea about the future prospects of the neighbourhood, or that it is one thing to manage an existing building and another to pull it down and replace it by another of a different kind.   Nor is our analogy with the circulation of the blood idle. For the first complete analysis of the static economic process, Quesnay's, was directly inspired by Harvey's discovery.   The analytic apparatus or theoretic point of view of statics is presented by the concept of a determined equilibrium, the use of which, however, is not absolutely confined to the explanation of the circular process, as temporary equilibria occur outside of this process.

Because a set of facts, which form a coherent whole and are, in many cases, capable of statistical separation from the rest, corresponds to static theory, the static state is not merely a methodological device, still less a pedagogical one.   And its range is much widened by the fact that it is not a state of rest.   It is first, of course, no state of absence of motion, as it implies the ever-changing flow of productive services and consumers' goods, although this flow is looked upon as going on under substantially unchanging conditions.   But, secondly, conditions need not be entirely constant.   We can allow seasonal oscillations.   We can also allow, without leaving the precincts of statics, chance variations, provided reaction to them is merely adaptive, in the sense of an adaptation *capable of being brought about by infinitesimal steps*.   And we can, finally, deal with the phenomenon of mere growth of population, of capital and, consequent thereupon, of the National Dividend.   For these changes occur continuously, and adaptation to them is essentially continuous.   They may

[1] Of course, only a minority of economists are aware of the fact.   And some of those who are, spoil the edge of the tool by speaking of a " stationary " state. Some of these, again, construct a state of harmonious progress to occupy the ground between "statics" and what too obviously lies outside of it.   There is no objection to such a construction.   But it is not always recognised that, owing to the fact that it implies consideration of long periods, the "normal," which pertains to it, is much bolder and much more dangerous an abstraction than the static one.

condition discontinuous changes; but they do not, directly and by their mere presence, bring them about. What they do bring about automatically are only variations at the margins.[1] Increase of population, for instance, will, by itself, merely tend to make labour cheaper, and diagnosis of the state of any particular nation in any particular point of time will have to recognise this as a real and distinct element of the situation, however much it may be compensated by other factors. From this it follows that mere growth is not in itself a source of instability of either the System or the Order of Capitalism, within the meaning given to " stability " in this paper. This disposes of some, if not most, theories of " disproportionality," past and present, and gives further help towards " localising " causes of instability.

II. *Stability and Progress*

§ 5. This might very well be all: Economic life, or the economic element in, or aspect of, social life might well be essentially passive and adaptive and *therefore, in itself, essentially stable.* The fact that Reality is full of discontinuous change would be no disproof of this. For such change could without absurdity be explained by influences from without, upsetting equilibria that would, in the absence of such influences, obtain or only shift by small and determined steps along with what we have called continuous growth. We could, of course, even then fit trend lines through the facts succeeding one another historically; but they would merely be expressions of whatever has happened, not of distinct forces or mechanisms; they would be statistical, not theoretical; they would have to be interpreted in terms of particular historic events, such as the opening up of new countries in the nineteenth century, acting on a given rate of growth—and not in terms of the working of an economic mechanism *sui generis.* And if analysis could not detect any purely economic forces within the system making for qualitative and discontinuous change, we

---

[1] Although, therefore, even these influences do not work within a given state of equilibrium and do not tend towards a given centre of gravitation, but displace this centre and propel the economic organism away from the old position, the static apparatus is admirably competent to deal with them. Treatment of such questions has been called " dynamics " by some authorities, foremost among whom was E. Barone. It would, perhaps, be best to drop the terms statics and dynamics altogether. Certainly they are misnomers, when used in the sense given to them in the text, and care should be taken not to think of them by way of analogy with their meanings in mechanics and not to confuse the different meanings attached to them by different writers. All the different meanings, I suppose, lead back to John Stuart Mill, who owes the suggestion to Comte, who, in his turn, expressed indebtedness to the zoologist de Blainville.

should evidently be driven to this conclusion,[1] which can never lack verification, as there are always outside influences to point to, and as a great part of the facts of non-equilibrium must in any case be explained largely on such lines, whether there be a definite piece of non-static mechanism in them or not.

Now it is always unsafe, and it may often be unfair, to attribute to any given author or group of authors clear-cut views of comprehensive social processes, the diagnosis of which must always rest largely on social vision as distinguished from provable argument. For no author or group of authors can help recognising many heterogeneous elements, and it is always easy to quote passages in proof of this. The treatment of the history of the analysis of value, cost and interest affords examples in point,[2] and it must be left to the reader to form his own opinion about the correctness or otherwise of our thus formulating what seems to us to be received doctrine : Industrial expansion, automatically incident to, and moulded by, general social growth—of which the most important purely economic forces are growth of population and of savings—is the basic fact about economic change or evolution or " progress "; wants and possibilities develop, industry expands in response, and this expansion, carrying automatically in its wake increasing specialisation and environmental facilities,

---

[1] As a matter of fact, this is what the position of our highest authorities comes to. It is certainly the position of Ricardo and John Stuart Mill, whose discussion of " progress " mainly turns on the question of relative growth of population and capital, occasionally affected by improvement of methods of production, which they glance at in passing as a disturber of the normal course of things. Such is the position, too, of Walras or, for that matter, of Böhm-Bawerk, who both of them seem convinced that everything of a purely economic nature must needs fit into one homogeneous body of doctrine, which is frankly " static " with Walras, whilst Böhm-Bawerk always rejected the static conception precisely because it excludes some things which yet are undoubtedly "purely economic." John B. Clark is the one outstanding exception, but Marshall, although embracing within his wide horizons every one of the elements essential to a distinct theory of "dynamics," still forced all of them into a frame substantially "static." The present writer believes that some of the difficulties and consequent controversies about Prof. Pigou's argument in his *Economics of Welfare* are traceable to the same source, and his work on *Industrial Fluctuations* is a monument to the view that economic life, in itself essentially passive, is being continually disturbed and propelled by "initial impulses" coming from outside.

[2] Even within the narrower precincts of problems such as these, it has become a fashion—a justified reaction, perhaps, from the opposite vice—to interpret older authors so very broadly as to make them " *see* " everything and *definitely say* nothing, and to frown on another way of stating their views as ungenerous. I submit, however, first that whilst this attitude is the correct one in evaluating individual theorists—provided that the same generous broadness be vouchsafed to all—it is not useful in bringing out characteristics; secondly, that mere " recognition " of a fact means nothing unless the fact be welded into the rest of the argument and made to do theoretic work.

accounts for the rest, changing continuously and organically its own *data*.

Grounds for dissent from this view present themselves on several points, but I am anxious to waive objections in order to make stand out *the* objection. Without being untrue, when taken as a proposition summing up economic history over, say, a thousand years,[1] it is inadequate, or even misleading, when meant to be a description of that mechanism of economic life which it is the task of economic theory to explain, and it is no help towards, but a bar to, the understanding of the problems and phenomena incident to that mechanism. For expansion is *no* basic fact, capable of serving in the rôle of a cause, but is itself the result of a more fundamental " economic force," which accounts both for expansion and the string of consequences emanating from it. This is best seen by splitting up the comprehensive phenomenon of general industrial growth into the expansion of the single industries it consists of. If we do this for the period of predominantly competitive capitalism, we meet indeed at any given time with a class of cases in which both entire industries and single firms are drawn on by demand coming to them from outside and so expanding them automatically; but this additional demand practically always proceeds, as a secondary phenomenon,[2]

[1] Different sets of problems require different distances from the objects of our interest; and different propositions are true from different distances and on different planes of argument. So, *e.g.*, for a certain way of describing historic processes, the presence of a military commander of Napoleonic ability may truly be said to be of causal importance, whilst, for a survey farther removed from details, it may have hardly any importance at all. Our analytic apparatus consists of heterogeneous pieces, every one of which works well on some of the possible " planes " of argument and not at all on others, the overlooking of which is an important, and sometimes the only, source of our controversies.

[2] We may conveniently enumerate, partly anticipating and partly repeating, the more important types of those secondary phenomena, which we hold received opinion, neglecting the primary phenomenon, exclusively deals with, and which would not entirely, but almost entirely, be absent without the primary one.

(1) Expansion of some industries called forth by primary expansion in others, as stated above : If a new concern establishes itself, grocers' businesses will expand in the neighbourhood and so will producers of subsidiary articles. *The expansion of all industries, which do not themselves display any break in their practice during the time under consideration* is to be accounted for thus.

(2) If the primary change results in turning out better tools of production, naturally this will expand the industries which use them. This must be taken account of in judging the comparative success of some State-managed railways surrounded by private industries, which force on them improved engines, fittings, and so on.

(3) Every given change starts from a given environment, and would be impossible without its facilities. But every given environment embodies the results of previous primary change, and, therefore, cannot be taken, except within static theory, as an ultimate datum, acting autonomously, but is itself, in great part, a secondary phenomenon.

from a primary change in some other industry—from textiles first, from iron and steam later, from electricity and chemical industry still later—which does not *follow*, but *creates* expansion. It *first*—and by its initiative—expands its own production, thereby creates an expansion of demand for its own and, contingent thereon, other products, and the general expansion of the environment we observe—increase of population included—is the *result* of it, as may be visualised by taking any one of the outstanding instances of the process, such as the rise of railway transportation. The way by which every one of these changes is brought about lends itself easily to general statement : it is by means of new combinations of existing factors of production, embodied in new plants and, typically, new firms producing either new commodities, or by a new, *i.e.* as yet untried, method, or for a new

(4) So is, in great part, what we have called growth. This is specially clear in the case of saving, the amount of which would be very much smaller in the absence of its most important source, the entrepreneurs' profits. It is also true as to increase of population. And expansion, incident to what would be left of growth in the absence of primary change, would soon be quenched by a (physical) law of decreasing returns acting sharply. *This, then, is the main reason why we think so little of the autonomous—as distinguished from secondary—importance of external economies incident to mere expansion and of what is left of increasing returns,* if we exclude all that is either primarily or secondarily due to the cause we are about to consider.

(5) Industrial evolution inspires collective action in order to force improvement on lethargic strata. Of this kind was, and is, Government action on the Continent for improving agricultural methods of peasants. This is not " secondary " in the sense we mean it, but if it comes to creating external economies by non-economic influence, it has nevertheless been due so far mainly to some previous achievement in some private industry.

(6) Successful primary change is followed by general reorganisation within the same industry, more and more other firms following the lead of some, both because of the profits to be gained and the losses to be feared. During this process, what have at first been the internal economies of the leaders soon become external economies for the rest of the firms, whose behaviour need be no other than one of passive adaptation (and expansion) to what *for them* is environmental advantage. But for us, the observers, to look upon the process as one of adaptation to expanding environment is to miss the salient point.

(7) Incident to all the phenomena glanced at, are, among other things, secondary gains going to all kinds of agents, who do not display any initiative. There is, however, another, a secondary, initiative, stimulated by the possibility of such gains becoming possible—extensions of businesses, speculative transactions and so on, calculated to secure them. The periodic rise and fall of the level of prices—an essential piece, as we shall see, of the mechanism of change in competitive capitalism—carries in its wake extensions and, to finance them, applications for credit merely due to the fact of prices rising, which greatly intensify the phenomenon. And this secondary phenomenon is being as a rule realised much more clearly by observers than the primary phenomenon which gives rise to it.

Our analysis neither overlooks nor denies the importance of these things. On the contrary, it aims at showing their cause and nature. But in a statement of fundamental principles within so short a compass they cannot loom large in the picture.

market, or by buying means of production in a new market. What we, unscientifically, call economic progress means essentially putting productive resources to uses *hitherto untried in practice*, and withdrawing them from the uses they have served so far. This is what we call " innovation."

What matters for the subject of this study is merely the essentially discontinuous character of this process, which does not lend itself to description in terms of a theory of equilibrium. But we may conveniently lead up to this by insisting for the moment on the importance of the difference between this view and what I have called the received one. Innovation, unless it consists in producing, and forcing upon the public, a new commodity, means producing at smaller cost per unit, breaking off the old " supply schedule " and starting on a new one. It is quite immaterial whether this is done by making use of a new invention or not; for, on the one hand, there never has been any time when the store of scientific knowledge had yielded all it could in the way of industrial improvement, and, on the other hand, it is not the knowledge that matters, but the successful solution of the task *sui generis* of putting an untried method into practice—there may be, and often is, no scientific novelty involved at all, and even if it be involved, this does not make any difference to the nature of the process. And we should not only, by insisting on invention, emphasise an irrelevant point—irrelevant to our set of problems, although otherwise, of course, just as relevant as, say, climate—and be thereby led away from the relevant one, but we should also be forced to consider inventions as a case of external economies.[1]

[1] There is another point which arises out of the usual treatment of these things : Nobody can possibly deny the occurrence or relevance of those great breaks in industrial practice which change the data of economic life from time to time. Marshall, therefore, distinguishes these, which he calls " substantive " inventions and which he deals with as chance events acting from outside on the analogy, say, of earthquakes, from inventions which, being of the nature of more obvious applications of known principles, may be expected to arise in consequence of expansion itself. This distinction is insisted upon by Prof. Pigou in the paper quoted above. This view, however, cuts up a homogeneous phenomenon, the elements of which do not differ from one another except by degree, and is readily seen to create a difficulty similar to that of filling the empty boxes. Exactly as the failure to distinguish different processes leads, in the case of the boxes, to a difficulty in distinguishing between groups of facts—and leads, also, to that state of discussion in which some authors hold that most industries display *increasing*, others that most industries display *decreasing*, still others, that normally any industry shows *constant*, returns—so it is obviously impossible to draw any line between those classes of innovations, or, for that matter, inventions ; and the difficulty is not one of judging particular cases, but one of principle. For *no* invention is independent of existing data ; and *no* invention is *so* dependent on them as to be automatically produced by them. In the case of important invention, change in data is great ; in the case of unimportant invention it is small. But this is all, and the *nature* of the process and of the special mechanism set in motion is always the same.

Now this hides part of the very essence of the capitalist process. This kind of external economies—and, in fact, nearly every kind, even the trade journal must, unless the product of collective action, be somebody's business—characteristically comes about by first being taken up by one firm or a few—by acting, that is, as an internal economy. This firm begins to undersell the others, part of which are thereby definitely pushed into the background to linger there on accumulated reserves and quasi-rents, whilst another part copies the methods of the disturber of the peace. *That* this is so, we can see every day by looking at industrial life; it is precisely what goes on, what is missing in the static apparatus and what accounts both for dissatisfaction with it and for the attempts to force such phenomena into its cracking frame— instead of, as we think it natural to do, recognising and explaining this as a distinct process going on along with the one handled by the static theory. *Why* this is so, is a question which it would lead very far to answer satisfactorily. Successful innovation is, as said before, a task *sui generis*. It is a feat not of intellect, but of will. It is a special case of the social phenomenon of leadership.[1] Its difficulty consisting in the resistances and un-

---

[1] This does not imply any glorification. Leadership itself does not mean only such aptitudes as would generally command admiration, implying, as it does, narrowness of outlook in any but one direction and a kind of force which sometimes it may be hardly possible to distinguish from callousness. But economic leadership has, besides, nothing of the glamour some other kinds of leadership have. Its intellectual implications may be trivial; wide sympathies, personal appeal, rhetorical sublimation of motives and acts count for little in it; and although not without its romance, it is in the main highly unromantic, so that any craving for personal hero-worship can hardly hope for satisfaction where, among, to be sure, other types, we meet with slave-trading and brandy-producing puritans at the historic threshold of the subject.

Apart from this source of possible objections, there is a much more serious one in the mind of every well-trained economist, whom experience has taught to think little of such intrusions into theory of views savouring of sociology, and who is prone to associate any such things with a certain class of objections to received doctrine, which continually turn up however often they may have been refuted— sublimely ignorant of the fact—such as objections to the economic man, to marginal analysis, to the use of the barter hypothesis and so on. The reader may, I think, satisfy himself that no want of theoretic training is responsible for statements which I believe to tally fundamentally with Marshallian analysis.

No difficulty whatever arises as to verification. That new commodities or new qualities *or new quantities* of commodities are forced upon the public by the initiative of entrepreneurs—which, of course, does not affect the rôle of demand within the static process—is a fact of common experience; that one firm or a small group of firms leads in the sense meant above, in the process of innovation, thereby creating its own market and giving impulse to the environment generally, is equally patent (and we do not deny facts of other complexion—the secondary or " consequential " ones); and all we are trying to do is to fit the analytic apparatus to take account of such facts without putting its other parts out of gear.

certainties incident to doing what has not been done before, it is accessible for, and appeals to, only a distinct type which is rare. Whilst differences in aptitude for the routine work of " static " management only result in differences of success in doing what every one does, differences in this particular aptitude result in only some being able to do this particular thing at all. To overcome these difficulties incident to change of practice is the function characteristic of the entrepreneur.

Now if this process meant no more than one of many classes of " friction," it certainly would not be worth our while to dissent from the usual exposition on that account, however many facts might come under this heading. But it means more than this : Its analysis yields the explanation of phenomena which cannot be accounted for without it. There is, first, the " entrepreneurial " function as distinct from the mere " managerial " function—although they may, and mostly must, meet one another in the same individual—the nature of which only shows up within the process of innovation. There is, secondly, the explanation of entrepreneurs' gain, which emerges in this process and otherwise gets lost in the compound of " earnings of management,"[1] the treating of which as a homogeneous whole is unsatisfactory for precisely the same reason which, by universal consent, makes it unsatisfactory so to treat, say, the income of a peasant tilling his own soil, instead of treating it as a sum of wages, rent, quasi-rent and, possibly, interest. Furthermore, it is *this* entrepreneurs' profit which is the primary source of industrial fortunes, the history of every one of which consists of, or leads back to, successful acts of innovation.[2] And as the rise and

[1] The function in question being a distinct one, it does not matter that it appears in practice rarely, if ever, by itself. And whoever cares to observe the behaviour of business men at close quarters will not raise the objection that new things and routine work are done, as a rule, indiscriminately by the same manager. He will find that routine work is done with a smoothness wholly absent as soon as a new step is to be taken, and that there is a sharp cleavage between the two, insuperable for a very worthy type of manager. This extends far into the realm of what we are wont to consider as automatic change, bringing about external economies and increasing returns. Take the instance of a business letting out motor cars on the principle " drive yourself." A mere growth of the neighbourhood, sufficient to make such a business profitable, does not produce it. Someone has to realise the possibility and to found the firm, to get people to appreciate its services, to get the right type of cars and so on. This implies solution of a legion of small problems. Even if such a firm already exists and further environmental growth make discontinuous extension feasible, the thing to be done is not so easy as it looks. It would be easy for the trained mind of a leading industrialist, but it is not so for a typical member of the stratum which does such business.

[2] It is, as has been said in a previous note, not the *running* of a business according to new plan, but the act of *getting it* to run on a new plan, which accounts

decay of industrial fortunes is *the* essential fact about the social structure of capitalist society, both the emergence of what is, in any single instance, an essentially temporary gain, and the elimination of it by the working of the competitive mechanism, obviously are more than " frictional " phenomena, as is that process of underselling by which industrial progress comes about in capitalist society and by which its achievements result in higher real incomes all round.

Nor is this all. This process of innovation in industry by the agency of entrepreneurs supplies the key to all the phenomena of capital and credit. The rôle of credit would be a technical and a subordinate one in the sense that everything fundamental about the economic process could be explained in terms of goods, if industry grew by small steps along coherent curves. For in that case financing could and would be done substantially by means of the current gross revenue, and only small discrepancies would need to be smoothed. If we simplify by assuming that the whole circular process of production and consumption takes exactly one period of account, no instruments or consumers' goods surviving into the next, capital—defined as a monetary concept—and income would be exactly equal, and only different phases of one and the same monetary stream. As, however, innovation, being discontinuous and involving considerable change and being, in competitive capitalism, typically embodied in new firms, requires large expenditure previous to the emergence of any revenue, credit becomes an essential element of the process. And we cannot turn to savings in order to account for the existence of a fund from which these credits are to flow. For this would imply the existence of previous profits, without which there would not be anything like the required amount—even as it is, savings usually lag behind requirements—and assuming previous profits would mean, in an explanation of principles, circular reasoning. " Credit-creation," therefore, becomes an essential part both of the mechanism of the process and of the theory explaining it.

---

for entrepreneurs' profits, and makes it so undesirable to try to express them by " static " curves, which describe precisely the phenomena of the " running " of it. The theoretical reason for our proposition is, that either competition or the process of imputation must put a stop to any " surplus " gain, even in a case of monopoly, in which the value of the patent, the natural agent or of whatever else the monopoly position is contingent on, will absorb the return in the sense that it will no longer be profit. But there is also a " practical " observation to support this view. No firm ever yields returns indefinitely, if only run according to unchanged plan. For everyone comes the day when it will cease to do so. And we all of us know that type of industrial family firm of the third generation which is on the road to that state, however conscientiously it may be " managed."

Hence, saving, properly so called, turns out to be of less importance than the received doctrine implies, for which the continuous growth of saving—accumulation—is a mainstay of explanation. Credit-creation is the method by which the putting to new uses of existing means of production is brought about through a rise in price enforcing the " saving " of the necessary amount of them out of the uses they hitherto served (" enforced savings "—cp. Mr. Robertson's " imposed lacking ").

Finally, it cannot be said that whilst all this applies to individual firms, the development of whole industries might still be looked at as a continuous process, a comprehensive view " ironing out " the discontinuities which occur in every single case. Even then individual discontinuities would be the carriers of essential phenomena. But, besides, for a definite reason that is not so. As shown both by the typical rise of general prices and the equally typical activity of the constructional trades in the prosperity phase of the business cycle, innovations cluster densely together. So densely, in fact, that the resultant disturbance produces a distinct period of adjustment—which precisely is what the depression phase of the business cycle consists in. *Why* this should be so, the present writer has attempted to show else-where.[1] *That* it is so, is the best single verification and justi-fication of the view submitted, whether we apply the criterion of its being " true to life " or the criterion of its yielding explanation of a phenomena *not itself implied in its fundamental principle*.

If, then, the putting to new uses of existing resources is what " progress " fundamentally consists in; if it is the nature of the entrepreneur's function to act as the propelling force of the process; if entrepreneur's profits, credit, and the cycle prove to be essential parts of its mechanism—the writer even believes this to be

---

[1] " Theorie der wirtschaftlichen Entwicklung," 1911, 2nd ed. 1926. Cp. also " The Explanation of the Business Cycle," *Economica*, 1927. The failure of the price-level to rise in the United States during the period 1923–1926 will be seen to be no objection but a further verification of this theory. It has, however, been pointed out to the writer, by a very high authority, that prices did also fail to rise in the United States in the prosperity immediately preceding the War. It could be replied that the factors which account for the stability 1923–1926 had been active already before the War. But the U.S. Bureau of Labour figures for 1908–1913 are 91, 97, 99, 95, 101, 100. Cp. also Prof. Persons' chart in *Review of Economic Statistics*, Jan. 1927. It may be well to mention that constructional trades and their materials need not necessarily show their activity fully by *every* index. Iron, *e.g.*, being an international commodity, need not rise in price if the phases of the cycle do not quite coincide in different countries. As a matter of fact, they generally do. But the right way to deal with iron and steel is to use the Spiethoff index (production + imports − exports), and this has, so far, always worked satisfactorily.

true of interest—then industrial expansion *per se* is better described as a consequence than as a cause; and we should be inclined to turn the other way round what we have termed the received chain of causation. In this case, and as those phenomena link up so as to form a coherent and self-contained logical whole, it is obviously conducive to clearness to bring them out boldly; to relegate to one distinct body of doctrine the concept of equilibrium, the continuous curves and small marginal variations, all of which, in their turn, link up with the circuit flow of economic routine under constant data; and to build, alongside of this, and *before* taking account of the full complexity of the " real " phenomenon— secondary waves, chance occurrences, " growth " and so on—a theory of capitalist change, assuming, in so doing, that non- economic conditions or data are constant and automatic and gradual change in economic conditions is absent. But there is no difficulty in inserting all this. And it would seem to follow that the organic analogy is less adapted to express faithfully the nature of the process than many of us think; although, of course, being a mere analogy, it may be so interpreted as not to imply anything positively wrong and as to avoid the idea of an equilibrium growth *ad instar* of the growth of a tree, which it may, but need not necessarily, suggest.

Summing up the argument and applying it to the subject in hand, we see that there is, indeed, one element in the capitalist process, embodied in the type and function of the entrepreneur, which will, *by its mere working and from within*—in the absence of all outside impulses or disturbances and even of " growth "— destroy any equilibrium that may have established itself or been in process of being established; that the action of that element is not amenable to description by means of infinitesimal steps; and that it produces the cyclical " waves " which are essentially the form " progress " takes in competitive capitalism and could be discovered by the theory of it, if we did not know of them by experience. But by a mechanism at work in, and explaining the features of, periods of depression, a new equilibrium always emerges, or tends to emerge, which absorbs the results of innovation carried out in the preceding periods of prosperity. The new elements find their equilibrium proportions; the old ones adapt themselves or drop out; incomes are rearranged; prosperity inflation is corrected by automatic self-deflation through the repayment of credits out of profits, through the new consumers' goods entering the markets and through saving stepping into the place of " created " credits. So the instabilities, which arise from the process of innovation, tend to right themselves, and do not go on accumulating. And we may phrase the result we reach in our terminology by saying that there is, though instability of the *System*, no economic instability of the *Order*.

§ 6. The instability due to what we conceive to be the basic factor of purely economic change is, however, of very different importance in the two historic types of capitalism, which we have distinguished.

Innovation in competitive capitalism is typically embodied in the foundation of new firms—the main lever, in fact, of the rise of industrial families; improvement is forced on the whole branch by the processes of underselling and of withdrawing from them their means of production, workmen and so on shifting to the new firms; all of which not only means a large amount of disturbance as an incident, but is also effective in bringing about the result, and to change " internal " economies into " external " ones, only *as far as* it means disturbance. The new processes do not, and generally cannot, evolve out of the old firms, but place themselves side by side with them and attack them. Furthermore, for a firm of comparatively small size, which is no power on the money market and cannot afford scientific departments or experimental production and so on, innovation in commercial or technical practice is an extremely risky and difficult thing, requiring supernormal energy and courage to embark upon. But as soon as the success is before everyone's eyes, everything is made very much easier by this very fact. It can now, with much-diminished difficulty, be copied, even improved upon, and a whole crowd invariably does copy it—which accounts for the leaps and bounds of progress as well as for setbacks, carrying in their wake not only the primary disturbance, inherent to the process, but a whole string of secondary ones and *possibilities*, although no more than possibilities, of recurrent catastrophes or crises.

All this is different in " trustified " capitalism. Innovation is, in this case, not any more embodied *typically* in new firms, but goes on, within the big units now existing, largely independently of individual persons. It meets with much less friction, as failure in any particular case loses its dangers, and tends to be carried out as a matter of course on the advice of specialists. Conscious policy towards demand and taking a long-time view towards investment becomes possible. Although credit creation still plays a rôle, both the power to accumulate reserves and the direct access to the money market tend to reduce the importance of this element in the life of a trust—which, incidentally, accounts for the phenomenon of prosperity coexisting with stable, or nearly stable, prices which we have had the opportunity of witnessing in the United States 1923–1926. It is easy to see that the three causes alluded to, whilst they accentuated the waves in competitive, must tend to soften them down in trustified, capitalism. Progress becomes " automatised," increasingly impersonal and decreasingly a matter of leadership and individual initiative. This amounts to a fundamental change in many respects, some of which reach far out of the sphere of things economic. It means the passing out of existence of a system of selection of leaders which had the unique characteristic that success in *rising* to a position and success in *filling* it were essentially the same thing —as were success of the firm and success of the man in charge— and its being replaced by another more akin to the principles of appointment or election, which characteristically divorce success of the concern from success of the man, and call, just as political elections do, for aptitudes in a candidate for, say, the presidency of a combine, which have little to do with the aptitudes of a good president. There is an Italian saying, "Who enters the conclave as prospective pope, will leave it as a cardinal," which well expresses what we mean. The types which rise, and the types which are kept under, in a trustified society are different from what they are in a competitive society, and the change is spreading rapidly to motives, stimuli and styles of life. For our purpose, however, it is sufficient to recognise that the only fundamental cause of instability inherent to the capitalist system is losing in importance as time goes on, and may even be expected to disappear.

§ 7. Instead of summing up a very fragmentary argument, I wish to emphasise once more, in concluding, that no account whatsoever has been taken of any but purely economic facts and problems. Our diagnosis is, therefore, no more sufficient as a basis for prediction than a doctor's diagnosis to the effect that a man has no cancer is a sufficient basis for the prediction that he will go on living indefinitely. Capitalism is, on the contrary, in so obvious a process of transformation into something else, that it is not the fact, but only the interpretation of this fact, about which it is possible to disagree. Towards this interpretation I have wished to contribute a negative result. But it may be well, in order to avoid misunderstanding, to state expressly what I believe would be the positive result of a more ambitious diagnostic venture, if I may presume to do so in one short and imperfect sentence: Capitalism, whilst economically stable, and even gaining in stability, creates, by rationalising the human mind, a mentality and a style of life incompatible with its own fundamental conditions, motives and social institutions, and will be changed, although not by economic necessity and probably even at some sacrifice of economic welfare, into an order of things which it will be merely matter of taste and terminology to call Socialism or not.

JOSEPH SCHUMPETER

University of Bonn.

[3]

Schumpeter's *Business Cycles* Revisited

Christopher Freeman

Introduction

Nineteen eighty-nine marked the fiftieth anniversary of Schumpeter's *Business Cycles* (1939). It seems probable that Schumpeter thought of this, at least before publication, as his magnum opus. In fact, he himself made a direct comparison between the brilliant first vision of young creative economists and its full-scale mature elaboration in a major scholarly work. For Marx this first vision was the *Communist Manifesto* and the massive work of maturity was of course *Das Kapital*. For Keynes, Schumpeter was of the opinion that the *Economic Consequences of the Peace* was the work of young genius and the *General Theory* corresponded to *Das Kapital* (Elliott 1985).

There is general agreement that the *Theory of Economic Development* (1912) by the twenty-eight-year-old Schumpeter represented a brilliant contribution to economic theory although he had already published another book on economic theory (Schumpeter 1908). Publication of the *Theory of Economic Development* established Schumpeter's reputation as a wunderkind and enfant terrible of the Austrian economics profession. Although English and Japanese translations came only with considerable delay, this book also established his international reputation, opening the way for his later appointments as Professor of Economics in Bonn (1926) and Harvard (1930). As early as 1914 he had been invited to be Visiting Professor at Columbia University.

Business Cycles was of course also immediately recognized, at least in the United States, as a major contribution to business cycle theory and more generally to economic theory and was accorded a major review article by Kuznets (1940) in the *American Economic Review*. Schumpeter's work was often controversial and this was as true of his later work as of his earlier work. Yet, half a century later it certainly cannot be said that *Business Cycles* occupies a place in the history of economic thought comparable to the major works of Marx, Keynes, Marshall, or Walras, or even other works by Schumpeter himself.

18   Evolving Technology and Market Structure

The ambitious scope of the book is evident from the full title: *Business Cycles: A Theoretical, Historical, and Statistical Analysis of the Capitalist Process* and its two volumes, comprising more than a thousand pages, bear further witness to the magnitude of the enterprise. Schumpeter always regarded business cycles not as a sideline or a specialty, but as the major manifestation of his theory of economic development in capitalist economies. In the *Theory of Economic Development* he had included a chapter on business cycles that foreshadowed his later work. Moreover, although he greatly admired Marx's intellectual achievement and gave him credit for being one of the first theorists to recognize cycles and address these problems, he nevertheless chided Marx for supposedly failing to develop any systematic theoretical explanation of crises and for holding an eclectic view embracing many possible causes (Schumpeter 1939, 36–39). There is little doubt, therefore, that Schumpeter regarded *Business Cycles* as one of his most important contributions to economics, if not *the* most important.

Schumpeter remains the rogue elephant among twentieth-century economists and although he has commanded the respect of the profession, he certainly has not won its allegiance. Whereas some elements of his theory have earned a place at the center of economic debate, such as his ideas on concentration or on technological competition, it would still be difficult to make this claim for his business cycle theory.

This may, of course, simply be due to the myopic attitudes of much of the profession and to the continuing neglect of structural change. Even the central point of his whole lifework—that capitalism can only be understood as an evolutionary process of continuous innovation and "creative destruction"—is still not taken to the bosom of mainstream theory, although many now pay lip service to it. It is also true that after a long period of relative neglect, Schumpeter's *Business Cycles* is the subject of renewed interest in the 1980s. This can be verified by looking at the pattern of borrowing the book in almost any university library, or, more elaborately, by citation analysis of new books, or by looking at the explosion of international conferences on the subject of long cycles in which Schumpeter's theories are among the most conspicuous. The book was reprinted for the first time in 1982 although an abridged edition was published in 1964. So it may be that it is only a matter of time before the merits of the work are much more widely recognized, and that it will come to occupy a more central place in the history of economic thought.

However, it will be argued in this paper that, although Schumpeter was unlucky in the timing of the publication and certainly faced lack of receptivity for most of his major ideas, there were also some weaknesses in the book itself which have contributed to its relative lack of success. It is not necessary in a meeting of the Schumpeter Society to make any apology for a critical assessment of some of Schumpeter's main ideas, for this was indeed the spirit of his own work and was one of his main characteristics. Particularly in

Business Cycles, Schumpeter insisted that his ideas were a first approximation and that he hoped that others would verify and criticize them in the light of further evidence. Few have accepted this invitation but this paper may be regarded as one belated acceptance.

Background Aspects of "Business Cycles"

It is often said (e.g., Elliott 1985) that Schumpeter was unfortunate in the timing of the publication of *Business Cycles.* It appeared just at the outbreak of World War II in 1939, and three years after the publication of Keynes's *General Theory.* This meant that the professional debate on *Business Cycles* was largely dominated by Keynesian ideas at the time the book appeared. The war itself, while it provided greatly increased opportunities for the testing, dissemination, and application of Keynesian ideas, had no apparent relevance to Schumpeter's theories, and his book at first attracted little attention outside the United States.

This situation was aggravated by Schumpeter's stance on the issue of policy advice. While he accepted the need for this and, indeed, had himself been a Minister of Finance in Austria and had occupied various positions in the commercial world, he nevertheless drew a very sharp line between "scientific" work and economic policy-making. He did not move as easily as Keynes between the academic world and the world of policy-making throughout his life. Moreover, he disapproved of the efforts made by Keynes and others for popular dissemination of their ideas.

However, it was not simply a question of a different approach to the role of the academic in political life. Schumpeter *had* an ideological position that he *did* disseminate, although in a very different way from Keynes (Shionoya 1986). The difference lay in the fundamental approach to the business cycle. Whereas, even before World War I, Keynes was actively interested in policies for the social management of investment and for counteracting the depressive phase of the cycle, Schumpeter fundamentally regarded the business cycle as a natural and indeed healthy phenomenon, and as the normal mode of growth and development which should take its course. It is true that he modified this position a little in the 1930s when he developed his distinction between recession and depression further. Nevertheless, paradoxically he believed in the self-adjusting mechanism of the market over the long term in a way which Keynes did not. As we shall see, his commitment to Walrasian general equilibrium theory was not simply a mode of exposition or a way of making his ideas more palatable to his colleagues (a "parable" in Samuelson's description), but remained a central part of his theoretical apparatus throughout his life despite its apparent inconsistency with his theories of innovation and development.

Consequently, it was not just a question of "bad luck" during the 1930s.

20   Evolving Technology and Market Structure

Schumpeter took the position of the detached academic partly because he did
not think that there was very much that should be done about the depression
or, indeed, could be done. Keynes took the position of the scourge of laissez-
faire theories because he thought that there was a great deal which could be
done and should be done to counteract depressive forces in the British economy and in the world economy.

As early as the 1920s Keynes argued that:

> The world is *not* so governed from above that private and social interest
> always coincide. It is *not* so managed here below that in practice they
> coincide. It is *not* a correct deduction from the Principles of economics
> that enlightened self-interest generally *is* enlightened; more often indi-
> viduals seeking separately to promote their ends are too ignorant or too
> weak to attain even these.

In 1934 his BBC broadcast was even more explicit:

> On the one side are those who believe that the existing economic system
> is, in the long run, a self-adjusting mechanism, though with creaks and
> groans and jerks and interrupted by the time lags, outside interference
> and mistakes . . . on the other side of the gulf are those who reject the
> idea that the existing economic system is, in any significant sense, self-
> adjusting. . . . I range myself with the heretics. (quoted in Eatwell
> 1982)

Paradoxically, despite his own even stronger reputation as a heretic,
Schumpeter was in some respects closer to the "self-adjusting" school, although he believed that the equilibrating mechanism operated through cycles
of varying length.

Lack of immediate political applications would not in itself have prevented Schumpeter's theory of business cycles from becoming more influential, if the central ideas had proved themselves in the long term. Indeed,
whereas Keynesian theories dominated the stage for thirty years after World
War II, there has been a new wave of criticism of Keynesian theory in the
1970s and 1980s. Moreover, the slowdown in the world economy and the
resurgence of large-scale structural unemployment might reasonably be held
to vindicate at least some of Kondratiev's and Schumpeter's ideas about long
waves.

If the test of a theory in the social sciences is held to be predictive power,
then long cycle theories emerge from this test better than most other theories if
applied to the development of the world economy from 1948 to 1988.

And indeed, as has already been stated, there has been a resurgence of
interest in Schumpeter's theory of business cycles. Nevertheless, the accep-

tance of his ideas is still hindered by the mode of presentation in his book and, as I shall maintain, primarily by weaknesses in his basic theory. It is not just a question of style, although *Business Cycles* was not a well written book. The history of economic thought has conclusively shown that it is possible to write even longer and more indigestible books than *Business Cycles,* which nonetheless are influential both inside and outside the profession.

Nor is it just a question of statistics. The debate on the statistical evidence for long cycles is likely to continue indefinitely. Despite the best efforts of economic historians, the evidence for the first and second cycles is bound to remain weak and controversial and relates, in any case, mainly to one country. Schumpeter anticipated and answered critics such as Weinstock (1964) or more recently Solomon (1986) who maintain that aggregative statistical time series do not consistently demonstrate the existence of long cycles.

Schumpeter pointed out that his theory was concerned with the *qualitative* changes in the structure of the economy and that aggregative long time series could often obscure, rather than conceal, these changes:

> Since the development generated by the economic system is "cyclical" by nature, the task to be accomplished goes far beyond the description of spectacular breakdowns on the one hand, and of the behavior of aggregate quantities on the other, into the formidable one of describing in detail the industrial processes behind them. Historians of crises primarily talk about stock exchange events, banking, price level, failures, unemployment, total production and so on—all of which are readily recognised as surface phenomena or as compounds which sum up underlying processes in such a way as to hide their real features. (1939, 221)

In my view, Schumpeter cannot be faulted for this approach and for concentrating attention on this underlying explanation of the spring tides and ebb tides of economic development. As van der Zwan (1979) has pointed out, there have been periods of deep structural adjustment in the 1830s, 1880s, 1930s (and 1980s) which were regarded at the time and by historians since, as unusually difficult times for the economy. These periods cannot be treated in just the same way as the minor recessions of the 1950s and the 1960s or similar recessions in other periods of high boom, such as the 1850s and 1860s or the 1890s to 1913. Nor can the sense of these long boom periods as belles epoques or golden ages of growth be dismissed as collective self-deception because our untidy, uneven, and imperfect measures of aggregate growth do not always conform to the ideal requirements of some statisticians.

The criticisms of Schumpeter's *Business Cycles* that follow therefore do not refer to this "statistical" critique, nor to matters of style or presentation, but to fundamental concepts i.e., first to his theory of innovation and entrepreneurship and second to his theory of equilibrium.

Schumpeter's Theory of Innovation

It might seem strange to start by criticizing Schumpeter's concept of innovation and entrepreneurship which was, after all, his most distinctive contribution to economics generally and not only to the theory of business cycles.
There is no disagreement with his insistence that innovation incessantly revolutionizes the economic structure and that "this process of creative destruction
is the essential fact about capitalism" (1943, 83).

What is at issue is not this part of his vision, which does indeed give him
a unique position among twentieth-century economists. The problem lies
rather in the somewhat schematic and abstract generalizations about innovation and diffusion which predominate in his basic theory of business cycles,
although much less so in the historical sections. This abstract, "pure theory"
of innovation is closely related to his theory of entrepreneurship since an
entrepreneur is defined as the individual responsible for an innovation. His
theories both of innovation and of entrepreneurship were carried over directly
from the *Theory of Economic Development*.

In some ways Schumpeter's definition of innovation was a broad one. He
included not only technical innovations, but organizational and managerial
innovations, new markets, new sources of supply, financial innovations, and
new combinations. There are passages in *Business Cycles* where he appears to
accept the introduction of a new product into another country or another
region as *innovation* (1939, 374) rather than *imitation,* although elsewhere he
is dismissive of imitators as mere routine managers rather than genuine
entrepreneurs.

But, despite the breadth of his definition and the occasional extension of
the concept to some aspects of diffusion, his conceptualization of innovation
was, in other ways, very limited. He scarcely discussed the origins of innovation, had virtually nothing to say about the interactions of science and technology, and largely neglected the cumulative nature of technology, despite his
earlier recognition (1928) of the role of industrial R&D departments in large
corporations. He substituted a theory of entrepreneurship for a theory of the
firm and for a theory of innovation. It is almost as though his vision of
innovation and entrepreneurship was frozen at the level of the first formulation
in *Theory of Economic Development* in 1912. Shionoya was justified in criticizing this formulation for failing to explain the circumstances that determine
innovation and for his comment that "innovation remained an exogenous
factor to the economic system despite his contrary assertion" (1986). Ruttan
put the matter more bluntly when he said:

> Neither in *Business Cycles* nor in Schumpeter's other work is there
> anything that can be identified as a theory of innovation. The business

cycle in Schumpeter's system is a direct consequence of the appearance of clusters of innovations. But no real explanation is provided as to why innovations appear in clusters or why the clusters possess the particular types of periodicity which Schumpeter identified. (1959)

Instead of discussing the circumstances that may encourage or hinder innovations and why they cluster together, Schumpeter simply insists that they are the product of supernormal individuals with exceptional intelligence and energy. Innovation is described as an act of will rather than of intellect. While there is certainly an element of truth in Schumpeter's perception of the exceptional difficulties facing many innovators and the exceptional persistence that is often needed to see them through, this conceptualization is lacking in depth and, surprisingly, in historical perspective. Moreover, it leads to relative neglect of some of the elements that are actually essential for a satisfactory theory of the business cycle itself: the interdependence of many innovations both technologically and economically and the existence of technological trajectories. It also leads to a relative neglect of incremental innovations, which are less obviously the product of heroic entrepreneurship but whose cumulative effect is nevertheless extraordinarily important. Finally, it fails to focus attention on the specific features of each new wave of technical change, which are supposedly the driving forces of each long cycle of economic development.

These are harsh comments but it was these weaknesses that led Kuznets (1940) and others to make two basic criticisms of Schumpeter's *Business Cycles* to which he had no adequate response:

1. Which innovations were so big in their scale that they could possibly drive the cycles of the entire world economy? There are myriad innovations every year. Surely some theory of the clustering of innovations is necessary to relate innovations to major waves of investment and long cycles of development.
2. Why should a long cycle last about half a century? If it is entrepreneurial energy that drives the whole system, do the heroic entrepreneurs get tired every fifty years?

The answer to the first criticism is actually *implicit* in much that Schumpeter wrote in *Business Cycles* and *Capitalism, Socialism, and Democracy* and in some passages it is also explicit as, for example, in the following:

When some innovation has been successfully carried into effect, the next wave is much more likely to start in the same or a neighboring field than anywhere else. Major innovations hardly ever emerge in their final form

24   Evolving Technology and Market Structure

or cover in one throw the whole field that will ultimately be their own. The railroadization, the electrification, the motorization of the world are instances. (1939, 167)

But, although in this and other passages there is the embryo of a full-fledged theory of the long-term diffusion of interdependent clusters of technical and organizational innovations, elsewhere the approach is far more discursive and resembles a listing of various scattered innovations, rather than a more systematic account of constellations of technologically, economically, and socially interrelated innovations, connected by cumulative advances in science, technology, and knowledge accumulation in specific types of firms and in leading sectors.

To the best of my knowledge it was not until he wrote *Capitalism, Socialism, and Democracy* that Schumpeter used the expression "gales of creative destruction," and it was in *Capitalism, Socialism, and Democracy,* too, that he spoke of "successive industrial revolutions," an expression which, in my view, best conveys the pervasive nature of the changes in technology and in business organization that characterize each Kondratiev cycle. In *Business Cycles* he does use the expression "industrial revolution" both to describe the first Kondratiev wave in eighteenth-century Britain and to characterize the changes in the third Kondratiev cycle, but he does not develop the concept systematically in either case.

This failure may be attributed partly to the fact that he was actually far more interested in the financial side of business cycles than in the technology. Only about a hundred pages out of the thousand pages in the book deal primarily with inventions and innovations. But this was not the main problem. More important was his preoccupation with the individual entrepreneur and the individual innovation, and his reluctance to conceptualize invention, innovation, and technology accumulation as a social process. This is related to his theory of diffusion with its sharp distinction between truly original entrepreneurs and routine managers and imitators.

Schumpeter's Theory of Entrepreneurship

Schumpeter's threefold distinction between invention, innovation, and diffusion of innovations has been widely adopted by economists and there is no doubt that it has been analytically valuable. It is essential to distinguish between the original idea for a new product or process (which may often be patented) and the translation of this idea into a commercially realizable innovation. The capacity of an enterprise to design, develop, produce, and market a new product is *not* identical with inventive activities, nor do the two activities necessarily coexist in the same organization. Schumpeter's insistence on this point was a major contribution to the understanding of innovation, even though there is an important overlap and interaction between inventive and innovative activities, and the very process of design, development, production, and marketing may often give rise to further inventions.

Similarly, in the case of the distinction between innovation and the diffusion of innovations. There *is* a difference between the very first commercial introduction of a new product or process and the subsequent process of diffusion (or "swarming" as Schumpeter so aptly named it). But again this distinction can be overdone. Rosenberg (1976) has consistently emphasized that the process of diffusion is seldom if ever a simple process of replication and imitation. Rosenberg, Gold (1981), and several other economists who have studied diffusion processes in depth have emphasized very strongly that the product or process which is diffusing through an adopter population often bears little resemblance at the end of the diffusion to the one that started the whole process. We have only to think of the computer, the radio, or the bicycle to realize the truth of this proposition. The process of induced innovation, incremental innovation, and modification for various applications continues through the life of a product.

Schumpeter was certainly aware of this point. He himself emphasized that "the motorcar would never have acquired its present importance and become so potent a reformer of life if it had remained what it was thirty years ago and if it had failed to shape the environmental conditions—roads among them—for its own further development" (1939, 167).

Nevertheless, as so often in his work, there was a coexistence of two apparently contradictory elements. On the one hand, there was an insistence on looking at technical journals and company histories to understand the real process of technical change, and a real appreciation of many features of technical innovation. But on the other hand, this existed side by side with an a priori theory of entrepreneurship that is largely ahistorical.

If we look at the history of science, technology, invention, innovation, and diffusion of innovations, then we find, of course, recognition of the contribution of outstanding individuals in all parts of the system. But we also usually find recognition of innumerable minor contributions and of the role of institutions in the accumulation, dissemination, and application of new knowledge.

At one end of the spectrum are some historians who put the main emphasis on outstanding individuals, and at the other end of the spectrum are those who stress the innumerable, sometimes anonymous, contributions of a wide variety of scientists, technologists, engineers, workers, managers, and users. Examples of the approach of the latter are theories of "learning by doing" and "learning by using," such as Gilfillan's (1935) theory of invention, and Hessen's (1931) theory of scientific discovery. Examples of the former group are Jewkes, Sawers, and Stillerman's (1958) *The Sources of Invention* and

26   Evolving Technology and Market Structure

Schumpeter's theory of entrepreneurship (sometimes called "Schumpeter Mark I") in *Theory of Economic Development*.

In both these cases, there is, of course, some recognition that pygmies as well as giants play some part in the process, and that social institutions, such as research laboratories, design departments, universities, and firms may facilitate the activities of inventors and innovators.

Schumpeter did recognize (1939, 346) that the function of entrepreneurship could be performed within public institutions, and that it could be split among a number of individuals (1939, 327). Jewkes also recognized that some important inventions did emerge from the R&D laboratories of large firms and that it was sometimes hard to ascribe them to any single individual, or even to several. Schumpeter went further and maintained that large oligopolistic or even monopolistic firms would have a competitive advantage in research and innovation. It may therefore seem strange to classify him with the "heroic individualist" school. His position was contradictory since he also maintained that the bureaucratization of innovation would lead to the death of entrepreneurship and of capitalism itself.

Despite the later developments in his theory in the 1920s and 1930s (Schumpeter Mark II), Schumpeter's basic theory of entrepreneurship was scarcely modified in *Business Cycles* compared with that set forth in the *Theory of Economic Development*. He failed to develop the notion that the *function* of entrepreneurship could be exercised differently in different types of firms and with different types of innovation in each successive industrial revolution. He had a theory of entrepreneurship without a theory of the firm. This prevented him from recognizing the full significance of the "partnership" form of company organization in the first Kondratiev wave (the original industrial revolution) as well as later changes in company structure.

Numerous empirical studies of innovation have confirmed Schumpeter's recognition of the importance of the entrepreneurial function in taking an invention to the market. They have confirmed his view that an entrepreneur is not the same as a capitalist. But they have also shown that the way in which the function of entrepreneurship is performed varies across different types of firms, different countries, different technologies, and different historical periods. Characteristically they also show multiple sources of information inputs from within and from outside the innovating organization and the importance of a "national system of innovation"—the supporting network of scientific and technical institutions, the infrastructure, and the social environment. These things, surprisingly, are lacking in Schumpeter's theory of innovative entrepreneurship.

Thus, although his theory went beyond the mainstream theory of the firm as a rational profit-maximizing agency, operating with perfect information and foresight in any country, any culture, and any period of history, it suffered to some degree from the same tendency to postulate a single universal essence for entrepreneurship from pure logic.

This was important for his theory of business cycles because it meant that he made little or no attempt to examine the changing pattern of international technological leadership and related patterns of entrepreneurship or the influence of innovation on patterns of international trade. Thus, the disequilibrating effects of international technological competition were largely unexplored in *Business Cycles* as were the issues of underdevelopment and international trade.

Schumpeter's Theory of Equilibrium

Many people have puzzled over the apparent inconsistency of Schumpeter's statements on equilibrium. On the one hand, he said that the system never was and never could be in equilibrium and stressed the inherently disequilibrating effects of the stream of innovations characteristic of capitalism. On the other hand, he consistently praised Walras for his theory of general equilibrium and insisted not only that this was the greatest achievement of economic theory, but that it was close to reality. In Volume I of *Business Cycles* he insists that "Common sense tells us that the mechanism for establishing or reestablishing equilibrium is not a figment devised as an exercise in the pure logic of economics but is actually operative in the reality around us" (47).

Some critics have attempted to resolve this apparent inconsistency by arguing that Schumpeter used the model of static general equilibrium simply as an expositional device to contrast with his own dynamic model, and to make this more intelligible to the reader. But, as the quotation above suggests, this cannot be reconciled with the fact that Schumpeter constantly emphasized the importance of equilibrium throughout his life from the first chapter of *Theory of Economic Development* (and his earlier book on economic doctrine and method) to his final work (*History of Economic Analysis*). Shionoya (1986) is therefore right to insist that Schumpeter's admiration for Walras was no mere formal acknowledgment or passing phase, but was an integral part of his entire theory.

Both in *Theory of Economic Development* and in *Business Cycles* Schumpeter represents *boom* as a departure from equilibrium and recession as a return to equilibrium in largely Walrasian terms. In *Business Cycles* he also represents *depression* as a departure from equilibrium and the revival from depression as a return to equilibrium: "The phenomenon becomes understandable only if we start with the neighborhood of equilibrium preceding prosperity and end up with the neighborhood of equilibrium following revival" (156).

While Schumpeter regarded depression as an unnecessary and pathological departure from equilibrium (1939, 150–55) that could be aggravated by

28   Evolving Technology and Market Structure

scares or panics and whose depth could not be predicted, he nevertheless continued to stress the "natural" equilibrating tendencies of the system. Moreover, he believed that these equilibrating tendencies were inherent in the behavior of the economy. Paradoxically, therefore as we have seen, he had greater faith in the resilience of the economy than Keynes and devoted very little attention either to the role of institutions or to the role of technology in achieving either a more stable dynamic equilibrium or a recovery from depression.

The notion of revival as a return to equilibrium is actually inconsistent with the historical evidence in Schumpeter's own description of business cycles, in which he points out several times that major innovations that "carry" a long boom had their origins long before and induced many other innovations in the course of their development. Revival from depression cannot, therefore, be regarded as simply the absorption of the effects of a previous wave of innovations until a natural equilibrium is restored, as is suggested both in *Theory of Economic Development* (244) and in *Business Cycles*.

It is, of course, essential in any theory of cycles to account for the "glue" that holds the system together and keeps it on a growth path despite its fluctuations. It *is* essential to account for the continuities as well as the discontinuities. Walrasian equilibrium theory explains neither, and it was Schumpeter's misfortune that he attempted to marry it with his own theory of dynamic destabilizing entrepreneurship.

It is difficult to account for this, although Goodwin's essay (in this volume) is illuminating. Schumpeter is certainly not alone in the apparent inconsistency of some of his major ideas. There is scarcely a single social or natural scientist who has not been criticized for such paradoxes and Schumpeter was pioneering in a difficult field. It may be that he was seduced by the mathematical elegance of the Walrasian system. Or it may be that the paradox can partly be explained in terms of personal psychological factors in Schumpeter's own early development. These will doubtless remain interesting topics for speculation and debate among historians of ideas for many years to come. What is more interesting for those who wish to understand the relationships among innovation, investment, and business cycles is to see whether some of the weaknesses in Schumpeter's analysis have been, or could be, overcome by the more recent research which builds on his insights and on what he himself repeatedly described as tentative first approximations. This is indeed what Schumpeter himself hoped for.

Results of Some Recent Research on Innovation

It would be impossible in this paper to do justice to the enormous range of empirical and theoretical work on innovation, diffusion, entrepreneurship, and their relationship to business cycles, that has been carried out since Schumpeter's death. Much of it was inspired directly or indirectly by Schumpeter's own work and this is the best tribute to his achievement. It is possible here to select and condense only from a few contributions some of the results that seem most relevant to this discussion.

One of the difficulties that Schumpeter confronted was precisely the lack of empirical and theoretical studies in his field of investigation. Rogers (1962) and Rosenberg (1976) have pointed out that there were scarcely any studies of the diffusion of innovations in industry before the 1960s. There were also very few case studies of innovation which took into account technological, economic, and entrepreneurial aspects. The history of technology was a relatively neglected area even by comparison with the history of science.

Today, the situation is undoubtedly much improved although this improvement relates mainly to the period since World War II rather than to long-term historical studies. Nevertheless it is now possible to make tentative generalizations about some aspects of innovation, diffusion, and entrepreneurship with a little more confidence than was possible in Schumpeter's time.

First, numerous studies (e.g., Dosi 1984; Freeman 1982; Nelson and Winter 1977, 1982; Pavitt 1984, 1986; Rosenberg 1976, 1982; Teece 1988; von Tunzelmann 1978) point out the cumulative nature of much technological advance. They also point to the importance of tacit knowledge gained from the experience of production and marketing as well as from research, design, and development. The firm as an institution, rather than an individual entrepreneur, may often be the locus of this accumulation, even though an act of entrepreneurship by some individual or combination of individuals is still essential to use this accumulated knowledge to introduce new or improved products and processes. The articles on learning by doing (Arrow 1962) and learning by using (von Hippel 1976) represent two attempts to interpret and encapsulate this continuous process of technical advance.

Second, the accumulation of knowledge within firms or by individual entrepreneurs does not mean that major innovations are typically made in isolation from external sources. This may be true of some incremental innovations, but it is certainly not true of the most important innovations. On the contrary, all the evidence of numerous case studies demonstrates the importance of external sources of knowledge, information, and advice coming, on the one hand, from the market (actual or potential users of an innovation), and, on the other hand, from suppliers of materials, components, etc. and last, but certainly not least, from a variety of scientific and technical institutions. Lundvall (1988) and his colleagues have developed the theory of "learning by interacting" and of "national systems of innovation" to reflect this complex interaction. This means that the function of innovative entrepreneurship varies enormously, depending on the time and place of the interaction. It is always a function of creating new combinations, and it is

30   Evolving Technology and Market Structure

often a function of matching a new technological advance with a market possibility. The task of historical scholarship is to reveal how the exercise of this function varies in different historical periods, in different countries, and in different industries. The task of economic theory is to develop a theory of the firm that takes account of this variety and does not assume as its foundation either hyperrationality of individual entrepreneurs or groups, nor supernormal intelligence and energy (Dosi and Orsenigo, 1988).

Third, technical innovation emerges not only as a disequilibrating, uncertain, disturbing element, but also quite often as an element of continuity, with rather well-defined trajectories, and sometimes offering rather clear-cut investment opportunities for the future development of new products, processes, systems, and markets. It remains true that in other circumstances, described so vividly by Schumpeter, technical innovations and their diffusion can be a severe shock to the system. This means, however, that it is not necessary to base a theory of business cycles on the supposed dichotomy between the destabilizing effects of innovation and the supposed equilibrating effects of "normal" economic behavior in absorbing these shocks in recession and recovery periods. Rather, it is important to identify in what circumstances technical innovation itself may stimulate and restore business confidence, and in what circumstances the reverse may occur (Freeman and Perez 1988).

We have argued that analysis cannot be restricted to the level of the individual innovation or to counting innovations; the qualitative aspects and the systems interrelatedness of innovations must be taken into account. Furthermore it is diffusion of innovations that underlies waves of investment. Under favorable conditions, the Schumpeterian bandwagons roll and business confidence improves leading to an atmosphere of "boom" in which, although there are still risks and uncertainties attached to all investment decisions, animal spirits rise. Such favorable conditions include complementarities between innovations and the emergence of an appropriate infrastructure as well as some degree of political stability and institutions that promote, or at least do not hinder too much, the diffusion of new technologies. In these favorable circumstances the growth of new markets and the profitability of new investments appear to offer a fairly stable prospect of future growth, despite the uncertainties.

There are also circumstances, however, when technical change could have the opposite effect and could destabilize investment by undermining confidence in future prospects for some firms, industries, or economies. Moreover, as technologies and industries mature over a long period, diminishing returns and declining profitability may set in, leading to sluggish investment behavior. If this is at all widespread, it may take major social and political changes to restore confidence in the future growth of the system on the basis of new technologies. The "natural" equilibrating tendencies of the economy are not sufficient to handle the problems of adjustment as they involve a complex process of institutional and structural change.

It is not possible to do justice here to many other findings of neo-Schumpeterian research on innovations and their diffusion. A much fuller and more comprehensive survey by more than twenty authors from a dozen different countries can be found in Dosi et al. (1988).

A New Theory of Innovation and Long Cycles

In concluding this essay it is possible to indicate only briefly how these findings could lead to a reformulation of Schumpeter's theory of long cycles in a manner that would go some way to resolve the problems that I have raised.

Carlota Perez (1983, 1985, 1987) has made an important contribution to formulating a new and more plausible theory of the relationship between innovation and long cycles of development. In particular, she has provided a convincing answer to Ruttan's point about clusters of innovations and Kuznets's original criticisms of *Business Cycles,* by suggesting the notion of a pervasive change in technology underlying each of Schumpeter's "successive industrial revolutions." As we have seen, Schumpeter hinted at such a concept but failed to provide any empirical or theoretical foundation for his idea. A number of authors, such as Keirstead (1948) with his "constellations" of innovations or Freeman, Clark, and Soete (1982) with their "new technology systems" or Dosi (1982) with his "technological paradigms" have demonstrated both a technological and an economic basis for the clustering of innovations. But Perez went beyond these formulations in several important respects. Her concept is that of a "metaparadigm" change affecting all or almost all branches of the economy, directly or indirectly.

She uses the expression *techno-economic* rather than "technological paradigm" (Dosi 1982) because the changes involved go beyond engineering trajectories for specific product or process technologies and affect the conditions of production and distribution throughout the system, and because the "glue" that links the innovations together is not merely technology. Her concept corresponds to Nelson and Winter's concept of "general natural trajectories" and this concept, once established as the dominant influence on engineers, designers, and managers, becomes a "technological regime" for several decades. From this it is evident that she views Schumpeter's successive industrial revolutions as a succession of "techno-economic paradigms."

A new techno-economic paradigm develops initially within the old, showing its decisive advantages during the "downswing" phase of the previous Kondratiev cycle. However, it becomes established as a dominant technological regime only after a crisis of structural adjustment, involving deep social

32   Evolving Technology and Market Structure

and institutional changes, as well as the replacement of the motive branches of the economy. This is an important point as several theories have suggested that Kondratiev upswings were based on a cluster of innovations introduced immediately before the upswing (Mensch 1975). Schumpeter, on the other hand, pointed several times to the long gestation period for the diffusion of key innovations and to the fact that they were sometimes made long before the upswing in which they became predominant, as in the case of railways (1939, 254–55) or the related case of steam engines (von Tunzelmann 1978), which became the predominant technological regime only in the second and not the first Kondratiev cycle.

As has already been made clear, Perez's conception of a techno-economic paradigm is much broader than "clusters" of innovations or even of "technology systems." She is referring to a combination of interrelated product, process, technical, organizational, and managerial innovations, embodying a quantum jump in potential productivity for all or most of the economy and opening up an unusually wide range of truly new investment and profit opportunities. Such a paradigm change implies a unique new combination of decisive technical and economic advantages.

The organizing principle of each successive paradigm and the justification for the expression *techno-economic paradigm* is to be found not only in a new range of products and systems, but most of all in the dynamics of the relative cost structure of all possible inputs to production. In each new techno-economic paradigm, a particular input or set of inputs, which may be described as the "key factor" of that paradigm, fulfills the following conditions:

i) Clearly perceived low and rapidly falling relative cost. As Rosenberg (1976) and other economists have pointed out, small changes in the relative input cost structure have little or no effect on the behavior of engineers, designers and researchers. Only major and persistent changes have the power to transform the decision rules and common sense procedures of engineers and managers (Perez 1985; Freeman and Soete 1987).

ii) Apparently almost unlimited availability of supply over long periods. Temporary shortages may, of course, occur in a period of rapid buildup in demand for the new key factor, but it must be clear that there are no major barriers to an enormous long-term increase in supply. This is an essential condition for the confidence to take major investment decisions which depend on this long-term availability.

iii) Clear potential for the use or incorporation of the new key factor or factors in many products and processes throughout the economic system; either directly or (more commonly) through a set of related innovations, which both reduce the cost and change the quality of capital equipment, labor inputs, and other inputs to the system.

Perez maintains that this combination of characteristics holds today for microelectronics and few would deny this. Until recently, it held for oil, which underlay the postwar boom (the "fourth Kondratiev" upswing). She suggests that in the third Kondratiev the role of key factor was played by low cost steel. Schumpeter had commented that the universal availability of cheap steel facilitated an enormous range of innovations in machinery and metal products (1939, 372).

Clearly, every one of the inputs identified as "key factors" existed (and was in use) long before the new paradigm developed. However, its full potential was recognized and made capable of fulfilling the above conditions only when the previous key factor and its related constellation of technologies gave strong signals of diminishing returns and of approaching the limits of its potential for further increasing productivity or for new profitable investment. This point complements Schumpeter's analysis in terms of the erosion of profitability through the swarming process.

Perez argues that from a purely technical point of view, the explosive surge of interrelated innovations involved in a technological revolution could probably occur even earlier and in a more gradual manner. But there are strong economic and social factors at play that first serve as prolonged containment and later as unleashing forces. The massive externalities created to favor the diffusion and generalization of the prevailing paradigm act as powerful deterrents to change for a prolonged period. Paul David (1985) demonstrated some of the ways in which the economy may become "locked in" to a particular technology and Brian Arthur (1988) has provided convincing evidence of the strength of these "containment" forces in his theory of path-dependent processes. It is only when productivity along the old trajectories shows persistent limits to growth and future profits are seriously threatened that the high risks and costs of trying the new technologies appear clearly justified. And it is only after many of these trials have been obviously successful that further applications become easier and less risky investment choices.

The new key factor does not appear as an isolated input, but rather at the core of a rapidly growing system of technical, social, and managerial innovations, some related to the production of the key factor itself and others to its utilization. At first these innovations may appear (and may in fact be pursued) as a means for overcoming the specific bottlenecks of the old technologies, but the new key factor soon acquires it own dynamic, and successive innovations take place through an intensive interactive process, spurred by the limits to growth that are increasingly apparent under the old paradigm. In this way, the most successful new technology systems gradually crystalize as an "ideal" new type of production organization which becomes the common sense of management and design embodying new "rules of thumb," restoring confidence to investment decision makers after a long period of hesitation.

34   Evolving Technology and Market Structure

The full constellation, once crystalized, goes far beyond the key factor(s) and beyond technical change itself. It brings with it a restructuring of the whole productive system.

As it crystalizes, the new techno-economic paradigm involves, among other things:

(a) a new "best practice" form of organization in the firm and at the plant level;

(b) a new skill profile in the labor force, affecting both quality and quantity of labor and corresponding patterns of income distribution;

(c) a new product mix, in the sense that those products which use the low cost key factor intensively will be the preferred investment choices and therefore will represent a growing proportion of GNP;

(d) new trends in both radical and incremental innovation geared to substituting more intensive use of the new key factor(s) for relatively high cost elements;

(e) a new pattern in the location of investment both nationally and internationally as the change in the relative cost structure transforms comparative advantages;

(f) a particular wave of infrastructural investment designed to provide appropriate externalities throughout the system and facilitate the use of the new products and processes everywhere; and

(g) a tendency for new, innovator-entrepreneur small firms also to enter the new rapidly expanding branches of the economy and in some cases to initiate entirely new sectors of production.

From this it is evident that the period of transition—the downswing and depression of the long wave—is characterized by deep structural change in the economy and such changes require an equally profound transformation of the institutional and social framework. The onset of prolonged recessionary trends indicates the increasing degree of mismatch between the techno-economic subsystem and the old socioinstitutional framework. It shows the need for a full-scale reaccommodation of social behavior and institutions to suit the requirements and the potential of a shift that has already taken place to a considerable extent in some areas of the techno-economic sphere. This reaccommodation occurs as a result of a process of political search, experimentation, and adaptation, but when it has been achieved, by a variety of social and political changes at the national and international level, the resulting "good match" facilitates the upswing phase of the long wave. A climate of confidence for a surge of new investment is created through an appropriate combination of regulatory mechanisms that foster the full deployment of the new paradigm. Since the achievement of a good match is a conflict-ridden process and proceeds very unevenly in different national political and cultural contexts, this may exert a considerable influence on the changing pattern of international technological leadership and international patterns of diffusion. As we have seen, Schumpeter's theory failed to take into account these institutional and social changes.

The uneven and varied response of governments, firms, and industries to the threats and opportunities posed by a new wave of technology tends to accentuate the uneven process of development. Newcomers are sometimes more able to make the necessary social and institutional innovations than are the established leaders, hindered by their more arthritic social structures. Erstwhile leading countries such as the United Kingdom or the United States may become the victims of their own earlier success. On the other hand, countries lacking the necessary minimal educational, managerial, R&D, and design capability may be even more seriously disadvantaged in international competition (Perez and Soete 1988).

This means that changes of the techno-economic paradigm are likely to be associated with the temporary aggravation of instability problems in relation to the flow of international investment, trade, and payments. To take a contemporary example, the enormous Japanese trade surplus and the U.S. trade deficit reflect not merely exchange rate problems, but also the more successful Japanese exploitation and application of information technology outside the leading edge industries, and the introduction of many institutional innovations facilitating this process. The U.S. economy leads in military applications of information technology but lags in other areas. There is thus a major structural component in the international trade imbalances, as there was in the 'technological gap' that the United States opened up between the 1920s and the 1950s (Freeman 1987), or the United Kingdom opened up in the first industrial revolution.

It has been possible to give only a brief summary of some new developments in the theory of innovation and long cycles. But they do indicate a real possibility of overcoming some of the weaknesses in Schumpeter's pioneering formulation. To continue in this direction would be the best tribute to the spirit of his work.

REFERENCES

Arrow, Kenneth. 1962. "The Economic Implications of Learning by Doing." *Review of Economic Studies* 29(80): 155–73.

Arthur, Brian. 1988. "Competing Technologies: An Overview." *Technical Change and Economic Theory,* ed. Giovanni Dosi et al., chap. 26. London: Pinter Publishers.

36   Evolving Technology and Market Structure

David, Paul A. 1985. "Clio and the Economics of QWERTY." *American Economic Review* 75(2): 332–37.

Dosi, Giovanni. 1982. "Technological Paradigms and Technological Trajectories." *Research Policy* 11(3): 147–62.

Dosi, Giovanni. 1984. *Technical Change and Industrial Transformation*. London: Macmillan.

Dosi, Giovanni, Christopher Freeman, Richard Nelson, Gerald Silverberg, and Luc Soete, eds. 1988. *Technical Change and Economic Theory*. London: Pinter Publishers.

Dosi, Giovanni, and Luigi Orsenigo. 1988. "Coordination and Transformation: An Overview of Structures, Behaviour, and Change in Evolutionary Environments." In *Technical Change and Economic Theory*, ed. Giovanni Dosi et al., chap. 2. London: Pinter Publishers.

Eatwell, John. 1982. *Whatever Happened to Britain?* London: Duckworth.

Elliott, John E. 1985. "Schumpeter's Theory of Economic Development and Social Change: Exposition and Assessment." *International Journal of Social Economics* 12(6 and 7): 6–33.

Freeman, Christopher. 1982. *Economics of Innovation*. London: Pinter Publishers.

Freeman, Christopher. 1987. *Technology Policy and Economic Performance: Lessons from Japan*. London: Pinter Publishers.

Freeman, Christopher, John Clark, and Luc Soete. 1982. *Unemployment and Technical Innovation: A Study of Long Waves in Economic Development*. London: Pinter Publishers.

Freeman, Christopher, and Carlota Perez. 1988. "Structural Crises of Adjustment, Business Cycles, and Investment Behaviour." In *Technical Change and Economic Theory*, ed. Giovanni Dosi et al., chap. 3. London: Pinter Publishers.

Freeman, Christopher, and Luc Soete, eds. 1987. *Technical Change and Full Employment*. Oxford: Blackwell.

Gilfillan, S. 1935. *The Sociology of Invention*. Chicago: Follett Publishers.

Gold, Bela. 1981. "Technological Diffusion in Industry: Research Needs and Shortcomings." *Journal of Industrial Economics* 29:247–69.

Hessen, B. 1931. "The Social and Economic Roots of Newton's 'Principia'." In *Science at the Crossroads*, ed. N. Bukharin. London: F. Cass.

Hollander, S. G. 1965. *The Sources of Increased Efficiency: A Study of Du Pont Rayon Plants*. Cambridge, Mass.: MIT Press.

Jewkes, John, David Sawers, and John Stillerman. 1958. *The Sources of Invention*. London: Macmillan.

Keirstead, Brian. 1948. *The Theory of Economic Change*. Toronto: Macmillan.

Keynes, John Maynard. 1936. *General Theory of Employment, Interest, and Money*. New York: Harcourt Brace.

Kuznets, Simon. 1940. "Schumpeter's *Business Cycles*." *American Economic Review* 30(2): 257–71.

Lundvall, Bengt-Ake. 1988. "Innovation as an Interactive Process: User-Producer Relations." In *Technical Change and Economic Theory*, ed. Giovanni Dosi et al., chap. 17. London: Pinter Publishers.

Mensch, Gerard. 1975. *Das Technologische Patt: Innovationen Uberwinden die Depression.* Frankfurt: Umschau. English Edition. 1979. *Stalemate in Technology.* New York: Ballinger.

Nelson, Richard, and Sidney Winter. 1977. "In Search of a Useful Theory of Innovation." *Research Policy* 6(1): 36–75.

Nelson, Richard, and Sidney Winter. 1982. *An Evolutionary Theory of Economic Change.* Cambridge, Mass.: Harvard University Press.

Pavitt, Keith. 1984. "Sectoral Patterns of Technical Change: Towards a Taxonomy and a Theory." *Research Policy* 13(6): 343–73.

Pavitt, Keith. 1986. "Technology, Innovation and Strategic Management." In *Strategic Management Research,* ed. J. McGee and H. Thomas, chap. 26. London: John Wiley.

Perez, Carlota. 1983. "Structural Change and the Assimilation of New Technologies in the Economic and Social System." *Futures* 15(4): 357–75.

Perez, Carlota. 1985. "Microelectronics, Long Waves, and World Structural Change." *World Development* 13(3): 441–63.

Perez, Carlota. 1987. "Las Nuevas Tecnologias: Una Vision de Conjunto." In *La Tercera Revolucion Industrial,* ed. C. Omanarie. Buenos Aires: RIAL, Grupo Editor Latinoamericano.

Perez, Carlota, and Luc Soete. 1988. "Catching Up in Technology: Entry Barriers and Windows of Opportunity." In *Technical Change and Economic Theory,* ed. Giovanni Dosi et al., chap. 21. London: Pinter Publishers.

Rogers, Everett. 1962. *Diffusion of Innovations.* New York: Free Press.

Rosenberg, Nathan. 1976. *Perspectives on Technology.* Cambridge: Cambridge University Press.

Rosenberg, Nathan. 1982. *Inside the Black Box.* Cambridge: Cambridge University Press.

Ruttan, Vernon. 1959. "Usher and Schumpeter on Invention, Innovation, and Technological Change." *Quarterly Journal of Economics* 73:596–606.

Schumpeter, Joseph A. 1908. *Das Wesen und der Hauptinhalt der Theoretischen Nationalokonomie.* Leipzig: Duncker und Humblot.

Schumpeter, Joseph A. 1912. *Theorie der Wirtschaftlichen Entwicklung.* Leipzig: Duncker und Humblot. English translation, 1934. *The Theory of Economic Development.* Cambridge, Mass.: Harvard University Press.

Schumpeter, Joseph A. 1928. "The Instability of Capitalism." *Economic Journal* 38: 361–86.

Schumpeter, Joseph A. 1939. *Business Cycles: A Theoretical, Historical, and Statistical Analysis.* 2 volumes. New York: McGraw Hill.

Schumpeter, Joseph A. 1943. *Capitalism, Socialism, and Democracy.* London: Allen and Unwin.

Schumpeter, Joseph A. 1954. *History of Economic Analysis.* Edited from manuscript by Elizabeth Booty Schumpeter. New York: Oxford University Press.

Shionoya, Yuichi. 1986. "The Science and Ideology of Schumpeter." *Revista Internazionale di Scienze Economiche e Commerciale* 33(8): 729–62.

Solomon, Solomous. 1986. *Kondratiev Waves and Kuznets Swings.* Cambridge: Cambridge University Press.

38   Evolving Technology and Market Structure

Teece, David. 1988. "The Nature and Structure of Firms." In *Technical Change and Economic Theory,* ed. Giovanni Dosi et al., chap. 12. London: Pinter Publishers.

van der Zwan, Arnold. 1979. "On the Assessment of the Kondratiev Cycle and Related Issues." Rotterdam: Center for Research in Business Economics, Erasmus University.

von Hippel, Eric. 1976. "The Dominant Role of Users in the Scientific Instrument Innovation Process." *Research Policy* 5(3): 212–39.

von Tunzelmann, Nicholas. 1978. *Steam Power and British Industrialization to 1860.* Oxford: Clarendon.

Weinstock, Ulrich. 1964. *Das Problem der Kondratiev-Zyklen.* Berlin: Dunker & Humblot.

Part II
Economic Natural Selection and Firm and Industry Behaviour

[4]

UNCERTAINTY, EVOLUTION, AND ECONOMIC THEORY

ARMEN A. ALCHIAN[1]

University of California at Los Angeles

A MODIFICATION of economic analysis to incorporate incomplete information and uncertain foresight as axioms is suggested here. This approach dispenses with "profit maximization"; and it does not rely on the predictable, individual behavior that is usually assumed, as a first approximation, in standard textbook treatments. Despite these changes, the analytical concepts usually associated with such behavior are retained because they are not dependent upon such motivation or foresight. The suggested approach embodies the principles of biological evolution and natural selection by interpreting the economic system as an adoptive mechanism which chooses among exploratory actions generated by the adaptive pursuit of "success" or "profits." The resulting analysis is applicable to actions usually regarded as aberrations from standard economic behavior as well as to behavior covered by the customary analysis. This wider applicability and the removal of the unrealistic postulates of accurate anticipations and fixed states of knowledge have provided motivation for the study.

The exposition is ordered as follows: First, to clear the ground, a brief statement is given of a generally ignored aspect of "profit maximization," that is, where foresight is uncertain, "profit maximization" is *meaningless* as a guide to specifiable action. The constructive development then begins with an intro-

duction of the element of environmental adoption by the economic system of a posteriori most appropriate action according to the criterion of "realized positive profits." This is illustrated in an extreme, random-behavior model without any individual rationality, foresight, or motivation whatsoever. Even in this extreme type of model, it is shown that the economist can predict and explain events with a modified use of his conventional analytical tools.

This phenomenon—environmental adoption—is then fused with a type of individual motivated behavior based on the pervasiveness of uncertainty and incomplete information. Adaptive, imitative, and trial-and-error behavior in the pursuit of "positive profits" is utilized rather than its sharp contrast, the pursuit of "maximized profits." A final section discusses some implications and conjectures.

I. "PROFIT MAXIMIZATION" NOT A GUIDE TO ACTION

Current economic analysis of economic behavior relies heavily on decisions made by rational units customarily assumed to be seeking perfectly optimal situations.[2] Two criteria are well known—profit maximization and utility maximiza-

---

[1] I am indebted to Dr. Stephen Enke for criticism and stimulation leading to improvements in both content and exposition.

[2] See, e.g., J. Robinson, *Economics of Imperfect Competition* (London: Macmillan), p. 6, for a strong statement of the necessity of such optimal behavior. Standard textbooks expound essentially the same idea. See also P. Samuelson, *Foundations of Economic Analysis* (Cambridge: Harvard University Press, 1946).

tion.[3] According to these criteria, appropriate types of action are indicated by marginal or neighborhood inequalities which, if satisfied, yield an optimum. But the standard qualification usually added is that nobody is able really to optimize his situation according to these diagrams and concepts because of uncertainty about the position and, sometimes, even the slopes of the demand and supply functions. Nevertheless, the economist interprets and predicts the decisions of individuals in terms of these diagrams, since it is alleged that individuals use these concepts implicitly, if not explicitly.

Attacks on this methodology are widespread, but only one attack has been really damaging, that of G. Tintner.[4] He denies that profit maximization even makes any sense where there is uncertainty. Uncertainty arises from at least two sources: imperfect foresight and human inability to solve complex problems containing a host of variables even when an optimum is definable. Tintner's proof is simple. Under uncertainty, by definition, each action that may be chosen is identified with a *distribution* of potential outcomes, not with a unique outcome. Implicit in uncertainty is the consequence that these distributions of potential outcomes are overlapping.[5] It is worth emphasis that each possible action has a *distribution* of potential out-

comes, only one of which will materialize if the action is taken, and that one outcome cannot be foreseen. Essentially, the task is converted into making a decision (selecting an action) whose potential outcome *distribution* is preferable, that is, choosing the action with the *optimum distribution*, since there is no such thing as a *maximizing* distribution.

For example, let each of two possible choices be characterized by its subjective distribution of potential outcomes. Suppose one has the higher "mean" but a larger spread, so that it might result in larger profits or losses, and the other has a smaller "mean" and a smaller spread. Which one is the maximum? This is a nonsensical question; but to ask for the optimum distribution is not nonsense. In the presence of uncertainty—a necessary condition for the existence of profits —there is no meaningful criterion for selecting the decision that will "maximize profits." The maximum-profit criterion is not meaningful as a basis *for selecting* the action which will, in fact, result in an outcome with higher profits than any other action would have, unless one assumes nonoverlapping potential outcome distributions. It must be noticed that the meaningfulness of "maximum profits —a realized outcome which is the largest that could have been realized from the available actions"—is perfectly consistent with the meaninglessness of "profit maximization"—a criterion for selecting among alternative lines of action, the potential outcomes of which are describable only as distributions and not as unique amounts.

This crucial difficulty would be avoided by using a preference function as a criterion for selecting most preferred distributions of potential outcomes, but the search for a criterion of rationality and choice in terms of pref-

---

[3] In the following we shall discuss only profit maximization, although everything said is applicable equally to utility maximization by consumers.

[4] "The Theory of Choice under Subjective Risk and Uncertainty," *Econometrica*, IX (1941), 298–304; "The Pure Theory of Production under Technological Risk and Uncertainty," *ibid.*, pp. 305–11; and "A Contribution to the Nonstatic Theory of Production," *Studies in Mathematical Economics and Econometrics* (Chicago: University of Chicago Press, 1942), pp. 92–109.

[5] Thus uncertainty is defined here to be the phenomenon that produces overlapping distributions of potential outcomes.

UNCERTAINTY AND ECONOMIC THEORY 213

erence functions still continues. For example, the use of the mean, or expectation, completely begs the question of uncertainty by disregarding the variance of the distribution, while a "certainty equivalent" assumes the answer. The only way to make "profit maximization" a specifically meaningful action is to postulate a model containing certainty. Then the question of the predictive and explanatory reliability of the model must be faced.[6]

II. SUCCESS IS BASED ON RESULTS, NOT MOTIVATION

There is an alternative method which treats the decisions and criteria dictated by the economic *system* as more important than those made by the individuals in it. By backing away from the trees—the optimization calculus by individual units—we can better discern the forest of impersonal market forces.[7] This approach directs attention to the interrelationships of the environment and the prevailing types of economic behavior which appear through a process of economic natural selection. Yet it does not imply that individual foresight and action do not affect the nature of the existing state of affairs.

In an economic system the realization of profits is the criterion according to which successful and surviving firms are selected. This decision criterion is applied primarily by an impersonal market system in the United States and may be completely independent of the decision processes of individual units, of the variety of inconsistent motives and abilities, and even of the individual's awareness of the criterion. The reason is simple. Realized positive profits, not *maximum* profits, are the mark of success and viability. It does not matter through what process of reasoning or motivation such success was achieved. The fact of its accomplishment is sufficient. This is the criterion by which the economic system selects survivors: those who realize *positive profits* are the survivors; those who suffer losses disappear.

The pertinent requirement—positive profits through relative efficiency—is weaker than "maximized profits," with which, unfortunately, it has been confused. Positive profits accrue to those who are better than their actual competitors, even if the participants are ignorant, intelligent, skilful, etc. The crucial element is one's aggregate position relative to actual competitors, not some hypothetically perfect competitors. As in a race, the award goes to the relatively fastest, even if all the competitors loaf. Even in a world of stupid men there would still be profits. Also, the greater the uncertainties of the world, the greater is the possibility that profits would go to venturesome and lucky rather than to logical, careful, fact-gathering individuals.

The preceding interpretation suggests two ideas. First, success (survival) accompanies relative superiority; and, second, it does not require proper motivation but may rather be the result of fortuitous circumstances. Among all competitors, those whose particular conditions happen to be the most appropriate of those offered to the economic system for testing and adoption will be "se-

[6] Analytical models in all sciences postulate models abstracting from some realities in the belief that derived predictions will still be relevant. Simplifications are necessary, but continued attempts should be made to introduce more realistic assumptions into a workable model with an increase in generality and detail (see M. Friedman and L. Savage, "The Utility Analysis of Choices Involving Risks," *Journal of Political Economy*, LVI, No. 4 [1948], 279).

[7] In effect, we shall be reverting to a Marshallian type of analysis combined with the essentials of Darwinian evolutionary natural selection.

lected" as survivors. Just how such an approach can be used and how individuals happen to offer these appropriate forms for testing are problems to which we now turn.[8]

III. CHANCE OR LUCK IS ONE METHOD OF ACHIEVING SUCCESS

Sheer chance is a substantial element in determining the situation selected and also in determining its appropriateness or viability. A second element is the ability to adapt one's self by various methods to an appropriate situation. In order to indicate clearly the respective roles of luck and conscious adapting, the adaptive calculus will, for the moment, be completely removed. All individual rationality, motivation, and foresight will be temporarily abandoned in order to concentrate upon the ability of the environment to *adopt* "appropriate" survivors even in the absence of any adaptive behavior. This is an apparently unrealistic, but nevertheless very useful, expository approach in establishing the attenuation between the ex post survival criterion and the role of the individual's adaptive decision criterion. It also aids in assessing the role of luck and chance in the operation of our economic system.

Consider, first, the simplest type of biological evolution. Plants "grow" to the sunny side of buildings not because they "want to" in awareness of the fact that optimum or better conditions prevail there but rather because the leaves that happen to have more sunlight grow

faster and their feeding systems become stronger. Similarly, animals with configurations and habits more appropriate for survival under prevailing conditions have an enhanced viability and will with higher probability be typical survivors. Less appropriately acting organisms of the same general class having lower probabilities of survival will find survival difficult. More common types, the survivors, may appear to be those having *adapted* themselves to the environment, whereas the truth may well be that the environment has *adopted* them. There may have been no motivated individual adapting but, instead, only environmental adopting.

A useful, but unreal, example in which individuals act without any foresight indicates the type of analysis available to the economist and also the ability of the system to "direct" resources despite individual ignorance. Assume that thousands of travelers set out from Chicago, selecting their roads completely at random and without foresight. Only our "economist" knows that on but one road are there any gasoline stations. He can state categorically that travelers will *continue* to travel only on that road; those on other roads will soon run out of gas. Even though each one selected his route at random, we might have called those travelers who were so fortunate as to have picked the right road wise, efficient, foresighted, etc. Of course, we would consider them the lucky ones. If gasoline supplies were now moved to a new road, some formerly luckless travelers again would be able to move; and a new pattern of travel would be observed, although none of the travelers had changed his particular path. The really possible paths have changed with the changing environment. All that is needed is a set of varied, risk-taking

---

[8] Also suggested is another way to divide the general problem discussed here. The process and rationale by which a unit chooses its actions so as to optimize its situation is one part of the problem. The other is the relationship between changes in the environment and the consequent observable results, i.e., the decision process of the economic *society*. The classification used in the text is closely related to this but differs in emphasizing the degree of knowledge and foresight.

(adoptable) travelers. The correct direction of travel will be established. As circumstances (economic environment) change, the analyst (economist) can select the types of participants (firms) that will now become successful; he may also be able to diagnose the conditions most conducive to a greater probability of survival.[9]

IV. CHANCE DOES NOT IMPLY NONDIRECTED, RANDOM ALLOCATION OF RESOURCES

These two examples do not constitute an attempt to base all analysis on adoptive models dominated by chance. But they do indicate that collective and individual random behavior does' not per se imply a nihilistic theory incapable of yielding reliable predictions and explanations; nor does it imply a world lacking in order and apparent direction. It might, however, be argued that the facts of life deny even a substantial role to the element of chance and the associated adoption principle in the economic system. For example, the long lives and disparate sizes of business firms and hereditary fortunes may seem to be reliable evidence of consistent foresighted motivation and nonrandom behavior. In order to demonstrate that consistent success cannot be treated as prima facie evidence against pure luck, the following chance model of Borél, the famous French mathematician, is presented.

Suppose two million Parisians were paired off and set to tossing coins in a game of matching. Each pair plays until the winner on the first toss is again

[9] The undiscerning person who sees survivors corresponding to changes in environment claims to have evidence for the "Lysenko" doctrine. In truth, all he may have is evidence for the doctrine that the environment, by competitive conditions, selects the most viable of the various phenotypic characteristics for perpetuation. Economists should beware of economic "Lysenkoism."

brought to equality with the other player. Assuming one toss per second for each eight-hour day, at the end of ten years there would still be, on the average, about a hundred-odd pairs; and if the players assign the game to their heirs, a dozen or so will still be playing at the end of a thousand years! The implications are obvious. Suppose that some business had been operating for one hundred years. Should one rule out luck and chance as the essence of the factors producing the long-term survival of the enterprise? No inference whatever can be drawn until the number of original participants is known; and even then one must know the size, risk, and frequency of each commitment. One can see from the Borél illustration the danger in concluding that there are too many firms with long lives in the real world to admit an important role to chance. On the contrary, one might insist that there are actually too few!

The chance postulate was directed to two problems. On the one hand, there is the actual way in which a substantial fraction of economic behavior and activity is effected. On the other, there is the method of analysis which economists may use in their predictions and diagnoses. Before modifying the extreme chance model by adding adaptive behavior, some connotations and implications of the incorporation of chance elements will be elaborated in order to reveal the richness which is really inherent in chance. First, even if each and every individual acted in a haphazard and nonmotivated manner, it is possible that the variety of actions would be so great that the resulting collective set would contain actions that are best, in the sense of perfect foresight. For example, at a horse race with enough bettors wagering strictly at random, someone will win on all eight races. Thus individual random behavior does not eliminate the likelihood of observing "appropriate" decisions.[10]

Second, and conversely, individual behavior according to some foresight and motivation does not necessarily imply a collective pattern of behavior that is different from the collective variety of actions associated with a random selection of actions. Where there is uncertainty, people's judgments and opinions, even when based on the best available evidence, will differ; no one of them may be making his choice by tossing coins; yet the aggregate *set* of actions of the entire group of participants may be indistinguishable from a set of individual actions, each selected at random.[11]

Third, and fortunately, a chance-dominated model does not mean that an economist cannot predict or explain or diagnose. With a knowledge of the economy's realized requisites for survival and by a comparison of alternative conditions, he can state what types of firms or behavior relative to other possible types will be more viable, even though the firms themselves may not know the conditions or even try to achieve them by readjusting to the changed situation if they do know the conditions. It is sufficient if all firms are slightly different so that in the new environmental situation those who have their fixed internal conditions closer to the new, but unknown, optimum position now have a greater probability of survival and growth. They will grow relative to other firms and become the prevailing type, since survival conditions may push the observed characteristics of the set of survivors toward the unknowable optimum by either (1) repeated trials or (2) survival of more of those who happened to be near the optimum—determined ex post. If these new conditions last "very long," the dominant firms will be different ones from those which prevailed or would have prevailed under other conditions. Even if environmental conditions cannot be forecast, the economist can compare for given alternative potential situations the types of behavior that would have higher probability of viability or adoption. If explanation of past results rather than prediction is the task, the economist can diagnose the particular attributes which were critical in facilitating survival, even though individual participants were not aware of them.[12]

Fourth, the bases of prediction have been indicated in the preceding paragraph, but its character should be made explicit. The prediction will not assert that every—or, indeed, any—firm necessarily changes its characteristics. It asserts, instead, that the characteristics of the new *set* of firms, or possibly a set of new firms, will change. This may be

---

[10] The Borél gamblers analogue is pertinent to a host of everyday situations.

[11] Of course, the economic units may be going through a period of soul-searching, management training, and research activity. We cannot yet identify mental and physical activity with a process that results in sufficient information and foresight to yield uniquely determinate choices. To do so would be to beg the whole question.

[12] It is not even necessary to suppose that each firm acts as if it possessed the conventional diagrams and knew the analytical principles employed by economists in deriving optimum and equilibrium conditions. The atoms and electrons do not know the laws of nature; the physicist does not impart to each atom a wilful scheme of action based on laws of conservation of energy, etc. The fact that an economist deals with human beings who have sense and ambitions does not *automatically* warrant imparting to these humans the great degree of foresight and motivations which the economist may require for his customary analysis as an outside observer or "oracle." The similarity between this argument and Gibbsian statistical mechanics, as well as biological evolution, is *not* mere coincidence.

characterized by the "representative firm," a purely statistical concept—a vector of "averages," one dimension for each of the several qualities of the population of firms. A "representative firm" is not typical of any one producer but, instead, is a set of statistics summarizing the various "modal" characteristics of the population. Surely, this was an intended use of Marshall's "representative firm."

Fifth, a final implication drawn from consideration of this extreme approach is that empirical investigations via questionnaire methods, so far used, are incapable of evaluating the validity of marginal productivity analysis. This is true because productivity and demand analyses are essential in evaluating relative viability, even though uncertainty eliminates "profit maximization" and even if price and technological changes were to have no consciously redirecting effect on the firms. To illustrate, suppose that, in attempting to predict the effects of higher real wage rates, it is discovered that every businessman says he does not adjust his labor force. Nevertheless, firms with a lower labor-capital ratio will have relatively lower cost positions and, to that extent, a higher probability of survival. The force of competitive survival, by eliminating higher-cost firms, reveals a population of remaining firms with a new average labor-capital ratio. The essential point is that individual motivation and foresight, while sufficient, are not necessary. Of course, it is not argued here that therefore it is absent. All that is needed by economists is their own awareness of the survival conditions and criteria of the economic system and a group of participants who submit various combinations and organizations for the system's selection and adoption. Both these conditions are satisfied.[13]

As a consequence, only the method of use, rather than the usefulness, of economic tools and concepts is affected by the approach suggested here; in fact, they are made more powerful if they are not pretentiously assumed to be necessarily associated with, and dependent upon, individual foresight and adjustment. They are tools for, at least, the diagnosis of the operation of an economic system, even if not also for the internal business behavior of each firm.

V. INDIVIDUAL ADAPTING VIA IMITATION AND TRIAL AND ERROR

Let it again be noted that the preceding extreme model was designed to present in purest form only one element of the suggested approach. It is not argued that there is no purposive, foresighted behavior present in reality. In adding this realistic element—adaptation by individuals with some foresight and purposive motivation—we are expanding the preceding extreme model. We are not abandoning any part of it or futilely trying to merge it with the opposite extreme of perfect foresight and "profit maximization."

Varying and conflicting objectives motivate economic activity, yet we shall here direct attention to only one particular objective—the sufficient condition of realized positive profits. There are no implications of "profit maximization," and this difference is important. Although the latter is a far more extreme objective when definable, only the former is the sine qua non of survival and success. To argue that, with perfect competition, the two would come to the same thing is to conceal an important difference by means of a very implausible as-

[13] This approach reveals how the "facts" of Lester's dispute with Machlup can be handled with standard economic tools.

sumption. The pursuit of profits, and not some hypothetical undefinable perfect situation, is the relevant objective whose *fulfilment* is rewarded with survival. Unfortunately, even this proximate objective is too high. Neither perfect knowledge of the past nor complete awareness of the current state of the arts gives sufficient foresight to indicate profitable action. Even for this more restricted objective, the pervasive effects of uncertainty prevent the ascertainment of actions which are supposed to be optimal in achieving profits. Now the consequence of this is that modes of behavior replace optimum equilibrium conditions as guiding rules of action. Therefore, in the following sections two forms of conscious adaptive behavior are emphasized.

First, wherever successful enterprises are observed, the elements common to these observable successes will be associated with success and copied by others in their pursuit of profits or success. "Nothing succeeds like success." Thus the urge for "rough-and-ready" imitative rules of behavior is accounted for. What would otherwise appear to be merely customary "orthodox," nonrational rules of behavior turns out to be codified imitations of observed success, e.g., "conventional" markup, price "followship," "orthodox" accounting and operating ratios, "proper" advertising policy, etc. A conventionally employed type of behavior pattern is consistent with the postulates of the analysis employed, even though the reasons and justifications for the particular conventions are not.[14]

Many factors cause this motive to imitate patterns of action observable in past successes. Among these are: (1) the absence of an identifiable criterion for decision-making, (2) the variability of the environment, (3) the multiplicity of

factors that call for attention and choice, (4) the uncertainty attaching to all these factors and outcomes, (5) the awareness that superiority relative to one's competitors is crucial, and (6) the nonavailability of a trial-and-error process converging to an optimum position.

In addition, imitation affords relief from the necessity of really making decisions and conscious innovations, which, if wrong, become "inexcusable." Unfortunately, failure or success often reflects the willingness to depart from rules when conditions have changed; what counts, then, is not only imitative behavior but the willingness to abandon it at the "right" time and circumstances. Those who are different and successful "become" innovators, while those who fail "become" reckless violators of tried-and-true rules. Although one may deny the absolute appropriateness of such rules, one cannot doubt the existence of a strong urge to create conventions and rules (based on observed success) and a willingness to use them for action as well as for rationalizations of inaction. If another untried host of actions might have been even more successful, so much the worse for the participants who failed, and even for those who missed "perfect success."

Even innovation is accounted for by imitation. While there certainly are those who consciously innovate, there are those who, in their imperfect attempts

---

[14] These constructed rules of behavior should be distinguished from "rules" which, in effect, do no more than define the objective being sought. Confusion between objectives which motivate one and rules of behavior are commonplace. For example, "full-cost pricing" is a "rule" that one cannot really follow. He can try to, but whether he succeeds or fails in his objective of survival is not controllable by following the "rule of full-cost pricing." If he fails in his objective, he must, of necessity, fail to have followed the "rule." The situation is parallel to trying to control the speed of a car by simply setting by hand the indicator on the speedometer.

UNCERTAINTY AND ECONOMIC THEORY

to imitate others, unconsciously innovate by unwittingly acquiring some unexpected or unsought unique attributes which under the prevailing circumstances prove partly responsible for the success. Others, in turn, will attempt to copy the uniqueness, and the imitation-innovation process continues. Innovation is assured, and the notable aspects of it here are the possibility of unconscious pioneering and leadership.

The second type of conscious adaptive behavior, in addition to imitation, is "trial and error." This has been used with "profit maximization," wherein, by trial and ensuing success or failure, more appropriate actions are selected in a process presumed to converge to a limit of "profit maximization" equilibrium. Unfortunately, at least two conditions are necessary for convergence via a trial-and-error process, even if one admits an equilibrium situation as an admissible limit. First, a trial must be classifiable as a success or failure. The position achieved must be comparable with results of other potential actions. In a static environment, if one improves his position relative to his former position, then the action taken is better than the former one, and presumably one could continue by small increments to advance to a local optimum. An analogy is pertinent. A nearsighted grasshopper on a mound of rocks can crawl to the top of a particular rock. But there is no assurance that he can also get to the top of the mound, for he might have to descend for a while or hop to new rocks. The second condition, then, for the convergence via trial and error is the continual rising toward some *optimum optimorum* without intervening descents. Whether decisions and actions in economic life satisfy these two conditions cannot be proved or disproved here,

but the available evidence seems overwhelmingly unfavorable.

The above convergence conditions do not apply to a changing environment, for there can be no observable comparison of the result of an action with any other. Comparability of resulting situations is destroyed by the changing environment. As a consequence, the measure of goodness of actions in anything except a tolerable-intolerable sense is lost, and the possibility of an individual's converging to the optimum activity via a trial-and-error process disappears. Trial and error becomes survival or death. It cannot serve as a basis of the *individual's* method of convergence to a "maximum" or optimum position. Success is discovered by the economic system through a blanketing shotgun process, not by the individual through a converging search.

In general, uncertainty provides an excellent reason for imitation of observed success. Likewise, it accounts for observed uniformity among the survivors, derived from an evolutionary, adopting, competitive system employing a criterion of survival, which can operate independently of individual motivations. Adapting behavior via imitation and venturesome innovation enlarges the model. Imperfect imitators provide opportunity for innovation, and the survival criterion of the economy determines the successful, possibly because imperfect, imitators. Innovation is provided also by conscious wilful action, whatever the ultimate motivation may be, since drastic action is motivated by the hope of great success as well as by the desire to avoid impending failure.

All the preceding arguments leave the individual economic participant with imitative, venturesome, innovative, trial-and-error adaptive behavior. Most conventional economic tools and concepts are still useful, although in a vastly different analytical framework—one which is closely akin to the theory of biological evolution. The economic counterparts of genetic heredity, mutations, and natural selection are imitation, innovation, and positive profits.

VI. CONCLUSIONS AND SUMMARY

I shall conclude with a brief reference to some implications and conjectures.

Observable patterns of behavior and organization are predictable in terms of their relative probabilities of success or viability *if* they are tried. The observed prevalence of a type of behavior depends upon both this probability of viability and the probability of the different types being submitted to the economic system for testing and selecting. One is the probability of appearance of a certain type of organization (mutation), and the other is the probability of its survival or viability, once it appears (natural selection). There is much evidence for believing that these two probabilities are interrelated. But is there reason to suppose that a high probability of viability implies a high probability of an action's being taken, as would be implied in a system of analysis involving some "inner directed urge toward perfection"? If these two probabilities are not highly correlated, what predictions of types of action can the economist make? An answer has been suggested in this paper.

While it is true that the economist can define a profit maximization behavior by assuming *specific* cost and revenue conditions, is there any assurance that the conditions and conclusions so derivable are not too perfect and absolute? If profit maximization (certainty) is not ascertainable, the confidence about the predicted effects of changes, e.g., higher taxes or minimum wages, will be dependent upon how close the formerly existing arrangement was to the formerly "optimal" (certainty) situation. What really counts is the various actions actually tried, for it is from these that "success" is selected, not from some set of perfect actions. The economist may be pushing his luck too far in arguing that actions in response to changes in environment and changes in satisfaction with the existing state of affairs will converge as a result of adaptation or adoption toward the optimum action that should have been selected, if foresight had been perfect.[15]

In summary, I have asserted that the economist, using the present analytical tools developed in the analysis of the firm under certainty, can predict the more adoptable or viable types of economic interrelationships that will be induced by environmental change even if individuals themselves are unable to ascertain them. That is, although individual participants may not know their cost and revenue situations, the economist can predict the consequences of higher wage rates, taxes, government policy, etc. Like the biologist, the economist predicts the effects of

---

[15] An anomalous aspect of the assumption of perfect foresight is that it nearly results in tautological and empty statements. One cannot know everything, and this is recognized by the addendum that one acts within a "given state and distribution of the arts." But this is perilously close, if not equivalent, to saying either that action is taken only where the outcome is accurately foreseen or that information is always limited. The qualification is inserted because one might contend that it is the *"constancy* of the state and distribution of arts" that is necessary as a *ceteris paribus*. But even the latter is no solution. A large fraction of behavior in a world of incomplete information and uncertainty is necessarily directed at increasing the state of arts and venturing into an unknown sphere. While it is probably permissible to start with a prescribed "distribution of the knowledge of the arts," holding it constant is too restrictive, since a large class of important and frequent actions necessarily involves changes in the state and distribution of knowledge. The modification suggested here incorporates this search for more knowledge as an essential foundation.

environmental changes on the surviving class of living organisms; the economist need not assume that each participant is aware of, or acts according to, his cost and demand situation. These are concepts for the economist's use and not necessarily for the individual participant's, who may have other analytic or customary devices which, while of interest to the economist, serve as data and not as analytic methods.

An alternative to the rationale of individual profit maximization has been presented without exorcising uncertainty. Lest isolated arguments be misinterpreted, let it be clearly stated that this paper does not argue that purposive objective-seeking behavior is absent from reality, nor, on the other hand, does it indorse the familiar thesis that action of economic units cannot be expressed within the marginal analysis. Rather, the contention is that the precise role and nature of purposive behavior in the presence of uncertainty and incomplete information have not been clearly understood or analyzed.

It is straightforward, if not heuristic, to start with complete uncertainty and nonmotivation and then to add elements of foresight and motivation in the process of building an analytical model. The opposite approach, which starts with certainty and unique motivation, must abandon its basic principles as soon as uncertainty and mixed motivations are recognized.[16] The approach suggested here is intellectually more modest and realistic, without sacrificing generality. It does not regard uncertainty as an aberrational exogenous disturbance, as does the usual approach from the opposite extreme of accurate foresight. The existence of uncertainty and incomplete information is the foundation of the suggested type of analysis; the importance of the concept of a class of "chance" decisions rests upon it; it permits of various conflicting objectives; it motivates and rationalizes a type of adaptive imitative behavior; yet it does not destroy the basis of prediction, explanation, or diagnosis. It does not base its aggregate description on individual optimal action; yet it is capable of incorporating such activity where justified. The formalization of this approach awaits the marriage of the theory of stochastic processes and economics—two fields of thought admirably suited for union. It is conjectured that the suggested modification is applicable to a wide class of events and is worth attempts at empirical verification.[17]

[16] If one prefers, he may believe that the suggestions here contain reasons why the model based on certainty may predict outcomes, although individuals really cannot try to maximize profits. But the dangers of this have been indicated.

[17] Preliminary study in this direction has been very convincing, and, in addition, the suggested approach appears to contain important implications relative to general economic policy; but discussions of these are reserved for a later date.

[5]

SATISFICING, SELECTION, AND THE INNOVATING REMNANT *

SIDNEY G. WINTER

I

In the long skein of criticism and complaint that has entangled the orthodox theory of the profit-maximizing firm, two main strands are identifiable.[1] The first, or "managerial," strand emphasizes the fact that the large size, diffused stock ownership, and market power of the modern corporation leave the management with significant freedom to pursue its own goals, which are not correctly represented as maximization of profit on behalf of the stockholders. The second, or "behavioral," strand emphasizes the orthodox theory's neglect[2] of the characteristics of decision processes in individual firms, and argues essentially that this neglect is so serious as to make the theory unreliable for all but the crudest predictions.

Individual contributions to the heretical tradition are locatable, with only minor exceptions and ambiguities, on one strand or the other. Among early contributors to managerialism, one would name A. A. Berle and G. C. Means, R. A. Gordon, and A. G. Papandreou; more recent representatives include W. J. Baumol, O. E. Williamson, R. Marris, and the arch-heretic, J. K. Galbraith.[3] A distinguishing

* An earlier version of this paper was presented to the Econometric Society in December 1968. I am indebted to P. O. Steiner and O. E. Williamson for helpful comments on that version.

Financial support for the research reported here was provided at various times by the Ford Foundation, the RAND Corporation, and the Institute of Public Policy Studies of the University of Michigan. All of this is gratefully acknowledged. The views expressed here are, of course, those of the author.

1. As noted by O. E. Williamson, *The Economics of Discretionary Behavior: Managerial Objectives in a Theory of the Firm* (Englewood Cliffs, N.J.: Prentice Hall, Inc., 1964), pp. 10–11.

2. Or "misrepresentation," if the critic does not accept the argument that the theory was not intended to relate to decision processes.

3. A. A. Berle, Jr., and G. C. Means, *The Modern Corporation and Private Property* (New York: The Macmillan Co., 1933). R. A. Gordon,

trait of a behavioralist is a strong emphasis on the role of simple decision rules in business behavior; relying on that test, one identifies R. L. Hall, C. J. Hitch, and R. A. Lester as early behavioralists,[4] but the attempt to go beyond criticism to an actual reconstruction of the theory on behavioralist principles is associated with the names of H. A. Simon, R. Cyert, and J. G. March.[5] Of course, the behavioralists' interest in decision processes leads them to inquire as to how firm goals enter the process and from there to a critique of the preeminence of the profit goal. Similarly, a managerialist may cite, e.g., the difficulties of an objective determination of the profit-maximizing course of action as a factor permitting the pursuit of other goals. On many questions, the two strands of heresy pull in the same direction.

There is one significant issue, however, on which the managerialists stand closer to orthodoxy than to behavioralism. That issue is the merit of the orthodox analysis of competitive industries. As F. Machlup has recently stated,

> Many of the proponents and protagonists of a more realistic theory of the firm are quite aware of the fact that the managerial extension and enrichment of the concept of firm was not needed except where firms in the industry were large and few, and not under the pressure of competition.[6]

Indeed, the leading managerial models include the traditional profit maximization analysis as a special case that prevails when the environmental pressure is sufficiently severe, and competition is ordinarily presumed to supply that pressure.[7] By contrast, Simon sug-

Business Leadership in the Large Corporation (Washington: The Brookings Institution, 1945); and "Short Period Price Determination in Theory and Practice," *American Economic Review*, Vol. 38 (June 1948), pp. 265–88. A. G. Papandreou, "Some Basic Problems in the Theory of the Firm," *A Survey of Contemporary Economics*, Vol. 2 (1952), pp. 183–219. W. J. Baumol, *Business Behavior, Value and Growth* (New York: The Macmillan Co., 1959). O. E. Williamson, "Managerial Discretion and Business Behavior," *American Economic Review*, Vol. 53 (Dec. 1963), pp. 1032–57, and *The Economics of Discretionary Behavior, op. cit.* R. Marris, *The Economic Theory of "Managerial" Capitalism* (New York: Macmillan Co., 1964). J. K. Galbraith, *The New Industrial State* (New York: New American Library, Inc., 1968).

4. R. L. Hall and C. J. Hitch, "Price Theory and Business Behavior," *Oxford Economic Papers*, Vol. 2 (May 1939), pp. 12–45. R. A. Lester, "Shortcomings of Marginal Analysis for Wage-Employment Problems," *American Economic Review*, Vol. 36 (March 1946), pp. 63–82.

5. H. A. Simon, "A Behavioral Model of Rational Choice," this *Journal*, Vol. 69 (Feb. 1955), pp. 99–118, and *Administrative Behavior*, 2nd ed. (New York: The Free Press (paperback), 1965). R. Cyert and J. G. March, *A Behavioral Theory of the Firm* (Englewood Cliffs, N.J.: Prentice Hall, Inc., 1963).

6. F. Machlup, "Theories of the Firm: Marginalist, Behavioral, Managerial," *American Economic Review*, Vol. 57 (March 1967), p. 11.

7. There are a great many offhand comments in managerial and or-

gested in his well-known survey article that traditional competitive theory might perhaps yield correct predictions about equilibrium situations, but would be unsatisfactory under conditions of continuing change:

> . . . the equilibrium behavior of a perfectly adapting organism depends only on its goals and its environment; it is otherwise completely independent of the internal properties of the organism. . . . to predict the short-run behavior of an adaptive organism, or its behavior in a complex and rapidly changing environment, it is not enough to know its goals. We must also know a great deal about its internal structure and particularly its mechanisms of adaptation.[8]

The present paper sets forth a model of a competitive industry that is very much in the spirit of Simon's suggestion. The short-run behavior of individual firms is characterized in a manner that is consistent at least with the general tenor of the empirical literature on firm decision making. Sufficient conditions are set forth under which the industry's long-run equilibrium position will be identical with that predicted by orthodox theory, even though no single firm may be a traditional profit maximizer. It is emphasized, however, that the adjustment processes leading to these traditional equilibrium positions differ radically from those usually envisaged, and that even the validity of the sufficient conditions for the equilibrium results is far from self-evident. These considerations make it clear that there is an important difference between a theory in which "firms maximize profits" is a theorem derived from specific assumptions and a theory in which it is an axiom applicable under all conceivable circumstances.

The next section argues that the proposition "firms establish decision rules and apply them routinely over extended periods" is sufficiently significant, obvious, and well documented to deserve a prominent place in theoretical characterizations of firm behavior. Section III sets forth the general argument exemplified by the theorem subsequently proved. Sections IV and V set up a specific theoretical structure, and Section VI proves the main theorem. Possible extensions of this result are discussed in Section VII. The eighth section illustrates how the model may be viewed, allegorically, as a partial formalization of Schumpeter's view of the process of

thodox literature to the effect that under competition, survival requires maximization. As will be seen, this is a bit oversimplified — unless the case considered is that of a lonely nonmaximizer in an industry full of maximizers.

8. "Theories of Decision Making in Economics," *American Economic Review*, Vol. 49 (June 1959), p. 255.

economic development. The final section considers the broader implications for the theory of the firm.

II

There is probably unanimous agreement in the economics profession today that theoretical analyses of profit-maximizing behavior are not to be taken as a literal account of the *processes* by which firms make significant economic decisions. The proposition "firms behave *as if* they were seeking rationally to maximize profits"[9] is part of the professional credo; doctrinal and methodological disputes relate primarily to the problem of defining the range of phenomena that can safely be dismissed by appeal to the "as if" qualification. At one extreme, this loophole may be exploited only in connection with, for example, claims by business executives that they seek only a "fair return" on investment, or evidence that the terms "marginal revenue" and "elasticity of demand" are not employed in intrafirm discussions of pricing decisions. The assumption of profit maximization is construed as leading, in principle at least, to definite quantitative predictions about the market behavior of individual firms, and would stand refuted if a careful study showed these predictions to be incorrect. At the other extreme, only a significant violation of qualitative comparative statics results by an entire competitive industry might cast doubt on the validity of traditional analysis. A forthright statement of the latter view is to be found in Professor Machlup's presidential address to the American Economic Association.[1]

Given the methodological consensus that largely exempts the theory of the firm from testing by data descriptive of decision processes, it is not surprising that there exists nothing that could be regarded as a coherent orthodox view of how firms actually make decisions. Orthodoxy involves at least a tentative judgment that the question lies outside of economics. However, the testimony of those who have taken business decision processes as an object of study (whether misguidedly or not) is virtually unanimous in support of the following generalization: Most of the decisions with which economic theory is concerned are derived, at least in the short run, from a routine application of established rules, procedures,

---

9. This is Friedman's phrase, except that I substituted "profits" for "their expected returns." (M. Friedman, "The Methodology of Positive Economics," *Essays in Positive Economics*; Chicago: University of Chicago Press, 1953, p. 22.)
1. *Op. cit.*

and policies. Whatever rationality or irrationality firm behavior possesses must therefore be embodied, at least in the short run, in these rules, procedures, and policies. Space does not permit extensive documentation of this point. Most economists presumably are willing to accept it as true on the basis of casual empiricism. Rather than leaving the matter at the level of bald assertion, however, I will cite illustrative evidence.[2]

In 1956, James Earley reported results of a survey of manufacturing companies rated as "excellently managed" by the American Institute of Management.[3] His results included, for example, the following: 29 out of 106 respondents replied "yes" to the question, "Is it your policy to try to maintain, as among products and market areas, more or less equal percentage margins between prices and 'full costs'?"[4] Of course, Earley's general conclusion was that "Marginal accounting and costing principles have a strong hold among these companies," and he anticipated that this pattern would become stronger, among "excellently managed" firms and in the economy as a whole, over time. But it is worth noting that (a) "marginal accounting and costing principles" here refers to making a distinction between fixed and variable costs and to separating costs according to product, division, etc. — not to anything with the conceptual subtlety of the economist's notion of marginal cost; (b) even on this rather weak criterion, attention to marginal costing principles was by no means a necessary condition for being "excellently managed" in the mid-1950's; and (c) in any case, the switch from crude standard cost and full cost principles to somewhat more sophisticated principles was a matter of replacing one set of routine procedures by another set. Earley's research was an effective retort to anyone who entirely deprecated the relevance of marginal principles in business decision making, but it certainly lends no support to the view that the characteristics of firm decision processes are matters than can safely be left outside of economics.[5]

The second piece of evidence is the department store pricing study done by R. Cyert, J. March, and C. G. Moore.[6] Detailed

---

2. I resist the temptation to repeat Friedman's famous survey phrase, "countless applications of the hypothesis. . . ."

3. J. S. Earley, "Marginal Policies of 'Excellently Managed' Companies," *American Economic Review*, Vol. 46 (March 1956), pp. 44–70.

4. *Ibid.*, question 8, p. 69.

5. This seems quite consistent with Earley's own views. See, for example, his comments on a paper by Simon, "The Impact of Some New Developments in Economic Theory: Discussion," *American Economic Review*, Vol. 47 (May 1957), pp. 330–35, esp. p. 331.

6. Reported as ch. 7 in Cyert and March, *A Behavioral Theory of the Firm, op. cit.*

study of pricing decisions in a single department of a large retail department store led to the construction of a computer model for "normal," "regular sale," and "markdown" pricing decisions. In normal pricing, for example, the rule for items that are neither imported items nor exclusives is "divide wholesale price by 0.6 and move the result to the nearest $0.95." The authors comment that "mark-up is probably subject to long run learning," but "the statement is frequently made in the industry that mark-ups have remained the same for the last forty or fifty years." Tests of the three models yielded predictions that were correct to the penny in, respectively, 188 out of 197 cases, 56 out of 58 cases, and 140 out of 159 cases.[7] It would be difficult to cite a quantitative empirical study in economics that yielded more accurate predictions on independent data. There can be no doubt that the rules described in the computer program actually governed behavior in the firm. To the extent that traditional economic analysis of the same behavior is relevant at all, it must be because, in the long run, the considerations it emphasizes shape the decision rules.

It can be argued that, even in the short run, firms' reliance upon relatively crude "rules of thumb" or "standard operating procedures" does not necessarily indicate that they do not maximize profits, whether "maximize" means "try to maximize" or "succeed in maximizing." If the task posed is that of providing a rationale for the existence of decision routines, plausible responses that run in terms of traditional economic logic are available. W. J. Baumol and R. E. Quandt have pointed out the basic fact that "The more refined the decision-making process, the more expensive it is likely to be, and therefore, especially where a decision is not of crucial importance, no more than an approximate solution may be justified."[8] Once it is recognized that decision making, treated as free in conventional theory, is actually costly, reliance upon simple rules is seen as an aspect of cost minimization. Such rules yield economies in information gathering, computation, and intrafirm communication; they set sharply defined tasks so that performance may be improved through learning, make possible consistency and continuity in the face of personnel changes, and increase the bargaining power of low-level employees vis-à-vis customers and suppliers. One might say that while firms behave "as if" they are

---

7. *Ibid.*, pp. 138–39, 147.
8. W. J. Baumol and R. E. Quandt, "Rules of Thumb and Optimally Imperfect Decisions," *American Economic Review*, Vol. 54 (March 1964), p. 23.

creatures of habit, applying the same simplistic rules for decades on end, "in reality" they are sophisticated maximizers!

This line of argument has great appeal to those with an unshakable a priori commitment to the use of maximization assumptions in theory building, but it muddies rather than clarifies the issue in the "realism of assumptions" controversy.

In almost all of orthodox theoretical and applied economics as it exists today, the implicit or explicit premise is that the characteristics of decision processes are a matter of negligible importance relative to the motivational and environmental forces in the situation. Perfect information and costless computation assumptions are typical, for cogent reasons of analytical tractability and empirical content. When these assumptions are challenged, the "as if" argument is invoked in defense. To embellish this defense by adding "In any case, the (disregarded) characteristics of decision processes conform to economic logic" is not to supplement the basic methodological argument, but to subvert it. To an economist, a theory that admits to disregarding or falsifying the *economic* features of intrafirm reality should presumably be at least as suspect as one that admits merely to dismissing psychological, sociological, and miscellaneous complications.

Whatever the future success may be of attempts to explain the characteristics of decision processes, in economic or noneconomic terms,[9] the branches of economic theory that disregard processes entirely will — if they continue to play a role in the discipline — continue to require some defense against the charge of "unrealism." It seems safe to assume that these branches will in fact continue to be taught and employed as a source of first approximations, limiting cases, and "ideal types." The model of competitive equilibrium under certainty, for example, is probably indispensable as an organizing device in the corpus of economic theory, though it may eventually be entirely superseded for prediction purposes by a variety of special purpose models.[1] For some, the "as if" principle may continue to provide adequate symptomatic relief for the feelings of intellectual discomfort produced by expounding the implications of

9. The theory of teams provides the theoretical structure for economic explanation. See, for example, J. Marschak, "Theory of an Efficient Several-Person Firm," *American Economic Review*, Vol. 50 (May 1960), pp. 541–48. Some of the work in team theory may be interpreted as an attack on the problem of "optimal rules of thumb" posed by Baumol and Quandt, "Rules of Thumb," *op. cit.*

1. In my view, the role of the competitive model is perfectly described in Nagel's discussion of the general role of "limiting case" theories. (E. Nagel, "Assumptions in Economic Theory," *American Economic Review*, Vol. 53 (May 1963), pp. 215–16.)

faultless, perfectly informed maximizing behavior in a world in which routinized decision is prevalent. The present paper prescribes, for the difficulty as it derives from the theory of the firm, a more radical treatment. It proposes to open the theory to a more realistic view of decision processes, while retaining the equilibrium results of existing theory as a possible special case.

III

In his classic methodological statement, Friedman did not rest the case for the "as if" principle merely on his general "irrelevance of assumptions" argument. Rather, he noted the existence of a systematic mechanism that tends to force conformity between the ultimate results of the complex realities of firm decision making and the predictions of traditional theory:

unless the behavior of businessmen in some way or other approximated behavior consistent with the maximization of returns, it seems unlikely that they would remain in business for long. Let the apparent immediate determinant of business behavior be anything at all — habitual reaction, random chance, or whatnot. Whenever this determinant happens to lead to behavior consistent with rational and informed maximization of returns, the business will prosper and acquire resources with which to expand; whenever it does not, the business will tend to lose resources and can be kept in existence only by the addition of resources from outside. The process of "natural selection" thus helps to validate the hypothesis — or, rather, given natural selection, acceptance of the hypothesis can be based largely on the judgment that it summarizes appropriately the conditions for survival.[2]

As I have argued elsewhere,[3] there are several very important objections to this sweeping form of the "natural selection" argument. The most crucial of these is that the processes by which successful firms drive out unsuccessful ones do not take place instantaneously, but over a period of time. If there is no more consistency over time in the behavior of individual firms than the phrase "random chance, or whatnot" suggests, then success in any individual time period implies nothing about success in a future time period; cumulative success is fortuitous and not a reflection of a sustained closs approximation to the profit-maximizing norm. The argument is stronger if the immediate determinant of behavior is "habitual reaction," but is qualified by the observation that habits leading

2. Friedman, "The Methodology of Positive Economics," *op. cit.*, p. 22.
3. S. G. Winter, Jr., "Economic 'Natural Selection' and the Theory of the Firm," *Yale Economic Essays*, Vol. 4 (Spring 1964), pp. 225–72, esp. pp. 239–42.

to approximately profit-maximizing behavior under one set of market conditions would not necessarily do so under another.[4]

To make a "natural selection" argument plausible in economics, some mechanism playing the role of genetic inheritance must be discovered.[5] And, if such a mechanism is found, its implications for short-run behavioral predictions must be accepted: The very continuity that makes evolutionary adjustment possible in the long run may produce short-run responses to changed conditions that are significantly maladaptive. Thus, if the "natural selection" argument is valid at all, its validity cannot be established without observations of behavior in individual firms, and its support for traditional theory must be limited to the prediction of responses to familiar, recurrent situations.

Interestingly enough, the results of direct observation of firm decision behavior seem to suggest precisely the sorts of empirical propositions that are needed in the (appropriately qualified) natural selection argument. First, the generalization discussed in the previous section — that decisions in firms are governed, over extended periods, by the routine application of relatively simple decision rules — indicates that we are not contending with decisions made by "random chance or whatnot." Second, although firms do change their decision rules from time to time, another empirical generalization suggests that such changes are likely to be timely from the point of view of the operation of the selection mechanism: Firms *satisfice* with respect to decision rules. That is, if existing rules are functioning well, the firm is unlikely to change them; if not, search for better rules will be stimulated. The search process itself may be governed, in part, by established routines. Generally speaking, however, it is less systematic, and has more of the characteristics of creative problem solving than the routine decision process to which it relates. Thus, while decision rules themselves are the economic counterpart of genetic inheritance, the failure-stimulated search process apparently has no analogue in biological evolution — it would correspond to a mechanism that automatically generates a burst of mutations when they are needed.

4. The assumptions subsequently made in this paper could be viewed as coming under the "habitual reaction" heading.

5. Essentially this point was made by E. T. Penrose in her comment, "Biological Analogies in the Theory of the Firm," *American Economic Review*, Vol. 42 (Dec. 1952), pp. 804–19. It is curious that such a gross discrepancy between Friedman's argument and the biological theory that inspired it was overlooked by him — and also by A. A. Alchian in his classic article, "Uncertainty, Evolution and Economic Theory," *Journal of Political Economy*, Vol. 58 (June 1950), pp. 211–22.

Seeking ways of modifying received theory to make it more consistent with decision process realities, we find that those realities are roughly of the sort needed to make natural selection work. Perhaps behavioralism will provide to orthodoxy the materials to make partial repairs in its favorite "we can get along without behavioralism" argument, while that argument comes to serve as the basis for a convincing demonstration that orthodox analysis is "really just a special case of behavioralism." This would be a happy, if paradoxical, circumstance. But caution is in order: The equilibria described by traditional competitive theory are very special configurations of behavior, and if some of the conditions for a valid natural selection argument have been satisfied, others remain to be mentioned.

For selection to be operative, the market's signals of profit and loss must correspond to "selective advantage"; that is, the group of profitable firms must, as an aggregate, have a higher growth rate than the group of unprofitable ones. This in turn requires that there be a difference between the two groups with respect to the ability to expand, or the inclination to expand, or both. A difference in the ability to finance expansion is a direct consequence of profit performance, insofar as internal funds are a dominant consideration in the financing of investment. To the extent that external suppliers of investment capital respond directly rather than perversely to past performance, capital markets also operate in the required direction. The existence of the inclination to expand poses a more troublesome issue: For traditional competitive equilibria to be generated, rates of return in excess of "normal" must always induce expansion. One possible rationale for this rule is provided by traditional theory itself. Individual firms must consider that they are small enough to be able to expand without significant effect on market prices, and thus be willing to take their own past performance as an indication of the returns to investment. And, they must be sufficiently interested in profits to take the opportunity. But a "managerialist" rationale is even more direct: Growth-oriented managements will expand as long as the normal rate of return can be realized on new investment.

A further question is, how does it happen that the expansion of the firm does not alter the firm's behavior in unfortunate ways, so that, even at constant prices, the expanding firm becomes less profitable? In general, the reply is that the principle of satisficing on the decision rules applies in the case of new capacity as well: The successful firm creates new productive units in the image of the old ones. This has sufficient behavioral plausibility to justify its tentative acceptance, but it is clear that this is a problem area requiring further investigation. A large multiplant firm is not precisely equivalent to a collection of single-plant firms, all following the same decision rules.

Finally, there remains the problem of the optimality of the equilibrium positions achieved. Traditional theory asserts that techniques employed in equilibrium will actually maximize profits over the set of techniques known to the firm. Whether the concept of such a set of "known" techniques has behavioral content at the level of the individual firm appears dubious to me.[6] In any case, it is not strictly necessary for an "as if" argument leading to traditional equilibrium results. The production set concept is replaced by the following: There is a set of decision rules, including production rules, which includes all the rules ever employed by any firm, and over which there is persistent search. By "persistent search" is meant a search process that continues indefinitely, regardless of how satisfactory or unsatisfactory performance may be — although the search may be slow, sporadic, or both. It is further assumed that, if the search process turns up a rule that is more profitable than rules currently employed at prevailing prices, some firm will adopt it (at which point its persistence becomes subject to the usual satisficing principle). It is *not* implied that any single firm searches the entire set of possibilities, or even that the persistent search process is entirely a matter of the behavior of *firms*. These assumptions assert the existence of a remnant, not of maximizing behavior, but of innovative behavior motivated by calculation of the profit consequences of a contemplated course of action. The crucial distinction is that, in contrast to the behavior patterns previously discussed, the "innovating remnant" assumption requires that some behavior derive from hypothetical calculations rather than realized results.

Here, in summary, are the general assumptions that might plausibly yield a class of theorems reconciling behavioral realism in short-run decision processes with "as if" profit maximization in the long run. The assumption that firms have decision rules, and retain or replace them according to the satisficing principle, provides both genetic stability and an endogenous mutation mechanism. The assumption that profitable firms expand by adding new ca-

6. Assuming, that is, that the set in question is supposed to be much more than a summary of current and recent practice, much less than a summary of all physically possible technology, and is supposed to have sharply defined boundaries separating "known" and "unknown."

pacity, operated according to the old rules, and that unprofitable firms contract, provides the selection process by which the fit replace the unfit. Finally, persistent search and the innovating remnant serve to eliminate as possible equilibrium positions situations in which possible but untried decision rules would yield higher profits than those currently utilized.

Intuitively, the chances that there are interesting theorems of the indicated type seem good. Systematic demonstration is another matter; even the simplest assumptions about firm decision processes yield dynamic systems of considerable complexity. Fulfilling the promise of behavioral realism in the assumptions on individual firms will require substantial further effort. The result proved in Section VI below does, at least, suggest that the basic logic of the proposal is sound.

IV

This section sets forth an orthodox partial equilibrium model of a competitive industry. A modified version of it will serve as the basis for the satisficing–selection–innovating-remnant model of the following section.

Assumption 1 (Technology). Each firm has the same convex, constant returns to scale technology, represented by a closed convex cone Y in N-dimensional Euclidean space $(N \geq 2)$. A vector $y \in Y$ is a list of single-period input and output flows that constitutes a feasible production plan. Thus, durable capital inputs are reflected as single-period flows of services. Negative components of y correspond to input quantities, positive components to output quantities.

Assumption 2 (Demand Price Function). The industry faces a continuous demand price function, $h(y)$, defined on Y, which maps the list y of input and output quantities into a list of nonnegative prices at which the outputs demanded and inputs supplied by the rest of the economy will just equal y. Prices corresponding to durable capital services are the prices that would be charged by a competitive industry that owned all the durables and rented them out.

The fact that the function $h(y)$ is defined independent of the distribution of industry output by firm is one indication of the partial equilibrium character of the analysis; the fact that h is constant over time (independent of past use of durables) is another.

Assumption 3 (Extreme Values of Industry Size). If the industry is small enough, some technique in Y will yield a profit. Given the continuity of h, this is implied by A3.1.

A3.1. There is a $y \, \epsilon \, Y$ such that $h(0) \cdot y > 0$.

If the industry is large enough, no technique in Y will yield a profit. That is:

A3.2. There is a positive scalar β such that $y' \, \epsilon \, Y$ and $\| \, y' \, \| \geqq \beta$ implies $h(y') \cdot y < 0$ for all $y \, \epsilon \, Y$, $y \neq 0$. Here, $\| \, y \, \| = \sqrt{y \cdot y}$.

Assumption 4 (Firms). Firms are price takers and profit maximizers at least in the limited sense that no firm will continue indefinitely to produce net outputs y' and sell at prices p unless $p \cdot y' \geqq p \cdot y$ for all $y \, \epsilon \, Y$.

The number of firms in the industry is assumed to be large enough that the assumption of price-taking behavior is plausible.

Assumption 3 assures that the industry has a place in the economy; given A4, equilibrium at industry output zero is not possible. It also assures that the industry cannot grow indefinitely; at a sufficiently large size, prices of inputs will rise, or those of outputs decline, or both, to a point where profits would be maximized by withdrawing. Incidentally, A3.2 implies the impossibility of producing output without using some input.

Since the demand price function is continuous, and neither zero industry output nor arbitrarily large output is consistent with profit maximization by individual firms, it is plausible that there exists a long-run competitive equilibrium position for the industry. That is, there is a feasible industry input-output list, $y^* \, \epsilon \, Y$, and a corresponding price vector, $p^* = h(y^*)$, satisfying $p^* \cdot y^* = 0$, $y^* \neq 0$, and $p^* \cdot y \leqq 0$ for all $y \, \epsilon \, Y$. A proof based on the Kakutani fixed-point theorem may be found in the Appendix.

It is worth noting that this definition of equilibrium would, if embedded in a dynamic model of the industry's behavior, have some implications for the price expectations of firms. The simplest assumptions consistent with those implications would be that firms act in period $t+1$ on the assumption $p_{t+1} = p_t$.

V

In the proof of a theorem illustrating the general arguments of Section III, the mathematical tools employed will be the theory of *finite* Markov chains. The first steps in constructing the required framework are to introduce a discrete version of the technology characterized in A1, and a basis for an explicit short-run–long-run distinction.

Assumption 1' (Technology). Each firm has the same technology, characterized as follows: There is an N by K matrix A; each column is a list of input and output flows that is feasible in a single "plant" in a single time period, and at least one row is strictly negative. In each time period, a firm operates a nonnegative integral number of plants. Denote the kth column of A by a_k, $k=1, \ldots, K$; let f_{jt} be the number of plants operated by firm j in time period t, and let x_{jkt} be the number of plants of firm j using technique k in time period t. Then the set of technologically feasible lists of input and output flows for firm j in period t — the short-run production set — is

$$Y_{jt} = \{y_{jt} : y_{jt} = \sum_{k=1}^{K} x_{jkt} a_k, \ (x_{jkt}) \text{ are nonnegative integers;} \\ \sum_k x_{jkt} = f_{jt}\}.$$

From period to period, firms may change the number of plants operated. Thus, the long-run production set, identical for all firms, is

$$Y = \{y : y = \sum_k x_k a_k, \ (x_k) \text{ are nonnegative integers}\}.$$

It is assumed, essentially, that there is only one type of plant, which suggests that in the rows of A corresponding to services of durable equipment, all columns are identical (unless the item is rented). The generalization to more than one type of plant would involve more notational complexity than substantive difficulty.

If the numbers x_k could be arbitrary nonnegative numbers, instead of being restricted to integral values, the production set Y characterized above would again be a convex cone — a convex polyhedral cone, to be precise. Thus, to the extent that input and output flows in individual plants are small relative to industry totals, the technological assumptions of the present section approximate a special case of those of the previous section.

Assumptions 2 and 3 will remain in force. Because "number of plants" is integer-valued, A1', A2, and A3 do not assure the existence of a competitive equilibrium. However, it is clear that one "almost" exists if plant sizes are small enough relative to industry output. Pleading substantive rather than mathematical plausibility, we will assume that there is an equilibrium. Since A4 is no longer appropriate, this will be introduced as A4'.

Assumption 4' (Existence of Equilibrium). Under A1', A2, and A3, there exists a long-run competitive equilibrium. That is, there are nonnegative integers $x_k{}^*$ such that

$$y^* = \sum_k x_k{}^* a_k, \text{ and}$$

$$p^* = h(y^*)$$

satisfy $p^* \cdot y^* = 0$, $y^* \neq 0$, and $p^* \cdot y \leq 0$ for all $y \in Y$.

The simplest possible assumption about firm decision rules for short-run production decisions will be made.

Assumption 5 (*Decision Rule*). In each time period, each firm has a *decision rule* (for production decisions). This rule is represented simply by one of the columns of A; all of the firm's plants are operated with this technique. Denote this rule for firm j in period t by the vector r_{jt}. Then the firm's input-output list in the period is simply $y_{jt} = r_{jt}f_{jt}$.

A *state of firm* j is now defined as a pair $(r_{j.}, f_{j.})$. An industry state is simply a list of firm states $[(r_{1.}, f_{1.}), \ldots, (r_{M.}, f_{M.})]$. (Here M is the number of firms potentially in existence; it is finite but "large enough" for purposes of subsequent arguments.) On the assumption that equilibrium in the "very short run" is successfully achieved, there corresponds to each industry state a definite price vector $p = h(y)$, where $y = \Sigma y_j$.

It will be notationally convenient to define the column K vectors

$$x_t = \begin{pmatrix} x_{1t} \\ \cdot \\ \cdot \\ \cdot \\ x_{Kt} \end{pmatrix}, \text{ where } x_{kt} = \Sigma x_{jkt} = \sum_{\substack{j \\ (j:\ r_{jt} = a_k)}} f_{jt}$$

and

$$x^* = \begin{pmatrix} x_1^* \\ \cdot \\ \cdot \\ \cdot \\ x_K^* \end{pmatrix}.$$

Thus, $y_t = Ax_t$ and $y^* = Ax^*$. It will be said of technique k that it is an "equilibrium technique" if $x_k^* > 0$, and that it is "represented at time t" if $r_{jt} = a_k$ for some j.

Given an industry state at time t and its corresponding price vector p_t, the states of individual firms are classified in five groups, designated P, B, L, Z, and Z_P. Here P is mnemonic for "profit," B for "breakeven," L for "loss," and Z for "zero plants." Firm j is classified in a group at time t according to the accompanying tabulation.

		$p_t \cdot r_{jt}$ is		
		negative	zero	positive
f_{jt} is	zero	Z	Z	Z_P
	positive	L	B	P

The qualitative characteristics of the transition probability rules now to be described are the representation, in this specific model, of the satisficing–selection–innovating-remnant concepts of Section III.

Assumption 6 (Transition Rules). Given the industry state at time t, individual firm states at time $t+1$ are determined, independent of the past sequence of industry states, by probability rules that depend on the group the firm is in at time t.

A6.1 (Group P). Firms in group P do not change decision rules. They expand probabilistically. That is,

$r_{j,\,t+1}=r_{jt}$ with probability one.

$$f_{j,\,t+1}=f_{jt}+\delta \text{ with probability} \left.\begin{Bmatrix} 0 \\ >0 \\ \geqq 0 \\ 0 \end{Bmatrix}\right. \text{for} \left.\begin{Bmatrix} \delta<0 \\ \delta=0,\,1 \\ 1<\delta<\Delta \\ \delta\geqq\Delta \end{Bmatrix}\right..$$

A6.2 (Group B). Firms in group B do not change state. That is,

$r_{j,\,t+1}=r_{jt}$ with probability one.

$f_{j,\,t+1}=f_{jt}$ with probability one.

A6.3 (Group L). Firms in group L contract probabilistically and search for an alternative decision rule in a manner described by a K by K matrix S. Here, S is a nonnegative matrix with positive diagonal and column sums equal to one. Let s_{uv} be a typical element of S. Then,

if $r_{jt}=a_v$, $r_{j,\,t+1}=a_u$ with probability s_{uv}.

$$f_{j,\,t+1}=f_{jt}+\delta \text{ with probability} \left.\begin{Bmatrix} 0 \\ \geqq 0 \\ >0 \\ 0 \end{Bmatrix}\right. \text{for} \left.\begin{Bmatrix} \delta<-f_{jt} \\ -f_{jt}\leqq\delta<-1 \\ \delta=-1,\,0 \\ \delta>0 \end{Bmatrix}\right.$$

A6.4 (Group Z). Group Z comprises potential entrants who are "contemplating" a technique that does not yield positive profits. They do not enter, but "contemplate" different techniques in a manner described by a K by K matrix $C=(c_{uv})$. This matrix is nonnegative and irreducible, with column sums equal to one and a positive diagonal.

If $r_{jt}=a_v$, $r_{j,\,t+1}=a_u$ with probability c_{uv}.

A6.5 (Group Z_P). Firms in group Z_P are potential entrants considering currently profitable techniques. They act like Z firms with some positive probability less than one, and like P firms with the complementary probability. Thus, if they enter they retain the same decision rule; if they change rules they do so according to the matrix C probabilities and do not enter.

The foregoing rules define probability distributions of individual firm states at $t+1$, conditional on the industry state at t, and independent of prior industry states. Since the industry state is just the list of firm states, the probability distribution of industry state at $t+1$ is determined, conditional on industry state at t and independent of prior industry states. Thus, a Markov process on the set of industry states has been defined. Note that since "no change of state" is a positive probability outcome for each individual firm, there is a positive probability that the industry state will not change in any given time period.

Consider the set E of industry states with the following characteristics. First, all firms are in group B or group Z. Second, at the corresponding prices p, $p \cdot a_k \leqq 0$ for $k=1, \ldots, K$. By A3.1, the number of firms in group B is not zero. Thus, industry states in E correspond to competitive equilibria; no firm is realizing profits or losses and the techniques actually employed are breaking even, hence are maximizing. Furthermore, under the transition rules of A6, a state in E will be followed, with probability one, by another state in E, and one that implies the same y and p vectors. Firms in group B will not change at all. Firms in Z will continue to "contemplate" different decision rules, but the set of techniques actually profitable at prevailing prices being empty, they will never shift to group Z_P, and never operate a plant. In the language of the theory of Markov processes, E is a "closed set of states." Assumption 4' assures us that it is a nonempty set. All we need do to define a state in E is to choose, for example, the first K firms and set $r_{k.}=a_k$, $f_{k.}=x_k^*$ for $k=1, \ldots, K$, and $f_{j.}=0$ otherwise. Obviously, there are many states in E corresponding to *any* competitive equilibrium for the industry as a whole.

Industry states not in E clearly do not represent competitive equilibria — actual profits and losses are being realized, or a technique that is profitable at prevailing prices is not in operation, or both. Assumption 6 implies that the probability is zero that the industry input-output list associated with any such non-E state will persist indefinitely. For there clearly is a positive probability that (1) a single firm in group P will expand, or (2) a single firm in L will contract, or (3) a firm in Z will (in fewer than K periods) come upon a profitable technique and then expand, all other firm states remaining unchanged in each case. Any one of these developments changes the industry input-output list.

Thus far the intuitive logic of Section III successfully carries us. An industry input-output list that gives rise to competitive equilibrium will persist; one that does not must eventually change. But there remains a question to which the intuitive argument provides no satisfactory answer: Given an initial industry state not in E, what assures that the system does not remain indefinitely in the non-E states? It seems that the patterns of change decreed by A6 should be "in the right direction," i.e., toward equilibrium, but to establish this rigorously requires another assumption. Discussion of the significance of this assumption is deferred to Section VII.

Assumption 7 (Weak Revealed Preference).

$$\text{If } h(y') \cdot y' \geqq h(y') \cdot y'', \text{ then } h(y'') \cdot y'' \leqq h(y'') \cdot y',$$
$$\text{and } h(y'') \cdot y'' = h(y'') \cdot y' \text{ implies } h(y'') = h(y').$$

The difference between this and the familiar proposition of the same name is attributable to the fact that $h(y)$ is a single-valued demand *price* function, whereas the standard revealed preference axiom is appropriate for single-valued demand functions. A function $h(y)$ that reflects preferences that are smooth and convex, but not necessarily strictly convex, may satisfy A7.[7]

By A4', we have $0 = p^* \cdot y^* \geqq p^* \cdot y$ for all $y \in Y$. Thus, the hypothesis of A7 is always satisfied if $y' = Y^*$, and we have the conclusion that, for all $y \in Y$,

$$h(y) \cdot y \leqq h(y) \cdot y^*, \text{ and}$$
$$h(y) \cdot y = h(y) \cdot y^* \text{ implies } h(y) = p^*.$$

That is, for any industry input-output list, the associated prices imply a value for that list no greater than they impute to the equilibrium list y^*. If the value is the same, the demand prices are the same as they are at y^*. An immediate consequence is that p^* is the unique competitive equilibrium price vector — but it remains possible that there are equilibrium net output vectors other than y^*.

VI

The main result of this paper can now be proved.

Theorem: Under A1', A2, A3, A4' and A5–A7, and given an arbitrary initial state, the following holds: With probability one, an industry state in E will eventually occur, and all subsequent states will lie in E.

---

7. Consistent with the partial equilibrium character of the analysis, the actors whose behavior is reflected in $h(y)$ are not constrained to particular values of their net transactions with the industry under examination. As a result, some further assumptions on preferences would be required before all the properties thus far attributed to $h(y)$ would be logically implied.

Briefly, the technique of the proof is this: First it is shown that only a finite number of industry states can be reached from the initial state. It then suffices to show that, given any state attainable from the initial state, a positive probability exists that E will be reached in finite time.[8] This demonstration appeals repeatedly to the fact that, under A6, individual firm states can succeed themselves with positive probability, and hence that it is valid to assume feasible transitions for any subset of the firms while the states of the others remain unchanged. It is shown first that, at any time, there is positive probability that every equilibrium technique will be represented K periods later. Then it is shown that, at any subsequent time, either there is positive probability that the industry state will move closer to equilibrium in the sense that the number $\Sigma \mid x_{kt} - x_k^* \mid$ will decrease, or else the industry state is in E. Since only finitely many industry states need be considered, and since (as already noted) the system will not leave E once it is reached, this proves the theorem.

The number of firms and the number of techniques both being finite, the set of industry states is infinite only because the number of plants operated by any individual firm can in principle be any nonnegative integer. There is, however, a number η such that Max $(\eta, \Sigma f_{j0})$ is an upper bound on the number of plants that can ever be operated in the industry if the initial firm sizes are f_{j0}. For, let μ be the smallest of the absolute values of the elements in a strictly negative row of A (see A1'). If y is an industry input-output list produced with π plants, then $\parallel y \parallel \geq \pi\mu$. Hence, if $\pi \geq \beta/\mu$, then $h(y) \cdot a_k < 0$ for all k (by A3.2). That is, if there are more than a certain number of plants operated, all techniques are sure to yield losses. Under the transition rules of A6, an increase in the number of plants can occur only if some technique yields a profit, and no single firm can increase its number of plants in a single period by more than Δ. Thus, $\eta = \beta/\mu + \Delta M$ is surely an upper bound on the number of plants that could exist in the industry at any time after the first period in which any technique would be profitable. Prior to that time (if it is not time 0), the number of plants does not exceed its initial value of Σf_{j0}. Given a particular initial state, therefore, industry size is bounded above, and the number of industry states that can be reached from the initial state is finite.

Consider any industry state within the indicated bound on industry size. It will be shown that, starting from this state, there is

8. See W. Feller, *An Introduction to Probability Theory and Its Applications* (New York: John Wiley and Sons, Inc., 1957), pp. 352–53, 364.

a finite sequence of positive probability transitions leading to a state in E.

Since the number of firms potentially in existence, M, has been assumed "large enough," it may be assumed that there are at least K firms in groups Z and Z_P. Pick K of these arbitrarily, and assume that all other firms maintain their states while the K chosen change their decision rules but not (if in Z_P) their scale. Given the transition rules of A6.4 and A6.5, particularly the irreducibility and aperiodicity of the matrix C, there is positive probability that at the end of at most $K-1$ periods each equilibrium technique will be the rule of at least one of these K firms. And, of course, there is positive probability that none of these firms changes its decision rule during any subsequent finite period. In sum: Given any industry state at time t, there is positive probability that every equilibrium technique will be represented at time $t+K$ and for any finite period thereafter.

Attention may now be focused on industry states in which every equilibrium technique is represented. Assuming such a state to occur at time t, let

$$V(t) = \sum_k |x_{kt} - x_k^*|.$$

Then, either there is a positive probability that $V(t+1) < V(t)$, or else the industry state at time t is in E.[9] For, on the assumption that there is zero probability that $V(t+1) < V(t)$, the following must hold:

(i) $p_t \cdot a_k > 0$ implies $x_{kt} \geqq x_k^*$. This is trivial if k is not an equilibrium technique. If it is, it is represented, and at least one firm is in group Z_P or P. With positive probability, such a firm can add one plant while all else remains the same. This would reduce V unless $x_{kt} \geqq x_k^*$.

(ii) $p_t \cdot a_k < 0$ implies $x_{kt} \leqq x_k^*$. For $x_{kt} > x_k^*$ would imply that k is represented, and by a firm in L. Such a firm could contract by one plant, all else remaining the same, with positive probability. This would imply $V(t+1) < V(t)$ with positive probability, contrary to hypothesis.

Combining (i) and (ii) and including the cases $p_t \cdot a_k = 0$, we find

$$p_t \cdot a_k \, x_{kt} \geqq p_t \cdot a_k \, x_k^* \text{ for all } k.$$

Sum over k:

___

9. Note that it is possible for the industry state to be in E even if $V > 0$, since neither y^* nor x^* is necessarily the unique equilibrium vector of its type.

$$p_t \cdot (Ax_t) \geqq p_t \cdot (Ax^*), \text{ or}$$

$$p_t \cdot y_t \geqq p_t \cdot y^*.$$

Appealing to A7 and the discussion immediately following, we conclude that $p_t \cdot y_t = p_t \cdot y^*$, and hence that $p_t = p^*$ and $p^* \cdot y_t = 0$. Since p^* prevails, no technique is profitable and no firm can be in P. Since industry profits $= p^* \cdot y_t = 0$, there can be no firms in L either. The assumption that $V(t+1) < V(t)$ has zero probability thus implies that the state at time t is in E.

It now suffices to remark that, given the finiteness of the set of industry states that are ever reached, there is some maximum value that V can ever take on. A finite number of unit reductions of V, each having positive probability, will therefore result in $V = 0$ if E is not reached first. Hence E is reached with positive probability in any case. This conclusion holds starting from any industry state within the upper bound on industry state. Thus, according to the previously cited passages in Feller,[1] there is probability one that E will eventually be reached.

VII

Several opportunities exist for modifying the foregoing argument in ways that, either obviously or as a plausible conjecture, do not affect the conclusion of the theorem. First, the weak revealed-preference assumption could be replaced by the conclusion derived from it: $h(y) \cdot y \geqq h(y) \cdot y^*$ implies $h(y) = p^*$. The latter statement may be interpreted, "No net output vector is revealed preferred (by market demand) to the equilibrium vector." This interpretation may perhaps make the need for some such assumption plausible: A certain amount of consistency in what the market indicates it "wants" may be needed if the selection process is to reach the conventional equilibrium position.[2] Intuitively, it seems that weaker "consistency" assumptions on $h(y)$ might be adequate if one were to compensate by strengthening the assumptions concerning the scale changes of firms in groups P and L: If firms were occasionally to expand or contract by large amounts in a single period, this might make it impossible for the system to get "hung up" indefinitely in some set of non-E states.[3]

1. *Op. cit.*
2. It is not easy to describe the relationship between the role revealed preference plays here and the one it plays in one proof of the stability of the general equilibrium tâtonnement process — except perhaps by saying that the relation is that of Marshall to Walras.
3. A theorem of essentially this type was proved in the earlier version of this paper.

It is interesting to note that the theoretical difficulty to which the demand price function and its revealed preference property respond does not (so far as a casual and inexpert observer can tell) appear to have been squarely confronted in the biological literature on evolution. The problem, stated for the two contexts in parallel, is this: The comparative (fitness of genotypes, profitability of decision rules) determines which (genotypes, decision rules) will tend to become predominant over time. However, the (fitness, profitability) clearly depends on the (characteristics of the environment, market prices) confronting the (species, collection of firms with similar decision rules). The (environment, price vector) in turn depends, however, on the (genotypes, decision rules) of all of the individual (organisms, firms) therein — a dependence discussed in the subdiscipline called (ecology, market theory). Therefore, no theory of long-run evolutionary change can logically take the environment of the individual (species, collection of firms) as exogenous. Hence, the notion of (fitness, profitability) contributes much less to the understanding of the long-run pattern of change than might at first glance appear. And what does play a crucial though obscure role is the character of the whole evolving system's interaction with the truly exogenous environment, represented in the present paper by the market demand-price function and in biological theory by . . . ? A theory that omits to explain how significant properties of that interaction affect the changing requirements for (fitness, profitability) over time cannot be regarded as an explanation of the evolution of the system.

The easiest path to generalization of the theorem is through weakening the restrictions that have been placed on firm state transition probabilities in A6. For example, the various probability distributions could all depend quantitatively on the firm's identity (its index j), provided that the qualitative properties previously stipulated were retained.

Even the qualitative behavior of individual firms could be greatly different in the case of the assumptions on persistent search. What is required, as noted previously, is that *some* firm eventually try each technique, not that each firm eventually try each technique. Also, persistent search could be an activity of existing firms as well as potential entrants — provided that the decision rules discovered in the process are not implemented if they yield losses.

A more ambitious change would involve the introduction of a profit aspiration level for each firm, as part of the firm state description. The firm would behave in the group P, B, or L fashion according to whether profit per plant exceeded, equaled, or fell short of aspiration. It seems very likely that the main theorem would continue to hold, provided (a) aspiration level could not be forced below zero, and (b) sustained negative or zero profits would force aspiration level to zero. A further complication would be to make both aspiration level and search behavior in each individual firm depend upon the realized profits and decision rules in other firms. A simple version of this situation might be the "trade association model": In addition to the market price, various "industry norm" functions might be defined as a function of industry state, and individual firm behavior could then depend on past behavior of the same firm, aspiration level, market price, and industry norms.

VIII

Imagine now that the number of techniques, instead of being a finite number K, is denumerably infinite. Suppose further that the techniques are ordered roughly in terms of technological sophistication and productivity. In the initial state, all firm decision rules are techniques early in the infinite list. Now the long-run competitive equilibrium disappears and continuing technological progress replaces it; the passage of time will always see the discovery of ever more advanced techniques.

However, by imputing a special structure to the matrices S and C, one can convert the model into a sort of formalized allegory for Schumpeter's *Theory of Economic Development*.[4] Let the rows and columns of C be partitioned in identical fashion, and let C_{uv} be a typical submatrix. Recalling that each column of C gives probabilities that various (row) techniques will be examined, conditional on the column technique being currently examined, suppose C has this general structure:

$$C = \begin{bmatrix} C_{11} & C_{12} & C_{13} & C_{14} & \dots \\ \epsilon & C_{22} & C_{23} & C_{24} & \dots \\ 0 & \epsilon & C_{33} & C_{34} & \dots \\ 0 & 0 & \epsilon & C_{44} & \dots \\ & \dots & \dots & \dots & \dots \\ & \dots & \dots & \dots & \dots \end{bmatrix}$$

Here, ϵ's denote matrices of very small positive numbers, 0's matrices of zeroes; the C_{uu} matrices involve fairly large probabilities, and C_{uv}, for $u < v$, involves probabilities of intermediate size.

4. J. A. Schumpeter, *The Theory of Economic Development* (Cambridge, Mass.: Harvard University Press, 1955).

If the ϵ's are sufficiently small, each submatrix on the diagonal will successively play the role of C in the theorem of Section VI. Suppose that initial firm decision rules are in the first block of techniques; equilibrium relative to this block of techniques may be established before the first transition to a technique in the second block occurs. Then, an entrepreneur takes the calculated profitability of a technique in the second block as a basis for action, expands, and forces losses on his competitors. Some of these search and perhaps imitate the new technique; others are forced out of business. The rest of the second block of techniques is tried, and adopted if profitable, over a relatively short period (a rush of secondary innovations linked to the main one). Gradually, something like equilibrium is again established, relative to the technology represented by blocks one and two combined. Then, a new entrepreneur adopts a technique in block three. . . .

IX

The simple decision rules postulated in the formal analysis were chosen for tractability, not realism. The behavior imputed to firms is, as a result, considerably less sophisticated than the most dedicated behavioralist would suggest. But even the most sophisticated rules — proposed by the best of management consultants — do not come to the firm certified "objectively rational." Such rules decide for the future on the basis of data from the past, manipulated according to some simplistic view of the causal structure of the environment, and they involve an enormous amount of implicit or explicit conjecture about the behavior of other actors. Beyond the rules themselves lies the realm of processes modifying rules — where we encounter such questions as which consulting firm to hire, whether the linear programming solution developed by the brash young man is likely to beat the "judgment" solution of the old hand, and so forth. In this realm, prejudice, false analogy, personalities, bargaining, and politics play a powerful role.

Thus, the model's story of simple rules modified by stochastic search processes may make the rules too simple and the search processes too stochastic, but conceptually it bears a much closer resemblance to the world of experience than the story of faultless maximization over sharply defined opportunity sets. At the same time, it remains a theory of market processes, in which "as if" profit maximization is a theorem with identifiable assumptions. If similar results can be achieved at a higher level of behavioral realism, it may eventually become possible for students of firm and market behavior to live in one reality rather than two.

APPENDIX

Proof of the Existence of Competitive Equilibrium under the Assumptions of Section IV.

Consider the convex, compact set $Y^* = \{y \; \epsilon \; Y : \| y \| \leqq \beta\}$ where β is the scalar whose existence is assured by A3.2. Define a correspondence ϕ from Y^* to itself by

$$\phi(y) = \{y' \; \epsilon \; Y^* : h(y) \; \cdot \; y' \geqq h(y) \cdot y'' \text{ for all } y'' \; \epsilon \; Y^*\}.$$

It is clear that $\phi(y)$ is convex and nonempty for each $y \; \epsilon \; Y^*$; also the continuity of h implies the upper semicontinuity of ϕ. Thus, by the Kakutani theorem, there is a $y^* \; \epsilon \; Y^*$ such that $y^* \; \epsilon \; \phi(y^*)$. We now verify that y^*, $h(y^*)$ is the required equilibrium.

(i) 0 is not in $\phi(0)$, since $h(0) \; \cdot \; 0 = 0$, while A3.1 assures that there is a y in Y, hence in Y^*, for which $h(0) \; \cdot \; y > 0$. Therefore $y^* \neq 0$.

(ii) If $\| y \| = \beta$ then y is not in $\phi(y)$. For, according to A3.2, $\| y \| = \beta$ implies $h(y) \cdot y' < 0$ for all $y' \epsilon Y$ except $y' = 0$, so $\phi(y) = \{0\}$. Therefore $0 < \| y^* \| < \beta$.

(iii) $h(y^*) \cdot y^* < 0$ is impossible because $y^* \epsilon \phi(y^*)$ implies that y^* maximizes $h(y^*) \cdot y$ over Y^*, and $0 \epsilon Y^*$, so $h(y^*) \cdot y^* \geqq h(y^*) \cdot 0 = 0$.

(iv) For any $y \neq 0$ in Y, $(\beta \| y \|^{-1}) y \; \epsilon \; Y^*$. Therefore, by the maximizing property of y^* again,

$$h(y^*) \cdot y^* \geqq (\beta \| y \|^{-1}) h(y^*) \cdot y \text{ for all } y \epsilon Y.$$

Taking $y = y^*$ and recalling (ii), we find that this implies

$$h(y^*) \cdot y^* \leqq 0.$$ Hence, by (iii), $h(y^*) \cdot y^* = 0$.

Then the previous inequality implies that $h(y^*) \cdot y \leqq 0$ for all $y \epsilon Y$. Thus y^* is an equilibrium input-output vector, and $h(y^*)$ the corresponding price vector.

UNIVERSITY OF MICHIGAN

[6]

FIRM AND INDUSTRY RESPONSE TO CHANGED MARKET CONDITIONS: AN EVOLUTIONARY APPROACH

RICHARD R. NELSON and SIDNEY G. WINTER*

This paper describes an evolutionary theory of the response of firms in a competitive industry to changed market conditions. Search and selection replace the more orthodox assumptions of profit maximizing and zero profit long run equilibrium. The particular assumptions needed to assure that the direction of response of such an evolutionary system is the same as that predicted by more orthodox theory are explored. While an evolutionary theory and a more orthodox one yield many of the same positive qualitative predictions, they differ sharply in a number of other respects, and these are considered in detail.

A central task of microeconomic theory is to explain and predict the effects of changes in market conditions upon the behavior of firms and industries — their inputs, outputs, and prices. From Smith, Ricardo, Mill, Marx, Marshall, Schumpeter, Knight, to Allen and Hicks and Samuelson, theoretical reasoning about the key relationships involved has been based on two central ideas. One of these is that firms seek profits and changes in market conditions influence the relative profitabilities of different production techniques and levels. The other is that competition among firms tends to drive profits toward a "normal" level. The basic ideas are venerable. However, it is only relatively recently that they have come to be formalized as they now are in the textbooks and treatises. In contemporary formal theory, profit *seeking* behavior is typically represented as profit *maximizing* behavior with choice sets precisely known and given. Competitive pressure is typically represented by its idealized consequence — price taking, zero profit equilibrium.[1]

Many contemporary economists seem to believe that the older ideas and the contemporary mathematical ones amount to the same thing, save that the latter are sharper and more rigorous. This is a misconception. Many earlier writers clearly meant to include, as an important component of response of firms to changed market conditions, the phenomenon that contemporary economists would call induced innovation. And in many of the classical statements, competition was viewed as a dynamic

---

*Professors of Economics, Yale University. We are indebted to Richard Levin, Jack Hirshleifer, John Quigley and the referee for very helpful comments.

1. For discussion of the evolution of thinking by economists about competition see McNulty (1968) and Stigler (1957).

process involving uncertainty, struggle and disequilibrium, not as a tranquil equilibrium state.[2]

Many economists today also seem to believe that contemporary formalism is the only way that profit seeking behavior and competitive pressure can be formalized. This is not so. Some years ago, in his now classic paper, Alchian (1950) recognized that a natural selection formulation was possible, and conjectured that models built on this design would generate many of the same predictions as neoclassical models. More recently, we have developed a number of models (Nelson and Winter (1974), (1975), (1976), (1977), (1978)) which while orthodox to the core in the sense of being based on profit seeking behavior and competitive pressure, formalize these in ways drastically different from those contained in contemporary textbooks and treatises.

The purposes of this paper are first, to argue that the contemporary orthodox formalization of the old ideas of profit seeking behavior and competitive pressure makes it difficult to treat phenomena that many economists recognize as extremely important, at least in their policy-oriented research, and second, to sketch a route to an alternative and richer formalization of these ideas. We will proceed as follows. A discussion of this sort must address the argument that contemporary theory yields qualitatively reliable predictions at least in many circumstances; Section I opens the lid and peers into the box where the "as if" argument lives. Section II develops a way of accounting for substitution and supply response to changed prices that recognizes the components included in the contemporary formalization and additional ones which are dealt with only within a broader theoretical perspective. The concluding section explores the difference it makes if one adopts the evolutionary perspective we propose rather than the contemporary orthodox mode of theorizing.

I. JUDGING THE ADEQUACY OF THEORIES

The key question is the standard by which one judges the adequacy of a formal theoretical structure. While we want to focus on particular issues relating to the theory of firm and industry response to changed market conditions, a few general remarks seem necessary to clear the air, and prevent the discussion from getting bogged down in the old debate about the weight that should be put on "accuracy of predictions" versus "realism of assumptions" as criteria by which to evaluate a theory. We

---

2. Consider for example the following discussion of the effect of an increase in price from an existing "equilibrium" on output supplied, taken from Marshall (1948) p. 343. "That is, let us assume that this is the price the expectation of which will just suffice to maintain the existing aggregative amount of production; some firms meanwhile rising and increasing their output, and others falling and diminishing theirs; but the aggregate production remaining unchanged. A price higher than this would increase the growth of the rising firms and slacken, though it might not arrest, the decay of the falling firms; with the net result of an increase in the aggregative production."

trust that most of the profession has gotten beyond the rather shallow dispute about "as if" theorizing that marked the fifties, and is now in agreement on the following.

First, the economic world is very complex and no theory ever is going to be exactly and completely right (whatever that might mean). Thus the aim of theorizing is to find fruitful simplifications and abstractions.[3] This will require focusing on certain phenomena and causal factors and neglecting others. Specification of the mechanisms linking causes to consequences, which is the intellectual heart of any theory, must abstract at least in part from what really is going on. There are some fundamental issues of "trade-off" involved in theory construction and evaluation. While there is value in having the theory that explains more and better, treats a wider range of causal elements, and characterizes mechanisms with greater realism, there is a trade-off between versimilitude and complexity of the theory that at some point becomes adverse to further complexity.

Second, the question of whether a theory is "good enough" or not can not be considered independently of the purposes of the theory. If the purposes are defined in terms of explaining and predicting a particular class of variables, it makes sense to devote special attention to how well the theory does regarding these. If the purpose of inquiry is relatively narrow, this almost certainly justifies different kinds of abstractions and stronger simplifications than would be called for in a theoretical scheme of broader applicability. An important consequence of this is that special theories aimed at one narrow class of phenomena may involve different assumptions, have a different structure, than theories aimed at another narrow class of phenomena. However, there are intellectual costs of having a collection of somewhat disparate special purpose theories or models. There are great advantages in having a unifying framework within which most of the special purpose models can be interpreted as special cases. This in fact is the way theory is structured in economics.

Third, certainly in the broader theories but also in the more focussed and narrow ones, one should aim for theoretical understanding that goes beyond the ability to make predictions of a specified type. While understanding is admittedly an elusive concept, the interpretation of it that seems to be common now in economics refers to a characterization of causal structure at a level significantly deeper than that required for the predictions of immediate concern. The objective is correct structural equations rather than merely adequate "reduced forms". While the modern theorist despairs of ever finding the "ultimate" structural equations, he recognizes the value of searching for something more than mere "good fits".

Understanding, in this sense, obviously is a fundamental intellectual

---

3. Friedman (1953) of course presents the sharpest contemporary articulation of this position, but economists long have understood and accepted it.

value: Its quest is what pure science is all about. But understanding also is of pragmatic value. The variables of interest may change over time and the range of the theory is an important disideratum; if the structural relations are understood it often is possible to examine their implications in a new arena of interest. Conditions may change so that old reduced forms no longer apply; if reduced forms are treated as structural relations the analyst will not be alert to this problem. Even if the reduced forms are satisfactory, so far as range and durability are concerned, lack of understanding or incorrect understanding of what lies behind them can lead to uncertainty, or error, when thought is given to the feasibility or desirability of trying to influence the relationships. Symptoms may be regarded as causes and causes overlooked. Factors that can not be manipulated by policy may be viewed as attractive targets, and factors that can be manipulated treated as constants.

Perhaps the central reason why discussion of the adequacy of the theory of firm and industry response to changed market conditions is so chronic, and marked by parties seeming to talk past each other, is the complex, multi-faceted role of that theory within economics. On the one hand it is a special purpose theory to be evaluated in terms of specific predictions; on the other hand it is a master theory serving as the organizer for a large class of models concerned with firm and industry behavior more generally and a major building block in still larger theoretical structures, both positive and normative. It is at once a set of reduced forms that are regarded as providing reliable predictions and the formal repository of the basic ideas of what molds firm and industry behavior under competitive conditions. Of course, it is only in its narrow role that the theory, or at least its derived hypotheses and models, can be considered empirically testable. Our remarks and proposals are concerned with the theory of firm and industry response both in its broad role and in its narrower one. The issues we want considered are, first, are the current formalizations of profit seeking behavior and competitive pressure structurally solid and deep enough for a theory of broad intended scope? Second, are these specific formal assumptions adequate for special purpose applied research on firm and industry response to changed market conditions?

There have been many different attacks on profit maximization as a formal theory of what firms do. Some of these posit that profits are one but not the sole objective of the policies of firms, and that to neglect other objectives is a theoretical mistake. The criticism stressed here, however, is not concerned so much with whether the idea of a quest for profit is a good first approximation of a firm's objectives, but rather with the formalization of behavior that strives towards profits as profit *maximization*. Maximization of profits presumes that the choice set is given, and that the firm knows this set and the profit consequences of choosing any element. As an objective fact it is clear enough that firms act as if they are aware of only a limited number of alternatives, and that their justifications for doing what they do seem more often to involve hunch or precedent than to be well argued analytically and empirically. The question, of course, is whether that portion of the choice set to which firms do attend contains the best elements, and whether choices actually made, for whatever articulated or tacit reason, are the best (profit maximizing) given market conditions. This is the presumption of orthodox theory.

But such a presumption makes it virtually impossible to deal with innovation, the discovery or creation of previously unconsidered alternatives, in a serious way. To deal seriously with innovation one may allow that at any time firms operate with technologies and policies as good as any they know about; however to admit innovation one must presume that there exist better choices that they do not know about. One may attempt to capture the processes by which firms look for better techniques by assuming that firms dedicate research and imagination to searching for better things to be doing. But the fact that innovation is a continuing activity should also be recognized. In particular it must not be presumed that the process is so effective that the full set of alternatives can be explored quickly and cheaply; the phenomenon of sustained technical progress is testimonial to the fact that the "best" (however that might be defined) always seems to be far away from "the best firms know". We suggest that "searching" is especially important and fruitful when market environments change. Searching and groping for a satisfactory or a better response — induced innovation — is, we propose, an essential part of a firms' response to changed market conditions.

The stress on innovation as an important component of firm behavior is closely affiliated with criticism of price taking, zero profit equilibrium as a formalization of competitive pressure. Recognition of the importance of induced innovation points one toward trying to model competition as a dynamic process rather than in terms of an equilibrium state. In particular, the Schumpeterian view of competition involves a quite different appreciation of the nature of technological alternatives and the character and benefits of competition that that contained in contemporary price theory texts. From this perspective a key characteristic of any present economic situation is its potential improvability. Since the search for better techniques is uncertain, and it is not clear *ex ante* what are the best new things to be doing, an important function of competition is to stimulate experimentation and to select on the most appropriate responses. This theoretical appraisal of competition is structurally different from the formal orthodox one. While we have associated the view above with Schumpeter, who today is viewed as not in the "main line" tradition, this same view of competition clearly was held by Smith, Marshall, and Knight.

In a number of recent papers we have developed a way of modeling firm and industry behavior that involves innovation and Schumpeterian competition in an essential way. We have called our models "evolutionary". In these models firms "search" for better techniques and policies then they currently have, and when they find them, adopt them. But we do not model the search for improvement as a maximizing strategy by firms because we believe that the real problem of devising an optimal innovation policy is far too complicated for firms to solve, and that this fact should be recognized explicitly in the modeling of search. Our discussion in the following two sections of firm and industry response to changed market conditions will employ the language and concepts of our evolutionary models.

However, appreciation of the limitations of traditional theory of firm and industry response does not depend on agreement with our particular alternative modeling proposal. Any model that does not take the production choice set as given and constant is likely to lead to an analysis that contains the same elements as ours. This is so for contemporary induced innovation models that assume optimizing strategies, if one admits uncertainty with respect to outcomes and differences among firms in the luck of the draw. This is so for contemporary optimal search models, if the search is viewed as over the space of production techniques. It is a rather curious fact that few of the optimal innovation models treat outcomes as stochastic, and few of the search models focus on search for new techniques as contrasted with search for the right price or trading partner.[4] This probably explains why these literatures have not spawned discussion akin to that presented here.

Our rejection of the optimizing framework represents a major difference in style from the literature above. In a broader context we would stress the importance of that difference. Here, however, we wish to emphasize that a large part of the substance of the present discussion would remain relevant even if the specific models considered were constructed on the orthodox plan. Grant that search is costly and uncertain, that as a result at any time firms do different things, and that differential success is reflected in differential growth; the situation thus characterized is one to which our discussion is largely applicable, regardless of the detailed modeling. In particular, the "accounting" analysis of the following section, and our concluding remarks on normative analysis, remain relevant whether actors are viewed as optimizers or not.

II. ACCOUNTING FOR FIRM AND INDUSTRY RESPONSE

We turn now to the development of an evolutionary accounting for firm and industry response to changed market conditions, an accounting that treats induced innovation and Schumpeterian competition explicitly, along with the mechanisms treated in contemporary neoclassical for-

---

4. Evenson and Kisleve (1973), Kohn and Shavell (1974) are exceptions. Radner (1975) takes a perspective on these matters quite close to our own.

malisms. We develop the class of arguments needed for standard prediction of the direction of response, recognizing this broader class of response mechanisms. Our central proposition is that while the mechanisms considered by formal orthodox theory tend to go in the direction of the full set of mechanisms, to the extent that the orthodox response is only a small or variable part of the story, orthodox theory is at best a useful "reduced form". It is not adequate as a structural model.

The following propositions about the behavior of firms are consistent with both an orthodox and an evolutionary view, although the emphasis and connotation would be different: At any time firms in an industry can be viewed as operating with a set of techniques and policies (we shall lump these together and call them "decision rules"), keyed to conditions external to the firm, prominently prices, and to various internal state conditions, in particular the firms' stocks of capital. Expansion or contraction of firms is related to the profitability of such moves. Firms also may have procedures for hunting for better decision rules.

In the orthodox formulation, the decision rules are assumed to be profit-maximizing over a sharply defined opportunity set that is taken as a datum, the firms in the industry and the industry as a whole are assumed to be at equilibrium size, and innovation (if it is treated at all) is absorbed into the traditional framework rather mechanically. Within what we call evolutionary theory, the decision rules are viewed as a legacy from the firm's past and hence appropriate, at best, to the range of circumstances in which the firm customarily finds itself, and unresponsive, or inappropriate, to novel situations or situations encountered irregularly. Firms are viewed as expanding or contracting in response to disequilibria, with no presumption that the industry is near equilibrium. Innovation is treated as stochastic, and variable across firms.

These differences in perspective mean that when analysis is on the effects of changed market conditions upon behavior, the focus is on different things. The following analysis of the behavior of firms and the industry is at once general enough to encompass both perspectives, and designed to highlight the differences.

Let X_i be the vector of firm i's outputs and variable inputs, the latter taken as negative. Assume for simplicity that the levels of inputs that are fixed in the short run can be represented by a scalar, K_i, the size of the firm's capital stock. And assume firm i's decision rule governing output and variable input levels has the following general form:

$$(1) \qquad \left(\frac{X}{K}\right)_i = D(P, d_i)$$

186   ECONOMIC INQUIRY

Here, P is the vector of output and variable input prices, corresponding to X, and d_i is a vector of decision rule parameters. (For notational convenience we treat all differences among alternative possible decision rules, among firms and over time, as parameter differences.) Let $X = \sum_i X_i$, and $K = \sum_i K_i$. Then, for the industry:

$$(2) \qquad \left(\frac{X}{K}\right) = \sum D(P, d_i)\left(\frac{K_i}{K}\right)$$

Under any market regime $\dfrac{X}{K}$ may evolve over time. The traditional comparative statics approach of price theory represses what happens to $\dfrac{X}{K}$ over time for a given set of market conditions and focuses on the variation associated with different market conditions. In what follows we will be explicit about *both* kinds of differences.[5]

Consider two different market regimes. In regime zero prices are at P_0 forever. Under regime one prices are at P_0 until time t and at P_1 after that time. Consider some time T greater than t. Then, under regime zero we can "account for" $\left(\dfrac{X}{K}\right)$ at time T as follows:

$$
(3) \qquad \left(\frac{X}{K}\right)_0^T = \sum D\left[P_0, d_i^t\right]\left(\frac{K_i}{K}\right)^t
$$

$$
+ \sum \left(D\left[P_0, d_{i0}^T\right] - D\left[P_0, d_i^t\right]\right)\left(\frac{K_i}{K}\right)^t
$$

$$
+ \sum D\left[P_0, d_{i0}^T\right]\left(\left(\frac{K_i}{K}\right)_0^t - \left(\frac{K_i}{K}\right)^t\right)
$$

In the accounting the superscripts T and t are used to identify the time at which the variables are measured. The subscript zero has been used to tag variables that may be different at time T under regime zero than under regime one. Given this notation, the first term is, of course $\left(\dfrac{X}{K}\right)^t$.

---

5. The above formulation implies that the level of X_i, is proportioned to K_i, given P and d_i. A more general formulation is of course possible. However, the particular assumption is analytically convenient in that it permits decomposition of the effect of a change in market conditions into a relative intensity effect defined in terms of what happens as a ratio to total industry capital, and a "scale" effect defined in terms of what happens to industry capital. The contrast between the two theories can be seen most sharply if we focus on the former part. In the analysis below of the evolution of $\dfrac{X}{k}$ under different "market regimes" we define these regimes in terms of prices, repressing the partial endogeneity of prices. As with the simplification involving proportioning X to k, the purpose here is to sharpen the focus on the differences between neoclassical and evolutionary explanations.

The second term accounts for the effects of the evolution of rules between t and T, weighted by capital stocks initially (at time t). The final term accounts for selection effects which change capital share weights on the final rules.

Under regime one, $\dfrac{X}{K}$ at time T can be accounted for as follows:

$$
(4) \quad \left(\frac{X}{K}\right)^T_1 = \sum D\left[P_1, d_i\right]\left(\frac{K_i}{K}\right)'
$$

$$
+ \sum \left(D\left[P_1, d_{ii}^T\right] - D\left[P_1, d_i\right]\right)\left(\frac{K_i}{K}\right)'
$$

$$
+ \sum D\left[P_1, d_{ii}^T\right]\left(\left(\frac{K_i}{K}\right)^T_1 - \left(\frac{K_i}{K}\right)'\right)
$$

By subtracting equation 3 from equation 4 one can "account for" the difference in $\dfrac{X}{K}$ at time T under the two market regimes.

(5)

$$
\left(\frac{X}{K}\right)^T_1 - \left(\frac{X}{K}\right)^T_0 = \sum\left(D\left[P_1, d_i\right] - D\left[P_0, d_i\right]\right)\left(\frac{K_i}{K}\right)'
$$

$$
+ \sum\left(D\left[P_1, d_{ii}^T\right] - D\left[P_1, d_i\right] - D\left[P_0, d_{io}^T\right] + D\left[P_0, d_i\right]\right)\left(\frac{K_i}{K}\right)'
$$

$$
+ \sum\left(D\left[P_1, d_{ii}^T\right]\left(\left(\frac{K_i}{K}\right)^T_1 - \left(\frac{K_i}{K}\right)'\right) - D\left[P_0, d_{io}^T\right]\left(\left(\frac{K_i}{K}\right)^T_0 - \left(\frac{K_i}{K}\right)'\right)\right)
$$

The first term (or, properly, the terms under the first summation) can be viewed as the result of firms' moving along the decision rules at time t in response to a change in price from P_0 to P_1. The second term reflects that decision rules may evolve differently under the two regimes. The final term accounts for the difference in selection effects.

The above decomposition of the difference made by a price change could be regarded as merely a matter of accounting, without causal significance. We believe however that the separation we propose is useful analytically, because the three terms correspond to the operation of analytically distinguishable mechanisms. Thus in what follows we will analyze separately *along the rule effects*, induced *changes in decision rules*, and *selection effects*, of a change in price regimes. While what is essential to the *theorizing* is that separable mechanisms are involved, we put forth as a tentative *empirical* proposition that the three effects occur at different speeds, and it is convenient to think of the "along the rule" effect as occurring promptly, followed by the appearance of differential innovation effects, followed by differential selection effects.

Our identification of the three terms of our accounting with distinct causal mechanisms rests on this image of the sequence of events. But our discussion of the individual mechanisms is relevant whether they are assumed to operate in this sequence, some other sequence or — realistically — concurrently.[6]

In any case, the prototypical question of positive economic theory is: What is the sign of the difference analyzed in (5) (say the sign of the response of intensity of use of an input to a rise in its price)? In deference to tradition and the weight of empirical evidence we shall call the results that accord with neoclassical qualitative predictions "standard" and results that fail to accord "perverse."

Orthodox theory derives its "standard" results from the assumption of profit maximization over a given choice set. In terms of the accounting framework above, orthodox theory may be interpreted as a theory about decision rule-governed response. The second and third terms are not considered. Our analysis involves both rejection of the orthodox view of the derivation of decision rules, and emphasis on the second and third terms as likely to be important. For overall industry response to be standard, it would be sufficient for each of the three terms in our accounting to carry the sign of standard response. We shall consider each mechanism in turn.

Consider the movements along prevailing decision rules, accounted for in the first term. It is implicit in both the behaviorist and the orthodox notion of a "decision rule" linking input and output quantities to prices that at any particular time there is a certain set of action alternatives open to the firm. For an orthodox economist this set is a technological "given" and the decision rule is derived by optimization over it. For us, the rules are what they are because they have evolved that way over time. The concept of known "possible actions" has no standing independent of the actions invoked by decision rules. These rules are themselves observable (in principle) by looking "inside" the firm.[7] Indeed, this may be the only way to actually find out what they are. Since some of the responses invoked by rules take time to work out, and since over time the rules may change, it is risky to try to infer rules from observed market responses which take place over time. In any case, under an orthodox interpretation of decision rules or under ours, it is implicit that if a firm takes one action under one market condition and another action under another market condition, it could have done exactly the reverse.

---

6. A referee of this paper has drawn our attention to the fact that the distinctions here made among adaptive mechanisms, and our appraisal of their relative speeds, resembles the discussion in the biological literature of mechanisms and their rates of adaptation to changed environmental conditions. See E.O. Wilson (1975) pp. 144-45.

7. That is, the *processes* by which actions can be chosen can be directly observed, and the results of such observations recorded in some systematic form, e.g., in the form of a computer model of the decision process. Although little of this sort of research has been done, we believe that its feasibility was adequately established by the "Carnegie School". See Cyert and March (1963).

Given this interpretation, we propose that a prediction of a standard sign of the "along-the-rule" change can be derived from the assumption that the rules reflect sensible profit-seeking behavior. The specific assumption is that routinized responses to price changes are not worse, in profitability terms, than no change at all. Let $\left(\dfrac{X}{K}\right)_{i0} = D(P_0, d_i^t)$ denote the full vector of input and output flows under regime P_0. Holding the decision rule constant but changing the price, $\left(\dfrac{X}{K}\right)_{i1} = D(P_1, d_i^t)$. Treat K as a constant. Then (repressing both K and the i subscript): Profit under regime one equals $P_1 \cdot X_1 \geqslant P_1 \cdot X_0$, or else the firm would have done better to stick with X_0. Similarly

$$P_0 \cdot X_0 \geqslant P_0 \cdot X_1$$

Familiar algebra yields the conclusion

$$\Delta P \cdot \Delta X \geqslant 0.$$

Hence, if ΔP has a single non-zero component, the corresponding element of ΔX cannot carry the opposite sign from the component.

Although the conclusion and its derivation are familiar and orthodox, the interpretation is not. This is a hypothesis about decision rules, involving no commitments regarding the existence of an independently specified set of "known" or "possible" production methods, or about the characteristics of the processes that introduced these methods in the firm and established the decision linkages between them and the prices. The argument rests on the assumption that X_0 is an "available" behavior when P_1 prevails, and similarly for X_1 and P_0. The hypothesis is that the decision rules are plausibly responsive to changed conditions, not that they are "optimal" among the set of all "possible" decision rules (whatever that might mean).[8]

The hypothesis that the "along-the-rule" response is standard certainly is not true by definition. There are several reasons why it might prove false. It could be that the firm does not consider changing its inputs in response to changing prices; then decision rule "response" would not be strictly perverse but it would not be strictly standard. It could be that the profit calculation does not adequately reflect the structure of the firm's

8. In a sense, our interpretation here involves a "revealed technology" approach to the firm, analagous to the "revealed preference" approach to the consumer. However, in sharp contrast to the revealed preference approach, we do *not* take actual choices to provide the sole operational content of the posited existence of the rules. Rather, as mentioned above, we take the rules to be directly observable (in principle). A formal statement of a "revealed technology" approach may be found in a paper by D. McFadden (1969) on the theory of second best; he calls a decision rule "orthodox pseudocompetitive" if it can be rationalized as the result of price-taking maximizing behavior over the set of alternatives revealed by the rule to exist, i.e., the codomain of the rule.

goals. For example, the firm (or rather its managers) might have a distaste for a relatively profitable activity which employs a particular input intensively; but be bound by a minimum profit constraint. Then a rise in the price of the input might, by decreasing the profitability of its current mix of activities, lead the firm, perversely, to undertake its disliked activity more intensively. It could be that there are errors built into the rules, that one behavior is employed when another is more profitable. However, the proposition that the routinized component of response to price change is standard seems likely to be of sufficiently broad validity to warrant its tentative acceptance as a theoretical commitment. (In passing, we note that the purposes of equation (5), the relevant question is whether the appropriately weighted *average* of routinized response is standard, so there is room for some exceptions.)

The second term of our accounting reflects the consequences of changes in decision rules under regime P_1 compared with what would have happened under P_0. We use the term "search" as a rubric for the variety of processes, mostly intentional but some not, by which rule changes take place. The question is, will the effect of the changed price regime on search be "standard"?

Search differs from routinized response in three fundamental respects. First, inasmuch as it involves the acquisition of information, it is intrinsically an irreversible process. The irreversibility is rooted in the familiar economic fact that the costs of retention and use of a given item of information are typically much lower than the costs of initial acquisition or production. An immediate implication of irreversibility is that a prediction of a "standard" response of search outcomes to price changes cannot be derived by the same theoretical argument just used for the case of rule-governed response. While it remains plausible that rule changes will tend to enhance profitability, there is no reaon why the new decision rules yielded by search should not dominate the old, and be more profitable at the old prices as well as at the new.

The second fundamental characteristic that distinguishes search is uncertainty. The scene surveyed by a decisionmaker inside the firm may well include identifiable "alternatives" that could be explored, but these may be only dimly perceived and it may not be at all clear which will turn out to be best. The process of exploring perceived alternatives, or exogenous events, may bring to light other alternatives, not even contemplated in the original assessments. As argued earlier, uncertainty and individual differences are structural aspects of search. It is clearly appropriate to conceptualize and model search as a stochastic process. And it is clearly *inappropriate* to apply uncritically, in the analytical treatment of that process, formalisms that posit a sharply defined set of perceived alternatives, to which no behavioral reality corresponds.[9]

Lastly, search is distinguished by what we may term its *contingent* character. Real search processes take place in specific historical contexts, and their outcomes clearly depend in part on what those contexts contain in the way of problem solutions that are available to be "found". What there is to be found consists in large part of the fruits, by-products and residues of information producing activities elsewhere in the society. The flow of general social history thus impinges directly on the firm through its search activities, and searching at t is not the same thing as searching at $T > t$.

We have probably exaggerated here the extent to which the conceptual distinctions among irreversibility, uncertainty and contingency are clear-cut. Rather, these are three, interrelated aspects of the single central fact that search processes are historical processes, not repetitive and not readily separable from other processes of historical change. Awareness of that central fact should perform the valuable function of keeping the ambitions and pretensions of economic theorizing under realistic control; there is reason not to expect too much. Distinguishing among the three characteristics is helpful in a more specific sense; it provides the basis for a taxonomy that clarifies the contribution and limitations of particular modeling approaches.

For example, one approach to modeling the firm's search for superior techniques involves taking input coefficients (or changes therein) as the objects of the search. This approach suppresses the contingent aspect of search at the outset; it loses contact immediately with the fact that the realities of search for techniques involve questions of improved machine design, work arrangement, etc., and that answers or partial answers to such questions are generated by processes external to the firm. But, at the price of accepting this rather extreme abstraction, we can construct simple models that illustrate the "tendency" for search outcomes to be deflected in the "standard" direction by input price changes. "Standard" results are obtainable in a simple "search and test" model where the direction of search is not influenced by factor prices. A searching firm draws on a random distribution of technological coefficients in the neighborhood of its current techniques; it compares the cost of the alternative technique it "finds" with costs associated with the *status quo* and switches if the alternative is less costly. The distribution may be such that there is a coefficient drift in one direction or another under a wide range of factor prices. However, the expected change in input coefficients

---

9. As indicated earlier, the orthodox literature on technical change contains a number of models that reflect the irreversibility of search, but few that reflects its uncertainty. Most of those that do attempt to deal with uncertainty typically treat it entirely in *ex ante* terms, as an aspect of a decision problem facing the individual enterprise. They rarely attempt to trace the implications of the fact that, *ex post*, the firm winds up in a position it did not specifically choose.

resulting from search is deflected in the standard direction by a change in relative input prices. (see Nelson and Winter (1975))[10]

It is plausible, of course, to assume that input prices affect the search process in more subtle ways than merely by providing parameters of a test applied to a discovered result. For example, the expected gains from an array of different R and D projects may be reordered by a change in prices so that the nature of what is attempted by the firm is changed. This too can be modeled, and the standard result may again be obtained. There are also relevant mechanisms traceable to certain descriptive regularities of behavior. Cyert and March (1963) advanced, some time ago, the generalization that organizational search is "problemistic"— it is stimulated by a particular problem and the symptoms of the problem define a neighborhood in which the search takes place. If the "problem" is a profit reduction associated with the rise of a price of an input, and the symptoms (cost increase) show up most vividly in certain activities or product lines that make intensive use of that input, one might expect that the firms' problem-solving activities will be directed to those areas. It is also plausible that search will be structured by the question; how can we reduce our use of this input? If a search process thus directed and structured is successful, it will likely reduce use of the input.

So the hypothesis that price change-induced changes in search outcomes are standard is plausible. But proper interpretation of the hypothesis requires some delicacy. First, insofar as the simple models treat search (appropriately) as stochastic, the hypothesis necessarily relates to "tendencies," or average results. An individual outcome may easily be perverse. Secondly, since search may take place even in a constant market regime, the hypothesis about the consequences of a change in regime necessarily involves a comparison with "what might have been," i.e., the path of technique change that would have occurred under the original regime. There is no reason why search outcomes might not be strongly biased in one way or another, reflecting the relative ease, or visibility, of certain kinds of innovations. For example, under some circumstances it may be that ways to save labor are obvious to see and easy to develop relative to other kinds of innovation, and that the evolution of technology (decision rules) will show a labor-saving bias under a wide range of possible factor price ratios. Under these circumstances, search may reduce labor input over time in a regime of constant wage rates, and lower wages would simply mean a slower drift in that direction than higher ones.

Even with delicacy of articulation, the hypothesis that the results of search are standard certainly isn't a tautology. Intelligent profit seeking

10. Actually, this proposition is valid as stated only if there is no rule-governed change in input coefficients. In the general case, we must allow for the fact that the distribution of input coefficient changes may be different depending on the initial values from which the change occurs. Additional, and quite restrictive, assumptions are then needed to establish the standard result.

behavior does not necessarily imply it. Consider, for example, the following scenario. A metal fabricating firm confronts a sudden rise in the price of its raw material. It makes routine adjustments to this change by, e.g., making greater use of odd-shaped pieces of material that were formerly treated as scrap. After this adjustment, a severe profit pinch remains, and triggers off a search for ways to deal with this situation — a search which would not have been undertaken had the price increase and cost crisis not occurred. The result of the quest is the discovery that new types of *labor* saving machinery, adaptable to the firm problems, have become available. The firms buys such machinery and eases its profit problem — but the new machinery is less tolerant of odd-shaped pieces of material than were the workers who previously performed the relevant operations. As a result, the raw material intensity of the output increases. Search triggered by the price rise has contributed a "perverse" component to the total response of the firm. The decision rule change moved the firm in the direction opposite to that in which its routine decision rule moved it. Because search would have been less, the firm would not have discovered this decision rule change in the different factor price regime.

The third term in the decomposition captures the effect of different price regimes on growth or decline of firms that have different time T decision rules. Again, under a variety of assumptions selection effects will be standard. For example, assume that routinized and search responses occur sufficiently rapidly so that capital shares can be considered as practically constant while these changes are going on. Then the reweighting effect is a pure selection effect on decision rules that have been established shortly after t, and which are constant over the selection period. It can be shown that under these assumptions the selection effect of a change in the price of a single input is standard, if firm growth rates are linearly related to gross rents per unit of capital and the slope coefficients are the same for all firms.

Again, there is nothing tautological about this. Timing effects can make the selection term perverse. For example, if firms that by time T have most adapted their decision rules to accommodate the change in prices do their adaptation late in the game relative to firms that only adapt a little, the selection term can have the wrong sign. Or, a perverse effect is possible if the marginal relationship between (quasi-rent) returns to capital and the firm growth rate is different for different firms, and systematically related to interfirm differences in intensity of use of the input whose price has changed. Imagine, for example, that there are two groups of firms, the first with a ten per cent lower labor-capital ratio than the second. Suppose that initial total capital in the two groups is the same, but investment by labor-intensive firms hardly responds to profitability at all, while in the other group half of any "excess return" to capital is reinvested. A fall in the wage rate will encourage investment by both groups. Although the capital-intensive group enjoys a smaller increase in profitability, its investment policies translate this into a larger increase in growth rate. Thus, abstracting from rule-induced changes and the effects of the wage rate decline on search, considering only selection effects, the average labor-capital ratio in the industry falls with a decline in the wage.

Obviously, our accounting scheme does not do full justice to the richness of the possible behavioral relationships and dynamic interactions linking routinized response, search and selection. Formal dynamic models incorporating routinized response, search and selection effects can be constructed, and explored analytically or with simulation. In the exploration of a particular dynamic model, our accounting scheme may retain heuristic value, but the specific assumptions of the model would necessarily take over the center of the stage.

The discussion above has been quite general. We have demonstrated, we think, that it is plausible to think of "along the rule," "search," and "selection" as involving different aspects of firm behavior, and that under plausible models the effects of each of these mechanisms would be standard. Indeed, it may be difficult to produce a plausible model in which an overall perverse result would hold in general, independent of particular initial conditions and parameter values. An evolutionary theory then is consistent with the same qualitative comparative statics as orthodox theory. But explicit recognition of the search and selection components of adjustment brings a whole new range of phenomena into theoretical view.

III. WHAT DIFFERENCE DOES IT MAKE?

In the preceding section we developed a way of accounting for the response of firms and the competitive industry as a whole to change market conditions that included the mechanisms stressed in orthodox formalism but others as well. We concede that what we presented was a way of theorizing rather than an explicit formal theory; we will argue in a moment however that the lines between these are somewhat blurry. The central question we want considered is this: Are search and selection components of response merely complications abstracted away in orthodox formalism which can be ignored or "tacked on" to a basic orthodox analysis? Or, are they so large a part of the response mechanisms involved and so different in kind from "along the rules" response that orthodox theory should be regarded as not merely oversimplified but a misleading, structurally inadequate explanation?

Conventional wisdom has it that the answer to this question should be derived from a critical "empirical test" in which the predictions of the two theories are contrasted and the differences confronted with data. However, this is far too simple a way of looking at the issue. In the first place, the way we have posed an evolutionary theory, it is unambiguous-ly more complicated than the orthodox one, including neoclassical considerations as one but only one of its components. It has "more degrees of freedom" than orthodox formalism, and therefore will fit any body of data at least as well. Furthermore, almost everybody agrees that automatic "along the rule" response is not *all* of the story. A theory that encompasses induced innovation and selection responses as well as along the rule responses clearly has an advantage. But it is a more complex theory. It appears that one is driven back to the question — is the added predictive power (degrees of freedom) worth the added complexity. But our argument is that this is *not* the only question. The issue needs to be posed in terms of the relative merits of the structural equations of the two theoretical perspectives. To the extent that search and selection are important components of firm and industry behavior, the problem with the orthodox formulation is not merely that it is oversimplified. Impor-tant mechanisms are disregarded or dealt with shallowly.

Earlier we noted that the requirement for abstraction means that models — little theories — aimed at different phenomena will stress different things. We also posited that, given the inevitable diversity of special purpose models, it is of high value that the different models be recognized special cases of a broader "master theory". The theory of firm and industry response to changed market conditions is viewed by the profession not merely as a special theory but as, in some sense, the master theory. As such it has been proving structurally inadequate. As one prominent example, consider the attempted extension of that theory, during the 1950's and 1960's, to encompass phenomena related to long term economic growth. Empirical research on economic growth demon-strated overwhelmingly that technical advance — innovation — is a central part of the growth story. This "difficulty" was handled within an extended orthodox theory by tacking on a "technical advance" term to the accounting, to make things add up right. But to the extent that technical advance is important, the set of ideas built into the formulation that individual firms are maximizing profits over a common (if moving) choice set, and that the industry is in moving competitive equilibrium, can be seen as serious structural misspecifications. It is exactly that some firms see alternatives that others do not, and that imitation is costly and takes time, that provides the incentive to try to innovate. It is a key structural characteristic, therefore, of growth in a competitive market economy that there is a diversity of behavior (technologies used) by firms in the industry at any time. A chronic disequilibrium is what is driving the growth process. To assume moving equilibrium is to structurally misspecify the process.

There are a variety of other phenomena relating to firm and industry behavior, not merely long run time paths of outputs, inputs, and factor prices, that have defied analysis based on maximization — equilibrium theory. Analysis of the diffusion of particular innovations is one example. Analysis of the size distribution of business firms is another. To deal with these phenomena, special purpose models which contain behaviorist and evolutionary ideas have been created and employed. The standard theory of firm and industry response does not extend to guide and discipline the development of these special purpose models. We have argued elsewhere that an evolutionary theory can do so. (Nelson and Winter (1974), (1977), (1978)).

A response might be that while limitations of this kind unhorse contemporary orthodox as a master theory of firm and industry behavior, that formalism still is useful as a special theory of short and medium term response of firms and industries to changed market conditions. We would like to argue that even on these narrow grounds, the theory is proving to be, and implicitly is recognized to be, structurally inadequate. If one backs off, for reasons we have stated above, from debating the merits of a neoclassical versus an evolutionary theory in terms of accuracy of prediction, and if defenders of orthodox formalism retreat to the argument that it is a useful "special case" theory, then surely the helpfulness of a theory in guiding applied work should be a, perhaps *the*, central criterion of merit. We observe that economists doing applied work with the intention of influencing policy choices (rather than testing, or calibrating theory) often find it necessary to stray far beyond the boundaries of orthodox formal theory. They recognize, implicitly or explicitly, all the mechanisms described in our evolutionary accounting for response.[11]

Consider, for example, the argument in favor of letting petroleum or natural gas prices rise to induce substitution or conservation by energy consuming firms. Few economists really believe, or have stated, that firms have built-in optimizing decision rules that will achieve the most efficient possible substitution. While a number of utilities (for example) are capable of using different fuels and switch among fuels routinely as prices vary, it seems apparent that these built-in decision rules are not expected to account for the bulk of the response of the economy to higher prices. Rather, it is presumed that higher fuel prices will stimulate firms (and buyers generally) to think more about possibilities for substitution, conserving, or doing without. Discussion of the supply-response aspects of energy pricing is similarly eclectic. Many economists have argued that higher prices will induce greater supply, over both the short and long runs. It is apparent that many suppliers do have built-in procedures guaranteeing positive short run response. However, long run supply response is explicitly understood to involve search, in a literal sense. The expectation is that higher prices will induce more search for new oil and

---

11. In econometric work the constraints of orthodox theory are evaded, and something like an evolutionary perspective implicitly accepted, through the device of distributed lags. See Nerlove (1972) for a thoughtful discussion.

gas fields, more R and D on ways to get more oil out of the ground, etc. It is not, of course, assumed that all of the oil companies will make the same adaptations, search in the same directions, and succeed or fail together. Rather, some will be smarter, luckier, or have more favored initial positions than others; they will tend to prosper, to grow, and to be at the focus of the imitative efforts of others. Clearly, a story about firms responding to changed prices by picking a different point in a given choice set is an inadequate metaphor for all of this activity, and few economists, if any, would rely entirely on that metaphor to structure the analysis.

It is not merely that formal orthodox theory is not helpful in guiding thinking about concrete cases, and that a broader conceptualization in fact is used. The problem is that because the broader conceptualization tends to be implicit and *ad hoc*, rather than explicit and systematic, a number of important issues tend to be neglected. As a prominent example, consider concepts like "elasticity of substitution" or "the elasticity of supply". Contemporary formalism takes these variables as "technologically determined data" and not variables which themselves can be "explained" by a deeper structural analysis that may also reveal them to be manipulable. An evolutionary theory of firm and industry response would suggest that substitution and supply responsiveness would be a function of the quantity and quality of "searching" and "innovating" that higher prices draw forth. Some of the key parameters of orthodox theory thus become endogenous in an evolutionary theory.

This, and other differences between orthodox and evolutionary way of theorizing, lead to different perspectives on the policy issues involved. Suppose the policy question is how to induce desirable levels of substitution and supply response. From an orthodox point of view, this question is likely to be treated as involving the relationship between the price signals received by the relevant economic actors and the social objectives that ultimately determine the desirability of various responses. The elasticities of supply and substitution will be regarded as technological data. From an evolutionary point of view, since these variables are not taken as given, the analyst can begin to think about how they can and perhaps should be manipulated by governmental policies. In particular, the question of the appropriate role of government in facilitating or guiding the R and D endeavor might become a topic of inquiry. Questions like whether certain important R and D projects generate significant externalities, or require support on the scale beyond the resources of the firms in the industry, are naturally called forth. This is not to say that these issues are easy to think through. But one of the advantages of evolutionary theory is that they are signalled, and both general and specific research would tend to be focused upon them. A serious indictment of the orthodox perspective is that in almost all analyses by economists of the energy policy question they are ignored.

Indeed there is a peculiar schizophrenia about R and D in some of the more formal energy models, focused on identifying the optimal mix of technologies over time. Many of the "technologies" in the model are recognized as not now operational. Yet somehow these technologies are assumed to become operational at the appropriate or assumed time. The uncertainty about the cost of developing these technologies and their economic attributes tends to be repressed. With this repression, the possible desirability of developing and exploring multiple alternatives is obscured. But the heart of the R and D — innovation problem is that reasonable people will disagree about what technologies will be best when. This is a major reason why it makes sense to have R and D largely conducted by competitive business firms who make their own bets, rather than under centralized control. But then there is the question of R and D incentives and the R and D portfolio the incentives will draw forth. The technologies that will get developed at various times depend on that portfolio. Thinking about the role of government should hinge on assessment of how active policies can modify incentives or fill out the R and D endeavor so that the portfolio makes sense from a social point of view, given both the "best bet" characteristics of the technologies and the uncertainties. Neoclassical formalism does not lead applied researchers to build applied models that explore these questions.

Why the tacit admission of ideas of search and selection in applied policy work and the holding to ideas of maximization and equilibrium in formal theorizing? We confess we don't know for sure, but we have some conjectures. One of these relates to the strongly held beliefs that simplicity and neatness are important characteristics of good theory, and that optimization and equilibrium models possess these characteristics. Samuelson's Nobel lecture (1972) is perhaps the clearest and most emphatic statement of the appeal of parsimony, but the argument recurs, with varying emphases, throughout the economic methodology literature. And when we query our colleagues about the puzzle, we find that some variant of the parsimony argument is the most common response.

We certainly agree that parsimony, and related considerations of aesthetics and intellectual economy, deserves some weight. We would argue, however, that once one recognizes the family of special purpose models that are cropping up that are not tied together by the maximization — equilibrium overview, and the tendency for much empirical research to proceed outside the formal framework afforded by that theory, the argument for the parsimony of prevailing orthodox thinking is less than persuasive. Perhaps the net "parsimony benefits" of contemporary neoclassicism seem large to some people because a significant fraction of the costs are externalized. An alternative theoretical scheme, more congruent to the disequilibrium, groping character of real economic activity, might well offer a much broader overview, and stronger systematic guidance to empirical research. In this sense, a greater readiness to accommodate complexity at the foundations of the theory might be the distinguishing mark of a truly parsimonous approach.

Another part of the explanation for the adherence to neoclassical formalism is the failure of many economists to distinguish between profit seeking behavior spurred by competitive pressures and incentives, and the standard formal way of stylizing such behavior involving sharply defined opportunity sets, optimization, and price-taking equilibrium. The fact that the former need not be stylized as the latter has been a central theme in this essay. We hope we have been persuasive not only that contemporary orthodox formalization of the venerable qualitative ideas is not necessary and that there is an evolutionary alternative, but that the advantages of trying to develop that alternative would be very considerable.

Still another reason clearly is the linkage of conventional positive theory of firm and industry behavior to conventional normative theory. Contemporary normative theory, as neoclassical positive theory, takes as its basic premises that technology (or the rule of its evolution) is given and known, and the economic problem is to make the best possible use of resources. As in positive theory, in modern welfare economics the idea of making the best possible use of resources is translated into optimization within given choice sets. Abandonment of optimization notions in positive theory, would, at once, eliminate the neat fit between positive and normative theory and throw into question the basic formulation of the normative problem.

But if the remarks about positive theory are accepted, contemporary normative theory may incorporate the wrong kinds of abstractions as well. In the particular case of energy policy, discussed above, we suggested that conventional theory may be quite inadequate for an important normative purpose — calling the analyst's attention to interesting policy alternatives. But the normative issues at stake clearly are larger than this. They involve the whole way that the benefits and costs of market competition are viewed.

It should be noted, however, that the formalism of contemporary welfare economics is of a quite recent vintage, contrary to what much contemporary discussion seems to imply. Economists from Smith to Marshall to Knight and Schumpeter viewed the economic problem as involving the experimental opportunity and task in a fundamental way. This did not prevent these economists from believing in the merits of markets and market competition. But their perceptions of the strengths, and weaknesses, of markets differed fundamentally from those of neoclassical welfare economics.

These differences are nicely highlighted by the Hayek criticism of Lange's proposal for operating a socialist economic through simulated markets. Hayek (1945) proposed that the central problem of economic organization was to respond to change — change in demands, change in factor supply conditions. He argued that a socialist regime, even one guided by Langeian rules, would be slow and cumbersome in response. To get rapid response one needs "real" markets, real profit incentives. It should be emphasized that his argument was not about "optimality"; it was about effective and speedy adaptation. This is not what the modern theory of welfare economics is about. Note also that Hayek was not arguing that the competitive market system was ideal in any sense. Rather, he was implicitly arguing the demerits of large governmental bureaucracies.

There are strong similarities in the Schumpeterian arguments that competitive capitalism is a good system for generating and screening innovation (Schumpeter (1950)). There is no argument that one can find in Schumpeter to the effect that the R and D generated by a regime of competitive (rivalrous) enterprise would be, in some sense, optimal. Rather, he appreciated the creativity and zeal that could be generated by competitive capitalism. And he doubted the efficiency in these respects of the socialist alternative. If the world is as Schumpeter saw it, and as we have argued it is, detailed economic planning is impossible. Attempts to plan will tend to smother the creative fires, if a premium is placed on keeping actual economic events in line with those of the plan. Schumpeter saw the socialist alternative as innately tied to trying to make planning work.

We do not want to take a stand here on the merits of Hayek's or Schumpeter's, normative arguments in favor of free enterprise. Rather we only want to stress that their normative arguments rest on a view of firm and industry behavior that resembles our evolutionary approach more than it resembles orthodox theory. It is not true that the adoption of an evolutionary theory means that contact with normative theory is lost. What is true is that the contact must be with a different kind of normative theory.

Instead of using theory to generate conclusions on the first or second best Pareto optimal choices of some hypothesized set of institutional arrangements of the system as a whole, we should use it to inform and guide the *comparative* analysis of the alternative incremental institutional changes that are realistically before us. That this is the most — or the only — useful style for normative economics has been urged by many economists before us.[12] An evolutionary theory provides firm conceptual underpinnings for these views. To view policy and institutional design questions in this manner — i.e., to recognize the adaptive, searching character of the "rationality" involved — is entirely natural in an evolutionary framework. Exploring a poorly defined choice set is a

---

12. The following is from Coase (1960) "A better approach would seem to be to start our analysis with a situation approximating that which actually exists, to examine the effects of a proposed policy change and to attempt to decide whether the new situation would be, in total, better or worse than the original one. In this way, conclusions for policy would have some relevance to the actual situation."

vastly different activity than optimizing over a given one, whether the searching is for a better technique or decision rule for a profit oriented firm, or for a more effective public policy.

While the "selection" aspects of an evolutionary model perhaps could be viewed as providing support for normative as well as positive tenets of orthodox competitive theory, *if* all alternatives were given and known, selection forces provide support neither for normative nor positive competitive equilibrium arguments if innovation is important. Some of our predecessors in proposing positive evolutionary models in economics may not have recognized this adequately. Some contemporary population biologists, as well as economists, seem rash in their willingness to impute optimality properties to the outcomes of selection processes, and correspondingly oblivious to the ambiguity of optimality concepts when the set of available alternatives (mutations) is not well defined. The argument, that of extant genotypes (techniques, policies) selection will weed out the inferior, says nothing about what genotypes (techniques, policies) will emerge. And often the latter issue is dominant, from both the positive and normative points of view.

An evolutionary theory and prevailing orthodoxy in economics yield many of the same positive conclusions, but they are structurally different. And the differences matter.

REFERENCES

Alchian, A.A., "Uncertainty, Evolution, and Economic Theory," *Journal of Political Economy*, June 1950, *58*, 211-22.

Coase, R., "The Problem of Social Cost," *Journal of Law and Economics*, October 1960, *3*, 1-44.

Cyert, R.M., and March, J.G., *A Behavioral Theory of the Firm*. Englewood Cliffs, N.J.: Prentice Hall, 1963.

Evenson, R.E., and Kislev, J., *Agricultural Research and Productivity*. New Haven: Yale University Press, 1975.

Friedman, M., "The Methodology of Positive Economics," Chap. 1 in *Essays in Positive Economics*. Chicago: The University of Chicago Press, 1963.

Hayek, F.A. von., "The Use of Knowledge in Society," *American Economic Review*, September 1945, *35*, 519-30.

Kohn, M. and Shavell, S., "The Theory of Search," *Journal of Economic Theory*, October 1974, *6*.

Machlup, F., "Theories of the Firm: Marginalist, Behavioral, Managerial," *American Economic Review*, March 1967, *57*, 1-33.

Marshall, A., *Principles of Economics*, 8th ed. New York: Macmillan, 1948.

McFadden, D., "A Simple Remark on the Second Best Pareto Optimality of Market Equilibria," *Journal of Economic Theory*, June 1969, *1*, 26-38.

McNulty, P.J., "Economic Theory and the Meaning of Competition," *Quarterly Journal of Economics*, November 1968, *82*, 639-56.

Nelson, R.R. and Winter, S.G., "Neoclassical vs Evolutionary Theories of Economic Growth: Critique and Prospectus," *The Economic Journal*, December 1974, *84*, 886-905.

Nelson, R.R. and Winter, S.G., "Factor Price Changes and Factor Substitution in an Evolutionary Model," *The Bell Journal of Economics*, Autumn 1975, *6*, 466-86.

Nelson, R.R., Winter, S.G. and Schuette, H.L., "Technical Change in an Evolutionary Model," *The Quarterly Journal of Economics*, February 1976, *90*, 90-118.

Nelson, R.R. and Winter, S.G., "Dynamic Competition and Technical Progress," Chapter 3 in Balassa, B., and Nelson, R., (eds.), *Economic progress, private values and public policy: essays in honor of William Fellner*. Amsterdam: North-Holland, 1977.

Nelson, R.R. and Winter, S.G., "Factors Generating and Limiting Concentration Under Schumpeterian Competition," *The Bell Journal of Economics*, Autumn 1978, 9, 524-48.

Nerlove, M., "Lags in Economic Behavior," *Econometrica*, March 1972, *40*, 221-51.

Radner, R., "A Behavioral Model of Cost Reduction," *Bell Journal of Economics*, 1975, *6*.

Samuelson, P.A., "Maximum Principles in Analytical Economics," *American Economic Review*, June 1972, *62*, 249-262.

Schumpeter, J.A., *Capitalism, Socialism and Democracy*. New York: Harper & Brothers, 1950.

Stigler, G.J., "Perfect Competition, Historically Contemplated," *Journal of Political Economy*, February 1957, *65*, 1-17.

Wilson, E.O., *Sociobiology*, Cambridge, Belknap Press of Harvard University, 1975.

[7]

Journal of Economic Behavior and Organization 5 (1984) 159–190. North-Holland

SCHUMPETERIAN DYNAMICS

An Evolutionary Model of Innovation and Imitation

Katsuhito IWAI*

University of Tokyo, Tokyo 113, Japan

Final version received October 1983

This paper develops a simple evolutionary model of innovation and imitation. It analyzes how dynamic interactions between equilibrating force of imitation and disequilibrating force of innovation mold the evolutionary pattern of an industry's state of technology, and shows that in this Schumpeterian world the industry will never approach a neoclassical equilibrium with perfect knowledge even in the long run. The paper also examines the steady-state efficiency distribution of firms that characterizes the industry's long run and obtains some comparative dynamics results.

1. Introduction

'The essential point to grasp ... in dealing with capitalism' is, according to Joseph Schumpeter (1950, p. 82), that 'we are dealing with an evolutionary process'. The evolutionary character of the capitalist process is due to the fact that 'the fundamental impulse that sets and keeps (its) engine in motion comes from the new consumers' goods, the new methods of production or transportation, the new markets, the new forms of industrial organization that capitalist enterprise creates' (p. 83). Such 'innovation' then creates a market power which enables the innovator to earn a monopoly profit or what is called an entrepreneurial profit, and it is this prospect of gaining entrepreneurial profit that in turn supplies the motives for innovative activities. But the innovator's monoply position is only temporary. As soon as an innovation is made, 'the spell is broken' and the way for others to imitate is opened up. The first innovation draws followers, and then successful imitation again makes it easier for more imitators to follow suit, until finally the innovation becomes familiar and the associated entrepreneurial profit is wiped out, or until the appearance of another innovation renders it obsolete [Schumpeter (1961)]. This process of 'Creative Destruction' — the process that 'incessantly revolutionizes the economic

*I am grateful to Sidney Winter for his discovery of a serious error in the first draft of this paper. Thanks are also due to Neil Ericsson for his valuable comments and to Andrew Joskow for his skillful computational assistance. The remaining errors and inadequacies are, of course, exclusively mine. This research is partly financed by the ministry of education in Japan.

structure *from within*, incessantly destroying the old one, incessantly creating a new one' — is what Schumpeter regarded as 'the essential fact about capitalism' [Schumpeter (1950, p. 83)].

The orthodox theory of competitive equilibrium consists precisely of assuming this 'fundamental fact about capitalism' *away*. The notion of competitive equilibrium in its most basic form is defined to be a state of affairs in which a set of prices, one for each commodity, balances demand and supply of all commodities and co-ordinates the actions of all market participants who take prices as given and determine demands and supplies accordingly. There is thus no one *within the system* who has any motivation to change the reached position, not to mention the one who strives for creation or destruction. Indeed, from the perspective of the orthodox analysis, the existence of entrepreneurial profit which arises inevitably from successful innovation must be treated as an example of the 'imperfection' of competition; the wave of imitations which relentlessly follows the first success must be classified as an 'externality' to markets; and the entire process of creative destruction is merely an 'adjustment process' which transfers the economy from one equilibrium to another. What Schumpeter considered to be 'the essential fact about capitalism' is regarded here as an aberration from the competitive equilibrium — a slip of the Invisible Hand.

This is the first of a series of papers whose major objective is to develop a simple theoretical framework which is capable of placing the evolutionary process of creative destruction at its central analytical core.[1] It is an attempt to analyze the phenomena of innovation, imitation and growth, not as equilibrium outcomes of the far-sighted choices of optimizing economic agents, but as the dynamic processes moved by complex interactions among individual firms which are constantly striving for survival and growth by their competitive struggle against each other.[2] Indeed, underlying the whole series of papers is a premise that even for the analysis of such 'long-run' economic phenomena it is essential to begin with the study of disequilibrium processes working at the micro level of firms and to trace out carefully the manner in which they interact with each other and cause the aggregate economy to move from one position to the next. Such a 'disequilibrium' view of technological change and economic development has certainly been foreign to the orthodox economists who tend to identify 'long run' with 'equilibrium' and dismiss 'disequilibrium' as mere 'short-run' problems.[2a]

---

[1] For recent attempts at formalizing the 'vision' of schumpeter, see Winter (1969), Nelson and Winter (1982) and Futia (1980). Our indebtedness to their works ought to be obvious.

[2] Our Schumpeterian dynamics should therefore be distinguished from the so-called neo-Schumpeterian models of Scherer (1967), Kamien and Schwartz (1972, 1975), Loury (1979), Dasgupta and Stiglitz (1980a, 1980b) and others. Their analyses treat the firm's R&D activity as a one-shot game and fail to situate it in a long-run evolutionary process of industrial development. We, however, intend to incorporate the firms' long-term decisions on innovation and imitation policies in our future studies.

[2a] See Iwai (1981) for another attempt to introduce 'disequilibrium' view into economics.

2. The state of technology

No one fails to notice a wide gap between the industrial structure we observe in the real economy and the idealized world of neoclassical economics in which all firms are supposed to have free access to the most efficient technological knowledge. Fig. 1 exhibits how the ratio of payroll to value added (a good index of the reciprocal of labor productivity) is distributed across establishments in metal stampings industry (SIC no. 3461) in 1958 and 1963. Establishments with a remarkably wide range of productivities co-exist in an industry, and this wide dispersion of productivities has no tendency to disappear over time. The state of technology in this industry appears to be in perpetual disequilibrium. In fact, the metal stampings industry is chosen as an example (almost) arbitrarily among over four hundred industries classified by SIC, and the similar pattern can be discerned in most other industries.[3]

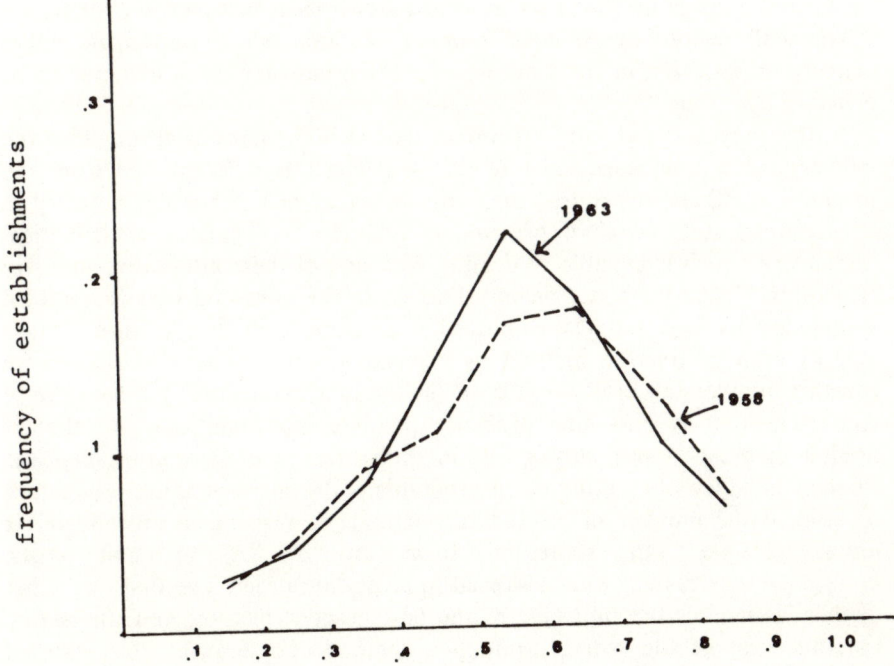

Fig. 1. The frequency distribution of efficiency in metal stampings industry. [*Source*: U.S. Department of Commerce (1968).]

[3]See U.S. Department of Commerce (1968). Sato (1975) analyzed the efficiency distributions reported in this census in detail. He also found similar patterns in Japanese cotton-spinning industry and Norwegian fish-food products and non-electrical machinery industries.

We start from this simple (but by no means the only possible) observation that the state of technology in most industries appears to be in a state of perpetual disequilibrium. And one of the aims of this paper is to develop, with the guidance of Schumpeterian vision, a simple mathematical model which is capable of demonstrating that the state of technology will be forever in disequilibrium.

Consider an industry which consists of a large number of firms competing with each other. Some firms are taking active part in the workings of the industry by turning out products; others may be passive participants that are not engaged in production at the moment but ready to start it when the right time comes. Some of the firms are leaving the industry for good, while some new firms are making an entry into it. In the present paper, however, we are not concerned with the firms' production decisions nor with the process of turnover of firms. Instead, in order to lay out the basic framework of our Schumpeterian dynamics as simple as possible, we shall abstract from the former and ignore the latter in what follows. (See, however, section 8.)

We shall denote by M total number of firms which participate either actively or passively, in the working of a given industry. M is assumed to be constant over time.

A firm may be producing a product that is homogeneous throughout the industry, or a unique product of its own which is differentiated from the products of others, depending upon the structure of a particular industry in question. In fact, we shall present, in this series of papers, a theoretical framework which is capable of dealing with any of these alternative industry structures. Unless there is a universal access to the same and best technology, production method actually employed is different from firm to firm. Let us identify each production method by a positive real number c. Although we call this number the firm's 'unit cost' (in terms of numeraire) for the sake of concreteness, it is only one of many possible interpretations. All that is needed in most of our subsequent investigations is a convention that the smaller the value of c is, the more profitable is the corresponding production method. If the number of production methods co-existing in an industry is finite (n) we can represent them by a list of unit costs, $c_n < c_{n-1} < \cdots < c_i < \cdots < c_1$, arranged in ascending order. The first in the list c_n then designates the unit cost of the best practice method and the last c_1 the unit cost of the worst production method. To describe the 'state of technology' of an industry at a point in time, it is therefore necessary to stipulate how these different production methods are distributed across firms.

Let $f_t(c)$ represent the relative frequency of firms whose unit cost equals c at time t. It is, in other words, the frequency function of unit costs at time t. Since only the production methods with unit costs $c_1, c_2, \ldots, c_n$ are actually employed at time t, the value of $f_t(c)$ is zero for any other value of unit cost. [By convention we have $f_t(c_1) + \cdots + f_t(c_n) = 1$.] Let $F_t(c)$ represent the relative frequency of firms whose unit costs are equal to c *or less* at time t. It is, in other words, the cumulative frequency function of unit costs at time t. Needless to say, $F_t(c)$ can be formally defined as

$$F_t(c) \equiv f_t(c_i) + f_t(c_{i+1}) + \cdots + f_t(c_n) \tag{1}$$

for $c_{i-1} < c \le c_i$. [We set, as convention, $F_t(c) = 0$ for $c < c_n$ and $F_t(c) = 1$ for $c \ge c_1$.] Fig. 2 illustrates the relation between $f_t(c)$ and $F_t(c)$.

The frequency function $f_t(c)$ or alternatively, the cumulative frequency function $F_t(c)$ represents how a variety of production methods from the most profitable to the least, are distributed across firms at a given point in time. Either of them gives us a snapshot picture of the industry's 'state of technology' at a given point in time. Unlike the paradigm of the orthodox economics, however, the state of technology is not a given datum to the industry. As time goes by and future unfolds itself, dynamic competition among firms for technological superiority constantly changes it from one configuration to another. The state of technology is never static and never exogenous in a capitalist economy.

The main aim of the following sections is to describe how the state of technology evolves over time in a Schumpeterian industry.

3. Imitation or diffusion process of technology

In the world of Schumpeterian competition, each firm is constantly striving for a better production method. There are basically two means by which that aim can be achieved. A firm may succeed in putting a new production method into practice by its own R&D effect; i.e., it may succeed in 'innovation'. The firm can also direct its eyes towards outside; it may indeed 'imitate' one of the more profitable methods which are currently employed by other firms. The evolution of the state of technology is therefore determined by the interaction of these two dynamic forces. In order to give an orderly exposition of this complex evolutionary process, however, we shall devote the present section exclusively to the study of the process of imitation, postponing that of the process of innovation until the next section.

Schumpeter wrote:

'[T]he carrying out of new combinations is difficult.... However, if one or a few have advanced with success, many of the difficulties disappear. Others can then follow these pioneers, as they will clearly do under the stimulus of the success now attainable. Their success again makes it easier, through the increasingly complete removal of the obstacles..., for

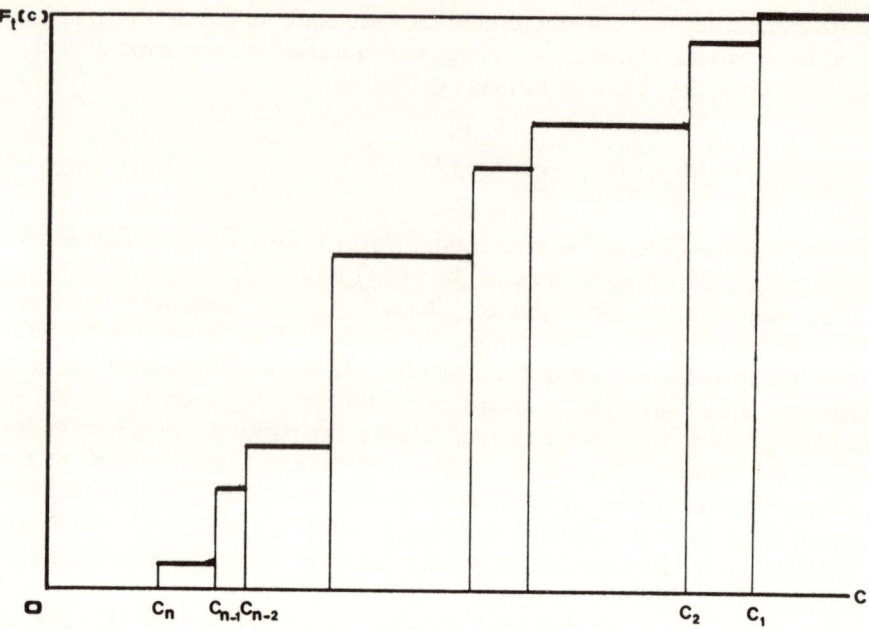

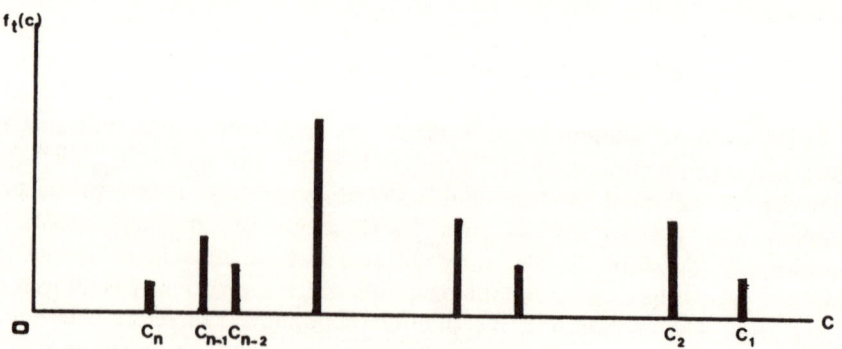

Fig. 2. The relation between $F_t(c)$ and $f_t(c)$.

more people to follow suit, until finally the innovation becomes familiar and the acceptance of it a matter of free choice.' [Schumpeter (1961, p. 228).]

For our purposes it is, however, necessary to translate this somewhat picturesque description of the process of imitation into a much more prosaic mathematical language. Indeed, there exist several alternative models which can do this, but the particular one chosen in this paper is characterized by the following extremely simple hypothesis:

Hypothesis (IM'). The probability that a firm is able to copy a particular production method is proportional to the frequency of firms which employ that method in the period in question. The firm, of course, implements only the method whose unit cost is lower than the one currently used by it.[4]

Formally, it will be assumed that the probability that a firm of unit cost c_i imitates a production method of unit cost c during a small time interval between t and $t + \Delta t$ is equal to

$$\mu f_t(c)\Delta t \quad \text{for} \quad c < c_i$$

and

$$0 \quad \text{for} \quad c \geq c_i,$$

where $\mu > 0$ is a parameter which summarizes the effectiveness of the firm's imitation activity.

The value of the imitation parameter μ should be influenced by the particular imitation policy the firm has come to adopt in its long-run pursuit of survival and growth. Indeed, in recent years a small but growing body of literature has been concerned with empirically indentifying factors which influence the value of the imitation parameter or something of the kind. [See, for instance, Mansfield (1968, ch. 8), Davies (1979), Mansfield, Schwartz and Wagner (1981) and papers quoted therein.] The present paper, however, is not concerned with the analysis of how each firm shapes up its imitation policy and chooses (or at least influences) the value of the imitation parameter μ. The main objective here is rather to work out formally the dynamic mechanism through which a given long-run imitation policy of the firms (along with a given long-run innovation policy, to be discussed in sections 6 and 7) structures the evolutionary pattern of the industry's state of technology. We shall, therefore, assume in this paper that the imitation parameter μ is a given constant whose value is a legacy from the past. We shall also assume that the value of μ depends neither on the current unit cost of the firm nor on the unit cost of the production method it wishes to imitate.[5] We shall assume further, for the sake of simplicity, that a new

---

[4]In the next paper which takes an explicit account of the process of capacity growth, this hypothesis will be modified into *Hypothesis (IM)*: The probability that a firm is able to copy a particular production method is proportional to the share of total productive capacity which employs that method in the period in question.

[5]It is, however, possible to replace this assumption by another: that the firm imitates only the best practice production method, or $\mu f_t(c)\Delta t$, for $c = c_n$ (the unit cost of the best practice method), and 0 otherwise, and then to reproduce qualitatively most of the results obtained under this. We intend to report our analysis under this alternative assumption in a forthcoming paper. Yet another alternative specification would be that the firm is able to imitate the production method whose efficiency is one rank above the one it is currently using, or the probability that a firm with a unit cost c_i imitates a production method of unit cost c is $\mu f_t(c)\Delta t$, for $c = c_{i+1}$, and 0 otherwise. Unfortunately, this alternative model has so far resisted our analysis.

production method once copied can be implemented to the entire productive capacity within a firm without any cost and without any delay. Indeed, throughout this series of papers, all technical changes are supposed to be of the disembodied type. The problem of intra-firm diffusion process of new technical knowledge [as is analyzed, for instance, by Mansfield (1968, ch. 9)] is thus set aside from our investigation.

Now, under hypothesis (IM') it is possible to analyze the evolutionary pattern of the industry's state of technology in the following simple manner. Consider the way in which $F_t(c_i)$, the relative frequency of firms with unit cost c_i or less, changes its value from time t to $t + \Delta t$. It is clear that this relative frequency increases whenever one of the firms whose unit cost is higher than c_i succeeds in imitating one of the firms with unit cost c_i or less. [Of course, even among firms whose unit costs are lower than c_i, the relatively higher cost firms are imitating the production methods of the lower cost firms. It is, however, plain that these intra-marginal imitation activities result only in intra-marginal transfers of frequencies and do not affect the value of $F_t(c_i)$ itself.] Now the relative frequency of firms whose unit costs are higher than c_i equals $f_t(c_{i-1}) + f_t(c_{i-2}) + \cdots + f_t(c_1)$, which can be conveniently rewritten as $1 - F_t(c_i)$ by (1). On the other hand, hypothesis (IM') tells us that the probability that *each* of these firms succeeds in imitating one of the production methods with unit cost c_i or lower during a time interval between t and $t + \Delta t$ is equal to $\mu f_t(c_i)\Delta t + \mu f_t(c_{i+1})\Delta t + \cdots + \mu f_t(c_n)\Delta t$, which can be conveniently rewritten as $\mu F_t(c_i)\Delta t$ by (1). (Here, the probability that a firm succeeds in copying two or more production methods simultaneously can be ignored so long as the time interval Δt is small.) We can therefore compute the *expected* increase in $F_t(c_i)$ during a time interval between t and $t + \Delta t$ as the product of these two expressions: $\{\mu F_t(c_i)\Delta t\} \cdot \{1 - F_t(c_i)\}$. In fact, if the total number of firms M is very large, the so-called law of large numbers allows us to use this expression for a good approximation for the *actual* increase in $F_t(c_i)$. In what follows, we assume this is indeed the case and treat the above expressions as representing the actual increase in $F_t(c_i)$.[6]

We have thus obtained an equation which describes the change in the relative frequency of firms of unit cost c_i or less, from time t to $t + \Delta t$, effected by the firms' imitation activities in an industry:

$$F_{t+\Delta t}(c_i) - F_t(c_i) = \mu F_t(c_i)(1 - F_t(c_i))\Delta t. \tag{2}$$

Furthermore, if we divide the both sides of this equation by Δt and let Δt approach zero, we can transform it in the following differential equation:

---

[6]If M is not large enough, what follows can be interpreted as the analysis of the 'expected' behavior of the state of technology. Note further that the analysis of the long-run average behavior of the state of technology to be given in sections 6 and 7 is independent of the largeness of M.

$$\dot{F}_t(c_i) = \mu F_t(c_i)(1 - F_t(c_i)),\tag{2'}$$

where $\dot{F}_t(c_i)$ represents the time derivative of $F_t(c_i)$. Since the same argument can be applied without any modification to any value of unit cost, we have, in fact, obtained the following series of differential equations:

$$\dot{F}_t(c_n) = \mu F_t(c_n)(1 - F_t(c_n)),$$
$$\vdots$$
$$\dot{F}_t(c_i) = \mu F_t(c_i)(1 - F_t(c_i)),\tag{3}$$
$$\vdots$$
$$\dot{F}_t(c_1) = \mu F_t(c_1)(1 - F_t(c_1)).$$

It requires only a moment's reflection to recognize that each of the above differential equations is nothing but a well-known 'logistic differential equation', which appears frequently in population biology and mathematical ecology. [See, for example, Pearl and Reed (1924), Lotka (1925), or any modern textbook on these subjects. Samuelson (1947, pp. 291–294), also contains a useful discussion on this form of differential equation.] It is very easy to show that this logistic differential equation has the following form of explicit solution, which is called the 'logistic growth curve':

$$F_t(c_i) = 1/[1 + (1/F_T(c_i) - 1)\exp[-\mu(t - T)]], \qquad i = 1, 2, \ldots, n,\tag{4}$$

where $\exp(\cdot)$ stands for exponential, and $F_T(c_i)$ represents the cumulative frequency function at a given time $T(\leq t)$ in the past.

Fig. 3 illustrates the foregoing result. Each of the S-shaped curves traces a logistic growth curve that represents the growth pattern of the cumulative frequency function of firms. In particular, the one at the lowest layer depicts the growth pattern of the relative frequency of firms with the least unit cost c_n. When only a small number of firms employ this production method, its growth is hesitant and slow. But as this number gradually increases, imitation activities of the less efficient firms become more and more successful. 'The spell is broken', and a bandwagon sets in motion. The growth rate then accelerates, until a half of total population comes to adopt this method. Once this median point is passed, the effect of saturation steps in and the growth rate starts decelerating. But the growth itself continues until the whole population of firms is swamped by this best practice method. The fate of the less efficient production method, on the other hand, can be easily read by tracing out the changing width of a strip formed by two adjacent logistic curves. Initially its number may expand by absorbing the firms with less efficient techniques. But sooner or later it will lose ground to the more efficient techniques, and will find its way to the eventual extinction.

The idea of using the logistic curve to describe a bandwagon phenomenon that can be commonly observed in a variety of diffusion process of a new

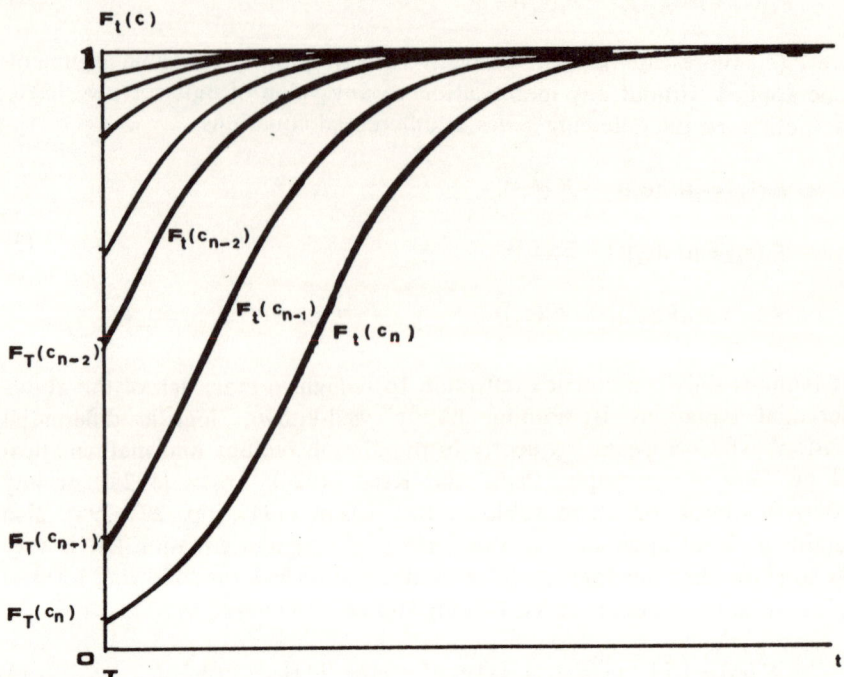

Fig. 3. The evolution of the state of technology under the pressure of imitation process.

idea, new technique, new instrument, and so forth is not new. Indeed, there is an abundant literature on this application in economics and other social sciences. [See, for example, Coleman, Katz and Menzel (1957), Griliches (1957), Ozga (1960) and Mansfield (1968, ch. 8).] Outside of social sciences the so-called 'models of epidemics' deal with mathematically similar problems. [See, e.g., Bailey (1957).] What seems novel about our foregoing analysis is its application of the logistic law to the description of the evolutionary pattern of the whole array of production methods co-existing side by side at the same time. And it is this small innovation which allows us to study the dynamic interaction between processes of imitation and innovation in an integrated manner, as we shall soon see.

4. Innovation

As is shown in the preceding section, firms' imitation activities will gradually upgrade their production techniques, and, if other things are equal, all the firms will eventually succeed in adopting the best practice method. This limiting state must be the paradigm of neoclassical economics in which every market participant is supposed to have complete access to the best technical knowledge of the society. Other things, however, do not forever remain the same. The tendency towards technological uniformity among firms is bound to be upset by a sudden introduction of a new and better production method by one of the firms. Indeed, to destroy the stalemate brought about by the imitation process and to create a new industrial structure is the role our capitalist economy has assigned to Schumpeterian entrepreneurs or to innovative firms. It is this 'process of creative destruction' that is 'what capitalism consists in and what every capitalist concern has got to live in' [Schumpeter (1950, p. 83)]. Let us now turn to the formal analysis of this perennial gale of creative destruction.

Suppose that at some point in time one of the firms finally succeeds in implementing a new production method whose unit cost equals $c_{n+1}(<c_n)$. We denote by $T(c_{n+1})$ the time at which this method is introduced for the first time and call it 'the innovation time' for the production method with unit cost c_{n+1}. (This somewhat clumsy notation will make more sense in section 6.) Since the total number of firms is M and hence each firm's share is $1/M$, this innovation creates a new relative frequency of the magnitude of $1/M$ at the new and lower unit cost c_{n+1}. That is, we have

$$F_{T(c_{n+1})}(c_{n+1}) = 1/M. \tag{5}$$

No sooner does this innovation occur than do all the other firms start struggling to imitate it. A firm or two will eventually make a headway, and a wave of imitation will then follow. Under hypothesis (IM'), this sets in motion a new logistic growth curve of $F_t(c_{n+1})$ from the initial condition (5) given above. Hence, we have for $t \geq T(c_{n+1})$

$$F_t(c_{n+1}) = 1/[1 + (M-1)\exp[-\mu(t - T(c_{n+1}))]]. \tag{6}$$

How does this innovation affect the evolutionary pattern of the state of technology of the industry as a whole? The answer to this question depends upon whether or not the innovator has used the best practice production method before innovation. We first examine a special case.

Let us suppose that the innovator of c_{n+1} has employed the then best practice method c_n before the innovation time $T(c_{n+1})$. In this case, the size of $f_t(c_n)$ declines by $1/M$ at the time of $T(c_{n+1})$, but this decline is recouped at the same time by the new creation of an equal magnitude of $f_t(c_{n+1})$, as shown in (5). Obviously, this exchange of an equal mass of frequency leaves unaffected the cumulative frequency $F_t(c_n)$, for it is nothing but the sum of $f_t(c_n)$ and $f_t(c_{n+1})$. It then follows that even after the innovation time $T(c_{n+1})$, the cumulative frequency $F_t(c_n)$ keeps moving along the same old logistic growth curve (4). Indeed, since the innovation in question involves no other production method, all the other cumulative frequencies must follow the same old logistic curves as well. Part of fig. 4 around the innovation time

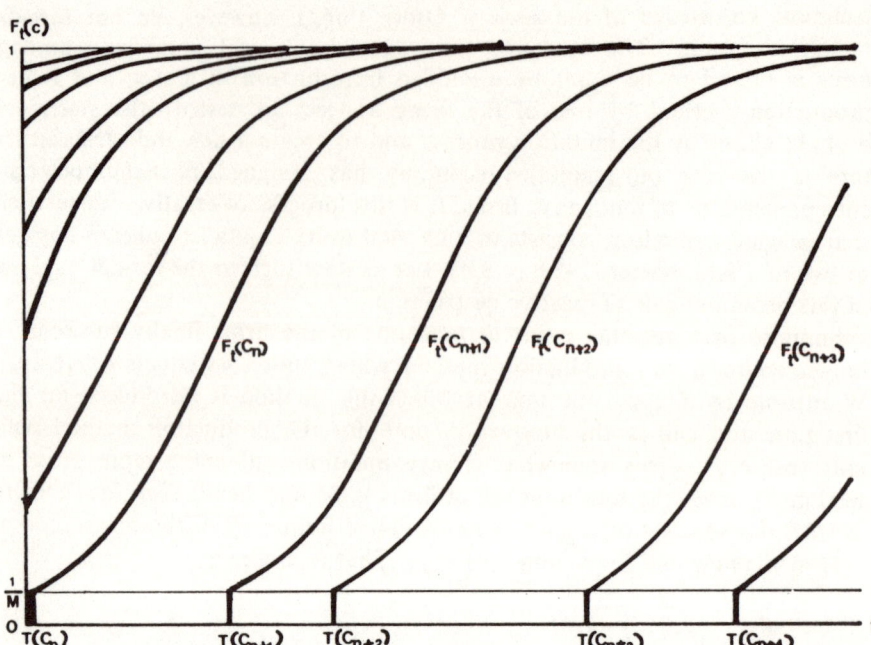

Fig. 4. The evolution of the state of technology under the joint pressure of innovation and imitation — the case where only the technologically most advanced firms can innovate.

$T(c_{n+1})$ illustrates all this. By comparing it with fig. 3, the reader can immediately see that the only alteration we made to the latter is to superimpose a new logistic growth curve that starts with an initial mass $1/M$ at time $T(c_{n+1})$.

Innovation is not a single-shot phenomenon. No sooner than an innovation occurs, a new round of competition for a better production method begins. And no sooner than a winner of this game is named, another round of competition for a still better production method is set out. And so forth. Innovation is by nature a recurrent process.

Accordingly, let $T(c_{n+2})$, $T(c_{n+3}),\ldots,T(c_N),\ldots$, denote times at which production methods with unit costs $c_{n+2}>c_{n+3}>\cdots>c_N>\ldots$ are introduced for the first time into an industry, respectively. We call $T(c_N)$ the 'innovation time' of the production method with unit cost c_N and $T(c_N)-T(c_{N-1})$ the 'waiting time' for a new method with c_N. (There is, of course, no reason to believe that these innovation times are evenly distributed over time.) Then, at each innovation time $T(c_N)$ a new cumulative frequency $F_t(c_N)$ starts its logistic growth path from the (suddenly created) initial frequency $1/M$.

If, as in the case of the first innovation, innovations always emerge from the class of firms which have practiced the then best production method, we can repeatedly apply the same argument as was given earlier and claim that none of these successive innovations perturb the logistic growth patterns of all the cumulative frequencies of the currently practiced production methods. They only add a new logistic growth curve one by one from the bottom at each innovation time. This process is explained in fig. 4.

We are now in a position to examine the more general case by removing the supposition so far made that innovations always emerge from the class of technologically most advanced firms. Then, the evolutionary pattern of the state of technology becomes slightly more complex.

Suppose, at time $T(c_{n+1})$, new production method with unit cost c_{n+1} is introduced by a firm whose pre-innovation unit cost was not the smallest in the industry but was equal to a somewhat outdated value, say c_{n-2}. Just as before, this innovation sets out a logistic growth process of the cumulative frequency of $F_t(c_{n+1})$ from a newly created initial frequency $1/M$. [See eq. (6).] But, unlike the previous special case, growth paths of some of the already existing cumulative frequencies have to undergo a certain adjustment at the time of innovation $T(c_{n+1})$. For instance, $F_t(c_{n-1})$, the cumulative frequency of c_{n-1}, which was the sum of $f_t(c_n)$ and $f_t(c_{n-1})$ before the innovation, has now to add to itself a frequency $f_t(c_{n+1})$ whose value suddenly jumps from zero to $1/M$. Similarly, $F_t(c_n)$ experiences a discrete jump in its value by $1/M$. Both $F_t(c_n)$ and $F_t(c_{n-1})$ then resume their logistic growth paths from these adjusted values from then on. The rest of the cumulative frequencies, $F_t(c_{n-2}), F_t(c_{n-3}), \ldots$ remain unperturbed by the innovation of c_{n+1} and keep the same logistic growth paths even after that. For, in the case of these cumulative frequencies, the emergence of the new frequency $f_t(c_{n+1})$ is offset by the decline of the frequency $f_t(c_{n-2})$ by the same magnitude $1/M$. The set of logistic growth paths thus began at $T(c_{n+1})$ will continue until some of them are again upset by another innovation at the next innovation time $T(c_{n+2})$. At time $T(c_{n+2})$, yet another set of logistic growth paths will be set off only to be upset once again at the next innovation time $T(c_{n+3})$. And so forth. Fig. 5 presents an evolutionary pattern of the state of technology in this general case.

5. A specific model of innovation

In the preceding sections we have seen how the process of imitation and the process of innovation interact with each other and mold the evolutionary history of an industry's state of technology. The process of imitation works essentially as an equilibrating force that continually but slowly tends the industry towards a static equilibrium, in which all firms employ the same and best production technique available. The function of innovation, on the other hand, lies precisely in upsetting such an equilibrating tendency. It is a disequilibrating force which breaks up the existing order of an industry and forces the state of technology to become more progressive but more volatile.

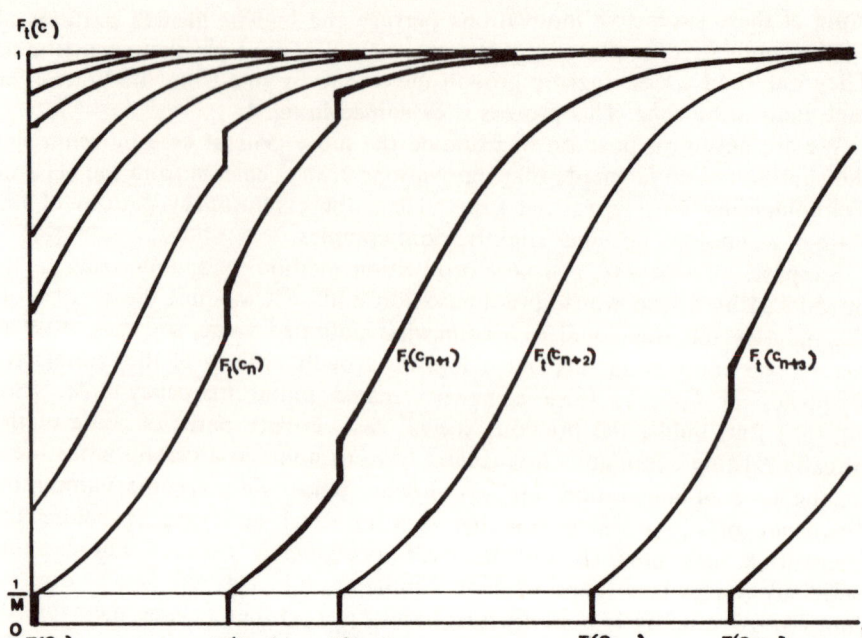

Fig. 5. The evolution of the state of technology under the joint pressure of innovation and imitation — the general case.

The purpose of this section and the next two is to study how the dynamic interaction of these opposite forces will determine the course of the development of the state of technology in the long run. To this end we have to specify the structure of firms' innovation activities in more detail.

Basic or applied scientific researches in private firms, governmental institutions and academia, weekend experiments of amateur inventors in their backyard garages, and so forth continuously expand the stock of technical knowledge potentially applicable to industrial production. But such a continuous inflow of new technical knowledge or 'inventions' does not necessarily lead to a corresponding improvement of production methods actually employed in an industry. 'As long as they are not carried into practice, inventions are economically irrelevant' [Schumpeter (1961, p. 88)]. For the purpose of industrial production, the potentiality must be transformed into the actuality; a production method hitherto untried must be put into industrial practice. This is what we mean by the word 'innovation', which must be conceptually distinguished from 'invention'.[7]

---

[7]This Schumpeterian dichotomy is, of course, a much oversimplified conceptualization of the inherently complex process of technical activities of modern corporations. We shall stick to this scheme solely for the sake of formalization.

Let us denote by $C(t)$ the unit cost of the best production method that is 'technologically possible' at time t but has thus far resisted the actual use in the industry. (For the sake of simplicity we ignore all the problems associated with the uncertainty as well as fuzziness inherent in delineating what is technologically possible from what is not.) We call $C(t)$ the unit cost of the potential production method or, more simply, the 'potential unit cost' at time t. It is then reasonable to suppose that the continuous inflow of technological knowledge or continuous supply of inventions constantly reduces the potential unit cost of the industry, so that we have

$$\dot{C}(t) < 0. \tag{7}$$

This paper, however, does not probe into the mechanism of inventive activity itself; inventions are supposed to occur outside the industry and beyond the control of the individual firms. This is, of course, a heroic assumption to maintain.

It then becomes possible to characterize the notion of 'innovation' formally as the activity by which a firm puts into practice the potential production method and thus succeeds in reducing its unit cost to the level of potential unit cost. Now, let $T(c)$ denote the inverse function of $C(t)$, defined by

$$T(C(t)) \equiv t \quad \text{or} \quad C(T(c)) \equiv c. \tag{8}$$

[Because of the monotone decreasingness of $C(T)$ with respect to T, as is assumed in (7), $T(c)$ is also a monotonically decreasing function of c.] We know that if an innovation occurs at time t it introduces a production method with $C(t)$ unit cost for the first time into an industry. It then follows that if a particular production method with unit cost c is presently in use it must have been introduced into the industry at time $T(c)$, for in view of the inverse relation (8) we have $c = C(T(c))$. The function $T(c)$ can then be interpreted as the 'innovation time' for a given production method with unit cost c, and this interpretation and notation are perfectly consistent with the definition of the same concept we introduced in the preceding section.

Later we shall find it useful to introduce the following hypothesis which further specializes the dynamics of the potential unit cost $C(t)$.

Hypothesis (PC). The potential unit cost is declining at a constant rate over time.

More formally this hypothesis supposes that

$$C(t) = \exp(-\lambda t), \tag{7'}$$

where λ is a positive constant. [For convenience, we set $C(0) = 1$.] Under this special hypothesis, the innovation time $T(c)$ — the inverse of $C(t)$ — can be expressed simply as a logarithmic function of c, or

$$T(c) = -\frac{1}{\lambda} \ln c. \tag{8'}$$

This special hypothesis will simplify our later exposition.

We have seen above what innovation consists of. But we have not seen who does innovation. It is now the time to specify in more detail the process that characterizes the way innovation occurs. We shall indeed consider two alternative models, which can be regarded as two polar cases spanning more realistic situations as their convex combinations. Let us explore these two models separately.

6. The state of technology in the long run (I)

In the first case, we postulate the following hypothesis concerning the stochastic nature of innovative activity.

Hypothesis (IN-a). Every firm has a small but equal chance for successful innovation at every point in time.

Let $v \cdot \Delta t$ be the probability that a firm succeeds in carrying out an innovation during a small time interval Δt; where v is a positive constant which is supposed to be of the much smaller order of magnitude than the imitation parameter μ. Then, the probability that an innovation is successfully carried out by *one of* the firms during a time interval Δt becomes equal to

$$vM\Delta t. \tag{9}$$

The probability that two or more firms simultaneously succeed in innovation is extremely small and hence ignored. Hypothesis (IN-a) amounts to saying that the occurrence of innovation is subject to the law of rare events or to the Poisson law which supposes that whether or not an innovation occurs in any time interval is independent of whether or not an innovation occurs in any time interval preceding it. (This is called the lack of memory property of the Poisson process.)

The innovation parameter v represents the effectiveness of each firm's innovation activity. Its value should, therefore, reflect a particular innovation policy the firm has come to choose as a critical pillar of its long-run growth strategy. In the present paper, however, we are concerned only with analyzing how the evolutionary pattern of the industry's state of technology is causally determined by a given innovation policy of the firm, together with its imitation policy. The study of how the firm selects a particular innovation policy in the long run and how this long-run decision process reflects the evolutionary pattern of the industry's state of technology is left for the future research.[8]

The state of technology of an industry is a historical outcome of the dynamic interaction between the process of imitation and the process of innovation. The process of imitation is an equilibrating force which moves the entire state of technology along the family of logistic growth curves, whereas the process of innovation is a disequilibrating force which disturbs this smooth journey and restructures the state of technology from time to time. As time goes on, however, innovation takes place over and over again. After a long period of time, it is expected that a certain statistical regularity will emerge out of this random pattern of the occurrence of innovations. [For instance, it is not difficult to show that after a long passage of time the average rate of innovation tends to approach a constant value vM, under the Poisson hypothesis (IN-a).] Indeed, not only the dynamic pattern of innovation but the entire state of technology is also expected in the long run to exhibit a tendency towards certain statistical regularity as a long-run averaging result of the dynamic balance between the forces of imitation and of innovation.

Let $F_t^*(c)$ represent the *expected* cumulative frequency function of unit costs at time t. We shall now turn to the study of the behavior of this expected cumulative frequency function. Since we are concerned only with describing the industry's state of technology 'in the long run', this is all that we have to do.

Now, we know from (3) that the cumulative frequency function $F_t(c)$ *increases* by $\mu F_t(c)(1 - F_t(c))\Delta t$, if no innovation occurs during a time interval, $[t, t + \Delta t]$. If, on the other hand, an innovation occurs during the same time interval, it creates a new cumulative frequency $F_t(C(t))$ of the size equal to $1/M$. When the innovator has belonged to the class of firms whose unit costs are higher than c, it automatically raises the value of $F_t(c)$ by the same magnitude $1/M$ in addition to the effect of imitation $\mu F_t(c)(1 - F_t(c))\Delta t$. When, however, the innovator is from the class of firms whose unit costs are less than or equal to c, the innovation effects only an intra-marginal exchange of an equal mass of frequency and leaves the value of $F_t(c)$ unaffected. Since by hypothesis (IN-a) the probability of an innovation during a time period of Δt is $vM\Delta t$ and the fraction of firms whose unit costs are higher than c is $1 - F_t(c)$, the expected number of innovators whose unit costs are higher than c can be calculated as $vM(1 - F_t(c))\Delta t$ during $[t, t + \Delta t]$.

---

[8]Empirical literature on the factors which influence the innovation policy of firms is enormous. Excellent surveys are Kamien and Schwartz (1975 and 1982; ch. 3), and Scherer (1979, ch. 15).

We can thus conclude that the cumulative frequency function $F_t(c)$ increases *on average* by $\{\mu F_t(c)(1 - F_t(c)) + \nu M(1 - F_t(c))(1/M)\}\Delta t$ from time t to $t + \Delta t$. In terms of expected cumulative frequency function $F_t^*(c)$, we can state this result as

$$\dot{F}_t^*(c) = \mu F_t^*(c)(1 - F_t^*(c)) + \nu(1 - F_t^*(c)). \tag{10}$$

This is indeed a logistic differential equation of $F_t^*(c) + \mu/\nu$, which has an explicit solution of the form

$$F_t^*(c) + \frac{\nu}{\mu}$$

$$= (1 + \nu/\mu) \Big/ \left(1 + \left[\frac{1 + \nu/\mu}{F_{T(c)}^*(c) + \nu/\mu}\right] \exp\left[-(\mu + \nu)(t - T(c))\right]\right) \tag{11}$$

for $t \geq T(c)$; where $T(c)$ is the innovation time for a given unit cost c and $F_{T(c)}^*(c)$ is the expected value of the cumulative distribution at that point of time. Although $F_{T(c)}(c)$ equals $1/M$ when an innovation occurs, the probability of an innovation at a particular instant is of course equal to zero. Hence, $F_{T(c)}^*(c) = 0$, which also implies $\dot{F}_{T(c)}^*(c) = \nu$, and we can simplify (11) as

$$F_t^*(c) = \frac{1 + \nu/\mu}{1 + (\mu/\nu)\exp\left[-(\mu + \nu)(t - T(c))\right]} - \frac{\nu}{\mu}. \tag{11'}$$

In order to proceed further, it is necessary at this point to keep in mind the obvious fact that unit costs of firms in the industry has a tendency to decline over time under the joint pressure of the forces of imitation and innovation. It is therefore futile to expect that the shape of the expected cumulative frequency function itself will exhibit a tendency towards any statistical regularity. If there exists any statistical regularity at all, it must be of the form which is relative to the declining tendency of the unit costs as a whole in the industry. In order to capture this relative nature of the possible statistical regularity, let us introduce the following new variable:

$$z \equiv \ln c - \ln C(t). \tag{12}$$

This variable measures how the unit cost c of a given production method is proportionally in excess of the potential unit cost $C(t)$ prevailing at time t. We call this the 'cost gap', for short. By definition, the value of cost gap becomes zero for the production method which has been just innovated; it takes a positive value for any other production method actually in use. As we shall see shortly, the use of this new measure of efficiency will enable us to neutralize the declining tendency of unit costs.

Indeed, if we recall the logarithmic relation (8') between a unit cost c and its innovation time $T(c)$, the gap between t and $T(c)$ in eq. (11') can be rewritten in terms of the cost gap as z/λ. Hence, we obtain a relation

$$F_t^*(c) = \tilde{F}(z) \equiv \frac{1 + v/\mu}{1 + (\mu/v) \cdot \exp[-(\mu+v)z/\lambda]} - \frac{v}{\mu}, \tag{13}$$

which is independent of the calendar time t! $\tilde{F}(z)$ above is the 'long-run average cumulative frequency function' of the cost gap we have sought to deduce under the hypothesis (IN-a). It is a function only of the cost gap, $z \equiv \ln c - \ln C(t)$, and not of the value of the potential unit cost $C(t)$ itself. Fig. 6 illustrates the structure of this long-run average cumulative frequency function. It has the shape of a truncated logistic growth curve, with growth parameter $(\mu+v)/\lambda$ and initial slope v/λ.

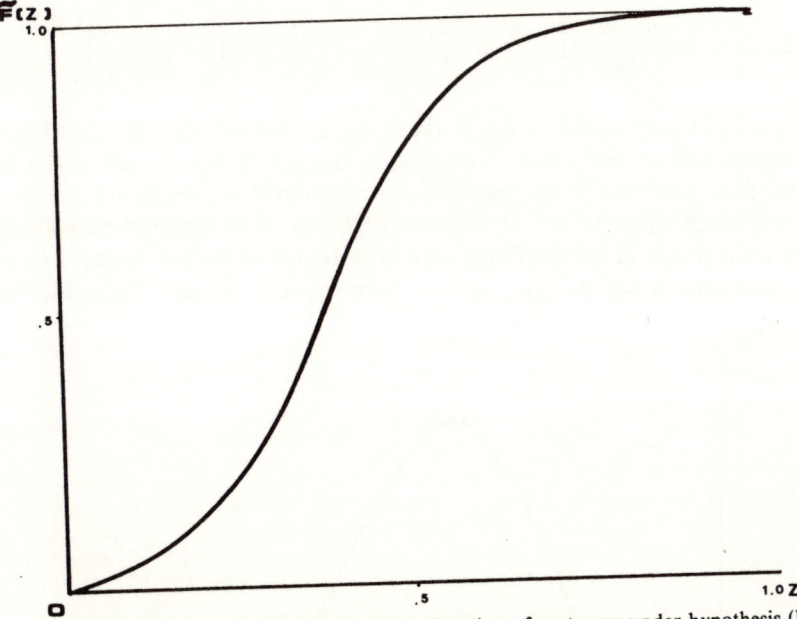

Fig. 6. The long-run average cumulative frequency function of cost gaps under hypothesis (IN-i), when $\lambda = 0.05$, $v = 0.01$ and $\mu = 0.50$.

The long-run average cumulative frequency distribution obtained above is a long-run statistical summary of the way in which firms in the industry are distributed over a multitude of diverse production methods with different unit costs. It shows that while the continuous inflow of new technological knowledge constantly reduces the potential unit cost over time, the industry will never be able to enjoy its fruits fully and unit costs of a majority of firms will always lag behind the potential one. The industry's state of technology will thus never approach a neoclassical equilibrium of uniform technological knowledge. Indeed, it is only the relative shape of the distribution of firms over different cost conditions which exhibits any tendency for a statistical regularity over the long-run course of events in the industry.

The dynamic interaction between the forces of innovation and imitation, together with the exogenous inflow of new technological knowledge, is what maintains the relative configuration of the state of technology in a statistical equilibrium in the form of (13). In order to study how a change in each of these forces will shift this delicate statistical balance, it is easier to examine the density form of the long-run average frequency function, given by

$$f(z) \equiv \frac{\mathrm{d}\tilde{F}(z)}{\mathrm{d}z}$$

$$= \frac{(\mu+v)^2}{\lambda\mu} \bigg/ \left[\sqrt{\frac{v}{\mu}} \cdot \exp\left(\frac{\mu+v}{2\lambda}z\right) + \sqrt{\frac{\mu}{v}} \cdot \exp\left(-\frac{\mu+v}{2\lambda}z\right) \right]^2 \qquad (14)$$

for $z \geq 0$. As is depicted in fig. 7, the long-run average density distribution is a smooth bell-shaped curve, truncated at the left. It has a peak of the height equal to $(\mu+v)^2/4\lambda\mu$ at the value of cost gap equal to $[\lambda/(\mu+v)] \cdot \ln(\mu/v)$, and the intercept equal to v/λ at the zero cost gap. It is thus not difficult to see that an increase in the declining rate of potential unit cost, λ, tends to widen the cost gaps of the industry and at the same time disperse their distribution

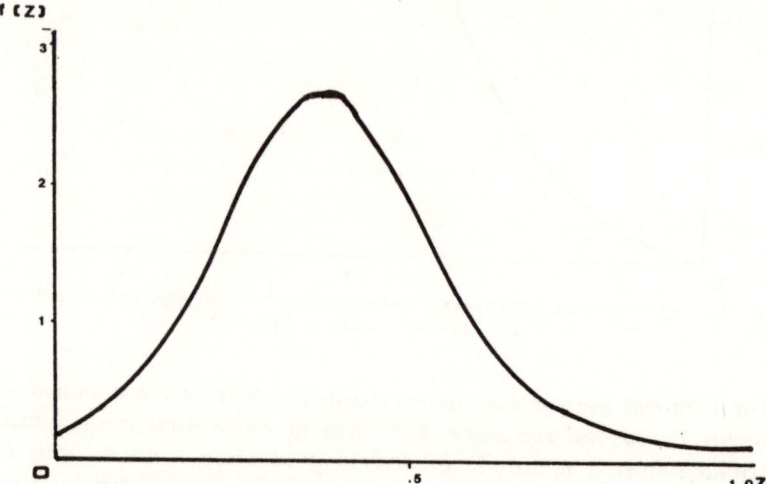

Fig. 7. The long-run average density function of cost gaps under hypothesis (IN-i).

across firms; that an increase in the rate of innovation, v, tends, albeit weakly, to narrow the cost gaps and concentrate their distribution; and that an increase in the rate of imitation, μ, also tends to narrow the cost gaps and concentrate their distribution.[9] Figs. 8, 9 and 10, respectively, illustrate these comparative statics results numerically. [The base values of parameters, $\lambda = 0.05$, $v = 0.01$, $\mu = 0.50$ mean, if the number of firms in the industry is 20, (i) that the potential unit cost declines 5% annually, (ii) that the average lag between invention and innovation is 5 years, and (iii) that it takes on average 5.89 years for half of the firms to succeed in imitating an innovation.]

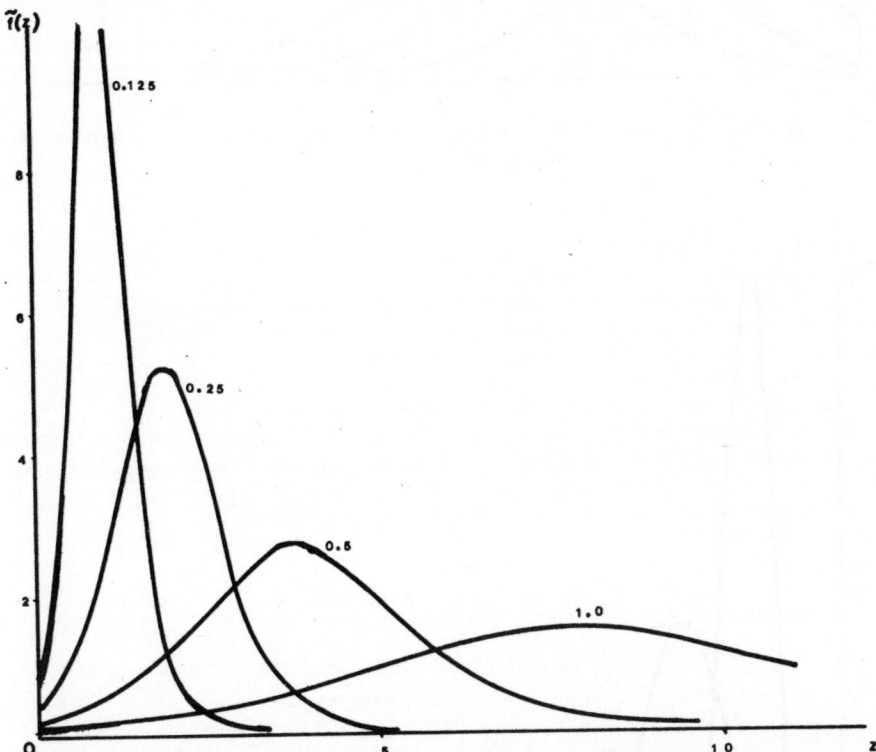

Fig. 8. The long-run average density functions under hypothesis (IN-i) for various values of λ (where v and μ are fixed at 0.01 and 0.50 respectively).

Note in passing that, while the occurrence of an innovation disrupts the existing order of the industry and makes its state of technology more disperse than before, an increase in its probability tends to increase the technological efficiency of the industry as a whole in the long run. This apparent conflict between short-run effect and long-run consequence of

---

[9]An increase in μ may widen the average cost gap if $1 + v/\mu < \ln(\mu/v)$. But this somewhat perverse case can be ignored as long as v is sufficiently small relative to μ.

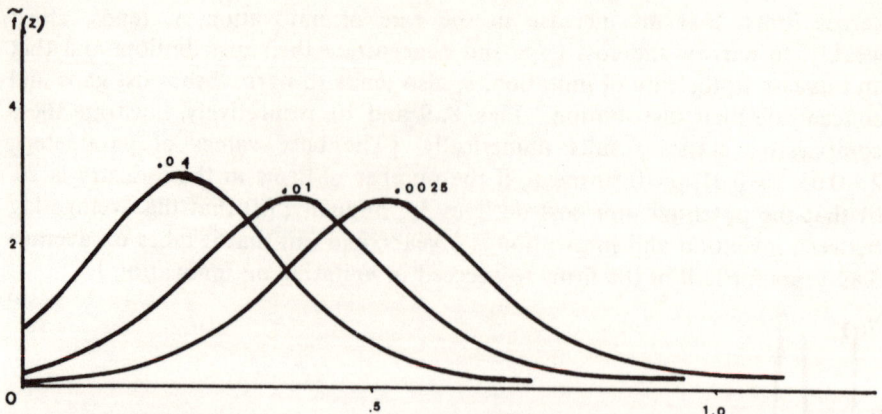

Fig. 9. The long-run average density functions under hypothesis (IN-i) for various values of v
(where $\lambda = 0.05$ and $\mu = 0.10$).

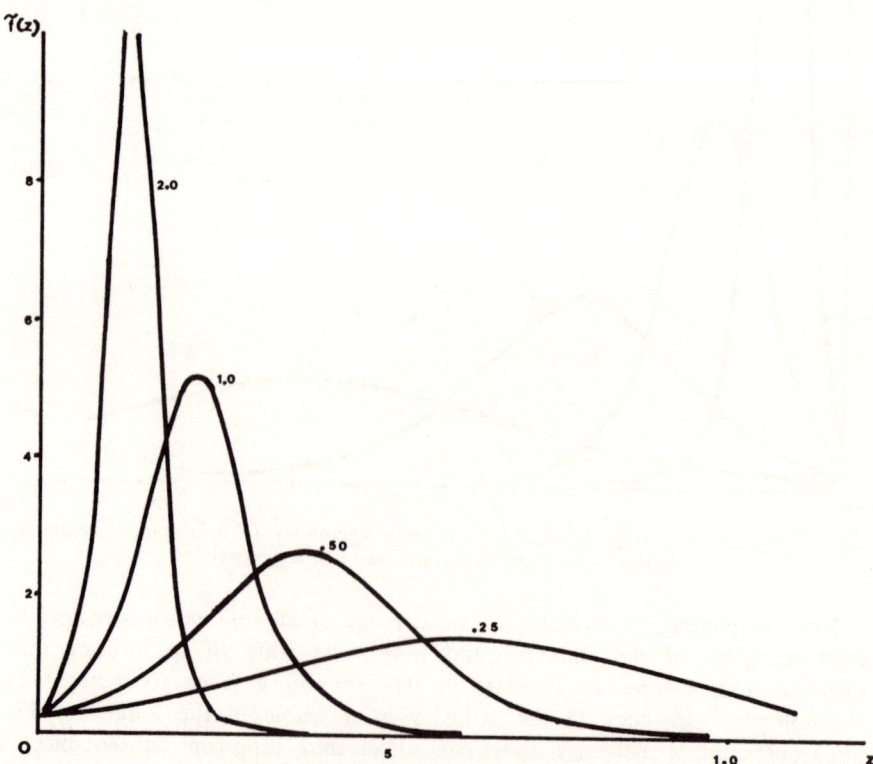

Fig. 10. The long-run average density functions under hypothesis (IN-i) for various values of μ
(where $\lambda = 0.05$ and $v = 0.01$).

innovation is exactly what Schumpeter tried to capture by the word 'creative destruction'.

In order to avoid the possible confusion, let us emphasize once again that the long-run average frequency distribution of cost gaps, $\widetilde{F}(z)$ or $\widetilde{f}(z)$, is no more than a long-run statistical summary of the evolutionary pattern of the state of technology. It never implies that the industry's state of technology will, in the long run, converge to a static equilibrium. Far from it, the state of technology is a state of constant flux. As was vividly pictured in figs. 4 and 5, it is continuously moved by the force of imitation and discontinuously disrupted by the force of innovation. Its year-to-year or decade-to-decade evolution exhibits no tendency towards equilibrium. All that is claimed here is merely that if the long history of the development of the industry's state of technology is patiently studied, it is possible to detect the existence of certain statistical regularities out of its seemingly irregular evolutionary pattern.

7. The state of technology in the long run (II)

In the second special case, we introduce the following hypothesis concerning the nature of innovative activities.

Hypothesis (IN-b). Innovation is always carried out by a firm technologically most advanced at the time of innovation. Among those firms which are potentially capable of carrying out innovation the chance for success is equal at every point in time.

This hypothesis is, of course, an opposite extreme of hypothesis (IN-a) which insisted that every firm, whether technologically advanced or not, is potentially capable of striking innovation. Needless to say, it corresponds to the special case we examined in section 4. Although we found it easy to illustrate, by means of a diagram, the evolutionary pattern of the state of technology in this case, the analysis of its long-run average performance turns out to be slightly more involved.

Let $\xi \Delta t$ represent the probability that one of the technologically most advanced firms succeeds in carrying out an innovation during a small time interval Δt; where ξ is a very small positive constant. Then, the foregoing hypothesis can be restated more formally in the following manner. Suppose that the best practice production method at time t has unit cost equal to c_N which was introduced into an industry at time $T(c_N)(\leq t)$. Then the number of firms which employ this production method at time t can be computed as $F_t(c_N) \cdot M$. Since the hypothesis (IN-b) insists that only those firms whose unit cost is c_N are potentially capable of introducing a new and better production method c_{N+1} and that any of those potential innovators has an equal chance for success, the probability that an innovation occurs during a small time interval between t and $t+\Delta t$ must be equal to $\xi \Delta t$ times the number of those firms given above, or

$$(\xi \Delta t) \cdot (F_t(c_N)M) = \frac{M\xi \Delta t}{1+(M-1)\exp\left[-\mu(t-T(c_N))\right]}. \tag{15}$$

Consider the sequence of successive waiting times for innovation, $T(c_2) - T(c_1)$, $T(c_3) - T(c_2), \ldots, T(c_N) - T(c_{N-1}), \ldots$. Under hypothesis (IN-b) they can be regarded as random variables which are identically distributed and independent of each other. In fact, that hypothesis enables us to compute explicitly the probability distribution of each waiting time. Let $U(s)$ denote the cumulative probability distribution of the waiting time $s \geq T(c_N) - T(c_{N-1})$. Then a calculation whose detail is relegated to the appendix shows that it has the form of

$$U(s) = 1 - \left[\frac{M-1}{M} + \frac{1}{M}\exp(\mu s)\right]^{-\xi M/\mu} \tag{16}$$

for $s \geq 0$. From this we can also calculate the expected waiting time for innovation τ as

$$\tau \equiv \mathrm{E}\{T(c_N) - T(c_{N-1})\} = \sum_{n=0}^{\infty} \left(\frac{M-1}{M}\right)^n \frac{1}{\mu n + \xi M}, \tag{17}$$

which is a decreasing function of ξ and μ. (See the appendix for the derivation.) The waiting time for innovation is thus expected to shorten as the effectiveness of innovative or imitative activity tends to increase.

In contrast to the first case, the probability of an innovation is uneven under hypothesis (IN-b). The probability of the next innovation is very small immediately after the occurrence of one innovation (for there is only one firm capable of striking it), but, as more and more firms succeed in imitating the best practice method and become potential innovators, this probability rises accordingly until almost the whole population of firms become capable of innovation. As time goes on, however, innovation takes place over and over again. After a sufficient number of years, therefore, a certain statistical regularity is expected to emerge out of the seemingly uneven pattern of the occurrence of innovations. In fact, the sequence of waiting times $\{T(c_{N+1}) - T(c_N)\}$ constitutes what is in the probability theory called a 'renewal process', which is known to have well-behaved asymptotic properties. [See, for example, Feller (1966, ch. XI) for an excellent discussion of the theory of renewal process.] For instance, it is possible to show that the expected number of innovations per unit of time will in the long-run converge to a constant rate $1/\tau$, which is nothing but the reciprocal of the expected waiting time. (This is what is called the renewal theorem.)

The fact that the dynamic pattern of innovations will in the long run settle down to a statistical uniformity suggests to us that even under hypothesis (IN-b) the industry's state of technology as a whole will also exhibit a certain statistical tendency towards regularity. In order to show this, let us consider the behavior of $F_t^*(c)$, the expected cumulative frequency function at time t.

Under hypothesis (IN-b), we can indeed directly calculate $F_t^*(c)$ as follows. The cumulative capacity share $F_t(c)$ of a given unit cost c is zero before its innovation time $T(c)$ and remains so as long as no innovation occurs at and after $T(c)$. Its value jumps to $1/M$ at the time of the first innovation to occur at or after $T(c)$, and then follows a logistic growth path from that time on, independently of the pattern of innovations that follow. (Recall fig. 4.) Now, let $H_x(y)$ denote the probability that the length of time measured from a given time x to the first innovation to occur at or after x is equal to or less than $y(\geq 0)$. We may call this the 'residual waiting time distribution'. In terms of this distribution, it is therefore easy to see that

$$F_t^*(c) = \int_0^{t-T(c)} \frac{1}{1+(M-1)\exp\{-\mu[t-(T(c)+y)]\}} \cdot dH_{T(c)}(y) \qquad (18)$$

for $t \geq T(c)$.

The residual waiting time distribution $H_x(y)$ in general depends upon the calendar time x from which the residual waiting time y for the next innovation is measured. But, as time goes by, it will gradually get rid of this dependency and approach asymptotically to a steady-state distribution. More specifically, we have that

$$H_x(y) \to \int_0^y \frac{1-U(s)}{\tau} \cdot ds \qquad (19)$$

for a sufficiently large x. [See Feller (1966, p. 355) for the proof.] Accordingly, if we let both $T(c)$ and $t(\geq T(c))$ grow large and substitute the explicit expression (16) for $U(s)$, we can in fact show that

$$F_t^*(c) \equiv \int_0^{t-T(c)} \{1+(M-1)\exp[-\mu(t-T(c)-y)]\}^{-1} \cdot \frac{1}{\tau}$$

$$\cdot \left[\frac{M-1}{M}+\frac{1}{M}\exp(\mu y)\right]^{-(\xi M/\mu)} \cdot dy \qquad (20)$$

for $t \geq T(c)$. Finally, if we note the relation: $z \equiv \ln c - \ln C(t) = \lambda(t - T(c))$ under hypothesis (PC), we can rewrite the asymptotic form of the expected cumulative capacity share function given above as follows:

$$F(z) \equiv \int_0^{z/\lambda} \left\{ 1 + (M-1)\exp\left[-\mu\left(\frac{z}{\lambda} - y\right) \right] \right\}^{-1} \cdot \frac{1}{\tau}$$

$$\cdot \left[\frac{M-1}{M} + \frac{1}{M}\exp(\mu y) \right]^{-(\xi M/\mu)} \cdot dy, \tag{21}$$

which is independent of the calendar time t.

Fig. 11 illustrates a typical shape of $\tilde{F}(z)$.[10] As is seen from this diagram, the long-run average cumulative frequency function of cost gaps has a shape similar to the logistic growth curve even under hypothesis (IN-b). But, as is indicated by its density form $\tilde{f}(z) \equiv d\tilde{F}(z)/dz$ illustrated in fig. 12, it is, unlike the true logistic growth curve, skewed to the left. Figs. 13, 14 and 15 then illustrate numerically the influence of a change in each parameter value on the shape of the density form of the long-run average frequency function of cost gaps. The first diagram shows that an increase in the declining rate of

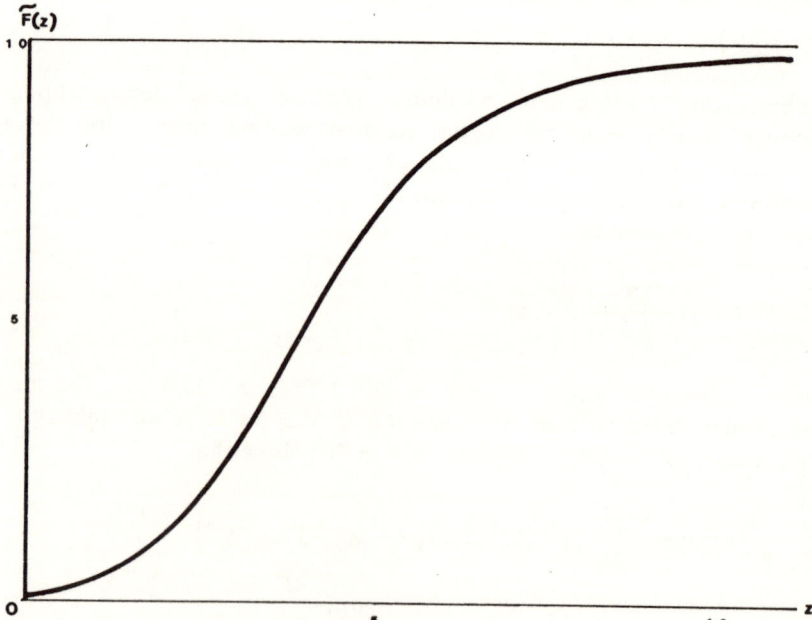

Fig. 11. The long-run average cumulative frequency function of cost gaps under hypothesis (IN-ii), when $\lambda = 0.05$, $\xi = 0.01$, $\mu = 0.50$ and $M = 20$).

[10]For this illustration, we have chosen the values of parameters as $\lambda = 0.05$, $\xi = 0.01$, $\mu = 0.50$ and $M = 20$.

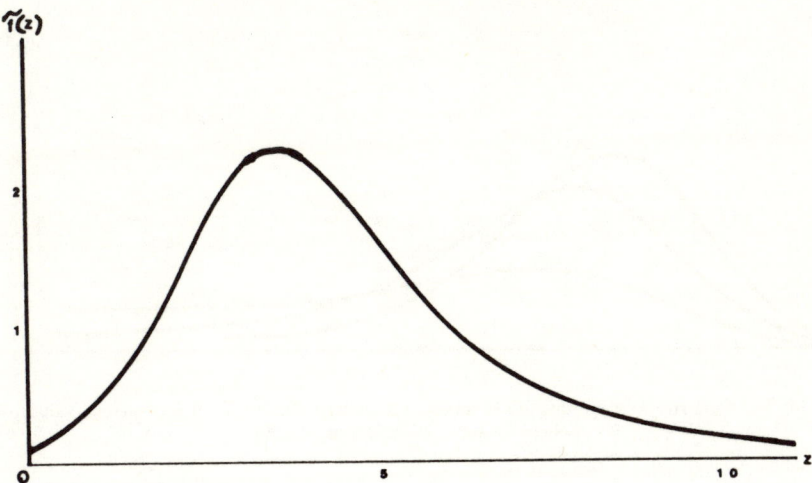

Fig. 12. The long-run average density function of cost gaps under hypothesis (IN-ii).

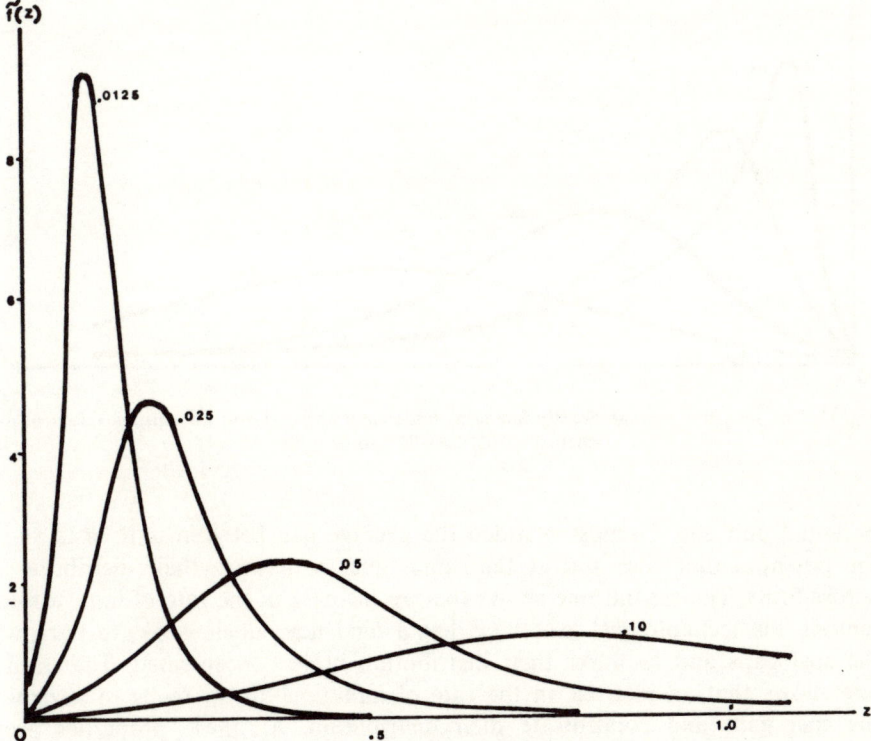

Fig. 13. The long-run average density functions under hypothesis (IN-ii) for various values of λ (where $\xi = 0.01$, $\mu = 0.50$ and $M = 20$).

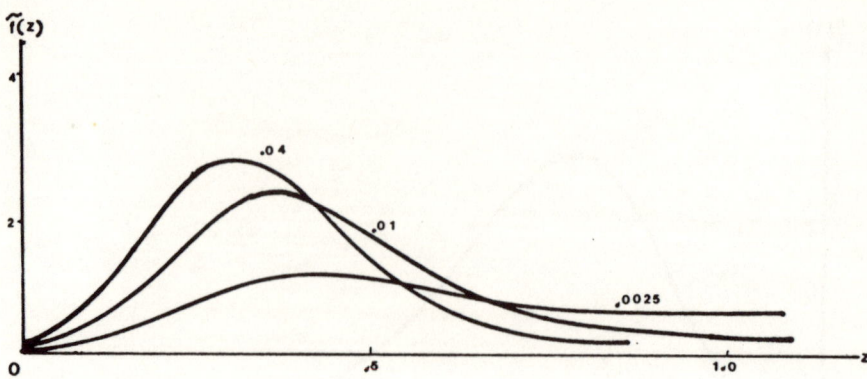

Fig. 14. The long-run average density functions under hypothesis (IN-ii) for various values of ξ (where $\lambda = 0.05$, $\mu = 0.50$ and $M = 20$).

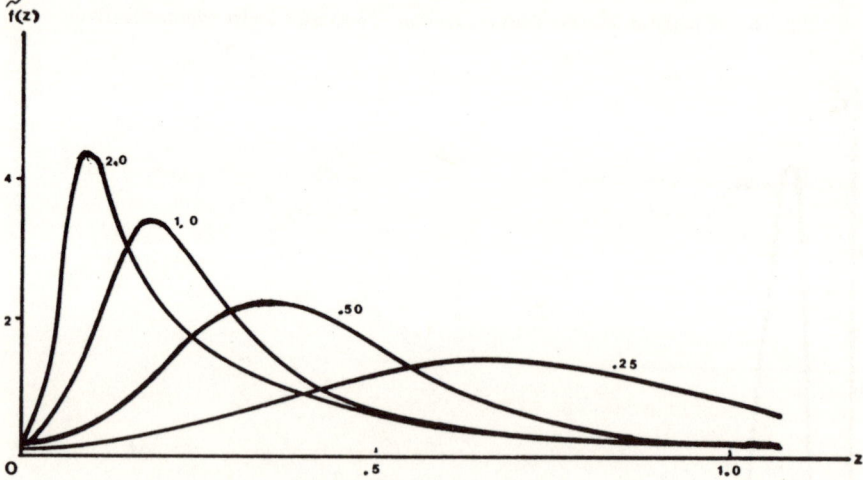

Fig. 15. The long-run average density functions under hypothesis (IN-ii) for various values of μ (where $\lambda = 0.05$, $\xi = 0.01$ and $M = 20$).

potential unit cost λ tends to widen the average gap between unit costs and the potential unit cost and at the same time to disperse their distribution across firms. The second one shows that an increase in the rate of innovation (among the technological leaders) ξ has a tendency, albeit weak, to narrow the cost gaps and to make their distribution more concentrated. The third one shows that an increase in the rate of imitation μ also tends to narrow the cost gaps and concentrate their distribution. All these properties are similar to those of the long-run average density function of cost gaps under hypothesis (IN-a).

8. Turnover of firms

So far our analysis has supposed that there is no turnover of firms into and out of the industry and that the same M firms forever stay in it. It is, however, not so difficult to show that the models developed in this paper require no modification even if the process of turnover of firms is incorporated into them *as long as* (i) both entry and exit occur only within the class of firms employing the industry's worst practice production method and (ii) entry and exit just balance each other so that the total number of firms remains constant over time. Indeed, all the results we have obtained here are totally independent of the existence of firm-turnover under these assumptions.

In general, however, the process of turnover of firms does make a difference.

9. Concluding remarks

Our conclusion is our starting point. Let us recall the efficiency distribution of the metal stampings industry we presented in fig. 1. This paper began with a 'casual empiricism' that the state of technology in this industry (and in almost all industries in the U.S.) appears to be perpetually out of equilibrium, and then proceeded to demonstrate 'theoretically' that the state of technology will indeed be in perpetual disequilibrium under the Schumpeterian hypotheses on innovation and imitation. We have seen that while firms' imitation activities constitute an equilibrating force of technology which tends the industry's state of technology (not uniformly but logistically) towards a neoclassical equilibrium in which all the firms have full access to the most efficient production method available, the function of innovation lies precisely in upsetting this equilibrating tendency. It is the dynamic interaction between the continuous and equilibrating force of imitation and the discontinuous and disequilibrating force of innovation which governs the evolution of the industry's state of technology. In fact, we have been able to show how these two opposite forces will work hand in hand to generate a certain statistical regularity in the way in which the relative configuration of the distribution of efficiencies across firms develops itself over time. Under the joint pressure of imitation and innovation, the industry will not reach a neoclassical equilibrium with perfect technological knowledge even in the long run. While new technological knowledge constantly flows into the industry, actual production methods of a majority of firms always lag behind it, and a multitude of diverse production methods with a wide range of efficiencies will co-exist forever. Indeed, it is merely the statistical regularity of the relative pattern of these micro-scopic disequilibria that characterizes 'the long run' of the industry. We find it somewhat remarkable that the 'theoretical' shape of this statistical regularity we presented in fig. 7 or fig. 12 does resemble the 'empirical' shape of the efficiency distribution in fig. 1.

The only economic principle we have employed in the present paper is that of efficiency, namely, that firms always desire to adopt the more efficient or more profitable production method, whenever possible. (That they are not always able to do so is, of course, the basic premise of this paper.) All the results we have obtained here are therefore founded ultimately on this weakest of all economic principles. The task of the sequels is to introduce more specifically economic principles into the basic model and to work out their implications for our Schumpeterian dynamics. In particular, in the forthcoming paper (part II: Technological progress, firm growth and 'economic selection') we shall introduce another simple economic principle, that firms successful in innovation and imitation grow relatively faster than less successful ones, and study how the interplay of the process of firm growth and the process of technological innovation and imitation will mold the evolutionary pattern of the industry's state of technology.

Appendix

Let $U(s)$ be the cumulative probability of the waiting time for innovation $T(c_{N+1}) - T(c_N)$. Suppose that none of the firms have been successful in innovation during a time interval $[0, s]$ after the last innovation time $T(c_N)$. Clearly, the probability of this occurrence is given by $1 - U(s)$. On the other hand, by (15) the probability that one of the firms will introduce a new production method with c_{N+1} unit cost during the succeeding small time interval $[s, s + \Delta t]$ equals $\xi M \Delta t / \{1 + (M-1) \exp[-\mu s]\}$. Since the probability that the production method with c_{N+1} unit cost will be introduced *for the first time* during the same small interval is the probability that no firms have been successful in $[0, s]$ *and* one of the firms becomes successful during $[s, s + \Delta t]$, we have the following equation:

$$U(s + \Delta t) - U(s) = (1 - U(s)) \cdot \{\xi M \Delta t / [1 + (M-1) \exp(-\mu s)]\}. \quad (A.1)$$

By letting $\Delta t \to 0$, we obtain

$$\frac{dU(s)}{dt} = (1 - U(s)) \cdot [\xi M / \{1 + (M-1) \exp(-\mu s)\}]. \quad (A.2)$$

This differential equation is not hard to solve, and we have

K. Iwai, Evolutionary model of innovation and imitation

189

$$U(s) = 1 - \exp\left[-\xi M \int_0^s \frac{1}{1 + (M-1)\exp(-\mu t)} dt \right]$$

$$= 1 - \left[\frac{1}{M}\exp(\mu s) + \frac{M-1}{M} \right]^{-\xi M/\mu}. \tag{A.3}$$

The expected waiting time is then calculated as

$$\tau \equiv \mathrm{E}\{T(c_{N+1}) - T(c_N)\} = \int_0^\infty s \cdot dU(s). \tag{A.4}$$

By integrating the right-hand side by parts, we have

$$\int_0^\infty s \cdot dU(s) = \int_0^\infty [1 - U(s)] \, ds = \int_0^\infty \left[\frac{M-1}{M} + \frac{1}{M}\exp(\mu s) \right]^{-\xi M/\mu} ds$$

$$= \frac{1}{\mu} \cdot \int_0^1 t^{(\xi M/\mu)-1} \cdot \left(1 - \frac{M-1}{M} t \right)^{-1} \cdot dt$$

$$= \frac{1}{\mu} \cdot \sum_{n=0}^\infty \left[\left(\frac{M-1}{M} \right)^n \cdot \int_0^1 t^{n-1+(\xi M/\mu)} \, dt \right]$$

$$= \sum_{n=0}^\infty \left(\frac{M-1}{M} \right)^n \cdot \frac{1}{\mu n + \xi M}.$$

References

Bailey, N.T.J., 1957, The mathematical theory of epidemics (Griffin, London).
Coleman, J., E. Katz and H. Menzel, 1957, The diffusion of an innovation among physicians, Sociometry 24, no. 1.
Dasgupta, P. and J. Stiglitz, 1980a, Industrial structure and the nature of innovative activity, Economic Journal 90, no. 2.
Dasgupta, P. and J. Stiglitz, 1980b, Uncertainty, industrial structure, and the speed of R&D, Bell Journal of Economics 2, no. 1.
Davies, S., 1979, The diffusion of process innovations (Cambridge University Press, Cambridge).
Feller, W.J., 1966, An introduction to probability theory and its applications, Vol. 2 (Wiley, New York).
Futia, C., 1980, Schumpeterian competition, Quarterly Journal of Economics 94, no. 4.
Griliches, Z., 1957, Hybrid corn: An exploration in the economics of technological change, Econometrica 25, no. 4.
Iwai, K., 1981, Disequilibrium dynamics (Yale University Press, New Haven, CT).
Kamien, M. and N. Schwartz, 1972, Timing of innovations under rivalry, Econometrica 40, no. 1.
Kamien, M. and N. Schwartz, 1975, Market structure and innovation: A survey, Journal of Economic Literature 13, no. 1.
Kamien, M. and N. Schwartz, 1982, Market structure and innovation (Cambridge University Press, Cambridge).

Loury, G., 1979, Market structure and innovation, Quarterly Journal of Economics 93, no. 3.

Lotka, A., 1925, Elements of physical biology (William and Wilkens, Baltimore, MD).

Mansfield, E., 1968, Industrial research and technological innovation (Norton, New York).

Mansfield, E., M. Schwartz and S. Wagner, 1981, Imitation costs and patents: An empirical study, Economic Journal 91, no. 346.

Nelson, R. and S. Winter, 1982, An evolutionary theory of economic change (Harvard University Press, Cambridge, MA).

Ozga, S., 1960, Imperfect markets through lack of knowledge, Quarterly Journal of Economics 74, no. 1.

Pearl, R. and L.J. Reed, 1924, Studies in human biology.

Samuelson, P.A., 1947, Foundations of economic analysis (Harvard University Press, Cambridge, MA).

Sato, K., 1975, Production functions and aggregation (North-Holland, Amsterdam).

Scherer, F.M., 1967, Research and development resource allocation under rivalry, Quarterly Journal of Economics 81, no. 3.

Scherer, F.M., 1979, Industrial market structure and economic performance, 2nd ed. (Rand McNally, New York).

Schumpeter, J.A., 1950, Capitalism, socialism and democracy, 3rd ed. (Harper and Row, New York).

Schumpeter, J.A., 1961, The theory of economic development (English translation of Theorie der Wirtschaftlichen Entwicklung, 1912) (Oxford University Press, Oxford).

Simon, H.A., 1957, Models of man (Wiley, New York).

Simon, H.A., 1978, Rationality as process and as product of thought, American Economic Review 68, no. 2.

U.S. Department of Commerce, 1968, 1963 Census of manufactures, Establishments classified by ratio of payrolls and value added, 1958 and 1963, Mc 63(S)-8 (Government Printing Office, Washington, DC).

Winter, S., 1969, Satisficing, selection and the innovative remnant, Quarterly Journal of Economics 85, no. 2.

Part III
Broader Biological Analogies

[8]

DARWINISM AND ECONOMIC CHANGE*

By R. C. O. MATTHEWS

AMONG the most inspiring characteristics of John Hicks's work are its range and its capacity to cast new light on old problems by bringing together ways of thinking normally regarded as separate. In that spirit I propose to consider a topic on which he has made outstanding contributions—the theory of enonomic change, more particularly the theory of long-run histori-cal change—in the light of an approach which as far as I know he has *not* much used, that of evolutionary biology. I shall consider one possible part of the mechanism of economic change, namely competitive selection, the economic equivalent of Darwinian natural selection in biology. In so doing, I shall make comparisons at some points with the biological selection process, the study of which is much more advanced both theoretically and empirically (though it remains a highly controversial subject). I do not mean to imply that the economic and biological processes are exactly analogous.[1]

1. Optimization and competitive selection

1.1. *Basic concepts*

Suppose that, in a given type of situation confronting an economic agent, there exist two alternative modes of behaviour, A and B. The economic agent may, for example, be an entrepreneur, and A and B alternative techniques of production. What is the process, other than chance, that may cause A to become generally adopted? Two possibilities may be distin-guished.

(1) *Optimization.* Economic agents are rational and well informed. Be-fore acting, they correctly perceive that A is the preferable course, and they adopt it. A distinction may be drawn between two sub-cases.

(1A) The choice in favour of A is made by perfectly *rational foresight* as soon as the option becomes available.

(1B) The choice in favour of A results from *learning*, that is to say by inference from the consequences of A and B in the past, as practised either by the economic agent himself or by others whose experience he can observe. The choice is this sub-case is subject to lags.

(2) *Competitive selection.* Economic agents, or at least some of them, are unable to discern the relative merits of A and B *ex ante*. Some choose A,

* I am much indebted for helpful comments to M. M. Bray, F. H. Hahn, R. E. Rowthorn, A. K. Sen, and to the participants in a seminar at Churchill College, Cambridge. Responsibility for remaining faults is entirely my own.

[1] In particular, although reasonably appropriate parallels can be drawn between economic processes and Darwinian ones, there is no counterpart in economics to the Mendelian theory of sexual reproduction which lies at the basis of classical genetics. Nor is there anything in economics corresponding to the sharp distinction that exists between animal species. For a general survey of biological approaches in economics, see Hirshleifer (1977).

some *B*. Those who choose *A* out-perform those who choose *B*. In the ensuing competition, *B*-users are presently eliminated by *A*-users, and option *B* is eliminated with them. The choice is indirect in the sense that the social choice between *A* and *B* results from the relative overall success of their practitioners, just as selection between genes occurs through the relative fitness of the organisms that embody them. Optimization is direct choice by the economic agent, competitive selection is indirect social choice through changes in the relative weights of different decision-makers, brought about through the working of the system.

Many choices are, of course, quite easy. So it would be absurd to suppose that optimization is ever unimportant. Equally, there cannot be such perfect foresight that people never make mistakes. Thus, although optimization and competitive selection are in themselves quite different processes, the question about their relative importance in practice must always be one of degree. Moreover, although the difference between optimization and competitive selection may reflect a difference in the mental processes of economic agents, it need not necessarily do so. People may always be trying their best to make the right choices, but their best may not be at all good, either because their powers are so feeble or because the problems are so difficult. Their attempts at optimization may then have no more than random chances of success.

I shall throughout use the term optimization to refer to *successful* attempts to make the right choice, where the success, moreover, is not just a matter of chance, like guessing rightly between heads and tails (I shall revert shortly to the question of the meaning of the distinction between chance and non-chance success). Attempts at optimization are liable to be unsuccessful in so far as there is defective knowledge. In circumstances where defective knowledge prevents rational foresight and learning from achieving the right decisions, adoption of the right choice throughout the economy will come about only, if at all, through competitive selection.

It will be noted that the criteria of choice are not identical in the two mechanisms, in that optimization maximizes utility and competitive selection maximizes survival. For the time being I shall disregard this distinction. Some of its consequences will be encountered in Section 2.1 below. One consequence is that selection processes may affect the outcome even in the absence of defective knowledge, by selecting against the modes of behaviour of those economic agents who deliberately choose to maximize something other than their survival (e.g. because of indolence or moral scruples).

A distinction may be drawn between two sub-cases of situations where knowledge is defective and where there is therefore scope for competitive selection:

(2A) *Uniformly defective knowledge* prevails among economic agents. They are all equally liable to make mistakes. Competition rewards those who happen by chance to choose the right mode of behaviour and selects in favour of that mode. This is the sub-case closest to genetic selection.

(2B) *Differentially defective knowledge* prevails among economic agents. Some of them are regularly more likely to make the right choices than others are. This case perhaps corresponds more nearly to the popular (political) notion of competitive selection, in which the able prosper and the less able go to the wall, carrying their inefficient modes of behaviour with them. Optimization and competitive selection here interact, in that the right choices made by the more able may be the consequence of optimization rather than luck, with competitive selection being required over only part of the field of economic agents.[2]

Even the less able will make some correct decisions by chance (e.g. they may have located their operations in the right region), and even the most able will find that some choices are too difficult to get right except by chance (e.g. choices dependent on future mineral discoveries). So sub-case (2B) will always be combined to some extent with elements of the kind of selection that occurs in sub-case (2A).

Since competitive selection between modes of behaviour works indirectly through the economic agents who practise them, it will not be effective unless there is consistency over time in the choices made by individual economic agents (this has similar effects to the requirements of 'heritability of traits'). If you sometimes choose A and sometimes B, and so do I, with neither of us more disposed in one direction than the other is, competition between us will not serve to eliminate the less efficient mode. A chance run of wrong choices, or a wrong choice on an important occasion, may eliminate one of us, but it will not affect the direction of future choices. The hypothesis of consistency can be justified by the assumption of *inertia*. People tend to go on doing what they were doing before, subject to stochastic variation. The postulate of inertia is itself quite a plausible one, capable of being derived from a variety of assumptions about the underlying mental processes. Thus inertia may reflect risk-avoidance or bounded rationality or satisficing (some interesting anthropological instances are described in Lumsden and Wilson (1981), pp. 72–4). However, the postulate will not always be valid. The fact that it is a necessary pre-condition of competitive selection is one of the reasons why competitive selection may not always work. For the same reason, the fact that competitive elimination of firms is observed to occur does not necessarily mean that competitive selection is going on between modes of behaviour.

Stochastic inertia also serves to explain how a new mode of behaviour (equivalent to a mutation), if it happens to be introduced, is able to gain a foothold and does not instantly disappear. However, inertia by itself would allow a new mode of behaviour to persist only through the life of one individual economic agent (whether an individual or a firm or other collec-

---

[2] Other forms of interaction are possible. One form is that postulated in satisficing models, in which the degree of competitive pressure affects the amount of care that people put with choices between options. Many authors have developed this kind of model; an early example was Downie (1953).

tive body). Longer persistence and transmission require *imitation*. Imitation of the kind most familiar to economists—Schumpeterian imitation—amounts to conscious learning, the deliberate choice of a new mode of behaviour because it looks better than an old one, and it therefore needs to be left aside in considering what may happen in circumstances where optimization fails. There are other forms of imitation, however. The introduction of a new mode of behaviour increases the repertory of modes from which other economic agents may make their choices, whether those choices are themselves based on optimization or whether they are random. In the latter case we may speak of non-optimizing imitation. A major example from outside economics of imitation that has no optimization characteristics is provided by the development of a spoken language over time—Latin evolved into Italian without any one consciously thinking that it was an improvement.

1.2. *The background in economic thought*

In the history of economic thought, pride of place has sometimes been given, as an explanation of reality, to optimization, and sometimes to competitive selection. Notions of competitive selection were prominent in Marshall, whose admiration for Darwin is well known, as is that of Marx. As economic theory became more formal, optimization gained ground, particularly optimization in the form of perfectly rational foresight. Its assumption of perfect knowledge obviously required qualification, but its other assumption, perfectly rational utility maximization, was and is more tenaciously adhered to. Most often, the assumption of rational utility maximization is seen as a substantive, refutable, assertion about economic behaviour; particularly has this been so in the work of the so-called economic imperialists, who have extended the application of economic concepts to traditionally alien domains like crime and the family. Sometimes the assumption has been seen merely as the definition of the kind of behaviour that falls within the scope of economics (Knight (1942)). In that case non-economic considerations may have to be adduced for the explanation of behaviour that is 'economic' in the broader sense of Marshall, that is to say concerned with the ordinary business of life. Either way, the assumption of rational optimization is commonly viewed as a distinctive feature of the economist's approach—and this is sometimes seen as a weakness in economics. Thus a leading biologist, seeking to explain what he sees as the surprising fact that game theory has proved to be more readily applicable to biology than to economics, has commented, 'there are good theoretical grounds to expect populations to evolve to stable states, whereas there are grounds for doubting whether human being always act rationally' (Maynard Smith (1982), p. vii).

Reaction against the optimization hypothesis among economists has come mainly from concern about bounded rationality. It can scarcely be disputed

R. C. O. MATTHEWS   95

that rationality *is* bounded, because of the limitations of our mental pow-ers.[3] Organization of individuals into teams for purposes of decision-making may overcome some of these limitations but introduces others. The effects of bounded rationality may be difficult to distinguish, even in principle, from the effects of incomplete information: if someone acts on incomplete infor-mation, what does it matter whether the reason is that the information is not in his mental files or that he is incapable of extracting it from the files at the moment of decision? Anyway, a central place has to be given to incomplete information, due to one or both of these causes, in order to explain some leading economic phenomena. Without it, the competitive struggle—what is meant by competition in popular parlance—would be over before it started (Kirzner, 1964). So would economic growth, except in so far as it consisted purely of capital accumulation or population increase.

These objections apply with less force to optimization by learning than they do to optimization by rational foresight. But they do still apply there to some extent. Learning about the relative merits of alternative options may be a good deal more difficult in practice than it looks in theory. A producer may know that his marketing or his industrial relations are not going well, but it is a long step from that of knowing what (if any) specific change in policy would improve matters. If he has a piece of equipment that is always giving trouble, is the reason that its design is fundamentally faulty or that it needs some minor adjustments? Learning from the experience of com-petitors is even more difficult than learning from his own experience. He may know that a competitor is doing better than he is, but unless he knows why he will not be in a position to learn and imitate. The costs of individual processes and the profitability of individual product lines are commonly treated as matters of commercial secrecy just for that reason, to keep rivals guessing. Independently of incompleteness of information, imitation may be hampered by sunk costs, either because they cause a firm to go bankrupt before it can adapt or because of the demolition costs of existing physical, human or organizational capital.

Economists have been led by considerations such as these to invoke competitive selection as a supplement to optimization. Some economists have sought in competitive selection an alternative route to the conclusions that would follows from optimization by itself, and thereby to reinforce those conclusions. This is what Friedman did in his famous essay on methodology (1953). Competitive selection tends to be invoked particularly in connection with modes of behaviour that are too complex to be plausibly attributable to conscious optimization by the economic agents in question. Thus the leader of the economic imperialists, in a book that postulates some

[3] More controversially, it is sometimes suggested that apparent manifestations of bounded rationality reflect not only limited intellectual power but also certain deep-seated psychological tendencies to act in a particular way—tendencies which may have been conducive to fitness during the millennia when *homo sapiens* was evolving but are not necessarily conducive to it now (Lumsden and Wilson, (1981) and (1983)). For an enumeration of tendencies that appear to imply systematic irrationality, see Tversky and Kahneman (1974), Reijnders (1978).

very complicated maximizing operations, writes that, while utility maximization is central to his approach, he does not assume that human beings
consciously maximize (Becker, 1981, p. x). A similar view is often taken,
with varying degrees of explicitness, by writers of the school of the 'new
economic history' (such as many of the contributors to Floud and McCloskey (1981)).

Quite different is the approach of such writers as Boulding (1981) and
Nelson and Winter (1982),[4] who have used competitive selection models in
order to arrive at results that differ in important ways from those of
mainstream orthodoxy. These writers have seen competitive selection as one
part of a broader evolutionary approach to economic change.

1.3. *Modes of behaviour*

The more formal applications of competitive selection to economics in
recent times at first had reference to the theory of the firm (Alchian (1950)).
More relevant to general economic change, however, and closer to the
biological analogy, is its application to modes of behaviour, embodied in the
firm or other economic agent in the same sort of way that genes are
embodied in an organism. The term 'modes of behaviour' has so far been
used in this paper without much explanation. The concept now needs to be
looked at more closely.

The concept of modes of behaviour is taken from the broader field of
cultural evolution. Various names have been used in that literature, with
broadly similar meanings—memes (Dawkins (1976)), culturgens (Lumsden
and Wilson (1981)), and, in the economic context, routines (Nelson and
Winter (1982)). I shall stick to the neutral sounding term modes of behaviour, or modes for short. Modes of behaviour are, of course, an abstraction, in a way that genes are not, and the use of this kind of abstraction to
break down behaviour into a bundle of characteristic attributes (rather
reminiscent of Hume's treatment of personal identity) has been considered
objectionable reductionism by some social scientists (Leach (1981)). This
objection is perhaps likely to be less strongly felt by economists, who are
quite accustomed to the notion of discrete activities or discrete innovations
and techniques of production. Mode of behaviour is a better term in the
present context than technique, because it is broader, not so exclusively
suggestive of engineering. According to the purpose in hand, a mode of
behaviour can be defined either very broadly, so as to allow scope for
sub-modes within it, or else very narrowly. Some modes of behaviour may
be directly equivalent to decisions about production or consumption: using
diesel locomotives, or working nights, or relying on frozen food. Others may
affect production or consumption decisions more indirectly, though not

---

[4] Nelson and Winter's book, which incorporates and develops earlier published work by its
authors, is a major contribution on the subjects treated in the present paper and my
indebtedness to it will be apparent in many places.

necessarily to a less important extent: having a multi-divisional corporate structure, being a member of a craft union, or using insurance. An important class of modes of behaviour, possibly the most important class, are those concerned with responses to externally originating stimuli or signals. Some modes, like some genes, are directly translated one for one into observable traits; other modes may influence a variety of observable traits (the biological equivalent is known as pleiotropy) or else may produce observable traits only when in conjunction with other modes (polygenic inheritance).

The consideration that modes of behaviour may have broad applications or narrow ones is related to the question mentioned earlier about how to distinguish between cases where success in attempts at optimization is or is not due merely to chance. Whether the adoption of a correct decision on a single occasion was due to chance or skill is an unanswerable question in practice, and perhaps even in principle. The same may be said of correct decisions that are habitually made, as a result of inertia, in respect of a single narrowly defined class of choices. However, to the extent that an economic agent habitually makes right choices in a number of different types of decision, or in a number of different types of environment, then it is reasonable to say that he manifests skill rather than good luck. He will be enabled to do this if he is using certain modes of behaviour that have a good effect over a wide area—whatever the reasons for his adopting them in the first instance. Such modes may relate to the individual (he uses double-entry book-keeping, he avoids alcohol at lunch-time) or to groups of people co-operating in an organization (they have a good committee system or good promotion procedures). Greater or less success in optimization may thus itself result from the adoption of the right or wrong choice among certain wide-ranging (pleiotropic) modes of behaviour. In so far as such modes exist, and firms differ in their use of them, the situation will conform to sub-case (2B), differentially defective knowledge, rather than to sub-case (2A), uniformly defective knowledge. One might even regard successful optimization as itself a mode of behaviour, but this is unlikely to be a helpful way of looking at things unless one can be more specific about what makes for the success.[5]

---

[5] Throughout this paper I disregard strictly genetic factors and assume that there are no changes that are economically significant in the genetic make-up of *homo sapiens* over the periods we are concerned with. This assumption is safe enough in relation to a period of, say, 250 years, though perhaps not quite so safe in relation to a period of, say, 2,500 years. In this connection, reference to the apparently contrary belief held by Marshall may be of interest, not least because Appendix A of the *Principles* ('The Growth of Free Trade and Enterprise') covers much the same theme as Hicks's *Theory of Economic History* to which I shall be referring below. Marshall's treatment has the same grand sweep as Hicks's and, like Hicks, he assigns large importance to changes in institutions and to liberation from the rule of custom. The peculiar feature is the stress that Marshall puts on national character, using frequently such words as race and natural selection. In some passages the meaning is clearly not intended to be genetic and refers rather to the set of modes of behaviour that have been fostered by a nation's historical circumstances (including particularly its geography and climate, rather than in the manner of Braudel's *La Méditerranée*). But he also makes such remarks as a 'process of natural selection brought to [England's] shores those members of each successive migration

98   DARWINISM AND ECONOMIC CHANGE

1.4. *Competitive selection and the evolutionary view of economic change*

We are interested in economic change rather than stationary equilibrium. Competitive selection is only one phase of the process of change. Three phases may be distinguished: the origin of a new mode of behaviour; its persistence beyond the moment of origin; and competitive selection between it and other modes. The following table shows how each of these phases is treated in an optimization model and in the kind of evolutionary model of which competitive selection forms a natural part, with the biological equivalent shown for comparison.[6] Optimization and evolution in this sense are, of course, to be understood as extreme cases, with reality always likely to be a mixture.

Phases in the process of change

| | Economic change | | |
Phase	Optimization	Evolution	Biological change
1. Origin		Chance	Chance (mutation, combination, random genetic drift)
2. Persistence	Ratiocination (including optimizing imitation)	Inertia + non-optimizing imitation	Intergenerational reproduction
3. Spread		Competitive selection	Darwinian selection (relative fecundity and mortality)

It should be noted at this point that economic change, in the present sense, is not the same thing as economic growth. Economic change means change in modes of behaviour, comparable to changes in the traits of a species brought about by evolution. Economic growth means increase in real national income (the conceptual ambiguities created by index-number problems, income distribution, income per head versus total income, and so on,

---

wave who were most daring and self-reliant' (p. 740). This can be interpreted as the perfectly tenable hypothesis that the individuals concerned made especially valuable contributions to shaping modes of behaviour, either themselves or through the education of their children, a hypothesis that could also be put forward for the United States (though Marshall does not choose to say so, rather surprisingly). But it is difficult in reading Appendix A to resist the conclusion that Marshall also had in mind that these people's superior qualities were transmitted to their descendants genetically. That hypothesis would be regarded as unsound by most present-day biologists, on the grounds that the relevant attributes are polygenic and would rapidly regress to the mean, in the absence of selective breeding in *each successive generation* of the kind practised by stockbreeders. It has to be remembered that, although Marshall was so much influenced by Darwin, his thought was formed at a time when genetics was in its infancy. There is a further ambivalent and visibly uneasy discussion in *Industry and Trade*, p. 163 n.

   [6] This table may be compared, both for similarities and difference, with the more comprehensive table in Hirshleifer (1977), p. 50.

need not concern us in the present context). Its analogy is with an increase in the population of a species—enlargement of its niche—whether or not this is accompanied by changes in its traits. In principle, growth can occur without change and change can occur without growth. Growth can occur without change because of capital accumulation or simply because it takes time to reach the equilibrium level of income associated with any set of modes; also, of course, it can occur through changes in sub-modes if the modes are defined broadly. It is a little more paradoxical that change can occur without growth, since change in modes will on the face of it occur only if the change is in the interest of their practitioners, though interest is, of course, ambiguous (utility, survival, income). The reasons why it may do so, even disregarding that ambiguity, are off-setting adverse changes in the environment and externalities. Externalities and their significance are a major topic that will be considered at length presently; for the time being I shall disregard them.

My main consideration in this paper is with Phase 3, but, as will be seen presently, considerations relating to the three phases cannot be entirely separated from one another. The relative importance of optimization and evolution need not be the same at each of the three phases. But circumstances making for a predominance of the evolutionary process at one phase are likely also to do so at the others. Thus competitive selection will be important relatively to ratiocination at Phase 3 in circumstances where it is difficult to make *ex ante* judgements on the relative merits of alternative modes of behaviour. Such circumstances will also make difficult the application of ratiocination at Phase 1—they will make it more likely that chance should play an important part in that phase. Similar considerations apply in Phase 2.

It does not follow, however, that in an economy with a high degree of substantive and procedural rationality there is bound to be little scope left for competitive selection. Indeed, the opposite may hold. In such an economy the rate of innovation (Phase 1) is likely to be rapid. But since the future is unknowable, a lot of economic agents will make the wrong moves, or no moves, at Phase 1. The fast rate of innovation makes for a fast rate of change in everybody's environment. A high degree of rationality means that a high proportion of the adaptation process at Phase 3 will be achieved by optimization (imitation) rather than by competitive selection; but it also means there will be a large amount of adaptation to be done. Hence the prevalence of a high degree of rationality throughout the economy may serve to increase, rather than decrease, the absolute amount of competitive selection going on at any time.

I have focused attention on competitive selection, going on to consider what are its natural concomitants at the other phases of the process of economic change. It would be possible to approach matters from a different angle. For some purposes, the distinctive feature of an evolutionary view of economic change might be better thought of as the hypothesis of inertia, whether accompanied by competitive selection or not. Inertia means that the *status quo* has a unique importance as the starting point for further developments. This is to be contrasted with the consequences of out-and-out optimization, where economic agents are conceived of as surveying all the alternatives open to them, without treating the initial position as of any special significance. As far as change is concerned, the distinction is then equivalent to that between a technical progress function and a production function. The consequence of inertia is that each step starts where the last one stopped: *natura non facit saltum*. Each step is likely to affect subsequent changes, both their rate and their direction.[7] This approach would give a different emphasis from that of the present paper but would involve many of the same issues. Towards the end of the paper I shall refer to some aspects of the process of change that are certainly evolutionary yet can hardly be regarded as subject to competitive selection.

2. The selection process and its preconditions and speed

2.1. *Selective contraction and expansion*

How does the process of competitive selection actually work as applied to economic behaviour? It is not good enough to take it for granted, nor will it do to rely on vague Darwinian analogies, since the processes are quite different. Darwinian natural selection works through the relative ability of organisms with given characteristics to survive and reproduce themselves, as a result of differential mortality and fertility. It is true that much the same might perhaps be said of economic behaviour during much of the history of *homo sapiens*. But competitive selection between modes of behaviour, in even moderately advanced economies, is not literally a matter of life and death in the physiological sense. When we consider how the process may actually work, the main conclusion that emerges is that its speed and even its occurrence depend very much on circumstances.[8]

Consider first the negative side (equivalent to mortality). In the course of time competition will bring about a fall in the relative weight of users of an inefficient mode. The quantitative importance of the inefficient mode in the economy will thereby be reduced. The speed and extent of this decline will depend on a variety of circumstances. Some are obvious, such as the severity of competition (the amount of slack provided by rents) and the nature of bankruptcy law. Two, more basic, circumstances require comment.

The first is the division of labour. Many modes of behaviour are specific to particular activities, that is to say the production of particular goods or services. Thus handloom weaving is a mode of behaviour specific to the

---

[7] As is well known, this can result also from models that are not explicitly evolutionary at all but are based on learning processes (Atkinson and Stiglitz (1969)).

[8] How complex it may be to model the process exactly is shown by the treatment in Farrell (1970) of one of the examples cited by Friedman, the alleged tendency for competitive selection to ensure that speculation in net stabilizes prices.

textile industries. If competition forces an economic agent to give up an activity and take up another one instead, he loses the opportunity to practise the modes of behaviour specific to his old activity; as far as he is concerned, those modes disappear altogether instead of merely becoming less important quantitatively. The extent to which this happens will depend on the extent and nature of the division of labour. If everybody practises all activities, as under a regime without any exchange, there will be little scope for movement. Of course even if the scope does exist, an economic agent may choose instead to accept less pay or work harder, as the handloom weavers in the cotton industry actually did in nineteenth-century Britain, and in that case competitive selection will be correspondingly slow.

The second is the extent to which production is organized into firms, that is to say undertakings with hired factors and an internal command system. Internal command introduces an element of gearing into decision-making. Certain individuals—entrepreneurs or managers—control modes of behaviour relating to the use not only of their personal labour and capital but also of resources bought or hired from other people. The effects of their decisions are thus magnified. At the same time the employment of factors remunerated at a fixed rate increases the sensitivity of survival to the modes chosen. The firm needs to break even; if it ceases to do so, it will in due course cease to exist and so will the modes of behaviour embodied in it. In addition, scope exists for competitive selection of individuals within firms, by promotion, takeovers, and amalgamations. Space prevents this important aspect from receiving more than a mention here—the processes involved are not identical to those in competition in product markets.

All these circumstances may vary. They will affect not only the speed of selection but also the form that it takes—for example, whether the elimination of the less fit is confined to the very unfit or else applies according to some proportional rule to all economic agents of below-average fitness. There are some circumstances in which it will not operate at all. One important example is that the process will not have any tendency to eliminate inefficient modes of behaviour within a *country*, if those modes are general there and apply with equal effect in all activities (though it will diminish the weight of the country's distinctive modes in the world economy). Another is that it will not have any tendency to eliminate inefficient modes of behaviour relating to consumption, unless inefficiency as consumer is such that it leads also to inefficiency as producer or in the reproduction of surviving offspring. This is because inefficiency in consumption reduces utility rather than economic survival.

Now consider the other side of the coin, the position of the practitioners of the more efficient mode. How does their above-average prosperity cause them, and hence the mode they practise, to become more important? This side is not symmetrical with the previous one, because there is no equivalent to bankruptcy or to giving up an activity. One possibility is that their greater efficiency simply enables them to increase their market share, especially

102   DARWINISM AND ECONOMIC CHANGE

since the less efficient firms are withdrawing from the scene. Alternatively, or in addition, ploughing back of profits may be important. This indeed is the mechanism of competitive selection that is closest to Darwinism, with saving—reproduction of capital—taking the place of reproduction of off-spring and operating symmetrically on gainers and losers. It presupposes that growth is capital-constrained.

The relatively unfit must be replaced by the more fit. The negative side and the positive side are both necessary in order for competitive selection to work, though their relative importance will depend on the rate of growth of the economy. The two sides are not fully symmetrical and the process will not work properly unless there is sufficient urge to expand. This condition may not be met to the same extent in all periods and places. Edith Penrose (1952) argued that although losses do indeed impose stringent imperatives, the urge to expand is less reliable; if successful firms are content to sit on their laurels, the space that might be created by the elimination of the unfit will not necessarily be filled.[9]

A strict Darwinist might reply that a propensity to sit on one's laurels, even if quite deliberately adopted, is itself a relatively unfit mode of behaviour that will be selected against. It is quite true that it *will* be selected against (a further consequence of the non-identity of utility and survival, and one which is in principle independent of defective knowledge). But what if firms that have an urge to expand are inefficient in other respects? This is a particular instance of an important general problem, to which we shall turn in a moment (Section 2.2).

How might one seek to measure empirically the relative contributions made by optimization and competitive selection to the diffusion of a given mode of behaviour, say a new technique of production? A first approxima-tion might be sought in the relative magnitudes of intra-firm change and of changes in the relative weights of firms. Writing Q and q respectively for the proportion of output produced by the new technique in the industry and in the firm respectively, and w for proportion of industry's output produced by a firm, the sources of diffusion over a period are given by summing across firms:

$$\Delta Q = \sum w \, \Delta q + \sum \Delta w (q - Q) + \sum \Delta w \, \Delta q$$

The first term on the right hand side could be taken as the result of optimization and the second and third terms as the result of competitive selection (reflecting the gain in weight of firms that respectively employ the new technique to an above-average extent initially and shift towards the new technique in the course of the period).

Such measures can in principle be calculated quite readily from data of the Census of Production kind, at least in respect of unambigously identifi-

---

[9] The corresponding problem in biology is dealt with by the assumption that all species tend to multiply unless in some way constrained.

able techniques. But they are not necessarily an accurate measure, even apart from stochastic elements. On the one hand, the contribution of optimization will be underestimated in so far as Δw is itself the result of optimization rather than of past success—as most obviously if new entrants systematically choose to put resources into production by the new mode. On the other hand, the contribution of competitive selection will be underestimated in so far as (a) intra-firm changes reflect the outcome of competitive selection between individuals or sections within firms, or (b) some new entrants die as the result of competitive selection and so do not appear in the figures for either the opening or the closing year. For these and similar reasons a serious empirical study would be unlikely to get far without detailed industrial history.

2.2. *Multiple loci and Haldane's dilemma*

The overall behaviour of an economic agent is composed of a large number of different modes of behaviour; it is determined by the choices made in respect of a large number of different aspects of behaviour, just as the genetic composition of an organism depends on the 'choice' between alleles at a large number of loci. There is no necessary presumption that an economic agent who practises one efficient mode of behaviour also practises others: a firm that had good engineering practices may be bad at industrial relations, or a firm that is well located weak in design or marketing. The elimination of each of a number of inefficient modes separately is a much larger task for competitive selection to perform than the elimination of a single inefficient mode would be in a situation where fitness depended only on that one aspect of behaviour. If there is little or no correlation in efficiency between the different modes of behaviour adopted by a single firm, it is likely that competitive selection will not be able to work fast enough, relatively to the rate of change in the environment, to eliminate all the relatively unfit modes that exist at any particular time. The most that can then be reasonably expected is that it should eliminate those modes of behaviour that either are gravely unfit in a particular environment or else are to some degree unfit in all environments.

This problem and its biological counterpart can be considered further in relation to the social costs of the selection process.

Some of these costs are of an obvious kind. In so far as selection takes time, there will be a loss of potential output during the period while the unfit modes are being eliminated. Calling this a cost does not mean that it is necessarily avoidable: optimization may be an unattainable ideal. These are costs comparable to the costs of R & D. More relevant in the present context are the costs involved by the fact that economic agents are eliminated in the process of selection. In part those costs are a matter of the distribution of income between the economic agents who are in the course of being elimated and the rest. But account must also be taken of capital costs. Production uses physical capital, human capital, and also organizational capital in the form of the experience, information, contacts, and so on that enable people to co-operate effectively as a group. Competitive selection will cause some of this capital to be scrapped. In so far as the capital is inherently specific to unfit modes of behaviour, capital depreciation is admittedly not necessarily any greater under selection than under optimization. But competitive selection implies more *ex post* non-malleability of capital than does optimization, particularly in respect of organizational capital. It therefore requires more gross investment in order for any innovation to be diffused throughout the economy.

There is a corresponding problem in biology, and a serious one. J. B. S. Haldane (1957) defined the cost of a genetic change as the ratio of the sum of 'selective deaths', over all generations, to survivors. On reasonable assumptions this ratio turns out to be high, even in the case of a single genetic change (change at a single locus). If changes are required at many loci—the realistic case—the ratio becomes astronomical. The population will become extinct if there are more than a limited number of selective deaths in each generation. Hence the rate of genetic change seems to have to be exceedingly slow (even apart from continuing changes in the environment). This is known as Haldane's dilemma. It does not seem to have been entirely resolved by biologists, though various resolutions have been offered (Maynard Smith (1968); Hartl (1980), pp. 377–8, and references there).

The economic parallel may be illustrated by an extreme example. Productivity growth is commonly believed to come about more from a combination of small advances than for a few spectacular breakthroughs, and likewise, in econometric cross-section studies, differences in performance almost always have to be traced by a considerable number of variables (see, for example, Caves (1980)). So suppose that productivity improvement in a particular industry at a given time is available from improvements in ten modes of behaviour, that the choice at each of the ten loci is bipolar (right or wrong), and that there is no correlation between the choices that have initially been made at each locus. If the number of firms is small, it is unlikely that any one firm ever has the right mode at every locus. In that case, competitive selection can never get rid of all the inefficient modes. If there are many firms, a few of them may by chance have all the right answers. In order for the normal distribution to yield one such firm, the number of firms must be 2^{10}, i.e. 1024. The capital stock in this one firm will comprise only a tiny proportion of the capital stock in the industry. If all capital is specific to particular modes, almost the whole of the industry's capital will then have to be eliminated in order for competitive selection to do its job completely, even on the supposition that all the replacement investment takes place in the one best firm. If we suppose a capital-output ratio of 4, and a gross-investment ratio of $\frac{1}{4}$, the process will take 16 years. Not too bad, perhaps. But this greatly understates the problem. On natural assumptions, the replacement investment will be spread over all the firms of above-average fitness, and a large part of it will therefore be in firms that will themselves fail to be eliminated. The industry's capital stock will therefore have to be replaced several times over, probably taking many decades, far longer than the period for which the environment can be expected to remain unchanged.[10] Faster elimination of the unfit firms would lead to a decline in the size of the industry—equivalent to the second horn of Haldene's dilemma—on account of the constraint on gross investment.[11]

Haldane's dilemma will, of course, not exist in circumstances where the choice of mode of behaviour at a single locus is of overwhelming importance, as may sometimes happen, for example, in an industry at an early stage of its development where technology is still very unsettled and there are many one-product firms each trying to find a decisive breakthrough. In the more normal case, where more than one locus is important, the dilemma will be made less acute in so far as the modes of behaviour that matter are few in number, or there is correlation between choices at different loci, or the efficiency of a mode survives changes in the environment. All these are characteristic of sub-case (2B), where there is differentially defective knowledge and economic agents differ from one another in modes of behaviour that are pleiotropic. It will also help if capital is not too specific to particular modes of behaviour; the elimination of inefficient modes of behaviour can then be achieved by takeover, with the entrepreneurs being eliminated without the need to scrap their physical assets.[12] Notwithstanding these qualifications and the other unrealistic features of the arithmetic example, Haldane's dilemma does constitute an important reason why competitive selection is unlikely to produce the same results as optimization. The two processes cannot be regarded as equivalent.

2.3. *Growth models*

The foregoing relates to once-for-all adaptation towards a certain set of models of behaviour. Why does it come out so differently from the ordinary 'vintage' model of economic growth, in which, likewise, capital equipment is assumed to be wholly specific to particular techniques yet growth is not thereby constrained to a snail's pace? The underlying difference (details apart) is that the vintage model assumes that there is *a continuous change for the better* at an independently given rate in the techniques available for

[10] This may be compared with the very long periods found in growth theory to be needed to execute the 'traverse' called for by a once-for-all change such as the rise in the saving ratio (Sato (1963); Hicks (1965), ch. 16).

[11] There is evidence of something like this happening on the 1970s. Despite a much lower rate of investment than previously, the rate of increase in the proportion of output produced by means of certain new technologies turned out, surprisingly, to be no slower than before. This was achieved by a combination of more rapid than previous scrapping of old-technology plants and a decline (or slow-down in the rate of increase) of total capacity (Ray (1984), pp. 77–9).

[12] Agriculture is a prominent example. Not much scrapping of capital was involved in the takeover of neighbours' farms by kulaks in the USSR in the 1920s or in the takeover of East Anglian farms by Scottish farmers in the 1880s.

embodiment in new equipment. As a result, the rate of replacement does not affect the steady state growth rate, since if replacement occurs only after a long interval there is a correspondingly large improvement in productivity when it does finally occur. The continuous technical advance is a source of growth separate from competitive selection. To postulate that it occurs is an assumption about Phase 1 of the process of change, the phase relating to the origin of changes in modes of behaviour. Thus the working of competitive selection (Phase 3) is not independent of what is going on at Phase 1.

The hypothesis that chance-based competitive selection predominates at Phase 3 does not sit easily with the hypothesis that there is continuous exogenous improvement in the modes of behaviour available. The latter hypothesis would be analogous to continuous mutations all for the better (orthogenesis), an unlikely case. It is perfectly possible, however, to devise models in which a more congenial combination of assumptions—competitive selection plus random changes in the range of available modes of behaviour—does lead to continuous growth in productivity (whether such a model is realistic is a separate matter). The following is an example. Suppose that initially there exists a dispersion in the efficiency of firms and that proportional changes from one period to the next in each firm's efficiency are randomly distributed about a mean of zero (that is to say, some of the changes are positive, some are negative).[13] Because of these random changes, dispersion in efficiency has a tendency to become greater in period 2 than in period 1. Suppose, however, that competition imposes a limit on dispersion. The tendency to increasing dispersion will be checked by contraction or elimination of the firms nearer the bottom of the distribution in period 2 and relative expansion of those nearer the top. The average efficiency will thus come to be higher than in period 1. Random changes in the next round start from a higher base. So there is continuous growth, at a rate dependent on the severity of competition at the bottom and on the limits to gross investment at the top. In one limiting case, where competition is so weak that there is no selection at all, the tendency to increasing dispersion will remain unchecked and there will be no advance in the average. At another extreme, where, say because of low average profitability, there is severe selection at the bottom but a limited rate of expansion at the top, the average efficiency of the industry will rise but total capacity will diminish, with danger of extinction of the industry. Further complications may arise if the relative fitness of modes of behaviour is itself a function of the severity of competition (thus the mode of having industry run by accountants may conduce to fitness in a context of severe selection but to inefficiency in other contexts). Continuous growth is, however, at least a possibility.

Yet if the changes in modes of behaviour were entirely random, the scope

---

[13] Growth will be slowed but not prevented if, as supposed by Leibenstein (1976), changes in the negative direction tend to preponderate, on account of lethargy, in the absence of some specfic stimulus.

for further improvements might surely become exhausted after a while. Modes of behaviour would then settle into equilibrium, just as biological phenotypes settle into equilibrium in the absence of changes in the environment. Continuous economic change at a non-negligible pace appears unlikely without the interposition of some success in optimization [14] or else of some entirely separate process making for improvement in the range of modes available. Such a source of improvement might be the growth of scientific knowledge, subject to its own independent evolutionary process.

Over much the greater part of human history, of course, the average rate of increase of income per head—or of population, for that matter—*was* very slow; and it was punctuated by long periods of stagnation or retrogression. To explain that sort of growth largely in terms of competitive selection is not necessarily so absurd.

3. Externalities, institutions, and governments

3.1. *Non-invadability and optimality*

A mode of behaviour is evolutionarily stable if, in the language of biologists, it is uninvadable, that is to say if no alternative would have any tendency to displace it via competitive selection. Evolutionary stability thus corresponds to Nash-equilibrium in game theory. It is not necessarily an optimum, in any sense, for the population (species) as a whole. It may fail to be an optimum for either of two reasons: because it is only a local optimum, a concept familiar to biologists; or else because there are externalities, a concept not explicitly used by biologists, doubtless because they regard them as the rule rather than the exception. In this section I shall consider some aspects of externalities and how they affect economic change under a system of competitive selection.

Necessary conditions for externalities to be precluded in a competitive system are that there are complete markets and that all the effects of the actions of one agent on another are internalized by a complete system of property rights. The existence of property rights enforced by law (external compulsion) is unique to *homo sapiens*. It would appear to follow that nature must be full of non-optimalities, even if attention is confined to a single species and we disregard the raw externality that exists between predator and prey.[15] Admittedly evolution has produced some modes of behaviour that have the effect of internalizing externalities, most obviously in the relation between parents and their offspring; and property rights are also to some extent simulated e.g. by the propensity to fight more vigorously in defence of one's own territory than in attack on another's. But there are

---

[14] Corresponding to what Winter (1971) calls 'the innovating remnant'.

[15] 'A race of wolves that has well organized plans for hunting in packs is likely to survive and spread; because those plans enable it to catch its prey, not because they confer a benefit on the world' (Marshall (1923), p. 175). For treatment of non-optimalities in nature from an economic standpoint, see Hirshleifer (1978).

very large areas of behaviour in which the externalities remain. The result is that there are indeed very large non-optimalities, contrary to what was supposed by naive early Darwinists. The quasi-optimizing unit is the gene, or possibly groupings of genes, not the species. For example, traits may develop that are uninvadable because they are useful in competition for mates (and therefore confer negative externalities on other members of the same sex) but at the same time hamper foraging or escape from predators; stock examples are the peacock, with its inconvenient tail, and the so-called Irish elk, which apparently had antlers seventeen times the weight of its skull (Dobzhansky *et al.* (1977), p. 244). Likewise, the interests of the species may be prejudiced by fighting among its members; there is some reason to believe that evolution has been less effective in mitigating this than was once supposed.[16]

The consequences of such non-optimalities may be merely that the niche of the species is smaller, or less rapidly expanding, than it would otherwise have been. However, if the disadvantages are sufficiently great, the species may become extinct. Whether or not this happens depends on the severity of the environment. If it does, the traits are invadable in the large though not in the small. It is believed that some 90 per cent of all species that have ever existed are extinct, some of them, doubtless, for that kind of reason.

The human economic analogies are obvious. Groups of economic agents may get trapped in modes of behaviour which are collectively harmful, as in the Prisoner's Dilemma type of situation. The result may merely be that their income is lower or less rapidly growing than it would otherwise have been. In more extreme cases it may lead to absolute decline, say of a region or an industry, or even its extinction, notwithstanding that it is not in the interests of any individual economic agent to alter his mode of behaviour. Likewise, on the borderline of economics and politics: for example, corruption may merely make the organs of the state work inefficiently, or it may ultimately lead to the collapse of the state itself.

3.2. *The role of institutions*

The extent and nature of externalities in economic behaviour depend on a particular class of modes of behaviour that I shall call *institutions*. Institutions are defined as those modes of behaviour that (a) are concerned with inter-personal relationships and (b) are, and are understood and expected to be, generally adopted in certain types of situation. Property rights are a prime example. They may be enforced by law but they do not necessarily have to be: their sanction may instead lie in religion or morality, in custom, or simply in self-interest (long-term or short-term). In this sense even endemic Hobbesian war can be regarded as one kind of institution.

In the normal way, however, institutions regulate the grossest forms of

---

[16] It has been estimated that a quarter of all gorillas meet their death from other gorillas (Hrdy (1981), p. 91).

externality, such as arise from the use of force or threats (in the sense of Boulding).[17] At a more sophisticated level, they may, for example, permit the use of money, or insurance, enforce or prohibit slavery, provide for the operation of monasteries, or limit the liabilities of share-holders in joint-stock companies. They may regulate the mutual relations between people who have formed an alliance or organization for particular purposes (monks or shareholders); or they may regulate the relations between those groups and third parties. Institutions have varied over time and place both in the modes of behaviour they have prescribed and in the categories of people to whom those modes have been made applicable. The need for an adequate theory of institutions has been an increasingly common theme in economic literature in recent years.

It is at this point, rather belatedly, that there emerges the connection between the present paper and Hicks's *Theory of Economic History*. The contention advanced by Hicks there may be summarized, in vastly oversimplified outline, as consisting of two propositions. First, a major part in economic history was played by institutional changes, especially changes that facilitated or inhibited market exchange. Secondly, the institutional changes were themselves largely the product of the incentives offered by changing economic circumstances to certain classes of economic agents, including governments (rulers), though this process was not inevitable. Mutual feedback occurred between the two causal relationships.

There are two separate ways in which institutions involve externalities. The first relates to the effects of given institutions, corresponding to the first of Hicks's propositions. The second relates to the evolution of the institutions themselves, relevant to Hicks's second proposition. Let us now consider the two sides, from the evolutionary standpoint adopted in the present paper.

3.3. *The effects of alternative institutions*

Institutions differ in the extent to which they internalize or otherwise regulate externalities in economic behaviour. As far as the institutions themselves are concerned, this is a matter of comparative statics. But alternative institutions will affect the way in which the economy grows under its own momentum and responds to other forces making for change.

Not all institutions, of course, are primarily concerned with the correction of potential externalities and the establishment of property rights. In many cases their chief function is informational, to reduce transaction costs by establishing standard terms of dealing between economic agents and so avoid the need to spend time and effort on working out everything from first

---

[17] A threat is a proposition of the form: if you do something nice to me, I shall refrain from doing something nasty to you. It is contrasted with the offer of exchange, which has the form: if you do something nice to me, I shall do something nice to you (Boulding (1962), pp. 223–8).

principles on each occasion.[18] Moreover, although a complete system of property rights would in theory eliminate externalities, it is impossible to conceive of a truly complete system, such as would govern literally every form of interaction between economic agents (Schelling, 1978, ch. 1). Hence a complete system of property rights may not be the most helpful yardstick by which to judge institutions. Indeed, for second-best reasons, it cannot be taken for granted that every (partial) expansion of the realm of property rights conduces to Pareto-efficiency. Alternative incomplete systems of property rights have each to be considered in detail before drawing any conclusions; and importance may attach to institutions that deal with the underlying problems otherwise than by property rights.

The comparative statics of institutions will affect the path of economic change whether the forces for change operate mainly through optimization or through competitive selection. But the effects will not necessarily be the same in the two cases. Change by means of competitive selection, as noted above, is achieved most readily if expansion and contraction in the activities of economic agents are closely tied to their success or failure. The following are some examples of the implications (intended to be suggestive rather than rigorously worked out). Under optimization, capital market imperfections that force firms to rely exclusively on internal finance hamper the process of change; but those imperfections might actually facilitate competitive selection, by trying future expansion or contraction tightly to past success or failure. By contrast, a land tenure system that makes it difcult for individual cultivators to expand their holdings is a more serious obstacle to the diffusion of technical change under competitive selection than under optimization. Stringent bankruptcy laws facilitate competitive selection but may hamper change through optimization by inducing excessive caution. Institutionalized monopoly is a serious obtacle to competitive selection but does not as such prevent *technical* efficiency under optimization. And so on.

3.4. *Sources of changes in institutions.*

Externalities attend activities which, by compulsion, precept, or example contribute to bringing about changes in institutions (indeed the mere act of behaving in compliance with an existing institution may have externalities, by strengthening the hold of that institution). This is comparable to the externalities that attend technological innovation.

The evolution of institutions over time is part of cultural history and also, in so far as government is involved, part of political history. The externalities are so blatant that it scarcely seems plausible to postulate that institutions tend to an optimum, certainly not to a global optimum as opposed to a local one. The contrary belief has, however, been influential, as

---

[18] The two aspects are combined together by North (1981), whose interpretation of historical change is based on the postulate that zero transaction costs are a prerequisite of a complete system of property rights.

exemplified alike by the Whig theory of history and by the Marxist doctrine of the ultimate inevitability of communism.

At the same time it would obviously be wrong to overplay the externalities and to deny that institutions will evolve that do serve essential purposes, even in the absence of government. This is clearest in cases where the scope for co-operation in interpersonal interaction is large relatively to the scope for conflict—such cases as driving on a specified side of the road. It is to be noted that a limited amount of free-riding by some people does not make the rule cease to be worth following by others, i.e. the institution is not invadable in the small; at the same time the danger is apparent that such cooperative institutions will get stuck at local optima because it is in no one's interest to take the initiative in altering them. More interestingly, it has been shown theoretically that there is room for at least a limited degree of optimism about the probable outcome even of situations like the Prisoner's Dilemma, where the scope for conflict is large. Hobbesian war is not necessarily the outcome that will emerge from unrestrained self-interest. In the so-called Hawk-Dove problem in game theory, it is not the best strategy always to behave like a Hawk if the cost is large relative to the gain from winning a fight (Maynard Smith (1982), ch. 2). Closer to economics, perhaps, is the time-hallowed second-best institution that Hirshleifer (1978) calls the Silver Rule—return good-for-good and evil-for-evil. It was found in a laboratory experiment that the Silver Rule was the most successsessful strategy in long series of Prisoner's Dilemma games played between the same pair of opponents, the Silver Rule being defined as above but with the good-neighbourly supplement that the opening move in a game should be 'good' (Axerod and Hamilton (1981)).[19]

What role can competitive selection play in the evolution of institutions? Much of what was said in Section 2 about modes of behaviour generally continues to apply. If the gains from acting in accordance with one mode of behaviour are sufficiently great, those who adopt other modes will be tend to find their position eroded. The gains in question are those of the people whose actions shape the institutions, and if there are externalities these are not necessarily gains for the economy as a whole, or indeed even of those people themselves collectively. A mode of behaviour that is contrary to Nash-equilibrium will not have a chance to establish itself as an institution; in that sense competitive selection is largely the history of what did not happen. Once the mode of behaviour is established as an institution, however, it will be correspondingly difficult to alter; in order to act against it, an economic agent will not only have to overcome his own inertia but also will find himself swimming against the stream and upsetting other people's expectations. The auto-regressive properties of the system are thus

---

[19] Important contributions to the general theory of the internal evolution of institutions have been made by Schotter (1981) and, from the standpoint of moral philosophy, by Ullman-Margalit (1978).

especially pronounced where institutions are concerned. Special considerations are involved in relation to the kind of institution that takes the form of an alliance to overcome a potential conflict of interest. Alliances are vulnerable to free-riders, but if they become established and suitably reinforced by sanctions, they may be difficult to depart from (Olson 1965), (1982)). There are many possible groupings of economic agents between whom alliances may be formed and the particular alliance pattern evolving may therefore owe a good deal to chance.[20]

No consideration of the forces governing the evolution of institutions is likely to get very far unless it takes account of differences between the circumstances of different groups of economic agents, broadly equivalent to polymorphism in the biological context. Rather than attempt to pursue all the implications of economic polymorphism, I shall concentrate on the most extreme case, that involving governments—the difference between rulers and ruled that plays such a large part in Hicks's book. The compulsory powers of government remove it from the realm of voluntary exchange and make the presence of externalities almost inevitable. The externalities may be negative in so far as rulers use their powers to advance their personal interests; they may be positive in so far as rulers' laborious (and well-advised) efforts advance the public good. Governments play a major part in shaping economic institutions: by using their powers to reinforce institutions originating in the private sector, to prohibit or amend them, and to maintain institutions of their own, such as taxation.

There is no historical reason to suppose that governmental economic institutions tend to any equilibrium that is stable in the long run. Their evolutionary changes, moreover, are an aspect of economic life where competitive selection applies rather little. This conclusion is perhaps scarcely controversial. But it is worth indicating the reasons.

The distinctive feature of competitive selection is that competition between traits occurs indirectly through the fortunes of their carriers. In the present context this would mean that the choice between alternative governmental policies regarding economic institutions is shaped by their effects on the relative success of the governments that espouse them. This is an unpromising hypothesis, if only because so many of the main developments in governments' policies have historically continued irrespective of who happened to be in power (Hicks (1969), pp. 99–100). More specifically, there are two obstacles to the hypothetical process happening.

In the first place, competitive selection depends on there being a range of alternative modes of behaviour, embodied in different agents.[21] But there is

---

[20] An interesting example is given by Kocka (1981), who contrasts the historical solidarity of low-level white-collar workers in Germany with that of skilled manual workers in Britain. Neither phenomenon had much counterpart in the other country and both were directed to underlining the distinction between the group concerned and the generality of workers. Similar purposes have been and are served by alliances based on race, religion, language, sex, and so on.

[21] Compare the so-called fundamental theorem of natural selection: the rate of evolution is proportional to the genetic variance of the population.

only one government—that is of its essence, since the basic characteristic of government is that it has a monopoly, viz. a monopoly of the use of legitimate force. Admittedly, there are alternative governments, possibly numerous ones, but as they are not in power there is no opportunity for their policies to prove their fitness or otherwise. Alternative policies can be adopted only in sequence, as governments alter. Competitive selection could therefore work only if the environment remained unchanged for a sufficiently long period for the effects of alternative policies on the fortunes of successive governments to work themselves out.

In the second place, policies in the sphere of economic institutions are, at most, only one of the causes of the rise and fall of governments. Many other forces are involved, alike in palace revolutions and in electoral defeats, these being the main sources of fall of governments in non-democratic and democratic regimes respectively. Selection between economic institutions is thus gravely subject to Haldane's dilemma. This is well-known as an objection to the optimistic interpretation sometimes placed on 'social choice' theories of democracy, according to which vote-maximization will cause governments' policies to correspond exactly with the interests of the electorate (Downs (1957); Atkinson and Stiglitz (1980), pp. 307–10).

Of course, one should not exaggerate. The foregoing applies rather less strongly, for example, in forms of governments in which individual ministers or advisers have responsibilities for formulating specified parts of policy and are liable to dismissal if their policies turn out badly (this is an aspect of the question of competitive selection within bureaucracies, which I am not attempting to treat in this paper). Moreover, some governments and systems of government *have* fallen in consequence of their economic policies, either because they failed to attain their own objectives or else because the associated adverse externalities proved fatal. But, in general, policies relating to economic institutions have proved a poor discriminator between governments. And governments have proved unreliable vehicles of policies.

None of the above is intended to belittle the importance of the two-way connection between economic change and the institutions that are due to government. Nor do I mean to deny the evolutionary character of the connection, with each step in the process of change affecting all subsequent steps. The model remains that of a random walk. There is a difference, compared with the evolution of modes of behaviour that are not directly connected with government, that the direction of the walk is less likely to be guided by competitive selection. Sometimes the situation is sufficiently clear for optimization, including learning, by rulers to guide them in much the same direction in all countires that are similarly placed; some of the cases considered by Hicks are of that kind. In others, governments are free to diverge from one another and produce disparate national patterns. In all cases, the path is influenced by political dynamics, which, being expressed in the currency of power, do not necessarily resemble closely the dynamics of purely economic change.

The above relates to single countries taken in isolation. In a world of many countries, interactions between them introduce new considerations. The institutions created by the government of any one country may be invadable in the literal sense (war was recognized by Darwin himself as one possible instrument of natural selection). The institutions of the defeated country may then be displaced by those of its conqueror. There is no doubt that this constitutes competitive selection between alternative military arrangements; but whether it is competitive selection between economic institutions (governmental or non-governmental) depends on how far economic institutions are associated with military superiority. This has perhaps been most nearly true of colonial wars, where the antagonists have been at very different stages of economic development. However, military superiority has many sources other then economic institutions—not least the mere relative size of the antagonists—and history shows many examples of wars won by the economically less advanced contender. Military selection is therefore capable of being economically retrogressive.

At the same time, the rise and fall of dominant countries have obviously been among the most important sources of change in modes of economic behaviour in the woɪld as a whole. The sources have not been exclusively military. Sometimes the effects have been felt through increase in the weight of an economically advancing country in world production, as with Great Britain in the nineteenth century and the U.S. in the twentieth—a straight case of competitive selection. Sometimes the effects have been felt through induced changes in modes of behaviour in the rest of world. The induced changes have in turn been brought about in a variety of ways (in addition to imposition of institutions by military force): imitation of the advancing country's institutions or its other modes of economic behaviour; adaptation by means of optimization to changes in comparative advantage brought about by events in the advancing country; adaptation by means of competitive selection to those changes in comparative advantage; and competitive selection achieved by emigration of entrepreneurship and management from the advancing country (Venetians in the Levant, multi-national corporations). All these effects may be brought about by the advance of a single country; they may also be brought about by improvement of transport and communications. Such improvement enlarges the scope both for optimization by imitation and for competitive selection, by enlarging the size of the world over which competition occurs and thereby increasing the relevant variance of modes of behaviour.

4. Conclusions

In briefest outline, the conclusions suggested by this paper may be summarized as follows.

The prevalance of limited information and bounded rationality restricts the scope for optimization. In some spheres, therefore, competitive selection—the economic equivalent of Darwinism—may be the only systematic mechanism directing the course of economic change. More typically, optimization and competitive selection will coexist and interact.

Competitive selection is an entirely different kind of process from optimization. A variety of considerations prevent them from leading to the same outcome, so they should not be regarded as equivalent. Competitive selection by itself is unreliable and stochastic and the movement it leads to has the character of a random walk.

A major characteristic of competitive selection is its slowness—slowness, that is to say, compared with optimization, not necessarily compared with the actual pace of historical change before modern times. It has often been suggested that processes of change can be arrayed in a hierarchy according to their speed. Thus genetic selection is very much faster than random recombination of the molecules that existed when the earth began, and cultural selection, in which traits can be transmitted non-genetically, is much faster than genetic selection. Competitive selection of an economic kind may, in favourable circumstances, be more rapid than other forms of cultural selection. Optimization, in turn, is likely to be much faster than competitive selection. A further conclusion suggests itself, that an important long-run contribution of competitive selection may be the extent to which it selects in favour of modes of behaviour that facilitate optimization.

Competitive selection, like optimization, is subject to externalities, though the effects of externalities do not work out identically under the two processes. Competitive selection therefore does not necessarily lead to social Pareto-efficiency, any more than natural selection, as nowadays understood, necessarily leads to the best possible outcome for the species as a whole. The extent and nature of externalities are affected by institutions, which constitute one class of modes of behaviour; institutions therefore affect the path taken by an economy in which competitive selection plays a part. Moreover, institutions themselves are subject to evolution over time, and their evolution may be affected by competitive selection of one sort of another. It is doubtful whether competitive selection of an economic kind will be very effective in shaping that part of the evolution of institutions— likely to be a significant part—that is determined by governments.

A complete model of economic change would have to take account of the nature of the different kinds of process that determine economic and political evolution and how they interact. It would also have to incorporate the effects of their interaction with yet another element, itself subject to evolutionary principles of its own, the development of ideas (both in ideology and religion and in science). As it requires computer simulation to work out random walks along even a single dimension, there is no prospect of actually constructing such a model in a way that would be intuitively understandable and have any claim to validity. The most one can do is to extract snippets, for particular purposes, from one's own notion of what it might look like.

Clare College, Cambridge

116   DARWINISM AND ECONOMIC CHANGE

REFERENCES

ALCHIAN, A. A. (1950), 'Uncertainty, evolution, and economic theory', *Journal of Political Economy*, 211–22.

ATKINSON, A. B. and STIGLITZ, J. E. (1969), 'A new theory of technological change', *Economic Journal*, 573–8.

ATKINSON, A. B. and STIGLITZ, J. E. (1980), *Public Economics* (London).

AXELROD, R. and HAMILTON, W. D. (1981), 'The evolution of cooperation', *Science*, 1390–6.

BECKER, G. S. (1981), *A Treatise on the Family* (Harvard, Mass.).

BOULDING, K. E. (1962), *Conflict and Defense* (New York).

BOULDING, K. E. (1981), *Evolutionary Economics* (Beverly Hills, Calif.).

CAVES, R. E. (1980), 'Productivity differences among industries', in R. E. Caves and L. B. Krause (eds), *Britain's Economic Performance* (Washington, DC): 135–198.

DAWKINS, R. (1976), *The Selfish Gene* (Oxford).

DOBZHANSKY, T., AYALA, F. J., STEBBINGS, G. L. and VALENTINE, J. W. (1977), *Evolution* (San Francisco).

DOWNIE, J. (1958), *The Competitive Process* (London).

DOWNS, A. (1957), *An Economic Theory of Democracy* (New York).

FARRELL, M. J. (1970), 'Some elementary selection processes in economics', *Review of Economic Studies*, 305–19.

FLOUD, R. C. and McCLOSKEY, D. N. (eds.) (1981), *The Economic History of Britain since 1700* (Cambridge).

FRIEDMAN, M. (1953), 'The methodology of positive economics', in *Essays in Positive Economics* (Chicago).

HALDANE, J. B. S. (1957), 'The cost of natural selection', *Journal of Genetics*, 511–24.

HARTL, D. L. (1980), *Principles of Population Genetics* (Sundelland, Mass.).

HICKS, J. R. (1965), *Capital and Growth* (Oxford).

HICKS, J. R. (1969), *A Theory of Economic History* (Oxford).

HIRSHLEIFER, J. (1977), 'Economics from a biological viewpoint', *Journal of Law and Economics*, 1–52.

HIRSHLEIFER, J. (1978), 'Natural economy versus political economy', *Journal of Social Biological Structures*, 319–37.

HRDY, S. B. (1981), *The Woman that Never Evolved* (Harvard).

KIRZNER, I. M. (1973), *Competition and Entrepreneurship* (Chicago).

KNIGHT, F. H. (1942), 'Some notes on the economic interpretation of history' in *Studies in the History of Culture* (Menasha, Wisc.).

KOCKA, J. (1981), 'Competition and bureaucracy in German industrialisation before 1914', *Economic History Review*, 453–68.

LEACH, E. (1981), Review of Lumsden and Wilson (1981) in *Nature*, 267–8.

LEIBENSTEIN, H. (1976), *Beyond Economic Man* (Harvard).

LUMSDEN, C. J. and WILSON, E. O. (1981), *Genes, Mind, and Culture* (Harvard).

LUMSDEN, C. J. and WILSON, E. O. (1983), *Promethean Fire* (Harvard).

MARSHALL, A. (1920), *Principles of Economics*, 8th ed. (London).

MARSHALL, A. (1923), *Industry and Trade*, 4th ed. (London).

MAYNARD SMITH, J. (1968), 'Haldane's Dilemma and the rate of evolution', *Nature*, 1114–16.

MAYNARD SMITH, J. (1982), *Evolution and the Theory of Games* (Cambridge).

NELSON, R. R. and WINTER, S. G. (1982), *An Evolutionary Theory of Economic Change* (Harvard).

NORTH, D. C. (1981), *Structure and Change in Economic History* (New York).

OLSON, M. (1965), *The Logic and Collective Action* (Harvard).

OLSON, M. (1982), *The Rise and Decline of Nations* (New Haven).

PENROSE, E. T. (1952), 'Biological analogies in the theory of the firm', *American Economic Review*, 804–19.

RAY, G. F. (1984), *The Diffusion of Mature Technologies* (Cambridge).

R. C. O. MATTHEWS   117

REIJNDERS, L. (1978), 'On the applicability of game theory to evolution', *Journal of Theoretical Biology*, 245–47.

SATO, A. (1963), 'Fiscal policy in a neo-classical growth model: an analysis of time required for equilibrating adjustment', *Review of Economic Studies*, 16–23.

SCHELLING, T. C. (1978), *Micromotives and Macrobehaviour* (New York).

SCHOTTER, A. (1981), *The Economic Theory of Institutions* (Cambridge).

TVERSKY, A. and KAHNEMAN, D. (1974), 'Judgment under uncertainty: heuristics and biases', *Science*, 1124–31.

ULLMAN-MARGALIT, E. (1978), *The Emergence of Norms* (Oxford).

WINTER, S. G. (1971), 'Satisficing, selection and the innovating remnant', *Quarterly Journal of Economics*, 237–61.

[9]

EVOLUTIONARY THEORY AND ECONOMIC THEORY: SOME METHODOLOGICAL ISSUES*

By JOHN M. GOWDY**
Rensselaer Polytechnic Institute

Economic theory and evolutionary theory in biology have much in common both in terms of their origins and in terms of the nature and complexity of their subject matter. It is well-known that Charles Darwin refined his idea of natural selection after a reading of British political economists, particularly Thomas Malthus. [Schweber, pp. 229-316] One of the founders of modern economics, Alfred Marshall, contended that biology, not mechanics, is the true Mecca of economics. In a recent book, Ernst Mayr [Mayr, 1982] argues that physical scientists have difficulty understanding evolutionary biology because, among other things, they fail to appreciate that living systems possess the characteristics of (1) uniqueness and variability, (2) complexity and organization, (3) indeterminacy, and (4) irreversibility. These characteristics make the reductionism that has been the hallmark of the physical sciences inappropriate in the study of evolutionary biology. In the present paper, we show that Mayr's arguments have great relevance to economics, particularly regarding the role of assumption and prediction in economic theory.[1]

Mayr notes that many of the major thinkers in the philosophy of science have been trained in the physical sciences, a point widely discussed in the economic literature. [Georgescu-Roegen; Hirsh; Weisskopf; Hutchinson; and Caldwell] Their physical science, or mechanistic, viewpoint has led to a widely held definition of "true" science that does not necessarily apply to evolutionary systems. In economics the dominance of positivism is an example of this phenomenon. [Caldwell, pp. 53-76]

THE MECHANISTIC PROGRAM

Positivism's most forceful statement in terms of economic theory is Milton Friedman's "Methodology of Positive Economics." [Friedman,

*0034-6764/85/1001-316/$1.50/0.

[1]It should be pointed out that many of Mayr's arguments below were made earlier and, in many cases, more convincingly by Nicholas Georgescu-Roegen. [1966, 1971] The purpose of this essay is to show that the same controversies are also present in the field of biology.

pp. 3-43] Two critical issues raised by Friedman are (1) the role of prediction in economic theory, and (2) the falsifiability of economic postulates. In Friedman's view, the task of economics is "to provide a system of generalization that can be used to make correct predictions about the consequences of any change of circumstances." [Friedman, p. 4] The validity of the underlying assumptions is unimportant. According to Friedman, "the only test of the validity of a hypothesis is a comparison of its prediction with experience." [Friedman, p. 7] Following Popper, Friedman states that "factual evidence can never prove a hypothesis; it can only fail to disprove it." [See Blaug, pp. 104-111; and Webb, pp. 912-916]

The importance positivist economists place on prediction follows from the importance of laws in the physical sciences. In mechanics, an event is explained when it can be shown to be due to causal factors consistent with general laws. [Mayr, p. 37] By contrast, laws in the evolutionary sciences are explained in terms of past events but are not predictive except in a loosely probabilistic sense. In economics this indeterminacy has to do with history as well as uncertainty. [See Weisskopf; Rothbard, pp. 313-314] History is important because evolutionary phenomena are near-unique events. Alfred Marshall recognized this when he referred to the irreversibility of the long-run supply curve. J. R. Hicks [Hicks, 1979] argues in his later work that, in economics, history and casuality are related in ways not found in the physical sciences.

As regards falsifiability, it is impossible to provide absolute proof for many scientific conclusions. With this problem in mind, Popper proposed that the test of "scientific" be whether or not it can be falsified. Similarly, the more attempts to discredit a theory that are successfully paried, the more credible that theory becomes. Any theory that cannot in principle be falsified is considered to be outside the realm of science. As Mayr points out [Mayr, p. 27], this shifts the burden of proof to the opponents of a given scientific theory. Positivist economists make falsification nearly impossible by saying that prediction is the only test of a theory. If the predictions of a particular theory do not seem to be correct, one can always say that the *ceteris paribus* conditions were violated. Neoclassical economists place the burden of proof on their critics.

WHY EVOLUTIONARY SCIENCE IS DIFFERENT

The mechanistic model/pattern model debate in economics is

advanced by Mayr's discussion of the differences between evolutionary science and traditional science.

(1) Uniqueness and Variability — The uniqueness of evolutionary phenomena in biology and economics makes the study of these subjects particularly unsuitable for the application of the sort of reductionism that has been so successful in classical mechanics. There are no absolute phenomena in evolutionary processes. Economic systems are complex structures of hierarchical systems with a large number of possible options at each evolutionary step.

Variability and interdependence within evolutionary processes are other reasons why reductionism is inappropriate in explaining economic behavior. Once a particular step in evolution or in economic development takes place, the effect ripples to other entities (organisms or firms) in the system. The "Red Queen" principle operates in both biology and economics. [Van Valen] Firms in a market system and organisms in an ecosystem are under constant pressure from competitors. Like Alice's Red Queen they must run as fast as they can just to stay in the same place. Because of this interdependence and competitive pressure, a multitude of responses and solutions to the problem of economic or biological survival are possible. The resulting variability means that postulates about a "Robinson Crusoe" economy shed little light on the study of real economic systems.

Evolutionary systems show much greater variability in their rates of change than do physical phenomena. Rates in physical phenomena are fairly constant, at least on a time scale relevant to humans. On the other hand, biological or economic evolution is characterized by periods of relative stasis interrupted by bursts of rapid change.

One lesson here is that absolute models, such as those based on applications of the calculus, are inappropriate for describing evolutionary behavior. In particular, certain forms of mathematics are sterile in both evolutionary biology and economics. Many current applications of mathematics begin by assuming away the phenomena we really need to be looking at.

The following assessments of current uses of mathematics in biology by Mayr, and in economics by Leontief, are strikingly similar:

> Two years ago I saw a paper in the *Proceedings of the National Academy of Sciences*, and the author wrote, "Let's assume the gene has a constant selective value, let's assume there is no gene flow from any other population." He made about five such assumptions, each of which was equally unrealistic, and then

EVOLUTIONARY THEORY AND ECONOMIC THEORY   319

he went on to prove something very beautiful mathematically, but it was meaningless. [Mayr, quoted in Lewin, p. 718]

Page after page of professional economic journals are filled with mathematical formulas leading the reader from sets of more or less plausible but entirely arbitrary assumptions to precisely stated but irrelevant theoretical conclusions. [Leontief, pp. 104, 107]

(2) Complexity and Organization — One important characteristic of an evolutionary system is variously called holism, wholeness, Gestalt, etc., all meaning that elements in the system should be considered in interaction. In an economic system, every individual firm and consumer is the product of a long history, and unforeseen changes can occur because of complex past interactions between the individual units. Georgescu-Roegen has called this "novelty by combination." [Georgescu-Roegen, 1981, pp. 14-15] Scientific knowledge of an evolutionary system cannot be reduced to the whole alone or to the sum of its parts.

Complexity by itself is not a fundamental difference between organic and inorganic phenomena. Many inanimate systems such as galaxies or weather systems are highly complex. The difference is that organic systems (including social systems) are always characterized by highly elaborate feedback mechanisms not present in inanimate systems. The complexity of an evolutionary system is not random but highly organized. [Mayr, p. 53] Most economic entities — the firm, the credit or futures market — derive meaning only in the context of the whole system.

Neoclassical economics accepts the idea of interaction between the parts — oligopoly theory has a prominent place in all microeconomic texts — yet little theoretical work has been done since the early formulations of Robinson, Chamberlin, and Sweezy. Oligopoly theory has not been integrated with general equilibrium theory. Much more time and effort has been spent creating a more and more elaborate mathematical superstructure to support neoclassical models of perfect competition with its independent actors.

In this regard, Georgescu-Roegen's contribution to the epistemology of an evolutionary science should be mentioned. This contribution is the demonstration of the correct analytical representation of a dialectical process. [Georgescu-Roegen, 1966, 1971, 1979; see also Daly, 1968; and Miernyk, 1982] The word dialectical is used in the sense that there are always overlapping boundaries or penumbrae between categories. The existence of such penumbrae violates a necessary attribute of an analytical representation. An element α in the boundary between two categories A and B, for example, can be both A ($\alpha \epsilon$ A) and not-A ($\alpha \epsilon$ B). Analysis cannot allow penumbrae. To examine a process analytically, we must make some heroic assumptions and isolate the relevant partial process by constructing a boundary delineating distinct categories. There are two distinct components to this boundary. There must be a frontier which sets the process off from the rest of the universe, and there must be a duration bounding the process in time. It can be argued that the failures of neoclassical theory (for example, the inadequacy of the theory when applied to peasant economies) arise from a failure to appreciate that the boundary must be drawn to serve the particular purpose at hand.

(3) Indeterminancy — Because evolutionary processes are not absolute, and evolutionary events are relatively unique, indeterminacy matters more than in mechanics. Certain aspects of indeterminacy, namely risk and uncertainty, have received considerable attention in the economic literature. The work of Frank Knight, for example, is considered anti-positivist because of the importance it gives to uncertainty. [Knight, 1933] With evolutionary phenomena, however, uncertainty lies outside the individual firm or organism. Economic agents must continually make binding decisions based on an unknowable and ever changing future.

Selection, whether in the ecosystem or in the market, works to select the fittest whether or not the individual knows it is the fittest. [See Alchian, pp. 211-221] The problem is that the unit selected today may not be the fittest tomorrow. Firms, like species, are victims of the historical burden they inherit. [See Wiley and Brooks] A successful firm in one economic environment may suddenly become singularly unfit when economic conditions change. Because dramatic changes in the economic environment cannot be predicted, it is inaccurate to say that existing firms are necessarily the most efficient according to some universal maximizing criteria. [See Gould and Lewontin, pp. 581-598]

Part of the indeterminacy in economics comes from social constraints. Frequently, the best solution in terms of technological efficiency is not possible because of such non-economic constraints. Spengler argues that the rate of economic growth depends upon the compatibility between economic and non-economic components of the respective culture. [Spengler, 1949] Changing social conditions, then, may also be a threat to a successfully adapted firm.

(4) Irreversibility and Irrevocability — Irrevocability is another fea-

ture of evolutionary systems that has been ignored by standard economics. Following Georgescu-Roegen [Georgescu-Roegen, 1967, pp. 81-82], a distinction should be made between an *irreversible* process, which, while not reversible, can pass through the same stage twice, and an *irrevocable* process, which can pass through the same state no more than once. The processes that make up biological evolution and the evolution of economic systems may be irrevocable as well as irreversible.

Evolution may be seen as the history of a system undergoing irrevocable changes. [Lotka, p. 26] Once again, the distinction between mechanistic processes and evolutionary processes is clear. The models of physical science are based on reversible concepts. All the stars and planets could reverse their motions without disrupting the system. There is no "time's arrow" in mechanical processes. At the heart of irreversibility and irrevocability is the presence of selection mechanisms in evolutionary systems. In biology it is natural selection and in economics it is the profit motive. These are synergistic processes without exact equivalents in mechanics. [See Thoben, pp. 292-306; and the work of Nelson and Winter]

The above characteristics of evolutionary systems makes prediction in the sense of "temporal prediction" [Mayr, p. 57] impossible. Temporal prediction is the meaning of prediction in common usage. It is an inference from the past to the future such as the prediction of a solar eclipse. Several features of economic systems make such predictions impossible. One is complexity. Economic systems are so rich in feedbacks, multiple pathways, and interactions that a complete description and thus a prediction of the future state must be highly tentative. Another feature is emergency; the unexpected appearance of new and unpredictable qualities in economic systems or "novelty by combinations." Finally, the characteristic of uniqueness also precludes temporal prediction.

Economics does allow what is referred to as logical prediction. By this is meant conformance of individual observations with a theory or a scientific law. Examples of this sort of prediction are the law of demand, the law of supply, and the law of diminishing marginal utility. So, the factors discussed above do not weaken the principle of causality in a "post-dictive" sense. [Mayr, p. 863]

SOME RELEVANT CONTROVERSIES IN
EVOLUTIONARY THEORY

Thus far it has been argued that the methodology and subject matter of evolutionary biology have much in common with those of economics. In particular, evolutionary biology shows that explanations of the past are possible even when they do not contain laws; even when they are not predictive in the mechanistic sense. It is useful to examine the relevance to economics of some current controversies in evolutionary theory.

Punctuated Equilibrium — According to the "modern synthesis" in evolutionary biology, the pace of evolutionary change is slow and gradual. The direction of evolutionary change is determined by natural selection among myriad small variations within a population. Changes above the species level, or macroevolution, are seen to be a consequence of microevolution within populations. According to the modern synthesis, evolution moves at a steady pace with small changes accumulating gradually.

Recently this view has been challenged by several schools of thought. The challengers point to the unevenness of the fossil record, which does not show a smooth transition from one form to another. According to Gould, "for millions of years species remain unchanged in the fossil record and they then abruptly disappear, to be replaced by something that is substantially different but closely related." [Quoted in Lewin, p. 883][2]

This same sort of process, punctuated equilibrium, is common in economic history. Economic entities persist more or less intact for relatively long periods only to be replaced by sweeping new innovations. Macroeconomic change is not one of gradual change at the margin. Schumpeter has written:

> In capitalist reality . . . it is. . . competition from the new commodity, the new technology, the new source of supply, the new type of organization (the largest scale unit of control for instance) — competition which commands a decisive cost or quality advantage and which strikes not at the margins of the profits and the outputs of existing firms but at their foundations and their very lives. [Schumpeter, p. 84]

Related to this is the idea that efficient firms may be "selected" by market forces under one set of rules, only to be bankrupted when unexpected forces such as a war or a recession suddenly change the rules of selection. The rules of the game may be constant for a long period of time, then change abruptly, favoring new economic forms.

[2]Georgescu-Roegen's approach also illuminates the concept of biological species. Species necessarily overlap in space and time. Just because species is the seat of evolution does not mean that the concept can be defined arithmomorphically. [Georgescu-Roegen, 1966, p. 83; this issue is discussed in more detail in Georgescu-Roegen's forthcoming book *Bioeconomics*]

Constraining Channels — Another important concept in evolutionary theory is that of constraining channels. Gould and Lewontin, in a critique of the modern synthesis in biology, write:

> We . . . reassert a competing notion (long popular in continental Europe) that organisms must be analysed as integrated wholes, with Bauplane so constrained by phyletic heritage, pathways of development and general architecture that the constraints themselves become more interesting and more important in delimiting pathways of change than the selective force that may mediate change when it occurs. [Gould and Lewontin, p. 147]

The implication of this idea is that current utility must not be mistaken for the reason for origin. In economics, too, systems must be analyzed as integrated wholes. Profit maximization is, in a sense, the editor of economic change but not the composer. Which types of firms enter the market and which types of economic and social organization they represent are a product of history. Internal factors are an equal partner with selection in the marketplace. Supply and demand may be the ultimate source of economic evolution, but most actual economic arrangements are just as likely the result of non-adaptive, pre-existing features.

In biological evolution, there appears to be considerable latitude at the molecular level for changes that do not affect the fitness of the organism. [King and Jukes, pp. 788-798] The same is true in the economy. The editor cannot remove characteristics it cannot perceive. If there is leeway in the profit motive, as many have argued, then there is more room for social features not related to economic survival. There is more room for constraining channels than the neoclassical model allows.

Over the years, neoclassical microeconomic theory has withstood many criticisms. Among the most serious challenges have been those related to the neoclassical treatment of economic change. This paper has attempted to suggest an alternative to the mechanistic model of neoclassical economics. This alternative framework is based on the explanatory, but not predictive, methodology of Charles Darwin.

324   REVIEW OF SOCIAL ECONOMY

REFERENCES

Alchian, Armen.   "Uncertainty, Evolution and Economic Theory," *Journal of Political Economy*, 58, June 1950.

Blaug, Mark.   *The Methodology of Economics*, Cambridge, 1980.

Caldwell, Bruce.   "Positivist Philosophy of Science and the Methodology of Economics," *Journal of Economic Issues*, 14, March 1980.

Daly, Herman E.   "On Economics as a Life Science," *Journal of Political Economy*, 76, May/June 1968.

Friedman, Milton.   "The Methodology of Positive Economics," in *Essays in Positive Economics*, Chicago, 1953.

Georgescu-Roegen, Nicholas.   *Analytical Economics*, Cambridge, MA, 1966.

_____.   *The Entropy Law and the Economic Process*, Cambridge, MA, 1971.

_____.   "Methods in Economic Science," *Journal of Economic Issues*, 13, June 1979.

Gould, Stephen and Roger Lewontin.   "The Spandrels of San Marco and the Panglossian Paradigm: A Critique of the Adaptationist Programme," *Proceedings of the Royal Society of London*, B 207, 1979.

Hicks, J. R.   *Causality in Economics*, New York, 1979.

Hirsh, Abraham.   "The Assumptions Controversy in Historical Perspective," *Journal of Economics Issues*, 14, March 1980.

Hitchinson, T. W.   *Knowledge and Ignorance in Economics*, Chicago, 1977.

King, Jack and Thomas Jukes.   "Non-Darwinian Evolution," *Science*, 164, 16 May 1969.

Knight, Frank.   *Risk, Uncertainty and Profit*, London School Reprints of Scarce Works, No. 16, 1933.

Leontief, Wassily.   Letter to *Science*, 217, 9 July 1982.

Lewin, Roger.   "Biology is not Postage Stamp Collecting," *Science*, 216, 14 May 1982.

Lotka, Alfred.   *Elements of Mathematical Biology*, New York, 1956.

Mayr, Ernst.   *The Growth of Biological Thought*, Cambridge, MA, 1982.

Miernyk, William H.   *Regional Analysis and Regional Policy*, Cambridge, MA, 1982.

Nelson, Richard and Sidney Winter.   "Simulation of Schumpeterian Competition," *American Economic Review*, 67, February 1977.

Rothbard, Murray.   "Praxeology as the Method of Economics," in *Phenomenology and the Social Sciences*, 2, Maurice Natanson, ed., Evansdale, IL, 1973.

Schumpeter, Joseph.   *Capitalism, Socialism and Democracy*, New York, 1950.

Schweber, Silvan.   "The Origin of the Origin Revisited," *Journal of the History of Biology*, 10, Fall 1977.

Spengler, J.   *Problems in the Study of Economic Growth*, National Bureau of Economic Research, 1949.

Thoben, H.   "Mechanistic and Organistic Analogies in Economics Reconsidered," *Kyklos* 35, 1982.

Van Valen, L.   "A New Revolutionary Law," *Evolutionary Theory*, 1, 1973.

Webb, James.   Review of Mark Blaug, *The Methodology of Economics*, in *Journal of Economic Issues*, 16, September 1983.

Weisskopf, Walter.   "The Method is the Ideology: From a Newtonian to a Heisenbergian Paradigm in Economics," *Journal of Economic Issues*, 13, December 1979.

Wiley, E. O. and Daniel Brooks.   "Victims of History — A Nonequilibrium Approach to Evolution," *Systematic Zoology*, 31, 1982.

[10]

EVOLUTIONARY MODELS IN ECONOMICS AND LAW:

COOPERATION VERSUS CONFLICT

STRATEGIES

Jack Hirshleifer

Attempting to address the combined topics of economics, law, and evolution in a single paper is hubris indeed. All the more so, as I will be adopting very broad interpretations of what we might mean by both economics and law. Economics, as understood here, is *not* limited to selfish, rational "economic man" interacting with his fellows only through impersonal market relationships. For my purposes, all human motivations and interactions constitute the subject matter of economics, so long as they respond to the pervasive fact of resource scarcity. As for law, I shall take that term as covering essentially all modes of *coercive social control* of behavior, thus including much of what might conventionally be considered under the headings of politics or sociology. How-

Research in Law and Economics, volume 4, pages 1–60
Copyright © 1982 by JAI Press Inc.
All rights of reproduction in any form reserved.
ISBN: 0-89232-266-7

2   JACK HIRSHLEIFER

ever, the evolutionary standpoint sets some bound upon the field of discussion. Also, I will be considering only one aspect of interpersonal interactions—though that is perhaps the most important of all—to wit, the determinants of *cooperation versus conflict* in human affairs.

I. ECONO-LEGAL THINKING AND THE MISSING TREND TOWARD HARMONY

In recent years there has been growing intellectual interchange between legal and economic scholars. The dominant influence, it seems fair to say, has been economics, in the sense that economic propositions have been borrowed or applied to provide new or more fundamental explanations of certain legal phenomena.[1] The influential economic ideas in question, together with their seeming legal implications, can be stated rather baldly (shorn of needed qualifications and possible adornments) as follows:

    1. *Smith's Theorem* (60), Book I, ch. 2. Voluntary exchange is mutually advantageous for participants. Implication: The law ought, presumptively at least, to promote trade—negatively, by removing artificial legal barriers, affirmatively, by facilitating and enforcing private exchange agreements.

    2. *Coase's Theorem* (11). All available mutually advantageous exchanges will be voluntarily undertaken by the parties involved. Even where individuals impose what are said to be "external" injuries upon others, as when an upstream user of water degrades the quality of the flow to a downstream user, a resolution of the conflict will tend to take place through the exchange process. This conclusion does not depend upon the initial assignment of property rights, provided the entitlements are well defined. If the upstream user has the legal right to degrade quality, the downstream party can offer him compensation for not doing so. If on the other hand the downstream user has a legal right to unimpaired quality, the upstream party can purchase the other's tolerance of damage. Either way, the upstream use will continue to take place if and only if it can pay its way in comparison with the downstream damage. Given such an assignment of property rights, and if there are no transaction costs, the final outcome will be *efficient* (in a sense to be made more precise below). Implication: In addition to removing artificial barriers to transactions, the law ought to assign well-defined property rights to all resources of economic value. And if transaction costs (barriers to exchange) are absent, the law need not otherwise concern itself with regulating external damage.

3. *Posner's Theorem* (49).[2] Where unavoidable transaction costs (that is, barriers other than those due to the law itself) preclude achievement of a fully efficient result by private negotiation, some particular initial assignments of property rights may constitute or lead to more nearly efficient outcomes than others. Implication: Recognizing the presence of unavoidable transaction costs, the law ought to choose the most efficient of the possible assignments of property rights.

I have in each case stated the seeming legal implication in *normative* terms, the operative phrase being: "The law ought to . . ." An alternative *positive* interpretation would be indicated by the assertion: "The law will in fact tend to . . ." In its normative version, this entire line of econo-legal thinking might be summarized: "Market transactions among individuals operate in the direction of economic efficiency, and the law *ought to* aid and where necessary supplement this trend." The positive version would be: "Market interactions tend toward economic efficiency, and the law *will in fact tend to* assist and supplement this tendency."

On either interpretation, a generally Panglossian aura surrounds the entire discussion. In the positive version, it would seem, we scholars need only chronicle the unfolding harmonious progress of law and economy toward the best (most efficient) of all possible worlds. The normative version of the argument, while it suggests some doubt as to the matter (why else concern ourselves with what *ought* to be done?), has the offsetting advantage of providing a more muscular role for savants like us. Whatever blemishes may mar its present complexion, the law can be improved, and we are the ones who know how to do so! Indeed, it seems reasonable to suppose, as scholarly understanding advances and as education of the public broadens and deepens over time, the various mistaken ideas that have in the past interfered with sound econo-legal thinking should have decreasing sway.

I have injected a note of sarcasm, for we know that there must be something seriously wrong with this picture. On the most fundamental matter, the rule of law has always fallen short of universal coverage of mankind. The potential mutual gains from cooperation have not abolished war, crime, or politics. Turning to less cataclysmic though still momentous issues, the advanced systems of law that are the proud possessions of Western nations have in fact been changing for at least a century in directions that are on the whole pernicious from the viewpoint of economic efficiency. Rather than increasingly supportive of property and exchange, the trend has clearly been in the direction of harassment, increasing uncertainty, and even confiscation. Parallel developments taking place in other aspects of life—rising crime rates, increasingly grave

4   JACK HIRSHLEIFER

race-class conflicts, growing political polarization—suggest that these
pernicious legal trends are due not simply to errors in the design of laws,
but rather to deeper social realities. The forces promoting harmonious
reciprocal exchanges among individuals and leading toward legal structures supporting and facilitating such exchanges are evidently weaker
than recent econo-legal thinking might have led us to suppose. The
central thrust of this paper will be an attempt to see how far this unfortunate fact is explained by evolutionary theory.

Evolutionary ideas are relevant to our question of the scope of harmonious interaction among men in two main ways. *First,* regarding the
nature of man. What capacities for cooperation or for conflict lie innate
within members of the human species, either as universal tendencies of
life or as the particular results of the evolution of mankind? In short,
are we humans essentially fighters or lovers? *Second,* regarding social
institutions. Whatever the intrinsic pattern of individual human drives
may be, the overall outcome is also a function of the social constraints
regulating personal interactions. Adam Smith's (60), Book IV, ch. 2,
principle of the Invisible Hand has shown us how even selfish individuals
may be led by appropriate social institutions to cooperate to their mutual
advantage. Conversely, even selfless generosity may sometimes be sub-
verted for lack of supportive social arrangements. The first element, our
innate make-up, constitutes a background which has been largely constant over the evolutionarily brief span represented by the historical
experience of mankind. Furthermore, it is also largely uniform over the
human species. The second element, the institutional or cultural fore-
ground, is in contrast highly volatile over historical time and amazingly
varied among different human societies. Both elements are essential for
understanding the prospects for and limits upon cooperative versus conflictual interactions among men.

II.   EFFICIENCY

It is time to address the problem of "efficiency," to ask whether this
concept is robust enough to bear the weight placed upon it in recent
econo-legal thinking.

The root idea is *Pareto-preference.* A social configuration Γ is said
to be Pareto-preferred to another social configuration Ω if no affected
member of the society prefers Ω to Γ, and at least one member actually
prefers Γ. (As we shall see, the proper interpretation to be placed upon
"affected" raises difficulties, but let us set this problem aside for the
moment.) Any *voluntary* transaction, if the participants can be assumed
to be rational, leads to a Pareto-preferred outcome. In particular, since

an act of voluntary exchange is mutually beneficial (the Smith Theorem), its outcome is Pareto-preferred to the pre-exchange situation—provided no other members of the society are adversely "affected" thereby. Furthermore, rational decision makers will eventually execute *all* mutually advantageous transactions available to them. The final outcome, when there are no further opportunities for mutual gain, is called *Pareto-efficient*. Note that only a small subset of the outcomes that are Pareto-preferred to some initial situation are Pareto-efficient (that is, leave no room for further improvement in the way of mutual gain). Conversely, there will generally be Pareto-*efficient* configurations that are not Pareto-*preferred* to some particular initial situation. That is, there may be outcomes which could not be improved upon (in terms of mutual gain) once arrived at, but which are not achievable by mutually advantageous transactions from a given specified starting point. Nevertheless, the Coase Theorem asserts, any starting point will eventually lead to *some* Pareto-efficient outcome—if existence of property rights and absence of transaction costs permit unrestricted exchange.

Practically all important social issues, however, involve comparisons among situations that cannot be ranked by Pareto-preference considerations. That is, almost always, social changes make some parties better off but others worse off. This even holds for "voluntary" exchange, since in general third parties will be affected. Suppose that women were previously barred from some line of employment, and now the barrier has been removed. The females who enter that line of employment gain from the increased scope of exchange, as do their employers. But the previously protected (male) employees will be adversely affected, yet do not have any legal entitlement to retain their old terms of employment. It is a standard proposition of economics that such pecuniary externalities balance out in aggregate value terms. The loss to the male workers (of receiving a lower wage) is exactly counterbalanced by the gain to their employers (in not having to pay a higher wage). Nevertheless, absent compensation it remains true that some parties are now worse off; removal of an artificial barrier to trade is thus *not* in general a strictly Pareto-preferred change.

To get around this difficulty, the concept of "potentially Pareto-preferred" (PPP) social changes has been proposed.[3] Suppose everyone's well-being could simply be scaled in terms of the amount of pie he consumes. Then any way of increasing the overall size of society's aggregate pie meets the PPP criterion. For a larger pie can *potentially* be redivided so that everybody gains (or, at least, so that some gain while nobody loses). Put more generally, the PPP criterion is satisfied by any change such that the gainers could (even *if they do not*) compensate the losers. Any such change is, in the modern econo-legal literature, called a movement in the direction of "efficiency." A final position in which no such PPP changes remain to be made is called simply "efficient."

In terms of changes from an arbitrary initial position, not every potentially Pareto-preferred change (movement in the direction of efficiency) will generally be strictly Pareto-preferred. In particular, the PPP criterion would (subject to some qualifications to be mentioned below) give a favorable response to our example of removing barriers to employment of women, where the strict Pareto criterion does not. Since the losses to the male employees are exactly counterbalanced by the gains to their employers, with a further net gain flowing to the new female workers and their employers, clearly the losers from the change could be compensated. The PPP criterion, if we accept it, thus justifies exchange even where pecuniary externalities are imposed on other parties (as almost always they will be).

Our discussion has suggested that there are a number of ethical or ideological problems associated with efficiency criteria, and it is time to mention three of these explicitly.

1. *Voluntarism:* The key issue in approving only strictly Pareto-preferred (SPP) changes versus approving all potentially Pareto-preferred (PPP) changes is voluntarism. The PPP criterion overrides dissent. There is an irony in the history of thought here: proponents of the market process usually contend that it is a way of achieving economic efficiency without compulsion or dictation, yet we have seen that market transactions will be unambiguous movements in the direction of efficiency only if we depart from a strictly voluntaristic interpretation of what "efficiency" means. Indeed, excessive emphasis upon the saliency of the efficiency criterion, in the nonvoluntaristic PPP sense, would seem to open the gates even to rather brutal social processes that might conceivably still operate in accordance with a PPP rule.

2. *Enshrining the status quo:* Matters may appear in a somewhat different light, however, once we appreciate that voluntary changes are necessarily relative to some starting point. Why should the starting point, the initial distribution of wealth and talents, be given such a privileged position in our social thinking? This objection holds with greatest force against the strict Pareto criterion. The PPP criterion is somewhat less bound to the status quo, as it allows some nonunanimistic departures therefrom. Nevertheless, even what is potentially Pareto-preferred may still depend upon the initial position.

One example which has received some attention is the so-called reversal paradox [Scitovsky (59)]. Consider an initial social configuration Γ, with its vector of produced goods and associated income distribution.

It may be that a change to some other configuration Ω with a different vector of produced goods and income distribution is PPP-indicated, in that compensating payments *could* make everybody better off in comparison with Γ. That is, Ω makes possible some other configuration Ω' which *would* be strictly Pareto-preferred to Γ. But it might also be the case that Γ meets the PPP criterion relative to Ω! That is, there might be a Γ' that is strictly Pareto-preferred to Ω. (It is the change in income distribution, shifting the market weights assigned to individuals' preferences, that makes this possible.) Probably a much more significant phenomenon is the paradox put in inverted form: starting at Γ a change to Ω may be ruled out as a PPP-inferior movement, yet starting at Ω the move to Γ may also be PPP-inferior! A nontrivial example: an enslaved person might not be able to afford buying his freedom from his master, yet were he free to begin with he might not be willing to sell himself into slavery at any price the master would pay. Which configuration is then the more efficient?

3. *Meddlesome preferences:* Suppose that some individuals have preferences that are not "self-regarding." For example, lowering the barriers to female employment in coal mines might be found disturbing by some third parties even though the latter are unaffected in material terms. Ought such preferences to be taken into account, under either the strict Pareto (SPP) or potential Pareto (PPP) criterion? Assuming that individuals are actually willing to pay (to sacrifice their own resources or potential consumption) in order to further such "meddlesome" goals, I see no basis for excluding them from consideration. However, when non-self-regarding tastes are taken into account, it no longer follows that voluntary exchange necessarily leads to efficiency even in the PPP sense.

What is the upshot of this discussion? If you now find yourself less than fully confident as to the normative validity of efficiency (either in the SPP sense or the PPP sense) as a criterion for social policy, you are in agreement with me. And notice that I have nowhere diverged from the premises of utilitarian individualism—the idea that the proper social goal can be expressed entirely in terms of the achievement of individual desires, rather than (for example) the pursuit of abstract ideals like justice or service to God—though in fact I do have reservations about strict utilitarianism. Nor have I attempted to bring in paternalistic arguments— to the effect that some individuals (or all individuals at some times) do not really know their true desires or are not able to choose what is best for them—and I would not entirely reject paternalism either. For all these reasons efficiency criteria fall short of being fully attractive. This is less threatening a thought for those of us who are doubtful in any case about the prospects of purposive social reconstruction in the pursuit of efficiency (or indeed in pursuit of any social goal); a doubt which is, for reasons that will become clear at the end of the next section, more or less consistent with an evolutionary approach to societal phenomena. But, as a matter of *positive* analysis, the difficulties that have been revealed may partially explain the seeming recalcitrance of the politically influential public to the efficiency argument of modern econo-legal thinkers.

Finally, one underemphasized aspect of the efficiency criterion is crucial for our purposes: efficiency is always relative to the boundaries of the society or group envisaged. An act of voluntary reciprocal exchange is beneficial for the "society" comprised by the two participants; it is when we consider third parties that questions begin to arise. If competing merchants were to form a cartel the move would be efficient from their point of view, though not so when consumers are taken into account. Or consider theft. If we set aside long-term effects upon the incentive to produce, theft as such would be purely redistributive. It is only the resources consumed in defenses erected against theft, and the consequent increased costs of thieving, that reduce the aggregate size of society's pie. Would it then be PPP-efficient to ban defenses against theft? Presumably, the answer would be yes (apart from the aforesaid long-run problems) if the thieves are considered members of the society, but no, if as *outlaws* they have placed themselves outside the social unit. (I myself prefer the latter answer!) In a broader context, outcomes efficient for our nation as a whole may be adverse to the well-being of other nations; even gains for the whole human species may be achieved at the expense of other species. My point is that no one, probably, favors efficiency in a totally universalistic sense. We all draw the line somewhere, at the boundary of "us" versus "them." *Efficiency thus is ultimately a concept relating to group advantage over other competing groups.*

III.   ELEMENTS OF EVOLUTIONARY MODELS

The word "evolution" primarily suggests to us the biological succession of living types, but the underlying concept is of course much broader. Stars evolve: initially a localized concentration of gases in space, a star goes through several stages as it burns its nuclear fuel, ending up eventually as a white dwarf or black hole. According to current cosmological theories the universe as a whole is evolving, under the sway of the second law of thermodynamics, to an eventual steady state of maximum entropy—a uniform distribution of energy throughout space. On the human level we know also that languages evolve, though following what course I am not prepared to suggest. Thus it is by no means illegitimate to argue that patterns of economic interaction and legal structures may evolve. Yet, I want to say, not everything that changes can usefully be said to *evolve*. Evolution represents a particular type or pattern of change.

1. *Evolution versus randomness:* Evolution is not random variation (totally inexplicable change). The outcomes of successive spins of a roulette wheel vary, but do not evolve. Yet random change on a micro or component level may be an element of evolutionary change at the level of a larger entity or collection. In biology genetic mutations occur randomly, yet they contribute to the evolutionary development of species.

2. *Evolution versus cyclicity:* Regular cyclical change, which plays a role in certain theories of social processes, is best not regarded as evolution. Cyclicity is a kind of generalized stationarity. Put another way, evolutionary changes have an *irreversible* element, so that things are never quite the same afterward [Lotka (38), ch. 2].

3. *Evolution versus revolution:* In evolutionary models, transitions on the macro level result from the accumulation of small changes in microelements over time. Species evolve through the gradual working of forces contributing to variations in the characters of individual organisms, and to differential multiplication thereof. Stars evolve via a multitude of infinitesimal changes operating over the eons on their atomic or subatomic constituent particles. Where custom is the dominant element, law tends to follow an evolutionary course: the law emerges from a host of small transactions. But a Moses or a Solon hands down the law from above, all at once as a *revolutionary* change. Similarly, in earlier times the economic system changed mainly through the gradual discovery and slow diffusion of new techniques and new social relationships. In modern times, of course, revolutionary economic transformations are occurring with increasing frequency, often (though not necessarily) imposed from above.

Whether a change is revolutionary or evolutionary is sometimes a matter of relevant time span or scope of unit. Fusion of a pair of hydrogen atoms within a star is a revolutionary change for the specific atoms involved, but only a tiny component of the evolutionary process for the star. In primitive times, within a small human band the invention of the bow, or the promulgation of a successful new law, may have been revolutionary. But among the larger group of related bands comprising what we now perceive as a single culture, the change may have progressed only at an evolutionary pace, perhaps being repeatedly reinvented or slowly diffusing before becoming characteristic of that culture.

4. *Evolution versus design:* When we speak of evolutionary changes in human affairs, we generally have in mind "unintended" ones. Once again, we must distinguish different levels of analysis. Purposive planning

by individuals, or by small groups, might be consistent with unintended evolutionary change on a macro level. The inventor of the bow had an intention, but it was only to help himself or his band; the spread of a new technique of hunting, not to mention the more remote social consequences following upon that spread, was surely beyond his purpose. Or, modern statute writers may intend some purposive redesign of the social order—but, since "legislation is based on folk notions of causality" [Moore (44), p. 7], the result may be very different from that planned.

One of the inferences I draw from this discussion is that the applicability of evolutionary models ought not be oversold; evolution is not the sole important pattern of social change. In particular, with the increasing connectivity of the human world-system—due mainly to advances in communication and to the development of technology with worldwide impact (most notably, military technology)— "revolutionary" and "designed" changes are playing larger and larger roles. Nevertheless, models of evolutionary change have not lost all relevance. First, many areas of life continue to be subject to evolutionary principles. Language, custom, the sphere of private economic activity, and the common law can still be said to evolve. Second, the *present-day* starting point, even for revolutionary or designed change, is in large part the product of *past* genetic and cultural evolution. The social evolution of the human species places constraints upon the nature and pace of planned future change.

Evolutionary models share certain properties. First of all, they concern populations. Even where we seem to be speaking of single entities, if the course of change is evolutionary it can be described in terms of changing populations of micro-units. Thus, the evolutionary course of a disease within a single human body is a function of the relations among populations of bacteria, antibodies, cells, and so on. Or the evolution of a single nation's economy is the result of changing relations among populations of individuals, trading units, and the like.

Evolutionary models represent a combination of constancy ("inheritance") and variation. There must be an unchanging as well as a changing element, and even the changing element itself must be heritable if a system can be said to evolve. In biological evolution, the emphasis is upon differential survival and reproduction of organismic types or characters from one generation to the next. Here the constancy is due to Mendelian inheritance of permanent patterns of coded genetic instructions (genes). Variation stems from a number of forces, including internal mutations of these instructions (genetic copying errors), recombination of genes in sexual reproduction, and the external pressure of natural selection. Socioeconomic evolution mainly concerns the differential growth and survival of patterns of social organization. The main "inheritance" element is the deadweight of social inertia, supported by intentionally taught tradition. As for variation, there are analogs to mutations ("copying errors" as we learn traditions). Also, natural selection is still effective. Finally, *imitation* and *rational thought* constitute additional nongenetic sources of socioeconomic variation.

Biologists have been much interested in the question of the "direction" of evolution. The main principle recognized is *adaptation*. That is, organisms and their lines of descent over the generations tend to fit themselves into niches of viability offered by their environments. They do so mainly under the pressure of selective competition from other organisms and species, all of which have an irrepressible Malthusian tendency[4] to multiply so as to fill any unsaturated places in the environment.

A number of philosophers have perceived a directional trend toward "complexity" in biological, cultural, and even cosmological evolution. I believe this is mistaken. If complexity is adaptive, the trend of development will be in that direction, but often the direction of adaptation may be toward simplicity. We see movement toward complexity when, for example, a few "founders" enter and proliferate within a new environment that contains many different yet-unfilled niches. We see movement toward simplicity, on the other hand, whenever homogenization of the environment reduces the number of distinct niches available.

The adaptation principle suggests that the external environmental determinants must ultimately govern in the evolutionary process.[5] But biological evolution is opportunistic, and must work with the internal materials at hand. The available internal materials—the genetically coded instructions—will have been shaped by a variety of past irreversible transformations. These transformations were perhaps responsive in their own day to then-current environmental requirements, but persisting today they remain more or less recalcitrant constraints upon adaptive change. Despite this, there are extraordinary examples of parallel evolution in Nature, for example, where traits usually associated with fishes have been independently evolved by quite different biological taxa moving into aquatic environments, among them the mammals (seals, whales), birds (penguins), and lizards (sea-going iguanas). There are also failures of parallel evolution, however. Nothing like the kangaroo has evolved outside Australia, despite large geographical regions where kangaroo-like qualities would seem to be highly adaptive.

The second qualification of the adaptation principle is of greater interest for our purposes. What is adaptive for the individual organism (and its descendants) may or may not be adaptive for the species. Fleetness of foot helps the gazelle escape the lion, but the gain to being exceptionally fleet may largely be that some other gazelle is eaten instead. If the gazelles were making a cooperative group adaptation, presumably somewhat less fleetness than what has actually evolved would be optimal. A different type of imperfect species adaptation is illustrated by the peacock. The enormous tail pleases the female's fancy and so its bearer sires more offspring, yet a heavy price is paid. As a group adaptation, it seems that the peacocks ought to have found a mode of sexual competition involving less energy loss and vulnerability to predators. In economic terms we would say that these forms of biological competition impose *adverse externalities* upon other members of (what we perceive as) a larger potentially cooperating group—in this case, the species.

Group adaptation remains imperfect in such cases because the biological payoff in reproductive competition depends mainly upon *relative* achievement. An organism can get ahead in evolutionary terms either by pulling itself up or by pushing its competitors down:

> It is crucial to understanding the behavior of organisms, including ourselves, that in evolutionary terms success in reproduction is always *relative;* hence, the striving of organisms is in relation to one another and not toward some otherwise quantifiable goal or optimum. [Alexander (1), p. 17]

The evolutionary emphasis upon *relative* reproductive competition has important implications for the question of efficiency discussed in Section II. If it were strictly true that only relative status counted, the efficiency concept would be meaningless. If one party's advance automatically means that other parties lose, there is no scope for *mutual* gain, actual or potential [see Becker (6), pp. 1089–1090, and Hirshleifer (30), pp. 329–330]. In the case of the peacock, other males' reproductive survival is not even a neutral but probably on balance a harmful consideration; the descendants of other cocks will use up resources and multiply to the disadvantage of its own descendants.[6]

At the end of Section II it was argued that efficiency must be interpreted as relative to the boundaries of the group. We can now see that for group efficiency to be economically meaningful as a criterion, the group must be one within which individuals do *not* compete mainly in terms of relative achievement. In nature, *species are mainly fields of relative reproductive competition*. This is why, so often, adaptations tend to be selected that are harmful to the species as a whole.

Nevertheless, truly cooperating groups within species[7] are also often evolved by Nature. Among the more evident examples are families, packs, and insect communities, extending on the human level to tribes and nations. What is happening here, insofar as evolutionary reproductive competition is controlling, is that some individuals have allied to achieve a mutual gain *relative to* other members of their species.

That intragroup cooperation and mutual gain typically take place within a larger context of intergroup competition and conflict is essential to keep in mind in speaking of efficiency. Failure to appreciate this fact is an important weakness of modern econo-legal thinking, which the evolutionary approach has exposed. Even within an actual or potential alliance there remain, however, mixed motives—individual advantage is generally not wholly consistent with group advantage. The theoretical approach to the viability of cooperation strategies in such mixed-incentive situations is the topic of the next two sections.

IV. PATTERNS OF CONFLICT AND COOPERATION: EVOLUTIONARY EQUILIBRIUM

Cooperation and conflict are not simple opposites. The two are complexly intertwined, but in ways that fall into a limited set of mixed-incentive patterns. I shall illustrate some of these patterns here in terms of game theory matrices.[8] (I will be considering only the especially simple class of two-person binary-strategy interactions at this point.)

The most famous of these patterns is the game known as Prisoners' Dilemma. It will be helpful to start with a simpler pattern, a game I shall call Tender Trap (Matrix 1).[9] Tender Trap illustrates the binding force of convention (of an agreed rule) even where all players realize that the wrong convention has been chosen. We tacitly agree upon many conventions to order our daily lives: for example, rules of the road, rules of language, rules of courtesy. Their function is to coordinate activities, so that any person can reasonably anticipate what others will do.

In Matrix 1 the parties can agree on either convention #1 or convention #2; the first is superior to the second in that each party gains 5 units of income instead of 2, but either is superior to following opposite strategies (such that each party receives 0). For example: everyone might agree that it would be better if Americans spoke Esperanto rather than English, but in any case all Americans are better off speaking the same language. I begin with this pattern because *here there is no conflict of interests* whatsoever; the problem is purely one of coordination. (The game of Tender Trap can be generalized to allow a degree of conflict of interest, however, by having the off-diagonal elements display different returns to the two players—see below.)

The standard solution concept which mathematicians employ for such "non-zero-sum" games is the *Nash equilibrium* (NE) [Nash (45)]. A strategy pair is an NE if, taking the strategy of the other party as given, neither player can improve his position by revising his own strategy. In

14   JACK HIRSHLEIFER

	Matrix 1 Tender Trap	
	C_1	C_2
R_1	5,5	0,0
R_2	0,0	2,2

		Matrix 2a Chicken	
		C_1 (Coward)	C_2 (Hero)
(Coward)	R_1	0,0	$-10,20$
(Hero)	R_2	$20,-10$	$-100,-100$

		Matrix 2b Hawk-Dove	
		C_1 (Dove)	C_2 (Hawk)
(Dove)	R_1	2,2	0,10
(Hawk)	R_2	10,0	$-5,-5$

		Matrix 3 Prisoners' Dilemma	
		C_1 (Omertà)	C_2 (Fink)
(Omertà)	R_1	$-1,-1$	$-20,0$
(Fink)	R_2	$0,-20$	$-10,-10$

	Matrix 4 Generalized Symmetrical Game	
	C_1	C_2
R_1	1,1	y,x
R_2	x,y	0,0

	Matrix 5 Battle of the Sexes	
	C_1	C_2
R_1	2,1	0,0
R_2	0,0	1,2

Matrix 1 the two agreed "conventions" (the two cells on the main diagonal) are both Nash equilibria. If the players had chosen the first convention (Row 1 and Column 1), either would lose by shifting, but the same holds if they had initially chosen the inferior second convention (Row 2 and Column 2).

A subtly different solution, which we will call the *evolutionary equilibrium* (EE), has been proposed by the biologist John Maynard Smith.[10] The idea is that the two parties are members of a homogeneous population meeting randomly in pairwise interactions. One strategy may be "defeated" by another, and therefore eventually be driven out in the evolutionary sense, if it yields on average a lower return than the other. The average returns received will be a function of the proportions of the population choosing each of the strategies, so that we are dealing with possible equilibria of a dynamic process.

In Matrix 1 it may be verified that if the proportion p of the population choosing strategy #1 were initially greater than 2/7, the average return from choosing #1 will exceed the return from #2. In this circumstance strategy #1 will tend to drive out #2. Then the "efficient" solution, in the potentially Pareto-preferred (PPP) sense of maximizing the "pie" of aggregate income[11] —the upper-left corner outcome (5,5)—will be attained as an evolutionary equilibrium EE. Furthermore, the efficient solution here is also strictly Pareto-preferred in comparison with any other starting point (it is *unanimously* preferred over any alternative outcome cell of Matrix 1). If, on the other hand, the initial proportion were less than 2/7, the attained EE would be at the lower-right corner.[12] So the two NE's are also both EE's. The dividing line p = 2/7 is a kind of threshold or critical mass for reaching the mutually preferred solution. Something like a shift from a generally less-preferred to a more-preferred EE actually occurred among Jews of Palestine, who managed to put together a critical mass for shifting from Yiddish (mainly) to Hebrew as a common language. But it is unlikely that a population could shift from driving on the left to driving on the right, or from the English to the metric system of units, without support by the force of law.

Moving now to mixed-incentive interactions, Matrix 2a illustrates the famous game of Chicken. The two players drive toward one another at full speed, the one who turns aside (Coward) becoming an object of contempt. If it turns out that each plays Hero, the result is death (-100 for each). Or, both might be Cowards (0 return for each). The really desirable situation, of course, is for the other to be a Coward (-10) and you a Hero ($+20$).

The Nash equilibrium (NE) is double here again, but occurs at the two *off*-diagonal outcomes. That is, from an initial position at either off-diagonal cell, it does not pay either party to change his strategy. The numbers in Matrix 2a are such that the off-diagonal outcomes are also jointly efficient (maximum sum of returns), though in this case neither NE is strictly Pareto-preferred in comparison with *all* the other possibilities. However, the essential features of Chicken would persist even if the sum of incomes in the off-diagonal cells were *not* maximal. For example, if the ($+20, -10$) cells were changed to ($+5, -10$) the off-diagonal outcomes would remain the Nash equilibria (NE's). But, whether or not the off-diagonal outcomes are efficient, these solutions are not available as evolutionary equilibria (EE's) in a homogeneous population! The reason is that they require *complementary* pairing of strategy choices, which is not possible in random encounters within a homogeneous population.

Let us now find the evolutionary equilibrium for Chicken. We can do so by calculating the average returns to each of the strategies as a function of the population fraction p choosing strategy #1 (Coward). In Matrix 2a the evolutionary equilibrium occurs at p = 9/11. The population being homogeneous, the interpretation is that each player chooses the Coward strategy 9/11 of the time and the Hero strategy 2/11 of the time. (This is known as a "mixed" as opposed to a "pure" strategy choice.) The average return will then be $-20/11$ to each player.[13] Even if the off-diagonal outcomes cannot be attained, there evidently remains a potential cooperative gain from both being Cowards (each receiving 0 rather than a negative amount). But this cooperative outcome is not an evolutionary equilibrium; if Cowards became too numerous, they would lose out on average to those making choices closer to the EE mixed strategy.

My picturesque description may perhaps suggest that the game of Chicken is a somewhat pathological class of social interaction. Such an inference would be quite false. The pattern of Chicken, in the more interesting version characterized by positive efficiency gains if the off-diagonal outcomes can be achieved, fits the *very* common situation of two parties in a position of potential conflict over a prize. Using a different ornithological metaphor, Maynard Smith calls what is essentially the same game "Hawk-Dove." In Matrix 2b a Hawk player encountering a Dove player wins a prize of 10, Dove receiving nothing. But Hawk-Hawk encounters involve a big loss (-5) to each. Dove-Dove encounters yield a modest gain (2) to each; the two do not suffer injury, but some potential gain (e.g., nutrition) is lost from lack of aggressivity. The EE here has the proportion $p = 5/13$ playing the Dove strategy. (Rather than assuming that every individual follows a mixed strategy, we can equally well interpret the EE as a population balance of individuals each of whom separately has a fixed Hawk or Dove nature.)

There are, of course, many examples in Nature of organisms faced with Hawk-Dove choices (whether to fight or retreat). Nor is it at all hard to imagine human analogs in the realms of warfare, politics, business, or anywhere that jockeying for position is important.[14] The essential feature is that each player must balance "cowardly" loss of the prize against the even greater loss should potential conflict become actual.

In Tender Trap, putting together a *critical mass* provided a way of escaping the inferior of the two solutions. In Chicken or Hawk-Dove (I will more usually employ the latter metaphor from now on), the trap takes the form of the EE mixed strategy with some positive probability of inefficient mutual losses due to Hawk-Hawk interactions. Critical mass does not provide any route out of Hawk-Dove. Instead, the obvious mode of escape is to somehow arrange that at each meeting one party will take the role of Hawk and the other the role of Dove. Any means of doing this would be PPP-efficient, but for the method to be viable each organism would have to be able to play each role about half the time. In effect, a convention is needed to assure that when two parties meet their behavior will be *nonparallel,* in contrast with the parallelism convention needed under Tender Trap.

If the two parties can be regarded as arriving randomly (as in search or exploration situations) at the location of the prize, "first come first served" would provide such a convention. Each organism would be first about half the time. Remarkably, this precursor of ownership or property rights has evolved in Nature in a number of ecological circumstances.[15]

Mathematically, the convention last come first served would do as well, but I know of no examples of this in Nature (and few in human affairs).[16]

First come first served as the basis for conventional avoidance of conflict is an example of what Maynard Smith (43) calls an *uncorrelated asymmetry*. Another example might be sex (for example, males defer to females). At least as important are *correlated asymmetries*[17] —for example, differences in the parties' adeptness at Hawking or Doving behaviors, or differences in their valuations of the prize. Perhaps the most obvious such convention would be "weaker defers to stronger." In Nature it is very commonly observed that after only a test of strength (taking the form of *limited combat,* in which the parties do not use their most lethal weapons or tactics) the weaker party does give way [Lorenz (37), Maynard Smith (43)].

Now for the Prisoners' Dilemma (Matrix 3). The tale is probably familiar. Two prisoners, held incommunicado, can be convicted only of a misdemeanor and suffer mild punishment (-1) if they both refuse to confess; they can be convicted of a felony and will suffer heavier punishment (-10) if they both confess. But if one confesses and the other does not, the authorities will release the first (0 penalty) and throw the book at the second (-20). Here mutual choice of the omertà strategy #1 provides a large efficiency gain. Yet, it is in each party's selfish interest to choose the fink strategy #2—regardless of what the other does! (That is, strategy #2 "dominates" #1.) The fink-fink outcome is the sole Nash equilibrium (NE) and the sole evolutionary equilibrium (EE). It might be regarded as a tough trap, in contrast with the tender trap of Matrix 1.

The Prisoners' Dilemma model has a wide range of applicability. The typical economic "externality" or "commons" problem falls into this pattern. If all nations were to cut back whaling activities, there would be a collective benefit (efficiency gain) to be shared from preservation of this valuable resource. Yet, it pays each alone to engage in whaling without regard to long-run considerations. Note that this is not a merely "defensive" policy made necessary by others' greed; even if other nations practiced restraint, each separate nation is motivated to engage in unrestrained whaling. (Indeed, it may often be the case—though not for the particular numbers shown in our Matrix 3—that restraint on the part of others *increases* the gains of the selfish or fink strategy.) On the other hand, Prisoners' Dilemma need not be socially disfunctional in the larger sense; the cooperation it subverts may be a conspiracy against the public.[18] This is presumably the case for the two prisoners of the initial example. And similarly for cartel agreements to restrict production.

Before turning to the large question of possible escapes from the Prisoners' Dilemma trap, it will be very useful to note that all three classes of mixed-motive games considered to this point can be put in the general format of Matrix 4. A generalized Tender Trap would have $x < 1$, $y < 0$. (In this generalized form, Tender Trap will not be a pure game of coordination; there is *some* conflict of interest whenever $x \neq y$.) Hawk-Dove has $x > 1$, $y > 0$ (with $x + y > 2$ in the more interesting case for which the off-diagonal cells are efficient outcomes). And Prisoners' Dilemma has $x > 1$, $y < 0$. I do not mean to suggest that all two-person symmetrical games with mixed conflict/cooperation incentives can be put in this format; Matrix 5, known as "Battle of the Sexes" [see Luce and Raiffa (39), ch. 5] represents a mixed-incentive game characterized by a somewhat different kind of symmetry. But I will consider only the generalized Matrix 4 pattern here, in order to explore a little more rigorously the nature and determinants of evolutionary equilibrium.

The evolutionary equilibrium (EE) strategy is one that, broadly speaking, will drive others out of existence by "defeating" them in binary encounters. If the population can be regarded as of infinite size, the average return α to the first strategy in Matrix 4, where p is the population fraction adopting that strategy, is:[19]

$$\alpha = (p)1 + (1 - p)y. \tag{1}$$

Similarly, the average return β to the second strategy is:

$$\beta = (p)x + (1 - p)0. \tag{2}$$

The first strategy will on average defeat the second, and therefore drive it out, whenever $\alpha - \beta$ exceeds zero, where:

$$\alpha - \beta \equiv p(1 - x) + (1 - p)y. \tag{3}$$

There are three qualitatively different types of situations, as illustrated by the three lines in Figure 1. The dotted line I corresponds to the generalized Tender Trap ($x < 1$, $y < 0$). As can be seen, for p sufficiently large $\alpha - \beta$ is positive, and so the proportion adopting the first strategy tends to grow. But for p sufficiently low, $\alpha - \beta$ is negative and the dynamic trend goes the other way. Thus, the two evolutionary equilibria are the extreme final situations C (where $p = 0$) and D (where $p = 1$); which one is attained depends upon the starting point. (At point K the two strategies are in balance, but K represents an unstable equilibrium.) The dashed line II corresponds to Chicken or Hawk-Dove ($x > 1$, $y > 0$). Here the *less* prevalent strategy has the advantage, the result being a mixed or interior solution at point L. Finally, line III represents Prisoners' Dilemma ($x > 1$, $y < 0$) for which the first (cooperative) strategy never has the advantage.[20]

I would have liked to claim that these simple curves represent *the* three ways in which potential cooperation may fail: (1) where lack of a critical mass traps the population at an inferior corner solution; (2)

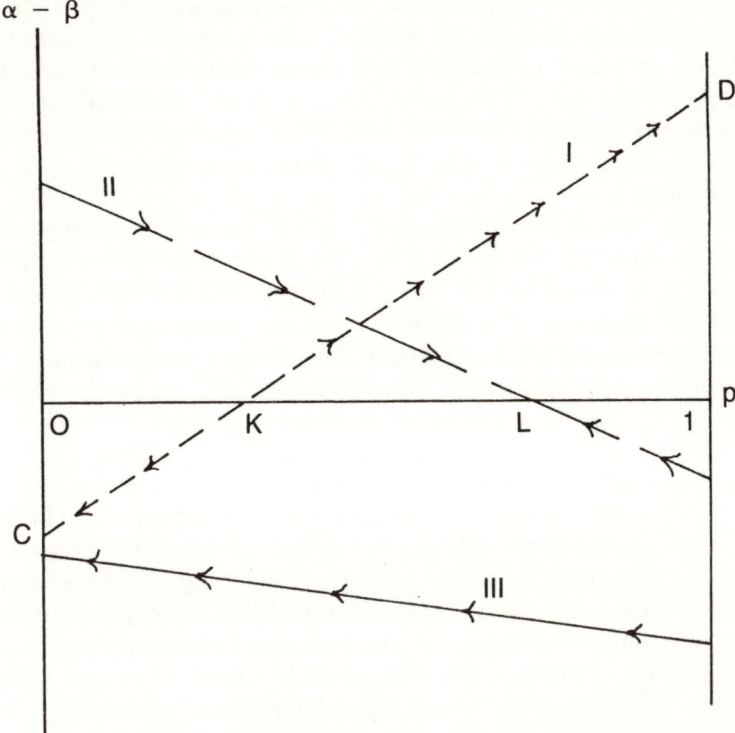

Figure 1. Three Classes of Cooperation Failures

where inability of a homogeneous population to arrive at a complementary pairing convention leads to an inferior mixed solution;[21] (3) where the "selfish" strategy is strictly dominant in terms of private calculations, despite the potential gain from mutual adoption of the cooperative strategy. While these three patterns do cover a surprising amount of territory,[22] it would be absurd to claim full generality. The underlying model remains excessively restrictive, in *at least* the following respects:

1. Not all symmetric patterns of mixed cooperation-conflict incentives have been covered (see, for example, Matrix 5).
2. The symmetry restriction (equivalent to assuming a homogeneous population) is severely limiting. More generally, at any moment of time a population would be characterized by a probability distribution along many relevant dimensions. For example, as already mentioned in connection with the Hawk-Dove game, some individuals may be better fighters than others, or may need the food more, etc.

3. Equally severe, perhaps, is the limitation to *dyadic* interactions. This is particularly relevant for us here, since the law is (at least in part) a way of converting dyadic into *triadic* social interactions. (There are the two contending agents, plus a third "uncommitted" party to decide between them.)

4. We have considered only binary-strategy situations (2×2 game matrices).

5. Finally, we have implicitly been ruling out any structuring of the interactions among individuals that might make possible binding agreements to cooperate, as by exchange. The difficulty is that contractual agreement does in general require some kind of outside (third party) enforcement, for example, law. What I am trying to do here, in effect, is to get a better focus upon the need for law by exploring the obstacles that cooperation encounters without it.

It follows that there are more complex forms of mixed-incentive cooperation/conflict interactions than we have yet gone into. Indeed, the number of qualitatively different mixed-incentive cases increases at a frightening rate when we depart from the simplifying assumptions of this section, which is undoubtedly why the problem of cooperation versus conflict remains so baffling. In the next section I shall mainly pursue one particular line of inquiry, into the possible modes of escape from the Prisoners' Dilemma—the "tough trap" for potential cooperators. These escape routes typically involve relaxing one or the other of the restrictive conditions mentioned above. Yet, as we shall see, a plausible escape route often leads toward other, more intricate traps that subvert cooperation in subtler ways.

V.   ESCAPES, MAINLY FROM THE PRISONERS' DILEMMA

The Prisoners' Dilemma has been by far the most studied pattern of cooperation failure—failure to achieve a potential mutual benefit in the strict Pareto sense, or possibly even an aggregate "efficiency" gain in the potentially Pareto-preferred (PPP) sense. Also, as we have seen, the Prisoners' Dilemma does represent the toughest trap, mainly because the noncooperator strategy is actually *dominant* (preferred whatever the choice of the other participant).

However, it will be of interest to show more rigorously how the ownership (first come first served) convention mentioned in the preceding section can actually provide an escape route from cooperation failures of the Chicken or Hawk-Dove type. Following Maynard Smith (43) we can suppose that the Hawk-Dove game (Matrix 2b) is expanded by the

Matrix 6
Hawk-Dove-Bourgeois

		C_1 (Dove)	C_2 (Hawk)	C_3 (Bourgeois)
(Dove)	R_1	2,2	0,10	1,6
(Hawk)	R_2	10,0	−5,−5	+2 1/2,−2 1/2
(Bourgeois)	R_3	6,1	−2 1/2,+2 1/2	5,5

Matrix 7
Prisoners' Dilemma
(Cost-Benefit Format, b > c)

		C_1 (Helper)	C_2 (Nonhelper)
(Helper)	R_1	−c+b,−c+b	−c,b
(Nonhelper)	R_2	b,−c	0,0

Matrix 8
Prisoners' Dilemma with Retaliators

		C_1 (Helper)	C_2 (Nonhelper)	C_3 (Retaliator)
(Helper)	R_1	−c+b,−c+b	−c,b	−c+b,−c+b
(Nonhelper)	R_2	b,−c	0,0	0,0
(Retaliator)	R_3	−c+b,−c+b	0,0	−c+b,−c+b

addition of a third "Bourgeois" strategy (Matrix 6). The Bourgeois rule is: When you are the first-comer in possession of the resource, play like a Hawk; when the late-comer, play like a Dove. That is, when an owner, fight to defend your property; when an interloper, defer to others' ownership.

The elements of the R_3,C_1 interaction (Bourgeois encountering Dove) in the lower-left cell of Matrix 6 are derived as follows. On average, half the time Bourgeois will be in an ownership situation against Dove, thus reaping the 10 units of income that Hawk would obtain against Dove; the other half of the time, Bourgeois as nonowner would receive only the 2 units of income that Dove would obtain against Dove. Averaging the two, the return to Bourgeois against Dove is 6. By analogous reasoning, the second element of the lower-left cell (the return to Dove against Bourgeois) is 1. The elements in the other new cells can be derived in the same way.

How about efficiency? Note that the maximum aggregate income of 10 units is attained at the old off-diagonal outcomes (R_1,C_2 and R_2,C_1) as well as at the Bourgeois-Bourgeois (R_3,C_3) outcome. All three solutions are therefore equally efficient in the PPP sense. Furthermore, each is a Nash equilibrium (NE).

But it still has to be shown which, if any, is an *evolutionary* equilibrium EE. The first step is to calculate the expected returns α, β, and γ to the three strategies Hawk, Dove, and Bourgeois, respectively—as functions of the corresponding population proportions p,q,r (where, of course, r = 1 − p − q). Then we have to find the ranges of values for p,q,r in which each strategy defeats the others, and the implied dynamic directions of change in those proportions. The algebra is rather tedious, but the result can be shown in Figure 2 (which is a kind of generalization of Figure 1). As the arrows indicate, there is a dynamic convergence toward the origin—that is, toward p = q = 0, which implies r = 1. In other words, only the Bourgeois strategy survives in the evolutionary equilibrium. (In Figure 2, at point A the gains from the three strategies are in balance, but this is a dynamically *unstable* equilibrium like point K in Figure 1.)

There is a fly in the ointment, however. Ability to play a Bourgeois strategy would seem to require a more complex mentality, or at least

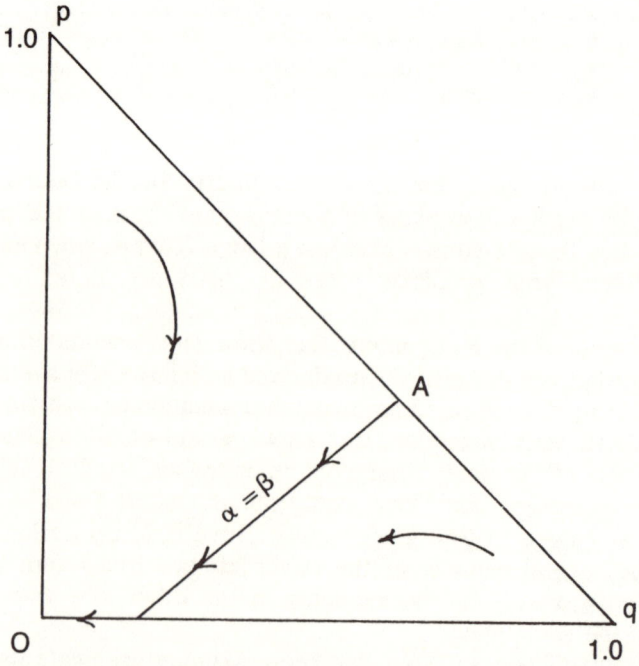

Figure 2.   Convergence to "Bourgeois" EE (Hawk-Dove-Bourgeois Game)

biochemistry: the Bourgeois strategist must be able to distinguish between owner and interloper situations, and must be able to execute the appropriate behavioral maneuvers of both Hawk and Dove. It seems reasonable to suppose that these capacities impose a certain burden; if so, the elements of the R_3,C_3 cell might become (for example) 4,4 rather than 5,5. This would mean, first, that a population of Bourgeois players is definitely a less efficient solution than complementary pairings of Hawk and Dove. In Figure 2, it also suggests that point A would become a stable rather than unstable equilibrium. Thus, making due allowance for the costs of a more elaborate behavioral repertory, the overall result might be an analog of Tender Trap—the population might tend toward either an evolutionary equilibrium at pure-Bourgeois, or a stable Hawk-Dove mixture, depending upon the starting point. This theoretical result need not surprise us. Since it seems plausible that not every population in a Hawk-Dove environment has succeeded in finding the Bourgeois way out of the trap, we would have proved too much in demonstrating that pure-Bourgeois is the *only* evolutionary equilibrium.

Nevertheless, there are many fascinating examples of respect for ownership in nature. Robert Ardrey (3), in a well-known popular work, attributed this to a somewhat mystic force which serves the good of the species by minimizing the scope of inefficient combat. The Maynard Smith development, in contrast, shows that respect for ownership is a possible evolutionary emergence that need not call upon any force other than private advantage. What is required (apart from the critical mass problem just alluded to) is only that the environment provide the particular patterns of mixed individual incentives for cooperation versus conflict represented by the underlying Hawk-Dove game. On the human level, a corresponding environmental situation might be expected to lead to a "social ethic" supporting a system of property rights [Hirshleifer (31)]. (For our purposes, it is not essential whether this ethic is a genetically implanted or a culturally learned pattern.)

We can now turn to the tougher cooperation trap represented by the Prisoners' Dilemma (PD). In this section it will be convenient to set up the PD matrix in a cost-benefit format (Matrix 7). Each act of "helping" costs the donor organism c, and benefits the recipient organism by the amount b, where $b > c$. Mutual helping is evidently efficient, but the parties are trapped at the Nonhelping (0,0) equilibrium. Critical mass provides no escape route here; even if 99 percent of the other organisms one is likely to encounter are behaving as Helpers, it still pays to play Nonhelper.[23] Nor is there a possible gain from any kind of ownership convention—Nonhelping remains dominant no matter what the other player does.

There is, of course, the valid escape route through reciprocation or contractual exchange: each party promises to act cooperatively, *provided* the other does. Smith's Theorem is potentially at work in Prisoners' Dilemma as it is in *all* mixed cooperation-conflict situations.

In what follows, a number of escape routes *not* requiring third party intervention or support will be discussed in turn. There is a certain sense in the sequence of topics, though no attempt will be made at a taxonomy of escape modes apart from a major division between symmetrical and asymmetrical strategy games.

A. Symmetric Strategies

1. The Silver Rule

Determined uncontingent Helpers are following the *Golden Rule* of social interaction; selfish Nonhelpers, the *Brass Rule*. How about the *Silver Rule*—responding to help with help, to nonhelp with nonhelp? Matrix 8 represents an expansion of Matrix 7 by addition of such a "Retaliator" strategy. This game has two symmetrical Nash equilibria— Nonhelper-Nonhelper and Retaliator-Retaliator. The latter, if it can be attained, would be just as efficient as the ideal Helper-Helper outcome. Both these NE's are "weak," in that there is in each case a second equally attractive strategy available for either player. Consequently, in an evolutionary model we might expect some random drift away from each of the NE's. The dynamic calculations to obtain the evolutionary equilibria (EE's) are rather troublesome but the results are pictured in Figure 3. Here α,β,γ represent the expected returns to Helper, Non-helper, and Retaliator, respectively. In Zone I (above the line where $\beta = \gamma$), there is strong convergence toward point K ($q = 1$, or an all-Nonhelper population). But point K, while a stable equilibrium with respect to Zone I, is unstable with respect to Zone II. So drift into Zone II and consequent convergence toward the origin O ($r = 1 - p - q = 1$, or an all-Retaliator population) then occur. However, O is only neutrally stable along the dotted range of the vertical axis (up to point L where $p = 1 - c/b$). If a sufficiently large fraction of the population consists of Retaliators, any individual organism can do as well being a pure Helper. (But if the proportion of Helpers ever exceeded $1 - c/b$, we are in Zone II where it becomes profitable for Nonhelpers to enter.) At point L itself all three strategies yield equal returns, and so this endpoint of the dotted range is unstable. Subject to a fuller study of the dynamics, it seems reasonable to conclude that after a possible initial transient the population proportions would, almost all the time, lie some-

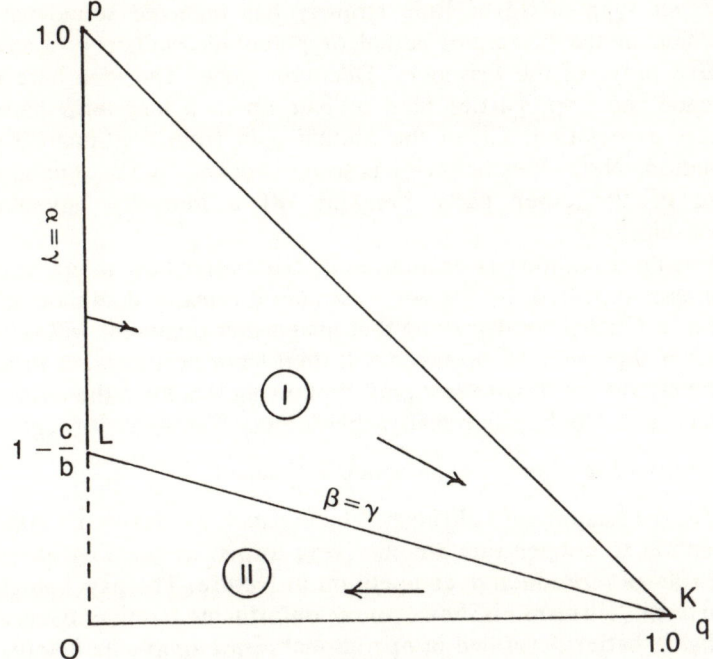

Figure 3. Neutral EE Range (Prisoners' Dilemma with Retaliator Strategy)

where on the dotted interval in Figure 3. That is, the population would be a mixture of Retaliators and pure Helpers.

So far, so good, but this otherwise attractive escape from the Prisoners' Dilemma has a flaw analogous to that discussed in connection with the Bourgeois strategy. The Retaliator must be able to recognize Helpers and Nonhelpers, and must also possess both helping and nonhelping capabilities in its repertory of feasible actions. These capacities again probably impose a certain cost upon being a Retaliator rather than pure Helper. Then, in an all-Retaliator population ($r = 1$), it would be *strictly* more profitable (rather than only equally profitable) to be a pure Helper instead. Thus the all-Retaliator population is not an equilibrium, and in fact the final outcome will be an all-Nonhelper population. We are back in the Prisoners' Dilemma. Note that the "cost of complexity" difficulty subverts the Bourgeois strategy in a Hawk-Dove environment situation only to the extent of requiring a critical mass before Bourgeois can become an EE, whereas it entirely destroys any hope of a Retaliator EE in a Prisoners' Dilemma environment.

Another type of Silver Rule strategy has received somewhat more discussion in the literature: actual or potential retaliatory behavior in *repeated plays* of the Prisoners' Dilemma game. The idea here is that to escape the trap, parties tend to pair up in a long-term pattern of business association. Given the mutual gain from continuance of the association, Nonhelper behavior is to be checked by the retaliatory response of the other party breaking off a mutually advantageous relationship.[24]

But again a paradox is encountered. No matter how many times the PD game is repeated, on the *very last* play it remains dominant strategy to act as a Nonhelper. Knowing that his partner-opponent will rationally behave in this way, each player will then have no incentive to act cooperatively on the *next-to-last* play. Following this logic the entire game unravels, and Nonhelper remains the dominant strategy throughout.[25]

2. *Nepotism and Other Discrimination Techniques*

Under the heading of "altruism," biologists have devoted a great deal of attention to cooperation among living forms, as seeming exceptions to the rule of reproductive competition in Nature. The psychological or ethical term "altruism" is, however, an unfortunate terminological choice for what is better described in operational terms simply as *helping*. The clearest instances of helping behavior are associated with kinship (nepotism). That parents care for offspring, that blood is thicker than water, is commonly though by no means universally observed in Nature or in human affairs. To some extent at least, relatedness seems to provide a way out of the Prisoners' Dilemma. My purpose here is to explore how this mechanism works, and more generally to understand how analogous mechanisms can apply to other forms of mutual aid.

We can think of a population in which a "gene for helping" H is in competition with a "gene for nonhelping" N. It might be thought that Nonhelpers will always be free riders upon Helpers, so that the H gene could never be viable.[26] But, as we shall see, helping can be viable despite free-riding if the ecological circumstances provide for a sufficient degree of *discrimination* in which aid is preferentially directed toward fellow Helpers. Kinship is one mechanism that provides the basis for such discrimination.[27]

The basic kin-selection model is due to Hamilton (25), but a more tractable version has been put forward by Charnov (9).[28] Quite generally, before bringing in nepotism, we can ask under what conditions W_H will exceed W_N—the "fitness" or viability of the helping gene H will exceed that of the nonhelping gene N. Let b and c be the benefit conferred and cost incurred of each helping act, let p be the proportion of the population bearing the helping gene, and finally let m be the discrimination factor—

the fraction of helping acts received by fellow Helpers. Then, the viability condition $W_H > W_N$ can be expressed as:

$$-c + bm > b(1 - m)\frac{p}{1 - p}. \tag{4}$$

On the left-hand side, the first term $-c$ is the cost incurred by the Helper (measured in fitness units, and normalized so that there is one helping act per time period). The second term, bm, represents the average per-Helper benefit of helping acts (per time period) that are directed at *fellow Helpers*. The right-hand side, analogously, shows the average *per-Nonhelper* (free rider) benefit of helping acts per time period. Inequality (4) reduces to:

$$\frac{c}{b} < \frac{m - p}{1 - p}. \tag{5}$$

Thus we see that for helping to be competitively superior to nonhelping, a *necessary* (though not sufficient) condition is $m > p$—helping acts must be disproportionately directed to fellow Helpers.

All that has been said so far is perfectly general; kinship has not entered specifically at all. Still deferring the specifics of kinship, we can use Matrix 9 to gain a better understanding of the role played by the discrimination factor m. Matrix 9 is in the standard form of Matrix 7 except for the introduction of new "recognition coefficients" v_H and $\bar{v}_N$. The first of these, v_H, is the conditional probability that an encountered Helper will be recognized as such by a fellow Helper and therefore will be "correctly" granted aid (in the form of the benefit b). The conditional probability that an encountered Nonhelper will be helped (because of being *incorrectly* recognized as a fellow Helper) is denoted $\bar{v}_N$. These two coefficients are in principle independent; for example, an organism might never fail to recognize a fellow Helper yet often treat Nonhelpers as Helpers. The discrimination factor m will generally be functionally related to v_H and $\bar{v}_N$, as well as to p. More specifically, $m/(1 - m)$—the ratio of correctly to incorrectly directed helping acts—can be expressed as:

$$\frac{m}{1 - m} = \frac{p\, v_H}{(1 - p)\bar{v}_N}. \tag{6}$$

Or,

$$m = \frac{pv_H}{pv_H + (1 - p)\bar{v}_N}. \tag{7}$$

Example: If $v_H = .8$, $\bar{v}_N = .4$, and $p = .25$, then $m = .4$. Evidently, m will rise as v_H increases, and fall as $\bar{v}_N$ increases.

Matrix 9
Prisoners' Dilemma
with Recognition

		C_1 (Helper)	C_2 (Nonhelper)
(Helper)	R_1	$v_H(b-c), v_H(b-c)$	$\overline{v}_N(-c), \overline{v}_N b$
(Nonhelper)	R_2	$\overline{v}_N b, \overline{v}_N(-c)$	0,0

Matrix 10
Prisoners' Dilemma
with Asymmetrical Commitment

		C_1 (Helper)	C_2 (Nonhelper)
(Helper)	R_1	$-c+b, -c+b$	$-c, b$
(Nonhelper)	R_2	$b, -c$	0,0
(Committer)	R_3	$-c+b, -c+b$	0,0

We now want to compare the expected returns α and β to the Helper and Nonhelper strategies, respectively:[29]

$$\alpha = p v_H(b - c) - (1 - p)\overline{v}_N c = p v_H b - c[p v_H + (1 - p)\overline{v}_N] \quad (8)$$

$$\beta = p\overline{v}_N b. \quad (9)$$

The condition for α to exceed β is then:

$$p > \frac{\overline{v}_N c}{(b - c)(v_H - \overline{v}_N)}. \quad (10)$$

We see that the ratio on the right-hand side is a kind of critical mass. Should p ever exceed it, Helping will grow until the population consists exclusively of Helpers. The critical mass will be more difficult of attainment the higher are c and $\overline{v}_N$ and the lower are b and v_H.

The incorporation of constant recognition factors thus converts the Prisoners' Dilemma into a Tender Trap situation, as discussed in Section IV above, for which the stability considerations are as pictured by the line labeled I in Figure 1. But, unfortunately, if the population is initially in a Nonhelping mode, putting together the critical mass needed to escape the trap will not be easy.

Example: Using our previous numbers $v_H = .8$; $\overline{v}_N = .4$, and supposing that b = 10 and c = 5, the critical value for p is 1! Thus, if the population were already all Helpers, they might remain so—but any smaller initial proportion of Helpers would spiral downward to the pure Nonhelper situation p = 0. And this despite a favorable 2:1 benefit-cost ratio b/c, and a similarly favorable recognition ratio $v_H/\overline{v}_N$.

While constant recognition coefficients v_H and $\bar{v}_N$ lead to a Tender Trap type of situation as in line I in Figure 1, a constant discrimination factor m would lead to a Hawk-Dove class of solution with a stable interior equilibrium as in line II of Figure 1.[30] That is, in equilibrium a certain proportion p* of the population would be Helpers and the remainder Nonhelpers. A stable m implies varying v_H and $\bar{v}_N$. In particular, for m to be actually or nearly constant, it must be that as p rises either v_H falls or $\bar{v}_N$ rises (or both). This might characterize a "mimicry" situation, in which Nonhelpers try to cheat by disguising their identities. Then, it seems reasonable to believe, as the proportion of true Helpers rises it is easier for the few cheaters to successfully disguise themselves.

Now we can turn to *kinship* as a means of escape from the Prisoners' Dilemma trap. We may note from Eq. (7) that, for any *constant* recognition coefficients (however favorable), the discrimination factor m approaches zero as p goes to zero. This is what makes it hard for a critical mass of Helpers to evolve. But, for kinship helping, there is a considerably better lower bound on m. Suppose we are talking of siblings, for whom genetic relatedness is r = 1/2. (The probability of two siblings having received the same gene at any given haploid locus—that is, of both having inherited the mother's gene or both the father's gene—equals 50 percent.) What happens when p approaches zero? We can imagine that the helping gene arose as a single new mutation in one parent. Then, if a given offspring of that parent is a Helper, there is a 50 percent chance that its sibling is a fellow Helper. Thus, at the limit, m = r = 1/2. And in fact, for sibling helping the relation between m and p is:

$$m = \frac{1 + p}{2}. \tag{11}$$

Even when p approaches zero, the proportion of helping acts directed at fellow Helpers never goes below 50 percent, and m rises toward unity as p increases.[31]

It follows immediately that the population will evolve toward cooperation (p = 1) of the Help-your-sibling variety if and only if:

$$c/b < 1/2. \tag{12}$$

Or, more generally for any degree of relatedness r, if and only if:

$$c/b < r. \tag{13}$$

Thus, helping relatives will be more viable in evolutionary terms than nonhelping whenever the cost-benefit ratio of the helping act is less than the degree of relatedness. For efficiency in the PPP sense, however, the rule "should" be to help whenever c/b < 1. Thus, *even within the kinship group* the kin-selection process provides only a partial escape from the Prisoners' Dilemma.

3. Group Selection

A topic much debated among biologists is the degree to which evolution of cooperative behavior may be due to *group selection*. Under kin selection, the favorable discrimination factor m needed to make helping viable is achieved because helping one's relatives is likely to mean helping fellow carriers of one's own helping gene H. In the genetic sense, a relative *is* partially one's self. Under group selection, the discrimination needed for viability of H is supposed to be achieved simply by propinquity, combined with improved survival of groups containing helpers.

In anthropological terms, it seems reasonable to infer that the shift from small kinship-based bands to large nations has been associated with a corresponding shift from kin selection to group selection as the major winnowing process in human evolution. Kin selection still, it is evident, retains importance today for eliciting helping actions within the family. But we are much more interested in the viability of cooperative behaviors among *unrelated* individuals in the group structures of modern life.

Kin selection and group selection are often hard to distinguish in practice. Neighbors are more likely than random members of a population to share common ancestry. To illustrate the power and limitations of group selection, we will analyze a simple model containing no element of kinship.

Suppose an entire population swarms together at mating time, but otherwise divides itself quite randomly into propinquity subgroups. Then, by sheer chance, certain subgroups will be characterized by higher-than-average fractions of help-your-neighbor H genes—even though members of a given subgroup are not otherwise any more closely related than average. The mechanism of group selection postulates that the viability of subgroups will be strongly correlated with the proportions of helpers they contain. Differential subgroup survival will then tend to raise the overall fraction of H genes in the population. The problem, however, is that *within* each subgroup containing Helpers, it pays Nonhelpers to free ride upon them. It has been shown that it is nevertheless mathematically possible for the proportion p of Helpers in the population to increase; the intergroup gain from helping may overcome the intragroup loss. But the dominant opinion among biologists is that the conditions for this to occur are so special that, *factually* speaking, group selection essentially never operates[32] in Nature—at least, below the level of *Homo sapiens*.

Analysis in terms of the discrimination factor m sheds some additional light upon the difficulty with group selection. If in fact a population broke up merely randomly into binomially distributed samples of unrelated carriers of H and N genes, then propinquity alone would dictate that m—the overall proportion of helping acts directed at fellow Helpers— would just equal p! Condition (5) could not be met, and helping would not be viable. To make it viable, some other conditions would have to be modified. For example, it might be that the per-act benefit b is not a constant but increases with the number of Helpers per group, thanks to some kind of increasing returns. Alternatively, it might be that group-ing causes the recognition coefficients v_H and $\overline{v}_N$ to take on more fa-vorable values.

Whatever the mechanism may be, it can only work through differential survival of Helper and Nonhelper genes as a function of the number of cooperative individuals falling into any given subgroup. To take the simplest case, suppose that after the initial mating swarm the population divides into subgroups of exactly two members each. With random seg-regation, if the proportion of H genes in the population is p then the proportion of groups containing two Helpers will be p^2, the proportion containing just one Helper will be 2pq (where $q = 1 - p$), and the proportion containing zero Helpers will be q^2.

Let s_{2H} be the per-capita survival probability of Helper individuals in groups of two H's, let s_{ON} be the per-capita survival probability of Non-helper individuals in groups of two N's, and let s_{1H} and s_{1N} be the respective survival chances of each type of individual in mixed groups. We would expect the survival probabilities to rank as follows: $s_{1N}, s_{2H} > s_{1H}, s_{ON}$. That is, the more profitable situations are (1) to be a free rider upon a Helper partner (s_{1N}), or (2) to be one of the two Helpers in an all-H group (s_{2H}). The less profitable situations are (3) to be a Helper with a Nonhelper partner (s_{1H}), or else to be one of two Nonhelpers (s_{ON}). (The proper rankings within the upper and the lower pairs will be left open for the moment.)

After the differential selection of H and N genes[33] represented by these survival probabilities takes place, in the next mating swarm the new Helper/Nonhelper ratio $(p/q)'$ in the overall population will be:

$$(p/q)' = \frac{p^2 s_{2H} + pq s_{1H}}{q^2 s_{ON} + pq s_{1N}}. \tag{14}$$

At equilibrium, $(p/q)'$ would have to equal p/q, so:

$$1 = \frac{p s_{2H} + q s_{1H}}{q s_{ON} + p s_{1N}}.$$

Or,

$$\frac{p}{q} = \frac{s_{1H} - s_{ON}}{s_{1N} - s_{2H}}. \tag{15}$$

It may be verified that this is a stable interior solution if both numerator and denominator on the right-hand side of Eq. (15) are positive. The H gene will remain present in the population at large if $s_{1H} > s_{ON}$, and the N gene if $s_{1N} > s_{2H}$. When these conditions are met, *within* each subgroup we have a Hawk-Dove type of game (as described in Section IV). If we had instead a true within-subgroup Prisoners' Dilemma, so that it *always* paid to be a Nonhelper whatever the other party played, the survival probabilities would show $s_{1N} < s_{ON}$ as well as $s_{2H} < s_{1N}$—the H gene would not be viable at all in the population. Put another way, for the H gene to survive in this model despite the advantage of being a free rider when one's partner is a Helper (that is, where the denominator in Eq. (15) is positive), it must be that when one's partner is a Nonhelper it is *selfishly* advantageous to be a Helper (that is, the numerator must be positive). This seems rather implausible; we would probably expect the numerator in Eq. (15) to be negative. But there is another route to viability of helping—the denominator might be negative. If *only* the denominator were negative, q would go to zero and all the population would be Helpers in equilibrium. In what is probably the most interesting case, where *both* numerator and denominator are negative, the interior equality will be unstable—the population will go to all-H or all-N depending upon the initial situation. Then, a critical mass would be necessary for viability of helping behavior. (Compare the Tender Trap game in Section IV.)[34]

If we think in terms of selection operating among (and within) human groups, the increasing-returns factor mentioned earlier tends to make s_{2H} very big, thus contributing to a negative denominator in Eq. (15). One arena where increasing returns to within-group cooperation are particularly effective is warfare,[35] and warfare among humans has been a potent selective force [Alexander (1), ch. 4]. Suppose it is the case that $s_{2H} > s_{1N}$. That means your survival chances, if your partner is a Hero, are better fighting alongside him than running away. If in addition $s_{1H} > s_{ON}$ (even if your partner runs away, it is still better to fight on), the numerator in Eq. (15) is positive and the Nonhelper gene will be driven out. This does seem implausible. But even if the latter condition fails, there will still be a critical mass for p beyond which only helping behavior is viable so long as s_{2H} exceeds s_{1N}. And the critical mass is the more easily achieved the greater is this difference.

The other force tending to raise the discrimination factor m is improved recognition within groups, which allows carriers of the H gene to modify their behavior so as to reward fellow-H's and punish N's. This seems a likely result of human intelligence. In particular, suppose it really does not make sense to fight on if one's partner runs away ($s_{1H} < s_{ON}$). Then, a smart Hero will act accordingly—that is, will run away himself. If his recognition coefficient for Nonhelper partners were perfect ($\overline{v}_N = 0$), his recognition-adjusted survival probability would then be $s'_{1H} = s_{ON}$ rather than $s_{1H} < s_{ON}$. Even short of this, any improved s'_{1H} relative to s_{ON} would reduce the negative balance in the numerator of Eq. (15) and thus tend to make Helping more viable.

B. Nonsymmetric Strategies

We have already seen how a kind of asymmetry may lead to *complementary* strategic choices in the Hawk-Dove game—converting the solution from an interior mixture of Hawks and Doves to fully efficient Hawk-Dove pairing. We are here considering possible asymmetries in the Prisoners' Dilemma context. There are, of course, many possible dimensions along which some degree of asymmetry may obtain: the payoffs might diverge from the fully symmetrical form of Matrix 7, or there might be differential knowledge of these elements, or differential communication capacities, or the players might vary in their ability to recognize fellow Helpers, and so on. In this section, however, I will mainly consider an asymmetry in ability to employ threat or promise strategies.

A more general statement is in order first. We have so far been considering only interactions within homogeneous populations, encounters where the player choosing Row comes from the same population as the player choosing Column. In all such cases Nonhelpers are free riders on Helpers. A bird that endangers itself by calling out to others when a predator appears would be subject to free-riding on the part of those who never call warnings. In Matrix 7, this feature is represented by the advantage of Nonhelpers over Helpers in the off-diagonal cells. But when the interacting players come from *different* populations, free-riding disappears. A bee following a Nonhelper strategy of refusing to pick up pollen from a flower does not gain thereby; the flower loses, but so does the bee. Evidently, there is no Prisoners' Dilemma trap here at all; if a mutual benefit exists, the Helper strategy is dominant for both players. It is quite generally easier, therefore, to convert potential into actual cooperation when the players come from *different* populations, or are otherwise in less direct competition with one another. One advantage of sexual over asexual reproduction, perhaps, is that sex divides the population into largely noncompeting halves. Males compete with males, and females with females, but the male-female interaction is complementary.[36]

Turning back to the Prisoners' Dilemma, I shall consider a particular form of nonsymmetrical strategy—*commitment to a threat or a promise.* Commitment is very much like the Retaliator strategy represented in the symmetric Matrix 8: the player cooperates with Helpers but not with Nonhelpers. But here we allow only *one* of the players to adopt such a strategy, as shown in Matrix 10.

The type of commitment strategy dealt with here represents adoption of a fixed *conditional-reaction function*. Its essence is restricting in advance one's freedom to select a response to the other party's choice.[37] It is first an engagement to do something one would otherwise not do in order to influence the behavior of the other party. Second, the difference between commitment to a threat versus a promise is not fundamental. Threat, strictly speaking, would involve Committer in a self-damaging "punishment" response to Nonhelper behavior; promise, in a self-damaging "reward" response for Helper behavior.[38] Third, threats or promises involve *communication* as well as commitment. If the other party does not know of the commitment, or does not believe it, his behavior will not be affected. But only one-way communication is required, and indeed threats and promises may typically be more effective if only one-way communication is possible.

Incorporation of a Commitment strategy into the options of one player allows achievement of the efficient outcome. In Matrix 10, upon Row's commitment to R_3 and communication of that commitment, Column player will choose the Helper strategy C_1 so long as $b > c$—that is, whenever mutual helping satisfies the criterion of efficiency.

To achieve this result in pairwise interactions, the players would have to combine into subordinate-superordinate teams. For larger groupings, this form of teaming generalizes to a hierarchical ranking system in which each player makes a commitment-plus-communication move in relation to those below him.[39] One further implication may be of interest for our purposes. It was suggested above that law could be thought of as an institutionalized "impartial" third party whose function is to enforce agreements between members of potentially cooperating dyads. This left open the question of who is to play that role, and what would be his incentive. The present discussion illustrates another institutional model of law: hierarchy. Here the suggestion is that one possible basis of law is the threat (or promise) on the part of superordinate parties to mete out punishment should subordinates engage in noncooperative behavior (or to grant rewards for cooperative behavior). As an interesting point, it is not logically necessary that the superordinate player actually ends up any better off than do the subordinates! And, in fact, in our otherwise symmetrical Matrix 10 the two players do equally well. (In such a situation there might be unanimous agreement on the *principle* of hierarchy, even if the actual ranks were to be randomly chosen.) However, as a practical matter it seems likely that only an initial asymmetry of power will lead to this form of solution to the Prisoners' Dilemma, and consequently that the superordinate player will set up the terms of the association (the elements of the payoff matrix) so as to reap the superior outcome [see Section VII(B) below].

The Committer in Matrix 10 is promising to reward the other player by not playing his Nonhelper strategy R_2 if the latter plays the cooperative strategy C_1, but the other player knows that if he should play C_1, the Committer would be better off reneging (choosing R_2 anyway). How can threats (or promises) be made credible? As a means of providing the needed guarantee, Nature has evolved "uncontrollable" emotions—of loving gratitude or vengeful rage as the case may be. Put another way, it sometimes pays off to be irrational, to lose the capacity for optimizing choice. Even on the human level, emotions limit the possible scope of rational behavior—not always to our disadvantage.[40]

One interesting example of these ideas is the "Rotten Kid" model.[41] A selfish individual (the Rotten Kid) can be induced to engage in cooperative behavior by an appropriate promise of reward. One way of guaranteeing such reward is for the other member of the dyad (Big Daddy) to evolve a sufficient degree of benevolence for Rotten Kid. The strategic situation must be asymmetrical, in that Big Daddy must be able to *commit* himself to rewarding cooperation by distributing enough of the gain back to Rotten Kid. (And of course he must be able to communicate the fact of that commitment.) The emotion of love provides the needed guarantee. The crucial point is that *Big Daddy himself also ends up better off*. And better off not merely in terms of emotional satisfactions, but in terms of the actual material gains needed to make the commitment-to-benevolence strategy a viable one.

In Figure 4, on axes representing Daddy's income I_D versus Kid's income I_K, Rotten Kid simply wants to attain a position highest up in the I_K direction. (In effect, Kid's indifference curves are horizontal.) Daddy's degree of love and concern for Kid is illustrated by his normal-looking indifference curve U_D. We now must suppose that Kid makes the first move, and Daddy the second: Kid proposes, but Daddy disposes.[42] If Kid were short-sighted as well as selfish, he would choose point R*. But, knowing Daddy's emotion-based commitment, Kid in his long-run self-interest should choose position J*—which is jointly optimum (efficient) in the sense of achieving the highest sum $I_K + I_D$. From J*, Daddy makes a love-induced transfer along the 135° line SS to his indifference-curve tangency optimum A*. Kid's "pragmatic" cooperation has been repaid, since A* is higher up (involves larger I_K) than R*. But, what is more remarkable, Daddy's "hard-core" cooperation[43] has also paid off in material terms: I_D too is higher at J* than at R*. And

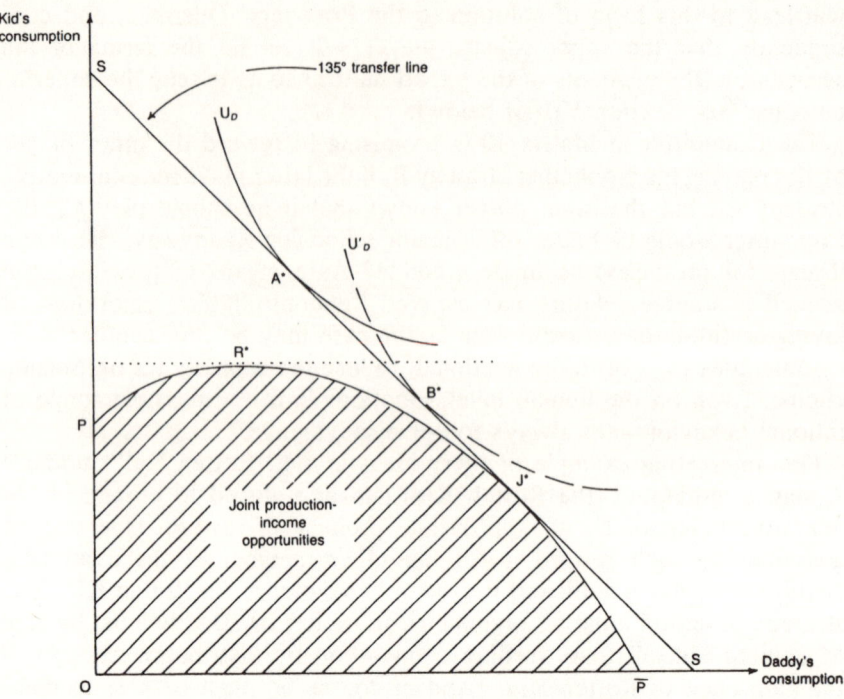

Figure 4.   Rotten Kid and Big Daddy

in fact, if Big Daddy were somewhat less loving, as represented by his alternative indifference curve U'_D, he would only react to Kid's cooperative move by more limited income transfers to point B*, which would be insufficient to motivate Kid to cooperate in the first place.

Benevolence or love on the one hand, rage or jealousy on the other, are the sorts of preferences or "tastes" that the economist is likely to regard as arbitrary brute facts. The evolutionary approach, in contrast, suggests that at least some aspects of preferences are not accidental, but have evolved as ways of restraining freedom of choice where such restraint can conduce to advantageous cooperation. More broadly speaking, it suggests (as will be brought out later) that social ethics, such as ingrained respect for property rights or obedience to constituted leaders, may also have evolved to aid group efficiency by allowing the Prisoners' Dilemma to be overcome.

A number of econo-legal scholars have suggested that "altruism" is a partial substitute for law in eliciting cooperative behavior.[44] The thrust of our theoretical development in Sections IV and V has been to the effect that the situation is far, far more complex than that. The likelihood that cooperative behavior will be viable depends on the details of the ecological situation (summarized, in our simple models, by the game matrices). Furthermore, helping can emerge among organisms evidently incapable of altruism in any ethical or psychological sense of the word. On the other hand, among more advanced animals, including man, emotions like benevolence and love can indeed serve to promote helping interactions—but it may well be that emotions like hate and rage are at least equally important (to induce, for example, "irrational" efforts to punish noncooperators).

Summarizing at this point: in Sections IV and V we have explored a number of alternative routes along which cooperation might evolve. In a binary-strategy world of random dyadic encounters between members of a homogeneous population, the possible payoff patterns (environmental situations) fall into a limited set of classes. In Tender Trap all the motivation is to cooperate, yet the population might (depending upon the initial situation and the required critical mass) not end up in the *best* cooperative solution. In Hawk-Dove there are mixed motives. The cooperative strategy (Dove) can be the more advantageous, up to a point, but not to the extent of driving out Hawk. (That is, each strategy is the more profitable once sufficiently rare in the population.) Thus, the result tends to be a mixed population (or a homogeneous population playing a mixture of strategies). What was rather significant is that some structuring of the possible encounters in Hawk-Dove may allow fully complementary efficient pairing. In particular, the evolutionary equilibrium achievable under the rule "first come first served" is a possible precursor of territoriality and property rights. This solution is associated with a Bourgeois strategy: playing Hawk against intruders, but Dove against possessors.

But if the environmental circumstances correspond to the game of Prisoners' Dilemma, where the cooperative strategy is always dominated by the noncooperative, evolution of mutual-aid interactions will be much more difficult. A Retaliator strategy would be the analog to Bourgeois in the Hawk-Dove game. Like Bourgeois, Retaliator represents self-enforcement of cooperation: Retaliator reacts favorably to good behavior, while punishing bad behavior committed against himself. But Retaliator seems not to be viable under Prisoners' Dilemma. Various other routes to cooperation do promise a degree of success. Nepotism (aiding only one's kin) facilitates cooperative interactions, but not so far as to achieve full efficiency even within the kinship group. Much the same can be said for other "discrimination" techniques, as in group selection, which focus aid upon individuals more likely to be fellow helpers. Ability to interact repeatedly with the same partner may also provide a partial escape. More interesting for our purposes here is the asymmetrical or hierarchical route out of the Prisoners' Dilemma. A player in a superordinate role

can make a pattern of cooperation effective by becoming *committed* to
a threat of punishment for bad behavior (or, what is essentially equivalent, a promise of reward for good behavior).

VI. COMPETITION AND EFFICIENCY

For ecobiologists in the Malthus-Darwin tradition, competition—in the
ruthless sense of the struggle for existence—is the fundamental principle
of Nature's economy. The source of competition is the limited resource
base of the globe in the face of the universal tendency of populations
to multiply. By natural selection the biosphere has come to teem with
life forms successful at pressing upon one another to obtain the nutrients
needed to sustain life.

Biologists have found it useful to distinguish three main classes of
competitive strategies: *scramble, interference,* and *predation.*[45] *Scramble*
competitors interact only through depletion of resources. The winning
organisms are those most effective at extracting energy and other needed
inputs from the external environment. *Interference* competitors, in contrast, gain and maintain control over resources by attacking (or otherwise
reducing the efficiency of) other contenders, mainly, though not exclusively, of their conspecifics. (Members of the same species, having a
higher overlap zone of resource needs, are typically closer rivals than
members of different species.) *Predation,* finally, is mainly interspe-
cific[46]—the competitor organisms have been made part of the resource
field.[47]

Competition in Nature, in all these forms, tends to be both antisocial
and wasteful of resources. And yet the economist views market competition as a harmonizing force, one that leads to productive efficiency.
What are the special features of market competition making this possible?
First, under idealized institutions of political economy only the more
innocuous form of scramble competition is permitted in the market.
When one businessman finds a customer for his output or a supplier for
needed input, he does indeed deplete the resource field for other businessmen. But he is not permitted to blow up his rival's shop (interference), or to stock his own store by raiding the other's inventory (predation). Second, again under idealized conditions, the adverse externalities
that the businessman imposes on his competitors are only pecuniary, as
discussed in Section II above. A less successful business competitor may
have to lower his product price quotation to customers, or raise his hire-
price offer to input suppliers, but in efficiency terms the effects of such
price adjustments cancel out. Another way of looking at this is to note
that market competition for the economist is not a two-sided but a three-

sided interaction. The market competitor vies not just *against* a rival, but *for* the opportunity to engage in mutually advantageous exchanges with other parties. The gain to third parties in this "vying competition" counterbalances any loss suffered by competitors. In simple two-sided "taking competition," in contrast, there is no such offsetting gain. The really useful distinction (so far as efficiency is concerned) is therefore not along the scramble-interference-predation dimension but rather is the dichotomy of competitive *vying versus taking*.

While the more downright *taking* form of competition is far more common in Nature, important instances of vying competition have evolved as well. In sexual competition there are two main modes of resolving rivalry for females:[48] (1) male combat and (2) female choice.[49] The latter comes close to what the economist would regard as mutually advantageous exchange. Where female choice obtains, males defer to the female's "property right" in her own reproductive capacity, which she will dispose of at her option to the most desired partner.

On the human level, *taking* in its extreme interference version is clearly the mode of competition in duels for survival such as Rome versus Carthage, or Ike Clanton versus Wyatt Earp. Such competition obviously tends to adopt inefficient or even violent methods. Turning back to male combat as an example of taking competition in Nature, the wasteful results include not only the direct damage which one or both combatants may suffer, but the consequent misdirected evolutionary trends, such as sexual dimorphism (the development of excessive male size, or weapons like horns and claws, that serve only for fighting other males). The consequences of human interference competition are entirely parallel, whether we speak in terms of genetic or cultural evolution.[50] But even the scramble form of taking competition is inefficient in the absence of property rights. An organism chancing upon a food source will consume it until the marginal benefit to itself falls to zero, even though stopping earlier might be more efficient for the species or other larger group, that is, might provide greater nourishment for the next searcher.

What has come to be known as *rent-seeking* is a less violent scramble form of competition in human affairs.[51] Where an asset exists that has not been reduced to recognized property, an inefficient struggle for the resource (or for the fruits thereof) tends to take place. This struggle takes two main forms. If the asset can be sequestered (for example, if it can become legally protected property), its value will thereafter be maintained even though valuable goods or services may have been initially wasted in the two-sided competition for it. An example would be a political struggle for a television channel or an airline route. Where the asset cannot be or is not sequestered at all, as in the case of common property resources like hunting grounds or underground aquifers, unlimited taking competition tends to sharply reduce the net social yield.

To achieve an ideal state of efficiency, property rights in all resources would have to be preassigned and perfectly respected. Absent these conditions there will be "excessive" efforts to acquire assets (if they can be sequestered) or to seize their fruits (if they cannot be sequestered). Such efforts include unlawful activities like theft (but recall that defending against theft is also inefficient).[52] Resource-taking may also occur because there is no relevant law, as when nations contend for power or territory. Or, finally, taking competition may take place even under law (which may or may not be regarded as an "imperfection" of the legal order). One example is the search for undiscovered resources like petroleum, fish, or ideas (whether patentable or not). Such search is, evidently, not totally wasteful. The increments to the community's stock of resources are socially useful, but it remains true that the degree of effort devoted to searching tends to be excessive.[53] The costly contests that take the form of redistributive politics, on the other hand, are unqualifiedly inefficient.[54]

We are not surprised that male combat for females, or struggles for territory, or pecking-order dominance (and their human analogs) represent wasteful forms of competition. Much more puzzling is why highly inefficient competition has evolved in Nature even in cases where the equivalent of preassigned and respected "property rights" does exist, specifically, in male competition for mates *even where female choice governs*. The peacocks with their burdensome tails are an obvious instance. Another case is that of the bower bird males, who toil at constructing attractive (rather than merely utilitarian) domiciles for prospective spouses. Two explanations have been offered. First, that the evolution of attractive sexual characters is a self-sustaining pattern, rather on the order of a chain letter or a speculative bubble [see Fisher (18), p. 152; Dawkins (15), p. 170]. It pays a peahen in the current generation to choose the cock with the largest tail, because her male offspring will then also tend to have big tails, thus attracting the next generation's peahens, who will prefer big-tailed cocks so that *their* sons will have big tails, and so on indefinitely. Alternatively, it has been suggested [Zahavi (75)] that we have here what the economist would call a "signalling equilibrium" [see Spence (61); Riley (51)]. The big tail is a kind of advertisement. It does not *contribute* to the male cock's quality as a mate, but it *signals* quality, since only a very strong bird can successfully carry a big tail.[55] Note that this explanation also has a rather fragile or unstable "self-sustaining" element; it pays for hens of this generation to respond to this signal only to the extent that future hens will read the signal the same way.

VII. EVOLUTION AND LAW

Man's laws are subject to the deeper rules of Nature. The first of these rules is that all living forms are in reproductive (Malthusian) competition with one another. However, and here we come to what might be called the second rule of Nature: it is often more effective for separate organisms to come together and engage in cooperative association. But such alliances are merely secondary and contingent, in at least two respects: (1) in-group cooperation is only a means for more effectively and ruthlessly competing against outsiders; and (2) there is never perfect parallelism of interest among the members of a group, hence cooperation must generally be supported by sanctions to punish "antisocial" behavior. Indeed, one of the greatest obstacles to cooperation is the fact that those individuals having the best opportunities to engage in mutual aid—because they are nearest in terms of propinquity or similarity or relatedness—are commonly the most closely competitive in their needs for resources.

A. Forms of Association, and Precursors of Law

Forms of association vary widely in degree of cooperativeness. What seems to be a social unit may be only a "selfish herd" [Hamilton (26)]: the term refers to animals who seek protection against predators by moving toward the center of the crowd, thus placing others at risk on the periphery. Here the element of cooperation is entirely lacking. Then there are cases of merely parallel mutual interests, as when birds return annually to a mating area where they can expect to find other birds. In patterns of association like territoriality or dominance hierarchies there is at least a negative cooperative element, a tendency to avoid strife. And, finally, there are true communities, most notably families, characterized by more or less intense positive helping.

The theoretical analysis in Sections IV and V suggested two possible situations serving as precursors of *law*, interpreted as a system of retaliation that deters noncooperative behavior: (1) Bourgeois strategies under Hawk-Dove and (2) Hierarchy under Prisoners' Dilemma. In the relatively benign environment corresponding to the conditions of the Hawk-Dove game, the regulation of behavior is egalitarian and decentralized. In the severer environment corresponding to Prisoners' Dilemma, it is hierarchical and centralized. In each case a "social ethic" is also involved, in the sense that one or more of the parties is required to engage in behavior that is not in its private interest in terms of the immediate situation. In Matrix 6, playing Bourgeois (R_3) means foregoing the more profitable Hawk strategy (R_2) upon encountering a Dove (C_1), as well as the more profitable Dove strategy (R_1) upon encountering a

Hawk (C_2). And in Matrix 10 the superordinate Committer strategist (R_3) foregoes the more profitable Nonhelper choice (R_2) against Helper (C_1), that is, he rewards cooperative behavior. (Compare also Big Daddy in Figure 4.)

The Bourgeois solution under Hawk-Dove can be generalized to a population of any size, in which everyone possesses some property or territory which he is prepared to defend. The Committer solution under Prisoners' Dilemma also extends to a group of any size, each member being ranked relative to all others. Nevertheless, the limitation of the analysis in Sections IV and V to binary-strategy dyadic encounters in a homogeneous population remains very restrictive, and I do not mean to imply that there are not other archetypes or primitive forms of law that arise out of more complex interactions. And in particular I believe that another source of law arises out of the balance-of-power or coalitional considerations that emerge when more than two parties interact.

More specifically, this other source corresponds to what biologists have called *moralistic aggression* [Trivers (66)]: intervention of "uninvolved" third parties on the side of the victim of hostile or uncooperative behavior [on this see also Hamilton (27); Aubert (4)]. I am not prepared to provide a formal analysis, but I conjecture that moralistic aggression will be a viable strategy, at least, as part of a mixed solution, in multiparty Prisoners' Dilemma interactions. If moralistic aggression is operative, coalitional power in an egalitarian social structure serves essentially the same role as the dominant power of a superordinate player in a hierarchical structure. Like the other sources of law, moralistic aggression also involves a social ethic; the intervenor foregoes the short-run advantage of shirking the third-party enforcer role.

Finally, we should keep in mind that forces promoting cooperation may amplify and support one another. Kin selection and group selection are perhaps weak forces regarded separately, but they tend to be mutually reinforcing since members of propinquity groupings are almost always more closely related than average in the population. Parent-child nepotism may also support a cooperative superordinate-subordinate commitment interaction (Big Daddy in our example above). And similarly, parents might be more inclined than mere outsiders to play the "moralistic aggressor" role so as to enforce mutual helping among their offspring.

B.   On the Historical Evolution of Law

A number of legal historians and philosophers have viewed the law as following an evolutionary course of change. Before commenting on these interpretations, it is elementary though perhaps still useful to notice that the evolution of law must be considered in conjunction with the evolution of societal forms. Very primitive men lived in small bands based primarily upon a hunting economy. Later on pastoralism and agriculture emerged, followed ultimately by industry. To bring out a slightly less familiar point, at least one other economic way of life has been important probably in all historical periods: predation upon other human groups. In response to accumulated technological advances and other forces (climatic change, population growth, pressure of nonhuman and human predators), the typical *scale* of human association has gradually increased over time, culminating eventually in the large modern nation-state based upon diversified economic activity and the division of labor.

The characteristic laws of an era when most of the world's population lived in sparsely distributed hunting bands must have diverged from the types of law in force now, when most people live in urban environments within huge national states. There is a question of cause versus effect here. I am suggesting that the law responds to larger social changes governing forms of economy and state. But, to some extent at least, legal systems tend to bring about these larger changes. For example, Marxist communism as a system of law has not proved to be very conducive to economic advance, but its effectiveness in organizing and using military strength against internal and external enemies has led to its enormous extension over the face of the globe.

Returning to the traditional legal historians,[56] they have—not surprisingly, in the light of the foregoing—tended to agree that the dominant evolutionary trend is from laws suitable for an intimate face-to-face community to a legal system capable of governing impersonal public life among strangers (from *Gemeinschaft* to *Gesellschaft*.)[57] More specifically, Sir Henry Maine contended that the directions of historical change were from family responsibility to individual obligation, and from legal relations based on family status to those based upon contract. Max Weber emphasized progress toward abstract rationality, decisions being made in accord with logic and principle rather than personality, magic, or emotion. A somewhat similar position was taken by Roscoe Pound, who tended to emphasize moral as well as procedural improvements in this unfolding development. Somewhat more specifically, primitive law was said to be characterized by strict liability, self-help, and collective responsibility; modern law by liability only for moral fault, recourse via impartial public law rather then self-help, and individual rather than collective responsibility for behavior.[58]

There is considerable disagreement among scholars on both the broad sweep and the finer details of these trends. For instance, important elements of strict liability remain in modern American law, and their scope may even be expanding (as in workmen's compensation). But, far

more importantly, the drastic events suffered by humanity in the twentieth century cast a dubious light upon the generally optimistic tone of
this entire line of thinking, and especially upon the implied trend toward
ethical as well as procedural progress in systems of law governing the
majority of men.

Thrasymachus in Plato's *Republic* says that "Justice is the interest
of the stronger." If we interpret this as a positive statement (rather than
as a principle of normative ethics), it is difficult not to concede a degree
of validity to the Sophist's contention.[59] A revisionist interpretation of
past legal trends might seek to explain why the more powerful groups
have been led to favor collective responsibility in some areas and times,
individual responsibility in others, and so forth. Or perhaps more correctly, why the *balances* of power among groups of varying strength
brought about such developments.

C.   Social Ethics and Systems of Law

While I will not be able to tie things all together in a neat package,
I will begin to connect the theoretical development in Sections IV and
V above with actual legal trends.

First, consider the hierarchical Committer solution to the Prisoners'
Dilemma. This has a rather close correspondence to the power structures
sometimes observed among animals and men. I have called it elsewhere
[Hirshleifer (31)] the "Iron Rule" of social order.[60] One odd feature of
the previous analysis (see Matrix 10) was that the superordinate or dominant individual did not end up any better off than the subordinate. And
curiously enough, something like this does occasionally occur among
animals, where it is found that the dominant male in the band does not
always father the most offspring. Nevertheless, we would be quite surprised if this were normally the case. Equality of *result* despite inequality
of *role* is, I want to suggest, a special case due mainly to the assumption
of a homogeneous population in the theoretical analysis. When there are
strong asymmetries of power in the population, even before the form of
association is fixed, it is more than likely that the stronger will be able
to set up a hierarchical system in which he reaps most of the mutual
gain, as Thrasymachus suggested. (On the other hand, since individuals
striving for dominance may not achieve it, and may suffer damage in
the process, the *average* payoff of a "seek power" strategy may be no
greater than that of an "accept inferiority" strategy.)

There is a social ethic associated even with the Iron Rule of dominance.
In our simple Matrix 10, we saw that good behavior by the subordinate
must be rewarded, even though it is against the Committer's immediate
interest to do so. In more general contexts (where injury strategies are

allowed in the contest for the top position), it has been observed also that animals typically fight by conventional means, often not using their most lethal weapons [Lorenz (37); Tinbergen (65)]. The defeated animal does not fight to the death, and his submission is accepted.

Let us now consider the more egalitarian precursors of law mentioned earlier. If the environment corresponds to the conditions of the Hawk-Dove game, we saw that a Bourgeois strategy (under our assumed conditions) was an evolutionary equilibrium. The strategy of fighting to defend your own property but deferring to the corresponding rights of others was superior to always seeking short-run gain (Hawk) or always deferring (Dove). The territoriality observed in Nature is such a social structure. Members of many animal species, humans among them, have either a fixed or a mobile bubble of personal space, invasion of which will be resisted. The supporting social ethic here involves both willingness to defend and reluctance to intrude, each action being (at least under the assumed conditions of Matrix 6) against the immediate interest of the territory holder. This is indeed what occurs. "Irrational" fury on the part of property owners and corresponding fearfulness or timidity on the part of intruders lead to the defeat of most incursions [see especially Ardrey (3)].

However, while the Bourgeois ethic undoubtedly plays a role even on the human level, it does not conduce to more affirmative forms of group cooperation. Egalitarian *coalitions,* we suggested above, enforce good behavior through the social ethic of moralistic aggression. Again, emotions like indignation [see Trivers (66); Willhoite (70)] may have evolved to overcome the short-run disadvantage of becoming involved in third-party punishment of offenders. Moralistic aggression is open-ended in its scope of application; it can be used to support a variety of different social norms. Among the many possibilities observed among mankind are sharing, reciprocation, and heroism. Human beings seem able to learn alternative ideologies, but once learned the support for any particular ideology stems probably at least in part from an innate pattern of behavior.

The social behavior of human beings is subject to many other influences, some mentioned in the preceding analytical discussions. In particular, *kinship* as a source of cooperative or even self-sacrificial behavior has always been of great historical importance; as a biologically determined universal, it is unlikely ever to lose its sway. Early human societies were very largely made up of close kin (though exogamy provided a counterbalancing force setting some bound upon xenophobia).[61] Associations broader than family groupings tend to be supported by ideologies *simulating* family relationships: the dominant individual in a hierarchical society becomes "the father of his country"; in an egalitarian society,

46   JACK HIRSHLEIFER

participants become "brothers." Culture, it seems, permits humans to learn to fool themselves, in ways that are often, though by no means always, socially productive.

D.   Does the Law Evolve toward Efficiency?

It follows from Coase's Theorem that, *given* any initial assignment of property rights, there will be a trend toward efficient use of resources. All possibilities for mutually advantageous exchanges will gradually be discovered and consummated, except as prevented by the barrier of transaction costs.

As indicated in Section II, however, it is not in general true that trade makes *all* affected parties better off; the result of exchange is only potentially rather than strictly Pareto-preferred to the pre-exchange situation. Still, the net balance of such losses must be less than the gain to the contracting parties. (Otherwise, the Coasian argument goes, these third parties would enter the transaction and induce a change in its terms.)

Recent thinking has suggested that the process by which the law itself changes, so as to *redistribute* established property rights, is not essentially different from the Coasian process of *exchange* of rights that is conditional upon an initial structure of property entitlements. This is clear enough when a change in the law is unanimously approved, either because it benefits everyone directly or because appropriate compensations are paid. A possible instance is the privatization of hunting rights for fur-bearing animals that took place among certain Indian tribes in North America. This change came about after the arrival of European traders opened up a larger market for furs, thus increasing the social gains achievable by shifting away from the previous inefficient regime of common property rights.[62]

The more difficult case, which is (with only rare exceptions) the one of practical concern, is when the law changes in ways that clearly help some individuals while injuring others. Traditional "welfare economics" implicitly viewed this process as a benign one in which a paternalistic government apparatus balances considerations of equity against efficiency in the light of changing external circumstances. A degree of optimism seemed warranted, since ongoing improvement in analytical understanding could be expected to aid performance in this regard, with the added nice feature of suggesting that lots of economists should be hired at all levels of government.

The "new political economy"[63] literature, in contrast, is much more pessimistic. It regards all the actors on the political scene—voters, legislators, bureaucrats, and even judges—as making choices so as to maximize personal utility subject to the constraints imposed by laws and institutions (and the behavior of other actors). While it might theoretically be possible to redesign the constraints of duties and rights so as to lead to more efficient outcomes, there seems to be no particular reason to suppose that any such improvements are likely to come about.

One of the most exciting new ideas in recent years has been the proposition that the law does after all tend to evolve in the direction of efficiency. (This is the positive, rather than normative, version of Posner's Theorem as described in Section I above.) It supposedly does so evolve not because of the wise benevolence of lawmakers, but as an inevitable result of the conflictual process of litigation.[64] The basic idea is quite simple. Suppose we are dealing with a situation where mutually advantageous *exchanges* of entitlements are partially or wholly unfeasible, so that the initial assignment of property rights may make a real efficiency difference. An inefficient assignment leaves more scope for improvement; that is, the net balance of gains and losses will be greater in shifting from an inefficient to an efficient set of rights than for the reverse change.[65] It follows that, other things equal, those individuals and groups whose interests will be served by legal changes in the direction of efficiency will be motivated to bring more pressure and strength to bear than will their opponents in the contest for judicial determination of rights.[66]

Different models have been proposed for the actual mechanism of this process. In the original version of Rubin the emphasis is upon relitigation. If precedents are not absolutely binding, attempts will be made repeatedly to overturn an inefficient one. Even if judges never become any more enlightened, intellectually speaking, as long as there is a random element in their decisions the efficient outcome will eventually be hit upon so as to become the new precedent.[67] In an alternative version, those standing to benefit from the efficient precedent will be induced to make the greater investment (for example, hire more able lawyers) so as to influence the outcome of the action [Goodman (22)].

Finally, what is very important, the thrust of this efficiency-through-strength argument is by no means limited to the arena of common law litigation. With minimal modifications the same logic can be applied also to the forces determining statute law and constitutional interpretation.[68] For that matter, since the process is essentially one of "trial by combat," why not apply it also to civil wars and international conflicts? Dr. Pangloss, it seems, may have been right after all!

To refute the idea that strife and contention lead to efficiency in any all-encompassing sense we need only look about us. Still, it is important to appreciate how and to what degree the argument goes wrong, at least in its application to the evolution of law. I see three major flaws, which I will try to explain in order of increasing importance.

First, while I would support the contention that judicial or political results are ultimately determined by *strength* (by pressures brought to bear upon decision makers), the link is weak between result-relevant strength and the underlying costs and benefits imposed upon individuals. Rubin mentions that there is a "public good" situation here; others who may gain from overturning the precedent are free-riding upon the actual litigant. Put more generally, each side has the problem of *mobilizing* its strength. Among the forces favoring the ability of one side or the other to mobilize so as to bring potential strength to bear are such familiar considerations as compactness (small numbers, geographical concentration), perceived unity of interest, cheapness of communications, and perhaps a group-centered social ethic. In this model, it is interesting to note, litigation emerged in the first place because of negotiation breakdowns[69] between the interests on each side. And yet, negotiations *within* each side aiming at mobilizing forces so as to present a common front are quite essential for winning the contest. The overall conclusion, then, is that there are at least two sets of forces at work in this conflictual process: on the one hand the balance of efficiency considerations, but on the other hand comparative effectiveness at mobilization.

Second, and in part a related consideration, once the outcome is seen to depend in part upon ability to mobilize we would expect to observe a kind of arms race between the contenders. Each would be motivated to trade off some of the potential efficiency gain in order to increase the chance of defeating the other. In the animal world, we have seen, male combat for females leads to the diversion of resources to the development of otherwise unproductive weapons of contest. The same effect is highly visible in the sphere of international conflict. Thus, any trend toward efficiency gains from improved precedents (or, more generally, from reallocation of resources in accordance with the outcome of contests) must be weighed against losses due to the pressure to "meet the competition" by adding to combative capacity. Increased armaments, furthermore, may raise the costs of the process of coming to a decision (determining who wins and who loses). In warfare among nations, the costs of producing armaments are generally minor in comparison with the direct damage should war actually come about.

Third, and most important, is the question of *whose* efficiency? That is, what are the boundaries of the relevant group? Even if economic benefits and costs translate directly into combat strength, even if no resources are wasted in arms races or direct damage, the loss to the defeated can be said to be outweighed by the gains to the victors only if the transaction changing the structure of rights is internal to the group, which thereby gains collective power for the purpose of competing against others. An example might be military conscription of a particular age-cohort. If an external enemy presented a sufficiently urgent threat, many of us might think that such a drastic revision of rights was nevertheless warranted in the interests of national survival. But suppose it were a question of one nation enslaving another. Even if the enslavers were willing and able to "bid higher" than their victims in a military contest, we would be disinclined to regard the transaction as improving efficiency in any meaningful way.[70] (Conceivably, this process of "efficient enslavement" might aid the entire human species in its competition for survival against other species, but such competition is not sufficiently urgent at this time to be a major consideration.)

VIII. CONCLUSIONS

I will not attempt any general summary of the paper but instead will present a number of the more interesting or noteworthy implications of the evolutionary approach as it applies to conflict versus cooperation strategies in human affairs.

  1. The central tradition of economic reasoning emphasizes the harmony of interests among men. Under the guidance of the Invisible Hand, even entirely self-interested individuals are led to cooperate so as to achieve the mutual gains of trade. Economists have paid much less attention to conflict and aggression, to attempts to reap one-sided gains at the expense of others, although this aspect of behavior is also entirely amenable to economic analysis.

  2. Recent economic approaches to the study of political interactions reflect a similar harmonistic tilt in viewing the political problem as one of "collective choice" rather than as fundamentally a contest for power and domination. And, analogously in the legal sphere, recent economic approaches have viewed the main function of law as that of facilitating (and possibly supplementing) the process of market exchange in its triumphant progress toward economic "efficiency." The alternative view which has some claim to our attention is that law is a system of coercion imposed on the weaker by the stronger party, or at least that it represents a balance of pressures among parties each contending to achieve or resist such domination.

  3. The evolutionary approach suggests that this darker picture is the true one. As a generalization holding over the entire realm of living forms, *reproductive competition* is the first imperative of Nature. Furthermore, in the last analysis no holds are barred—all means of struggle

will be employed in this competition, so long as one contender or another finds it advantageous to do so.

4.   Nevertheless, it is true that in a multitude of ways and on all levels of life organisms have found it profitable to come together in patterns of cooperative association. But such cooperation is always secondary and contingent, in at least two respects: (1) in-group cooperation is only a means for more effectively and ruthlessly competing against outsiders, and (2) even within the group there will not be perfect parallelism of interests, hence cooperation must generally be supported by sanctions.

5.   From this point of view, the ultimate test of any group's constitutive law is whether it makes the group a more effective collective competitor. A very major concern of law must always be to prevent internal subversion of the collective effort by members pursuing their private interests.

6.   *Efficiency,* on this interpretation, is meaningful only as a measure of group strength or advantage relative to competing groups in the struggle for life and resources. Forming a cartel may be an efficient course of action for a group of firms, even if the net balance is adverse when the interests of consumers are also counted in. Outcomes efficient for our nation may be inimical to the well-being of other peoples; gains for the entire human species may be achieved at the expense of other forms of life. A totally universalistic measure of efficiency is pointless; we must draw the line somewhere, at the boundary of "us" versus "them."

7.   Whether in fact cooperative or helping behavior will be elicited from individuals with mixed motivations depends ultimately upon the ecological situation (the payoffs from hostile versus friendly interactions). This paper provided a systematic analysis for the simplest case: random dyadic encounters in a homogeneous population, individuals having only a binary choice between a more and a less cooperative strategy. Three qualitatively different sets of environmental circumstances (payoff matrices) each led to a characteristic result: (a) In the Tender Trap class of interaction, the gain from choosing either strategy *increases* with the proportion of the population adopting it. The more cooperative (more mutually advantageous) strategy will then be unanimously adopted if the proportion following it comes to exceed a critical mass in the population; otherwise, the result goes the other way. (b) In the Chicken or Hawk-Dove class of interaction, the gain from either strategy *decreases* with the proportion adopting it. The characteristic result is then a mixed equilibrium, with the more and the less cooperative option each being pursued a given fraction of the time (or by a given percent of the population). In both Tender Trap and Hawk-Dove, typically the potential efficiency gain from cooperation is only partially realized. (c) In the Prisoners' Dilemma class of interaction the selfish strategy *always* dom-

inates, and cooperation will not be viable at all despite the potential mutual gain.

8. In extending the analysis beyond this very simple case, innumerable analytical variations become possible. Among the cases of greatest interest for our purposes are the following: (i) Generalization of the Hawk-Dove game to allow a Bourgeois strategy—defense of one's own established control over resources, while deferring to the corresponding priority of others—can lead to an equilibrium characterized by a high degree of cooperation. This suggests how a sense of *property*, one of the possible preconditions supporting a system of law, might have evolved. (ii) With regard to the Prisoners' Dilemma, biologists have been much concerned with evolutionary solutions that turn upon ability to direct helping acts preferentially toward fellow cooperators. Aiding only one's relatives (kin selection) or only members of one's own propinquity group (group selection) may, under certain conditions, provide partial ways out of the trap—that is, some but typically not all of the efficiency gains can be thus achieved. This analysis again is suggestive of major features of human cooperative association, to wit, that observed helping largely takes place within kinship or other closely knit groups. (iii) If an asymmetrical environmental situation permits one player to commit himself to a threat-promise strategy relative to the other, full cooperation can in principle be induced even in the Prisoners' Dilemma context. Curiously, it does not necessarily follow that the individual in the superordinate hierarchical role reaps more gain than the other from the interaction. Nevertheless, in practice the circumstances making an asymmetrical strategy choice possible are likely to coincide with an inequality of power and thus of realized gain. This analytical model can therefore be regarded as patterning the Sophist view of law as the imposed will of the stronger. (iv) In a more egalitarian environmental context, coalitional power of the majority can serve a function analogous to that of the dominant individual in an unequal situation. Cooperative behavior is enforced by moralistic aggression on the part of third parties against malefactors. This interaction mode therefore provides the elementary pattern for a democratic structure of law.

9. To the extent that these systems of eliciting cooperation or punishing subversion require organisms to act in ways opposed to their immediate interests (for example, when a superordinate player has to carry out a threat or deliver on a promise), a social ethic in the form of ingrained emotional drives may provide the overriding motivation. Rage on the part of the victim and/or indignation on the part of third parties, for example, each irrational in terms of the direct interest of the party affected, may serve to raise the costs of cheating or other group-subversive activities. Or, equally "irrational" love and gratitude may

lead to enough unenforced reciprocation to make mutual helping viable. Different social ethics are required according to whether the structure is hierarchical or egalitarian. Among more advanced animals, and humans in particular, typically each individual will have a mixture of ingrained "hard-core" cooperativeness (appropriate for the social context in which he is placed) as well as merely prudential "pragmatic" cooperativeness based upon immediate considerations of cost and benefit.

10.   Turning specifically to economics, the following are among the suggestive implications:

(a) The image of "economic man" has been much denounced, but the evolutionary approach suggests that self-interest is ultimately the prime motivator of human as of all life. This theme is, however, subject to several qualifications, among them that one's kin are in the genetic sense partly one's own self. Also, as just indicated, even economic man's behavior is constrained by inbuilt emotions and tastes. While these no doubt contain accidental elements, they are not completely arbitrary. What tastes sweet to us is mainly what serves our own interest, and even our "irrational" or "unselfish" drives have largely met the evolutionary test of enabling us the better to compete via group membership.

(b) "Economic imperialism"—the use of economic analytical models to study all forms of social relations rather than only the market interactions of "rational" decision makers—is similarly entirely consonant with the evolutionary approach. All aspects of life are ultimately governed by scarcity of resources. But our use of the powerful tools of economic analysis must not lead us to unconsciously carry over harmonistic preconceptions, valid for the domain of mutually advantageous market exchanges, to the sphere of struggles for power and dominance. It is with that sphere that politics and law are mainly concerned.

(c) I find this thought somewhat disconcerting, but the evolutionary approach also suggests that, after all, the mercantilists were really not so wrong! Failing to appreciate the significance of the *mutual* advantage of exchange, they viewed trade essentially as an instrument in the international struggle for power. Mutual advantage is very nice, but trade still must be looked at with suspicion if it strengthens a potential enemy in war. This point is not without topical interest, for example when we consider the sale of industrial technology to the Soviet Union.

11.   And now, turning to law:

(a) In the great debate between natural law and social contract philosophies—that is, between those who view association under law as fundamental and intrinsic in man as against those who regard it as merely a contingent and pragmatic option—the evolutionary approach suggests an intermediate position. Human social behavior is enormously variable. That man is a social animal, often capable of great heroism and self-sacrifice, is true for some and perhaps true in part of all men. It is also true of other men, or perhaps the same men at other times, that they will help others only to the extent that they thereby serve themselves. And indeed the latter is the deeper truth, since ingrained social ethics are themselves viable only if ultimately of selfish advantage.

(b) The analysis here suggests that law, in the sense of coercive social control of group-subversive behavior, has two elementary forms, each of which corresponds to an associated social structure. The first form is hierarchical, control being achieved by the superordinate player's commitment to a threat-promise strategy. The second is egalitarian, with control effected by third-party moralistic aggression. Of course, these elements are interwoven in highly complex ways in any actual society. The circumstances making one or other form more effective in the competition among groups remain to be explored.

(c) As to the historical evolution of law itself, such alleged trends as the movement from status to contract or the shift from strict liability to moral fault do not seem valid except over limited segments of human history. The only really clear unidirectional trends are the fairly obvious developments associated with the greatly increased scale of human societies over historical time. The law necessarily became more impersonal, systematic, predictable, and professionalized as bands and tribes gradually gave way to huge industrial nations.

(d) The adversarial processes of law themselves engender a certain tendency toward efficient solutions, since supporters of the more productive legal rule can "bid higher" in the struggle to establish precedents. But too much ought not be claimed. For one thing, the struggle itself is likely to lead to a wasteful "arms race" as each side attempts to mobilize its strength. Even more fundamental is the question of *whose* efficiency is being achieved: is it really meaningful to balance off the loss of some parties against the gains to others? Are these redistributions only internal to that group whose competitive viability is of valid concern for the contending parties?

12. What might be called "the Smith-Coase message" tells us that, under a system of perfectly effective law, there will be a continuing tendency to seek out and achieve all mutually advantageous exchanges. How generalizable is this message to transactions in a world of imperfect law, or subject to no law at all? The harmonistic or Panglossian argument, which economists are perhaps predisposed to favor, is that wherever mutual advantage is present we can expect continual progress toward its achievement. Refuting that contention has been the main concern of this paper. At every point in time, each decision-making agent will be weighing the relative attractiveness of cooperation and conflict strategies—of seeking *mutual* advantage on the one hand, or on the other

hand *unilateral* advantage even at the expense of others. And indeed, the latter is the more fundamental evolutionary force; ultimately, co-operative association is only a means for more effectively competing *against* others in the struggle for reproductive survival.

NOTES

1. Professionals in both fields, most notably the double-threat economist-legist Posner [see especially (49)], have contributed to these developments.

2. See also Calabresi (8).

3. Also known as the "Kaldor criterion" [Kaldor (33)].

4. As is well known, reading Malthus' *Essay on Population* played a key role in the shaping of Darwin's thought.

5. As emphasized, for example, by Alexander (1), ch. 4.

6. This is somewhat of an oversimplification. For one thing, descendants of other cocks would provide less-inbred mates for one's own descendants.

7. There are also many fascinating examples of across-species cooperation, but these are only means whereby individual members of both species compete more effectively against their own conspecifics.

8. My analysis is in the spirit of Schelling (56,57) and Luce and Raiffa (39), ch. 5.

9. In these matrices one player chooses a Row strategy, the other a Column. The first number in each cell is the income return to Row-player, the second the return to Column-player.

10. Maynard Smith (42); the biologists call this solution an "evolutionarily stable strategy" or ESS. For economic interpretations of the ESS concept, see Hirshleifer and Riley (32), Cornell and Roll (13), Schotter (58).

11. Since there is only a single "income" commodity, no reversal paradox can arise.

12. If the proportion were exactly $p = 2/7$ the two strategies would yield equal returns, so that neither would tend to drive out the other. But this is an unstable situation; any small accidental shift of p in one direction or the other would be self-reinforcing.

13. Since the zero point is arbitrary, the negativity of average achieved returns need cause no concern.

14. Cornell and Roll (13) suggest a number of examples in economic affairs, including seniority ladders and stock market analysis.

15. Maynard Smith (42) cites several instances: for example, male hadmadryas baboons recognize conventional prior "ownership" of females by other males. For a more general discussion of the emergence of property rights among animals, see Fredlund (20).

16. A possible explanation is that "last come first served" conflicts with the adaptive incentive to search diligently for resources. A large fraction of the time, diligent searchers can expect to find and consume the prize before any competitors even put in an appearance. [For a different explanation see Cornell and Roll (13).]

17. For an economic discussion of uncorrelated versus correlated asymmetries, see Cornell and Roll (13).

18. Recall the argument in the section above about the relativity of the efficiency criterion with regard to the boundaries of the group.

19. The analysis that follows derives in part from Hirshleifer and Riley (32).

20. An important complication arises, however, where the populations are taken as of finite rather than of infinite size [Riley (52)]. Once only a single member of the population

Evolutionary Models in Economics and Law 55

is following a given strategy, it can no longer encounter any other playing the same strategy. For small populations (by no means uncommon in Nature, or in human affairs) this effect can be significant. In Figure 1, the cross-over cases I and II are affected. What can happen, essentially, is that the cross-over point can come so close to either end of the p scale that one strategy *is* driven out even though the infinite-population model calls for a mixed solution (line II) or for a possible Tender Trap EE at that strategy (line I).

21. Recall that the interesting case is where $x + y > 2$. In such a situation the mixed solution is more "efficient" (in the PPP sense) than either of the diagonal outcomes, but still falls short of what could be achieved by complementary pairing.

22. For example, a large fraction of the problems analyzed in Schelling's fascinating *Micromotives and Macrobehavior* (57) can be fitted under these headings.

23. Schelling (57), ch. 7, is perhaps misleading on this score. He shows that with a sufficient proportion p of Helpers in the population there may be an absolute expected gain to playing Helper—that is, for large p it may be that $p(-c + b) + (1 - p)c = -c + pb > 0$. Nevertheless, the absolute gain from playing Nonhelper is even greater (it is in fact pb), and so the Helper strategy remains nonviable in the evolutionary sense.

24. The saliency of this threat in actual modern business practice has been discussed by Macaulay (40).

25. This paradox can be overcome if there is no "last play"; for example, if the game is to be played an infinite number of times. Or, more realistically, if at each play there is a certain constant probability of the game continuing further. See Luce and Raiffa (39), p. 102, and Telser (62).

26. See Tullock (68), and the countering arguments of Frech (19), Hirshleifer (30), and Samuelson (55).

27. In the previous discussion, the presence of Retaliators provided in effect a degree of discrimination in the population as a whole.

28. I have used Charnov's simplest "sexual haploid" model.

29. To reconcile these expected returns in Eqs. (8) and (9) with condition (4), note that in (4) one helping act was supposed to occur per time period. To renormalize α and β in this way, divide both α and β by the bracketed expression at the right of Eq. (8). From Eq. (7), this expression equals pv_H/m. The results are the "fitnesses" compared in inequality (4):

$$\alpha\frac{m}{pv_H} = W_H = -c + bm$$

$$\beta\frac{m}{pv_H} = W_N = b\frac{p\bar{v}_N}{pv_H + (1-p)\bar{v}_N} = b\frac{p(1-m)}{1-p}$$

30. If m is constant, the left-hand side in Eq. (4) is a constant. But the right-hand side will be an increasing function of p. So $W_H - W_N$ is a *decreasing* function of p, from which $\alpha - \beta$ must behave similarly—leading to a picture like that of line II in Figure 1. (But in this case $\alpha - \beta$ will be a negatively sloped curve rather than a line.)

31. In terms of the underlying recognition coefficients, if $m = \frac{1+p}{2}$ then it follows from Eq. (6) that $\frac{1+p}{p} = \frac{v_H}{\bar{v}_N}$. So the ratio $v_H/\bar{v}_N$ falls as p rises, but never goes below 2.

32. See Williams (71), Maynard Smith (41). The major instance of group selection commonly cited is the tendency toward reduced virulence of disease germs [Barash (5), ch. 4]. But even this is not a pure group-selection case, as there is a kin-selection element involved [Alexander and Borgia (2)].

33. The standard biological literature on this subject [see, for example, E. O. Wilson (73), ch. 5; Barash (5), ch. 4] places undue emphasis upon differential *group extinction* as the critical factor in group selection. This is somewhat misleading. Differential rates of group extinction play an important role, but are by no means a sufficient statistic for determining the proportions of H and N genes in the next generation; it is also necessary to take account of differential H and N survival *within* groups, both those going extinct and those not doing so. In the biological literature, the model here is generally consistent with that of D. S. Wilson (72), and (I believe) with the views of Hamilton (27).

34. More complicated models, involving groups larger than two, or partial in-group mating rather than simple swarming, will of course have more complex stability conditions. But the simple model here lays bare the key issues.

35. "God is on the side of the bigger battalions." —Voltaire

36. This is not entirely true, of course. For one thing, at the genetic level, a "gene for having male offspring" can be regarded as being in competition with a "gene for having female offspring." But given that the population is sexually divided, intrasex competition is much more intense than intersex competition.

37. For a fuller discussion, see Schelling (56), chs. 2, 5.

38. In these terms, R_3 in Matrix 10 represents a promise rather than a threat. (Row promises not to play his more advantageous R_2 *if* Column plays C_1.)

39. This situation is analyzed in detail in Thompson and Faith (63, 64).

40. The difficulty of guaranteeing to behave in a way that is ex post irrational is exemplified by the "Mutual Assured Destruction" (MAD) problem in nuclear deterrent strategy. The underlying theory is that a potential attacker will be deterred if the target nation can retain enough strength to impose sufficient retaliatory damage. Yet, having suffered the attack, the victim's "rational" incentive to retaliate is not very strong. One's own losses are no longer remediable, and it seems pointless to engage in mass murder of the other population. A semi-whimsical solution for the problem is the "Doomsday Machine," which would make retaliation automatic rather than subject to human control or recall.

41. Becker (7). Becker's discussion is in the context of the family, so there is some danger of confounding this route to cooperation with mutual aid due to relatedness (kin selection). The mechanisms are entirely separate, and relatedness plays no role in the present analysis.

42. The necessity for this "hierarchical" asymmetry is emphasized in Hirshleifer (29).

43. For further discussion of pragmatic versus hard-core cooperation, see E. O. Wilson (74).

44. See, for example, Kurz (35), Landes and Posner (36).

45. This classification represents only one of the dimensions along which distinctions might be made. One might distinguish also strategies of competing by high survival versus high fertility, by adventurous versus risk-avoiding behavior, by specializing versus generalizing in use of resources, by adaptation to mountain or desert or polar conditions, etc. Another strategic dimension which is very crucial for our purposes is competition via isolated versus group struggle.

46. Cannibalism occurs widely in nature, but is still far less common than eating other species. Conceivably, this is the result of group selection.

47. The predator-prey interaction has a cooperative aspect, though a one-sided one. A rational predator would be concerned to promote the survival of its prey species, but generally speaking the prey would do better without the predator.

48. Males are essentially always in severer competition for females than females for males. The female's more costly investment in facilities for reproduction is the scarce

resource sought after by males. (On the other hand, females may compete for higher quality males, especially where monogamy governs.)

49. In Darwin's words, males strive "to conquer other males in battle" or, alternatively, "to charm the females."

50. Culturally, humans learn that a degree of willingness to fight for resources does pay off in this world. Whether this message has become _genetically_ implanted in the human species may be left an open question for the moment. As to sexual competition, male superiority in size and strength suggests that the principle of male combat may have governed even in human evolution. (On sexual competition as a cause of possible masculine intellectual as well as physical superiority, see _The Descent of Man_, ch. 19.)

51. See Krueger (34), Tullock (67), Posner (48). The term "rent-seeking" is another unfortunate terminological choice. All economic agents are seeking "rents" —that is, returns to resources under their control. The loss of efficiency is not due to _rent-seeking_, but to effort expended in _resource-taking_.

52. At least in the short run, and if the thief is regarded as a member of the group within which efficiency is calculated; see Section II.

53. For the fishery case, see Gordon (23). On the possibility of "excessive" searching for ideas, see Cheung (10) and Hirshleifer (28).

54. Again, only if both gainers and losers are considered part of the group within which efficiency is calculated. From the point of view of the gainers alone, the losers may merely constitute a resource field—like a prey species.

55. For an analogous theory of advertising, see Nelson (46,47).

56. For citations and discussion, see Friedman (21); Moore (44).

57. Ferdinand Tonnies, cited in Friedman (21), p. 282.

58. For a general discussion, see Moore (44), especially ch. 3.

59. That law is whatever serves the interest of the Soviet state is (I believe) openly professed as the main principle of Soviet justice.

60. For an analysis of dominance patterns among humans and other primate species, see Willhoite (69).

61. The origin of exogamy is subject to some question. Close inbreeding leads to expression of more genetic defects, but on the other hand a more closely related group will tend to be more cooperative and thus more effective. It has been suggested that exogamy is of "political" advantage in enabling groups to form alliances with others.

62. See Demsetz (16). For a somewhat analogous treatment of the enclosure movement in England, see Dahlman (14).

63. I will cite only the major seminal work of Downs (17).

64. Rubin (54), and see also Gould (24), Priest (50).

65. Note that the "reversal paradox" problem discussed in Section II is being ignored.

66. Perhaps this is the prophetic meaning of the otherwise mysterious riddle of Samson: "Out of the eater came forth meat, and out of the strong came forth sweetness." (Judges xiv:14)

67. Rubin (54). Similarly motivated attempts to overturn even efficient precedents will also probably take place. In consequence, we would expect to observe both the more and less efficient precedents, each governing with a certain fractional probability or a corresponding fraction of the time—see Cooter and Kornhauser (12). However, the more efficient rule will tend to prevail more frequently, increasingly so the larger the efficiency improvement it represents.

68. As already suggested by Rubin (54) and Priest (50).

69. As emphasized by Cooter and Kornhauser (12).

70. A somewhat similar argument is put forward by Rothbard (53), though I am sure

58   JACK HIRSHLEIFER

he would reject my suggestion that military conscription might (even hypothetically) be said to be efficient.

REFERENCES

1. Alexander, Richard D. (1979) *Darwinism and Human Affairs*, Seattle, University of Washington Press.
2. ———, and Borgia, G. (1978) "Group Selection, Altruism, and the Levels of Organization of Life," *Annual Review of Ecology and Systematics*, Vol. 9:449–475.
3. Ardrey, Robert. (1966) *The Territorial Imperative*, New York, Atheneum.
4. Aubert, Vilhelm. (1963) "Researches in the Sociology of Law," *American Behavioral Scientist*, Vol. 7:16–21.
5. Barash, David P. (1977) *Sociobiology and Behavior*, New York, Elsevier.
6. Becker, Gary. (November/December 1971) "A Theory of Social Interactions," *Journal of Political Economy*, Vol. 82(6):1063–1093.
7. ———. (September 1976) "Altruism, Egoism, and Genetic Fitness: Economics and Sociobiology," *Journal of Economic Literature*, Vol. 14:817–828.
8. Calabresi, Guido. (1961) "Some Thoughts on Risk Distribution and the Law of Torts," *Yale Law Journal*, Vol. 70:499.
9. Charnov, Eric L. (1977) "An Elementary Treatment of the Genetical Theory of Kin-selection," *Journal of Theoretical Biology*, Vol. 66:541–551.
10. Cheung, Steven N. S. (1979) "The Right to Invent and the Right to an Invention," University of Washington, Institute of Economic Research Report No. 79–13.
11. Coase, Ronald H. (October 1960) "The Problem of Social Cost," *Journal of Law and Economics*, Vol. 3:1–45.
12. Cooter, Robert, and Kornhauser, Lewis. (1980) "Can Litigation Improve the Law without the Help of Judges?" *Journal of Legal Studies*, Vol. 9:139–163.
13. Cornell, Bradford, and Roll, Richard. (Spring 1981) "Strategies for Pairwise Competitions in Markets and Organizations," *Bell Journal of Economics*, Vol. 12:201–213.
14. Dahlman, Carl J. H. (1976) "The Economics of Scattered Strips, Open Fields, and Enclosures," Ph.D. thesis, University of California, Los Angeles.
15. Dawkins, Richard. (1976) *The Selfish Gene*, New York, Oxford University Press.
16. Demsetz, Harold. (May 1967) "Toward a Theory of Property Rights," *American Economic Review*, Vol. 57(2):347–360.
17. Downs, Anthony. (1957) *An Economic Theory of Democracy*, New York, Harper.
18. Fisher, Ronald A. (1958) *The Genetical Theory of Natural Selection*, New York, Dover Publications (original publication 1929).
19. Frech, H. E. III. (1978) "Altruism, Malice and Public Goods: Does Altruism Pay?" *Journal of Social and Biological Structures*, Vol. 1:181–186.
20. Fredlund, Melvin C. (June 1976) "Wolves, Chimps and Demsetz," *Economic Inquiry*, Vol. 14:279–291.
21. Friedman, Lawrence. (1975) *The Legal System*, New York, Russell Sage Foundation.
22. Goodman, John C. (1978) "An Economic Theory of the Evolution of the Common Law," *Journal of Legal Studies*, Vol. 7:393–406.
23. Gordon, H. S. (April 1954) "The Economic Theory of a Common Property Resource: The Fishery," *Journal of Political Economy*, Vol. 62:124–142.
24. Gould, John P. (1973) "The Economics of Legal Conflicts," *Journal of Legal Studies*, Vol. 2:279–301.
25. Hamilton, W. D. (1964) "The Genetical Evolution of Social Behavior, I," *Journal of Theoretical Biology*, Vol. 7:1–17.

26. ———. (1971) "Geometry for the Selfish Herd," *Journal of Theoretical Biology*, Vol. 31:295–313.
27. ———. (1975) "Innate Social Aptitudes of Man: An Approach from Evolutionary Genetics," in R. Fox, ed., *Biosocial Anthropology*, New York, Wiley.
28. Hirshleifer, J. (September 1971) "The Private and Social Value of Information and the Reward to Inventive Activity," *American Economic Review*, Vol. 61:561–575.
29. ———. (June 1977) "Shakespeare vs. Becker on Altruism: The Importance of Having the Last Word," *Journal of Economic Literature*, Vol. 15:500–502.
30. ———. (October 1978) "Natural Economy versus Political Economy," *Journal of Social and Biological Structures*, Vol. 1:319–338.
31. ———. (1980) "Privacy, Its Origin, Function, and Future," *Journal of Legal Studies*, Vol. 9:649–665.
32. ———, and Riley, J. (August 1978) "Elements of the Theory of Auctions and Contests," UCLA Department of Economics, Working Paper No. 118B.
33. Kaldor, Nicholas. (1939) "Welfare Propositions in Economics and Interpersonal Comparisons of Utility," *Economic Journal*, Vol. 49:549–552.
34. Krueger, Anne O. (June 1974) "The Political Economy of the Rent-seeking Society," *American Economic Review*, Vol. 64:291–304.
35. Kurz, Mordecai. (1977) "Altruistic Equilibrium," in Bela Balassa and Richard Nelson, eds., *Economic Progress, Private Values, and Policy*, Amsterdam, North-Holland Publishing.
36. Landes, William M., and Posner, Richard A. (May 1978) "Altruism in Law and Economics," *American Economic Review*, Vol. 68:417–422.
37. Lorenz, Konrad. (1966) *On Aggression*, New York, Harcourt, Brace, & World (original German publication 1963).
38. Lotka, Alfred J. (1956) *Elements of Mathematical Biology*, New York, Dover Publications.
39. Luce, R. Duncan, and Raiffa, Howard. (1957) *Games and Decisions*, New York, John Wiley.
40. Macaulay, Stewart. (February 1963) "Non-contractual Relations in Business," *American Sociological Review*, Vol. 28:55–67.
41. Maynard Smith, John. (March 14, 1964) "Group Selection and Kin Selection," *Nature*, Vol. 201:1145–1147.
42. ———. (January–February 1976) "Evolution and the Theory of Games," *American Scientist*, Vol. 64:41–45.
43. ———. (September 1978) "The Evolution of Behavior," *Scientific American*, Vol. 239:176–192.
44. Moore, Sally Falk. (1978) *Law as Process: An Anthropological Approach*, London, Routledge & Kegan Paul.
45. Nash, J. F. (1951) "Non-cooperative Games," *Annals of Mathematics*, Vol. 54:286–295.
46. Nelson, Phillip. (March–April 1970) "Information and Consumer Behavior," *Journal of Political Economy*, Vol. 78(2):311–330.
47. ———. (July/August 1974) "Advertising as Information," *Journal of Political Economy*, Vol. 82(4):729–755.
48. Posner, Richard A. (August 1975) "The Social Costs of Monopoly and Regulation," *Journal of Political Economy*, Vol. 83(4):807–829.
49. ———. (1977) *Economic Analysis of Law*, 2nd ed., Boston, Little, Brown.
50. Priest, George L. (1977) "The Common Law Process and the Selection of Efficient Rules," *Journal of Legal Studies*, Vol. 6:65–83.
51. Riley, John G. (April 1975) "Competitive Signalling," *Journal of Economic Theory*, Vol. 10:174–187.

52. ———. (1979) "Evolutionary Equilibrium Strategies," *Journal of Theoretical Biology*, Vol. 76:109–125.

53. Rothbard, Murray N. (1979) "Comment: The Myth of Efficiency," in Mario J. Rizzo, ed., *Time, Uncertainty, and Disequilibrium*, Lexington, Mass., D. C. Heath.

54. Rubin, Paul H. (1977) "Why Is the Common Law Efficient?" *Journal of Legal Studies*, Vol. 6:51–63.

55. Samuelson, Paul A. (1980) "Complete Genetic Models for Altruism, Kin Selection, and Like-gene Selection," mimeo.

56. Schelling, Thomas C. (1960) *The Strategy of Conflict*, London, Oxford University Press.

57. ———. (1978) *Micromotives and Macrobehavior*, New York, W. W. Norton.

58. Schotter, Andrew. (February 1979) "Evolutionarily Stable Market Equilibria," New York University, Department of Economics.

59. Scitovsky, Tibor. (1941) "A Note on Welfare Propositions in Economics," *Review of Economic Studies*, Vol. 9:77–89.

60. Smith, Adam. (1937) *The Wealth of Nations*, New York, Random House (original publication 1776).

61. Spence, A. Michael. (1974) *Market Signalling: Informational Transfer in Hiring and Related Processes*, Cambridge, Mass., Harvard University Press.

62. Telser, L. G. (January 1980) "A Theory of Self-enforcing Agreements," *Journal of Business*, Vol. 53:27–45.

63. Thompson, Earl A., and Faith, Roger L. (1980) "Social Interaction under Truly Perfect Information," *Journal of Mathematical Sociology*, Vol. 7:181–197.

64. ———. (June 1981) "A Pure Theory of Strategic Behavior and Social Institutions," *American Economic Review*, Vol. 71:366–380.

65. Tinbergen, N. (June 21, 1968) "On War and Peace in Animals and Men," *Science*, Vol. 160:1411–1418.

66. Trivers, Robert L. (March 1971) "The Evolution of Reciprocal Altruism," *Quarterly Review of Biology*, Vol. 46:35–58.

67. Tullock, Gordon. (June 1967) "The Welfare Costs of Tariffs, Monopolies, and Theft," *Western Economic Journal*, Vol. 5:224–233.

68. ———. (January 1978) "Altruism, Malice, and Public Goods," *Journal of Social and Biological Structure*, Vol. 1:3–10.

69. Willhoite, Fred H., Jr. (December 1976) "Primates and Political Authority: A Biobehavioral Perspective," *American Political Science Review*, Vol. 70:1110–1126.

70. ———. (1979) "Rank and Reciprocity: Speculations in Human Emotions and Political Life," mimeo.

71. Williams, George C. (1966) *Adaptation and Natural Selection*, Princeton, N.J., Princeton University Press.

72. Wilson, David S. (January 1975) "A Theory of Group Selection," *Proceedings of the National Academy of Sciences*, Vol. 72:143–146.

73. Wilson, Edward O. (1975) *Sociobiology*, Cambridge, Mass., Belknap Press.

74. ———. (Fall 1977) "Biology and the Social Sciences," *Daedalus*, Vol. 106(4):127–140.

75. Zahavi, A. (1975) "Mate Selection—A Selection for a Handicap," *Journal of Theoretical Biology*, Vol. 53:205–215.

Part IV
Path-Dependency and Bifurcations:
Aspects of Non-Linear Dynamics

[11]

Path-dependent processes and the emergence of macro-structure

W. Brian ARTHUR
F.R.I., Stanford University, Stanford, CA 94305, U.S.A.

Yu. M. ERMOLIEV and Yu. M. KANIOVSKI
Glushkov Institute of Cybernetics, Kiev, U.S.S.R.

Abstract: Path-dependent systems of the 'autocatalytic' or self-reinforcing type typically possess a *multiplicity* of possible asymptotic outcomes or structures, with early random fluctuations determining which structure is 'selected'.

We explore a wide class of such systems, which we call non-linear Polya systems, where increments to proportions or concentrations occur with probabilities that are non-linear functions of present proportions or concentrations. We show that such systems converge to outcomes (proportions or concentrations) that are represented by the stable fixed points of these functions. These limit theorems are strong laws of large numbers for path-dependent increments, and as such they generalize the standard Borel strong law for independent increments. They are powerful and easy to use.

We show applications in chemical kinetics, industrial location theory and in the emergence of technological structure in the economy.

Keywords: Stochastic processes, non-linear dynamics, strong laws, self-organizing systems, asymptotic theory, fixed points

1. Introduction

Of recent fascination to physical chemists, biologists, and economists are non-linear dynamical systems of the 'dissipative' or 'autocatalytic' or 'self-organizing' type, where positive feedbacks may cause certain patterns or structures that emerge to be self-reinforcing. Such systems tend to be sensitive to early dynamical fluctuations. Often there is a multiplicity of patterns that are candidates for long-term self-reinforcement; the cumulation of small events early on 'pushes' the dynamics into the orbit of one of these and thus 'selects' the structure that the system eventually locks into.

'Order-through-fluctuation' dynamics of this type are usually modelled by non-linear differential equations with Markovian perturbations [1,2]. Showing the emergence of *structure* in the sense of long-run pattern or limiting behavior then amounts to analyzing the asymptotic properties of particular classes of stochastic differential equations. But while these continuous-time formulations work well, their asymptotic properties must often be specially studied and are not always easy to derive. Moreover, for discrete events, continuous-time formulations involve approximations. In this paper we introduce an alternative class of models (developed in previous articles [3,4,5]) that we call *non-linear Polya processes*. These processes have long-run behavior easy to analyze, and for discrete applications they are exact. Within this class of stochastic processes we can investigate the emergence of structure by deriving theorems on long-run limiting behavior.

Received March 1985

In this short paper we survey our recent work on the theory of *non-linear Polya processes*. We avoid technicalities as far as possible, and present applications in industrial location theory, chemical kinetics, and the evolution of technological structure in the economy. The limit theorems we present generalize the strong law of large numbers to a wide class of path-dependent stochastic processes.

2. Structure and the strong law

If a fair coin is tossed indefinitely, the proportion heads tends to vary considerably at the start, but settles down more and more closely to fifty percent. We could say, trivially perhaps, that a *structure* — a long-run fixed pattern in the proportion of heads and tails — gradually emerges. Of course, it is perfectly *possible* that some other proportion might emerge — two heads followed by one tail repeated indefinitely, for example, would yield $\frac{2}{3}$ and is just as *possible* as any other sequence. But such an outcome is unlikely. Borel's strong law of large numbers tells us that repeated random variables (drawn from the same distribution) that are independent of previous ones have long-term averages that must approach their expected values. While other outcomes might in principle be possible, they have probability zero. Thus in coin-tossing, where the event 'heads' is certainly independent of previous tosses, the average of heads in the total — the proportion heads — must settle down to 0.5, the expectation of each toss being a head. The emergence of a 50% proportion has probability one. Further, the 'strong' part of the strong law tells us that once the proportion settles down it persists. If we were to repeat the coin-tossing experiment eventually all (but a zero-measure set of) repetitions would enter and remain corralled inside an arbitrarily small interval surrounding the expected 0.5 value. The standard Borel strong law then is a statement about the emergence of, the inevitability of, and the persistence of a unique structure in certain systems with independent increments subject to random fluctuations.

Coin-tossing examples are useful mainly as textbook abstractions. A more interesting dynamical system that illustrates the emergence of macrostructure under varying assumptions is the process by which firms in an industry concentrate in various regional locations [6]. Suppose that firms start-up one by one, and each in sequence chooses one location from N candidate regions and settles there. Randomness enters if the firms differ in type and we do not know which type of firm will come into being next to make its locational choice.

The simplest locational dynamics would have independent increments like the coin-tossing case. Suppose that probabilities are fixed, so that the probability is p_j that the next firm to choose is of a type that will prefer location j. Thus a unit — a firm — is added to region 1, or 2, or ..., or N at each time of choice independently of previous choices, with probabilities $p = (p_1, p_2, \ldots, p_N)$ where $\sum_j p_j = 1$. Starting from zero firms in any region, concentrations of the industry in the various regions will fluctuate, considerably at first; but again the standard strong law tells us that as the industry grows, proportions in the N regions must settle down to the expectation of each choice, that is, to a constant vector equal to p. Under our assumptions, a pre-determined unique structure — this time a long run fixed regional location pattern — must emerge and persist.

What happens in the more general case where firms' locational choices depend in part upon the numbers of firms in each region at the time of choosing? Here increments to the regions are not independent of previous locational choices. The standard strong law no longer applies. We now have a *path-dependent* process, where the probability p_j of an addition to region j becomes a function of the numbers of firms, or equivalently, of the proportions of the industry, in each region at each time of choice. Will such a process settle down to a fixed locational pattern of proportions? That is, will a macro-structure emerge in this path-dependent case, and if so, what will it look like? We seek, in other words, strong laws for systems of this path-dependent type.

We can see at once that path-dependence can create a dynamical system of the 'autocatalytic' or self-reinforcing type mentioned earlier. Suppose in our locational example there are now potential economies of agglomeration — so that firms choosing are attracted by the presence of other firms in a region. It will then happen that if one region by chance gets off to a good start, its attractiveness and the probability that it will be chosen become enhanced. Further firms may then choose this region; it becomes yet more attractive. If the economies of agglomeration are strong enough this region could end up with a share of the industry arbitrarily close to 100 percent [6]. Yet, by chance, a similar outcome might have obtained with one of the other regions becoming dominant. If the process were to be replicated under different random sequences of firms choosing, different locational patterns might well emerge. With self-reinforcing path-dependence, a *multiplicity* of possible structures can result.

It is not difficult to think of other examples of path-dependent systems where we might see the same phenomenon of multiple potential emergent structures. For example, chemical reactions form products at rates that depend upon current concentrations of the products. If there is more than one possible reaction product, and autocatalysis, so that products enhance their own formation, the resulting end concentrations — the macro-structure of the reaction outcome — may also have multiple possibilities. Similarly, in consumer economics, if tastes are endogenous so that people are influenced in their purchase of durable goods — cars, say — by the brands that others have purchased already, there will be path-dependence. The market can 'lock in' to one of a multiplicity of brands, with early events determining the brand that comes to dominate.

It turns out that it is useful to formulate path-dependent unit-increment processes of the type we are discussing as *generalized* urn processes of the Polya kind. Before we do this, however, let us pause to look at the *standard* Polya process.

3. The standard Polya case: A special path-dependent process

In 1923 Polya and Eggenberger [7] formulated a path-dependent process that has a particularly striking outcome. Think of an urn of infinite capacity to which are added balls of two possible colors — red and white, say. Starting with one red and one white ball in the urn, add a ball each time, indefinitely, according to the rule: Choose a ball in the urn at random and replace it; if it is red, add a red; if it is white, add a white. Obviously this process has increments that are path-dependent — at any time the probability that the next ball added is red exactly equals the propor-

tion red. We might then ask: does the proportion of red (or white) balls wander indefinitely between zero and one, or does a strong law operate, so that the proportion settles down to a limit, causing a structure to emerge? And if there is a fixed limiting proportion, what is it? Polya proved in 1931 [8] that indeed in a scheme like this the proportion of red balls does tend to a limit X, and with probability one. *But X is a random variable uniformly distributed between 0 and 1.*

In other words, if this Polya process were run once, the proportion of red balls may settle down to 22.3927...% and never change; if run again, it might settle to 81.4039...%. A third time it might settle to 42.0641...%. And so on. Moreover, the convergence is strong — given enough time the process is close to the limit, not *probably* close to it; it does not wander away from the limit from time to time.

Figure 1 shows 10 realizations of this basic process. We can see in this special case that the proportions do indeed settle down — a structure does emerge each time — but the structure that is 'selected' is perfectly random. In this case an uncountable infinity of possible structures can emerge. A particularly insightful and entertaining account of this standard Polya process and how it might apply to the emergence and also to the misinterpretation of structure in biology and physics is given by Joel Cohen [9]. In the more general case where the urn starts off from an arbitrary number of red and white balls, proportions once again tend to a limit X, but now X has a two-parameter Beta distribution [10]. Here are two examples of Polya-type path-dependence.

Example 3.1. *A dual autocatalytic chemical reaction.* A substrate molecule S is converted into an R-molecule if it encounters an R-molecule, or into a W-molecule if it encounters a W-molecule:

$$S + R \rightarrow 2R + \text{Waste Molecule } E,$$
$$S + W \rightarrow 2W + \text{Waste Molecule } F.$$

Thus the probability that an R-molecule is created at any time exactly equals the concentration of R-product. A standard Polya process operates. Starting with one molecule of R and W, the process settles to a fixed concentration of R-product, but one that is anywhere between 0 and 100%.

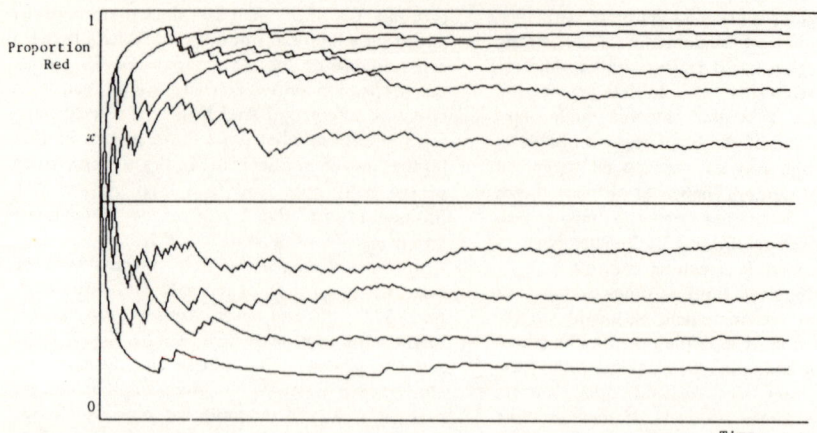

Figure 1. Ten realizations of the standard Polya process

Example 3.2. *Industrial location by spin-off.* An industry builds up regionally from some set of initial firms, one per region say, but this time new firms are added by 'spinning off' from parent firms one at a time. (David Cohen [11] has shown that such spin-offs have been the dominant 'birth' mechanism in the U.S. electronics industry.) Assume that each new firm stays in its parent location, and that any existing firm is as likely to spin off a new firm as any other. We again have Polya path-dependence — firms are added to regions incrementally with probabilities exactly equal to the proportions of firms in each region. Once again, a locational structure emerges with probability one — but it is a vector of proportions

that is *selected randomly* from a uniform distribution. (We could generate a representative outcome by placing $N - 1$ points on the unit interval at random, and cutting at these points to obtain N 'shares' of the unit interval.)

To get some intuitive feeling for this basic Polya urn process, notice that, as in Figure 2, the probability of adding a red always equals the proportion red. It is easy to show that this means, on an *expected motion* basis, that the process tends to stay where it is. There is no 'drift'. Of course, there are perturbations to the proportion red caused by the random sampling of balls; but unit additions to the urn make less and less difference to the proportions as the total number of balls grows, and therefore the effect of these perturbations dies away. The process then fluctuates less and less, and, since it does not drift, it settles down. Where it settles, of course, depends completely on its early random movements.

4. Non-linear path dependence

The standard Polya framework described above is too restrictive for our purposes. It requires a highly special path-dependence where the probability of adding a ball of type j exactly equals the proportion of type j. For a much wider set of applications we would want to consider a more

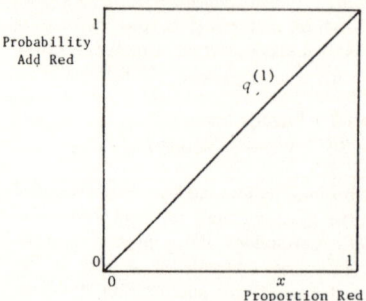

Figure 2. Urn function: Standard Polya process

general situation where the probability of an addition to type j is an arbitrary *function* of the proportions of all types. Moreover, to allow for realistic applications we would want more than two dimensions — two colors — and functions that may change with time. To describe our new process and the theorems that go with it, we will proceed a little more formally for a moment, drawing on our previous work [4,5], and that of Hill, Lane and Sudderth [3].

We now take an urn of infinite capacity that may contain balls of N possible colors and allow new units to be added at each time with probabilities that are not necessarily equal to but *a function of* the proportions in the urn. Let the vector $X_n = (X_n^1, X_n^2, \ldots, X_n^N)$ describe the proportions of balls of types 1 to N respectively, at time n (after $n - 1$ balls have been added). Let $\{q_n\}$ be a sequence of continuous functions mapping the proportions (of colors) into the probabilities (of an addition to each color) at time n. Thus, starting at time 1 with an *initial vector* of balls $b_1 = (b_1^1, b_1^2, \ldots, b_1^N)$, one ball is added to the urn at each time; and at time n it is of color i with probability $q_n^i(X_n)$. The scheme is iterated to yield the proportions vectors $X_1, X_2, X_3 \ldots$. Of interest is whether a structure emerges, chosen probabilistically from a multiplicity of possible structures — or, more technically, whether $\{X_n\}$ tends to a limit random vector X, with probability one, where X is selected from some set of possible limit vectors B.

Let the total balls initially be $w = \sum_i b_1^i$. At time

n, define the random variable

$$\beta_n^i(x) = \begin{cases} 1 & \text{with probability } q_n^i(x), \\ 0 & \text{with probability } 1 - q_n^i(x), \\ & i = 1, \ldots, N. \end{cases}$$

Then additions of i-type balls to the urn follow the dynamics

$$b_{n+1}^i = b_n^i + \beta_n^i(X_n), \quad i = 1, \ldots, N.$$

Dividing through by the total balls $(w + n - 1)$, the evolution of the proportion of i-types, $X_n^i = b_n^i/(w + n - 1)$, is described by

$$X_{n+1}^i = X_n^i + \frac{1}{(w+n)} \left[\beta_n^i(X_n) - X_n^i \right],$$

$$n = 1, 2, \ldots, \tag{1}$$

with $X_1^i = b_1^i/w$.

We can rewrite (1) in the form

$$X_{n+1}^i = X_n^i + \frac{1}{(w+n)} \left[q_n^i(X_n) - X_n^i \right]$$

$$+ \frac{1}{(w+n)} \mu_n^i(X_n), \tag{2}$$

$$X_1^i = b_1^i/w,$$

where

$$\mu_n^i(X_n) = \beta_n^i(X_n) - q_n^i(X_n). \tag{3}$$

Equation (2) is the basic dynamic equation of

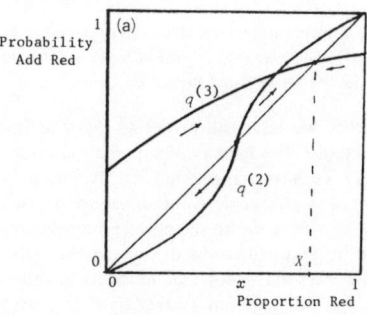

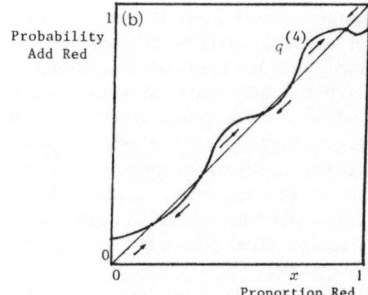

Figure 3. Urn functions: Non-linear Polya processes

our *N*-dimensional path-dependent process. It consists of a determinate 'driving' part (the first two terms on the right of (2)) and a perturbational part (the μ-term in (2)). Notice in (3) that the conditional expectation of μ_n^i with respect to X_n is zero, so that we can show that the expected motion of X_{n+1} is given by the 'driving' part of (2) as

$$E\left\{ X_{n+1}^i \mid X_n \right\} = X_n^i + \frac{1}{(w+n)}\left[q_n^i(X_n) - X_n^i \right].$$

$$(4)$$

Thus we see that motion tends to be directed by the term $q_n(X_n) - X_n$. In Figure 3a, for example, urn function 2 shows a tendency toward 0 or 1. Urn function 3 shows a tendency toward *X*. In each case there is an 'attraction' toward certain fixed points of *q*. Figure 3b shows a more complicated urn function in two dimensions, with attractions toward several fixed points.

The standard Polya process discussed earlier is represented by an urn function that is identically equal to *x*, and so has no expected motion driving it. Our more general process (2) has a non-linear driving part plus the Polya perturbational part. Hence we call it a *non-linear Polya process*.

5. Strong laws for non-linear path dependence

It is tempting to conjecture from Figure 3a that the dynamics must tend toward a fixed point of the urn function *q*. We might conjecture further from Figures 3a and 3b that not any fixed point will do. Some fixed points appear to be stable ones (they attract) — while others are unstable (they repel). A moment's thought, however, shows that without formal proof, it is hard to guarantee these conjectures. Notice from (4) that the attraction toward fixed points falls off at rate $1/n$ — so that the process may not have sufficient motion to be able to arrive at attracting fixed points. Notice also that while unstable points repel, they are nonetheless self-perpetuating — only perturbations can shake the dynamics away from them. Unless there are sufficient perturbations, and sufficient repulsion near these points, it might be the case that unstable fixed points can act as limit points for the process.

It turns out that (subject to certain technical conditions being fulfilled) our conjecture does go

through. The system must indeed end up with proportions that map into the identical probabilities; and it must end up only at stable fixed points. For two-dimensional processes with stationary urn functions, this was first proved in 1980 in the elegant article of Hill, Lane, and Sudderth [3]. The present authors proved this conjecture for the *N*-dimensional processes with non-stationery urn functions described here, in articles in 1983 and 1984 [4,5].

Before we quote the relevant theorems, here are two useful definitions. We will say that $\{q_n\}$, the set of urn functions, converges *reasonably rapidly* if it converges to a function *q* faster than $\{1/n\}$ converges to zero. We will also say following (4), that

$$X_{n+1}^i = X_n^i + \frac{1}{(w+n)}\left[q_n^i(X_n) - X_n^i \right]$$

$$(5)$$

is the *equivalent deterministic system* corresponding to our stochastic process. Now, a deterministic system like (5) might not itself converge — it might give rise to limit cycles or other more complicated asymptotic behavior. However, we can simplify matters by restricting (5) to be a *gradient system* — so that there exists a non-negative potential function whose downhill gradient gives the movements of our deterministic system. (This rules out cycles because no process can cycle forever downhill.) Given this restriction plus a technical requirement, our first result is that *non-linear Polya processes* have to converge to fixed points of *q*.

Theorem 1. *Suppose continuous urn functions* $\{q_n\}$ *that converge reasonably rapidly to a function q and suppose the equivalent deterministic system is a gradient system. Suppose also that the set of fixed points of q,* $B = \{x : q(x) = x\}$, *contains a finite number of connected components. Then the vector of proportions* $\{X_n\}$ *converges, with probability one, to a point z in the set of fixed points B.*

For proof we refer the reader to [5]. The full proof is lengthy, but by way of explanation notice that in (2) we have represented the dynamics in the form of a stochastic approximation process [12]. This allows us to use the powerful machinery of stochastic approximation theory together with martingale methods. Proof then amounts to showing that, for our gradient system dynamics with perturbations, expected increments in the value of the potential are less than some negative value (of order $1/n$) at points of q which are not fixed points. Unless the system settles to a local stationary point of the potential function — a fixed point of q — cumulations of negative increments would eventually drive the potential function negative, a contradiction.

Our next two theorems show that indeed not all fixed points can emerge as the eventual structure of the process. Attracting fixed points — stable ones — are candidates for 'selection' as the eventual outcome. Repelling fixed points — unstable ones — are not. Technically, given a fixed point z, we will say that it is a *stable point* if there exists a symmetric positive-definite matrix C such that

$$\langle C[x - q(x)], x - z \rangle > 0. \tag{6}$$

where x is any point in a neighborhood of z. Similarly, we will say z is an *unstable point* if there exists a symmetric positive-definite matrix C such that

$$\langle C[x - q(x)], x - z \rangle < 0. \tag{7}$$

where x is any point in a neighborhood of z. These criteria test whether expected motion is locally always toward z, or locally away from z respectively.

We will also say that point x is *reachable* if the process can arrive at it in finite time from the starting conditions with finite probability. (A sufficient condition for this is that the urn functions q_n map the interior of the unit simplex into itself.)

Theorem 2. *Let the urn functions $\{q_n\}$ converge reasonably rapidly to a function q. And let z be a reachable, stable point of q. Then the process has limit point z with positive probability.*

Again, we refer the reader to [4] or [5] for proof. The proof uses criterion (6) to construct a local Lyapunov function around z.

Theorem 3. *Suppose the functions $\{q_n\}$ converge reasonably rapidly to some function q, and suppose z is a non-vertex unstable point of q. Then the process cannot converge to z with positive probability.*

To prove this (see [5]) we use (7) to construct a suitable local Lyapunov function around z, then invoke stochastic asymptotic results of Nevelson and Hasminskii [12].

To use these theorems to study the emergence

of structure — the long-run behavior of proportions or concentrations — we need then only examine the fixed points of the limiting function q that maps the proportions of each type into the probabilities of adding an increment to each type. Unstable points will not emerge as the 'selected structure'. And there may be a multiplicity of stable points — each candidates for 'selection'. Referring back to the standard Polya process earlier, we now see that all points of the urn function $q^{(1)}$ are fixed points and all are reachable, so that all points are candidates for long-run selection. The standard Polya process is in fact a highly singular special case of our more general non-linear path-dependent process.

Notice that the conventional strong law (with unit independent increments) is a special case of our results above: Here we have $q(x) = p$ for all proportions x; the vector p is a fixed point and it is stable, reachable, and unique — p must therefore emerge as the ultimate proportions.

Here are two applications of our theorems outlined above.

Example 3. *A second dual autocatalytic reaction.* Consider a slightly different version of the chemical reaction given earlier.

$$S + 2R \rightarrow 3R + \text{Waste Molecule } E,$$
$$S + 2W \rightarrow 3W + \text{Waste Molecule } F.$$

In this case a single substrate molecule S is converted into either W or R-form (with waste molecules E and F) according to whether it encounters *two* W-molecules before *two* R-molecules. We may think of the process of 'sampling' the next *three* W- or R-molecules encountered and adding one to W or R according as two out of the three molecules sampled are W or R. Now, the probability that an R-molecule is added is

$$q_n = \sum_{k=2}^{3} H(k; n, n_R, 3)$$

where H is the Hypergeometric distribution parameterized by n and n_R, the number of R-molecules where there are n R- and W-molecules in toto, and by the sample size 3. In this scheme the urn functions have an S-shape as in $q^{(2)}$ in Figure 3a. There are stable fixed points at 0 and 1 and an unstable one at 0.5. Therefore, in contrast to the previous example where any intermediate concentration between 0 and 100% could emerge, only extreme 0 or 100% concentrations of R or of W can emerge.

Here is an example without multiple structures that generalizes our earlier location-through-spin-off example. This time a unique regional distribution pattern must emerge.

Example 4. *Locational spin-offs: A second mechanism.* There are N regions in a country. As before, firms are added to an industry by spinning off from parent firms. Again, any existing firm is as likely to spin off a new firm as any other. Now suppose that a firm in region j spins off a new firm that settles in region i with some positive probability $q(i, j)$ where $\sum_{i=1}^{N} q(i, j) = 1$ for all j. In this case we can write the vector of probabilities q_n given the proportions x as

$$q_n(x) = Qx$$

where Q is the matrix $Q = (q(i, j))$.

Our theory tells us that the regional structure that will emerge corresponds to a fixed point $z = Qz$. And from our condition that all $q(i, j)$ elements are greater than zero, we can show that there is a unique, stable, fixed point. Therefore, in contrast to the previous stay-put spin-off case where any locational shares are possible, in this case the regional shares of the industry must converge to a unique pre-determined structure.

Some remarks are necessary at this stage.

1. We can see from (3) that non-linear Polya processes have the property that initially they are dominated by stochastic motions — random unit increments early in the process make a large difference — but that later these dissolve away and the deterministic expected motions come to the fore. In fact, the possible structures that may emerge are completely given by the equivalent deterministic system — it is the role of the perturbations to 'select' from these. It is this property that makes these processes natural models for the emergence of (determinate) structure through (stochastic) fluctuation.

2. It is possible to generalize this non-linear Polya process further, to discontinuous urn functions, to cases where the equivalent deterministic system has limit cycles or more complex behavior, and to non-unit increments. But that is beyond the scope of this survey paper.

3. Notice that in the theory and examples given above, we are dealing with pure birth processes — only increments are allowed. A corresponding theory could be developed where decrements are allowed (that is, where balls may be taken from the urn). But in this case, in general we would no longer have strong laws: usually we would have convergence in distribution to the emergent structure.

4. We could usefully distinguish between processes that have a single stable fixed point, so that a unique structure or limit must emerge, and processes that have more than one reachable stable fixed point, where structure is 'selected' partly randomly. The former we can call *ergodic* — there is one possible outcome, and perturbations 'wash away'. The latter are *non-ergodic* — there are multiple outcomes and early perturbations become all-important in the 'selection' of structure.

An interesting and instructive case of non-ergodic path-dependence seems to determine the technological structure that emerges in the economy [13,14]. We briefly summarize this case now.

6. Path-dependence and the emergence of technological structure

Very often, individual technologies show 'increasing returns' to adoption — the more they are adopted the more is learned about them; in turn the more they are improved, and the more attractive they become [15]. Very often, too, there are several *technologies* that *compete* for shares of a 'market' of potential adopters. (In the 1890s, for example, the steam engine, the electric motor, and the gasoline engine competed — albeit unconsciously — as power sources for the new automobile.)

Adoption of technologies that compete can be usefully modelled as a non-linear Polya process. A unit increment — an individual adoption — is added, each time of choice, to a given technology with a probability that depends on the numbers (or proportions) holding each technology at that particular time. We can use our strong-law theorems to show circumstances under which *increasing returns to adoption* (the probability of adoption rises with the share of the market) may drive the adopter 'market' to a single dominant technology, with small events early on 'selecting' the technology that takes over [13,14,16].

Asymptotic theory is also important in showing three key features of the dynamics that arise in this non-ergodic 'increasing returns' case. First, *a priori* we cannot say with accuracy *which* technological structure will 'win' the market. In fact, gasoline was held to be the least likely option in the 1890s [14] and yet it emerged as the dominant technological structure for automobile propulsion. Second, the technology that comes to dominate — the structure that emerges — does not necessarily have to be the 'best' or most efficient; events early on can lock the system in to an inferior technological path. It has certainly been argued in the engineering literature that, had steam been developed to the same degree as gasoline, it might conceivably have been superior [17]. (The 1950s programming language FORTRAN, the U.S. color television system, and the QWERTY typewriter keyboard [18] are demonstrably inferior structures that seem to be locked in). Third, once a single-technology structure emerges and becomes self-reinforcing, it is difficult to change it. If it were desirable to re-establish an excluded technology — say steam propulsion — an ever-widening technical changeover gap would have to be closed.

For non-ergodic systems — like competing technologies with sufficient increasing returns to adoption — these properties of the macro-structure that emerges — *non-predictability*, potential *non-superiority*, and *structural rigidity* — appear to be common and to some degree inevitable [13].

7. Conclusion

We have defined 'structure' for the purposes of this brief survey as the long-run pattern in eventual proportions, concentrations, or shares of a market that emerges from a dynamic process. The conventional strong law of large numbers makes statements about the emergence of structure in processes where additions to the possible categories occur with independent, fixed probabilities. In the more general 'non-linear Polya' case we have examined, where additions to categories are influenced at each time by the proportions in each category — the process has dependent increments. We have shown that the Borel strong law (under certain technical conditions) can be generalized to this important dependent-increment case: such processes do indeed settle-down, with probability

one, to proportions that are fixed.

In certain simple cases non-linear Polya processes settle to unique pre-determinable proportions. But more generally they possess the familiar property of non-linear systems: a multiplicity of structures may be possible of which one will be eventually, dynamically 'selected'. We can identify these candidate structures as represented by the set of stable fixed points in the mapping from proportions into probabilities. Thus non-linear Polya processes may offer a useful alternative to the usual differential-equation formulations. And for particular, discrete path-dependent systems — in chemical kinetics, industrial location, and technological choice, for example — we can construct exact models that demonstrate how small fluctuations at the outset can cause quite different eventual structures to emerge.

References

[1] Nicolis, G., and Prigogine, I. (1971), *Self-Organization in Nonequilibrium Systems: From Dissipative Structures to Order through Fluctuations*, Wiley, New York.

[2] Mansour, M.M., Van den Broek, C., Nicolis, G., and Turner, J.W. (1981), "Asymptotic properties of Markovian master equations", *Annals Phys.* 131, 1–30.

[3] Hill, B.M., Lane, D., and Sudderth, W. (1980), "A strong law for some generalized urn processes", *Annals Prob.* 8, 214–226.

[4] Arthur, W.B., Ermoliev, Yu. M., and Kaniovski, Yu. M. (1983), "A generalized urn problem and its applications", *Kibernetika* 19, 49–57 (in Russian). Translated in *Cybernetics* 19, 61–71.

[5] Arthur, W.B., Ermoliev, Yu. M., and Kaniovski, Yu. M. (1984), "Strong laws for a class of path-dependent stochastic processes, with applications", in: Arkin, Shiryayev, Wets (eds.), *Proc. Conf. on Stochastic Optimization, Kiev 1984*, Springer, Lecture Notes in Control and Information Sciences.

[6] Arthur, W.B. (1984), "Industry location pattern and the importance of history: Why a Silicon Valley?", Stanford Univ., Center for Econ. Policy Research.

[7] Polya, G., and Eggenberger, F. (1923), "Ueber die Statistik verketteter Vorgaenge", *Z. Angew. Math. Mech.* 3, 279–289.

[8] Polya, G. (1931), "Sur quelques Points de la Théorie des Probabilités", *Ann. Inst. H. Poincaré*. 1, 117–161.

[9] Cohen, J. (1976), "Irreproducible results and the breeding of pigs (or non-degenerate limit random variables in biology)", *Bioscience* 26, 391–394.

[10] Johnson, N., and Kotz, S. (1977), *Urn Models and their Application*, Wiley, New York.

[11] Cohen, D. (1984), "Locational patterns in the electronics industry: A survey", Econ. Dept., Stanford Univ., mimeo.

[12] Nevelson, M.B., and Hasminskii, R.Z. (1972), *Stochastic Approximation and Recursive Estimation*, Amer. Math. Soc. Translations of Math. Monographs. Vol. 47, Providence, RI.

[13] Arthur, W.B. (1983), "Competing technologies and lock-in by historical small events: The dynamics of allocation under increasing returns", C.E.P.R. Research Publication No. 43. Stanford Univ.

[14] Arthur, W.B. (1984), "Competing Technologies and Economic Prediction", *Options*, April 1984, IIASA laxenburg, Austria.

[15] Rosenberg, N. (1982), *Inside the Black Box: Technology and Economics*, Cambridge Univ. Press, Cambridge.

[16] Hanson, W. (1985), "Bandwagons and orphans: Dynamic pricing of competing systems subject to decreasing costs", Ph.D. dissertation, Economics, Stanford University.

[17] Burton, R.L. (1976), "Recent advances in vehicular steam engine efficiency", Soc. of Automotive Eng. Preprint No. 760340.

[18] David, P.A. (1985), "Clio and the economics of QWERTY", *Am. Econ. Rev. Proc.* 75, 332–337.

[12]

Clio and the Economics of QWERTY

By Paul A. David*

Cicero demands of historians, first, that we tell true stories. I intend fully to perform my duty on this occasion, by giving you a homely piece of narrative economic history in which "one damn thing follows another." The main point of the story will become plain enough: it is sometimes not possible to uncover the logic (or illogic) of the world around us except by understanding how it got that way. A *path-dependent* sequence of economic changes is one of which important influences upon the eventual outcome can be exerted by temporally remote events, including happenings dominated by chance elements rather than systematic forces. Stochastic processes like that do not converge automatically to a fixed-point distribution of outcomes, and are called *non-ergodic*. In such circumstances "historical accidents" can neither be ignored, nor neatly quarantined for the purpose of economic analysis; the dynamic process itself takes on an *essentially historical* character. Standing alone, my story will be simply illustrative and does not establish how much of the world works this way. That is an open empirical issue and I would be presumptuous to claim to have settled it, or to instruct you in what to do about it. Let us just hope the tale proves mildly diverting for those waiting to be told if and why the study of economic history is a necessity in the making of economists.

*Department of Economics, Encina Hall, Stanford University, Stanford, CA 94305. Support provided for this research, under a grant to the Technological Innovation Program of the Center for Economic Policy Research, Stanford University, is gratefully acknowledged. Douglas Puffert supplied able research assistance. Some, but not the whole, of my indebtedness to Brian Arthur's views on QWERTY and QWERTY-like subjects is recorded in the References. I bear full responsibility for errors of fact and interpretation, as well as for the peculiar opinions abbreviated herein. A fuller version with complete references, entitled "Understanding the Economics of QWERTY or Is History Necessary?," is available on request.

I. The Story of QWERTY

Why does the topmost row of letters on your personal computer keyboard spell out QWERTYUIOP, rather than something else? We know that nothing in the engineering of computer terminals requires the awkward keyboard layout known today as "QWERTY," and we all are old enough to remember that QWERTY somehow has been handed down to us from the Age of Typewriters. Clearly nobody has been persuaded by the exhortations to discard QWERTY, which apostles of DSK (the Dvorak Simplified Keyboard) were issuing in trade publications such as *Computers and Automation* during the early 1970's. Why not? Devotees of the keyboard arrangement patented in 1932 by August Dvorak and W. L. Dealey have long held most of the world's records for speed typing. Moreover, during the 1940's U.S. Navy experiments had shown that the increased efficiency obtained with DSK would amortize the cost of retraining a group of typists within the first ten days of their subsequent full-time employment. Dvorak's death in 1975 released him from forty years of frustration with the world's stubborn rejection of his contribution; it came too soon for him to be solaced by the Apple IIC computer's built-in switch, which instantly converts its keyboard from QWERTY to virtual DSK, or to be further aggravated by doubts that the switch would not often be flicked.

If as Apple advertising copy now says, DSK "lets you type 20–40% faster," why did this superior design meet essentially the same rejection as the previous seven improvements on the QWERTY typewriter keyboard that were patented in the United States and Britain during the years 1909–24? Was it the result of customary, nonrational behavior by countless individuals socialized to carry on an antiquated technological tradition? Or, as Dvorak himself once suggested, had there been a conspiracy among the members of the typewriter oligopoly to suppress an invention which they feared would so increase typewriter efficiency as ultimately to curtail the demand for their products? Or perhaps we should turn instead to the other popular "Devil Theory," and ask if political regulation and interference with the workings of a "free market" has been the cause of inefficient keyboard regimentation? Maybe it's all to be blamed on the public school system, like everything else that's awry?

You can already sense that these will not be the most promising lines along which to search for an economic understanding of QWERTY's present dominance. The agents engaged in production and purchase decisions in today's keyboard market are not the prisoners of custom, conspiracy, or state control. But while they are, as we now say, perfectly "free to choose," their behavior, nevertheless, is held fast in the grip of events long forgotten and shaped by circumstances in which neither they nor their interests figured. Like the great men of whom Tolstoy wrote in *War and Peace*, "(e) very action of theirs, that seems to them an act of their own free will, is in an historical sense not free at all, but in bondage to the whole course of previous history..." (Bk. IX, ch. 1).

This is a short story, however. So it begins only little more than a century ago, with the fifty-second man to invent the typewriter. Christopher Latham Sholes was a Milwaukee, Wisconsin printer by trade, and a mechanical tinkerer by inclination. Helped by his friends, Carlos Glidden and Samuel W. Soule, he had built a primitive writing machine for which a patent application was filed in October 1867. Many defects in the working of Sholes' "Type Writer" stood in the way of its immediate commercial introduction. Because the printing point was located underneath the paper carriage, it was quite invisible to the operator. "Non-visibility" remained an unfortunate feature of this and other up-stroke machines long after the flat paper carriage of the original design had been supplanted by arrangements closely resembling the modern continuous roller-platen. Consequently, the tendency of the typebars to clash and jam if struck in rapid

succession was a particularly serious defect. When a typebar stuck at or near the printing point, every succeeding stroke merely hammered the same impression onto the paper, resulting in a string of repeated letters that would be discovered only when the typist bothered to raise the carriage to inspect what had been printed.

Urged onward by the bullying optimism of James Densmore, the promoter-venture capitalist whom he had taken into the partnership in 1867, Sholes struggled for the next six years to perfect "the machine." From the inventor's trial-and-error rearrangements of the original model's alphabetical key ordering, in an effort to reduce the frequency of typebar clashes, there emerged a four-row, upper case keyboard approaching the modern QWERTY standard. In March 1873, Densmore succeeded in placing the manufacturing rights for the substantially transformed Sholes-Glidden "Type Writer" with E. Remington and Sons, the famous arms makers. Within the next few months QWERTY's evolution was virtually completed by Remington's mechanics. Their many modifications included some fine-tuning of the keyboard design in the course of which the "*R*" wound up in the place previously allotted to the period mark "." Thus were assembled into one row all the letters which a salesman would need to impress customers, by rapidly pecking out the brand name: TYPE WRITER

Despite this sales gimmick, the early commercial fortunes of the machine, with which chance had linked QWERTY's destiny remained terrifyingly precarious. The economic downturn of the 1870's was not the best of times in which to launch a novel piece of office equipment costing $125, and by 1878, when Remington brought out its Improved Model Two (equipped with carriage shift key), the whole enterprise was teetering on the edge of bankruptcy. Consequently, even though sales began to pick up pace with the lifting of the depression and annual typewriter production climbed to 1200 units in 1881, the market position which QWERTY had acquired during the course of its early career was far from deeply entrenched; the entire stock of QWERTY-embodying machines in the United States could not have much exceeded 5000 when the decade of the 1880's opened.

Nor was its future much protected by any compelling technological necessities. For, there were ways to make a typewriter without the up-stroke typebar mechanism that had called forth the QWERTY adaptation, and rival designs were appearing on the American scene. Not only were there typebar machines with "down-stroke" and "front-stroke" actions that afforded a visible printing point; the problem of typebar clashes could be circumvented by dispensing with typebars entirely, as young Thomas Edison had done in his 1872 patent for an electric print-wheel device which later became the basis for teletype machines. Lucien Stephen Crandall, the inventor of the second typewriter to reach the American market (in 1879) arranged the type on a cylindrical sleeve: the sleeve was made to revolve to the required letter and come down onto the printing-point, locking in place for correct alignment. (So much for the "revolutionary" character of the IBM 72/82's "golf ball" design.) Freed from the legacy of typebars, commercially successful typewriters such as the Hammond and the Blickensderfer first sported a keyboard arrangement which was more sensible than QWERTY. Then so-called "Ideal" keyboard placed the sequence DHIATENSOR in the home row, these being ten letters with which one may compose over 70 percent of the words in the English language.

The typewriter boom beginning in the 1880's thus witnessed a rapid proliferation of competitive designs, manufacturing companies, and keyboard arrangements rivalling the Sholes-Remington QWERTY. Yet, by the middle of the next decade, just when it had become evident that any micro-technological rationale for QWERTY's dominance was being removed by the progress of typewriter engineering, the U.S. industry was rapidly moving towards the standard of an upright front-stroke machine with a four-row QWERTY keyboard that was referred to as "the Universal." During the period 1895–1905, the main producers of non-typebar machines fell into line by offering "the Universal" as an option in place of the Ideal keyboard.

II. Basic QWERTY-Nomics

To understand what had happened in the fateful interval of the 1890's, the economist must attend to the fact that typewriters were beginning to take their place as an element of a larger, rather complex system of production that was technically interrelated. In addition to the manufacturers and buyers of typewriting machines, this system involved typewriter operators and the variety of organizations (both private and public) that undertook to train people in such skills. Still more critical to the outcome was the fact that, in contrast to the hardware subsystems of which QWERTY or other keyboards were a part, the larger system of production was nobody's design. Rather like the proverbial Topsy, and much else in the history of economies besides, it "jes' growed."

The advent of "touch" typing, a distinct advance over the four-finger hunt-and-peck method, came late in the 1880's and was critical, because this innovation was from its inception adapted to the Remington's QWERTY keyboard. Touch typing gave rise to three features of the evolving production system which were crucially important in causing QWERTY to become "locked in" as the dominant keyboard arrangement. These features were *technical interrelatedness*, *economies of scale*, and *quasi-irreversibility* of investment. They constitute the basic ingredients of what might be called QWERTY-nomics.

Technical interrelatedness, or the need for system compatibility between keyboard "hardware" and the "software" represented by the touch typist's memory of a particular arrangement of the keys, meant that the expected present value of a typewriter as an instrument of production was dependent upon the availability of compatible software created by typists' decisions as to the kind of keyboard they should learn. Prior to the growth of the personal market for typewriters, the purchasers of the hardware typically were business firms and therefore distinct from the owners of typing skills. Few incentives existed at the time, or later, for any one business to invest in providing its employees with a form of general human capital which so readily could be taken elsewhere. (Notice that it was the wartime U.S. Navy, not your typical employer, that undertook the experiment of retraining typists on the Dvorak keyboard.) Nevertheless the purchase by a potential employer of a QWERTY keyboard conveyed a positive pecuniary externality to compatibly trained touch typists. To the degree to which this increased the likelihood that subsequent typists would choose to learn QWERTY, in preference to another method for which the stock of compatible hardware would not be so large, the overall user costs of a typewriting system based upon QWERTY (or any specific keyboard) would tend to *decrease* as it gained in acceptance relative to other systems. Essentially symmetrical conditions obtained in the market for instruction in touch typing.

These decreasing cost conditions—or *system scale economies*—had a number of consequences, among which undoubtedly the most important was the tendency for the process of intersystem competition to lead towards de facto standardization through the predominance of a single keyboard design. For analytical purposes, the matter can be simplified in the following way: suppose that buyers of typewriters uniformly were without inherent preferences concerning keyboards, and cared only about how the stock of touch typists was distributed among alternative specific keyboard styles. Suppose typists, on the other hand, were heterogeneous in their preferences for learning QWERTY-based "touch," as opposed to other methods, but attentive also to the way the stock of machines was distributed according to keyboard styles. Then imagine the members of this heterogenous population deciding in random order what kind of typing training to acquire. It may be seen that, with unbounded decreasing costs of selection, each stochastic decision in favor of QWERTY would raise the probability (but not guarantee) that the next selector would favor QWERTY. From the viewpoint of the formal theory of stochastic processes, what we are looking at now is equivalent to a generalized "Polya urn scheme." In a simple scheme of that kind, an urn containing balls of various colors is sampled with replacement, and every drawing of a ball of a specified color results

in a second ball of the same color being returned to the urn; the probabilities that balls of specified colors will be added are therefore increasing (linear) functions of the proportions in which the respective colors are represented within the urn. A recent theorem due to W. Brian Arthur et al. (1983; 1985) allows us to say that when a generalized form of such a process (characterized by unbounded increasing returns) is extended indefinitely, the proportional share of one of the colors will, with probability one, converge to unity.

There may be many eligible candidates for supremacy, and from an *ex ante* vantage point we cannot say with corresponding certainty which among the contending colors —or rival keyboard arrangements—will be the one to gain eventual dominance. That part of the story is likely to be governed by "historical accidents," which is to say, by the particular sequencing of choices made close to the beginning of the process. It is there that essentially random, transient factors are most likely to exert great leverage, as has been shown neatly by Arthur's (1983) model of the dynamics of technological competition under increasing returns. Intuition suggests that if choices were made in a forward-looking way, rather than myopically on the basis of comparisons among the currently prevailing costs of different systems, the final outcome could be influenced strongly by expectations. A particular system could triumph over rivals merely because the purchasers of the software (and/or the hardware) expected that it would do so. This intuition seems to be supported by recent formal analyses by Michael Katz and Carl Shapiro (1983), and Ward Hanson (1984), of markets where purchasers of rival products benefit from externalities conditional upon the size of the compatible system or "network" with which they thereby become joined. Although the initial lead acquired by QWERTY through its association with the Remington was quantitatively very slender, when magnified by expectations it may well have been quite sufficient to guarantee that the industry eventually would lock in to a de facto QWERTY standard.

The occurrence of this "lock in" as early as the mid-1890's does appear to have owed something also to the high costs of software "conversion" and the resulting *quasi-irreversibility of investments* in specific touch-typing skills. Thus, as far as keyboard conversion costs were concerned, an important asymmetry had appeared between the software and the hardware components of the evolving system: the costs of typewriter software conversion were going up, whereas the costs of typewriter hardware conversion were coming down. While the novel, non-typebar technologies developed during the 1880's were freeing the keyboard from technical bondage to QWERTY, typewriter makers were by the same token freed from fixed-cost bondage to any particular keyboard arrangement. Non-QWERTY typewriter manufacturers seeking to expand market share could cheaply switch to achieve compatibility with the already existing stock of QWERTY-programmed typists, who could not. This, then, was a situation in which the precise details of timing in the developmental sequence had made it privately profitable in the short run to adapt machines to the habits of men (or to women, as was increasingly the case) rather than the other way around. And things have been that way ever since.

III. Message

In place of a moral, I want to leave you with a message of faith and qualified hope. The story of QWERTY is a rather intriguing one for economists. Despite the presence of the sort of externalities that standard static analysis tells us would interfere with the achievement of the socially optimal degree of system compatibility, competition in the absence of perfect futures markets drove the industry prematurely into standardization *on the wrong system*—where decentralized decision making subsequently has sufficed to hold it. Outcomes of this kind are not so exotic. For such things to happen seems only too possible in the presence of strong technical interrelatedness, scale economies, and irreversibilities due to learning and habituation. They come as no surprise to readers prepared by Thorstein Veblen's classic passages in *Germany and the Industrial Revolution*

(1915), on the problem of Britain's undersized railway wagons and "the penalties of taking the lead" (see pp. 126–27); they may be painfully familiar to students who have been obliged to assimilate the details of deservedly less-renowned scribblings (see my 1971, 1975 studies) about the obstacles which ridge-and-furrow placed in the path of British farm mechanization, and the influence of remote events in nineteenth-century U.S. factor price history upon the subsequently emerging bias towards Hicks' labor-saving improvements in the production technology of certain branches of manufacturing.

I believe there are many more QWERTY worlds lying out there in the past, on the very edges of the modern economic analyst's tidy universe; worlds we do not yet fully perceive or understand, but whose influence, like that of dark stars, extends nonetheless to shape the visible orbits of our contemporary economic affairs. Most of the time I feel sure that the absorbing delights and quiet terrors of exploring QWERTY worlds will suffice to draw adventurous economists into the systematic study of essentially historical dynamic processes, and so will seduce them into the ways of economic history, and a better grasp of their subject.

REFERENCES

Arthur, W. Brian, "On Competing Technologies and Historical Small Events: The Dynamics of Choice Under Increasing Returns," Technological Innovation Program Workshop Paper, Department of Economics, Stanford University, November 1983.

Arthur, W. Brian, Ermoliev, Yuri M. and Kaniovski, Yuri M., "On Generalized Urn Schemes of the Polya Kind," *Kibernetika*, No. 1, 1983, *19*, 49–56 (translated from the Russian in *Cybernetics*, 1983, *19*, 61–71).

_____, _____, and _____, "Strong Laws for a Class of Path-Dependent Urn Processes," in *Proceedings of the International Conference on Stochastic Optimization, Kiev*, Munich: Springer-Verlag, 1985.

David, Paul A., "The Landscape and the Machine: Technical Interrelatedness, Land Tenure and the Mechanization of the Corn Harvest in Victorian Britain," in D. N.

McCloskey, ed., *Essays on a Mature Economy: Britain after 1840*, London: Methuen, 1971, ch. 5.

_____, *Technical Choice, Innovation and Economic Growth: Essays on American and British Experience in the Nineteenth Century*, New York: Cambridge University Press, 1975.

Hanson, Ward A., "Bandwagons and Orphans: Dynamic Pricing of Competing Technological Systems Subject to Decreasing Costs," Technological Innovation Program Workshop Paper, Department of Economics, Stanford University, January, 1984.

Katz, Michael L. and Shapiro, Carl, "Network Externalities, Competition, and Compatibility," Woodrow Wilson School Discussion Paper in Economics No. 54, Princeton University, September, 1983.

Veblen, Thorstein, *Imperial Germany and the Industrial Revolution*, New York: MacMillan, 1915.

[13]

Public Choice 61: 41–74 (1989)

Sparks and prairie fires: A theory of unanticipated political revolution

TIMUR KURAN*

Department of Economics, University of Southern California, Los Angeles, CA 90089–0035

Abstract. A feature shared by certain major revolutions is that they were not anticipated. Here is an explanation, which hinges on the observation that people who come to dislike their government are apt to hide their desire for change as long as the opposition seems weak. Because of this preference falsification, a government that appears unshakeable might see its support crumble following a slight surge in the opposition's apparent size, caused by events insignificant in and of themselves. Unlikely though the revolution may have appeared in foresight, it will in hindsight appear inevitable because its occurrence exposes a panoply of previously hidden conflicts.

1. Introduction

Certain political revolutions in modern history, including the French Revolution of 1789, the Russian Revolution of February 1917, and the Iranian Revolution of 1978–79, took the world by surprise. Consider the Iranian Revolution. None of the major intelligence organizations – not even the CIA or the KGB – expected Shah Mohammad Reza Pahlavi's regime to collapse. Right up to the revolution, they expected him to weather the gathering storm. Retrospective perceptions notwithstanding, the Shah's fall came as a surprise even to the Ayatollah Ruhollah Khomeini, the fiery cleric who, from exile, masterminded the revolutionary mobilization process that was to catapult him to Iran's helm.

In hindsight, these revolutions seem anything but surprising. The literatures they have spawned put forth a wealth of explanations: disappointments, governance failures, class conflicts, foreign exploitation, and so on. Plausible as at least some of these seem, they leave unanswered the question of why hindsight and foresight diverge. Why does a revolution that in hindsight seems to

* For valuable discussions, I am grateful to Gary Dymski, Richard Easterlin, and especially Bruce Thompson, who provided some key references on the French and Russian Revolutions. I also benefited from comments by Berhanu Abegaz, Robert Higgs, Viktor Kipnis, Daniel Klein, Mustapha Nabli, Jeffrey Nugent, Everett Rogers, Gordon Tullock, and several participants at seminars at USC and UCLA. Under grant no. SES-8509234, my research was partially supported by the National Science Foundation of the United States. I presented the paper at the March 1988 meetings of the Public Choice Society, held in San Francisco.

42

be the inevitable outcome of powerful social forces surprise so many of its leaders, participants, victims, and observers?

My objective in this paper is to resolve this paradox. I do so with the aid of a collective choice model that distinguishes between individuals' privately held political preferences and those they espouse in public. The central argument goes as follows. A privately hated regime may enjoy widespread public support because of people's reluctance to take the lead in publicizing their opposition. The regime may, therefore, seem unshakeable, even if its support would crumble at the most minor shock. A suitable shock would put in motion a bandwagon process that exposes a panoply of social conflicts, until then largely hidden. From these newly revealed conflicts, almost any writer with a modicum of imagination will be able to construct an elaborate explanation, consistent with almost any social theory, as to why the observed revolution took place.

Historians of revolution have *systematically* overestimated what revolutionary actors could have known. The reason, I argue in the final section, lies in the human mind's use of heuristics that project into the past trends that later developments have revealed.

The paper helps explain two other features of modern revolutions that do not fit into existing theories. One is that they tend to be spearheaded by leaders. Leaders enter naturally into the framework developed here, as individuals with an exceptional ability to detect and to help to expose the incumbent regime's vulnerability. The other feature is that revolutionary regimes invariably undertake campaigns of repression and indoctrination, whose targets include people who risked their lives for the revolution. A major reason, I suggest, is that the memory of how quickly the previous regime's support crumbled makes leaders of a revolution fear that if a counter-revolutionary movement were tolerated it would become unstoppable.

The term revolution has changed meaning over time; currently it covers several forms of change (see Zagorin, 1973: Sect. 1). Here I am using it to mean a fundamental change in the social order brought about in a short period of time through a massive shift in people's expressed political views. By this definition, a *coup d'état* involving the replacement of one set of leaders by another, with neither popular participation nor a major impact on the social order, is not a revolution. Whether or not an observed change in the social order is fundamental may, of course, be controversial. Some have argued that the Iranian revolution did not bring about a fundamental reorientation of the social order, because, they say, the Iranians are just as oppressed as they were under the Shah. But what matters, from the standpoint of the definition offered, is how a change tends to be perceived by the society in question at the time it comes about. In the case of Iran, therefore, the relevant criterion is whether in the winter of 1978−79 the Iranians themselves considered the end

43

of the monarchy to represent fundamental change; the retrospective assessments of outsiders are immaterial.

2. Three anticipation failures: Evidence

My objective in this section is to substantiate the claim that the three revolutions mentioned above took the world by surprise. Later, in Sections 3 through 5, I shall develop a model to explain why anticipation failures occur. Further on, in Section 6, I shall relate this explanation to the evidence presented here.

The most telling evidence that the French Revolution of 1789 startled the world appears in Alexis de Tocqueville's masterpiece, *The old régime and the French Revolution* (1856/1955: in particular, pp. 1 and 143). On the basis of pre-revolutionary documents, Tocqueville reports that on the eve of the revolution, Louis XVI had not the slightest clue that a violent eruption was in the making — let alone that he was about to lose his throne and his head. He saw in the middle class, which was to form the backbone of the insurgence, his strongest base of support. The aristocrats, meanwhile, were more preoccupied with royal encroachments on their political rights than with the mounting frustrations of the middle class. Outside observers did no better at predicting the King's fall. Not even Frederick the Great of Prussia, whose political acumen is legendary, had an inkling of the trouble brewing next door.

In retrospect, of course, it is easy to find signs of the impending revolution. Tocqueville himself suggests that

> Chance played no part whatever in the outbreak of the revolution; though it took the world by surprise, it was the inevitable outcome of a long period of gestation, the abrupt and violent conclusion of a process in which six generations had played an intermittent part. (p. 20)

How can the suggestion that the French revolution was long in the making be reconciled with the fact that it was not foreseen? Before we address this paradox, let us consider some evidence pertaining to the Russian and Iranian Revolutions.

The Russian Revolution of February 1917 was not totally unexpected. For one thing, there were the precedents of the French Revolution and of Russia's own revolution in 1905. For another, the preceding years witnessed numerous industrial strikes and peasant uprisings, as well as some terrorist acts. Neither supporters nor opponents of Tzar Nicholas II thought that his power was fully secure. Still, and in spite of Russia's large human and material losses in the war, the Tzar was widely believed to enjoy the allegiance of the army, without whose cooperation a revolution was deemed out of the question. In the early

44

days of 1917 Lenin told an audience in Switzerland that older men like himself would not live to see Russia's great explosion (Schapiro, 1984: 19). Nor did others working for a revolution see the fall of the monarchy as imminent. Not even the Bolsheviks and Mensheviks in Petrograd during the months leading up to the revolution were prepared for the fall of the Tzar (Schapiro, 1984: 39; and Chamberlin, 1935: 74–75). Foreign observers in the capital were also caught by surprise. Just three days before the Romanov dynasty was over-thrown, the British Ambassador cabled his Foreign Minister: 'Some disorders occurred to-day, but nothing serious' (Chamberlin, 1935: 76). Nor did the Tzar and his family realize what was in store. Two days before the end, the Tza-rina Alexandra had this to say about the general strike in the capital:

> This is a hooligan movement. Young people run and shout that there is no bread, simply to create excitement, along with workers who prevent others from working. If the weather were very cold they would probably all stay home. But all this will pass and become calm, if only the Duma [the parliament] will behave itself (Chamberlin, 1935: 73).

The Tzar, too, was optimistic. Until the very last day of his rule, he apparently believed that the movement against him was too weak to succeed (Paléologue, 1924: 221–225).

The most significant case from our standpoint is the Iranian Revolution, whose climax came in January 1979, with the Shah's self-exile. Because it happened so recently, readers will find it especially instructive to contrast their own explanations with the pre-revolutionary perceptions held by the world's leading intelligence organizations and the principal players in Iranian politics. Common *ex post facto* explanations rest on such matters as the people's hatred of the Shah, the corruption in his government, the brutality of his secret police, his apparent disdain for Iran's Islamic heritage, and the im-balances created by his economic policies.

In September 1977, only 16 months before the end of the monarchy, the CIA conducted a study on Iran, finding it to be an island of stability in a sea of turbulence and the Shah's position to be very secure. The demonstrations that were to lead to the revolution had already begun, but the study saw these as minor disturbances that the Shah's police was quite capable of handling. The Soviet Union was no more accurate in its assessment: since the Soviets did not withdraw their support from the Shah until the last few weeks of his reign, it appears that they, too, expected him to pull through, even as the street dem-onstrations grew by leaps and bounds. Every other significant state, including China, Great Britain, Turkey, and Pakistan, supported him almost to the end (see Hoveyda, 1979/1980: 15–17; and Zonis, 1983: 602).

The Shah and his entourage did no better in foreseeing the explosion. In

45

May 1978, eight months before the end, the Empress Farah first heard a name she is unlikely now ever to forget. 'For heaven's sake,' she asked, 'who is this Khomeini?' (Heikal, 1981: 123). In June 1978, according to inside accounts, the Shah continued to believe that the demonstrators belonged to the fanatic fringes of Iranian society and that their cause would not appeal to the wider masses (Hoveyda, 1979/1980: 33–38). This perception was shared by the leaders of Tudeh, the pro-Soviet Communist Party.[1] Most amazing, perhaps, is that Khomeini himself doubted that the Shah could be toppled. Although in public he thundered relentlessly that the monarchy was about to collapse, to his close associates he confided serious reservations. In the spring of 1978, he told them that the Shah would manage to extinguish the fire that had engulfed his regime (Bakhash, 1984: 45). It is revealing that as late as December 1978, Khomeini's lieutenants were looking for a country that would take him when his French visa expired in April 1979 (Heikal, 1981/1982: 157).

If there is any lesson in all this, it is that a revolution *can* come as a surprise even to those with exceptionally good access to information and with everything to lose from misjudgment. This does not mean that big social changes *always* come suddenly, or that they are *never* anticipated. There are, to be sure, fundamental social conflicts that reveal themselves gradually and are resolved over long periods. Changes of regime brought about by prolonged civil wars offer examples of this pattern. But although the framework here can, with suitable refinements, be applied to such changes of regime as well, they will not receive attention. In the spirit of medical research that focuses on why seemingly healthy individuals might die *suddenly* of a heart attack, I shall restrict my attention to unanticipated revolutions.

3. A framework for analysis

The analysis is based on a model developed in two earlier papers, Kuran (1987a, 1987b), where more elaborate justifications for the main features, as well as further details, may be found.

3.1 Preliminaries

Consider a society whose members have a unidimensional conception of the social order, represented by p. Specifically, every possible social order lies in the unit interval, [0,1]. Although social orders differ in reality along very many dimensions, individuals often collapse the differences to a single dimension. A case in point is the left-right political spectrum, which in this century has been used very widely to classify and compare even the most complex programs.

46

Two political parties are in competition over the social order. One, which initially governs the country, advocates p = 0; the other advocates p = 1. I shall call them Party 0 and Party 1, respectively. Neither party's position is influenced by changes in the popularity of its position, and the leaders of each are fully and unalterably committed to their party's fixed agenda.[2] The notion of a durable revolutionary organization with a fixed agenda suits the revolutions of the nineteenth and twentieth centuries better than those of earlier times. The French Revolution, in particular, was led by a hastily formed, loosely organized coalition of informal associations, whose goal was rather ill-defined.[3] But all that matters here is the existence of some nucleus of opposition to the government, around which a large movement for change can crystallize.

Society contains N individuals, indexed by i, who belong to neither party's leadership. In contrast to the *activists* within party leaderships, these *non-activists* are not publicly pre-committed to any particular social order: if the incentives they face make it advantageous to alter their political positions, they will do so.

Let the preference that non-activist i conveys in public – his *public preference* – be denoted by y^i. Individuals' public preferences matter, because their weighted average, which I shall call *collective sentiment*, determines the apportionment of power between the parties and, hence, the nature of the social order. The observation that the power to rule rests on collective sentiment goes back, of course, at least to Hume (1741–42/1963).[4] The weight associated with non-activist i's public preference, w^i, is a measure of his importance and influence in society. If he is a lieutenant stationed in the capital his weight is bound to be larger than if he is a peasant inhabiting some isolated region. As a rule, of course, there are numerous lieutenants stationed in the capital, and there exist many additional important and influential people, so the weight of even the most influential non-activist is likely to be very small.

In terms of the notation introduced, collective sentiment is given by

$$\hat{y} = \sum_{i=1}^{N} w^i y^i, \tag{1}$$

where the weights sum to 1. The closer collective sentiment is to 0, the freer Party 0 is to run the government as it pleases. A revolution, as we shall see further on, involves a sudden and massive shift in collective sentiment, which results in a huge transfer of power from Party 0 to Party 1.

3.2 Preference declaration

Let us turn now to the individual non-activist's preference declaration decision. Individual i's public preference depends on a tradeoff between two distinct considerations. The first is the sociological fact that he gains rewards and incurs punishments for his political stands. The second is the psychological fact that he suffers for compromising his integrity. He makes such a compromise, and incurs a commensurate opportunity cost, by conveying a preference that diverges from his privately held preference – by engaging, that is, in preference falsification.[5] The latter preference, which I am taking to be exogenous, corresponds to the position he would take in a secret ballot. Labelling it his *private preference*, I am denoting it by x^i.

Formally, the maximand of an individual with private preference x^i is represented by

$$V^i(y^i|x^i) = R(y^i) + N(y^i|x^i), \tag{2}$$

where $R(y^i)$ captures the individual's reputational utility, the utility he derives from being known as having preference y^i; and $N(y^i|x^i)$ is the utility he derives from integrity, given that his private preference is x^i. Conspicuously absent from (2) is the utility the individual derives from the social order itself. The weight of his public preference in collective sentiment being very small, his personal influence on the selection of the social order is negligible. Knowing this, he treats the order and his associated utility as given.

This feature of the model puts it into a class with Tullock's (1974) theory of revolution and sets it apart from almost all the others. In most theories, the individual's motivation to act is the promise of changing the social order. In both Tullock's theory and the present one, by contrast, the individual disregards the advantages and disadvantages associated with alternative political outcomes. Treating all possible outcomes as collective goods or bads, he bases his political choices on his personal gains and losses.

There is a crucial difference between the two theories. In Tullock's model the individual derives no utility from integrity, which means that (what I call) his private preference does not influence his political choices even indirectly. Accordingly, he jumps on the revolutionary bandwagon as soon as the reputational benefit of doing so rises above that of continuing to side with the government – this, even if he privately considers the revolutionary platform to be an abomination. Here, as we shall see, such an individual does not move over to the revolutionary camp until the reputational advantages of supporting the opposition exceed those of supporting the government by a sufficiently wide margin. To put this difference in perspective, think of Iran in the months leading up to the revolution. As it appeared increasingly probable that the Shah would lose the struggle, many of his supporters switched over to Khomeini's camp. This much is in line with Tullock's model. But the Shah's supporters did not all switch at once, and some held out, at great peril to themselves, even

48

after he had been deposed. The model being developed explains this fact, too. It suggests, as will become clear presently, that those who privately preferred the Shah most strongly stayed on his side longest, because their cost of preference falsification was greatest. In sum, the distinctiveness of the present theory lies in its emphasis on preference falsification. This emphasis will enable us to explain the paradox put forth at the outset — namely, that a revolution might catch everyone by surprise, yet in retrospect seem the natural outcome of a long chain of developments.

To return to the model, let s and S denote the weighted shares of the non-activists who publicly support the government and the opposition, respectively. In terms of these variables, the first additive component of (2) has the form

$$R(y^i) = \begin{cases} f(s) & \text{if} & y^i = 0 \\ 0 & \text{if} & 0 < y^i < 1 \\ F(S) & \text{if} & y^i = 1 \end{cases}, \tag{3}$$

where $f(0) > 0$, $F(0) > 0$, $df/ds > 0$, and $dF/dS > 0$. Two properties of (3) require attention. One is that the individual derives no reputational utility if he supports neither party's position. This is an extreme simplification, but as I have maintained in earlier work, it accords with the observation that, in the interest of discouraging factionalism, political parties deal harshly with free-thinking rebels against party discipline. The other feature is that the individual's utility from supporting a particular party's position is related positively to the party's weighted share of support. Its empirical basis is that participants in a political movement provide *each other* various subtle benefits, such as camaraderie, social support, and a sense of importance. The levels and shapes of $f(\cdot)$ and $F(\cdot)$ reflect the selective incentives available to the two parties, either directly through their leaders or indirectly through their supporters.

The second additive component of (2) has the form

$$N(y^i|x^i) = N(1 - |x^i - y^i|). \tag{4}$$

The function $N(\cdot)$ is increasing in $1 - |x^i - y^i|$, which assumes a value between 0 and 1. According to this formulation, preference falsification imposes a cost on the individual, which equals $N(1) - N(1 - |x^i - y^i|)$.

Inspection of the model reveals that (2), the individual's maximand, reaches a maximum when he chooses one of three options: $y^i = 0$, $y^i = 1$, or $y^i = x^i$.[6] To keep the model simple, however, I shall assume that the third option is always dominated, for every non-activist, by one of the other two. This assumption implies that an individual with $0 < x^i < 1$ is better off, in all possible situations, to support one of the parties than he is to remain independent and advocate the order he privately prefers. It is important to recognize that the assumption does not suppress the role of integrity in the individual's calculus: for reasons of integrity, an individual might withold his support from the party able to reward him most.

If all non-activists side either with the government or the opposition, it is reasonable to assume that their estimates of the weighted shares, s^e and S^e, will satisfy the condition

$$s^e + S^e = 1. \tag{5}$$

This implies that S^e equals $\hat{y}^e$, expected collective sentiment. Using (5), along with (2)–(4), one finds the levels of utility the individual expects to attain by supporting the government and opposition to be

$$V^i(0|x^i) = f(1-S^e) + N(1-x^i), \tag{6}$$
$$V^i(1|x^i) = F(S^e) + N(x^i). \tag{7}$$

Note the following: (i) $V^i(0|x^i)$ varies inversely, and $V^i(1|x^i)$ directly, with S^e; (ii) $V^i(0|x^i)$ varies inversely, and $V^i(1|x^i)$ directly, with x^i. From these relationships it follows that the value of x^i that makes the individual just indifferent between declaring $y^i = 0$ and $y^i = 1$ declines with S^e.[7] This relationship is illustrated in Figure 1, where the individual prefers to side with the government if the ordered pair $[S^e, x^i]$ lies below the depicted function, but with the opposition if it lies above.

3.3 The threshold function

To be able to focus on the implications of differences in private preferences, I shall assume that all non-activists form the same point expectations of the parties' shares of support, and in addition, that they all have the same reputation and integrity functions. The latter assumption means that the boundary curve in Figure 1 is shared by all. The curve can conveniently be reinterpreted, therefore, as a separator of the non-activists whose private preferences impel them to side with the government from those whose private preferences impel them to side with the opposition. In Figure 2, the downward-sloping segment of the heavy curve is the boundary curve depicted in Figure 1. This curve also has a horizontal segment, which signals that for sufficiently low values of S^e the non-activists support the government unanimously. (A horizontal segment along the bottom axis would indicate that for sufficiently high values of S^e all non-activists support the opposition.) I shall call this curve the *threshold function* and denote it by $\underline{x}(S^e)$. To each possible expectation of opposition support, the threshold function assigns a range of private preferences for which

50

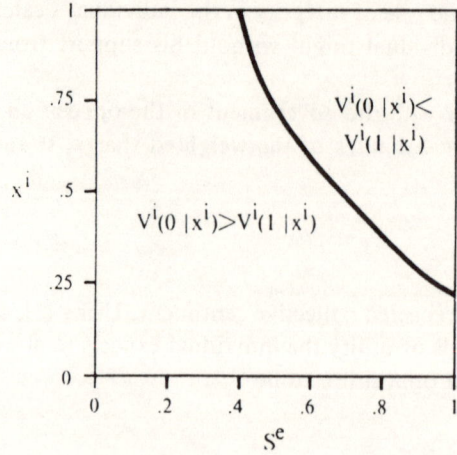

Figure 1.

ACTUAL SHARE OF OPPOSITION

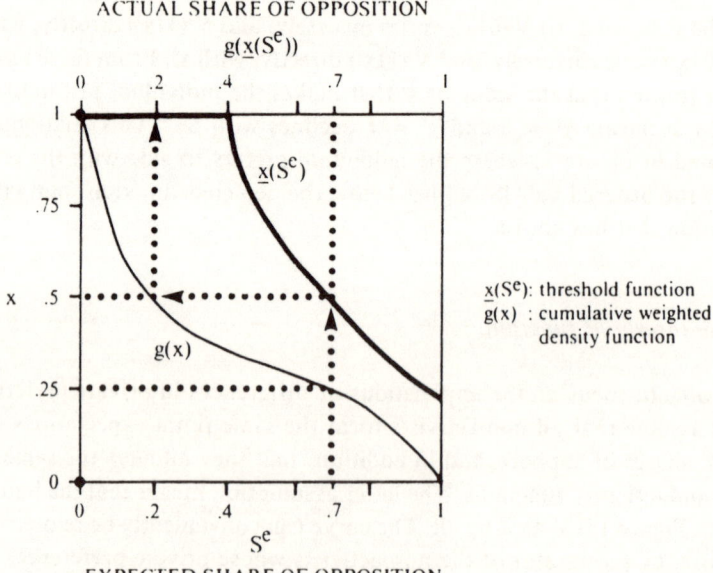

$\underline{x}(S^e)$: threshold function
$g(x)$: cumulative weighted
          density function

EXPECTED SHARE OF OPPOSITION

Figure 2.

supporting the opposition is optimal. It could be relatively steeper or flatter, relatively lower or higher, and with two, one, or no horizontal segments. But this particular example will do as a representation of initial tradeoffs.

3.4 *The cumulative weighted density of private preferences*

The light curve in Figure 2, g(x), represents the *cumulative weighted density* of

51

the non-activists' private preferences. The weights incorporated into it are the same as those in collective sentiment. Recorded along the top horizontal axis, it measures the weighted share of the non-activists with private preferences greater than any given x. The S-shaped density shown in the figure implies that, in weighted terms, half the non-activists have private preferences between 0.25 and 0.5.[8]

3.5 Equilibrium

Given S^e, the actual share supporting the opposition turns out to be

$$S = g(\underline{x}(S^e)). \tag{8}$$

If $S \neq S^e$, the system is obviously in disequilibrium. In Figure 2 this is the case for any $S^e > 0$. For $S^e = 0.7$, for instance, we see from the dotted arrows that the corresponding S is 0.2; only the non-activists with private preferences above 0.5, who form 20 percent of the population, support the opposition. If $S^e = 0$, the non-activists' expectations are self-confirming, and none has an incentive to alter his preference declaration. The system depicted in this figure features, therefore, a unique and stable equilibrium. An equilibrium, in the present context, does not mean absence of social change, for everyone might want some form of change. It means that collective sentiment is at rest, in other words, that the weighted average of people's public preferences, which governs *how* the social order will change, is fixed.

4. Revolution

There would be multiple equilibria if the threshold and cumulative density functions crossed more than once. The vertical projection of each crossing would constitute an equilibrium. Let us now examine the emergence of new equilibria and then turn to an analysis of the revolutionary process.

4.1 Disturbances and new equilibria

For additional equilibria to emerge, one or both of the curves in Figure 2 must shift. Suppose first that only the density of private preferences shifts, as shown in Figure 3, in favor of p = 1. Such a shift might arise in response to an economic downturn that makes certain groups feel relatively deprived and, hence more sympathetic than before to a new order. Alternatively, it might arise as new production methods cause people to desire fundamental political change.

52

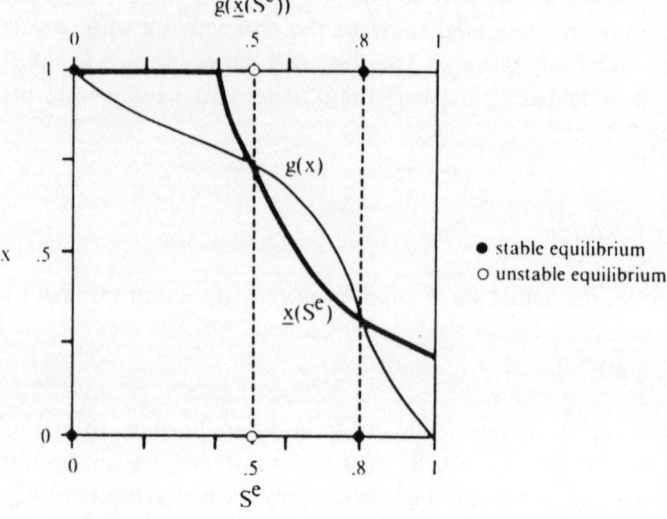

Figure 3.

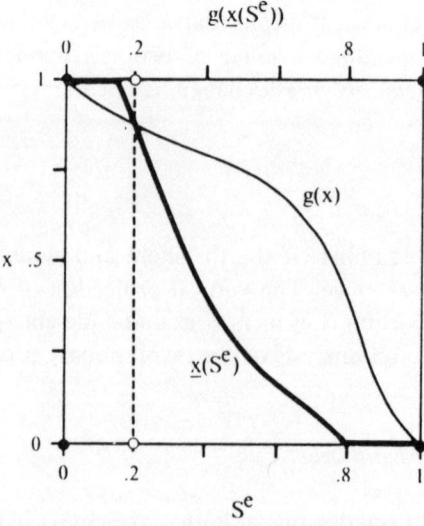

Figure 4.

53

Each of these factors plays a key role in a popular theory of revolution, the former in the relative deprivation theory, the latter in the Marxian theory.[9] But I see no reason why the possibilities should be limited to these. The advent of television, for instance, could alter people's political preferences by enhancing their awareness of how other societies are governed.

Figure 3 features three equilibria: a stable equilibrium at 0 (which constitutes the status quo), a new unstable equilibrium at 0.5, and a new stable equilibrium at 0.8. We see that if the opposition's expected share somehow became positive, but remained below 0.5, revisions would take place to drive it back to 0. On the other hand, if the expected share moved above 0.5, the ensuing revisions would drive it to 0.8. The status quo thus casts a *shadow* over the interval [0,0.5), and the new stable equilibrium casts one over (0.5,1].

In Figure 4, the threshold function has also moved leftward. The reason could be an improvement in the opposition's relative ability to deliver reputational utility – generated, say, by an upward displacement of F(S) in (3), made possible by funds provided by a foreign source. Here, too, there are three equilibria, the middle one unstable. But the status quo's shadow comprises a narrower interval, [0,0.2). Also, the new stable equilibrium lies further to the right, at 1, and it casts a wider shadow, (0.2,1].

4.2 Revolution defined

As noted above, collective sentiment determines how political power is apportioned between the two parties. Party 0 remains totally in control as long as all the non-activists support it publicly. As Party 1 gains support, Party 0 is forced to make increasingly large concessions to it – by giving its members positions in the government and altering policies in favor of its platform, among other possibilities. If Party 1's share of support rises above 0.5, it comes to dominate the government, and Party 0 moves into opposition. Observe that since collective sentiment is a weighted average of public preferences, it is possible for a revolution to be carried out by a small, but influential, share of the population.

According to this model, a revolution is a sudden and massive shift in collective sentiment which induces a fundamental transformation of the social order. Whether or not a change is fundamental may, as already mentioned, be a source of disagreement. But there are certain changes which most members of society would readily characterize as fundamental. In Iran, overthrowing the Shah constituted such a change. In the United States, to give another example, most people would characterize the establishment of a socialist regime as a fundamental transformation – although libertarians might argue that since the federal government is already very powerful, the changes instituted

54

would be symbolic. Returning to the model, I shall call a shift in collective sentiment a *revolution* if it exceeds 0.5 units. In Figure 3, therefore, a sudden rise in S from 0 to 0.8 constitutes a revolution; so does, in Figure 4, a sudden rise from 0 to 1.

Every political party responds, in varying degrees, to collective sentiment. But when it suffers a massive loss of support very suddenly, it generally cannot respond quickly enough to regain the people's confidence. Consider the Iranian government in 1978. As the demonstrations grew, the Shah tried to meet some of the opposition's demands. For instance, he abolished the Women's Ministry and jailed some of his former ministers.[10] But in the short period in which collective sentiment turned drastically against him, he could not possibly have met all the demands being voiced. Even if he had tried to do so, he would not have been taken seriously. Who would have believed him if, from one day to the next, he announced that he wished to run Iran according to the precepts of fundamentalist Shi'i Islam? Would the angry mobs in Tehran have turned down the opportunity to topple his regime just to give him a chance to prove he could outdo Khomeini? Another reason has to do with the fact that changes in a party's orientation require a measure of consensus within its leadership – which in pre-revolutionary Iran included the Shah's family, his generals, and his ministers. Forging a drastically different consensus is a notoriously difficult task, which can take a very long time.[11] Finally, there is a point beyond which an individual leader will not go. The Shah would probably not have been willing to embrace fundamentalist Islam even if by doing so he might have saved his throne.

We now have a justification for the assumption in the model that the parties have fixed positions. A political party cannot adapt quickly enough to reverse a sudden and massive shift in collective sentiment – the kind of shift with which we are concerned.

4.3 Long-term causes and precipitants of revolution

We can now explore what it would take to set a revolution in motion. Three factors may play a role, either in setting the stage for a revolution or in getting it started. These have to do with expectations of the collective sentiment, the threshold function, and the density of private preferences.

Turn back to Figure 4, recalling that the status quo is $S^e = 0$. A jump in the opposition's expected share of support to a point above 0.2 would precipitate a bandwagon toward $S^e = 1$. Such a jump might be generated by an exposition of the pervasiveness of preference falsification, which convinces the non-activists that over 20 percent of them (in weighted terms) actually support the opposition. Given the shape of the threshold function, the exposition would

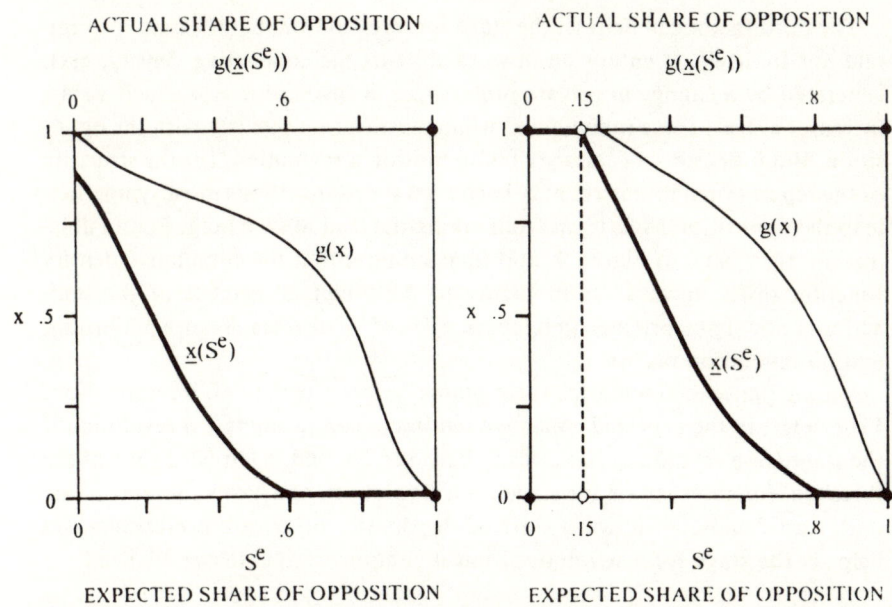

EXPECTED SHARE OF OPPOSITION   EXPECTED SHARE OF OPPOSITION

Figure 5.   *Figure 6.*

in the first instance affect the public preferences of individuals with private preferences around 1. Individuals with somewhat lower private preferences would follow suit, which would then induce those with even lower private preferences to make the switch, and the bandwagon would keep rolling until the opposition enjoyed unanimous support. I leave to Section 7 the issue of how the pervasiveness of preference falsification might get exposed. What needs to be noted here is that although an expectational shift might precipitate a revolution once the stage is set, it cannot start one by itself if the stage is not ready. In Figure 2, for instance, no expectational jump could start a revolution, however large.

If we now compare Figures 3 and 4, we see that a leftward shift of the threshold function makes a revolution more likely by narrowing the status quo's shadow. A second factor in getting a revolution started consists therefore of the long-term causes that move the threshold function, $\underline{x}(S^e)$, leftward. Such a move might be brought about by a rise over time in the opposition's relative effectiveness in rewarding its supporters, through an upward shift of F(S) or a downward shift of f(s). A leftward move of the threshold function can also serve as a precipitant. Suppose, to illustrate the point, that the threshold function were to move further leftward, as shown in Figure 5. The status quo of $S^e = 0$ would become unsustainable, and the expected share of the opposition would gravitate toward the sole remaining equilibrium, $S^e = 1$.

56

The third factor can help set the stage for a revolution, but it cannot precipitate one by itself. It entails an upward shift of the cumulative density, $g(x)$, generated by a change in private preferences in favor of $p = 1$. Such a shift increases at least some individuals' willingness to side publicly with the opposition. But it does not necessarily put in motion a revolution, for the structure of the reputational incentives may keep even the non-activists most sympathetic to the opposition's platform from taking the lead in switching. For an illustration, turn back to Figure 4, and then suppose that the cumulative density function shifts upward, as in Figure 6. Although 20 percent of the non-activists now have private preferences of 1, $S^e = 0$ remains an equilibrium, and no revolution occurs.

Let me pause to summarize these points before I turn to an interpretation. First, a rise in the expected collective sentiment can precipitate a revolution if the stage for a revolution has already been set. Second, a leftward shift of the threshold function can set the stage for a revolution, and it can also precipitate one. And finally, an upward shift of the density of private preferences can help set the stage for a revolution, but it cannot precipitate one by itself.

4.4 Discontent and revolution

The third point lends credence to the assertion, put forward in the Russian revolutionary journal *Narodnaya Volya*, that 'No village has ever revolted *merely* because it was hungry' (quoted by DeNardo, 1985: 17; My emphasis). For a hungry person to revolt he must not only attribute his misery to government policies but also believe that revolting is a remedy. If no one else is revolting, $F(S)$ is likely to fall way short of $f(s)$. This means, unless he derives immense satisfaction from integrity, that he would only compound his misery by following the call of his private political preference.

A nineteenth-century socialist is reputed to have exclaimed to a friend who was handing coins to a beggar: 'Don't delay the Revolution!' The logic underlying this cry is shared by the two most popular theories of revolution in the social sciences, the Marxian theory (according to which epochal changes in production methods and forms of exchange generate discontent, which then leads to an overthrow of the social order) and the relative deprivation theory (according to which gaps between economic expectations and outcomes produce frustration and revolt). Proponents of these theories believe that discontent leads automatically to change-oriented political action. They thus overlook the interdependence of people's political choices and fall victim to the fallacy of composition.[12] Given that in a wide class of plausible situations interdependencies make frustrated people refrain from revolutionary agitation, it is not surprising that neither theory accords with the historical record.

57

ACTUAL SHARE OF OPPOSITION

$g(\underline{x}(S^e))$

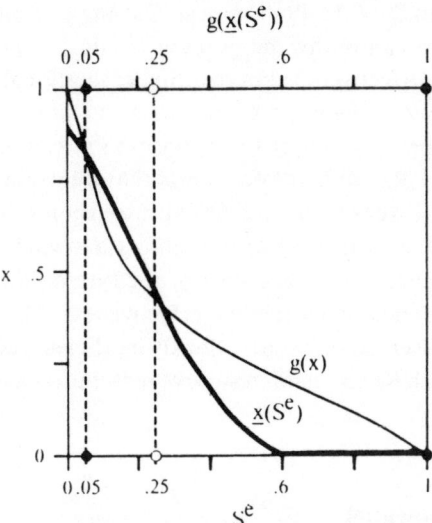

EXPECTED SHARE OF OPPOSITION

Figure 7.

If the Marxian theory (specifically, the best known of Marx's own versions) were correct, the early industrializers of Europe would all have experienced communist revolutions by the early twentieth century. Equally important, the first successful communist takeover would not have occurred in backward, semi-feudal Russia. As for the relative deprivation theory, it falters in the face of evidence that deep economic crises are not followed automatically by heightened agitation against the political status quo. Snyder and Tilly (1972) found that between 1830 and 1960 the level of collective violence in France was uncorrelated with the degree of mass discontent.[13]

None of this should be taken to mean that the opposition does not stand to gain from upward movements of private preferences. On the contrary, if the cumulative density of private preferences is too unfavorable to the opposition, then even a substantial leftward shift of the threshold function might not generate a revolution. To see why, return to Figure 2 and then suppose that the threshold function shifts dramatically to its position in Figure 7. The expectation $S^e = 0$ is no longer self-sustaining, so S^e will be revised upward. To which equilibrium will the revisions lead? One can easily check (in the manner shown in Figure 2) that they will lead to the leftmost equilibrium at 0.05 – the reason being that the pre-disturbance equilibrium at 0 provides the initial post-disturbance expectation. The shift from $S = 0$ to $S = 0.05$ entails a tiny increase in opposition support and, hence, a minuscule adjustment in the social order in the direction of the opposition's demands.

58

Of course, if the threshold function shifts sufficiently leftward, all equilibria other than $S^e = 1$ will disappear, putting into motion a major revolution. A revolution can always be brought about through a large change in the parties' relative effectiveness in providing reputational utility to their supporters. Interestingly, some writers have taken the position that a revolution does not occur in practice *unless* the opposition's relative effectiveness rises dramatically. In the *Republic*, Plato asserts that a revolution is possible only if the ruling class is weakened by internal dissension or defeat in war.[14] In terms of our model, a weakening of the ruling class would entail a downward shift of f(s) and, hence, a leftward shift of the threshold function, which implies a rise in the opposition's relative effectiveness. More recently, Tullock (1987: Ch. 4) has observed that horrendously inefficient regimes, such as those in Albania and North Korea, tend to survive indefinitely as long the ruling elite maintain their unity.

5. Revolutionary potential

In some of the examples considered above, revolution entails a larger shift in collective sentiment than in others, and/or it appears easier to accomplish. Take Figures 2 through 4, in all of which the status quo is by assumption $S^e = S = 0$. In Figure 2, revolution is not a possibility, since there is no self-sustaining alternative to $S = 0$. In Figure 3, there is a self-sustaining and stable alternative, $S = 0.8$, which would be established if the expected share of the opposition were to jump by over 0.5 units. Figure 4 differs from Figure 3 in two respects: the alternative stable equilibrium lies further away from the status quo (at $S = 1$ as opposed to $S = 0.8$), and the expectational jump required to start a revolution is smaller (0.2 units as opposed to 0.5).

It will be instructive to develop a continuously variable measure to quantify the joint effect of such changes. Since each of the examples considered contains at most two stable equilibria, I shall construct it for this class of cases. Some new notation is needed. So, let S^- represent that status quo; S^+ the alternative stable equilibrium; and S^{-+} the unstable equilibrium sandwiched between S^- and S^+. (In the unique equilibrium case, $S^- = S^{-+} = S^+$.) Further, let $d(S,S')$ denote the Euclidean distance between any two shares of the opposition S and S'; and $D(S)$ the largest possible jump in the opposition's share. In terms of this notation, a meaningful measure of revolutionary potential is

$$S^* = \frac{d(S^-, S^+) - d(S^-, S^{-+})}{D(S)}. \tag{9}$$

Table 1. The revolutionary potential stored in the status quo: Figures 2–7

Figure	S⁻	S⁻⁺	S⁺	S*
2	0	0	0	0
3	0	0.5	0.8	0.3
4	0	0.2	1	0.8
5	1	1	1	0
6	0	0.15	1	0.85
7	0.05	0.25	1	0.75

Since $0 \leq d(S^-,S^{-+}) \leq d(S^-,S^+) \leq D(S)$, the measure's range is $0 \leq S^* \leq 1$. Observe that on the right-hand side of (9), $d(S^-,S^+)/D(S)$ is the change in opposition support that a revolution would bring in relation to the greatest possible change. It enters the expression with a positive sign, which means that S* increases with the size of the potential revolution. The second term on the right-hand side, $d(S^-,S^{-+})/D(S)$, represents the jump in the opposition's expected support needed to get a revolution started. It enters the expression negatively, implying that the smaller it is, the larger is the revolutionary potential.

Let us evaluate S* for the each of the cases just reconsidered. For Figure 2 both terms in the numerator are 0, so S* = 0. For Figure 3, S* = (0.8−0.5)/1 = 0.3; and for Figure 4, S* = (1−0.2)/1 = 0.8. For each of the remaining figures, the value of S* can be found in Table 1.

A society featuring high revolutionary potential is liable to burst aflame following a minor shock. Yet it appears tranquil, because the status quo's overwhelming support conceals the existence of a latent bandwagon which, if unleashed, will cause this support to evaporate. This latent bandwagon rests on intra-individual tensions caused by preference falsification. In the pre-revolutionary transformation captured by Figures 2 through 4, these tensions are mounting. The shift of the cumulative density of private preferences raises individuals' integrity-associated losses from supporting the government; and the threshold function's shift then lowers their reputational gains. In Figure 4 the government still enjoys unanimous support, which means that, for all i, $V^i(0|x^i)$ continues to exceed $V^i(1|x^i)$. But the differences are smaller relative to Figures 2 and 3, and individuals' inner tensions correspondingly larger.

The notion that an outwardly stable social order might harbor inner tensions is not novel in itself. Hegel (1807/1949) and Marx (1867−94/1967) consider inner tensions (contradictions in Hegelian terminology) to be the driving force behind social transformations. While some of the tensions that Marx and his followers built into the Marxian theory of social change have upon careful reflection turned out to be spurious, the concept itself has proved useful outside of Marxian thought, too. A non-Marxian use is found in Thomas Kuhn's (1970) theory of scientific revolution. In the course of 'normal science',

60

Kuhn suggests, more and more facts emerge which the reigning paradigm cannot explain. The ensuing tensions within individual scientists set the stage for
a scientific revolution.

6. Unanticipated revolution

We are prepared now to explain why a long-standing regime that has survived
many challenges might collapse suddenly, to the bewilderment of all concerned.

The explanation hinges on preference falsification. Individuals who, for any
number of reasons, become increasingly sympathetic to the idea of change, do
not necessarily take actions that betray their changing private preferences. If
the government enjoys widespread support and, hence, is very powerful, such
individuals find it prudent to remain outwardly loyal to the existing order. In
the process, they keep the government, outside observers, opposition leaders,
and even each other in the dark as to the regime's vulnerability. Their silence
makes society appear stable, even though it would find itself in the throes of
revolution if there were even a slight surge in the size of the opposition. Sooner
or later, a relatively minor event makes a few individuals reach their boiling
point and take to the streets in protest. This kicks off the latent revolutionary
bandwagon, and the opposition darts into power. The magnitude and speed of
the revolutionary process come as an enormous surprise, precisely because the
masses had been concealing their growing frustrations.

The dynamics involved are captured beautifully by the old Chinese saying,
'A single spark can start a prairie fire' (cited by Mao Tse-Tung, 1930/1972).
Just as a normally ephemeral spark can, given the right combination of physical conditions, touch off a wildfire, an event that would normally lead to
mere grumbling can, given the right combination of social conditions, touch
off a revolutionary uprising.

Let us turn back now to the three revolutions considered in Section 2. Does
the explanation I have offered fit the facts?

In the decades leading up to 1789, many groups in France had reason to
resent the status quo: the cloth merchants faced increasing competition, seasonal laborers lacked job security, soldiers felt underpaid — and the list goes
on and on. From time to time, moreover, such groups took to the street in
protest. But virtually every segment of the population was watched and controlled by some specialized police, so the authorities were never unprepared.
Confident of their ability to control crowds, the King's men actually tolerated
some forms of disorder. They even allowed street riots, as long as the rioters
kept violence to a minimum and stayed clear of certain quarters. The rioters
invariably respected these rules of protest (Cobb, 1969: Chs. 8 and 20). This
is why riots were considered no more of a threat to the pre-revolutionary

monarchy than crowds of screaming football fans are to the Fifth Republic. What neither the King nor anyone else appreciated was that the preservation of order depended vitally on his regime's willingness and ability to enforce the established rules of protest. Everyone saw that most Frenchmen remained loyal to the regime, that they respected its rules even while letting off steam. No one saw, or could see, that multitudes were prepared to join a revolt against the regime if ever they felt it was safe to do.

In Russia, too, it was widely known that many segments of the population had grievances against the regime. The peasants were hungry for land, the urban working class felt exploited, and the soldiers hated the harsh conditions of military service. But the potential revolutionaries were divided — not least because the regime took measures to ensure this (see Chamberlin, 1935: 63–77). Equally important, there was a huge garrison in the capital, whose function it was to help the police in defending the regime. Both friend and foe of the Tzar considered the army to be a reliable protector of the regime (Chamberlin, 1935: 66). True, the soldiers were disgruntled, but when had they not been? And even if most would welcome a change in regime, who among them would take the lead in revolting? In 1848 Bismarck had managed to avert a revolution in Germany by retaining the support of the army. Why, people asked, shouldn't the same strategy work for the Tzar?[15] No one, it seems, expected the army to disintegrate upon contact with civilian protestors.

With respect to Iran, there is much evidence that the likelihood of revolution was distorted by people's propensity to engage in preference falsification. Four years before the revolution, when the Shah formed the Rastakhiz (Resurgence) Party, most politically significant Iranians rushed to join it. From post-revolutionary accounts, we know that in private many resented having to do so.[16] We also know that at least some high-level bureaucrats were critical of the sumptuous celebrations of the 2500th anniversary of the Persian monarchy, but only in the company of family and close friends (see Hoveyda, 1979/1980: 103 and 117). Meanwhile, numerous clerics who achieved prominence after the revolution, including the Ayatollah Beheshti, were quite restrained in their criticisms — until, that is, the eve of the revolution. In various capacities, some even served in organizations linked to the Shah's government (see Bakhash, 1984: 40–42). These examples, to which many more could be added, illustrate why neither the Shah nor others noticed the simmering trouble.

In terms of the model developed in this paper, the evidence just presented suggests the following. In all three pre-revolutionary periods, substantial numbers of people were privately opposed to the incumbent regime. At the same time, the regime appeared strong, which ensured that public opposition was, in fact, unalarming. What, then, happened to break the appearance of the invincibility of the regime and to start a revolutionary bandwagon rolling?

In the cases of France and Iran, the answer seems to lie, in large measure,

62

in a lessening of government repression – which in our model shifts the threshold function leftward. The French Revolution, Tocqueville (1856/1955: 175) notes, drew much of its strength from districts near Paris where 'the freedom and wealth of the peasants had long been better assured than in any other [district].' Under the influence of the democratic ideas in the air, King Louis XVI and his men had simply 'lost the will to repress'.[17] In Iran, the impetus for reducing repression seems to have come from U.S. President Jimmy Carter's human rights campaign. Aiming to preempt Carter to avoid the appearance of being pressured by the U.S., the Shah took some measures on his own initiative: he gave the press more freedom and permitted open trials for civilians brought before military tribunals (Bakhash, 1984: 13 – 14). Regardless of the merits of the measures themselves, it stands to reason that they helped the opposition grow. If hatred for the government is widespread, providing greater opportunities for criticism serves to publicize this fact, thereby encouraging more people to side openly with the opposition. Also significant no doubt is the Shah's vacillation with regard to the use of force against the growing crowds, perhaps because the cancer treatment he was receiving impaired his judgment. Inasmuch as vacillation is seen as a sign of weakness, it raises the relative attractiveness of joining the opposition.

As mentioned earlier, the Marxian and relative deprivation theories of revolution trace political explosions to policies and institutions that are unpopular. We have just seen, however, that both the French and Iranian Revolutions were precipitated by government measures that were popular. The following remarks by Tocqueville are apposite:

> [I]t is not always when things are going from bad to worse that revolutions break out. On the contrary, it oftener happens that when a people which has put up with an oppressive rule over a long period without protest suddenly finds the government relaxing its pressure, it takes up arms against it. Thus the social order overthrown by a revolution is almost always better than the one immediately preceding it, and experience teaches us that, generally speaking, the most perilous moment for a bad government is one when it seeks to mend its ways. (pp. 176–177)

The Russian Revolution, it appears, was ignited by a major strategic error on the part of the authorities, coupled with a series of coincidences. The Petrograd regiments normally responsible for protecting the Tzar were at the front in early 1917, and most of their replacements were new recruits who were not only less well trained and less experienced, but also more attuned to the mood of the civil population. This proved to be a grave error, since the new regiments fell apart as they came in contact with the crowds (see Chamberlin, 1935: 66, 74–80; and Walsh, 1975: 267–269). It is well worth reiterating in this connection that no one, not even Lenin and his fellow revolutionaries, foresaw that the regiments in Petrograd would melt away when called on to control the crowds.

But what brought the crowds into the street in the first place? Four factors seem to have played a role. On 23 February, the day the uprising began, many residents of Petrograd were standing in food queues, because of rumors that food was in short supply. 20,000 workers were in the streets after being locked out of a large industrial complex. Hundreds of off-duty soldiers were outdoors, looking for a distraction. And as the day went on, multitudes of women workers left their factories early to march in celebration of Women's Day (Chamberlin, 1935: 75; and Walsh, 1975: 267–273). The combined crowd quickly turned into a self-reinforcing mob. It managed to topple the Romanov dynasty within four days.

7. Revolutionary leadership

It was mentioned above that even when revolutionary potential is very great the typical member of society will not know this. While in principle he could find out by polling his fellow citizens for their private preferences, he is unlikely to do so, because polls cost time and money, and because the ensuing benefits would accrue largely to others. He will know his own private preference and possibly those of his relatives and close friends. But such limited information does not provide a reliable base for estimating the wider distribution.

How, then, do people seething with repressed resentments ever discover the vulnerability of the status quo? The information could emerge through a conjunction of events, as in the Russian Revolution of February 1917. Alternatively, it could be foisted on them by revolutionary leaders.

Before I go on to discuss the activities of revolutionary leaders, let me deal with a possible source of criticism, which is the distinction I am drawing between uninformed, politically ungifted masses on the one hand, and knowledgeable, skilled leaders on the other. This may seem an ad hoc distinction, but it does reflect reality. The production of information entails increasing returns to scale, which means that the intelligence specialists employed by political leaders can acquire information more cheaply. Also, political prowess differs across individuals, much like eyesight and mechanical ability. We do not have a full explanation as to why only certain individuals possess political prowess, but this is no reason to deny that differences exist. After all, we cannot explain why some people have exceptional mechanical ability, yet we do not pretend that this ability is distributed uniformly. Recognizing that differences are pervasive, we bring them into our explanations of the labor market.

That movements for change depend on leadership has, of course, been rec-

64

ognized. But as far as I can ascertain, there has been little systematic theorizing on what a revolutionary leader does; the most popular theories of revolution avoid the issue altogether. In the present theory, we can identify three distinct roles, which correspond to the three factors designated in Section 4.3 as a long-term cause or a precipitant.

One is to help break the appearance of the inevitability of the status quo. An opposition leader who senses that there is a great deal of hidden discontent will publicize this in an effort to raise S^e, the opposition's expected share of support. Going further, he will foster the belief that almost everyone privately wants change, and that in reality the government has only the smallest base of support. To succeed, the leader does not have to know exactly how private preferences are distributed. He needs only to sense that hidden discontent is pervasive. His task is akin to that of an entrepreneur who, knowing only that his new product has market potential, sets out to maximize his sales. Just as the entrepreneur discovers the demand curve facing him as the market unfolds, so too, the revolutionary leader improves his knowledge of the distribution of private preferences in the course of the revolution.

In the Iranian Revolution, the Ayatollah Khomeini played a crucial role in creating the image that an overwhelming majority was opposed to the Shah. His tactic was to organize strikes and demonstrations, in order to convince supporters of the status quo that the Shah's days were numbered. Fearing that the Shah would use his 700,000-man army to stop the revolutionary movement in its tracks, and knowing that a soldier carries a much greater weight in collective sentiment than a non-soldier, Khomeini devoted much energy to spreading the message that the soldiers' sympathies lay with the crowds. Don't be fooled by appearances, he said, pointing out that even though the army might seem loyal to the Shah, it was made up of men who were the strikers' and demonstrators' brothers. And he made every effort to keep his followers from firing at the soldiers, lest this turn them against the crowds. 'Do not attack the army in its breast, but in its heart,' he exhorted. 'You must appeal to the soldiers' hearts even if they fire on you and kill you' (Heikal, 1981/1982: 145–146). As already mentioned, Khomeini was not sure, until the battle was more or less won, that the movement would succeed. He sensed that the Shah was vulnerable, but the speed with which the opposition grew surprised him like everyone else. This is not to say that he picked the time to call for an uprising at random. In 1974, when he was still in Iraq, the Iraqi President proposed that they work together to topple the Shah. He declined the offer, quoting Prophet Muhammad: 'There is a right time for everything' (Heikal, 1981/1982: 140).

The uprising that brought down the Romanovs was not orchestrated by a tightly organized leadership. Many factions worked independently against the Tzar. It is significant, however, that the leaders of these factions directed their

65

efforts at winning over the troops rather than at arming the crowds (Chamberlin, 1935: 76).

The second role of a leader is to mold people's private preferences. To this end, he finds wrongs in the existing order, brings these to the non-activists' attention, and drums into their consciousness that the order advocated by the opposition would serve them better. His immediate objective here is to enhance the non-activists' willingness to join his movement. (Recall that a person's utility from siding with the opposition rises with the proximity of his private preference to the opposition's stand). Khomeini, students of the Iranian revolution agree, did a brilliant job of convincing Iranians of almost all walks of life that they would be better off under an Islamic regime that under the Pahlavi monarchy. He managed to be all things to all people: to the devout, an idol smasher; to the downtrodden, a deliverer of dignity; to the poor, an egalitarian redistributionist; to the Marxist, a democrat who would allow them to prepare for *their own* revolution.

The third role of a leader is to enhance the benefits of siding with the opposition. This can be done through a variety of means, ranging from social events to prayer meetings to physical intimidation. In the Iranian revolution, as in others, it was clear that if the movement succeeded, government supporters would be punished. The fear of retribution was undoubtedly instrumental in causing increasing numbers of government workers to go on strike as the opposition grew.

The view that leadership plays a crucial role in getting a revolution started was rejected by Marx, who saw political revolutions as the work of grand forces of history. One might expect, therefore, leading communist revolutionaries to have deemphasized its role. In reality, most, including all who were successful, have accorded it a vital role. Lenin (1902/1975), for instance, explicitly rejected the doctrine of historical inevitability, arguing that the revolutionary mobilization process depends crucially on sound political strategy, and on inculcating the workers with a revolutionary consciousness.

Engels managed to capture the reasoning behind Marx's position in one of the most famous sentences he ever wrote: 'In default of Napoleon, another would have been found.'[18] What he meant by this is that when historical trends bring a society to the brink of revolution, the leadership required to push it over will always be forthcoming. There are two reasons why this view is difficult to accept. First, the emergence of a great leader, or of a great cadre of leaders, depends on many complex factors — biological, psychological, and social. Since no one really knows how these factors come together, we have no way of ascertaining that a leader will necessarily be there when needed. Second, there is no guarantee that when a leader does emerge, the opposition will be the beneficiary. For reasons known fully not even to himself, the leader might choose to join the party in power, take its helm, and succeed in stemming the

66

revolutionary tide by outmaneuvering the opposition.

This should not be taken as an endorsement of the 'great man' theory of history, which ascribes to exceptional individuals a cardinal role in shaping the course of events. An entire generation of talented revolutionary leaders might fail so much as to dent the social order, even if they succeed in altering the criteria on which people base their public preferences. The reasoning that sustains this argument was outlined through Figures 2, 3, and 4. In practice, many generations of revolutionary leaders might come and go before the revolutionary potential is sufficiently high for a major change in the social order to become possible. One must also recognize that long-run developments impose limits on what leaders can accomplish. Local and global economic trends, for instance, influence revolutionary leaders' effectiveness in preparing people's minds for change.

The arguments just advanced are in line with Tocqueville's views on the role of leadership in the French Revolution. He observes that the ideas that turned the French peasantry and the middle class against the old regime came to them largely from above – from philosophers, the aristocrats, and surprisingly in retrospect, the King and his ministers. And he maintains that revolutionary leaders are likely to preach to deaf ears until people are ready to accept change. Here is a remarkably perceptive passage:

> In all periods, even in the Middle Ages, there had been leaders of revolt who, with a view to effecting certain changes in the established order, appealed to the universal laws governing all communities, and championed the natural rights of man against the State. But none of these ventures was successful; the firebrand which set all Europe ablaze in the eighteenth century had been easily extinguished in the fifteenth. For doctrines of this kind to lead to revolutions, certain changes must already have taken place in the living conditions, customs, and mores of a nation and prepared men's minds for the reception of new ideas. (p. 13)

8. Post-revolutionary repression and indoctrination

Major revolutions tend to be followed by massive campaigns of repression and indoctrination whose targets include many of the revolutionaries themselves. The revolutionary regime in France was obsessed with tearing the mask of mendacity and hypocrisy off the faces of all Frenchmen, including its own leaders. The thousands it sent to the guillotine included such figures as Danton and Robespierre.[19] Under Stalin, the Bolshevik regime engineered one of the worst calamities of the twentieth century, wiping out over ten million people,

67

including almost all of Lenin's closest comrades (see Medvedev, 1967/1973: Chs. 2–8). In Iran those executed or imprisoned by the Islamic regime include thousands who, before victory seemed assured, risked their lives by participating in the anti-Shah demonstrations. Meanwhile, immense efforts have been undertaken to control how people think and act. Universities remained closed for two years while professors redesigned their courses in accordance with ostensibly Islamic values. A clause was inserted into the constitution which makes criticism of Islam a punishable offense. Various organizations, like the Center for Combating Sin, have been created to enforce ideological and behavioral conformity (see Bakhash, 1984: esp. Chs. 4, 9, and 10).

How to explain these campaigns? And how, specifically, to explain that revolutionaries figure prominently among their targets? The Marxian and relative deprivation theories provide no answer. Each says that people revolt against an established order when they become convinced that a new order would serve them better. An implication is that while a revolutionary regime might gain security from terrorizing and indoctrinating its active opponents, it would have no reason to target its supporters. The theory developed here, however, provides an explanation. Since people's public and private preferences may differ, a revolutionary regime is justified in suspecting that its supporters include many would-be turncoats, people who participated in the revolution even though they privately favored the old regime.[20] Consider, once again, Figure 5, which features a single equilibrium that entails unanimous support for the revolution. Some supporters have private preferences close to 0, which means that if the revolutionary regime were to relax its grip over what people do and say, a counter-revolutionary bandwagon might form.

The leaders of the Iranian Revolution had a well-founded reason to fear that many who took part in the revolution would disapprove of forced Islamization. The uprising that brought down the Shah united the most disparate social groups: clerics and Westernized intellectuals, nationalists and pro-Soviet communists, wealthy industrialists and bazaar merchants, factory workers and bureaucrats, women with and without the concealing *chador* (see Arjomand, 1986: esp. 392 and 402). Among those who marched through Iran's major cities shouting 'Death to the Shah' and 'Allah is great' were many who had benefited handsomely from the Shah's rule and had everything to lose from a theocratic order. Moreover, there were substantial differences within the clergy as to what Islamization would entail. The Ayatollah Shariatmadari, for instance, was opposed to some key features of Khomeini's interpretation.[21] There was thus a very real possibility that after the excitement of the Shah's fall died down, some type of counter-revolution would gain momentum.

This is not to suggest that in the aftermath of a revolution the counter-revolutionary potential[22] will be assessed accurately. The typical member of society is likely to underestimate it, for the same reason that before the revo-

68

lution he underestimated the revolutionary potential. The fact that collective sentiment strongly favors the revolutionary order will hide the readiness of multitudes to participate in a counter-revolution should the political winds change. An additional reason why the counter-revolutionary potential is likely to be underestimated is that after the revolution it will be prudent for people to exaggerate their contribution to the revolution's success. Many will thus turn the clock back on when they lost faith in the old order and on when they exposed themselves to danger by siding with the opposition.[23] In restrospect, consequently, the revolutionary potential in the pre-revolutionary period will be overestimated. It might even seem that the revolution was inevitable, even if it would not have occurred at all in the absence of fortuitous circumstances.

Nevertheless, until the extent of the previous regime's one-time support and the suddenness of its disintegration recede from memory, many members of society will consider a counter-revolution to be within the realm of possibility. The revolutionary leaders will recognize, in this connection, that just as they forged a coalition of disparate elements to topple the previous regime, so too, could another group of aspiring leaders forge a similarly composed coalition to topple the new regime. In Iran, in fact, almost as soon as the Islamic order was established, the leftist Mojahedin Party set out to organize strikes and demonstrations, in the hope that these would stimulate an anti-Islamic uprising (see Bakhash, 1984: 219–224). The Mojahedin evidently sensed that the very process that destroyed the monarchy could be used to destroy the nascent theocracy. The Islamic regime's ongoing campaigns of repression and indoctrination stem from its well-founded fears that the anti-Islamic movement has a chance to succeed.

9. Explaining revolutions: Why we err

As mentioned, political revolutions are commonly explained through theories emphasizing such factors as socioeconomic trends and relative deprivation. So it is with regard to the latest great explosion, the Iranian Revolution of 1979. Scores of books and articles have appeared which attempt to explain it in terms of these theories. None, as far as I am aware, ascribes much significance to the fact that the revolution shocked almost everyone concerned. Nearly all explanations suggest that the Iranian revolution was inevitable and, hence, predictable. The objective of this final section is to explain why scholars tend to give the appearance of inevitability to revolutions that seemed anything but inevitable until they occurred.

The mind of a scholar, like that of anyone else, is limited in its ability to receive, store, retrieve, and process information. It is thus forced to use shortcuts, or judgmental heuristics, in trying to interpret, estimate, and infer. Two heuristics are relevant here. One is the *availability heuristic*, according to which the relative availability of information dictates which information is used. The other is the *representativeness heuristic*, which involves the application of resemblance criteria to tasks of causal explanation.[24] Cognitive psychologists have found that although these heuristics serve the mind rather well in many contexts, they generate serious judgmental errors in others.

The availability heuristic comes into play because information consistent with revolution gains salience, and information inconsistent with a revolution loses salience, with a revolution's occurrence. Experimental research suggests that whether a given piece of information is consistent or inconsistent with revolution will depend on the mental models that the historian brings to the task of explanation.[25] An historian who subscribes to the relative deprivation theory is apt to notice, and consider significant, different pieces of information from one who subsribes to the Marxian theory.

Noticing that there were many strikes in the decades preceding the revolution, Marxist historians trying to explain the revolution of 1917 infer that a proletarian revolutionary tide was in formation.[26] They tend not to notice that in the decade preceding the revolution the incidence of strikes was minuscule compared to the next-to-last decade, and that the war generated a wave of pro-Tzarist, nationalist sentiment (see Chamberlin, 1935: 62–63; and Malia, 1980: 92–93). For another illustration, take the relative deprivation explanation for the Iranian Revolution. It suggests that the revolution was fueled by disappointments caused by the post-1975 decline in Iran's oil revenues (see Walton, 1980). Writers who offer this explanation do not appreciate that throughout the 1960s and 1970s there were always groups in Iran who felt relatively deprived. Nor do they accord significance to the non-occurrence of revolutions in Turkey, Brazil, and India, in each of which certain groups suffered severely from the adjustments necessitated by the global economic shocks of the 1970s.

Writing with the benefit of hindsight, historians of revolution consistently exaggerate what anyone could have anticipated in foresight. Might historians who recognize that outcome knowledge distorts human perceptions overcome the bias that the availability heuristic introduces into their judgments? In experiments, trained subjects manage to reduce, but not to eliminate, the bias. Like their untrained counterparts, they tend to overestimate both what they knew before outcome knowledge was revealed to them and what others could have known (see Fischhoff, 1975; and Fischhoff and Beyth, 1975). This last result is especially significant, as it suggests that even historians who understand that perceptions are colored by outcome knowledge might overestimate the foresight of revolutionary actors.

Tocqueville's book on the French Revolution is a towering accomplishment partly because he took exceptional care to guard against the biases that out-

70

come knowledge introduces into historical analysis. His interpretations are based almost entirely on pre-revolutionary documents: minutes of meetings of the 'Estates' and provincial assemblies, written instructions given to deputies by their constituents, and confidential files of the government. Where he does use a post-1789 source, he remains alert to discrepancies between pre-1789 facts and post-1789 renderings of them. In this connection, he reports without equivocation that Frenchmen of all backgrounds tried systematically to conceal their pre-revolutionary dispositions – to obliterate, as it were, their former selves.

The representativeness heuristic biases historical interpretation by focusing the historian's attention on great forces, like epochal shifts in economic structures or massive disappointments. It keeps him from imagining that small forces, such as misjudgment on the part of a ruler, or a string of fortuitous circumstances, could explain why one country blew up while another remained stable. A *small* event, according to its logic, is not representative of a *great* outcome, so there can be no causal relationship between them. Thus, if country A experienced a revolution but not country B, this must be because a great force was at work in the former but not the latter. A great force, of course, is likely to be visible. One might fail to notice the prejudices that underlie the actions of a political leader, but it is hard to miss an epochal shift in relations of production.

Tullock (1974: Ch. 5) observes that post-revolutionary writers ignore people's personal incentives for revolutionary participation and greatly exaggerate their collective incentives. The two heuristics explain why. Collective incentives, such as the benefits that accrue to the nation at large from the toppling of a rapaciously corrupt regime, are more representative of a great revolution than are personal incentives, such as the lure of a job or the fear of ostracism. Also, they are more salient, or available, than personal incentives. It hardly helps that in their memoirs revolutionaries tend to conceal their selfish motives and stress their devotion to the common good.

The causal significance of the factors stressed in the theory presented here, namely preference falsification and the interdependence of public preferences, has tended to be overlooked. One reason is that these factors are perceived as unrepresentative of great events. The model will help, I hope, to alter this perception. Once it is recognized how preference falsification can keep a society's revolutionary potential from being assessed correctly, and how in an apparently tranquil society a small event can precipitate a cataclysmic upheaval, the representativeness heuristic need no longer be a factor in keeping the focus of analysis on relative deprivation and structural economic trends.

A complementary reason why the factors highlighted here have received little attention lies in the perception that the data necessary to detect preference falsification and latent bandwagons are not readily available. There is some validity to this charge. One must recognize, though, that the supply of data is driven largely by demand, and that the demand for data is driven by the existence of theories that suggest how they might be useful. Who would want to collect data that no one desires to use? Equally important, who would want to develop methodologies for collecting such data? Fortunately, the usefulness of data on preference falsification and the interdependence of public preferences is beginning to gain recognition. At the Allensbach Institute in Germany, some very promising work is underway to develop a methodology for detecting changes in the distribution of private preferences and for quantifying the factors that drive a wedge between private and public preferences (see Noelle-Neumann, 1980 / 1984). It may soon be possible to track the revolutionary potential of a society, as defined in this paper, thereby improving our ability to predict and explain future revolutions. But I do not want to sound overly optimistic, for social predictions interact with the phenomena they predict. The announcement that revolutionary potential is high may precipitate a revolution; or, by inducing the government to take decisive action, it may prevent one. Possibilities abound, as do questions calling for further research.

Notes

1. For this blunder, they were later sacked in a meeting held in Prague. See Heikal (1981 / 1982: 156).
2. Some leaders have no other option, as they cannot alter their political stands convincingly. See section 4.2 above.
3. On the emergence of durable revolutionary organizations, see DeNardo (1985: Ch. 1).
4. Noelle-Neumann (1980/1984: Chs. 4–12) provides an excellent survey of the pertinent writings by Hume and by others, including Locke, Madison, Rousseau, and Tocqueville.
5. For more on this tradeoff, see Kuran (1987a: Sects. 1–3).
6. Due to the form of (3), all other intermediate choices of y^i are dominated by $y^i = x^i$.
7. To obtain this result formally, equate $V^i(0|x^i)$ with $V^i(1|x^i)$, and implicitly differentiate x^i with respect S^e.
8. Observe that $g(0.25)-g(0.5) = 0.7-0.2 = 0.5$.
9. On the relative deprivation theory, see Davies (1962) and Gurr (1970). The Marxian theory has many variants, of which Skocpol's (1979) is the latest to receive substantial attention. Marx's most influential statement on the subject of revolution is in *A contribution to the critique of political economy* (1859/1970: 20–21). Elster (1985: 428–446) provides an excellent critique of Marx's pertinent writings.
10. See Bakhash (1984: Ch. 1). The chapter provides numerous additional examples of policy shifts in the waning days of the Shah's reign.
11. For a detailed explanation that rests on preference falsification, see Kuran (1987b). Some complementary explanations are surveyed in Kuran (1988).
12. Marx, unlike many of his followers, understood the fallacy of composition. He argued, for instance, that the capitalist class would self-destruct, against the wishes of individual capitalists. But, as Olson (1965 / 1971: 105–110) and Buchanan (1979) have pointed out, he nonetheless fell victim to the fallacy on the subject of socialist revolution.

72

13. The fallacy of composition does not afflict all arguments based on relative deprivation. A case in point is Easterlin's (1980) theory of fertility, in which the childbearing decisions of couples depend on how well off they consider themselves to be relative to their parents. Couples decide how many children to have largely independently of other couples, so if each of 100 households wishes to have one more child, it follows (in the absence of biological obstacles) that there will be 100 more children. In this context, therefore, the link between relative deprivation and childbearing is basically automatic.

14. Plato makes this assertion in the eighth volume. As cited by Popper (1957 / 1964: 62).

15. On the regime's efforts to follow Bismarck's strategy, see Malia (1980: esp. Ch. 1). An additional component of this strategy was to make concessions designed to moderate their opposition. One such concession was Alexander II's emancipation of the peasants.

16. One must keep in mind that those who served a toppled regime have a strong incentive after the revolution to say that they served only to avoid reprisals. See Section 8 below.

17. The phrase belongs to Cobb (1969: 272). Tullock (1987: 121) observes in this connection that at the time of the revolution the Bastille prison did not contain a single genuinely political prisoner.

18. F. Engels to H. Starkenburg, 25 January 1894. As quoted by Gardiner (1952: 100).

19. A brilliant analysis of the post-revolutionary terror in France is provided by Arendt (1963 / 1965: 88–109).

20. An analogous phenomenon has been detected in studies of technological diffusion. Rogers (1983: 172–174) cites cases of people choosing to adopt a new technology *before* becoming persuaded as to its superiority over the old.

21. See Akhavi (1980: 168–180). Bakhash (1984: 223) reports that in 1982 Shariatmadari was accused of treason and put under house arrest. In retrospect, it appears that the Shah might have avoided the revolution by exploiting the serious differences within the clergy.

22. If one redefines S^- as the share of the revolutionary party's support after the revolution, and S^+ its share in the event the counter-revolution succeeds, this potential, too, can be measured by (9).

23. Such systematic distortions are observed in non-revolutionary contexts as well. After elections, for instance, more people claim to have voted for the winning candidate or platform than actually did so. See Noelle-Neumann (1980 / 1984: 31–33) and Uhlaner and Grofman (1986).

24. These heuristics were first introduced by Tversky and Kahneman (1974). Other important articles on the subject can be found in a volume edited by Kahneman, Slovic, and Tversky (1982). A splendidly clear exposition has been provided by Nisbett and Ross (1980).

25. On the mechanisms by which preconceptions bias cognitive processes, see Taylor (1982).

26. The standard Marxian explanation and its flaws have been outlined by Malia (1980: 91–93).

References

Akhavi, S. (1980). *Religion and politics in contemporary Iran*. Albany: State University of New York Press.

Arendt, H. (1963 / 1965). *On revolution*. New York: Penguin Books.

Arjomand, S.A. (1986). Iran's Islamic Revolution in comparative perspective. *World Politics* 38 (April): 383–414.

Bakhash, S. (1984). *The reign of the Ayatollahs: Iran and the Islamic Revolution*. New York: Basic Books.

Buchanan, A. (1979). Revolutionary motivation and rationality. *Philosophy and Public Affairs* 9: 59–82.

Chamberlin, W.H. (1935). *The Russian Revolution 1917–1921*, Vol. 1. New York: Macmillan.

Cobb, R. (1969). *A second identity: Essays on France and French history*. London: Oxford University Press.

Davies, J.C. (1962). Toward a theory of revolution. *American Sociological Review* 27: 5–19.

DeNardo, J. (1985). *Power in numbers: The political strategy of protest and rebellion*. Princeton, NJ: Princeton University Press.

Easterlin, R.A. (1980). *Birth and fortune: The impact of numbers on personal welfare*. New York: Basic Books.

Elster, J. (1985). *Making sense of Marx*. Cambridge: Cambridge University Press.

Fischhoff, B. (1975). Hindsight ≠ foresight: The effect of outcome knowledge on judgment under uncertainty. *Journal of Experimental Psychology: Human Perception and Performance* 1 (3): 288–299.

Fischhoff, B., and Beyth, R. (1975). 'I knew it would happen' – remembered probabilities of once-future things. *Organizational Behavior and Human Performance* 13: 1–16.

Gardiner, P. (1952). *The nature of historical explanation*. London: Oxford University Press.

Gurr, T.R. (1970). *Why men rebel*. Princeton, NJ: Princeton University Press.

Hegel, G.W.F. (1807 / 1949). *The phenomenology of mind*. J.B. Bailke, transl. London: George Allen & Unwin.

Heikal, M. (1981 / 1982). *Iran: The untold story*. New York: Pantheon Books.

Hoveyda, F. (1979 / 1980). *The fall of the Shah*. R. Liddell, transl. New York: Wyndham Books.

Hume, D. (1741–42 / 1963). *Essays: Moral, political, and literary*. London: Oxford University Press.

Kahneman, D., Slovic, P., and Tversky, A., Eds. (1982). *Judgment under uncertainty: Heuristics and biases*. Cambridge: Cambridge University Press.

Kuran, T. (1987a). Chameleon voters and public choice. *Public Choice* 53 (1): 53–78.

Kuran, T. (1987b). Preference falsification, policy continuity and collective conservatism. *Economic Journal* 97 (September): 642–665.

Kuran, T. (1988). The tenacious past: Theories of personal and collective conservatism. *Journal of Economic Behavior and Organization* 10 (September): 143–171.

Lenin, V.I. (1902 / 1975). What is to be done? In R.C. Tucker (Ed.), *The Lenin anthology*, 12–114. New York: Norton.

Malia, M. (1980). *Comprendre la Révolution Russe*. Paris: Éditions du Seuil.

Mao Tse-Tung (1930 / 1972). A single spark can start a prairie fire. In *Selected military writings of Mao Tse-Tung*, 65–76. Peking: Foreign Languages Press.

Marx, K. (1859 / 1970). *A contribution to the critique of political economy*. New York: International Publishers.

Marx, K. (1867–94 / 1967). *Capital*, 3 vols. New York: International Publishers.

Medvedev, R.A. (1967 / 1973). *Let history judge: The origins and consequences of Stalinism*. C. Taylor, transl. New York: Vintage Books.

Nisbett, R., and Ross., L. (1980). *Human inference: Strategies and shortcomings of social judgment*. Englewood Cliffs, NJ: Prentice-Hall.

Noelle-Neumann, E. (1980 / 1984). *The spiral of silence*. Chicago: University of Chicago Press.

Olson, M. (1965 / 1971). *The logic of collective action: Public goods and the theory of groups*. Cambridge, MA: Harvard University Press.

Paléologue, M. (1924). *An ambassador's memoirs*. London: Doubleday.

Popper, K.R. (1957 / 1961). *The poverty of historicism*. New York: Harper Torchbooks.

Rogers, E.M. (1983). *Diffusion of innovations*, 3rd. ed. New York: Free Press.

Schapiro, L. (1984). *The Russian Revolutions of 1917: The origins of modern communism*. New York: Basic Books.

Skocpol, T. (1979). *States and social revolutions: A comparative analysis of France, Russia, and China*. Cambridge: Cambridge University Press.

74

Snyder, D., and Tilly, C. (1972). Hardship and collective violence in France. *American Sociological Review* 37: 520–532.

Taylor, S. (1982). The availability bias in social perception and interaction. In D. Kahneman, P. Slovic and A. Tversky (Eds.), *Judgment under uncertainty: Heuristics and biases*, 190–200. Cambridge: Cambridge University Press.

Tocqueville, A. de (1856/1955). *The old régime and the French Revolution*. S. Gilbert, transl. New York: Doubleday.

Tullock, G. (1974). *The social dilemma: The economics of war and revolution*. Blacksburg, VA: University Publications.

Tullock, G. (1987). *Autocracy*. Dordrecht, The Netherlands: Kluwer Academic Publishers.

Tversky, A., and Kahneman, D. (1974). Judgment under uncertainty: Heuristics and biases. *Science* 185: 1124–1131.

Uhlaner, C.J., and Grofman, B. (1986). The race may be close but my horse is going to win: Wish fulfillment in the 1980 presidential election. *Political Behavior* 8: 101–129.

Walsh, W.B. (1975). The Petrograd garrison and the February Revolution of 1917. In R.F. Weigley (Ed.), *New dimensions in military history: An anthology*, 257–273. San Rafael, CA: Presidio Press.

Walton, T. (1980). Economic development and revolutionary upheavals in Iran. *Cambridge Journal of Economics* 4: 271–292.

Zagorin, P. (1973). Theories of revolution in contemporary historiography. *Political Science Quarterly* 88: 23–52.

Zonis, M. (1983). Iran: A theory of revolution from accounts of the revolution. *World Politics* 35 (July): 586–606.

[14]

Excerpt from *Economic Evolution and Structural Adjustment*, 187–226.

Chapter 9

The Schumpeter Clock

G. HAAG, W. WEIDLICH & G. MENSCH

1. INTRODUCTION

It is a fundamental fact that the non-equilibrium behaviour of an economy consists of long-term and short-term cycles (Keynes 1973; Hicks 1956) and fluctuating components. As a first approximation, the long- and short-term phenomena can be treated separately (Figure 1). In this contribution, we shall focus on short-term motions of the economy which manifest themselves in the macroeconomic variables. We aim to provide a partial theory for the non-equilibrium motion of an industrial system of nations or regions.

The model differs from other existing models of industrial fluctuations in many of its design principles (Goodwin 1950; Chang and Smyth 1950). It is called "the Schumpeter Clock" here according to a proposal from Goodwin (1951), since its moving parts, driving mechanism and control devices are typically Schumpeterian and not, as in the case of other models, typically neo-classical or neo-keynesian. This post-Schumpeterian mathematical theory of short-term cycles is based on microeconomic concepts of the Schumpeterian variety (Schumpeter 1961). It refers to the functioning of the Schumpeter Goods Sector, which is essentially comprised of industry, and those parts of agriculture and services which are operating similarly to industrial organizations. Furthermore, this economic theory refers to dynamic change in major statistical units such as whole nations or regions, and is thus oriented towards the institutional user of applied macroeconomic theory.

The model is primarily designed to take into account hard-driving, microeconomic

188

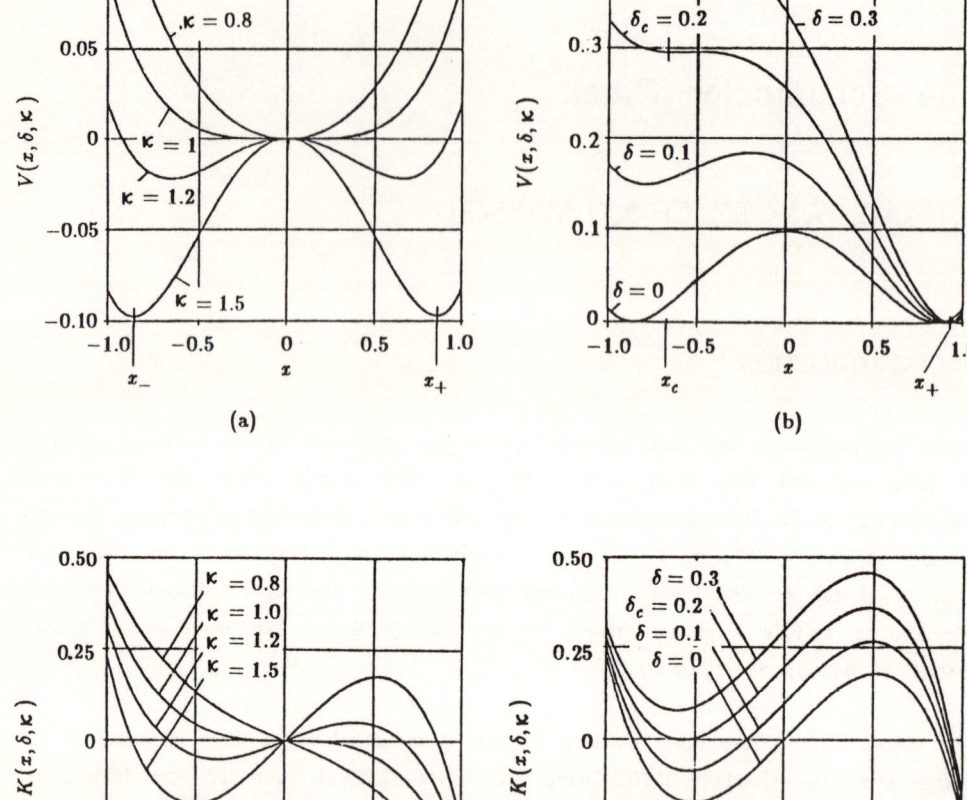

Figure 1 (a, b) Typical graphs of the configuration potential $V(x,\delta,\kappa)$
(c, d) The associated configuration driving forces $K(x,\delta,\kappa)$

189

forces and powerful supply side checks and balances, which combine to create short-term oscillations. The soft-driving macroeconomic forces, and the weak demand side checks and balances, are assumed to be mediated through microeconomic behaviour. In particular, the model operationalizes the Schumpeterian notion of the Prime Mover, i.e., innovators and imitators, who create and propagate microeconomic differences. The heterogeneity among products and production processes constitutes the force field for the creative and destructive energies which hold the economic process in motion. (In this sense, Schumpeter's Process of Creative Destruction can also be understood as the Process of Monopolistic Competition. E.H. Chamberlin has shown that this concept of the product as an economic variable leads Toward a More General Theory of Value (1957)).

Differences among products come into play at the disaggregate levels (firms, markets) of the economic system. The creation of such differences - leading to competitive advantages among rival producers - is the objective of the strategic investments of entrepreneurs. We classify strategic investments I(t) according to their respective competition purposes as expansionary E(t) and rationalizing R(t). These investments move the extensive and intensive frontiers of the economy.

The link between the newly introduced macroeconomic investment structure index and the microeconomic investor's configuration index can be made by introducing methods out of the field of synergetics (Weidlich and Haag, 1982). The investment structure index is a measure for the composition of the aggregate strategic investment, namely, of its expansionary (E) and rationalizing (R) shares. The investors' configuration describes all investors' propensities as either expansionary or rationalizing, as they make their strategic investments predominantly either for extensifying or for intensifying purposes; and the investors' configuration index describes the expansionary bias, or rationalization bias, prevalent in the combined population of investors in any one period of time. Because of the tight relationship between the investors' configuration index and the investment structure index, short-term shifts in bias for either expansionary or rationalizing investments translate directly into swings in the composition of total realized investment in the whole economy. E-type investments extend the capacity of firms, industries, and the economy as a whole. R-type investments have ambivalent macroeconomic effects. As they intensify cost factors, rationalizing investment projects have contractionary ramifications for the supply side of the economy on the whole. Thus, micro-shifts in

190

individual investment propensities combine in generating up- and down-swings of the economy.

The main argument for the cyclicity of industrial (short-term) development presented here is derived from the notion of a dynamics of the shifts between differentiation (innovation) and conformative behaviour (imitation). Over the years, the majority of industrial investors repeatedly shift from a predominantly expansionary investment portfolio to a rationalization bias, with innovators and pioneering entrepreneurs in search of monopoly profits taking the lead in the anticyclical redirection of investment strategies. This "band-waggon" effect results in industrial fluctuations.

In the following sections, equations of motion, which quantify the dynamics of economic change, will be set up and solved. The model simultaneously connects the relevant micro-economic and macro-economic concepts, although it is certainly partial, with its focus on the theory of industrial fluctuations, and in its abstraction of the impact of other substantive areas of economic theory.

According to Gold's managerial decision coefficient model, there are only two principal option types; those directed at either increasing sales volume S, or decreasing the cost level C, in return-on-investment (r.o.i.)

$$r.o.i = \frac{S-C}{output} \cdot \frac{output}{capacity} \cdots \frac{capacity}{fixed\ investment} \tag{1}$$

Thus, both expansionary (E-type) and rationalizing (R-type) investment can increase the r.o.i. by increasing the profits (S-C).

Accordingly, the total volume of strategic investment (Kalecki 1935)

$$I(t) = E(t) + R(t) \tag{2}$$

is defined as all fixed capital investment, replacement deducted, which is considered to be tactical, where

191

E(t)   is the <u>volume of expansionary investment</u> at time t and

R(t)   is the <u>volume of rationalizing investment</u> at time t.   (3)

We propose that there are considerable fluctuations in the volume of expansionary and rationalizing investment as a result of entrepreneurial innovation and imitation activities. The proportional distribution of the shares of E(t) and R(t) in I(t) shifts with time. As these fluctuations take place around long term average paths ($E_0(t)$ and $R_0(t)$) of the expansionary and rationalizing investment, it is first appropriate to decompose E(t) and (R(t)

$$E(t) = E_0(t) + B(t) \;\; \Big\rbrace$$
$$R(t) = R_0(t) - B(t) \;\; \Big\rbrace \tag{4}$$

where the oscillating shift B(t) around the average values E_0 and R_0 is of interest. While the long term behaviour of E_0 and R_0 displays positive semidefinite quantities by definition, B(t) can only vary within the range

$$-E_0 < B(t) < R_0. \tag{5}$$

An investment structure index is now defined as

$$Z(t) = [E(t) - R(t)] / [E(t) + R(t)] = [E(t) - R(t)] / I(t) \tag{6}$$

where Z(t) varies within $-1 < Z(t) < +1$. Inserting (4) into (6), Z(t) decomposes into

$$Z(t) = Z_0(t) + z(t) = (E_0 - R_0) / I(t) + 2 B(t) / I(t). \tag{7}$$

The performance of the Schumpeter Clock will be demonstrated by observing the non-equilibrium motion of the investment structure index Z(t), or preferably, its fluctuating part z(t), for the industrial sector in the Federal Republic of Germany during the period 1956-1979. This will be then explained by using micro-economically determined and supply side factor reinforced shifts of bias in the overall investment activities.

192

In principle, an industrial firm may plan and/or undertake any number of projects at a given time t, but since the "investor" is defined as the decision-making unit, one project per firm will be assumed. The total number of investment projects is large, say $2N \gg 1$, for it is convenient - but not decisive - for the equations to have an <u>even</u> number of projects. For simplicity, it will also be assumed that all projects have the same financial volume . This assumption has no effect on the mean value considerations of this chapter; differences in the size of projects would only influence the variances of the model parameters.

A fictitious "neutral" investor who behaves according to the average long term investment trend will be considered first. His investment project of volume $i = I/2N$ is composed of expansionary investment e_0 and rationalizing investment r_0 as follows:

$$i = I/2N = e_0 + r_0 \quad \text{where} \quad e_0 = E_0/2N, \quad r_0 = R_0/2N. \tag{8}$$

Real investors, however, behave differently to the neutral investor: there are <u>E-type investors</u> who favour the expansionary investment type rather than the average trend. Their projects of financial volume i are constructed as follows:

$$i = e_E + r_E \quad \text{where}$$

$$e_E = e_0 + b \quad \text{and} \quad r_E = r_0 - b, \quad \text{with } b > 0. \tag{9}$$

Evidently b is the surplus of expansionary investment in comparison with the neutral case.

On the other hand, <u>R-type investors</u> favour the rationalizing investment type rather than the average trend. The E/R type shares of their projects are such that

$$i = e_R + r_R \quad \text{where}$$

$$e_R = e_0 - b \quad \text{and} \quad r_R = r_0 + b, \quad \text{again with } b > 0. \tag{10}$$

b is now the surplus in rationalizing investment with respect to the neutral case. For simplicity, the same value for b in (9, 10) will be taken.

193

At a given point in time $n_E(t)$ E-type investors and $n_R(t)$ R-type investors, whose total number is 2N, where:

$$n_E(t) + n_R(t) = 2N(t) \tag{11}$$

are assumed.

The two numbers in the vector $\{E(t), R(t)\}$ characterize the investment structure at time t according to investment volume, and the two numbers $\{n_E(t), n_R(t)\}$ characterize the investors' strategic investment activities at time t (by head count). $\{n_E(t), n_R(t)\}$ is denoted as the investors' configuration.

The integer

$$n(t) = \{n_E(t) - n_R(t)\} / 2 \quad \text{where} \quad -N \leq n(t) \leq N \tag{12}$$

increases or decreases by one if the investors' configuration changes according to transitions

$$\{n_E, n_R\} \rightarrow \{n_E + 1, n_R - 1\} \tag{13a}$$

or

$$\{n_E, n_R\} \rightarrow \{n_E - 1, n_R + 1\}, \tag{13b}$$

i.e. if an R-type investor becomes an E-type investor or vice versa. Multiple unit motions (band-wagon effects) within the investors' configuration are also possible, for instance

$$\{n_E, n_R\} \rightarrow \{n_E + d, n_R - d\} \tag{14a}$$
$$n \rightarrow n + d.$$

Such transitions may indicate series of synchronized product variations or innovations, as often observed and described by the heuristic regularity usually called the product life cycle. Similarly,

$$\{n_E, \ n_R\} \ \rightarrow \ \{n_E - d, \ n_R + d\} \tag{14b}$$

$$n \quad \rightarrow \quad n - d$$

indicates series of synchronized process improvements or process rationalizations.

Instead of $n(t)$, a normalized variable, the investors' configuration index, can be employed so that

$$x(t) = \{n_E(t) - n_R(t)\} \ / \ \{n_E(t) + n_R(t)\} = n(t) \ / \ N(t) \tag{15}$$

with

$$-1 \leqq x(t) \leqq 1.$$

The relation between the investors' configuration index (15) and the investment structure index (6), characterizing strategic investment, now follows unambiguously by combining the postulated equations. The total expansionary investment $E(t)$ and the total rationalizing investment $R(t)$ at time t are given by

$$E(t) = n_E(t) \ e_E + n_R(t) \ e_R \tag{16}$$

$$R(t) = n_E(t) \ r_E + n_R(t) \ r_R \ . \tag{17}$$

Inserting (8-10) as well as (11, 12, 15) it follows that

$$E(t) = [n_E(t) + n_R(t)] \ e_0 + [n_E(t) - n_R(t)] \ b$$

$$= 2 \ Nc_0 + 2 \ n(t)b = E_0 + 2 \ Nb \ x(t) \tag{18}$$

and

$$R(t) = [n_E(t) + n_R(t)] \ r_0 - [n_E(t) - n_R(t)] \ b$$

$$= 2 \ Nr_0 - 2 \ n(t)b = R_0 - 2 \ Nb \ x(t) \tag{19}$$

$$Z(t) = (E_0 - R_0) \ / \ I(t) + [4 \ Nb \ / \ I(t)] \ x(t) = Z_0 + z(t) \tag{20}$$

or

$$z(t) = [4 \ Nb \ / \ I(t)] \ x(t) = g \ x(t) \quad \text{with} \quad g(t) = [4 \ N(t)b(t)] \ / \ I(t). \tag{21}$$

The result (21) shows that the fluctuating part $z(t)$ of the investment structure index

195

$Z(t)$ is proportional to the investors' configuration index $x(t)$. Thus, oscillations of the investors' configuration will show up in oscillations of the investment structure index. The variable $g(t)$ provides the link between the normalized $x(t)$ and the non-normalized $z(t)$.

The discussion of the investors' strategic choice set indicated that the model is consistent with the traditional profit seeking hypothesis. The investigation of the investors' configuration reveals that the model is also consistent with the rational expectation hypothesis. "Rational" expectations are model based, and the life cycle model and progress function model are frequently used by investors to form expectations about the timing of their rivals' next improvements, (Barzel 1968; Kamien and Schwartz 1972) i.e. of the current best practice frontier.

Rosenberg (1976) also pointed out the rationality of speeding-up or delaying product or process innovations under conditions of rivalry. This is done in the expectation of breakthroughs and rapid successions of product or process innovations, which hit the market as a series of capacity expanding or cost reducing investments. Also, in the "awareness context" (Glaser and Strauss 1964) of industrial investors "a firm must incur some positive expense just to maintain a constant level of production cost or efficiency" (Flaherty 1980).

This is especially true in times of cost inflation when the goal is one of "reducing cost in total, not particular costs such as labour costs or capital costs" (Salter 1960). This micro-economic theory of macro-economic contractions also suggests that - in times of cost inflation in which industrial firms try to combat a strong rationalization bias in their overall investment activities - heavy investment does not create higher employment, as the Phillips curve would suggest, but "stagflation".

2. THE EQUATIONS OF MOTIONS FOR THE INVESTORS' CONFIGURATION

It will be assumed that short term industrial investment cycles come about through dynamic interaction between industrial investors, or between two interrelated components of investment behaviour: a) the decision behaviour of managers and entrepreneurs who are making strategic choices about the kind of industrial investments to be implemented, and b) the actual total volume and composition of

196

realized investments. As these components are embodied in the investors' configuration, changes in the numbers $n_E(t)$ and $n_R(t)$ of investors undertaking expansionary or rationalizing investments can be taken as a proxy for the real socio-economic causes of the time path of all industrial activity. Changes in the investors' configuration $\{n_E(t), n_R(t)\}$ result in changes in the rate and direction of industrial investment, as indicated by the investment structure index $Z(t)$. These changes come about as investors change their propensities for E- and R-type investments in view of market opportunities, the revealed preferences of other investors, and their supply side conditions.

Thus, changes in the industrial economy can be formulated as equations of motions of these two components of investment behaviour. The equation of motion for the investors' configuration and the equation of motion for the investors' propensities, as presented in the next two sections, constitute essential parts of the Schumpeter Clock model being presented.

Is has been shown that the transition from one investors' configuration $\{n_E, n_R\}$ to another can be a single unit motion connected with a product innovation (13a) or a process innovation (13b) of one investor. It could also be a multiple unit motion (14a and b) which is most often an imitation process. As innovation is always, and imitation is sometimes, investment under uncertainty, it is doubtful that a deterministic modelling of the motion of the investors' configuration will succeed. But since all investment is risky, the stochastic approach is appropriate. Therefore the well founded master equation formulation will be adopted.

The micro-economic approach to changes in the investors' configuration $\{n_E, n_R\}$ adopted incorporates the notion of individual transition probabilities (per unit of time) for investors turning from an R-type investment to an E-type investment, and vice versa. These individual transition probabilities are denoted by:

$$P_{E \leftarrow R}[n_E, n_R] \equiv p\uparrow(n) = \text{probability per unit time for turning from} \qquad (22)$$
$$\underline{R}\text{-type to } \underline{E}\text{-type investment}$$

$$P_{R \leftarrow E}[n_E, n_R] \equiv p\downarrow(n) = \text{probability per unit time for turning from} \qquad (23)$$
$$\underline{E}\text{-type to } \underline{R}\text{-type investment.}$$

197

The individual transition probabilities yield the total probabilities for changes of the entire investors' configuration. The transition

$$\{n_E, n_R\} \rightarrow \{n_E+1, n_R-1\}$$

takes place with the total transition probability

$$w\uparrow(n) = n_R \; p\uparrow(n) = (N-n)p\uparrow(n) \tag{24}$$

as there are n_R investors who could turn from R-type to E-type investment with individual probability $p\uparrow(n)$. Analogously, the transition

$$\{n_E, n_R\} \rightarrow \{n_E-1, n_R+1\}$$

takes place with the total transition probability

$$w\downarrow(n) = n_E \; p\downarrow(n) = (N+n) \; p\downarrow(n) \tag{25}$$

as there are n_E investors who could turn from E-type to R-type investment with individual probability $p\downarrow(n)$. These transition probabilities (24, 25) of single unit motions of the investors' configuration $\{n_E, n_R\}$ are the fundamental inputs for formulating the master equation.

The master equation describes the motion of the <u>probability distribution</u> over the investors' configuration. This distribution function is denoted as

$$P[n_E, n_R ; t] \equiv P(n;t) \quad \text{for } -N \le n \le N. \tag{26}$$

By definition, the value of this function of n and t is the probability that at time t the investors' configuration $\{n_E, n_R\}$ is realized; the configuration relevant variable of the function $P(n;t)$ is $n=(n_E - n_R)/2$. Because one of the configurations $\{n\}$ is <u>always</u> realized, the sum of the probabilities has to be 1:

198

$$\sum_{n=-N}^{N} P(n;t) = 1. \tag{27}$$

The master equation is derived by a simple probability balance consideration: the probability $P(n;t)$ of the configuration n can <u>increase</u> by means of transitions from either one of the neighbouring configurations $(n-1)$ or $(n+1)$ into configuration n, while $P(n;t)$ may simultaneously <u>decrease</u> by transitions from configuration n into these neighbouring configurations. The transition probabilities per time unit for these processes have already been introduced in (24, 25). Incorporating them into the balance consideration immediately leads to the master equation

$$dP(n;t) / dt = [w\uparrow(n-1)P(n-1;t) + w\downarrow(n+1)P(n+1;t)] \tag{28}$$
$$-[w\uparrow (n) P(n;t) + w\downarrow (n) P(n;t)] .$$

The master equation (28) represents $2N + 1$ coupled linear difference differential equations for $P(n;t)$ with $n = -N , -N + 1, ...,N - 1,N,$ which are not easily solved in the general case when N is large. However, if it is assumed that the $P(n;t)$ are sharply peaked and uni-modal around their mean values $<n>_t$, then a set of closed equations of motion for the mean values can be derived. These are defined by

$$<n>_t = \sum_{n=-N}^{N} nP(n;t) \tag{29}$$

Taking the time derivative of (29) and inserting the master equation (28) in the rhs, one obtains

$$d<n>_t / dt = \sum_{n=-N}^{N} n [dP(n;t)] / dt = \sum_{n=-N}^{N} [w\uparrow(n) -w\downarrow(n)] P(n;t). \tag{30}$$

The rhs of (30) is the mean value $<w\uparrow(n) - w\downarrow(n)>_t$ of $w\uparrow(n) - w\downarrow(n)$. Equation (30) is not a closed equation for the mean value $<n>_t$ because the full distribution $P(n;t)$

199

has to be known in order to calculate $d<n>_t/dt$. But under the assumption that $P(n;t)$ remains sharply peaked and uni-modal around its mean value, an approximate closed equation of motion for the mean value $<n>_t$ can be obtained as

$$d<n>_t / dt = w\uparrow(<n>_t) - w\downarrow(<n>_t). \tag{31}$$

The mean value equation for x, the investors' configuration index, upon transition to variable $x = n/N$, (see (15) in (31)) then reads:

$$d<x>_t / dt = K(<x>_t) \tag{32}$$

$$K(<x>_t) = 1/N [w\uparrow(<n>_t) - w\downarrow(<n>_t)] =$$

$$(1-<x>_t)p\uparrow(N<x>_t) - (1+<x>_t)p\downarrow(N<x>_t). \tag{33}$$

From this point on the clumsy mean value brackets will be omitted and $x(t)$ written for $<x>_t$, thus (32) is

$$dx(t)/dt = K(x(t)). \tag{34}$$

According to (33), K depends on the actual configuration $x(t)$ of all the actors (investors) in the system at time t, and the transition probabilities for change of this configuration $p\uparrow(x)$ and $p\downarrow(x)$, which in turn depend upon all investors' propensities, which shall be parametrized by 6 and κ. Thus the driving force K, see (33), may be written as a function of x, 6 and κ as

$$K(x;6,\kappa) = (1-x)p\uparrow(x;6,\kappa) - (1+x)p\downarrow(x;6,\kappa). \tag{35}$$

A fairly general constructive specification of these transition probabilities which has already been shown to be sufficiently flexible takes the form:

$$p\uparrow(x;6,\kappa) = \nu \exp(6+\kappa x)$$
$$p\downarrow(x;6,\kappa) = \nu \exp[-(6+\kappa x)] \tag{36}$$

(Weidlich and Haag, 1983).

The technical parameter ν is a frequency which relates, according to (49), the abstract dimensionless time τ in formal modelling to real time t in empirical work, when the model is being applied to real economic data. The trend parameter δ is referred to as The Alternator. It initiates the reversal of strategic bias. To see this, first assume an increasingly positive value of δ in (36). It increases the value of $p\uparrow$, whereas the value of $p\downarrow$ is decreased. Therefore, a positive alternator favours individual strategy change over to E-type investment, and it disfavours transitions to R-type investment. The inverse holds for negative δ. In our model the alternator is viewed as a function of time $\delta(t)$. A dynamic equation of motion for the alternator shall be set up in section 3. It alternates between positive and negative values over time, and its oscillations produce periodic shifts of the probabilistic decision behaviour of investors. In other words, the alternator governs the propensity to switch the strategic direction of innovation.

The trend parameter κ represents the propensity to imitate. Thus, it is referred to as The Coordinator. It amplifies the strategic shifts. To see this, let us first focus upon a situation with $n_E > n_R$ or $x > 0$. This means that the majority of firms are currently investing with expansionary bias. Then, according to (36), the transition probability $p\uparrow$ of an R-type investor to switch over to E-type investment is larger than the transition probability $p\downarrow$ of an E-type investor to change from E-type to R-type investment. The converse is true in a situation where $n_E < n_R$, or $x < 0$. In both cases, however, the transition probability for change to the investment type of the majority is larger than that for a change to the minority type. Hence, the incumbent majority is stabilized and even extended by the effect of κ. This trend increases for increasingly positive κ. In other words, the coordinator represents the investors' inclination to conform to the behaviour of the majority of firms at the time. The coordination effect manifests itself as a synchronization effect of investments of the same type undertaken by a majority of investors. In general, the effects of the alternator and the coordinator superpose and thus determine the transition probabilities at any point in time. Since δ and x depend on time, the transition probabilities of investors are themselves functions of time. They simultaneously cause strategic changes, and depend on the effects of the changes which manifest themselves in the economic data.

201

Inserting (36) in (35) and using the standard definitions of the hyperbolic sine and cosine, a specific expression for the driving force

$$K(x;\delta,\kappa) = 2\nu[\sinh(\delta+\kappa x) - x \cosh(\delta+\kappa x)] \tag{37}$$

is obtained, which in turn yields an explicit form for the mean value equation of motion of the investors' configuration index

$$dx(t) / dt = K(x;\delta,\kappa) \tag{38}$$

by using (37) on the rhs of (38).

The dynamic behaviour of x can also be described in terms of a "potential" which stands in close relation to the driving force K· of x such that

$$K(x;\delta,\kappa) = -\partial V(x; \delta,\kappa) / \partial x, \tag{39}$$

which may be regarded as being the pace maker of the Schumpeter Clock. Integrating the force (37) yields the "configuration development potential"

$$V(x; \delta,\kappa) = (2\nu/\kappa^2) [\kappa x \sinh(\delta+\kappa x) - (1+\kappa) \cosh(\delta+\kappa x)]. \tag{40}$$

In the upper part of Figure 1, numerical values for $V(x; \delta,\kappa)$ are depicted:

(a) for δ = 0 and different values of κ

(b) for κ = 1,5 and different of values δ,

whereas in the lower part of Figures 1c and d, the quantified driving forces $K(x; \delta,\kappa)$ associated with the cases a and b, respectively, are shown. Comparing Figure 1a with c, and b with d for the same sets of parameters κ, δ it is seen that the force $K(x; \delta,\kappa)$ drives x into the minima of the potential $V(x; \delta, \kappa)$. In case a with κ = 1.5 for instance, the motion ends at the positive minimum $x = x_+$ (expansionary bias of the investors' configuration index x) or at the negative minimum at $x = x_-$ (rationalization bias of x). In case b with δ = 0.3 > δ_c , the potential has one minimum only at $x = x_+$

202

and the motion ends with the strong expansionary bias $x = x_+$.

It may be supposed that the motion of the investors' configuration index x always ends at a stable (expansionary or rationalizing) bias and that no Schumpeter Clock begins to tick. But this is only true as long as δ and κ are kept <u>constant</u> with time. In section 3, however, an equation of motion for the alternator $\delta(t)$ will be set up. In becoming a <u>dynamic variable</u>, the alternator $\delta(t)$ shifts and transforms the whole shape of the configuration development potential $V(x; \delta, \kappa)$ and of the driving force $K(x; \delta, \kappa)$. Hence x may never come to rest; in fact a periodicity in the motion of $x(t)$ can result from the coupling of the motion of $\delta(t)$ with that of $x(t)$, and so oscillatory shifts in the variable x in the course of this coupled motion have to be expected. In Figure 1b it can be seen that for given κ the shape of the potential varies from a two minima to a one minimum form as δ grows from 0 to $\delta > \delta_c$. The transition takes place at a critical value $\delta = \delta_c$ given by

$$\cosh^2 [\delta_c - \sqrt{\kappa(\kappa-1)}\ ] = \kappa \tag{41}$$

for which the left hand minimum of the potential disappears at

$$x_c = -\sqrt{\kappa(\kappa-1)} \tag{42}$$

Because of the symmetry of the potential

$$V(-|x|, -|\delta|, \kappa) = V(|x|, |\delta|, \kappa), \tag{43}$$

a similar transition takes place for $\delta = -|\delta|$ for which the right hand minimum disappears at $x = |x_c|$. If $x(t)$ is considered to start at the left minimum of $V(x; \delta < \delta_c, \kappa)$ – i.e. with a rationalizing bias – and if $\delta(t)$ moves from $\delta < \delta_c$ to values $\delta > \delta_c$ so that the left minimum of V disappears, $x(t)$ will quickly swing to the remaining right-hand minimum of $V(x; \delta > \delta_c, \kappa)$ at $x > 0$ (expansionary bias). This in turn can induce the motion of the alternator $\delta(t)$ to negative values $\delta(t) < -|\delta_c|$, leading to a sudden downswing of x(t) towards a rationalizing bias, and so on. It can be seen that the coupled dynamics of x(t) and 6(t) can, in principle, explain the upswings and downswings of x(t). In the next section the function of a time dependent alternator shall be explained in economic terms, and its equation of motion will be established.

3. THE EQUATION OF MOTION FOR THE INVESTORS' PROPENSITIES

The alternator 6, which is the investors' strategic choice parameter in the force K(x;6,к), and the variable for which an equation of motion is going to be introduced, plays the role of a "trend setting function".

If most investors tend to maximize profits at a given point in time by expanding their business operations so that x(t) > 0, then some innovators or pioneers (trend–setters) will try to improve their market position by adopting a non-conformist strategy in an attempt to capture quasi-rents due to differentiation. When an upswing is well under way due to expansionary investments undertaken by a majority of investors, these trend setters tend to redirect their effort and start pushing back the cost frontier by means of cost reducing investments. They thereby force others to imitate and also to undertake rationalizing investments in the expectation of further cost reductions along the progress function, descriptive of the least cost combination in the branch of industry under observation.

At other times when a downswing is well under way due to the contractionary effects of rationalizing investments undertaken by a majority of investors, the trend setters start moving towards the quality section of the best practice frontier, introducing better products and implementing investment plans for expanding their facilities. Thereby, others are forced to imitate this expansionary and quality updating behaviour, thus creating the synchronization to be observed in the occurrence of business cycles. Since Adam Smith, economists have viewed these entrepreneurial actions as one of the main sources of the wealth of nations. The equation of motion for the alternator 6(t), which describes the differentiation activities of entrepreneurs in various fields of industrial investment in aggregate terms, should generate switches under the circumstances stipulated above. A suitable specification of this dynamic behaviour is

$$d\delta(t)/dt = \mu \,[\delta_0 - \delta(t)] \, \exp[-\beta x(t)] - \mu \,[\delta_0 + \delta(t)] \, \exp[\beta x(t)] \qquad (44)$$

with $\mu > 0, \beta > 0$ and $\delta_0 > 0$.

The mathematical implication of (44) is such that: for $x = 0$, $\delta(t)$ relaxes towards $\delta = 0$; but for $x(t) > 0$ the rhs of (44) represents a strong restoring force so that $\delta(t)$ moves towards $-\delta_0$. The negative δ in turn leads to a force $K(x; \delta, \kappa)$ – see (37) – driving x to negative values. Alternatively, starting from $x(t) < 0$, the rhs of (44) yields a restoring force for a change in $\delta(t)$ towards $+\delta_0$; the positive δ, in turn, produces a force $K(x; \delta, \kappa)$ driving x to positive values again. It can be seen that (44) correctly describes the alternating dynamics of the strategic choice parameter $\delta(t)$ in terms of a non-conformist reaction to the investors' configuration index $x(t)$.

In order to achieve the alternating effects, parameter β, the trend reversal speed parameter, has to be much larger than unity. The strategic flexibility parameter μ describes the flexibility of the investors in turning their strategies from expansionary to rationalizing, and vice versa, whereas the strategic choice amplitude δ_0 is an operative scaling constant.

Using the definitions of hyperbolic functions, the general form of the equation of motion for δ is obtained from (44) as

$$d\delta(t)/d) = -2\mu \, \delta_0 \, \sinh[\beta x(t)] - 2\mu \, \delta(t) \, \cosh[\beta x(t)] \,. \qquad (45)$$

Introducing δ_1, a strategy bias parameter, which is positive if the entire trend period is heavily biased towards expansion (as the 1950's were), or negative when biased towards rationalization (as the 1970's were), (45) can be modified and generalized to a complete equation of motion for the alternator. This is both stable enough to hold the ongoing trend over considerable periods of inertia, and flexible enough to change expeditiously with the investors' propensities:

$$d\delta(t)/dt = -2\mu \, \delta_0 \, \sinh[\beta x(t)] - 2\mu \, [\delta(t) - \delta_1] \, \cosh[\beta x(t)] \,. \qquad (46)$$

205

Analogous to $K(x; \delta,\kappa)$, $L(x; \delta,\beta)$ is denoted as the <u>strategy reformulation driving force</u> by writing the equation of motion for the alternator in the form:

$$d\delta(t)/dt = L(x; \delta,\beta) \tag{47}$$

with

$$L(x_i \delta,\beta) = -2\mu[\ \delta_0 \sinh(\beta x) + (\delta - \delta_1) \cosh(\beta x)] \tag{48}$$

and denoting the parameters as follows:

β: trend reversal speed parameter,

μ: strategic flexibility parameter,

δ_0: strategic choice amplitude,

δ_1: strategy bias parameter.

4. THE CLOSED SET OF EQUATIONS OF MOTION

Collecting the equations of motion for the investors' configuration index $x(t)$ (38), and the equation of motion for the alternator $\delta(t)$ (47), then introducing scaled time τ as

$$\tau = 2\nu t \tag{49}$$

and γ, a scaled strategic flexibility parameter, as

$$\gamma = \mu/\nu, \tag{50}$$

scaled forms of the equations of motion

$$dx(\tau)/d\tau = \hat{K}(x; \delta,\kappa) \tag{51}$$

$$d\delta(t)/d\tau = \hat{L}(x; \delta,\beta) \tag{52}$$

are obtained with the (scaled) driving force K as

$$\hat{K}(x;\ \delta,\kappa) = \sinh(\delta + \kappa x) - x\ \cosh(\delta + \kappa x) \equiv [\tanh(\delta + \kappa x) - x]\ \cosh(\delta + \kappa x) \tag{53}$$

and the (scaled) strategy reformulation driving force L as

$$\hat{L}(x;\ \delta,\beta) = -\gamma[\delta_0\ \sinh(\beta x) + (\delta - \delta_1)\ \cosh(\beta x)]$$

$$= -\gamma[\delta_0\ \tanh(\beta x) + (\delta - \delta_1)]\ \cosh(\beta x). \tag{54}$$

It is worthwhile to note that the central equations of the model (51, 52) are invariant against

$$x \rightarrow -x, \quad \delta \rightarrow -\delta \quad \text{and} \quad \delta_1 \rightarrow -\delta_1. \tag{55}$$

This invariance condition also shows up in the symmetry condition (43) of the potential $V(x;\ \delta,\kappa)$.

5. STRUCTURAL ANALYSIS OF THE SYSTEM OF EQUATIONS

The first part of the analysis examines how many singular points $\bar{P}(\bar{\delta},\bar{x})$ of the equations of motion exist. <u>Singular points</u> are defined as points in the δ-x plane where the motion comes to rest, i.e. where

$$dx/d\ \tau|_{\bar{p}} = \hat{K}(\bar{x}\bar{\delta}) = 0 \tag{56}$$

and

$$d\delta/d\tau|_{\bar{p}} = \hat{L}(\bar{x},\bar{\delta}) = 0. \tag{57}$$

Inserting (53) and (54) into (56) and (57), respectively, it can be seen that the coordinates of a singular point $\bar{P}(\bar{\delta},\ \bar{x})$ have to satisfy the two transcendental equations simultaneously

207

$$F_1(\bar{\delta}, \bar{x}) \equiv [\tanh(\bar{\delta} + \kappa\bar{x}) - \bar{x}] = 0 \tag{58}$$

$$F_2(\bar{\delta}, \bar{x}) \equiv [\delta_0 \tanh(\beta\bar{x}) + (\bar{\delta} - \delta_1)] = 0. \tag{59}$$

These equations are easily solved graphically: the functions $F_1(\bar{\delta}, \bar{x}) = 0$ and $F_2(\bar{\delta}, \bar{x}) = 0$ can be represented in the $\bar{\delta} - \bar{x}$ plane and their intersection points, which are the singular points of the differential equations (51, 52), can be determined. Furthermore, it follows from the definitions that the graph of (58) is the locus of all horizontal - and the graph of (59) the locus of all vertical-fluxlines of the equation (51, 52). Restricting the analysis for the moment to the slightly simplified case of vanishing strategic choice bias, i.e. for $\delta_1 = 0$, Figure 2 shows a typical plot of (59) and three typical plots a), b) and c) of (58). This figure confirms that one, three or even five singular points can exist.

The marginal case b) with three singular points, is characterized by the fact that (58, 59) hold good at the singular points $P_+(\delta_+, x_+)$ and $P_-(\delta_-, x_-) = 0$ and $F(\delta, x) = 0$ agree at P_+ and P_- ; thus the condition

$$(dx/d\delta)^{(F_1)}_{P\pm} = (dx/d\delta)^{(F_2)}_{P\pm} \tag{60}$$

where $(dx/d\delta)^{(F_2)}$ and $(dx/d\delta)^{(F_2)}$ are the derivatives taken along the curves $F_1(\delta, x) = 0$ and $F_2(\delta, x) = 0$, is also satisfied. A straight-forward evaluation of (60) leads to the equivalent implicit condition

$$\kappa = \delta_0 \beta[1 - (\bar{\delta}/\delta_0)^2] + 1/(1 - \bar{x}^2) \tag{61}$$

which also has to be fulfilled by the parameters κ, δ_0 and β for this marginal case. In (61) the solutions δ_+, x_+ or $\delta_- = \delta_+, x_- = -x_+$ of (58, 59) have to be inserted for $\bar{\delta}$ and $\bar{x}$ with $\delta_1 = 0$.

208

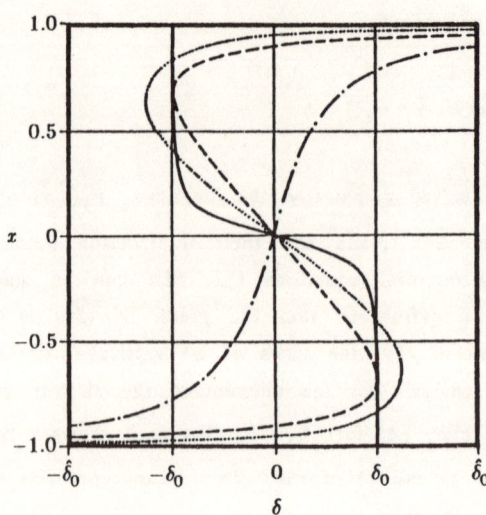

<u>Figure 2</u>   (————) $F_2(\bar{\delta},\bar{x}) = 0$

            (— · —)   (a) $F_1(\bar{\delta},\bar{x}) = 0$ for small κ (one equilibrium point -- the origin)

            (-------)   (b) $F_1(\bar{\delta},\bar{x}) = 0$ in the marginal case (3 equilibrium points)

            (············)   (c) $F_1(\bar{\delta},\bar{x}) = 0$ for very large κ (5 equilibrium points)

       Typical graphs of the transcendental functions

$$F_1(\bar{\delta},\bar{x}) = 0 \quad \text{and} \quad F_2(\bar{\delta},\bar{x}) = 0$$

The two-dimensional domain of parameters κ, δ_0 and β satisfying (61), for which there exist three singular points in the δ-x plane, will be denoted by $D_2^{(3)}$. The two-dimensional surface $D_2^{(3)}$ separates the three dimensional domain $D_3^{(5)}$ of the parameters $\kappa, \delta_0 \beta$ – for which <u>five</u> singular points exist – from the three dimensional domain $D_3^{(1)}$, for which only <u>one</u> singular point (namely the origin $\bar{\delta} = 0, \bar{x} = 0$) exists.

To discover the types of paths traversed by $x(\tau)$ and $\delta(\tau)$ it is also relevant to know their behaviour in the vicinity of the singular points. Therefore a <u>linear stability analysis</u> will be performed in order to see whether the singular points are <u>stable</u> or

209

<u>unstable</u> stationary points. With this objective, the behaviour with time of the solutions in a small neighbourhood of a singular point $\bar{P}(\bar{\delta}, \bar{x})$, is investigated by introducing deviations $\eta(\tau)$ and $\xi(\tau)$ from $\bar{\delta}$ and $\bar{x}$, so that:

$$x(\tau) = \bar{x} + \xi(\tau) \quad \text{and} \quad \delta(\tau) = \bar{\delta} + \eta(\tau). \tag{62}$$

The equation of motion (51, 52) can now be linearized with respect to $\xi(\tau)$ and $\eta(\tau)$. This leads to the following, which are valid only in the vicinity of $\bar{P}(\bar{\delta}, \bar{x})$:

$$d\xi(\tau)/d\tau = a_1 \xi + b_1 \eta \tag{63}$$

$$d\eta(\tau)/d\tau = -a_2 \xi - b_2 \eta \tag{64}$$

with the coefficients

$$a_1 = \cosh^{-1}(\bar{\delta} + \kappa\bar{x}) [\kappa - \cosh^2(\bar{\delta} + \kappa\bar{x})] \tag{65}$$

$$a_2 = \gamma \beta \delta_0 \cosh^{-1}(\beta\bar{x})$$

$$b_1 = \cosh^{-1}(\bar{\delta} + \kappa\bar{x})$$

$$b_2 = \gamma \cosh(\beta\bar{x})$$

where $a_2, b_1, b_2 > 0$, and a_1 is unrestricted. According to standard methods, (63, 64) can be solved using

$$\left. \begin{array}{l} \xi(\tau) = \xi(0) \exp(\lambda\tau) \\ \eta(\tau) = \eta(0) \exp(\lambda\tau) \end{array} \right\} \tag{66}$$

where the eigenvalues λ have to fulfill the determinant condition

$$\begin{vmatrix} a_1 - \lambda & b_1 \\ -a_2 & -b_2 - \lambda \end{vmatrix} = (a_1 - \lambda)(-b_2 - \lambda) + a_2 b_1 = 0. \tag{67}$$

This quadratic equation yields the eigenvalues

210

$$\lambda_{1/2} = 1/2[(a_1 - b_2) \pm \sqrt{(a_1 + b_2)^2 - 4a_2 b_1}].$$ (68)

The singular point is a __stable focus__ if the eigenvalues λ_1 and λ_2 both have negative real parts, since then both $\xi(\tau)$ and $\eta(\tau)$ approach zero with time. On the other hand, the singular point is __unstable__ if the real part of at least one eigenvalue is positive.

Of great interest is the stability of the singular point $\dot{P}_0(\bar{\delta}_0 = 0, \bar{x}_0 = 0)$ which is, however, slightly shifted from the origin for a non-vanishing strategic choice bias δ_1. With $\delta_1 = 0$, $\bar{\delta} = 0$ and $\bar{x} = 0$, the parameters a_1, a_2 and b_2 assume the simple forms:

$$a_1 = \kappa - 1, \qquad b_1 = 1,$$
$$a_2 = \gamma \beta \delta_0, \qquad b_2 = \gamma,$$ (69)

which leads to the eigenvalues

$$\lambda_{1/2} = 1/2[(\kappa - 1 - \gamma) \pm \sqrt{(\kappa - 1 + \gamma)^2 - 4\gamma \beta \delta_0}].$$ (70)

It is reasonable – and confirmed by the calculations presented in section 6 – to assume relative large values for the trend reversal parameter β and the strategic choice amplitude δ_0. Thus

$$(\kappa - 1 + \gamma^2) < 4\gamma \beta \delta_0$$ (71)

can be assumed. In this case the eigenvalues (70) become conjugate-complex and can be written as

$$\lambda_{1/2} = 1/2[(\kappa - 1 - \gamma) \pm i\sqrt{4\gamma \beta \delta_0 - (\kappa - 1 + \gamma)^2}].$$ (72)

211

From (72) it follows immediately that a **stable focus** exists at the origin of the δ-x plane under the condition

$$\kappa-1-\gamma < 0 \quad \text{or} \quad \kappa < 1 + \gamma \tag{73}$$

and that the origin becomes an **unstable focus** if condition

$$\kappa-1-\gamma > 0 \quad \text{or} \quad \kappa > 1 + \gamma \tag{74}$$

is fulfilled.

Finally, the solutions of the equations of motion (51, 52) have to be investigated. A complete survey of all the possible types of solution to the equations dependent on the parameters $\kappa, \delta_0, \delta_1, \beta$ and γ will not, however, be made. The immediate aim is to derive **sufficient conditions** for those parameters which lead to the existence of an asymptotically periodic type of solution; this is the type of solution which has been anticipated qualitatively in terms of the investment cycle, and in which the main interest lies. In other words, it is necessary for the substantial aspects of the model being considered to derive an **existence theorem** for **solutions approaching a "limit cycle"** under certain conditions of the parameters $\kappa, \delta_0, \delta_1, \beta$ and γ.

A limit cycle $C(t)$ is defined as a closed trajectory, i.e. a periodic solution to the equations of motion, with the property that there exists a domain D_c around $C(t)$, so that all trajectories starting within D_c approach $C(t)$ as $t \to \infty$. D_c can be denoted as the "domain of attraction"' and $C(t)$ as an "attractor". Before the existence theorem is stated, the famous **Poincaré-Bendixon theorem** should be formulated in a — in context — relevant version:

Consider two autonomous first order differential equations for the variables $\delta(\tau)$ and $x(\tau)$, and suppose that a finite domain D_c exists in the δ-x plane such that:

a)   no singular points are situated in D_c

b)   all trajectories $\delta(\tau), x(\tau)$ starting inside or on the boundary of D_c at time $\tau = 0$ remain in D_c for $0 < \tau < \infty$. In this case (at least one) limit cycle must exist within D_c

212

and all trajectories in D_c either <u>are</u>, or <u>approach</u> as $\tau \to \infty$ a limit cycle.

Suppose that the parameters $\kappa, \delta_0, \beta, \gamma, \delta_1 = 0$ satisfy the conditions

1) $\{\kappa, \delta_0, \beta\} \in D_3^{(1)}$.

    i.e. the origin is the only singular point   (75)

2) $(\kappa - 1 + \gamma)^2 < 4\gamma\beta\delta_0$

3) $\kappa > 1 + \gamma$.

These imply that the eigenvalues λ_1 and λ_2 belonging to $\bar{P}(\bar{\delta} = 0, \bar{x} = 0)$ are conjugate-complex with a positive real part, so the one singular point $P(0,0)$ is an <u>unstable focus</u>. D_c, of the δ-x plane is bounded internally by an infinitesimally small elliptical core enclosing the origin and externally by the straight lines $\delta = \delta_0$, $x = 1$, $\delta = -\delta_0$ and $x = -1$ (Figure 3). It fulfills the premise of the Poincaré-Bendixon theorem that: a) there are no singular points situated in D_c, and b) all trajectories starting from the boundary of D_c enter D_c and remain in D_c.

Premise a) follows from condition 1) of (75), according to which the origin is the <u>only singular</u> point.

Premise b) follows from the fact that according to conditions 2) and 3) of (75), the origin is an <u>unstable focus</u> with all trajectories spiraling out of it and therefore <u>entering</u> the core from its interior boundary C_i. Also, on the exterior boundary C_e:

$dx/d\tau = [\tanh(\delta + \kappa) - 1] \cosh(\delta + \kappa) < 0$ for $x = 1$
$dx/d\tau = [\tanh(\delta - \kappa) + 1] \cosh(\delta - \kappa) > 0$ for $x = -1$ (76)

$d\delta/d\tau = -\gamma[\delta_0 \tanh(\beta x) + \delta_0] \cosh(\beta x) > 0$ for $\delta = \delta_0$
$d\delta/d\tau = -\gamma[\delta_0 \tanh(\beta x) - \delta_0] \cosh(\beta x) > 0$ for $\delta = \delta_0$ (77)

and (76, 77) show that all trajectories crossing C_e are <u>directed inward</u> into D_c. From

213

the Poincaré-Bendixon theorem, it now follows that within a limit cycle, i.e. a periodic solution of the equations of motion, $C(t)$ must exist, and that all other solutions starting from any point within D_c approach this limit cycle. D_c is a domain of attraction for $C(t)$. Assumptions 1-3) are <u>sufficient</u> but <u>not necessary</u> conditions for the existence of a limit cycle. This means that there could also exist limit cycle solutions under more general conditions for the parameters $\kappa, \delta_0, \delta_1, \beta$ and γ. On the other hand, it can be shown that there are initially quasi-cyclic trajectories which break down into a stable solution after some oscillations.

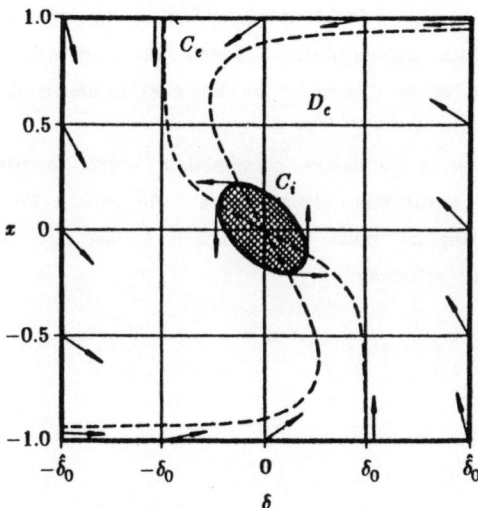

<u>Figure 3</u> Domain D_c with interior boundary C_i and exterior boundary C_e. All trajectories enter D_c and remain in D_c as the flux lines at the boundaries show.

If assumption 3) of the existence theorem is changed into

$$\kappa < 1 + \gamma \tag{78}$$

the case for which the origin is the only singular point and is a <u>stable focus</u> is obtained. The main importance of these two different types of solution lies in the implied proof that whether or not an economy tends towards a stationary state, or undergoes non-equilibrium oscillations, depends in a sensitive way on the decision psychology of the entrepreneurs as expressed by the decision psychology parameters exist. κ, δ_0, δ_1, β and γ. In particular "critical values" of these parameters exist. Crossing these critical thresholds elicits a transition from one type of solution into the other. (See $\kappa = 1.6$, which crosses the marginal case with a critical threshold value of the coordinator $\kappa_c = 1.5$).

In Figure 4 a parameter combination is chosen for which the origin $\bar{\delta} = 0$, $\bar{x} = 0$ is the only singular point, and a stable focus of the damping out of cyclic behaviour. This phenomenon which troubles disequilibrium models in situations of zero-growth, is but a special case among many others in the non-equilibrium model being discussed.

Sustained cycles occur for a parameter combination which satisfies the assumptions of the limit cycle existence theorem. Figures 5a and 5b exhibit the limit cycle. Again, the origin is the only singular point which, however, has now become an unstable focus of the motion of the economy.

215

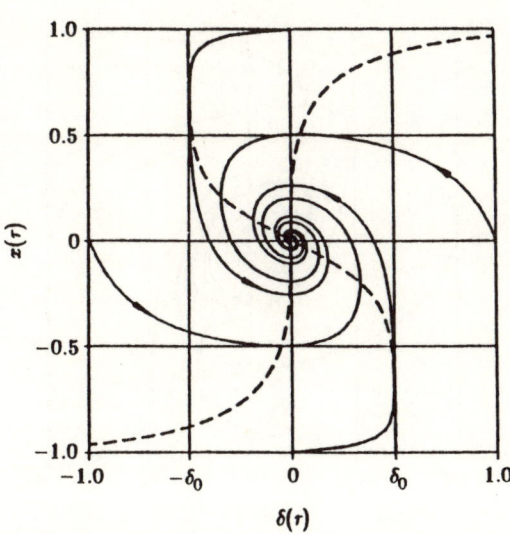

Figure 4 (a) Trajectories in the δ-x plane approaching the one stable focus at the origin $P_c(0,0)$ for $\kappa = 1.0$, $\delta_0 = 0$, $\beta = 4.0$ and $\mu = 0.5$.

(———) Trajectories; (------) $F_{1,2}(\dot{\delta},\dot{x}) = 0$

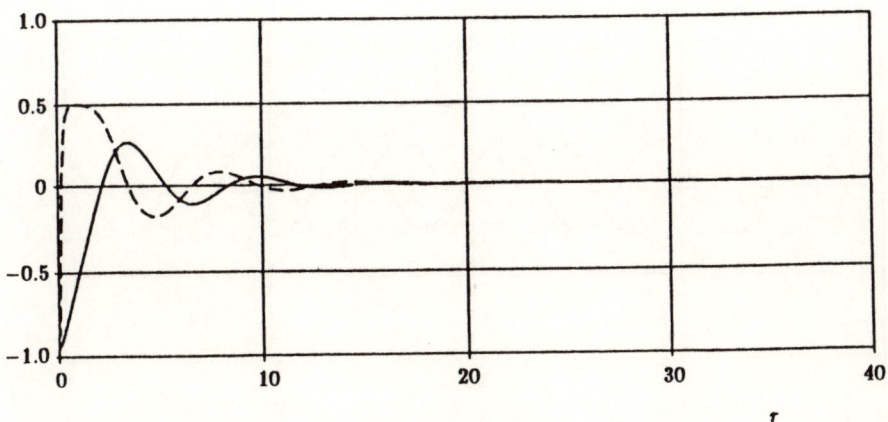

Figure 4 (b) Path of $x(\tau)$ (———) and $\delta(\tau)$ (------) for the parameters of 3.4a)

216

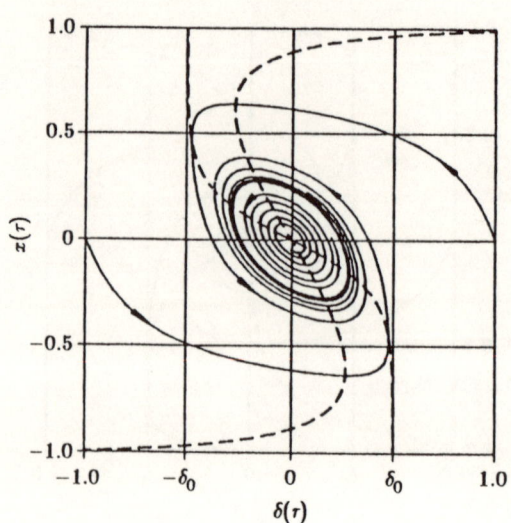

<u>Figure 5</u>   (a) Trajectories in the δ-x plane for one unstable focus at $P_e(0,0)$ and one
limit cycle for $\kappa = 1.6$, $\delta_0 = 0.5$, $\delta_1 = 0$, $\beta = 4$ and $\mu = 0.5$. These fulfill the condition (75) of the limit cycle existence theorem.
(————) Trajectories: (------) $F_{1,2}(\delta,\bar{x}) = 0$.

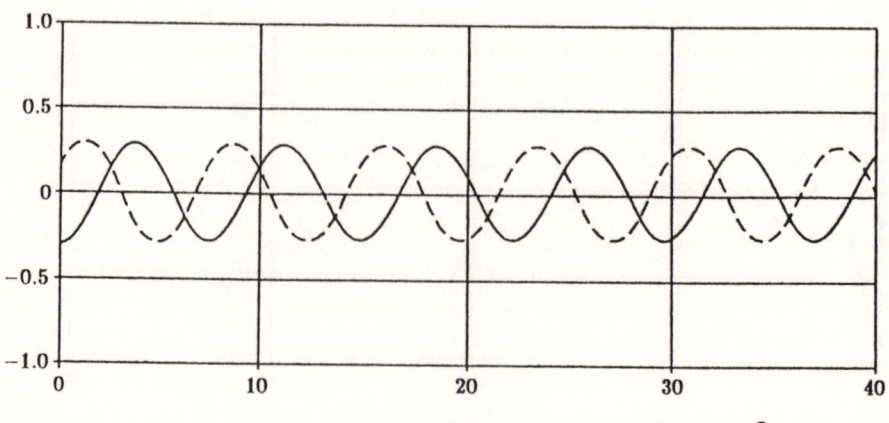

<u>Figure 5</u>   (b) Path of $x(\tau)$ (————) and $\delta(\tau)$ (------) for the parameters of (a). The
motion is periodic and traverses the limit cycle.

217

6. CHANGES IN INDUSTRIAL STRATEGIC INVESTMENT IN THE FEDERAL REPUBLIC OF GERMANY BETWEEN 1956 AND 1978

It has just been demonstrated numerically by means of parametrical variation of some of the influential factors in the model, that theoretical solutions can represent a whole range of types of economic motion. A variety of periodic, symmetric and asymmetric oscillations, and also some vanishing, accelerated and decelerated fluctuations that approach an existing mean value trend line, or diverge towards a new, higher or lower trend line, have been demonstrated. And it is exactly this variety of possible types of motion which has to be explained when theory is compared with the variety of economic motions observable empirically. It has therefore been shown that by incorporating the micro-economic strategic investment decisions of entrepreneurs into the model, macro-economic fluctuations can be interpreted, and that the influence of macro-economic change on the micro-economic level of entrepreneurship can be explained.

In devising a test for the model, with data for a real economy, two restrictions apply. The first restriction is __spatial__. The non-availability of time series on industrial strategic investments (expansionary and rationalizing) in some countries, narrows down the choice of national economies to which the model can be readily applied. But even in countries such as United States of America - where data are available, but only for one type of strategic investment (expansionary) and not for the other rationalizing type (the latter is reported with tactical investments or replacement) - some relevant empirical regularities could be predicted using the model. For example, modernization expenditures (Feldstein and Foot 1971) vary over time, while replacement itself may be regarded as a constant proportion of capital stock: (Jorgenson (1963), Jorgenson and Stephanson (1967)). On the other hand, the fluctuations in replacement and modernization expenditures are less pronounced than the fluctuations in expansionary investment, which, according to Eisner (1978), explain almost 80% of the variation in annual capital expenditures in the United States' business sector. Consequently, it can be predicted, using statistical methods, that the explanatory power of an investment analysis falls under the 80% line suggested by Eisner if the analysis mixes expansionary investment with investment for modernization and replacement, since the analysis of "strategic" investment would be "contaminated" with some "tactical" investment, namely for replacements.

218

Conversely, the explanatory power of an analysis of industrial investment in plant and equipment in the United States would probably exceed 80% if the analysis were restricted to "strategic" investment proper, i.e. expansionary and rationalizing investment (the latter now being buried under "modernization and replacement"). The availability of pertinent data is one of the reasons for the choice of the Federal Republic of Germany as the test unit for analysis.

The second restriction upon the application of the model as it stands in <u>temporal</u>. Times of discontinuity have been excluded from the test as these represent changes in economic regime, or phase transitions. Although such transitions can be handled by the model, additional theory (long term economic theory) would have to be incorporated — for instance, in the form of an equation of motion for the coordinator — in order to handle discontinuities systematically. It is well known that differential equation models of only three coupled dynamic variables (e.g. the Lorenz model) already possess "strange attractor" solutions side by side with those of the limit cycle type. Though fully deterministic, such solutions could represent quasi-chaotic economic motion. These questions of long term economic theory and mode architecture, and how they relate to possible phase transitions in times of discontinuity, will not be discussed further here (see, however, Mensch, Weidlich, Haag, 1987).

For the period 1955-1980 data are available on expansionary and rationalizing industrial investment in the Federal Republic of Germany, and moreover, this period appears to be void of a major discontinuity. Nevertheless, this period certainly does not build a continuum. In terms of economic policy and government regulation, it can be divided into two main sub-periods each of about eleven years. The first four or five years of the second sub-period can clearly be designated as "interventionistic". Investment activity was therefore under the influence of the "regulator" δ_1 to varying degrees, differing during the three periods 1955-1965, 1967-1971 and 1973-1980. The increasing $g(t)$ mainly reflects the general increase in the total number of investment projects. Furthermore, the technological base of German industry changed and matured during these years, in more or less the way suggested and modelled by Utterback and Abernathy (1975), as well as Mensch (1979), and Mensch, Kaasch, Kleinknecht, Schnopp (1980).

219

According to their findings, industries develop in terms of technology and market structure, by going through stages which depend on the age of the technology and other related factors in the particular industry concerned. The following regularity holds for the post-war growth industries in most western countries: the 1950s were dominated by product innovation in diversifying industry: the 1960s by process innovation in concentrating industry, and the 1970s by pseudo-innovations in nearly all industries; the 1980s are expected to be dominated by a cluster of basic innovations in some key industries. Therefore it can be maintained that these patterns in the rate and direction of innovation have created, and have been the consequence of, a high degree of conformity in strategic behaviour (namely, in the timing of innovation, synchronization of investment and imitation of business tactics) in the first sub-period under consideration. In the second sub-period, on the contrary, there appears to have been a low degree of conformity. This alteration is reflected in the relative values of the "coordinator" κ chosen in modelling the three periods . Similarly, in the three periods the value of the "accelerator" ν was chosen to be "small", "medium" and "large", because it reflected the shortening of successive product life cycles as major industries advanced out of a phase of large improvement effects (true product innovation) to minor improvement effects (mere pseudo-innovation) which did not last very long.

In Table 1 the chosen values of the parameters are listed for the reader, who may wish to replicate the empirical analysis that follows; the investment data for the Federal Republic of Germany is given in Table 2.

Table 1   Model Parameters for the Economy of the Federal Republic of Germany

Period	γ	β	δ_0	δ_1	g	κ	ν
1955-1965	0.13	10	0.5	-0.3	0.2	1.5	0.145
1967-1971	0.13	10	0.5	+0.3	0.5	1.5	0.225
1973-1980	0.13	10	0.5	-0.3	0.7	0.7	0.400

The original data were collected by a German institute for economic research (The IFO-Institute in Munich) by means of questionnaires sent to a (representative)

220

sample of German industrial corporations. They have been econometrically corrected for a stronger rationalization bias (Mensch et.al. 1980), so that the regression line of Figure 6a, which depicts the data, possesses a smaller intercept and a steeper descent than it would have in the original data version, which incorporates an expansionary bias. Figure 6b shows the investment structure data $z(t)$, which is the investment structure index $Z(t)$ cleaned of the linear trend. Weidlich and Haag (1982) have shown that the trend deviation pattern is robust, i.e. insensitive to the form of the trend functions. Also, since the investment structure index without trend is to be used, the difference in built-in biases between the original data version and the Mensch version should have no effect on the matching of the observed trend deviations with the theoretical values calculated from the model.

<u>Table 2</u>   Investment Data for the Federal Republic of Germany 1956-78

Year	R-investment [10^9 DM]	E-Investment [10^9 DM]	$Z = (E-R)/(E+R)$
1956	16.4	11.4	-0.183
1957	15.9	10.8	-0.197
1958	16.6	8.2	-0.342
1959	17.7	10.2	-0.274
1960	22.2	12.6	-0.282
1961	24.2	13.6	-0.282
1962	24.2	11.2	-.0369
1963	22.4	10.6	-0.360
1964	23.5	11.2	-0.360
1965	26.1	13.0	-0.342
1966	25.9	11.6	-0.388
1967	23.0	7.2	-0.527
1968	22.3	10.4	-0.369
1969	30.0	21.6	-0.162
1970	34.9	23.2	-0.205
1971	34.4	18.6	-0.298
1972	31.3	12.4	-0.439
1973	30.5	13.8	-0.379
1974	28.5	10.2	-0.471
1975	25.9	6.2	-0.626
1976	26.5	6.8	-0.626
1977	27.5	6.6	-0.613
1978	28.9	7.0	-0.613

221

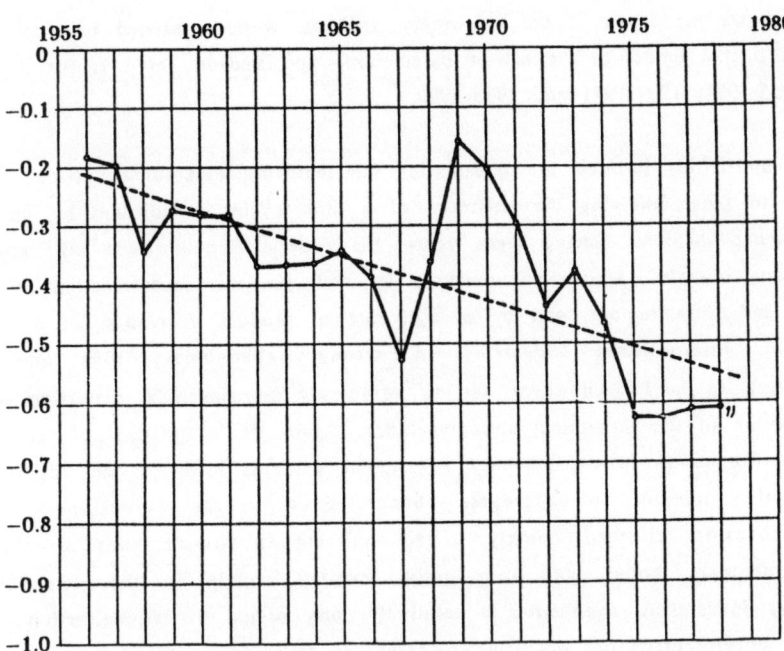

<u>Figure 6a</u> Investment structure index $Z(t) = Z_0 + z(t)$ in the Federal Republic of Germany 1956-1978 (data by IFO). A linear time dependence of the long-term component $Z_0(t)$ (------) is assumed.

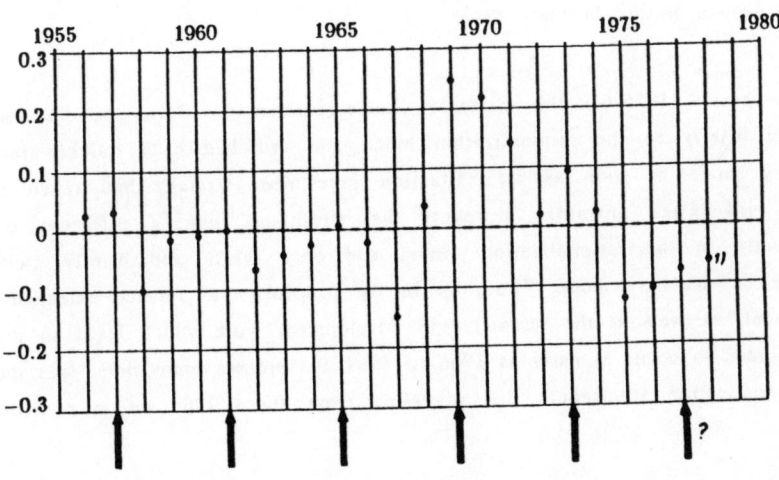

<u>Figure 6b</u> Short-term investment structure index $z(t)$. The long-term trend component $Z_0(t)$ of Figure 6a has been subtracted.

222

Figure 7 shows the result of the empirical analysis, which consisted of a piecewise application of the model to the set of parameters specified in Table 1, for the three periods 1955-1971, 1967-1971 and 1973-1980.

From the mid-fifties through the mid-sixties the matching external conditions chosen correspond to those implying the existence of a limit cycle as indicated by the limit cycle existence theorem. During these years, the Federal Republic was still enjoying its "economic miracle", which was nurtured by both post-war reconstruction of plant, equipment and infrastructure, and by a high rate of product innovation in a number of growing international industries. A strong expansionary bias and bias reinforcement ($\kappa = 1.5$), however, led to a strongly non-sinusoidal distortion of the periodic motion of the investment structure index. Again, as in the case of the United States, the fluctuation in expansionary investment explains most of the variation in the economic indicators of aggregate change. Even in the expansionary phase, industrial investors changed quickly to rationalizing investment after a relatively short expansionary boom, and they only reverted slowly in the direction of expansionary investment, even after a relatively long period of rationalization. Thus, the effects of entrepreneurial decision processes, as reflected by the path of $z(t)$ in Figure 7, reveal a persistent, and perhaps growing concern for rationalization and productivity advancement (even in the period 1955-65 when the economy expanded at a high rate). On the other hand, preparations for the "quantum leaps" which occurred were time-consuming. The development of new or better products, and the planning of new or bigger plants to produce them, took place during the preceding periods of growth in the business cycle.

During the period 1955-65, the strategic choice parameter $\delta(t)$, the "alternator", stayed only briefly in the rationalization mode and switched back quickly into the expansionary mode as soon as rationalization investment strategy had taken effect. From the mid-sixties onwards, however, the alternator took a different course, staying mostly in the rationalization mode, and only rarely and briefly switching over to the expansionary mode. The drop in the propensity to finance extended plant and equipment, as well as the research and development work which leads to growing business, is seen to occur as early as 1966 to 1967. As process innovation was the gist of the rationalization atmosphere that prevailed from about 1965 on, a confirmation

223

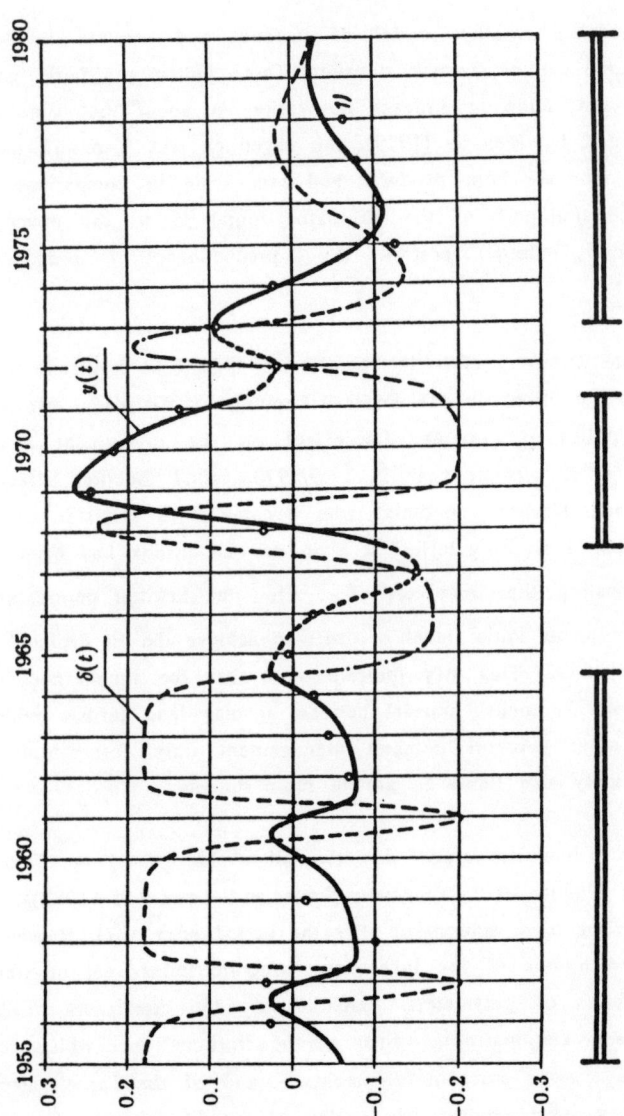

<u>Figure 7</u> Path of the short-term component z(t) of the investment structure index
(———) and of the alternator δ(t)   (------) for appropriate choices of
trend parameters in comparison with the observed investment structure
data, West German Industry 1956-1978.

224

of the Utterback-Abernathy model of product and process innovation has been obtained with the use of German statistics. This indicates a fairly general switch-over from product innovation to process innovation at about that time. Furthermore, as already suggested by Mensch (1979), the seventies was a period of relatively weak propensity to innovate both products and processing in comparison to the previous years, and the time-path of the alternator found to fit the observed investment behaviour does indeed portray the predominance of pseudo-innovation during the 1970s.

During the late sixties , after the neo-liberal incumbant government fell, the newly formed "Grand Coalition" in the Federal Republic of Germany resorted to a massive expansionary policy programme. Its effect on the investment structure index is clearly visible as an all-time peak in 1969/1970, called "Schiller Effect", after Schiller, the accomplished Keynes economist who became both minister of finance and of economic affairs. This irregularity in economic conditions has been adjusted for by temporarily boosting the "regulator" θ_1. After the Schiller period, the regulator had to be returned to its initial level in order to achieve the fit depicted in Figure 7 for the period after 1972. This may indicate more than the simple necessity to alter the regulator in order to model unusual periods. It may lend further evidence to the not unusual view that forceful demand management only forces industrial firms to consider the supply side limits to growth more quickly.

Although some economists argue that the oil shock caused the "slumpflation" after the hyperboom around 1970 (Freeman, Soete and Townsend (1982)), an evolutionary explanation may be more appropriate. For the period after 1971, it was not possible to fit the observed motion of the investment structure index (net of trend) with model data on the basis of parameters which satisfy the conditions of the limit cycle existence theorem. The matching values of the "inflator" g - which could not be set lower with the given price developments - and of the "accelerator" v - which reflects the short-ended product life cycles of pseudo-innovations - fit together only by using a "coordinator" value κ below unity, which is in the realm of damped fluctuations. Marketing managers speak of "a fluttering cycle" in reference to this quasi-stationary state, in which the low amplitude and high frequency of the branch cycles do not create either an upswing or a true downswing in macro-economic aggregate.

225

Obviously this is a state of high micro-economic friction and loss of activity, which already carries the seeds for a transition into another cyclic stage in which the investors' interaction parameter κ would exceed the critical value κ. Needless to say, the economy need not necessarily resume its cyclic motion with an upswing from the current intermediate level of investment activities.

This model is not designed to predict the investment structure index. But it can be used for diagnostic purposes. If the data are meaningful and the model is reasonable, (as the authors believe), then industry in the Federal Republic is in a state of de-phasing (asynchronization of micro-economic developments for the diverse firms, industrial branches and sectors). Thus, it is getting "ready" for a phase transition, and preparing itself structurally for the breakthrough of a whole set of basic innovations. Whether this will in fact take place, could only be answered by further investigations which encompass many more factors than the short-term business cycle theory presented here.

REFERENCES

Barzel, Y., 'Optimal Timing of Innovations', Rev. Economics and Statistics 50, 1968, pp. 348-355.

Chamberlin, E.H., Toward a More General Theory of Value, Oxford University Press, New York, 1957.

Chang, W. and Smyth, D., 'The Existence of Persistence of Cycles in a Nonlinear Model, Kaldor's 1940 Model Re-Examined', Rev. Economics and Statistics 32, 1950.

Eisner, R., 'Factors in Business Investment', National Bureau of Economic Research, General Series NO. 102, Ballinger, Cambridge, MA, 1978.

Feldstein, M.S., and Foot, D.K., 'The Other Half of Gross Investment: Replacement and Modernization Expenditures', Rev. Economics and Statistics 53, 1971, pp. 49-58.

Flaherty, M.T., 'Industry Structure and Cost-reducing Investment', Econometrica, 48, 1980, pp. 1187-1209.

Freeman, C., Soete, L., and Towsend, J., Fluctuations in the Numbers of Product and Process Innovations, mimeographed paper, Brighton, 1982.

Goodwin, R.M., ' A Non-Linear Theory of the Cycle', Rev. Economics and Statistics 32, 1950.

Goodwin, R.M., "The Nonlinear Accelerator and the Persistence of Business Cycles', Econometrica 19, 1951, pp. 1-17.

Glaser, O. and Strauss, L., 'Awareness Contexts and Social Interaction', Am. Sociological Rev., 29, 1964, pp. 669-679.

Hicks, J.R., A contribution to the Theory of the Business Cycles, 3rd ed., Clarendon Press, Oxford, 1965.

Jorgenson, D.W., 'Capital Theory and Investment Behaviour', Am. Economic Rev. 53, 1963, pp. 241-259.

226

Jorgenson, D.W. and Stephenson, J.A., 'Investment Behaviour in U.S. Manufacturing: 1947-1960', Econometrica 35, 1967, pp. 169-220.

Kalecki, M., 'A Macrodynamic Theory of Business Cycles, Econometrica 3, 1935, pp. 327-348.

Kamien, M.L. and Schwarz, N.L., 'Timing of Innovation Under Rivalry', Econometrica 40, 1972, pp. 43-60.

Keynes, J.M., 'The General Theory and After, Part II: Defence and Development' in Moggeridge, D. (ed.) Keynes Collective Writings, vol. 14, London 121, 1973.

Mensch, G., Stalemate in Technology, Ballinger, Cambridge, MA., 1979.

Mensch, G., Kaasch, K, Kleinknecht, A., and Schnopp, R., Innovation, Investment Trends and Switches Between Full- and Underemployment Equilibria, Berlin, International Institute of Management, Discussion Paper 10 (1980).

Mensch, G., Weidlich, W., Haag, G., Outline for a Formal Theory of Long-Term Economic Cycles, in (ed.) Vasko, T., The Long Wave Debate: Concepts, Results and Perspectives, IIASA-publication, 1987.

Rosenberg, N., 'On Technological Expectations', Economic J. 86, 1976, pp. 523-535.

Salter, W..G., Productivity and Technical Change, Ballinger, Cambridge, MA, 1960.

Schumpeter, J.A., Konjunkturzyklen eine theoretische, historische und statistische Analyse des kapitalistischen Prozesses, vol. 2, Vandenhoeck und Ruprecht, Göttingen, 1961.

Utterback, J.M. and Abernathy, W.J., 'A Dynamic Model of Process and Product Innovation', Omega. Intern. J. Management Sci. 3, 1975, pp. 639-654.

Weidlich, W. and Haag, G., An Indicator of Change in the Investment Structure, to appear in Proceedings of the Berlin Conference on "Modelling Innovation Processes and Structural Change" ed. by G. Mensch, International Institute of Management, Science Center, Berlin, 1982.

Weidlich, W. and Haag, G., Concepts and Models of a Quantitative Sociology – The Dynamics of Interacting Populations, Springer Series in Synergetics, vol. 14, Berlin, 1983.

Part V
Knowledge, Innovation and Competition

[15]

Excerpt from *Beyond Positive Economics?*, 104–21.

7 Knowledge, Learning and Enterprise

BRIAN LOASBY

Although there is no intention, here or elsewhere in this volume, to develop an extended critique of conventional microeconomic analysis, it is appropriate to begin by indicating the problems which seem to provide the opportunity for a new approach. These problems are associated with the concepts of equilibrium and production.

EQUILIBRIUM AND KNOWLEDGE

The equilibrium of an economy is normally defined in terms of a set of prices and quantities (or, in growth models, rates of change in these variables) which, in the absence of any outside disturbance, would persist indefinitely. G. B. Richardson (1960) has drawn attention to the dependence of such equilibria on assumptions about the knowledge and expectations of economic agents, and emphasised the inadequacy of perfect competition as a plausible justification for the kind of assumptions which are needed. More recently, Professor Hahn (1973) has proposed a definition of equilibrium in terms, not of prices and quantities, but of *theory* and *policy*. An agent's *theory* is a procedure for deriving predictions (which may take the form of a probability distribution) from information; his *policy* is a procedure for deriving decisions from predictions. An appropriate example would be the use of a specific econometric model to forecast demand each month, together with a production-scheduling technique which generates output plans from the forecasts thus produced. A less formal example is a theory which predicts that it is safe to cross the road at a controlled crossing when a green light is showing to pedestrians, and a policy to cross only under such conditions.

Rational decisions appear to require both theory and policy. Indeed, it is difficult to see how policy can exist without theory, though the converse is often true: cosmological theories, for example, are not usually associated with decisions. Professor Hahn offers the following definition (1973, p. 25): 'an economy is in equilibrium when it generates messages which do not cause agents to change the theories which they hold or the policies which they pursue'. But although he introduces notions of knowledge and decision into his definitions, Professor Hahn follows conventional practice by confining his attention to the conditions which will sustain equilibrium; he explicitly renounces any attempt to cope with learning. Thus his further analysis is of no direct help to us here; his concepts, however, will serve as a reference point for our discussion. What should be noted immediately is that equilibrium, so defined, does not necessarily depend on the truth of a theory: someone who (in this country) will never have honey in the house because honey attracts bears is unlikely to receive any messages from his environment which will cause him to change either his theory or his policy.

Professor Hahn's definition of equilibrium is an unconscious paraphrase of that advanced over forty years ago by Professor Hayek (1937, p. 41). Professor Hayek, however, was addressing himself precisely to the problem of the acquisition and use of knowledge in an economy. Interest in processes of adjustment through a sequence of human decisions which improve knowledge is characteristic of the Austrian School of economists, and has been effectively developed by Professor Kirzner in his *Competition and Entrepreneurship* (1973). A market in which prices and quantities are out of equilibrium offers profit opportunities to entrepreneurs; they formulate plans to buy and sell particular quantities at particular prices on the basis of their expectations. These plans are then tested in the market, and the results may confirm plans and expectations or cause them to be modified.

The economy thus, it is claimed, moves towards an equilibrium of both plans and prices, through a market process that seems to parallel the sequence of conjecture and exposure to refutation which is at the heart of Sir Karl Popper's (1972) theory of scientific progress. Now Sir Karl has written extensively about the difficulties involved in deciding whether a conjecture has been effectively refuted, and what should be done if it is. Professor Kirzner, however, discusses no such difficulties. Knowledge, in his original model, lies waiting to be discovered; an entrepreneur simply recognises a change in preferences or technology which has already happened. (In a recent (1981) paper, Professor Kirzner has allowed uncertainty into his analysis; but he does not consider this problem.) As he defines it, Professor Kirzner's model is therefore of limited applicability; this can be seen by contemplating some of the implications of production.

PRODUCTION AND ORGANISATION

Austrians and conventional microequilibrium theorists both start with the analysis of exchange. Production is then introduced as a special case of exchange — the exchange of inputs for outputs — by adding technology to preferences and resource endowments, either (for conventional theorists) as the basic data from which an equilibrium configuration of prices and quantities is to be derived, or (for Professor Kirzner) as the set of knowledge which is open to entrepreneurial perception. In a formal sense, production functions are closely analogous to preference functions, converting inputs into outputs just as the latter convert commodities into utilities.

But this simple theoretical extension entails a formidable increase in the knowledge attributed to economic agents. Not only is the requirement that technologies be available, and known to be available, a good deal more demanding than the requirement that consumers should know their own preferences; these preferences must now cover not just those commodities which currently exist but those which might be brought into existence. Although many potential objects of exchange may have no place in the equilibrium solution, yet they exist independently of that solution; but commodities which result only from production have to be included in the equilibrium production set in order to come into existence at all. Even Professor Kirzner's entrepreneurs will need to be extremely alert in order to perceive production technologies and consumer preferences for goods which can be brought into existence only by their own decisions.

The opportunity may arise only from a combination of perceptions. Consider, for example, the opportunity created by juxtaposing the realisation that fluorine compounds might well prove effective anaesthetics and the recognition that all existing inhalant anaesthetics had significant disadvantages. These two perceptions occurred in different divisions of ICI; but it was some time before they were combined to stimulate the search which led to the introduction of a superior and profitable new anaesthetic. They also occurred, separately, to a number of people outside the company, but these perceptions were never combined into a productive opportunity (Bradbury *et al.*, 1972). Nor is such a search bound to succeed, even in inventing a product with the desired properties; a profitable outcome will require active management, and in many instances, numerous further instances of creative imagination. To confine entrepreneurship, as Professor Kirzner does, to the exploitation of ready-made opportunities, and thereby to exclude the problems of management in complex organisations, is to impose severe potential restrictions on the applicability of his theory.

Since the time of Adam Smith, production has been associated in economic theory with the division of labour; and the division of labour produces most of its benefits through differentiation, which enhances specific skills but narrows the range of competence. Thus individual firms cannot have effective access to the known set of technologies within the economy, but are favourably placed to initiate, or to adopt, improvements within certain specific technologies. Nor can they possibly be well informed about all actual or potential products but they may be quick to perceive, or to create, opportunities in particular markets. A firm, like an individual, possesses specialised knowledge, and pays for it by limitations on its flexibility.

Similar conclusions follow from the analysis, pioneered by Professor Coase (1937), of the firm as an alternative to the market, avoiding some of the information- and transaction-costs of using the market by substituting administrative arrangements for the internal allocation of resources. Within the firm, the advantages of division of labour are sought through organisational design. The specialisation of function thus prescribed may also be thought of as a means of accommodating the constraints of bounded rationality, which have provided a foundation for Professor Simon's (1976) analysis of organisational behaviour. But these constraints will affect behaviour as well as structure. Members of an organisation will thus give selective attention to phenomena, both internal and external, and will learn from their own particular patterns of experience. Their theories and their plans will be influenced by their own situation and their own history.

INTERPRETATIVE FRAMEWORKS AND THE METHODS OF SCIENCE

Whether, or in what condition, such theories and plans might be roughly consistent, is, in the broadest sense, the question underlying the analysis of general equilibrium theorists and of the Austrians. However, neither come very close to the issues which have been raised in the last few pages. The Austrians, it is suggested, are right to think in terms of processes, but avoid many of the difficulties by considering only how individuals interact through the market, and by assuming, in effect, that such individuals acquire knowledge by perceiving the truth. The purpose of this paper is to explain, and to begin to apply, a method of analysing human understanding and human action – the theories that people hold and the policies that they pursue – which, although unfamiliar to most economists, seems particularly appropriate to the problems of knowledge, learning and enterprise. The method was proposed by an American psychologist, George Kelly, and this is now well known in the analysis of personality (to which it was originally directed) and in studies of consumer behaviour. Those familiar with the work of Lakatos (1970) will recognise many similar ideas, expressed in a different language; but there is no space here to consider the attractive notion of a firm's 'research programme'.

Kelly's fundamental proposal is to analyse human beings as scientists: that is, as people whose '*ultimate aim is to predict and control*' (1963, p. 5). This, we may note, is the obverse of Sir Karl Popper's conception of scientific method as a carefully designed version of human trial and error: people learn (imperfectly and inefficiently) from their mistakes; science attempts to discover mistakes quickly and efficiently. A detailed comparison between the two views might be very rewarding; but in this paper we shall attempt no more than a few passing observations.

The selection of data, and its interpretation in the light of both theory and experience – the latter either natural or contrived – are central issues for anyone seeking to predict and control, whether as professional scientists or as human being. Why this is so emerges from the confrontation between the limits of human rationality and the interconnectedness of all phenomena, as Kelly explains. 'The universe that we presume exists . . . is integral. By that we mean it functions as a single unit with all its imaginable parts having an exact relationship to each other' (1963, p. 6). That, of course, is a general equilibrium concept, with the scope of the equilibrium far wider than has been essayed by any economist. Kelly can afford such a wide conception because he is not concerned to offer any general equilibrium solution. In fact, he argues that since anything like a total comprehension of this interdependent system is far beyond our powers, every discipline must necessarily take a partial view, and, recognising that the view is partial, should be wary of making claims outside the realm thus (roughly) defined.

> Man looks at his world through transparent patterns or templets which he creates and then attempts to fit over the realities of which the world is composed. The fit is not always very good . . . Even a poor fit is more helpful to him than nothing at all. (1963, pp. 8–9)

Notice that these patterns, or theories, are created; they are neither perceived, nor derived in any simple way from the phenomena to which they are subsequently applied. Such a concept of theory-creation, and a similar explanation in terms of the desire to impose order on the unimaginable complexity of phenomena, is developed in Adam Smith's remarkable, though little known, early 'History of Astronomy' (1979), and is the key to Professor Shackle's account of the development of economic thought in *The Years of High Theory* (1967); Professor Skinner of Glasgow has examined Smith's ideas and their modern counterparts in a recent article (1979). Sir Karl Popper's rejection of induction as logically impossible has led him to emphasise the importance of imaginative conjecture in providing theories worth testing: however, he is primarily – though far from exclusively – concerned with the ways in which such conjectures may be exposed to possible refutation, whereas Smith, Shackle and Kelly all emphasise the defensive use of theories to accommodate experience. Sir Karl has persistently attacked such defensive uses as an impediment to the progress of knowledge; but they do appear to give a kind of security, even though it may be false. Moreover, as Kelly argues, it is necessary to close off some avenues of enquiry, if necessary by a theoretical fudge, in order to improve our understanding at all.

> We limit the *realm* and try to ignore, for the time being, the intransigent facts just outside the borders of that *realm* . . . For the time being we shall have to content ourselves with a series of miniature systems, each with its own realm or limited range of convenience . . . (1963, p. 10).

That such a strategy should gain even modest success requires that almost all interdependencies are of no significance almost all the time. In Professor Simon's (1969) phraseology, the universe is decomposable into a hierarchy of systems which for the most part interact only weakly. Kelly assumes this to be true within the human time-scale; Professor

Simon argues that complex systems are unlikely to evolve or to survive, unless they are nearly decomposable. But near decomposability is not identical with complete decomposability; and if the latter is assumed, as it has to be in order to construct miniature systems, then the theory embodied in these systems must be, to some extent, false. Two consequences should be noted. Not only are these systems unreliable beyond a limited range of application; they are liable to unsuspected collapse wherever the assumption of decomposability is falsified. Past performance is no guarantee of future success, either for a theory or for a firm which uses it. This inevitable fallibility is a good reason for possessing alternative structures of interpretation, even if they appear less immediately useful.

Kelly's analysis is intended to apply both to the discipline of psychology and to the behaviour of people trying to make sense of their situation. Since psychologists are, one presumes, people trying to make sense of the world, it should indeed apply to both – and to economists and managers also. But, as has been observed, any usable pattern must be incomplete and distorted – at least at the boundaries, where it necessarily denies connections which we believe to exist, and to matter; and it therefore follows that whatever pattern we happen to be using has no claim to exclusivity. 'The same event may be construed simultaneously and profitably within various disciplinary systems' (1963, p. 10). Alternative constructions may be profitable, not because they lead to similar conclusions, but because they do not. 'It is not a matter of indifference which of a set of alternative constructions one chooses to impose upon his world' (1963, p. 15) . . . 'often the facts assume their particular shapes only in the light of a certain theory' (1963, p. 26).

Like Kelly, I wish to use this argument at two levels. The underlying justification for this paper is the belief that by looking at firms in a different way from those employed either in the prevalent kinds of equilibrium theory or in Austrian theories, we can discover different interpretations which offer something additional to anything that the prevalent interpretations can provide. These prevalent interpretations, as was true of psychology when Kelly wrote, are based on theories of situational determinism and an experimental method of external observation. Economists and psychologists alike had reacted against introspection, and denied the relevance of personal testimony. Behaviour was all that mattered; knowledge and motivation, if used at all, appeared as conscious fictions. But the preference for behaviourism is a subjective preference, and even if it were – as it may be – the best single principle of selection, it must, like any other principle, have a limited range of convenience. An approach which leaves room for human initiative, human experimentation and human interpretation, as do several modern theories of scientific development, seems worth exploring.

That is the argument for using alternative methods of analysis. But the view of firms as organisations being explored here uses this argument for alternative frameworks as its core. Managers, like scientists, or any other person who wishes to predict and control, must impose some pattern on events. No single pattern can claim any exclusive rights, yet different patterns may lead to different interpretations, and possibly to different decisions. It is part of the 'perfect knowledge' assumption which is never more than slightly attenuated in standard theories that all firms would have the same perception of any given situation; by abandoning that assumption one can gain some understanding of the behaviour of firms.

EVENTS AND FRAMEWORKS

The focus of Kelly's analysis is the interaction between events and the frameworks which are used to interpret them. These events are of two kinds. First, there are those which impinge on a passive observer. 'The universe is continually changing with respect to itself. Within our universe something is always going on. In fact, that is the way the universe exists; it exists by happening' (Kelly, 1963, p. 7). Thus the passage of time generates a stream of events to be interpreted by the use of whatever patterns people use. 'Experience is made up of the successive construing of events. It is not constituted merely by the events themselves' (p. 73). It is the recipient of the data who converts it into information; and this conversion may involve the use of existing theory to make fresh predictions, or a revision of theory to accommodate recalcitrant data. Since the events which are observed depend upon the time period, and a variety of patterns may be used, the lessons of experience are not common to all, even within a single industry. Different events (at different times, or in different places) and different interpretations are each capable of producing different conclusions about both theory and policy. It is of course possible that a variety of events and a variety of patterns should all lead to similar conclusions. Indeed, if this never happened, human behaviour would no doubt be much less coherent than it is. But there are no logical reasons for

112 *Beyond Positive Economics?*

assuming that this will be generally true, and some fairly persuasive evidence that it is not. Our data rarely meets the requirements of sampling theory, and our interpretative frameworks are incomplete.

The passage of time gives us a chance to check the serviceability of the patterns which we use by testing them against subsequent events, either by the rigorous method of making explicit predictions before-hand, or by the more dangerous − but still quite often effective − method of seeing whether the new events can be accommodated within the currently-accepted framework. By either route, there is a presumption that the serviceability of a person's constructs will tend to improve over time, provided that the nature of the phenomena being observed is changing more slowly than he is able or willing to revise his inter-pretative framework − in particular that neglected interdependencies do not become significant − and furthermore that he does not seek to apply his interpretations to phenomena of a different kind. Both qualifications will be taken up later.

The second class of events are, at least in part, internal to the analysis. People do not simply observe and interpret; they also act. Agents have policies as well as theories. What happens in the universe is partly the result of human action, based on interpretations, and providing material for fresh interpretations − not only by the originat-ing actors. The outcome of one set of entrepreneurial decisions pro-vides opportunities for other entrepreneurs. Thus interpretations and decisions produce an interactive (but not closed) system which evolves over time. Whether this system moves towards some sort of equilib-rium is an open question. That it should reach a static equilibrium is incompatible with the conception of the universe employed here. This is not to deny that static equilibrium concepts may sometimes offer a useful scheme of interpretation, provided one remembers that, like any other scheme, it is incomplete.

ORGANISATION AND INTERPRETATION

Let us now begin to apply these ideas to the firm as an organisation. A firm is composed of a group of people who all, in varying ways and to varying extents, interpret what they observe and take decisions accord-ing to their interpretation. We will follow convention by concentrating on those people who are usually called managers, though we should not forget that much of what follows applies also to those usually called workers.

If a new firm is created, and staffed by people who are unfamiliar with the line of business which the firm has chosen to enter, its managers are likely to be ill-equipped with constructs which will help them to understand what is happening and to take good decisions; but, provided that the firm does not collapse as a result of their inexperience, they will learn from events and their own mistakes, and will eventually acquire a set of frameworks which proves serviceable for that line of business. Indeed, the danger of collapse before the minimum amount of learning has been achieved is so generally recognised that it is unusual to staff a new organisation with people who have no knowledge of the business area; even those with such experience will probably need to modify their constructs to accommodate the somewhat different circumstances of the new firm.

It is even more certain that before things can run fairly smoothly, there will be a need for the alignment of the constructs used by different members of the firm. Even within a particular kind of business, different constructs may be employed, and people moving between organisations — be they two universities, two government departments, two consultancy firms or two manufacturing firms — will usually find some differences in the way things are done, and will have to spend time learning how the system into which they have entered works. Thus, even if there were no need to learn about the technology or the market, there would still be the need to learn about the working style of other members of the organisation.

While the learning process continues it consumes managerial resources; indeed, in the early stages it may consume a great many, and long hours and frequent meetings may be the price even of survival; but as people gradually learn to develop and to use interpretative frameworks which not only seem to offer a satisfactory fit to the data but are reasonably compatible with the systems used by other people within the organisation, so the effort required diminishes. Resources are thus released, and may be used to increase the throughput of the organisation, if necessary by bringing in additional people, who will also need to learn and to be assimilated, at some cost both to old and new members of the organisation.

In this process of learning, organisational design plays an important part, in two major ways. First, it determines the flow of events which will come to the attention of each manager, and thus the material which his developing constructs will have to fit. This sets limits to the interpretative possibilities, but, by the arguments advanced earlier, does not fix them. Second, by defining the extent, and the limits, of responsibility, it prescribes what the constructs must accomplish, and what they need not — the kinds of policy models which the theories are required to serve. As Kelly observes (1963, pp. 9–10), 'when one limits the realm of facts, it is possible to develop a detailed system without worrying about the inconsistencies in the system which certain peripheral facts would reveal'. What inconsistencies would matter depends on how the periphery is defined; constructs which would suit a functional manager may be quite inadequate for a product manager. The policy requirements, and thus the theoretical requirements, are very different. Indeed, the redrawing of organisational boundaries is usually intended to invalidate old constructs which were thought to be leading to decisions that are now judged to be undesirable when assessed from some higher viewpoint. Restructuring is intended to improve policy through the use of more appropriate theories.

A successful organisational design is one that generates a stream of events for each manager which enables him to develop quickly an effective set of constructs. Effectiveness is here assessed by the decisions which result from the use of these constructs: they must be consistent both with the world outside, and with those decisions taken by other members of the organisation. Consistency between decisions does not necessarily require similar constructs. For good organisational design not only brings some kinds of people together; it also keeps other kinds of people apart. Partial insulation may allow the development of simpler constructs within each field of interest, making management more effective within those limits. The art of organisational design requires the creation of such insulating barriers where they will facilitate good and low-cost local decision-making, while maintaining a sufficient commonality of framework to ensure (if assurance is indeed possible) that the outcomes of local decisions are not disastrous — for example, that products designed to replace the existing range are not totally outside the manufacturing competence of the existing equipment and workforce.

The speed of learning depends on what it is desired to learn. As Burns and Stalker (1961) taught us twenty years ago, in a very stable environment a mechanistic system of management, in which functions are narrowly defined, is very effective in developing the skills for dealing with that environment. Simple interpretative frameworks with very narrow ranges of convenience may be perfectly adequate. But its effectiveness depends on that environment remaining stable; and the great danger is of a failure to recognise how limited is the range of convenience of the simplified frameworks to which everyone has become accustomed. The structure reflects an assumption that neither theory nor policy will require more than minor amendment; no innovations are called for. Professor Hahn's self-imposed restriction of theory to the examination of equilibrium conditions may likewise lead to a specification which is quite incapable of adjusting to unforeseen events. At the other extreme, an organic system, providing for interaction anywhere within the organisation, slows down learning by providing only small samples of each kind of phenomenon and requires the development of many different patterns to fit different situations (or, improbably, some elaborate pattern which fits them all). The release of managerial resources from such a system is not likely to be rapid; on the other hand, those resources which are released are likely to have a far wider range of use than the resources released by a mechanistic system – not least because managers are likely to realise that new circumstances may require the creation of new schemes of interpretation.

GROWTH AND ADJUSTMENT

This apparent trade-off between the rate at which spare managerial resources are generated and their applicability suggests that the most rapid growth of firms may occur by simple expansion within an existing field, with additional output being supplied to existing customers, or to new customers with similar characteristics. Of course, if the total market is not expanding, or expanding only slowly, such growth must be at the expense of other firms, which might be expected to have similar potential for growth (though we should be careful not to assume that all will have similar ambitions). Thus one might expect to find fairly bitter battles in such circumstances, with little scope for avoiding direct confrontation by way of diversification. Control over customers or sources of supply might suggest itself as a competitive tactic.

There will also clearly be differences between firms with different patterns of experience (and experience, remember, depends both on events and their interpretation) in the rate at which resources are released and in their applicability. Even within the same industry, different firms may develop different capabilities; between industries there are liable to be wide differences. Nor is the release of resources an irreversible process. A drastic change in the environment of a firm (for example, through the development of new technology or a new source of competition) may impose a need for relearning how to conduct its own business — a need which has proved beyond the powers of some organisations which were only too well adapted to their familiar circumstances. Too strong an assumption of convergence towards a state approximating to equilibrium is dangerous both for the theorist and for the manager.

Adjustment to new circumstances is not often easy. For what is required is often more than the revision of some local constructs in response to environmental change. Local constructs must be mutually compatible, at least to the extent that they impinge upon each other; and revisions in response to external events may disrupt that compatibility. The difficulty of adjustment may well be aggravated by the need to revise also the inter-relations between local constructs, so that some need to be more closely interlocked than before. As Kelly remarks (1963, p. 9), 'in seeking improvement [a person] is repeatedly halted by the damage to the system that apparently will result from the alteration of a subordinate construct'. We can all see how difficult it is for well-trained economists to give up a particular theoretical approach; but the difficulty is not peculiar to our discipline. Such a threat to a person's thought-system helps to explain why some people continue to make the same mistakes; any adequate response seems to them to require an adjustment of their ways of thinking which threatens their way of life — even, in the last resort, their personality. Kelly's professional interest in developing his theory was in fact to provide a better interpretative framework for the analysis of personality disorders.

Of course, this problem of maintaining one's personality applies directly to managers as to anyone else (to practitioners of an academic discipline, for example). But there is in addition the requirement to maintain some kind of working system for the organisation; and it may seem impossible to maintain that system if those adjustments are made which would permit more effective handling of particular problems. Thus learning, at a personal or an organisation level, may be impossible. For example, both management and union representatives in some firms may simply be incapable of changing their approach to industrial relations, despite the repeated failure of their current methods, because a more effective method would require so radical a change in their conceptions of the 'opposition' as to threaten their whole interpretation of the economic and social system. Chandler (1962) has explained how Du Pont's attempts to come to terms with the needs of a diversified business were agonisingly protracted by the company's devotion to the accepted practices of good management; and Burns and Stalker (1961) have shown how a deep-rooted belief in certain fundamental notions of orderliness frustrated the attempts of some Scottish firms to break into a new and technically-progressive industry. The history of British Rail, of British Leyland and its predecessors, the fate of AEI and BSA, are just a few instances of the appalling difficulty experienced by people and by organisations in abandoning well-confirmed theories and policies which have been carried by events far beyond the limits of their applicability. Some principles an organisation must have, if it is to remain an organisation; some principles of behaviour a person must cling to, whatever the evidence, if he is to remain a person. Some changes are simply not possible, even if the alternative is death.

GROWTH AND THE THEORY OF THE FIRM

The kind of analysis which has just been outlined may be used to add some detail to Penrose's (1959) treatment of the growth of firms. Penrose, like Coase (though she does not refer to him), regards the firm as an administrative framework which serves as an alternative to the market for the purposes of resource allocation: it is 'an autonomous administrative planning unit, the activities of which are interrelated and are coordinated by policies which are framed in the light of their effect on the enterprise as a whole' (Penrose, 1959, pp. 15–16). A feasible plan for the firm requires compatibility – not, we may repeat, identity – of interpretative frameworks between the component elements of the organisation.

These plans are derived jointly from its expectations – 'the way in which it interprets its environment' (p. 41) – and from its appraisal of its own internal resources. Its expectations, in the language of Professor Hahn, are generated by the theory which it holds; and among its own internal resources Penrose lays especial emphasis on managerial services, which we can now interpret as a well-validated set of constructs for selecting and interpreting data and for making effective and timely decisions. Perceived resources and expectations are brought together in the firm's '"productive opportunity"', which comprises all of the productive possibilities that its "entrepreneurs" see and can take advantage of' (p. 31); and this productive opportunity, as Penrose makes clear, exists in the imaginations of entrepreneurs, not in the world outside. (The resemblance to Professor Shackle's ideas should need no emphasis.) The more imaginative the entrepreneur, the greater the productive opportunity.

Penrose pays very little attention to the relationship between perception and reality. She does not choose, like Professor Kirzner, to restrict entrepreneurs to the perception − selective and incomplete − of opportunities which already exist, as consequences of changes in preferences or technology which have already taken place. Instead she contents herself with observing that if the productive opportunities are a mirage, then the firm's plans will not be successful, and disclaiming any interest in such firms. Her theory is explicitly designed for successful firms; but might it not be helpful to have a theory which can help to explain the difference between success and failure?

Though success is not guaranteed, it does not necessarily depend on the choice of one particular course of action. The firm's own action may change its environment − a point also made by Kelly about individual actions (1963, p. 8). Both authors provide much more scope for originative choice than do the behaviourist traditions of situational determinism in psychology and economics. This analytical recognition of alternative possible futures adds to the significance of entrepreneurial versatility, which not only widens the range of perception but augments creativity. Within Kelly's system, versatility requires either constructs with a very wide range of convenience, or, more likely, a range of constructs with different foci of application. It certainly implies the capacity, and willingness, to adapt constructs as circumstances change.

The application of Kelly's mode of analysis to Penrose's theory reinforces the latter's argument for the heterogeneity of firms. Heterogeneity has important theoretical uses. It provides a basis for an assumption which Professor Kirzner needs but does not explain: the assumption that a few entrepreneurs will perceive an opportunity which is hidden from everyone else. As Richardson (1960, p. 57) has pointed out, 'a general profit opportunity, which is both known to everyone and equally capable of being exploited by everyone, is, in an important sense, a profit opportunity for no one in particular'. If every individual has his own pattern of experience, mediated by his own interpretative framework, then each may have a slightly different perception; thus relatively few will recognise any particular change in the environment. (For the great majority, it will not be within their own environment that the change occurs.) If the profitable exploitation of that change requires the use of a pool of resources within an administrative framework, then some of those who see the possibilities will feel unable to take advantage of them. Barriers to the entry of most firms may be necessary to give confidence to the remainder. Such barriers may thus, contrary to the presumptions of static theory, contribute to economic welfare.

COMPETITION

In welfare economics, any departure from the conditions of perfect competition is still likely to be condemned as a violation of Pareto optimality. Strictly speaking, of course, both Pareto optimality and perfect competition are valid only for equilibrium, and are not appropriate for the analysis of adjustment processes. Something close to perfect competition might perhaps be appropriate for adjustment, if we could somehow avoid the paralysing criticism of Richardson, and if we could assume that we all knew where to search for the equilibrium configuration: in Kelly's terms, we would be certain that there was no need to stray beyond the range of convenience of a single, commonly-shared set of constructs. But this is to assume a far greater degree of knowledge than we can hope to possess. Within an economy, just as within academia, we need a variety of interpretative frameworks; indeed we need them within an industry as we need them within an academic discipline. Possibilities of intellectual and of economic progress will not all be envisioned within any single framework.

The adjustment of constructs – of theories and of policies – is facilitated by their subordination to a higher-level construct which is formulated sufficiently loosely to accommodate a variety of subordinate constructs, not necessarily mutually compatible. The permeability of superordinate constructs, to use Kelly's term (p. 79) confers resilience. Such permeability is desirable within any organisation which has to cope with change; but, as we have argued above, it is necessarily limited. Successful adaptation within an industry may therefore be dependent on the existence of a number of firms, with substantially different sets of constructs, and (quite possibly) different organisational arrangements which permit different kinds of permeability. Attempts to compel all firms within an industry to conform to a single best pattern, as judged by the perceived requirements of the current situation, may prove disastrous. However successful that pattern may presently be, we must not forget that its range of applicability is limited, and, the more closely it is tailored to contemporary circumstances (and therefore apparently the more efficient), the narrower is that range.

120 *Beyond Positive Economics?*

Sir Karl Popper reminds us that no amount of corroboration can immunise a theory against falsification. There can be no assurance that alternative conjectures will never be required; and alternative conjectures arise most readily from alternative frameworks. If we are to react effectively to the stream of events by which the universe exists (some of them the product of human action) we must avoid misguided attempts to stabilise low-level constructs, either within individuals or within firms. It is the attempt to preserve detailed subordinate constructs in the face of their growing inadequacy to cope with the phenomena which they are required to interpret which leads to human breakdown. Similarly, an attempt to preserve every firm within an industry, or even every industry within an economy, is less likely to succeed in that object than to destroy a superordinate structure which could have been preserved by greater permeability.

REFERENCES

Bradbury, F. R., McCarthy, M. C., and Suckling, C. W. (1972) 'Patterns of innovation: Part ii — the Anaesthetic Halothane', *Chemistry and Industry*, pp. 105–10.

Burns, T., and Stalker, G. M. (1961) *The Management of Innovation* (London: Tavistock).

Chandler, A. D. (1962) *Strategy and Structure* (Cambridge, Mass.: MIT Press).

Coase, R. H. (1937) 'The Nature of the Firm', *Economica* (N.S.), iv, 386–405.

Hahn, F. H. (1973) *On the Notion of Equilibrium in Economics* (Cambridge University Press).

Hayek, F. A. (1937) 'Economics and Knowledge', *Economica* (N.S.), iv, 33–54.

Kelly, G. A. (1963) *A Theory of Personality* (New York: W. W. Norton).

Kirzner, I. M. (1973) *Competition and Entrepreneurship* (University of Chicago Press).

Kirzner, I. M. (1982) 'Uncertainty, Discovery and Human Action', in I. M. Kirzner (ed.), *The Contributions of Ludwig von Mises to Economics* (Lexington, Mass.: Lexington Books).

Lakatos, I. (1970) 'Falsification and the Methodology of Scientific Research Programmes', in I. Lakatos and A. Musgrove (eds), *Criticism and the Growth of Knowledge* (Cambridge University Press).

Penrose, E. T. (1959) *The Theory of the Growth of the Firm* (Oxford: Basil Blackwell).

Popper, K. R. (1972) *The Logic of Scientific Discovery*, 6th impression (London: Hutchinson).

Richardson, G. B. (1960) *Information and Investment* (Oxford University Press).

Shackle, G. L. S. (1967) *The Years of High Theory* (Cambridge University Press).

Simon, H. A. (1969) *The Sciences of the Artificial* (Cambridge, Mass.: MIT Press).

Simon, H. A. (1976) *Administrative Behavior*, 3rd edn (New York: The Free Press).

Skinner, A. S. (1979) 'Adam Smith: an Aspect of Modern Economics?' *Scottish Journal of Political Economy*, 26, 109–26.

Smith, A. (1979) 'History of Astronomy', in W. P. D. Wightman (ed.), *Essays on Philosophical Subjects* (Oxford University Press).

[16]

Excerpt from *Technology and Economic Progress*, 54–85.

4 Evolution and Economic Change

STAN METCALFE

'The Mecca of the economist lies in economic
biology rather than in economic dynamics.'
(Marshall, *Principles of Economics*, 8th Variorum edn, p. xiv)

1 INTRODUCTION

The central theme of this paper is economic change and the mechanisms
by which it is generated. As befits a paper presented to the British
Association for the Advancement of Science, it draws its inspiration
from theories of evolutionary change, theories which over one hundred
years ago were the subject of debates of some ferocity at its meetings
(Jones, 1980). To be more precise the purpose of this paper is to outline
elements of a framework for the analysis of the relationship between the
development of technology and long-run economic change. Since Marx
and Schumpeter wrote, no one has seriously questioned the idea that
economic change is driven by the introduction and diffusion of
innovations either in technique or in organisation. In this they draw a
remarkable, if unnoticed, parallel with the process of change in the
natural world where speciation and selection are the driving forces
behind the changing patterns of plant and animal life.

Yet, since the publication of Marshall's *Principles of Economics*
(1920), the role of biological ways of thinking in economics has been a
source of genuine puzzlement and not infrequent outbursts of irritation
(Levine, 1980). The issue is not simply a matter of the appropriateness of
reasoning by analogy, for any analogy, mechanical, biological or
otherwise has its limitations and must always be treated with due
caution. Rather the issue is the precise nature of the insight which a
natural science can provide in a social science context.

In what follows I hope to illustrate some consequences of a special form of evolutionary thinking in economics, drawing attention to its role in making sense of variety in economic behaviour. Given the emphasis on variety and change, I hope that the ideas presented here will also be of some interest to the economic historians, since one of the principal products of their labours is precisely the delineation of the variety of forms of behaviour in an economic system. History is a rich tapestry of variety and change. Evolutionary economics is one of the frameworks which contribute to an understanding of that tapestry.

In its essentials the ensuing argument is deceptively simple. Economic change is driven by variety in economic performance between competing, alternative ways of meeting specific needs. In turn economic variety is contingent upon variety in technological and organisational forms. Innovations, whether they be incremental or radical, are akin to mutations, they introduce new varieties of technology and organisation into an existing economic structure. While innovation enhances variety, imitation and competition consume variety so that continued economic progress depends on there being a balance between the different mechanisms, a balance which may fluctuate over time. As Marshall emphasised, variety is the mainspring of economic progress within the context of competitive capitalism.

We find it helpful to analyse technology at two conceptual levels. In terms of artifacts, the products and process of production which firms reveal in the market-place; and in terms of the corresponding knowledge bases, the ideas, concepts and modes of enquiry which are necessary to generate a particular revealed performance (Layton, 1974). Bridging the two dimensions of technology is the firm, that organisation which articulates a knowledge base to design and implement a particular level of revealed performance. One immediate implication of this is that both the knowledge base and revealed technological performance are concepts inseparable from questions of organisational structure and activity. But, paradoxically perhaps, the competitive environment does not select directly with respect to organisations but rather with respect to the products they produce and their methods of production.

2 EVOLUTIONARY MODES OF THOUGHT

Before turning to a more detailed analysis of technological competition it is important to be clear on what it is that the biological analogy is contributing to the analysis. The fundamental point here is that the evolutionary framework is concerned with frequencies of events and

56   *Evolution and Economic Change*

phenomena rather than with ideal, representative types and there is a considerable shift in intellectual orientation in this change of emphasis. More is at stake here than epistemology. The shift from analysing ideal cases to examining frequencies and their distribution is central to the elaboration of an evolutionary perspective of the sort we are proposing. The shift from classical to distributional modes of explanation has occurred in biology in terms of the shift from typological to population thinking about species (Mavr, 1982; Sober, 1985). In typological thinking species are regarded as fixed and identifiable in terms of a few distinct characteristics which represent the essence of the entity. In this view all variations around the ideal type are accidental, and are to be interpreted as aberrations.

By contrast, in population thinking, species are described in terms of a distribution of characteristics and, whereas in typological thinking variation is a nuisance, in population thinking it is of all-consuming interest because it is the variety in the system which drives the evolutionary process. Moreover the changes over time in statistical moments derived from the characteristics distribution are an index of the rate and direction of evolutionary change, as we shall demonstrate below.

It will be as well to remind ourselves here of the essential mechanisms of evolutionary change. These are: the principle of variation, that members of the population vary with respect to at least one characteristic with selective significance; the principle of heredity, that there exist copying mechanisms to ensure continuity over time in the form of the species under investigation; and the principle of selection, that some forms are better fitted to environmental pressure and thus increase in relative significance compared to inferior forms.

To transfer these concepts uncritically to a social science context is correctly recognised to be untenable. None the less, applied carefully to the context of technological competition they prove to be remarkably fruitful, primarily because they are ideally suited to cope with two enduring historical facts, namely variety and change. Economic environments then provide the basis for selection between competing technologies, by establishing price structures which provide a direct evaluation of the performance characteristics of rival products and processes. While products and processes are the direct units of selection this necessarily entails indirect selection across the firms which articulate those technologies. But the two levels of selection must be kept quite distinct; the selection and survival of firms involves considerations beyond those which determine the selection and survival of technologies. Paraphasing Sober (1985, p. 100) there is selection for performance characteristics and selection of technologies and by implication firms.

Whenever there are economic differences betweeen competing technologies there is scope for selection. But variety itself is not sufficient; the differences must be stable relative to the speed with which selection operates. In a world of perfect adaptation there would be no scope for selection. Selection is quite consistent with random technological variation but what it does require are elements of inertia to hold competing varieties in a form long enough for selection to operate (Matthews, 1985; Hannan and Freeman, 1977). It is here that organisations become crucial, for one of their attributes is their ability to create structures of thought and activity which are impervious, in part, to adaptive pressures. (Itami, Hrebaniak and Joyce, 1985). Organisations generate variety and they hold variety sufficiently constant for selection to operate. As Hannan and Freeman put it, rather graphically, 'Failing churches do not become retail stores nor do firms transform themselves into churches' (p. 957). Similarly, within and between competing technologies, firms generate commitments and loyalties which are not easily shaken. Adaptation and selection both have a role to play. But we do insist that the ability to adapt depends in part on the past history of selective experience of the firm. Cases abound, for example, of firms where past success in the selection environment has lulled them into a false sense of security, minimising their adaptive response when adaptation was most needed.

Of course, to interpret the evolutionary argument solely in terms of Darwinian selection would be a crude error. Technologies are articulated by purposeful organisations capable of search activity and capable of reacting, although often erroneously and within limits, to anticipated events. There are plausible arguments for claiming that the nature and timing of inventions are random events but, equally, there are powerful inducement mechanisms at work in shaping the rate and direction of inventive activity. Certainly the transition from invention to innovation is guided by selective forces. In terms of evolutionary theory, there is a clear Lamarckian element to be incorporated here. Not only do innovations arise in response to perceived needs and opportunities, they are carried through time in the memory of firms and other institutions in such a way that the experience of the past shapes what they can achieve in the future. The fact that firms learn, have memory, and possess mechanisms for maintaining memory over time in the face of changes in personnnel is the source of the chief elements of irreversibility in the pattern of economic progress.

Finally one must not draw too sharply the distinction between firms and their selective environment. Alliances made with other firms to share the market, or to perform co-operative research are common phenomena, as are attempts to sway governments in favour of protective tariffs, production subsidies or advantageous technological standards. By acting in this way firms can change the selective pressures that they experience to their advantage.

However it is our view that these qualifications enrich rather than diminish the significance of evolutionary thinking in this area. The bedrock of competition remains variety and selection, and no mechanism for generating variety is more potent in the long run than that which stimulates technological change.

3   THE EVOLUTIONARY NATURE OF ECONOMIC CHANGE: SOME PRECURSORS

As is well known, throughout the *Principles*, Marshall makes frequent reference to the similarity between economic and biological methods of analysis, to the appropriateness of biological modes of thought for higher stages of economic analysis, and to the role of natural selection in economic affairs. However it is chiefly for the analogy which he draws between the growth of trees in a forest and the growth of firms in an industry that Marshall is remembered. This device was employed to capture the idea of a balance between the forces of progress and decay, as represented in the tendencies to increasing and decreasing returns. It was in brief a device to limit the historical growth of firms and maintain competitive conditions intact. Whether it is useful to treat organisations such as joint stock companies as living organisms is, of course, a contentious issue but it is not from our viewpoint the main issue. The principle implication of Marshall's resort to biological analogy is quite different. The inference which follows from this mode of reasoning is precisely that there is variety in behaviour and, in particular, variety in the cost conditions experienced by different firms. Thus Marshall's problem was how to reason in the presence of variety. How and why these differences change over time is a secondary question, to which an explanation based on the life cycle characteristics of organisations may or may not have much to contribute. It is this element of variety in Marshall's reasoning which leads directly to his device of the representative firm, that hypothetical firm with costs of production which in long-period equilibrium are the average for the industry as a whole. That hypothetical firm which in stationary conditions is also of constant size

(Robbins, 1928). The point is simple. Once Marshall had permitted variety in the behaviour of firms, he naturally sought a summary measure of the set of firms comprising an industry and chose the average firm as his index of representativeness. What Marshall did not successfully address, as Robbins and others have pointed out, was the analytic significance of the representative firm. In short, Marshall failed to establish the conditions under which the representative firm had an economic as distinct from a purely statistical meaning.

It was not until the appearance of Alchian's controversial paper in 1951 that the economic significance of diversity of behaviour began to be systematically explored. Alchian put forward the view that in a world of incomplete information and uncertain foresight individual behaviour is not predictable. Faced with changes in information, say a change in the price of an input, individual firms will typically react in different ways and may not even react in the same direction. None the less, Alchian argued, the effects of such changes can still be predicted at the aggregate, industry level, once it is recognised that the market mechanism is an adoption mechanism selecting across different forms of behaviour, and that realised profits are the criterion which drives the selection process. In elaborating this theme, he further argued that selective success is premised on results, not motivations, that random behaviour at the individual level may still be consistent with predictable behaviour at the system level, and that uncertainty results not in optimising behaviour but in various forms of learning behaviour related to imitation and individual experimentation. He expressed the fundamental point thus: 'As in a race, the award goes to the relatively fastest, even if all the competitors loaf. Even in a world of stupid men there would still be profits' (p. 213).

There is no question that this was a highly provocative argument, containing as it did the implication that it is fatal to base economic analysis upon the predictability of individual behaviour, and the corollary that methodological individualism should give way to holistic modes of reasoning. If optimality is relevant at all it should be considered as an attribute of system behaviour, not of individual choices. However it is important to make clear the limited scope of Alchian's argument. The central limitation for present purposes is its equation of economic selection with economic viability, the survival or the elimination of firms according to their profitability. To illustrate, consider a population of firms producing the same homogeneous product, facing common input prices but using methods of production with different capital: labour ratios. Assume all the firms are profitable, although they

60 *Evolution and Economic Change*

obviously enjoy different levels of profitability. Now impose an environmental change in the form of a higher wage rate. The traditional argument would now predict that firms would change their behaviour and choice of technique, to take the industry to a more capital-intensive spectrum of technology. However, Alchian argues, even if no firm adjusts its production method in response to the changed input prices there will still be predictable consequences at the industry level. At the higher wage, some firms will now be unprofitable and they will exit from the industry. Consequently, even though individual behaviours do not change, system behaviour does change and that the industry ends up with a higher capital:labour ratio and a different distribution of surviving capital:labour ratios embodied in the given methods of production. Moreover, for any given change in the wage, it would be possible for the omniscient economist to predict which of the methods of production would cease to be viable. Predictions are about systems not individual behaviours.

A number of difficulties arise from this argument (Penrose, 1952; Alchian, 1953). It clearly depends on assumptions about the intensity of competition and the rules governing exit from an industry, yet Alchian provided no clear indication of how intensity or exit rules are to be defined. If a criterion for the intensity of competition could be found how would the viability of firms be influenced by environments of differing competitive intensity? Secondly, his analysis of viability was unquestionably static. Missed was the opportunity to consider a further implication of variety in profitability, namely that it would underpin variety in the growth of firms and systematic changes over time in the *relative* weight of different firm behaviours within the overall distribution of behaviour. Interestingly enough, this link between growth and profitability subsequently played a central role in Mrs Penrose's own theory of the growth of firms (Penrose, 1961) and in the independently developed analyses of Steindl and Downie (see below). In other words relative viability ought to be distinguished from absolute viability. Thirdly, the issue of random versus purposive, motivated behaviour proved to be a particular source of difficulty. This is not an issue I wish to pursue here, save to note that Alchian was insistent upon the need to develop stochastic models of economic behaviour, and that any appraisal of the significance of random elements requires a fully articulated statement of their precise generating mechanism.

These difficulties notwithstanding, the central element in Alchian's argument is clear. Namely, that analysis should be switched from a focus on the behaviour of individuals to a focus upon the properties of distributions of economic behaviour. One may then describe these distributions via a number of shorthand statistics, including the notion of the representative firm, by which Alchian meant the modal firm. Thus Alchian had made that crucial switch from typological to population methods of analysis referred to above.

With the benefit of hindsight we can now see that the root cause of the controversy engendered by Alchian's argument was a dichotomy between economics as the study of individual adaptation and economics as the study of system selection. As so often happens, it was a controversy based upon a false dichotomy, for the two modes of reasoning are perfectly compatible (Matthews, 1985). The crucial issue remains the existence or otherwise of different individual behaviours. If there is no variety in behaviour there can be no scope for selection and all change can only be explicable as the result of uniform identical adaptations by all individuals. But such a world of homogenous adaptations is not the world of actual economics, and it surely represents a trivialisation of the historical record. Equally, if there is no element of adaptiveness in individual behaviour then a major source of variety would be eliminated at its source. Adaptation and selection play complementary roles. Thus, Alchian's argument hinges not upon the absence of individual adaptation but upon the presence of differential adaptation. Faced with a change in the market environment, firms may all adapt in the right direction as Penrose wishes them to, but if they adapt by different degrees or at different rates over time then some may not adapt enough to remain viable. Extending this line of reasoning to firms which adapt in the wrong direction may add historical relevance but it does not add analytic substance. Furthermore firms with superior adaptive behaviour will not only experience higher survival probabilities, they will also enjoy potentially superior growth prospects. Because it is precisely the existence of varieties of behaviour which is the central issue, the exact motivations underpinning these behaviours are of secondary importance. Adaptations may be maximising, they may be satisficing, they may be habitual, they may be unthinking. No matter, providing the relevant motivations result in consistently different behaviours then the scope is created for economic selection. To repeat, this is perfectly consistent with individual maximisation provided maximising behaviour is not equated with identical behaviour across individuals.

Accepting for the present the hypothesis that firms are intendedly rational, we may pose the question, 'What factors might lead to differential adaptiveness in response to changed circumstances?' The

62   *Evolution and Economic Change*

most obvious and well known answer resides in the phenomenon of bounded rationality. Individuals do not face the same choice sets because information is not distributed equally to all, and the capacity to translate information into knowledge differs between them. Differential capacities to acquire costly information and differential creativity in the use of that information are the twin pillars of variety in behaviour. Extending this argument to organisations reinforces it considerably. Firms are coalitions of thinking, information-processing individuals each with their own life experiences and accumulated stock of knowledge. Through its communication and decision-making structures the firm filters and combines the knowledge of its individual members. Different organisational structures then provide a further basis for differential adaptation to changing circumstances. The firms simply do not perceive the same choice sets: they know different things about the world they share. At best their optimisations are local and hence different (Loasby, 1976).

Of themselves these familiar arguments are suggestive of diversity in behaviour but they are not the complete picture. They imply that firms are expected to make mistakes and that they are continually discovering alternative patterns of behaviour. But discovery is not adaptation until we take account of the possibilities of response. It is here that the arguments relating to inertia become relevant (Hannan and Freeman, 1977; McElvey, 1982). Typically the responses of a firm are limited by many consequences of its past behaviour. Sunk capital investments, interrelatedness between the elements of its operations, which mean that responses must be system-compatible (Frankel, 1955), and the accumulated stock of knowledge and experience which underpins its 'world view' each act and interact to limit the time rate of response to newly perceived opportunities. Since there is no reason to expect the determinants of inertia to be the same in all firms, depending as they do in part upon personalities and the composition of management teams, it follows that even if two firms begin with identical behaviour they will subsequently develop different behaviour patterns, differences which will become cumulative and difficult to reverse.

Given the empirical significance of persistent differences in firm behaviour it is surprising how little economic analysis there is of the consequences of diversity. The evidence for diversity in unit cost and factor productivities, within the same industry and between the same industry in different countries, had been conclusively established by the pioneering studies of Rostas (1948), and others prior to 1950. Further evidence on this was subsequently provided by Salter (1961), and in the frontier production function method developed by Farrell (1957). If cost variety is important and persistent, surely so is product variety, otherwise it is difficult to see how theories of imperfect competition could have found such favour among economists. And yet the implications of product and process diversity were simply not developed. Even Chamberlin, it will be remembered, developed his theory of monopolistic competition under the assumption that all firms in the group produced the same product under identical cost conditions. Fortunately two authors stand out as counter-examples to this general picture.

The first is Joseph Steindl, who, in a remarkable book published in 1952, developed a theory of profitability and industrial competition based upon empirically observed differences in unit costs between firms in the same industry. Steindl sought to establish that net profits are the result of cost differentials between firms. By analogy with the Ricardian theory of rent, he defined the marginal producer as the highest cost producer who under conditions of acute competition would earn zero net profits. From this it follows that the distribution of net profits depends on the distribution of costs in the infra-marginal firms. Steindl went on to develop a dynamic picture of long-run competition, in which the aggregate of non-marginal firms deployed their cost-determined surpluses to accumulate capacity and gradually squeeze the existing marginal firms out of the industry. Not surprisingly we find frequent allusion in this work to biological metaphor. For Steindl, just as for Alchian, variety becomes the basis for selection across the given behaviours of the firms. Steindl also attempted, albeit in a limited fashion, to explain how cost variety evolved over time through process innovations made by the larger firms.

The second book, published by Downie in 1955, is no less remarkable for its intention to make economic sense of variety in behaviour. Downie started from two empirical observations, the co-existence of firms of different efficiency in the same industry, and the slow diffusion of technology and consequential efficiency gap between average practice and best practice unit cost. Unlike Salter, who later sought to explain this gap in terms of a vintage investment model, Downie traces variety in efficiency to differences in innovation performance, such that the more efficient a firm is relative to its rivals, the less likely it is at any time to be pressured into innovating to improve its efficiency. This pattern of innovative behaviour works to maintain variety in efficiency. In turn, this is the basis for an accumulation mechanism which is the same as that postulated by Steindl. Differences in efficiency are the basis for

64 *Evolution and Economic Change*

differences in net profitability, so that the more efficient firms can accumulate capacity and market share at the expense of their less efficient rivals. Selection acts as a 'transfer mechanism', bringing to economic dominance the most efficient firm, and it is only the offsetting innovation mechanism which prevents this dominance from becoming absolute. Again we find abundant resort to biological metaphor with, for example, the suggestion that the market economy is the mechanism for selecting the fit from the unfit (p. 60).

In comparison with the analysis of Alchian, it is immediately apparent that Downie and Steindl have developed a dynamic process rather than a static equilibrium version of the selection mechanism. It is differential growth rather than differential viability which is their central concern. But for all three authors the underlying logic is the same: differential cost conditions give rise to differential rents. For Alchian negative rents mean elimination of the firm. For Downie and Steindl positive rents are the basis for differential growth, and the changing relative importance, or weight, of firms over time. Thus it is not simply the existence of surpluses or rents but the uses to which firms deploy those rents which is relevant for competitive performance. High profits do not logically entail high growth, and so evolutionary theory must combine its explanation of differential rents with an explanation of differential behaviour in directing those rents to the accumulation over time of visible and invisible assets (Itami, (1987)).

The most recent developments in evolutionary thinking are contained in the authoritative work of Nelson and Winter (1983). To the analysis of selection processes, essentially of the kind described above, they have added models of search behaviour, the purpose of which is to generate the very variety on which selection operates. Because these models are stochastic, essentially Markov processes, they generate many of their conclusions through simulation techniques, illustrating the trade-offs which emerge between patterns of industrial concentration, rates of innovation and imitation and the distribution of input productivity in an industry. The crucial point, of course, is that these phenomena are generated simultaneously by a process of competitive selection across endogenously created technological variety.

4 A DIGRESSION ON ENTREPRENEURSHIP

At this point there are obvious connections with the analysis of entrepreneurship and endogenous economic change. We have no theory of individual entrepreneurship as such but the obvious consequence of entrepreneurship is to generate economic variety, to establish different ways of acting, each competing for economic significance. Schumpeter's contribution in this field remains dominant, with the emphasis on the 'new man' or 'new firm' introducing different combinations into the economic system, often in the face of inertia and sometimes outright hostility from fellow citizens. Now while Schumpeter was a saltationist, Marshall was a gradualist, an advocate of cumulative, incremental change. None the less, for Marshall too, 'variety was the chief source of progress' (Principles, 1920, p. 355) and the competitive industry the ideal institution for generating entrepreneurship and innovative experiments (Loasby, 1982). Both Marshall and Schumpeter had good reason to fear the growth of the modern joint stock company. Indeed, entrepreneurship is central to modern Austrian accounts of the competitive process, with the distinction between three categories of entrepreneurship (arbitrage, speculative and innovative) and the equation between alertness, that is, seeing things differently, and different behaviour (Kirzner, 1973).

5 COMPETITION AND EVOLUTIONARY CHANGE

Within the dominant schools of economic theory, competition is a state of equilibrium, based on two quite different and independent premises; that each firm has no power to influence market prices, and that actual or threatened entry establishes a position of normal profitability for each firm. From a business perspective this view of competition is all rather puzzling, as many scholars have argued (Hayek, 1948; McNulty, 1968; Klein, 1984). Indeed, Morgenstern (1972) goes so far as to claim that economists' use of the word 'competition' has lost touch with reality, precisely because it eliminates any connotation of struggle and rivalry. Whatever the merits of the equilibrium view, and they are considerable, they are simply inappropriate to the study of economic change. Here the appropriate perspective is of struggle and rivalry, of a process of competition between unequals. Superior product and process technology is a basis for superior profitability which in turn gives the firm potential advantages in all those competition-enhancing activities which require an investment of resources. Whether it be capacity expansion, marketing activity, training and skill-enhancing activity or innovation, all of these key competitive activities are resource-based. Command of resources is thus a necessary if not a sufficient condition

66   *Evolution and Economic Change*

for maintaining or enhancing a competitive position.

Nor are these idle theoretical distinctions. In their detailed study of competition in the mainframe computer market, Fisher and his co-authors reverted to precisely the process view of competition to assess the anti-trust implications of IBM's performance (Fisher, *et al.*, 1983). Just as Schumpeter had emphasised the dynamic gains which stem from departures from static competitive equilibrium, so Fisher *et al.* argue that the static framework can lead to quite false judgements, suggesting that competition is absent when in fact it is operating fiercely (p. 39). Indeed such judgements resulted in an abortive anti-trust case against IBM, a case in which the United States government failed to recognise that static notions of long-run competitive equilibrium could not be related to 'a dynamically changing competitive market whose basic feature was technology change' (p. 344). In similar vein, there is a long tradition of empirical work relating inter-firm differences in profitability to market power. As Manke (1974) has demonstrated such empirical tests are quite inconclusive. The hypothesis of a uniform propensity to accumulate across firms, combined with random returns to investment, leads to systematically positive correlations between profit rates and measures of firm size, market share and past growth. But these correlations are produced by a process operating over time, a process which jointly generates market structures and patterns of profitability.

Thus an evolutionary view of competition is concerned with a process of change, driven by technological differences between firms which has as its outcome continuous alteration in the relative economic significance of the competing technologies. This perspective on competition raises questions at three distinct levels. The first concerns the sources of technological variety across firms. Why do firms differ in their revealed technological performance at a particular point in time, and why do they differ in their creative ability to advance their revealed performance over time? The second set of questions concerns the operation of the selection environment. How are different technologies evaluated, and how quickly are the effects of this evaluation translated into changing economic weight? The third concerns the behaviour of firms. In particular, how do they translate profits into enhancement of market share, and why is it that they are not infinitely malleable in the face of competing technological advances? Why, in other words, is there loyalty and inertia so that technological differences can persist long enough to generate a distribution of co-existing technologies in an industry?

It is to some answers to these questions that our attention now turns.

6 UNDERSTANDING ECONOMIC CHANGE

In this section we shall outline a simple framework for interpreting economic change in terms of variety and selection. As with the analyses of Downie (1955) Steindl (1952) and Alchian (1951), we shall consider first a process of selection between a given number of unchanging technologies. The unit of selection is a process of productive transformation to which are attached a product and a process. As well as providing a clear elaboration of the elements driving technological competition, this section demonstrates how change at the industry level is quite compatible with stasis at the level of the individual technologies and firms. Evolutionary theory is, in this limited sense, anti-reductionist. From this analysis of selection we move on to questions of technological change proper, the mechanisms by which technological variety is generated over time, and the connections between selection and the endogenous development of technology.

It will be helpful to clarify some of our concepts. The analogue to a species is a set of products and their methods of production which are drawn from the same technological knowledge base. The economic weight of a product or process is measured by its prevailing share in economic activity within a specified selection environment. The market is defined as a homogeneous field within a selection environment, homogenous in the sense that all the products and processes competing in that market are subjected to the same selective pressure. A selection environment which consists of more than one market is said to be segmented. Each technology is specific to an individual firm so the two concepts are interchangeable. The firm is defined as an organisation articulating a knowledge base to generate a particular revealed technological performance in pursuit of certain objectives. This is not coterminous with the firm as traditionally defined in terms of control over the disposition of capital assets. Rather, in contemporary conditions, our 'firm' is to be interpreted typically as a sub-unit of a larger enterprise, the larger enterprise often being multi-technology. The relations between the 'firm' and the larger 'umbrella enterprise' often constituted an important part of the operating environment of the former. Indeed the identification of the boundary relationships between the operating sub-unit and the umbrella is one of the more important tasks which any empirical study of innovation or technology strategy must undertake. Note also that our treatment of the firm does not require that it maximise profits or any other performance attribute. All that we do require is that it seeks improved performance.

68   *Evolution and Economic Change*

Variety and the Competitive Selection

The first issue to be clear about in any evolutionary theory of technological competition is the shift in perspective from matters of equilibrium to matters of change, from the scale of production of competing commodities to the rates of growth of those scales of production. The second aspect to emphasise is that selection operates with respect to the performance characteristics of the competing products and processes. Products and their processes are selected jointly and directly, according to their overall performance. A single-product firm is naturally subject to the same selective process as is its technology, while the selective pressure on a multi-product organisation would depend on the balance of selective forces across its product and process portfolio. This established, we may assign to the firm three attributes. First, there is the efficiency of the firm as embodied in its revealed technological performance, the productivity with which it transforms inputs into products and the functional characteristics of those products. Secondly, there is the propensity of the firm to grow as measured by the relation between its growth rate and its profit margin. Growth depends upon access to internal and external finance, on the investment requirements to expand capacity and marketing activity, on the ability to manage growth without sacrificing efficiency, and on the simple willingness to grow (Penrose, 1961). In previous work (Metcalfe and Gibbons, 1986) we have summarised these factors with the term 'fitness', since, despite possible ambiguities, it captures the essential link between efficiency and growth. More simply we may summarise these factors as the propensity to accumulate. Finally, there is the creativity of the firm, the ability to improve revealed performance through knowledge base-enhancing activities: learning phenomena, formal R & D and superior design capabilities. Creativity depends upon the resources available to advance technology; the opportunities for advance within the chosen configuration; the incentives to advance in relation to scale of effort, the scale of application of advances and their appropriability; and the effectiveness with which the firm manages its creative activities. We expect that any two firms will differ in all three dimensions. Variety in creativity naturally leads to variety in efficiency, while variety in propensities to accumulate leads to different resource bases for financing subsequent technological advance. We also expect that these differences will not be eliminated easily. Inertia sustains variety in all three dimensions.

On the market environment side we have a number of difficulties to face. Firstly, the market environment generates a set of input prices and product characteristics valuations which translate technological variety into economic variety. This provides the basis for our constructing a selection set. However, while the input prices are normally explicit market data, the product performance valuations are almost always *implicit*, to be discovered by the firm through market research activities and interaction with its customers. In short, the environment generates a price structure which may, or may not, be the same for all firms, and certainly may be perceived differently by different firms. The second attribute of the environment is the rate of growth of the market, which is typically subject to retardation over time. The third attribute is the degree of selective pressure which the market imposes. This depends upon the frequency with which selective decisions are made, frequent selection generating fine-grained environments and occasional selection generating coarse-grained environments (Levins, 1968). It also depends upon the severity with which selection operates, how quickly firms are punished or rewarded by their deviations from average behaviour. Finally it depends upon the uniformity of selection, a uniform market being one in which all firms experience the same selective pressure, a segmented one being one in which pressure varies across firms, for example, because of goodwill or long-term contractual relationships. The fourth attribute of the environment relates to the manner in which it changes over time. A tranquil environment is defined as one with a given structure of product and process characteristic valuations, which grows at a constant compound rate. Degrees of turbulence may then be defined relative to various shocks to the growth rate and price structure, some of them being exogenous and some of them being endogenous to the selection process.

Selection and the Technology Set

In order to emphasise the central ideas we consider selection across a given selection set with a variety of products and associated production processs. This creates a multi-technology diffusion process converging upon a dominant design, and extends the arguments of Steindl and Downie by having firms with different products as well as different production processes. The market environment has a given price structure, independent of the selection process, and grows at the compound rate g_d. This selection environment is uniform and operates continuously. On the basis of the given price structure we can identify

70   *Evolution and Economic Change*

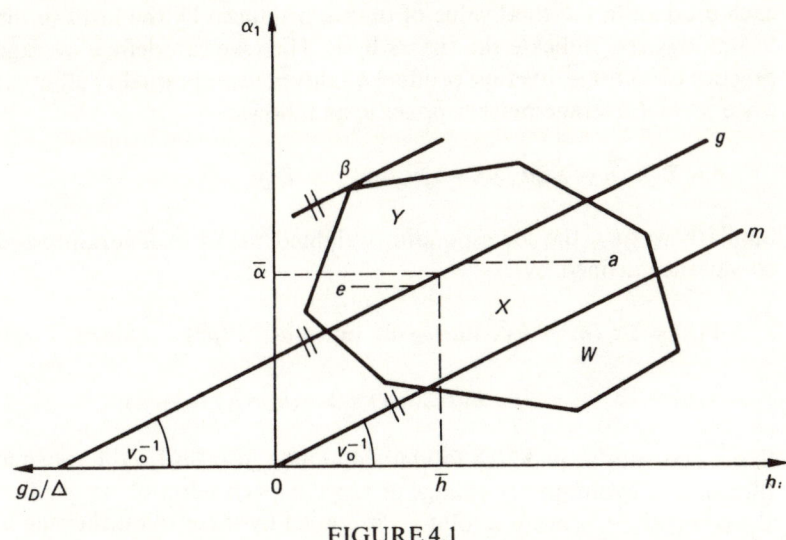

FIGURE 4.1

any product and its associated process with a unit cost of production, h_i, and a quality adjusted price, p_i^*. Unit costs we take as given and independent of the scale of individual firms and the industry of output. If w_j and v_k are the prices of the jth input and kth product characteristic respectively, then we can write $h_i = \Sigma w_j a_{ij}$ and $p_i^* = \Sigma \alpha_{ik} v_k$, with a_{ij} the input of j into a unit of i, and α_{ik} the output of characteristic k per unit of i. It will help to simplify the expression of p_i^* by choosing one of the v_k as an index of the entire price structure and writing $p_i^* = v_o \alpha_i$, α_i representing the 'quality' of the product in terms of the index characteristic. The actual price of a product we represent by p_i. On the basis of this information we then have the selection set in Figure 4.1. Each point in this set represents a product and its associated process of production, and the given variety of technologies is contained on or within the boundaries of this set. Notice that the technologies need not be evenly distributed over the set and that regions of the selection set may be empty. Any change in the price structures which define p_i^* and h_i will require this set to be redrawn and will generally change the relative location of different technologies within the set.

To explore the economics of selection in more depth we must now define various statistics which capture the variety contained in the selection set, and here we need to specify the economic weights of the different technologies. These weights we define by the market shares of

Stan Metcalfe   71

each product in the total value of output produced by the firms in the technology set. Indicate the shares by s_i. Then we can define, average practice unit cost, $\bar{h}$, average product quality $\bar{\alpha}$, average quality adjusted price $\bar{p}^*$ and average market price, $\bar{p}$, as follows,

$$\bar{h} = \Sigma s_i h_i, \ \bar{\alpha} = \Sigma s_i \alpha_i, \ \bar{p}^* = v_o \bar{\alpha}, \text{ and } \bar{p} = \Sigma s_i p_i$$

Similarly we have the corresponding weighted measures of variance and co-variance defined by,

$$V(h) = \Sigma s_i \ (h_i - \bar{h})^2, \ V(\alpha) = \Sigma s_i \ (\alpha_i - \bar{\alpha})^2, \ V(p^*) = v_o^2 V(\alpha),$$

$$V(p) = \Sigma s_i \ (p_i - \bar{p})^2, \text{ and } C(h,\alpha) = \Sigma s_i \ (h_i - \bar{h}) \ (\alpha_i - \bar{\alpha}).$$

These statistics provide the fundamental data to measure the rate and direction of evolutionary change across the given selection set. Within the competitive process, evolution is guided by three rules: the rule of survival, the rule of accumulation, and the rule of customer selection. Survival of a product requires that it earn non-negative profits, $p_i - h_i > 0$, and correspondingly the survival of single-product firms is equivalent to survival of their product. Bankruptcy we assume entails the immediate elimination of the product or process from the set of competing technologies. The rule of accumulation specifies that firms making above normal profits $(p_i > h_i)$ have the potential to grow, and do grow at a rate with depends upon their propensity to accumulate. We let each firm concentrate its capital investment entirely on its own product, even where it is not the best-practice technology, by reinvesting internally generated profits and supplementing this with external finance. The higher the firm's profit rate the greater its access to investible funds (Turner and Soete, 1984; Downie, 1955). If f_i represents the given propensity to accumulate, then the growth rate of the output and capacity of the ith product is given by

$$g_i = f_i(p_i - h_i) \tag{4.1}$$

where, f_i varies inversely with the investment/output ratio and positively with the ratio of internal and external funds to the capital stock (Metcalfe and Gibbons, 1986).

The rule of customer selection forms the demand side of the selection mechanism and is concerned with the factors which change the customer bases of the competing products. In this simple, unsegmented market

72 *Evolution and Economic Change*

environment each of the competing products supplies the same set of functional characteristics to customers and they are therefore perfect substitutes if they sell at their quality-adjusted prices. If this were not the case, the market would have to be divided into its appropriate segments. During the selection process there is no requirement that each product sells at its quality adjusted price, that is, that $p_i = p_i^*$. Any increase in the price of i, or fall in the price of j should be associated with some erosion of the customer base for product i. Similarly, an improvement in the quality of i (either it contains more characteristics, or some of the particular characteristics are more highly valued) or reduction in the quality of j should work to enhance the customer base for product i. One way to represent the dynamics of customer selection is to let customers switch products in proportion to their relative market shares and the price and quality advantages which the products offer (Phelps and Winter, 1970). Our representation gives a relation of the form

$$\frac{ds_i}{dt} = \Sigma_j s_i s_j \delta_{ij} \left[(p_j - p_j^*) - (p_i - p_i^*) \right]$$

where the δ_{ij} coefficients represent the probability of a demand switch upon 'contact' between customers of firms $_i$ and $_j$. Now in a uniform market environment, by definition, all the δ_{ij} coefficients take the same value, δ, from whence we obtain the following selection rule (taking account also of the definitions of p_i^* and $\bar{p}_i^*$).

$$\frac{1}{s_i} \frac{ds_i}{dt} = g_i - g_d = \delta[(\bar{p} - p_i) - v_o(\bar{\alpha} - \alpha_i)] \tag{4.2}$$

A product's share in market demand is increased if it has a below-average market price and above-average product quality, or some favourable combination of the two to make the bracketed expression in equation (4.2) positive. Notice that (4.2) represents only one possible rule for customer selection. However, it does capture plausible attributes of the selection process, and it does satisfy one necessary logical condition, namely that $\Sigma s_i g_i$ equals the growth rate of the aggregate market. A rule which does not meet this requirement is simply internally inconsistent. The clear advantage to be gained from (4.2) is that it relates the dynamics of selection to the distance of the particular product from the industry average. In this way it rests upon a very simple statistic of inter-product variety.

Two special cases come immediately to mind when considering this customer selection rule. When $\delta = \infty$, we have the analogue to perfect competition. A firm must set $p_i = p_i^*$ (and hence $\bar{p} = \bar{p}^*$), for if $p_i > p_i^*$ it immediately loses its entire customer base. Conversely, with $\delta = 0$, we have the analogue to monopoly, with the firm's customer base and market share quite independent of its position in the price and quality structure. In this case customer loyalty is absolute. In between are all the cases of dynamic imperfect competition, in which the rate of change of the firm's customer base does depend on how it prices relative to the average for the selection set. It should be clear that, under imperfect competition, the firm does not have a given demand curve but rather a demand curve which shifts over time with changes in its customer base in accordance with (4.2).

The question which must now be faced is how the two selection rules relating to accumulation and demand are to be brought together. Only one of several alternatives will be explored here. We consider the implications of a uniform propensity to accumulate, $f_i = f$, and concentrate solely on those situations of dynamic market balance where the growth rate of a firm's capacity equals the growth rate of its market. These balanced paths are illustrative of the secular trends of the evolutionary process. The implication is that deviations from the secular trend do not result in a redefinition of that trend.

Together, these assumptions imply that the market shares of different products evolve according to the following condition, obtained by combining (4.1) and (4.2).

$$\frac{1}{s_i} \frac{ds_i}{dt} = \frac{\delta f}{f + \delta} \left[(\bar{h} - h_i) - v_o(\bar{\alpha} - \alpha_i) \right]$$

$$= \Delta S_i$$

(4.3)

and $g_i > 0$ *iff* $p_i > h_i$.

Equation (4.3) is the fundamental equation of the evolutionary process. It indicates that the selective pressure acting on a technology is the product of the coefficient of selection and the selective force. In this expression, Δ represents the coefficient of selection, and it is increasing in both f and δ. The expression in brackets, S_i in equation (3) we term the selective force acting on i. Providing a product generates profits its output increases absolutely. But in a growing market this does not mean it grows in relative market significance. To increase in relative significance, a product must generate above-average profitability either by

74   *Evolution and Economic Change*

having unit costs below average ($h_i < \bar{h}$) or by having above-average
product quality ($\alpha_i > \bar{\alpha}$) or some appropriate combination of the two.
Hence the relative economic weight of a product changes according to its
distance from average performance within the technology set.

To explore these ideas further, we shall concentrate on showing how
the evolution of a technology's market share depends on its position in
the technology set. Along the horizontal axis of Figure 4.1 are measured
unit costs, while on the vertical axis are measured the real product
qualities (in terms of the index characteristic), α_i. The selection set may
be partitioned along the following lines. The implicit market price of the
index characteristic is measured by the slope v_o^{-1}. The two lines m and g
each have slope v_o^{-1} and intercepts at the origin and point $g_D\Delta$
respectively. They partition the selection set into three distinct areas.
Notice that the second of the lines passes through the average practice
point $(\bar{\alpha}, \bar{h})$. In area W are all the bankrupt products, products for which
$p_i < h_i$. These are no longer produced, if they ever were. In X are
profitable products but with less than average profitability, so that they
are declining in relative importance; $g_i < g_d$. In Y are products with
above-average profitability, which correspondingly increase their
market shares over time; $g_i > g_d$. Products located on m just break even,
while any lying on g are dynamically representative with $g_i = g_d$ and
constant market shares. Now the bracketed term in (4.3), measuring the
selective force operating on a technology, has a simple interpretation in
Figure 4.1. Take any profitable product point (a or e), then the length of
the horizontal line from this point to the average performance line g
measures the magnitude and direction of the selective force. For product
a this is negative, while for product e it is positive. Thus the evolutionary
principle that rate of selection equals the selective coefficient multiplied
by the selective force has a ready interpretation in this diagram. At a
glance we can see how the market position of rival technologies will
evolve, which technologies are viable and which will rise or fall in relative
economic importances.

Under conditions of balanced expansion it is a straightforward matter
to determine the relationship between the actual distribution of prices
and the corresponding distribution of quality adjusted price p_i^*. The clue
is to note that under balanced conditions, the price of the index
characteristic must satisfy the relation

$$\frac{1}{v_o} = \frac{\bar{\alpha}}{g_d/\Delta + \bar{h}} \tag{4.4}$$

For should v_o be higher we would have $g > g_d$ and should it be lower we would have $g < g_d$, neither being consistent with balanced conditions. But with v_o at this value we also find that

$$g_i = \Delta[v_o\alpha_i - h_i) \tag{4.5}$$

for each technology. Its rate of growth is equal to the selection coefficient multiplied by the hypothetical profit margin based on the difference between B_i^* and A_i.

On comparing (4.5) with (4.1) we find that p_i is a weighted average of p_i^* and h_i given by

$$p_i = \frac{\delta}{f+\delta} \; p_i^* + \frac{f}{f+\delta} \; h_i \tag{4.6}$$

For the firm on the margin of bankruptcy we have $p_i = p_i^* = h_i$ but for all other profitable firms p_i satisfies the inequality $p_i^* > p_i > h_i$. The relationship between the average values $\bar{p}, \bar{p}^*$ and h follows immediately from (4.6), and the variance of the price distribution is given by

$$V(p) = \frac{f}{f+\delta}^2 V(h) + \frac{\delta}{f+\delta}^2 V(p^*) + \frac{2f\delta}{(f+\delta)^2}2v_o \, C(h,\alpha) \tag{4.7}$$

Special cases then emerge in an obvious way. With $\delta = \infty$ perfect competition, we find that $V(p) = V(p^*)$ and unit costs have no effect on the dispersion of market prices. With $\delta = 0$, a world of independent monopolies, we find that $V(p) = V(h)$ and product quality has no effect on the dispersion of prices. In between lie all the cases associated with dynamic imperfect competition, for which the co-variance between unit costs and product quality becomes significant. Notice that these statistics are defined only with respect to the set of profitable, non-marginal technologies. These results are hardly surprising and reflect the obvious consequence of imperfect customer selection, namely that firms charge prices which differ from the corresponding quality-adjusted prices. On averaging the values of p_i we have

$$\bar{p} = \frac{g_d}{f} + \bar{h} \tag{4.8}$$

76   *Evolution and Economic Change*

so that the average profit margin (that of the representative technology) is just sufficient to finance aggregate output growth at a rate equal to the growth rate of the aggregate market.

Of course, Figure 4.1 can only represent a snapshot of the competitive process. As market shares change, so economic weight is redistributed within the selection set to redefine the statistical movements of the selection process. One way to measure and summarise these evolutionary trends is to focus on the rates of change of average unit cost and average product quality, which are governed by the relations

$$\frac{d\bar{h}}{dt} = \Delta[v_o C(h, \alpha) - V(h)]$$

(4.9)

and,

$$\frac{d\bar{\alpha}}{dt} = \Delta[v_o V(\alpha) - C(h, \alpha)]$$

(4.10)

Here we see a distinguishing feature of the evolutionary perspective, with the rates of change of average population characteristics being related to measures of variety within the population. The simplest special case, where all products are of the same quality, $V(\alpha) = V(p^*) = 0$, generates the famous Fisher Law that average practice unit cost declines at a rate proportional to the variance of unit costs within the technology set (Nelson and Winter, 1983, p. 245). More generally we see that if unit cost and product quality are negatively correlated, then selection always reduces average unit cost and increases average product quality. Furthermore in a world of monopoly relationships $\delta = 0$ evolution in this sense is not possible.

If the average practice technical coefficients are changing over time, then v_o must also change over time, to maintain balanced conditions. From (4.4) we have the condition

$$-\bar{\alpha}\frac{dv_o}{dt} = v_o\frac{d\bar{\alpha}}{dt} - \frac{d\bar{h}}{dt}$$

(4.11)

Now the right-hand side of this expression is an aggregate measure of the rate of selective change which from (4.9) and (4.10) is equal to

$$v_o\frac{d\bar{\alpha}}{dt} - \frac{d\bar{h}}{dt} = \Delta[V(h) + V(p^*) - 2v_o C(h, \alpha)]$$

(4.12)

Selection imposes an overall direction upon the evolutionary process, enhancing average product quality relative to average unit cost. Simplifying this expression further gives the required rate of change in v_o, namely

$$-\bar{\alpha}\,\frac{dv_o}{dt} = \frac{V(g)}{\Delta}$$

(4.13)

Where $V(g)$ is the variance of growth rates within the profitable areas of the selection set (areas X and Y). Since $V(g)$ is non-negative, it follows that v_o must fall over time.

We can now determine the properties of the final equilibrium appropriate to a given selection set, a key determinant of which is the growth rate of the market environment. The solid lines m and g in Figure 4.2 show the equilibrium consistent with growth rate g_d. It is a logical requirement that any equilibrium must fall on the boundary of the selection set, and so the price of the index characteristic, v_o must adjust to support the equilibrium position taking on a value lower than that shown in Figure 4.1. At the ruling market growth rate the dominant product is β, the market share of which approaches 100 per cent asymptotically. However, at the ruling growth rate there is also a survival region, X^1, in which are located all other technologies which remain profitable and yet have no economic significance in terms of their

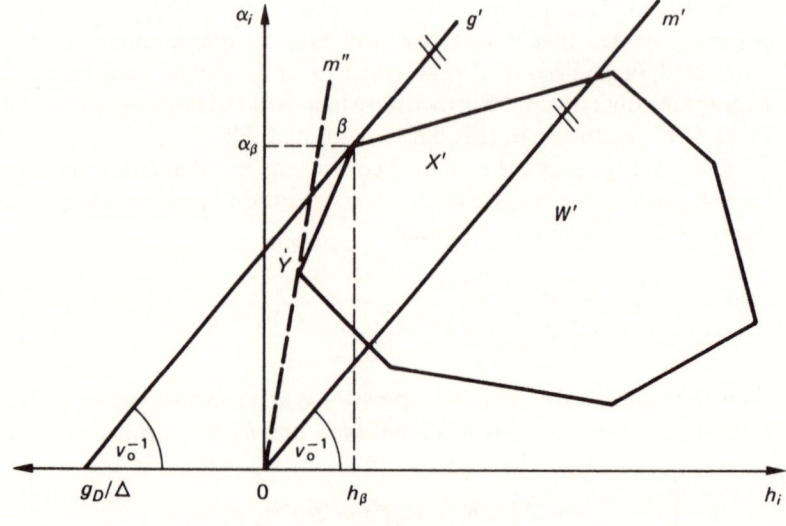

FIGURE 4.2

market share. It is thus vital to distinguish between survival and economic significance in a selection equilibrium. All products in W^i are eliminated during the course of the selection process. It follows immediately that a market environment which is static must result in the elimination of this survival region, for the lines g and m now coincide in the line m. Indeed with zero market growth only one technology survives and this is Y and not β. Thus the ultimate focus of selection depends upon the market environment in two ways, via its growth rate and via its relative price structures which evaluate the competing products and processes. We can obviously interpret this selection process as bringing to market dominance a particular product design but it does not follow that the dominant design is, in an economic sense, the best-practice design. Indeed, if we interpret best-practice as applying to the product with the highest ratio of quality to unit cost of production, α_i/h_i, then this is represented by product Y which only comes to dominance in a static market environment. In a dynamic environment best-practice does not dominate the selection equilibrium, and in the context of some technology sets it may not even survive.

While the notion of a selection equilibrium is analytically helpful there is no doubt that it is also rather fanciful. Numerous changes may be expected to occur during the selection process, changes which redefine the selection set and thus the balance of selective pressure across the different technologies. The entry of new firms, changes in customer valuations of the product characteristics and changes in the structure of input prices will each create turbulence and redefine what would be the equilibrium selection point. Thus it is Figure 4.1 and its snapshot partitioning of the selection set which perhaps provides the most useful tool in the analysis of competitive selection. A fuller treatment of selection would require a great deal more to be said: about the exit of bankrupt technologies; about different investment rules; about internal and external economies; about the consequences of the f and δ coefficients differing between firms, about cartels and price agreements between firms; and about situations of unbalanced growth. For the moment the reader must be referred to the literature for a discussion of some of these developments (Nelson and Winter, 1983; Silverberg, 1985; Metcalfe and Gibbons, 1986).

7 CREATIVITY AND THE GENERATION OF VARIETY

In the previous section we took the extent of technological variety as a given element and worked out the dynamics of competitive selection in this highly artificial context. In any historical context, of course, the set of technologies is not given but is generated by a sequence of innovations. The frequency with which inventions occur, the proportion translated into innovations, and the performance characteristics of innovations relative to the existing technology set become the vital elements in the picture of evolutionary change. Indeed the sequence in which innovations emerge can generate quite different historical patterns of development. At root these are questions concerning the creativity of firms and of individuals, questions which obviously permit no easy answer. None the less some progress in our thinking is possible.

As a first step we return to our distinction between technology as knowledge and technology as artifact. Every product and process has a knowledge base, and every knowledge base permits a sequence of 'improved' products and processes, improvements which are based upon the same design principles and set of performance characteristics but which differ in terms of the levels of performance embodied in each product and its process. It is convenient to call such a knowledge base a 'design configuration' and the set of different design configurations which produce products with the same application a 'technological regime' (Georghiou *et al.*, 1986). Innovations may then be grouped into two categories: those which entail cumulative incremental change and gradualistic advance within the limits of a given design configuration; and those which involve jumps to a different design configuration. The latter are sometimes called radical innovations and might equally be termed technological speciations. Now, since the agenda of any design configuration is limited and typically different from that of any other design configuration, the firm is faced with the difficult problem of knowing when diminishing returns to further innovation are pressing, and which alternative design configuration it should consequently switch to (Foster, 1987). Indeed these choices are vital aspects of any technology strategy for a firm.

If different firms operate with different knowledge bases and design configurations, there are powerful reasons for expecting inter-firm differences in technological creativity. This potent source of variety is enhanced by the nature of the innovation process. Firms differ in the resources they devote to advancing their knowledge base, in the effectiveness with which they conduct research, and in their ability to design out of their knowledge base. Firms also differ in their ability to learn from experience and apply those lessons to their revealed technological performance. Organisation and the quality of individuals matter tremendously and there is always uncertainty about the improvements in characteristics which users value, and the

80   *Evolution and Economic Change*

improvements in characteristics which can be achieved with a given
effort in a given time span. In many cases, part of the relevant knowledge
base lies, outside the firm. The degree to which it is open to flows of
external information, its links with this greater institutional structure
and the alliances it forms with other institutions and firms all play their
role in differential creativity (Carter and Williams, 1957). At the same
time there are apparent limits on the amount of variety which can coexist
at any time. There are limits imposed by what is possible within and
between design configurations. Some elements of knowledge bases are
held in common by the competing firms. Some knowledge is difficult to
appropriate, while movement of personnel between firms and informal
contacts between professional scientists and engineers all result in the
sharing of knowledge. Patents, even when they are significant, have a
limited duration. The generation of technology variety is therefore
influenced by a number of conflicting forces, the incidence of which will
change over time but in no obviously predictable way. Indeed it is
tempting to define a mature technology, not as one in which progress has
ceased, but as one in which it is extremely difficult for firms to
differentiate themselves technologically. Let us now see how these
questions of creativity relate to the previous discussion of selection.

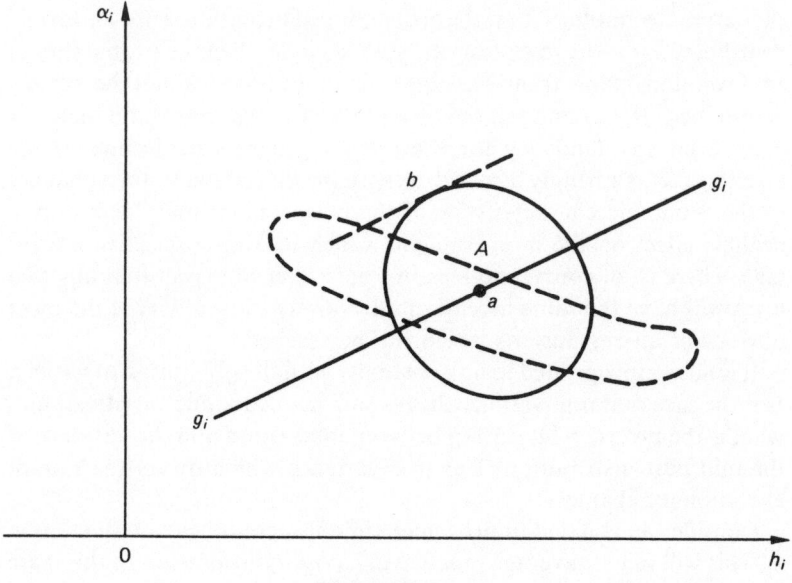

FIGURE 4.3

In Figure 4.3 we show the situation in a given firm, growing at a rate g_i and with current technology represented by point a. The firm's chosen design configuration determines the invention opportunities open to the firm, and they are represented by the circle centred on the current technology point a. For the purposes of this discussion it is assumed that all inventions are equally likely to occur and equally costly to produce within this circle. At the current price of the index characteristics we can immediately establish the following. The probability of an invention being translated into an innovation is exactly one half, since the g_i-g_i line cuts through the centre of the invention opportunity set. Only inventions which arise in area A are likely to be translated into innovations and this area is exactly half that of the whole circle. This probability is independent of the price of the index characteristic. The invention which generates the greatest selective advantage for the firm is given by b. Clearly, where b lies does depend on v_o, such that the smaller is v_o the more cost-saving rather than quality-improving is this optimum invention. If this invention set remains stationary over time, gradually the firm will converge but with decreasing probability on a point on the boundary such as b. At this point it will have exhausted its agenda for change.

One can see immediately how complex the question of creativity is when we reflect for a moment on the severe assumptions employed in the previous paragraph. If the centre of the invention opportunity set is not the current technology, or if the probability of invention is not uniformly distributed, or if the invention set is not a circle, then the probability of an invention being translated into an innovation cannot be readily determined. If, in contrast, the invention set moves over time then this may offset any tendency for the rate of progress to decline. If the invention set is strongly directed, as with the dotted space, then changes in the economic characteristics of the environment may have only a neglible effect on the improvements which maximise selective advantage. There is, of course, no reason whatsoever to expect that any two firms will have the same invention set. Variety in creativity is the most obvious of all conclusions which can be reached.

It is now appropriated to link creativity with the generation of variety. Is it the case that innovations always enhance economic variety? If not, what is the precise relationship between innovation and the variance of the unit cost distribution? For it is variance which drives the rate of evolutionary change.

Consider an isolated improvement in one technology, a reduction in h_j. This will reduce average practice unit cost in proportion to the share of that technology in total output, and it will reduce or increase the variance of unit costs according to whether $h_j \lessgtr \bar{h}$. This conclusion follows because

$$\frac{\delta V(h)}{\delta h_j} = 2s_j(h_j - \bar{h})$$

Generalising this to the selection set as a whole, we have

$$\frac{dV(h)}{dt} = 2\Sigma_j s_j(h_j - \bar{h})\frac{dh_j}{dt} \tag{4.14}$$

so that the effect upon the variance of unit costs depends upon the precise incidence of improvements across the selection set. No simple outcome can be expected. A tendency for improvements to be concentrated in technologies of above-average efficiency will increase this variance, and conversely if improvements are concentrated in technologies of below-average efficiency. Furthermore if all technologies are improved by the same absolute amount the variance of unit costs will not be affected.

If the incidence and magnitude of improvements is truly random then nothing more can be said; the variance of unit costs will itself behave in a random fashion. It is of interest, therefore, to consider the possibility of systematic elements in the innovation process. Suppose specifically that each firm reduces its unit costs by innovating in proportion to its current unit costs, and that it imitates other firms in proportion to its distance from average practice in the industry (Cavalli–Sforza and Feldman, 1981). Specifically, let

$$\frac{dh_j}{dt} = -[(1 - \beta)\lambda h_j + \beta\mu (h_j - \bar{h})] \tag{4.15}$$

where λ is the innovation parameter, μ is the imitation parameter, and β is the weight determining the relative significance of innovation and imitation. If these parameters of creativity are the same for all firms then we find

$$\frac{dV(h)}{dt} = -2[(1 - \beta)\lambda + \beta\mu]V(h) \tag{4.16}$$

In this particular formulation innovation and imitation are a conservative force, progressively reducing the dispersion of unit costs in the selection set. By no means can it be assumed that the generation of new technology will increase the economic variety on which selection operates. Indeed in the case of (4.16) variance declines exponentially to zero with time for any given set of market share weights. More complex mechanisms, no doubt, will yield different results, especially when we allow feedback from the selection process so that a firm's rate of innovation is directly related to its profitability. But these further developments are not the concern of this paper.

8 CONCLUSIONS

The central themes of this essay have been that economic change is driven by economic variety, and that the chief long-run source of economic variety is to be found in technological innovation. We have argued that to analyse these phenomena requires a major change in thinking, away from the search for ideal, representative types which can only mask the forces which drive progress and change, towards the search for distributions of phenomena. We have drawn attention to the work of other economists who have explored this mode of thought. The key elements in our evolutionary view are the mechanisms for generating economic variety and for selecting across that variety to produce economic progress and structural economic change. At a minimum, our analysis suggests that a progressive economy is one with a high rate of variety-enhancing experimentation and institutions which exert strong selective pressure on competing technologies. The evolutionary theme provides a rich framework of analysis, capable of encompassing the wide variety of ways in which organisations articulate technology, and yet capable of giving that variety causal significance in the process of change. Perhaps this essay will stimulate others critically to develop an evolutionary perspective on technological competition.

ACKNOWLEDGEMENTS

This paper draws heavily on ideas developed with my colleagues in the ESRC-financed programme on competitive performance in industry in the United Kingdom. I am particularly indebted to Professor Michael Gibbons for allowing me to draw upon jointly-authored writing on technological innovation. I also thank Dr Luke Georghiou, Janet Evans, Hugh Cameron, Brendan Barker, Mark Boden, Tim Ray and Jean–Jacques Chanaron for many helpful discussions on the ideas

84   *Evolution and Economic Change*

presented in this paper. Needless to add, none of the above are responsible for the interpretation contained in this paper.

REFERENCES

Alchian, A. (1951) 'Uncertainty, Evolution and Economic Theory', *Journal of Political Economy*, vol. 68, pp. 211–21.
Alchian, A. (1953) 'Biological Analogies in the Theory of the Firm: A Comment', *American Economic Review*, vol. 53, pp. 600–603.
Carter, C. and Williams, B. (1957) *Industry and Technical Progress*, Oxford University Press.
Cavalli-Sforza, L. and Feldman, M. W. (1981) *Cultural Transmission and Evolution: A Quantitative Analysis*, Princeton University Press.
Downie, J. (1955) *The Competitive Process*, London: Duckworth.
Farrrell, M. (1957) 'The Measurement of Production Efficiency', *Journal of Royal Statistical Society* (A), vol. 120.
Fisher, F., McGowan, J. and Greenwood, J. (1983) *Folded, Spindled and Mutilated*, London: MIT Press.
Foster, J. (1987) *Innovation*, London: Macmillan.
Frankel, M. (1955) 'Obsolescence and Technological Change', *American Economic Review*, vol. 55.
Georghiou, L., Metcalfe, J. S., Evans, J., Ray, T. and Gibbons, M. (1986) *Post-Innovation Performance*, London: Macmillan.
Hannan, M. T. and Freeman, J. (1977) 'The Population Ecology of Organisations', *American Journal of Sociology*, pp. 929–64.
Hayek, F. (1948) *Individualism and Economic Order*, Chicago University Press.
Hrebeniak, L. and Joyce, W. (1985) 'Organisational Adaptation, Strategic Choice and Environmental Determinism', *Administrative Science Quarterly*, pp. 336–49.
Itami, H. (1987) *Mobilising Invisible Assets*, Harvard University Press.
Jones, G. (1980) *Social Darwinsim and English Thought*, Brighton: Harvester Press.
Kirzner, I. M. (1973) *Competition and Entrepreneurship*, Chicago University Press.
Klein, B. (1984) *Prices, Wages and the Business Cycle*, London: Pergammon.
Layton, E. T. (1974) 'Technology as Knowledge', *Technology and Culture*, pp. 30–41.
Levine, A. L. (1980) 'Increasing Returns, the Competitive Model and the Enigma that was Alfred Marṣhall', *Scottish Journal of Political Economy*, vol. 27, pp. 260–75.
Levins, R. (1968) *Evolution in Changing Environments*, Princeton, University Press.
Loasby, B. (1976) *Choice Complexity and Ignorance*, Cambridge University Press.
Loasby, B. (1982) 'The Entrepreneur in Economic Theory', *Scottish Journal of Political Economy*, vol. 29, pp. 235–45.
McElvey, W. (1982) *Organisational Systematics*, University of California Press.

McNulty, P. J. (1968) 'Economic Theory and the Meaning of Competition', *Quarterly Journal of Economics*, pp. 649–56.

Manke, R. B. (1974) 'Interfirm Profitability Differences', *Quarterly Journal of Economics*, vol. 88, pp. 181–93.

Marshall, A. (1920) *Principles of Economics*, 8th variorum ed, London: Macmillan.

Matthews, R. C. O. (1985) 'Darwinism and Economic Change', in D. Collard *et al.* (eds), *Economic Theory and Hicksian Themes*, Oxford University Press.

Mayr, E. (1982) *The Growth of Biological Thought*, Harvard University Press.

Metcalfe, J. S. and Gibbons M.(1986) 'Technological Variety and the Process of Competition', *Economie Applique*, pp. 493–520.

Morgenstern, O. (1972) 'Thirteen Critical Points in Contemporary Economic Theory', *Journal of Economic Literature*, pp. 1163–89.

Nelson, R. and Winter, S. (1983) *An Evolutionary Theory of Economic Change*, Harvard University Press.

Penrose, E. (1952) 'Biological Analogies in the Theory of the Firm', *American Economic Review*, vol. 52, pp. 804–19.

Penrose, E. (1959) *The Theory of the Growth of the Firm*, Oxford: Basil Blackwell.

Phelps, E. and Winter, S. (1970) 'Optimal Price Policies under Atomistic Competition', in E. Phelps (ed.), *Micro Foundations of Employment and Inflation Theory*, New York: W. Norton.

Robbins, L. (1928) 'The Representative Firm', *Economic Journal*, vol. 28, pp. 387–404.

Rostas, L. (1948) *Productivity, Prices and Distribution in Selected British Industries*, Cambridge University Press.

Salter, W. E. G. (1961) *Productivity and Technical Progess*, Cambridge University Press.

Schumpeter, J. (1961) *The Theory of Economic Development*, Oxford University Press (first published 1934).

Silverberg, G. (1985) 'Technical Progress, Capital Accumulation and Effective Demand', in D. Batten (ed.), *Economic Revolution and Structural Change*, Berlin: Springer-Verlag.

Sober, E. (1985) *The Nature of Selection*, London: MIT Press.

Steindl, J. (1952) *Maturity and Stagnation in American Capitalism*, Monthly Review Press (1976), New York.

Turner, R. and Soete, L. (1984) 'Technology, Diffusion and the Rate of Technological Change', *Economic Journal*, pp. 612–23.

Winter, S. (1963) 'Economic "Natural Selection" and the Theory of the Firm', *Yale Economic Essays*, Yale University.

[17]

Excerpt from *New Studies in Philosophy, Politics, Economics and the History of Ideas*, 179–90.

CHAPTER TWELVE

Competition as a Discovery Procedure[*]

I

It is difficult to defend economists against the charge that for some 40 to 50 years they have been discussing competition on assumptions that, *if* they were true of the real world, would make it wholly uninteresting and useless. If anyone really knew all about what economic theory calls the *data*, competition would indeed be a very wasteful method of securing adjustment to these facts. It is thus not surprising that some people have been led to the conclusion that we can either wholly dispense with the market, or that its results should be used only as a first step towards securing an output of goods and services which we can then manipulate, correct, or redistribute in any manner we wish. Others, who seem to derive their conception of competition solely from modern textbooks, have not unnaturally concluded that competition does not exist.

Against this, it is salutary to remember that, *wherever* the use of competition can be rationally justified, it is on the ground that we do *not* know in advance the facts that determine the actions of competitors. In sports or in examinations, no less than in the award of government contracts or of prizes for poetry, it would clearly be pointless to arrange for competition, if we were certain beforehand who would do best. As indicated in the title of this lecture, I propose to consider competition as a procedure for the discovery of such facts as, without resort to it, would not be known to anyone, or at least would not be utilised.[1]

---

[*] This lecture was originally delivered, without the present section 2, to a meeting of the Philadelphia Society at Chicago on 29 March 1968 and later, on 5 July 1968, in German, without the present final section, to the Institut für Weltwirtschaft of the University of Kiel. Only the German version has been published before, first in the series of 'Kieler Vorträge', N.S. 56, Kiel, 1968, and then reprinted in my collected essays entitled *Freiburger Studien*, Tübingen, 1969.

[1] Since I wrote this my attention has been drawn to a paper by Leopold von Wiese on 'Die Konkurrenz, vorwiegend in soziologisch-systematischer Betrachtung', *Verhandlungen des 6. Deutschen Soziologentages*, 1929, where, on p. 27, he discusses the 'experimental' nature of competition.

Competition as a Discovery Procedure

This may at first appear so obvious and incontestable as hardly to deserve attention. Yet, some interesting consequences that are not so obvious immediately follow from the explicit formulation of the above apparent truism. One is that competition is valuable *only* because, and so far as, its results are unpredictable and on the whole different from those which anyone has, or could have, deliberately aimed at. Further, that the generally beneficial effects of competition must include disappointing or defeating some particular expectations or intentions.

Closely connected with this is an interesting methodological consequence. It goes far to account for the discredit into which the micro-economic approach to theory has fallen. Although this theory seems to me to be the only one capable of explaining the role of competition, it is no longer understood, even by some professed economists. It is therefore worthwhile to say at the outset a few words about the methodological peculiarity of any theory of competition, because it has made its conclusions suspect to many of those who habitually apply an over-simplified test to decide what they are willing to accept as scientific. The necessary consequence of the reason why we use competition is that, *in those cases in which it is interesting*, the validity of the theory can never be tested empirically. We can test it on conceptual models, and we might conceivably test it in artificially created real situations, where the facts which competition is intended to discover are already known to the observer. But in such cases it is of no practical value, so that to carry out the experiment would hardly be worth the expense. If we do not know the facts we hope to discover by means of competition, we can never ascertain how effective it has been in discovering those facts that might be discovered. All we can hope to find out is that, on the whole, societies which rely for this purpose on competition have achieved their aims more successfully than others. This is a conclusion which the history of civilisation seems eminently to have confirmed.

The peculiarity of competition – which it has in common with scientific method – is that its performance cannot be tested in particular instances where it is significant, but is shown only by the fact that the market will prevail in comparison with any alternative arrangements. The advantages of accepted scientific procedures can never be proved scientifically, but only demonstrated by the common experience that, on the whole, they are better

Competition as a Discovery Procedure

adapted to delivering the goods than alternative approaches.[2]

The difference between economic competition and the successful procedures of science consists in the fact that the former is a method of discovering particular facts relevant to the achievement of specific, temporary purposes, while science aims at the discovery of what are sometimes called 'general facts', which are regularities of events. Science concerns itself with unique, particular facts only to the extent that they help to confirm or refute theories. Because these refer to general, permanent features of the world, the discoveries of science have ample time to prove their value. In contrast, the benefits of particular facts, whose usefulness competition in the market discovers, are in a great measure transitory. So far as the theory of scientific method is concerned, it would be as easy to discredit it on the ground that it does not lead to testable predictions about what science will discover, as it is to discredit the theory of the market on the ground that it fails to predict particular results the market will achieve. This, in the nature of the case, the theory of competition cannot do in any situation in which it is sensible to employ it. As we shall see, its capacity to predict is necessarily limited to predicting the kind of pattern, or the abstract character of the order that will form itself, but does not extend to the prediction of particular facts.[3]

2

Having relieved myself of this pet concern, I shall return to the central subject of this lecture, by pointing out that economic theory sometimes appears at the outset to bar its way to a true appreciation of the character of the process of competition, because it starts from the assumption of a 'given' supply of scarce goods. But which goods are scarce goods, or which things are goods, and how scarce or valuable they are – these are precisely the things which competition has to discover. Provisional results from the market process at each stage alone tell individuals what to look for. Utilisation of knowledge widely dispersed in a society with extensive division

2 Cf. the interesting studies of the late Michael Polanyi in *The Logic of Liberty*, London, 1951, which show how he has been led from the study of scientific method to the study of competition in economic affairs; and see also K. R. Popper, *The Logic of Scientific Discovery*, London, 1959.

3 On the nature of 'pattern prediction' see my essay on 'The theory of complex phenomena' in *Studies in Philosophy, Politics and Economics*, London and Chicago, 1967.

Competition as a Discovery Procedure

of labour cannot rest on individuals knowing all the particular uses to which well-known things in their individual environment might be put. Prices direct their attention to what is worth finding out about market offers for various things and services. This means that the, in some respects always unique, combinations of individual knowledge and skills, which the market enables them to use, will not merely, or even in the first instance, be such knowledge of facts as they could list and communicate if some authority asked them to do so. The knowledge of which I speak consists rather of a capacity to find out particular circumstances, which becomes effective only if possessors of this knowledge are informed by the market which kinds of things or services are wanted, and how urgently they are wanted.[4]

This must suffice to indicate what kind of knowledge I am referring to when I call competition a discovery procedure. Much would have to be added to clothe the bare bones of this abstract statement with concrete flesh, so as to show its full practical importance. But I must be content with thus briefly indicating the absurdity of the usual procedure of starting the analysis with a situation in which all the facts are supposed to be known. This is a *state* of affairs which economic theory curiously calls 'perfect competition'. It leaves no room whatever for the *activity* called competition, which is presumed to have already done its task. However, I must hurry on to examine a question, on which there exists even more confusion – namely, the meaning of the contention that the market adjusts activities spontaneously to the facts it discovers – or the question of the purpose for which it uses this information.

The prevailing confusion here is largely due to mistakenly treating the order which the market produces as an 'economy' in the strict sense of the word, and judging results of the market process by criteria which are appropriate only to such a single organised community serving a given hierarchy of ends. But such a hierarchy of ends is not relevant to the complex structure composed of countless individual economic arrangements. The latter, unfortunately, we also describe by the same word 'economy', although it is something fundamentally different, and must be judged by different standards.

4 Cf. Samuel Johnson in J. Boswell, *Life of Samuel Johnson*, L. F. Powell's revision of G. B. Hill's edition, Oxford, 1934, vol. II, p. 365 (18 April 1775): 'Knowledge is of two kinds. We know a subject ourselves, or we know where we can find information about it.'

Competition as a Discovery Procedure

An economy, in the strict sense of the word, is an organisation or arrangement in which someone deliberately allocates resources to a unitary order of ends. Spontaneous order produced by the market is nothing of the kind; and in important respects it does not behave like an economy proper. In particular, such spontaneous order differs because it does *not* ensure that what general opinion regards as more important needs are always satisfied before the less important ones. This is the chief reason why people object to it. Indeed, the whole of socialism is nothing but a demand that the market order (or catallaxy, as I like to call it, to prevent confusion with an economy proper)[5] should be turned into an economy in the strict sense, in which a common scale of importance determines which of the various needs are to be satisfied, and which are not to be satisfied.

The trouble with this socialist aim is a double one. As is true of every deliberate organisation, only the knowledge of the organiser can enter into the design of the economy proper, and all the members of such an economy, conceived as a deliberate organisation, must be guided in their actions by the unitary hierarchy of ends which it serves. On the other hand, advantages of the spontaneous order of the market, or the catallaxy, are correspondingly two. Knowledge that is used in it is that of all its members. Ends that it serves are the separate ends of those individuals, in all their variety and contrariness.

Out of this fact arise certain intellectual difficulties which worry not only socialists, but all economists who want to assess the accomplishments of the market order; because, if the market order does not serve a definite order of ends, indeed if, like any spontaneously formed order, it cannot legitimately be said to *have* particular ends, it is also not possible to express the value of the results as a sum of its particular individual products. What, then, do we mean when we claim that the market order produces in some sense a maximum or optimum?

The fact is, that, though the existence of a spontaneous order not made for a particular purpose cannot be properly said to have a purpose, it may yet be highly conducive to the achievement of many different individual purposes not known as a whole to any single person, or relatively small group of persons. Indeed, rational action is

5 For a fuller discussion see now my *Law, Legislation and Liberty*, vol. II, *The Mirage of Social Justice*, London and Chicago, 1976, pp. 107–20.

[183]

Competition as a Discovery Procedure

possible only in a fairly orderly world. Therefore it clearly makes sense to try to produce conditions under which the chances for any individual taken at random to achieve his ends as effectively as possible will be very high – even if it cannot be predicted which particular aims will be favoured, and which not.

As we have seen, the results of a discovery procedure are in their nature unpredictable; and all we can expect from the adoption of an effective discovery procedure is to improve the chances for unknown people. The only common aim which we can pursue by the choice of this technique of ordering social affairs is the general kind of pattern, or the abstract character, of the order that will form itself.

3

Economists usually ascribe the order which competition produces as an equilibrium – a somewhat unfortunate term, because such an equilibrium presupposes that the facts have already all been discovered and competition therefore has ceased. The concept of an 'order' which, at least for the discussion of problems of economic policy, I prefer to that of equilibrium, has the advantage that we can meaningfully speak about an order being approached to various degrees, and that order can be preserved throughout a process of change. While an economic equilibrium never really exists, there is some justification for asserting that the kind of order of which our theory describes an ideal type, is approached in a high degree.

This order manifests itself in the first instance in the circumstance that the expectations of transactions to be effected with other members of society, on which the plans of all the several economic subjects are based, can be mostly realised. This mutual adjustment of individual plans is brought about by what, since the physical sciences have also begun to concern themselves with spontaneous orders, or 'self-organising systems', we have learnt to call 'negative feedback'. Indeed, as intelligent biologists acknowledge, 'long before Claude Bernard, Clerk Maxwell, Walter B. Cannon, or Norbert Wiener developed cybernetics, Adam Smith has just as clearly used the idea in *The Wealth of Nations*. The "invisible hand" that regulated prices to a nicety is clearly this idea. In a free market, says Smith in effect, prices are regulated by negative feedback.'[6]

6 G. Hardin, *Nature and Man's Fate* (1951), Mentor ed. 1961, p. 54.

Competition as a Discovery Procedure

We shall see that the fact that a high degree of coincidence of
expectations is brought about by the systematic disappointment of
some kind of expectations is of crucial importance for an understanding of the functioning of the market order. But to bring about
a mutual adjustment of individual plans is not all that the market
achieves. It also secures that whatever is being produced will be
produced by people who can do so more cheaply than (or at least as
cheaply as) anybody who does not produce it (and cannot devote his
energies to produce something else comparatively even more
cheaply), and that each product is sold at a price lower than that at
which anybody who in fact does not produce it could supply it.
This, of course, does not exclude that some may make considerable
profits over their costs if these costs are much lower than those of
the next efficient potential producer. But it does mean that of the
combination of commodities that is in fact produced, as much will
be produced as we know to bring about by any known method. It
will of course not be as much as we might produce if all the knowledge anybody possessed or can acquire were commanded by some
one agency, and fed into a computer (the cost of finding out would,
however, be considerable). Yet we do injustice to the achievement
of the market if we judge it, as it were, from above, by comparing it
with an ideal standard which we have no known way of achieving. If
we judge it, as we ought to, from below, that is, if the comparison
in this case is made against what we could achieve by any other
method – especially against what would be produced if competition
were prevented, so that only those to whom some authority had
conferred the right to produce or sell particular things were allowed
to do so. All we need to consider is how difficult it is in a competitive
system to discover ways of supplying to consumers better or cheaper
goods than they already get. Where such unused opportunities seem
to exist we usually find that they remain undeveloped because their
use is either prevented by the power of authority (including the
enforcement of patent privileges), or by some private misuse of power
which the law ought to prohibit.

It must not be forgotten that in this respect the market only brings
about an approach towards some point on that n-dimensional
surface, by which pure economic theory represents the horizon of all
possibilities to which the production of any one proportional
combination of commodities and services could conceivably be
carried. The market leaves the particular combination of goods, and

Competition as a Discovery Procedure

its distribution among individuals, largely to unforeseeable circumstances – and, in this sense, to accident. It is, as Adam Smith already understood,[7] as if we had agreed to play a game, partly of skill and partly of chance. This competitive game, at the price of leaving the share of each individual in some measure to accident, ensures that the real equivalent of whatever his share turns out to be, is as large as we know how to make it. The game is, to use up-to-date language, not a zero-sum game, but one through which, by playing it according to the rules, the pool to be shared is enlarged, leaving individual shares in the pool in a great measure to chance. A mind knowing all the facts could select any point he liked on the surface and distribute this product in the manner he thought right. But the only point on, or tolerably near, the horizon of possibilities which we know how to reach is the one at which we shall arrive if we leave its determination to the market. The so-called 'maximum' which we thus reach naturally cannot be defined as a sum of particular things, but only in terms of the chances it offers to unknown people to get as large a real equivalent as possible for their relative shares, which will be determined partly by accident. Simply because its results cannot be assessed in terms of a single scale of values, as is the case in an economy proper, it is very misleading to assess the results of a catallaxy as if it were an economy.

4

Misinterpretation of the market order as an economy that can and ought to satisfy different needs in a certain order of priority, shows itself particularly in the efforts of policy to correct prices and incomes in the interest of what is called 'social justice'. Whatever meaning social philosophers have attached to this concept, in the practice of economic policy it has almost always meant one thing, and one thing only: the protection of certain groups against the necessity to descend from the absolute or relative material position which they have for some time enjoyed. Yet this is not a principle on which it is possible to act generally without destroying the foundations of the market order. Not only continuous increase, but in certain circumstances even mere maintenance of the existing level of incomes, depends on adaptation to unforeseen changes. This necessarily

7 Adam Smith, *The Theory of Moral Sentiments*, London, 1759, part VI, chapter 2, penultimate paragraph, and part VII, section II, chapter 1.

Competition as a Discovery Procedure

involves the relative, and perhaps even the absolute, share of some having to be reduced, although they are in no way responsible for the reduction.

The point to keep constantly in mind is that *all* economic adjustment is made necessary by unforeseen changes; and the whole reason for employing the price mechanism is to tell individuals that what they are doing, or can do, has for some reason for which they are not responsible become less or more demanded. Adaptation of the whole order of activities to changed circumstances rests on the remuneration derived from different activities being changed, without regard to the merits or faults of those affected.

The term 'incentives' is often used in this connection with somewhat misleading connotations, as if the main problem were to induce people to exert themselves sufficiently. However, the chief guidance which prices offer is not so much how to act, but *what to do*. In a continuously changing world even mere maintenance of a given level of wealth requires incessant changes in the direction of the efforts of some, which will be brought about only if the remuneration of some activities is increased and that of others decreased. With these adjustments, which under relatively stable conditions are needed merely to maintain the income stream, no 'surplus' is available which can be used to compensate those against whom prices turn. Only in a rapidly growing system can we hope to avoid absolute declines in the position of some groups.

Modern economists seem in this connection often to overlook that even the relative stability shown by many of those aggregates which macro-economics treats as data, is itself the result of a micro-economic process, of which changes in relative prices are an essential part. It is only thanks to the market mechanism that someone else is induced to step in and fill the gap caused by the failure of anyone to fulfil the expectations of his partners. Indeed, all those aggregate demand and supply curves with which we like to operate are not really objectively given facts, but results of the process of competition going on all the time. Nor can we hope to learn from statistical information what changes in prices or incomes are necessary in order to bring about adjustments to the inevitable changes.

The chief point, however, is that in a democratic society it would be wholly impossible by commands to bring about changes which are not felt to be just, and the necessity of which could never be clearly demonstrated. Deliberate regulation in such a political system must

[187]

Competition as a Discovery Procedure

always aim at securing prices which appear to be just. This means in practice preservation of the traditional structure of incomes and prices. An economic system in which each gets what others think he deserves would necessarily be a highly inefficient system – quite apart from its being also an intolerably oppressive system. Every 'incomes policy' is therefore more likely to prevent than to facilitate those changes in the price and income structures that are required to adapt the system to new circumstances.

It is one of the paradoxes of the present world that the communist countries are probably freer from the incubus of 'social justice', and more willing to let those bear the burden against whom developments turn, than are the 'capitalist' countries. For some Western countries at least the position seems hopeless, precisely because the ideology dominating their politics makes changes impossible that are necessary for the position of the working class to rise sufficiently fast to lead to the disappearance of this ideology.

5

If even in highly developed economic systems competition is important as a process of exploration in which prospectors search for unused opportunities that, when discovered, can also be used by others, this is to an even greater extent true of underdeveloped societies. My first attention has been deliberately given to problems of preserving an efficient order for conditions in which most resources and techniques are generally known, and constant adaptations of activities are made necessary only by inevitably minor changes, in order to maintain a given level of incomes. I will not consider here the undoubted role competition plays in the advance of technological knowledge. But I do want to point out how much more important it must be in countries where the chief task is to discover yet unknown opportunities of a society in which in the past competition has not been active. It may not be altogether absurd, although largely erroneous, to believe that we can foresee and control the structure of society which further technological advance will produce in already highly developed countries. But it is simply fantastic to believe that we can determine in advance the social structure in a country where the chief problem still is to discover what material and human resources are available, or that for such a country we can predict the particular consequences of any measures we may take.

[188]

Competition as a Discovery Procedure

Apart from the fact that there is in such countries so much more to be discovered, there is still another reason why the greatest freedom of competition seems to be even more important there than in more advanced countries. This is that required changes in habits and customs will be brought about only if the few willing and able to experiment with new methods can make it necessary for the many to follow them, and at the same time to show them the way. The required discovery process will be impeded or prevented, if the many are able to keep the few to the traditional ways. Of course, it is one of the chief reasons for the dislike of competition that it not only shows how things can be done more effectively, but also confronts those who depend for their incomes on the market with the alternative of imitating the more successful or losing some or all of their income. Competition produces in this way a kind of impersonal compulsion which makes it necessary for numerous individuals to adjust their way of life in a manner that no deliberate instructions or commands could bring about. Central direction in the service of so-called 'social justice' may be a luxury rich nations can afford, perhaps for a long time, without too great an impairment of their incomes. But it is certainly not a method by which poor countries can accelerate their adaptation to rapidly changing circumstances, on which their growth depends.

Perhaps it deserves mention in this connection that possibilities of growth are likely to be greater the more extensive are a country's yet unused opportunities. Strange though this may seem at first sight, a high rate of growth is more often than not evidence that opportunities have been neglected in the past. Thus, a high rate of growth can sometimes testify to bad policies of the past rather than good policies of the present. Consequently it is unreasonable to expect in already highly developed countries as high a rate of growth as can for some time be achieved in countries where effective utilisation of resources was previously long prevented by legal and institutional obstacles.

From all I have seen of the world the proportion of private persons who are prepared to try new possibilities, if they appear to them to promise better conditions, and if they are not prevented by the pressure of their fellows, is much the same everywhere. The much lamented absence of a spirit of enterprise in many of the new countries is not an unalterable characteristic of the individual inhabitants, but the consequence of restraints which existing customs

[189]

Competition as a Discovery Procedure

and institutions place upon them. This is why it would be fatal in such societies for the collective will to be allowed to direct the efforts of individuals, instead of governmental power being confined to protecting individuals against the pressures of society. Such protection for private initiatives and enterprise can only ever be achieved through the institution of private property and the whole aggregate of libertarian institutions of law.

[18]

Economie appliquée, tome XXXVII - 1985 - Nᵒˢ 3/4, pp. 569-595

Coordination of Individual Economic Activities as an Evolving Process of Self-Organization

Ulrich Witt

Faculty of Economic Statistics, University of Mannheim, A 5, D-6800 Mannheim, FRG

I.

INTRODUCTION

This paper deals with a core problem in economics, the question of how, and to what extent, individual economic interactions in the markets are self-coordinating or — to use the classical metaphor — are guided by an «invisible hand». This old economic problem can, as here initially, be seen as an example of «self-organization», a phenomenon that is the subject of rapidly expanding interdisciplinary research. Although the connection appears valid, it is not clear what it implies for the development of economic theory. An attempt could, for instance, be made to construct an analogy so that some plausible economic variables replace the physical, chemical, or biological variables in some of the well-known, characteristic equations (as e.g. the Fokker-Planck equation) in the natural sciences. Alternatively, it could be tried to develop an independent, economic theory of the coordination process in markets and then to investigate whether some features of such a theory indeed display formal similarities to the established generic description of self-organization phenomena.

For reasons set out in Section II the present paper is in favor of the second procedure. Unfortunately, a satisfactory dynamic theory of the coordination process in markets does not exist. Ironically, this is so because of an older analogy with physics introduced by the neoclassical writers — the analogy of the static equilibrium analysis with classical mechanics. This is discussed in detail in Section III. The few attempts that have been made to underpin equilibrium analysis with some notions of a dynamic trading process, for a recent survey see

Fisher (1983), fail as a more generally valid description. Their very strong assumptions about the information available to the economic agents are hardly acceptable even as an approximation.

The criticism of the neoclassical misconceptions concerning the actual limitations of individual knowledge and the variety of ways it is acquired and used is not new. In the writings of the «Austrian» or subjectivist economists this criticism is made a central argument in supporting the notion of a permanently ongoing market process in contrast to the equilibrium concept (see, e.g. Lachmann 1976, Kirzner 1976). The approach to the coordination problem suggested in the Sections IV and V (an elaboration of some concepts introduced in Witt 1980) is much in the spirit of this tradition in that the notion of a continually evolving process plays a central role here. It is deduced from some properties of the interactions of the agents in the markets in attempting to cope with imperfect information and uncertainty. The properties are established without a precise specification of hypotheses on individual behavior since space limitations prevent a detailed discussion here of the appropriate assumptions. A selection argument and some reflections on the role of innovations in the coordination process provide a sufficient basis for the present purpose.

Both these elements, the idea of selectional forces operating in the market process and the emphasis on innovations are characteristics of an evolutionary theory. The suggested approach has, thus much in common with the work of Nelson & Winter (1982). In fact, it sketches a natural extension of evolutionary economics to the problem of the market process. In Section VI some features of the self-organizing coordination process which has been theoretically described before are outlined in a simple model. The intention is to take up the question of formal similarities or contrasts to self-organization phenomena in the natural sciences. Section VII, finally, draws some conclusions.

II.

A GENUINE CASE OF SELF-ORGANISATION

In the natural sciences, the term «self-organization» is frequently used to denote situations where collective macroscopic features of multicomponent systems emerge from and are sustained by the interactions between units of the system at the microscopic level. As an interpretative notion it underlines, e.g., the investigations in the newly developing interdisciplinary research branch of synergetics (see Haken 1978, Weidlich and Haag 1983). When the basic perspective is transferred to economics, it becomes evident that it paraphrases a long-standing, familiar idea. Most concisely, it is the notion of spontaneous order emerging as an unintended consequence of individual economic and social actions (see Hayek 1967 who traces back this idea to Carl Menger and to Adam Smith).

Indeed, the coordination of individual economic activities that comes out of the interactions in and between the markets, to which the present paper is confined, is a remarkable example of self-organization. None of the individual decisions on prices, qualities and quantities is designed to impose restraints on agents other than those directly confronted. Yet, they do affect all agents in functioning markets and may even induce other more distant agents to revise and adjust their decisions thus keeping the unintentional coordinating market process going.

Of course, the mere fact that, with the system of prices and its informational content, unintended collective, macroscopic features emerge from the individual interactions in the market should not distract attention from essential differences between self-organizing systems in the natural sciences and in economics. The former are characterized by a detailed theoretical understanding of the elementary units' behavior and of the kind of interactions that occur at the microscopic level. What is lacking there is precise knowledge of the particular state of the microscopic components at a certain point in space and time (e.g. the precise space coordinate and velocity of the particles in thermodynamics). Therefore only statistical descriptions of these states can be given. Nevertheless, this has not prevented the deduction of stable, often almost deterministic, properties of the macroscopic system as expressed by well-known, experimentally reproducable variations of single parameters (e.g. temperature, density, entropy, etc.) over time.

In economics, in contrast, it is not only precise knowledge of the states of the individuals that is lacking. Little is also known at present about the dynamics of the individual behavior and the interactions. Even more fundamental is the difference resulting from human intelligence being involved: microscopic units in physico-chemical systems do not change behavior as a consequence of systematic learning, thinking, and strategic reasoning, nor do they «innovate», i.e. create new ways of behaving. Correspondingly, it is an open question what precisely the reliable regularities on the macroscopic, interactive level in economics are and how actual observations are to be interpreted.

Trying to transfer specific concepts and formalisms of the phenomena of self-organization in the natural sciences to the problem of economic coordination would therefore run the risk of stretching the analogy too far. Indeed, in view of earlier experiences economists should in principle be sceptical with respect to such analogies. Many of the fictions and shortcomings in the present understanding of the market process seem to be the result of another analogy suggested by the neoclassical writers in economics in the second half of the last century: the analogy between their equilibrium approach to the economic coordination problem and classical mechanics.[1] A short digression into the problems involved in this still usual approach will be helpful in establishing the arguments for an alternative, evolutionary approach in Section IV.

---

[1]   For a discussion of the analogy see Georgescu-Roegen (1971). It is an irony of the history of science that with the first edition of Walras' «Elément» in 1874 ideas from classical mechanics started their victorious career in economics at a time in which the work of Maxwell and Boltzmann on thermodynamics and statistical mechanics — precursors of present day self-organization research in the natural sciences — began to replace classical (Newtonian) mechanics in physics. For more general reflections on analogies and interactions between the natural sciences and economics see Faber and Proops (1985).

III.

THE NEOCLASSICAL APPROACH:
PERFECT COORDINATION

Image a set of scales where a weight is placed on one side. A process of adjustment starts immediately in which any free potential caused by adding the weight is dissipated until, finally, a new state of equilibrium is reached. According to the analogy drawn by the neoclassical writers, the «mechanics of utility and self-interest» (Jevons) establish an equilibrium in markets in a similar manner. «Free potentials» in the markets — i.e. the desire to revise unsatisfied individual plans which are reflected by corresponding excess demands — vanish similarly.

As is well-known, this was expected to be achieved by an appropriate variation of prices alone. Initially, nobody seems to have doubted that the free potential would actually disappear and a new equilibrium be reached. Hence theoretical efforts were concentrated entirely on the equilibrium state and its properties. Instead of exploring how free potential is eliminated, that is, instead of investigating the complicated dynamics of market interactions which actually have to bring about coordination — if it occurs at all — the alleged final state was considered by static analysis.[2]

When later some efforts were made to introduce dynamics explicitly into the general equilibrium of perfect coordination framework, the result were the economically rather weakly founded tâtonnement and non-tâtonnement models in the fifties and sixties (see Negishi 1962). The artificial character of these models meant that their assumptions were not very convincing, and the efforts turned out to be rather short-lived. Indeed, the crude transaction rules in the models, in particular in the tâtonnement, invited obvious criti-

---

[2] Culminating eventually in Debreu (1959), static analysis was exclusively concerned with a system, or more precisely, a unique vector of prices which, if imposed, would alone be sufficient to *perfectly coordinate* all optimized individual plans.

cisms.[3] However, the more fundamental problem with any attempt
to add dynamics in a supplementary way to the neoclassical equilibrium approach went unnoticed: the fact that by some sort of «fram-
ing»-effect the basic analogy to mechanics deeply biases the resear-
cher's preconceptions of the dynamics.

The flow of economic events is submitted to a dichotomous view
in which, on the one hand, the occurrence of «free potential»
(excess demand) is exclusively attributed to «exogeneous shocks».
The state of perfect coordination is somehow disturbed so that this
aspect of the problem does not need to be explained by the theory.
On the other hand, once equilibrium has been disturbed and new
data have been created the theoretician feels called for. It is taken
for granted, then, that individual adjustments will take place which
bring about convergence to a new equilibrium or perfect coordination just as they do in the analogous classical mechanics.

Clearly, although this dichotomy has a reasonable basis in classical mechanics, it only makes sense in economics if individual behavior is purely reactive, adapting to exogeneously caused events. The
idea that dissatisfaction or anger may remain even after all adjustments have been made, inducing the individuals to look for new possibilities of behavior so that an equilibrium may be disturbed *endogenously* if the agents are only inventive enough has no role to play.
(Indeed, in the mechanical neoclassical view of individual economic
behavior as a maximization of a target function subject to given
constraints there is no place at all for dissatisfaction or anger as a
source of motivation.)

---

[3] A detailed, critical survey is given elsewhere (Witt 1980, chs. II-IV). The
non-tâtonnement models nevertheless entailed an unexpected outcome: the path-
dependence of individual adaptations due to redistributive effects of trading which
takes place before an equilibrium is reached. As a consequence, there is no guarantee that a unique *ab ovo*-equilibrium identified in the static analysis given some initial endowment distribution will result from the adjustment process in the market
starting from that distribution. (In the original analogy there is, of course, nothing
equivalent to such a «remanence effect».) However, under certain assumptions the
non-tâtonnement processes can be proved to converge at least to *some* equilibrium
and, in the meantime, the assumptions could even be weakened somewhat, see the
«No Favorable Surprise» — model in Fisher (1983). Thus, perfet coordination still
remains the ultimate idea.

COORDINATION OF INDIVIDUAL ECONOMIC ACTIVITIES 575

Furthermore, in order to really prove the idea of convergence to a state of perfect coordination, as implied by the dichotomous scheme, the strong assumptions, characteristic of the neoclassical approach, are required foremost among these the perfect information assumption. The need for perfect information, at least in the probabilistic sense, if a systematic equilibrium not a purely arbitrary random one is to result, can easily be grasped in the static version: if the optimizing agents did not correctly anticipate the true constraints they would be compelled to revise their plans, thus there would be no equilibrium established and «free potential» would not vanish. By the same logic, in the dynamic version, the process of convergence to equilibrium must involve the agents simultaneously acquiring perfect information, if they start with imperfect information.[4]

In view of the markets which the neoclassical writers obviously had in mind all the strong assumptions and perhaps even the neglect of the actual process of coordination might possibly be deemed to be acceptable. In fact, the neoclassical market paradigm was made up of markets which were highly organized with respect to trading times, places and rules so that equilibrium prices were instantaneously reached, easily observable, or even explicitly announced.[5]

---

[4]   In order to model uncertainty and ignorance it is, in a probabilistic setting, often assumed that the agents do not know the true probability distribution(s) but rather have subjective probabilities. For some arbitrary chosen state of affairs this may be a useful approximation. The equilibrium state, of course, requires more. Mutually compatible individual plans presuppose that subjective probabilities equal the true ones by the same argument as above. Hence, for to get from the arbitrarily chosen state to the equilibrium state, some mechanism of up-dating subjective probabilities (learning) must be introduced. And it must be ensured that with up-dating on the basis of additional information subjective probabilities approach the initially unknown true probability distribution(s) in the process of convergence to equilibrium. Usually, Bayesian up-dating (learning) procedures are suggested here, since they are known to satisfy these requirements. Prerequisite is, of course, that prior information needed to carry out the first up-dating is correct. Thus, even in the attempt to realistically take account of uncertainty and ignorance, the neoclassical approach is forced to let in an embryonic perfect information assumption through the back-door of prior information in order to secure the idea of perfect coordination.

[5]   For instance, Walras (1926), pp. 43-48 used the example of the Paris stock-exchange; Edgeworth's recontracting idea underlies the notion of perfectly inter-

Since then, of course, institutional settings of exchange activities in the economy have changed greatly. Industrial product markets have been extended. Decentralized retailing has grown strongly and has become more and more diversified. Traditional forms of competition have been complemented by various forms of innovative competition as already described by Schumpeter (1912, p. 100).

With the absence of centralized information, ignorance, error and other informational deficiencies on both sides of the markets become elementary facts. Economic theory tried to take account of these changes. However, even in the most recent extension, the theory of search markets designed to deal with the informational problems, the static equilibrium approach still predominates (see Hey 1979 for a survey, Chan and Leland 1982, Burdett and Judd 1983) although it is by no means evident when, or even if, an equilibrium is reached in a real search market. Indeed, the idea of a convergence to an equilibrium is far less convincing in the case of search markets than it is for the neoclassical market paradigm. Where agents on both sides of the market are searching for an acceptable offer and where so little is known about how information is actually acquired and processed in learning, it is hard to say what the aggregate outcome will be unless the dynamic interactions are in fact investigated.

Thus, the heuristic basis of the neoclassical to the coordination problem has lost relevance simply through the changes that have occurred in the nature of markets. Its dominant concern, the demonstration of perfect coordination in equilibrium — the fruit of several fictious assumptions — is, except in a partial sense in organized markets, itself a fiction and, apparently, it is not possible to restate, it more realistically. There is good reason to believe, however, that even if perfect coordination is never reached, a coordinating process is always going on, brought about in a self-organizing way by the individual efforts to find better arrangements. If this is true, a problem shift must be made as in the next section towards not only a

---

connected traders «collected at a point, or connected by telephones», Edgeworth (1881), p. 18; Marshall (1938), pp. 281-291 took reference to highly organized corn, wood and woollen trade markets.

dynamic instead of static analysis but also towards a theory of ongoing change instead of convergence to equilibrium. A way must be found to characterize less than perfect coordination and to show how it is sustained to varying degree by the self-organization taking place in markets. In that context, then, it may be useful to come back to the question of what self-organization regularities observed in the natural sciences can contribute to the understanding of the problem in economics.

IV.

COORDINATION WITHIN BOUNDS — AN ALTERNATIVE APPROACH

Let the number of goods and services, in short, commodities offered for exchange in an economy at time t which, at least in some respect, differ in quality be m(t). Then the quantities of each commodity which have effectively been exchanged in t together with their prices can be represented by a point in the 2 . m- dimensional space of real numbers. Less formally it will be labeled the price-quantity-quality (pqq hereafter) space. Furthermore consider the individuals in the economy only in their different roles on the supply and/or demand side of the markets as s-agents and d-agents respectively.[6] The exchange activity of each agent in t can be represented by a point in the pqq-space.

Finally, let us introduce time as an additional dimension. Assume as a first approximation in this section that from the present up to some future date T there are no new, qualitatively different commodities. Under these conditions the sequence of transactions carried out by each agent in the given markets can be represented by an individual time path or trajectory in the pqq-time space. Released from the neoclassical heuristical bias, there is no a priori reason to

---

[6] In order to simplify the exposition of the basic concepts it will be assumed that s-agents and d-agents act independently, i.e. a partial perspective is chosen here. The effect which the result that an individual achieves in one market as an s-agent has on his behavior as d-agent in another market and vice versa is ignored.

expect that some general tendencies such as, e.g. convergence, necessarily govern the individual trajectories. Rather simultaneous learning processes, information gathering, experimentation, negotiations, higgling and haggling exert complex influences on the time paths. Phases of unchanged behavior can alternate with changes due to reactivated search for profit or utility increasing pqq-recombinations (for instructive examples see the simulated time paths in Witt and Perske 1982, ch. 2).

From the subjective point of view, the individual trajectories may in each single case follow reasonable purposive designs. But looked upon from «outside» — without knowing all the individual intentions — they appear as more or less erratic movements. However, these movements are not entirely unbounded. According to the idea of self-organization, it can be expected that the agents in their individual efforts unintendedly impose mutually binding restrictions and sanctions on their pqq-activities in the markets. In order to explain this central tenet in more detail let us look more closely at the agents' situations.

Consider the d-agents. Lacking perfect knowledge on all current transaction possibilities and their consequences, they inspect or otherwise process information and perhaps negotiate on offers which come to their attention in t. Even without penetrating into the question of how the searching d-agents reach their decisions — optimizing or non-optimizing — it can be conjectured that whatever type of economic behavior they follow, they will not accept every offer they inspect or know of in t. Rather acceptance as well as quantity demanded will systematically vary with price and quality observed in the sense of some probabilistic version of the law of demand. As will become clear in a moment, this simple property is already sufficient to impose coordinating constraints on the efforts of the s-agents.

With respect to the s-agents the basic condition of informational imperfections must similarly by acknowledged. Consequently, they, too, inspect or experiment with several pqq-combinations which they are aware of if feasible, or which they try to make feasible. However they make decisions and whatever they aim at — maximizing profits or satisficing some aspiration level of profits, market share, or something else — the following basic fact will be upheld

COORDINATION OF INDIVIDUAL ECONOMIC ACTIVITIES 579

because of the simple property stated for the d-agents' behavior: the s-agents' attempt to realize their chosen targets cannot succeed with every imaginable pqq-offer.

Let, in the easiest case, the s-agents' supply be perfectly elastic, i.e. instantaneously adjustable to observed demand. Then, conditional on the present knowledge of the d-agents met with in t and the competitors' offers, there is for any chosen quality an upper bound for each s-agent's price. Once it is exceeded expected sales in t fall to a value at which price no longer covers average total costs or simply fall to zero. Furthermore, if at least one cost-covering price exists, there is also a lower bound for the price conditional on the s-agent's know-how and efficiency and the competitors' offers. For given quality, with the quantity an s-agent can expect to sell, prices below that bound no longer cover average total costs in t. (Of course, if not even one cost-covering price exists, this is a problem of the production, organization and selling technique employed. Such an s-agent has simply no competitive capacity.)

Together these bounds, if they exist, delimit a range of action profitable to an s-agent with competitive capacity, i.e. of pqq-offers for which at least non-negative profits can be expected in t. Since the often seemingly erratic behavior of other agents influences these bounds they will rarely remain invariant throughout the time until T. The notions developed so far lead to:

Hypothesis 1   For every s-agents with competitive capacity, there exists a corridor in the pqq-time space from the present to a date T as defined, the not necessarily invariant bounds of which are established by the activities of the d-agents and other s-agents in the economy.[7] For any pqq-policy or time path remaining within or at the bounds of the corridor expected profits will not become negative at any time up to date T.

---

[7] Strictly speaking the definition of the bounds given is confined to the case of an s-agent posting price and reacting perfectly elastically to demand. The case of inelastic supply is somewhat more complicated since additional bounds for the quantity produced and, possibly, inventories have to be observed. As a consequence, similar bounds with respect to the s-agent's quantities — simultaneously to be determined on the basis of expected demand given the s-agent's price — must be included in the definition of the corridor. Also, for the rather rare case of s-agents posting quantities and leaving the price to be quoted to the demand side similar bounds can analogously be defined for the quantities offered for sale.

Under random influences or systematic changes in the other agents' behavior it may be quite difficult for an s-agent to identify a satisfactory or even the most favorable pqq-behavior within the possibly shifting corridor. Hence, quite a lot of experimentation, perhaps intermittently or, alternatively, an early settling down to some particular pqq-combination — satisficing instead of searching for the optimum — is likely to occur. According to hypothesis 1 this does not cause serious consequences in the form of loss expectations as long as the corridor is not departed from. Things change substantially, however, once the bounds of the corridor are exceeded. Then losses have to be expected which take the form of a reduction in either the s-agents' wealth or that of his creditors.

Exceeding the bounds therefore creates strong incentives for the s-agent to try and get back into the corridor. Of course, an attempt to achieve this may not necessarily be successful. The s-agent's trajectory perhaps remains outside the corridor because he is just not capable of adjusting production appropriately. Or, if the corridor shifts downwards, the agent may not be able to lower costs sufficiently. In that case losses accumulate until either the s-agent gives up and shuts down or sanctions are taken by the creditors forcing him into bankruptcy. Put differently, a persistent pqq-time path outside the corridor is prevented by internally operating selection (search for and substitution by superior policies)[8] as well as externally generated selection (sanctions by creditors) forcing the unsuccessful agent out of business. Summarized in another hypothesis:

Hypothesis 2　　Though within the bounds of the corridor an s-agent's pqq-behavior may be subject to idiosyncratic moves, the endeavor not to exceed the bounds or to get back once they are exceeded is strongly enforced by individual incentives as well as by external sanctions. If nevertheless an s-agent is unsuccessful, he is forced out of business.

---

[8]　The internally operating selection of routines as a means of responding to changed market conditions in a scenario similar to the one discussed here is a central argument in the evolutionary approach suggested by Nelson and Winter (1982, esp. ch. 7). Of course, this kind of selection is not necessarily reactive, induced by the crisis arising when the bounds are in fact exceeded. It can also result from anticipatory intervention if, e.g. the danger of exceeding is announced by a profit decrease when the bounds of the corridor are approached.

COORDINATION OF INDIVIDUAL ECONOMIC ACTIVITIES 581

Obviously, it is the effort of the s-agents to avoid exceeding the bounds which ensures that a certain degree of coordination evolves in the market. That degree is certainly far removed from the one suggested by the neoclassical equilibrium approach — all the more so the less narrow the bounds within which any idiosyncratic pqq-behavior is tolerated.[9] Indeed, it becomes clear that the neoclassical idea of perfect coordination is but a limiting case of the present approach where no more learning is taking place: Once d-agents have acquired perfect information, and the s-agents all share a common knowledge, upper and lower bounds coincide. The corridor collapses into one single trajectory for which the selection argument for hypothesis 2 can be and in fact has been, claimed as implying support for, and only for, optimizing behavior (see Friedman 1953), We thus get:

Hypothesis 3   As long as the agents involved in market interactions lack perfect information, the bounds of the corridors of all s-agents do not collapse into a single trajectory. Consequently, coordination through markets is less than perfect, yet it is not completely missing. Compatibility of all individual plans is not established[10] but the fact that some imaginable gains from trade and division of labor are withheld does not threaten the economic existence of the agents.

---

[9]   On the other hand, this less definite proposition about coordination and, of course, allocation and welfare does not draw on the fictitious assumptions connected with the strong notion of convergence to equilibrium as criticized in section III above. Not more than the weak condition of boundedness is required, that is the condition of pqq-trajectories exceeding the bounds of the corridor only for a finite, sufficiently short time.

[10]   For that reason alone any attempt to connect the idea of weakly bounded pqq-trajectories with the notion of a stochastic equilibrium would lead astray. Furthermore, the hypothesis that all pqq-trajectories represent realizations of a stationary stochastic process, as implied by the definition of a stochastic equilibrium, would, of course, directly contradict the elementary facts which motivated hypothesis 1 above: learning, searching, experimentation etc. on both sides of the markets.

V.

THE ROLE OF INNOVATIONS
IN THE ALTERNATIVE APPROACH

Sofar we have been concerned with the coordination effect of the forces which bring about the self-organization phenomenon in the individual interactions. There is, however, another effect which is connected with innovation. The strong incentive to avoid exceeding the bounds of the corridor will often not only induce pqq-activities constrained to already known options. It may be that inventiveness, one of the most spectacular and exclusively human capabilities, is instigated resulting in the discovery of previously unknown options for actions and, possibly, their realization in the form of innovations.

In order to discuss this extension it is useful to distinguish between two kinds of innovations which have different consequences for the approach suggested here. The first includes diverse forms of innovative activities. They have in common the fact that they affect the bounds of the corridor in which the s-agent operates and, as a consequence, mediated by the d-agents' activities, those of the innovator's competitors producing the same commodity or a substitute. The second kind are commodity innovations. They call into question the assumption of a given number of qualitatively differing commodities underlying the previous section. Let us begin with the first kind.

Consider the introduction of a new, cost-saving production technique by one s-agent. As a consequence, the lower price bound is shifted downward and the agent may be induced to try a price-cut. In that case some of the d-agents inspecting the offers in the market will be inclined to make a transaction at the lower price instead of buying from the direct or indirect competitiors. The latter consequently lose potential customers. This not only influences the sales of the competitors, challenging their pqq-policy, but may also cause a downward shift of the *upper* bound for some competitor. Then endeavors to overcome the newly arisen crisis may be triggerd off which, perhaps, in turn, result in induced innovations elsewhere in the market. Similar effects can be expected to follow when some

COORDINATION OF INDIVIDUAL ECONOMIC ACTIVITIES 583

s-agent tries to invade new market segments along with a changed marketing policy; when new inputs and subcontractors are introduced, reducing those previously employed; or when organizational change arouses new motivation to reduce slack, thereby saving costs and/or improving selling success.

Thus, due to the self-organizational character of the market interactions, the effect of this kind of innovative activity will through the reaction of the d-agents spread through the market and affect even far distant agents. It certainly entails pqq-experimentation but, presumably, also successive innovations elsewhere. Hence, besides the coordinating first effect of the self-organizing forces, there is a second one which has an at least temporarily, «de-coordinating» character.[11] Both effects act on the market process at the same time as stated by the following hypothesis:

Hypothesis 4   The full effect of the self-organizing forces established unintentionally by the interacting activities of the agents in the market is composed of two simultaneous but opposed tendencies: a coordinating one, forcing the s-agents to keep to their shifting corridor according to hypothesis 2; and a de-coordinating tendency causing the bounds of the corridors to shift due to innovative activities which in turn seem to be motivated chiefly by the s-agents' attempt to cope with present or possible future shifts of the bounds of profitable action.

The occurrence of innovations thus supports the basic conjecture that the efforts taken simultaneously by the d-agents and s-agents in the markets will not result in pqq-trajectories definitely converging simultaneously to a state of equilibrium.

The message contained in hypotheses 4 is no less valid when taking commodity innovations into consideration. However, it is no longer possible then to confine the analysis to the time period up to T, that is, on the given set of qualitatively homogenous commodities which can be represented in a metric space of *given* dimension. Once time T is exceeded, the trajectories representing the agents' pqq-behavior will enter the $2 \cdot (m + 1)$- dimensional space and so on. Un-

---

[11]   The endeavor of the s-agents to keep track to the shifting pqq-corridor calls forth ongoing change and need to adapt also on the demand side, the possibility of innovations included. For simplicity innovative activity of the d-agents is neglected here although its empirical relevance should not be underrated.

fortunately, the precise date T cannot be determined, nor is it possible to say where the new commodity will be introduced or even what its specific properties will be — novelties will not disclose their nature before they have occurred and can be experienced.

This is a basic impediment for all theories where novelties play a crucial role. Such theories usually are called evolutionary and, consequently, the presently suggested approach is an evolutionary one![12] What can be done in such theories is to deduce necessary conditions which restrict the multiplicity of imaginable consequences of novelties, in the present context innovations, in such a way that not all these consequences are allowed to occur if the theory is valid. This will certainly not yield very strong predictions, but it was precisely this device that was used above in the discussion leading to hypothesis 4. By similar reasoning it can now be infered — and, in fact, that is all we need for the current concern — that commodity innovations also result in a de-coordinating effect, whatever, their properties are.

Indeed, it is not difficult to see why. Information on their availability and their characteristics diffuses throughout the market and causes additional information processing requirements on both sides of the market, i.e. at least transitory uncertainty. A way of persuasive presentation and appropriate pricing have to be found in order to induce d-agents to substitute something else for the purchases of the new commodities. If this succeeds, the demand side will have mediated the effect on the pqq-trajectories of some other s-agents, perhaps causing crises which, in turn, can induce further innovations. Thus, even though the case of commodity innovations complicates the formal representation of the corridor approach substantially, the conjectured basic features of the self-organizing market process as stated in hypothesis 4 are not affected in principle.

It can be argued then that economic coordination results from two opposing tendencies which emerge from the interaction of individual efforts in the markets. According to this notion the coordinating process is a permanently «evolving» one. It continues

---

[12]   For a detailed discussion on the role of novelty in evolutionary theories and the problems connected with the fact of non-predictability see Witt (1986, ch. 1).

without ever reaching the state of neoclassical perfect coordination except when: (i) the differentiation of commodities and the variety of markets is small enough for agents to be able to reach simultaneously a state of perfect information in their interfering adjustment efforts and (ii) innovative activity is absent, perhaps because of being suppressed.[13]

As predicated by hypothesis 3, there is no time in the evolving process of coordination when all individual plans are mutually compatible. There are disappointments and frictions and losses of efficiency (as compared to perfect coordination). By and large, however, the economic process of production and distribution of commodities works quite well; gains from trade and the extent of the division of labor admit wealth increases. Indeed, in a wider sense, the social gains from innovations presumably overcompensate the losses from imperfect coordination. Ongoing innovative competition, i.e. the entry of new agents as well as new commodities — which is often the only way of preventing or combatting monopolization — necessarily is to some extent de-coordinating. This is what the second effect discussed in this section purports.

VI.

SOME FEATURES
OF THE SELF-ORGANIZATION PROCESS

Some features of the evolving process of self-organization suggested by the alternative approach will now be outlined in a

---

[13] Without going into details here it can easily be imagined what kind of societies might be named where conditions (i) and (ii) are approximately fulfilled: mediaeval estates and guild societies in Europe, precolonial African and other native tribe economies etc., see, e.g., the contributions in Polanyi e.a. (1957). Certainly they are hardly what the neoclassical writers intended as domain of their theory. Moreover, in these societies social and economic positions, professions etc. are strongly regulated by custom and often ascribed by birth. Correspondingly, markets are strongly monopolized so that the state of perfect coordination, which perhaps is acieved, is not a perfect competition (or Walrasian) equilibrium but rather one of monopolistic equilibrium.

somewhat more definite form. This can be done with a simple model if, instead of the complicated dynamics of the pqq-processes and the evolution of the relevant bounds, only the patterns of change of the bimodal status of the s-agents are investigated. According to hypothesis 4, the two opposing effects or tendencies governing the coordination process, the coordinating and the de-coordinating, will result in a variety of different patterns. These can be followed up by the time evolution of a ratio-variable which indicates how the two opposing tendencies affect the s-agents' ability to remain within the corridor. For convenience, firms will be the only s-agents considered in the simple exposition.

Let n_t denote the relative frequency of firms within their corridor («*interior*») in period t and x_t the relative frequency of those outside («*exterior*») with $n_t = 1 - x_t$. A change in these frequencies in discrete time results when firms manage to get back into their corridor or drop out of it, i.e. from firms changing their bimodal status in the relevant period of time. Hence, the equation of motion

$$(1) \qquad x_{t+1} = x_t - f^i(x_t) + f^o(n_t),$$

can be used to describe the impact of each of the two effects evolving in the market process. On the right hand side of (1) the second (third) summand indicates the frequency change due to firms switching into (switching out of) their corridor.

According to hypothesis 2 firms have a strong incentive to stay in the corridor or to get back in again if they are outside.[14] Turning first to the *coordinating effect* it seems reasonable, therefore, that some of the firms previously not performing adequately manage to stop making losses in a period t by simply making an appropriate pqq-adjustment. Let us assume that, for a certain time, observations for the corresponding data are available. In order to simplify matters,

---

[14] Otherwise they risk shut-down or bankruptcy. Since we use relative frequencies in this model the exposition is made much easier if we adopt the following assumption in what follows: whenever a firm withdraws, a new firm enters the market which may or may not start a profitable business, so that this event is implicity taken account of in the specification of $f^i(x_t)$. Furthermore, exit or entry of firms for any other reason is assumed neutral with respect to the current frequencies x_t and n_t.

let us concentrate on the observed mean share α, $o < \alpha < 1$, of these firms among all firms outside. On the other hand, in every period t of the observation time period some of the firms previously performing satisfactorily may no longer be doing so. This can happen, e.g., if firms operating very close to the upper bound of their corridor suffer decreases in demand (may be systematically induced by business cycle fluctuations) so that the bound shifts and their pqq-time path leaves the corridor. Let us assume first that this group has been observed to have mean share $\beta = 0$, of all firms within the corridor, since there is no reason to assume that extrusive forces systematically result form the coordinating effect. ($\beta \geq 0$ can, however, be interpreted as an exogeneously varying factor, too, which represents e.g. political factors squeezing average profit margins among the low profit firms, see below.)

As far as the impact of the coordinating effect is concerned we thus get the linear specifications

(2)
$$f^{ci}(x_t) = \alpha x_t$$
$$f^{co}(n_t) = \beta n_t.$$

Inserting in (1) this leads to

(3) $$x_{t+1} = (1 - \alpha - \beta)x_t + \beta,$$

a simple linear first-order difference equation which describes the impact of the coordinating effect. Provided $0 < \alpha < 1$ and $\beta = 0$, (3) shows that the coordinating effect as the name implies is going to reduce the expected relative frequency of displaced firms to zero. Once x_t has been shifted to a positive value for whatever reasons, all firms can be expected to get back into their corridor with growing t since the only «attractor» (stable equilibrium point) is $x = o$ (see figure 1 where for purpose of demonstration a possible time path is displayed).

We turn now to the second, *de-coordinating effect* that is due to the occurrence of innovations as stated in hypotheses 4. Let the firms be classified by two criteria: being in or out of the corridor, with relative frequencies n and x as above; innovating or not in t, with relative frequencies p and 1—p respectively. Suppose it has turned out in the past that the proportion of innovating firms among

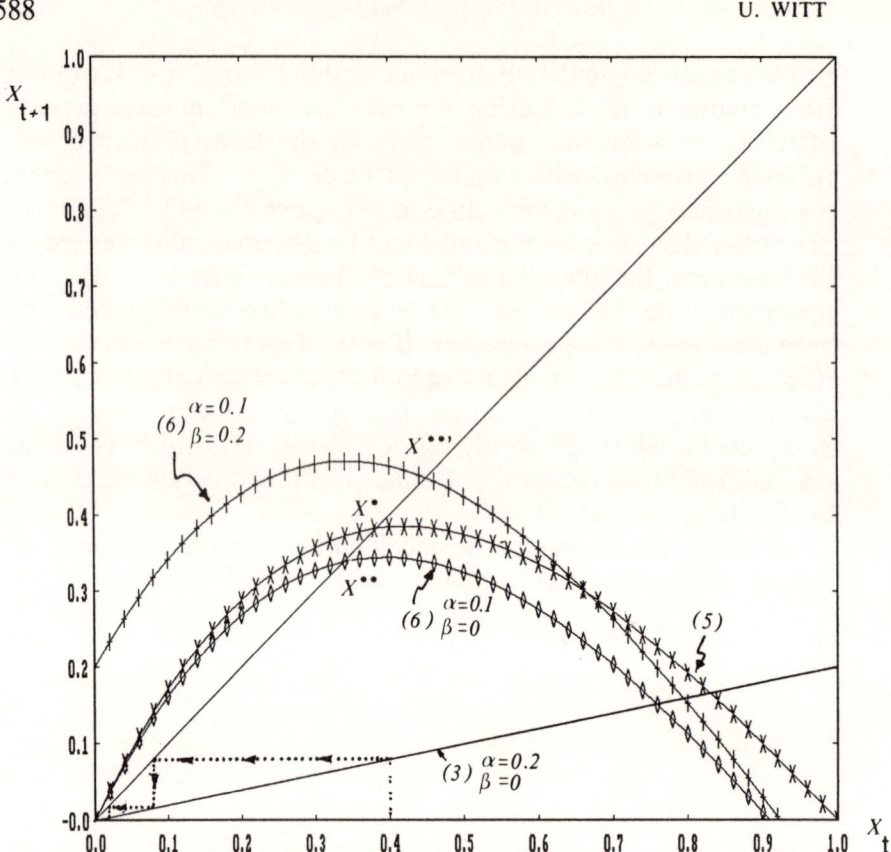

Fig. 1. — Impact of the Coodinating, the De-coordinating, and the Compound Effect on the Mean Frequency of Firms Outside their Corridor.

those in and out of their corridor is the same. Four classes of firms with their shares can then be distinguished (index t omitted for notational convenience): (i) out of the corridor and innovating, p · x; (ii) in the corridor and innovating, p · n; (iii) in the corridor and not innovating, (1—p) · n; (iv) out of the corridor and not innovating, (1—p) · x.

By assumption, firms in class (i) succeed in getting back into the corridor, thus causing increased competition particularly for class-(iii) firms. Take px · (1—p)n as a measure of conflicts arising and assume the observed frequency of class-(iii) firms which, as a consequence of these conflicts, on average exceed their bounds in the same period is directly proportional to this measure. Similarly, class-(ii) firms increase competition for class-(iii) firms, forcing some out of the corridor so that a frequency change pn · (1—p)n results. Summarized, this leads to the specification

(4)
$$f^{di}(x_t) = px_t$$
$$f^{do}(n_t) = px_t(1-p)n_t + pn_t(1-p)n_t.$$

Suppose, in addition, that the relative frequency of innovations increases the greater the number of firms in a crisis situation, in particular that the linear specification $p = x_t$ is a good approximation of this hypothesis for the time under concern. Inserting (4) into (1) while making use of this additional hypothesis we find

(5)
$$x_{t+1} = 2x_t - 3x_t^2 + x_t^3$$

as the difference equation which gives the impact of the de-coordinating effect. The graph of (5) in figure 1 displays that there is one and only one attractor (stable equilibrium point) x^*, $0 < x^* < 1$. As expected, the de-coordinating effect establishes and sustains a positive relative mean frequency of firms outside their corridor.

The *compound effect* of the two opposing tendencies which is expressed in the patterns of change of the bimodal status can easily be found by expanding (1) into

$$x_{t+1} = x_t - f^{ci}(x_t) - f^{di}(x_t) + f^{co}(n_t) + f^{do}(n_t).$$

Using (2) and (4) with hypothesis $p = x_t$ this yields

(6)
$$x_{t+1} = (2 - \alpha - \beta)x_t - 3x_t^2 + x_t^3 + \beta.$$

This non-linear first-order difference equation describes the regularity which governs the time path of the mean relative frequency of firms outside their corridor under the assumptions introduced above. (6) has a unique maximum in the interval (o, 1) and possesses an attractor x^{**} which for $\beta = o$ is the more to the left of x^* the greater α.[15]

---

[15]   Note, however, that for $\alpha > o$ and $\beta = o$ (6) is only valid for $x_{t+1} \geq o$. For very large, empirically irrelevant values of x_t there is thus a discontinuity where

The facts that some firms find their way back into the corridor under the coordinating tendency without innovating (indicated by the mean share α), lowers the impact of the de-coordinating tendency. On the other hand, if external forces displace firms from their corridor, e.g. as a consequence of political influences or of business cycle fluctuations as expressed by the parameter $\beta > o$, then this naturally shifts the attractor to the right with growing β. This means that the mean relative frequency x_t which is stabilized in the evolving process — the indicator of the strength of the de-coordinating effect — is increased beyond the value that is enforced by innovative activities (compare figure 1 for the graphs of some alternative numerical specifications of (6)). Without going into details it can be seen from (6) that there is nothing spectacular in the possible time-paths of x_t under the assumptions and hypotheses that have been chosen. The interplay of coordinating and de-coordinating forces in the self-organizing market process stabilizes into a regular pattern.

It is at this point that we can return to the question of what self-organization phenomena and their formal description in the natural sciences can contribute to the understanding in the present context. If the representation of the self-organization taking place in individual market interactions given above is contrasted with those phenomena a remarkable difference is found. At least on the level of analysis chosen for the above model, there is no phase transition phenomenon such as that characteristically connected with emerging self-organization in the domain of the natural sciences. There a structure not previously observed suddenly turns up if some external parameter is continuously changed (e.g. energy through-put). This is formally described by a potential function with a shape that displays several stable and unstable equilibria or by an alteration of the function itself so that its stability properties change.

In fact, some of the attractiveness which a possible analogy could have for some economists seems to be due to these discontinuity phenomena. (But notice, that no recourse to any such analogy has

---

x_{t+1} becomes zero, which is an unstable equilibrium. (If $\alpha > o$ and $\beta > o$ there even exists an interval for very large x_t where x_{t+1} is not defined.)

been necessary here in developing the idea of how self-organization comes about in the market process.) No doubt a model with such properties could also be developed for the present problem. Consider, for instance, the alternative specification

(7)
$$f'^{di}(x_t) = x_t n_t,$$
$$f'^{do}(n_t) = \mu \sqrt{x_t} \cdot f^{di}(x_t)$$

for the de-ccordinating effect.[16] If (7) is inserted into (1) and the coordinating effect (2) is added, the difference equation

(8)
$$x_{t+1} = \beta - (\alpha + \beta)x_t + x_t^2 + \mu(x_t^{3/2} - x_t^{5/2})$$

results. It has stability properties which change dramatically, when the parameter β and μ are varied. This is displayed exemplarily in figure 2.

If, e.g., $\alpha = 0.1$, $\beta = 0$, and μ is continually increased from 1 to 2, there is first a unique stable equilibrium $x = 0$. Then suddenly, an additional, unstable equilibrium x' at very high x-values occurs. If μ is increased further the latter bifurcates into a stable equilibrium $\bar{x}$ remaining at very high x-values and a slowly downward wandering unstable equilibrium point. If, in addition, for $\mu = 2$ β increases minimally, a catastrophic structural change occurs: the stable equilibrium in $x = 0$ vanishes as does the intermediate unstable one and an x-value close to 1 is the only attractor left.

It is by no means evident, however, that the «catastrophic» model resulting in (8) would indeed yield a better description of the economic process of coordination than the stable pattern of change implied by the model resulting in (6). It seems unlikely, therefore, that for the understanding of the coordination of individual market

---

[16] It might be motivated as follows: $x_t n_t$ can be interpreted as a measure for the ease with which those firms exterior can succeed with an innovation. If x_t is low, success rates are low because of the low capabilities of the then external firms; if x_t is high, success rates are low because of the high capabilities of the then internal firms; in between the success rates increase. $\sqrt{x_t} \cdot f^{di}(x_t)$ can be understood as a measure for the displacement effect on firms previously performing successfully which is caused by the firms which manage to get back into their corridor; μ is a «maturity» parameter (see Mensch 1985 for a background discussion) indicating how sensitively firms within the bounds react to competition by innovation.

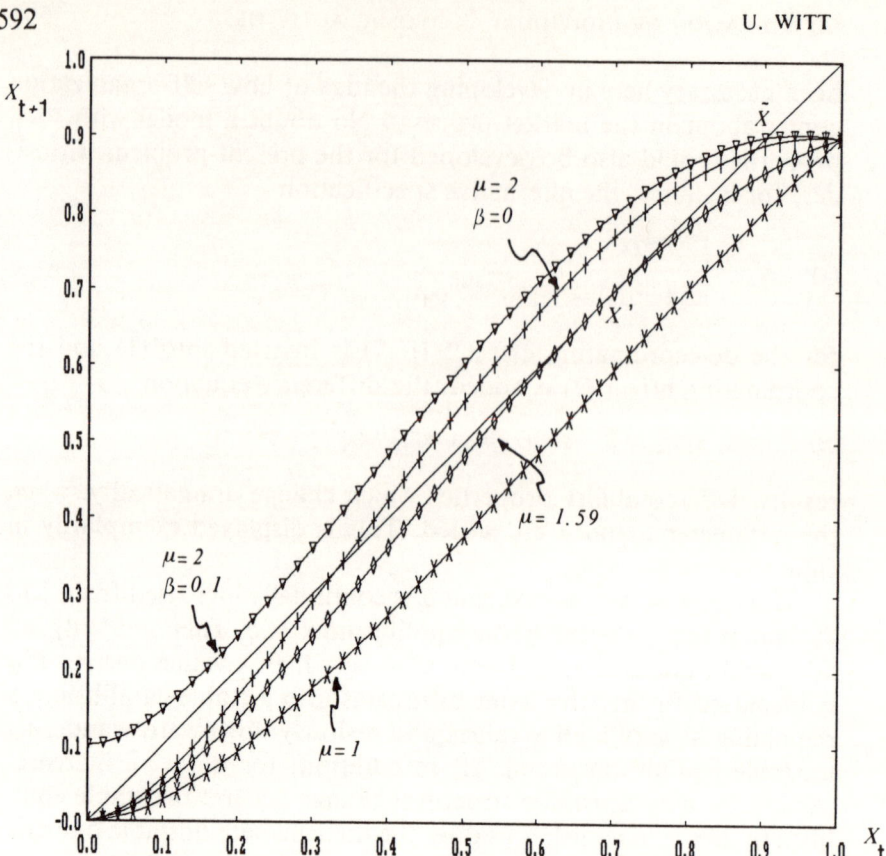

Fig. 2. — Impact of the Compound Effect in a «Catastrophic» Model.

activities there is much that can be contributed by studying the characteristic self-organization phenomena in the natural sciences.

VII.

CONCLUSIONS

In this paper a non-neoclassical approach to the economic coordination problem is sketched. The approach is not based on the fallacious heuristical analogy to classical mechanics and it is not con-

COORDINATION OF INDIVIDUAL ECONOMIC ACTIVITIES 593

strained to the notion of perfect coordination which is associated with an equilibrium point in the price-quantity-quality (pqq) space or a stationary pqq-distribution. The basic ideas are outlined in four hypotheses. Emphasis is given to uncertainty, fallibility, and inventiveness at the individual level and to selectional forces operating, on the individual as well as the market, level against a too strong variance in individual behavior. These are typical elements in an evolutionary theory and the present approach can therefore qualify as an evolutionary one.

Some features of the evolutionary process taking place in the market interactions are outlined in a simple model mainly to illustrate the notion that coordinating and decoordinating forces occur simultaneously in the market process. The model does not penetrate into the complicated dynamics of the individual interactions and their consequences in the pqq-space. Therefore the full implications of the suggested evolutionary approach cannot be surveyed here. For that purpose a more detailed version which directly shows the impact of the coordinating and the decoordinating tendencies shaping the individual corridors in the pqq-time space and working on the individuals to stick to them is required.

Nevertheless, the simple representation allows a tentative conclusion with respect to a possible analogy with self-organization phenomena in the natural sciences to be drawn. It does not seem likely that their characteristic, dramatic discontinuity phenomena have a plausible analogue in the coordination process established by the individuals which interact in the market, at least not on the level of analysis chosen in the model. This, of course, does not preclude the existence of similarities in other domains of economics, e.g. in the theory of group decision making, in the theory of preference formation and adaption of reliable standards of conduct, or, perhaps, on a more aggregate level.

ABSTRACT

An evolutionary approach to the economic coordination problem is suggested. Instead of the strong, neoclassical notion of perfect coordination represented by equilibrium points in the price-quantity-quality (pqq) space the notion of a corridor in the pqq-time space is developed. This corridor is established spontaneously by internal and external forces which control divergence. Within the corridor quite erratic individual pqq-movements are possible, but, due to those selectional forces, systematic changes occur if the bounds are exceeded. Some features of the alternative approach are outlined in a simple model and are compared with characteristics of self-organization phenomena in the natural sciences.

RÉSUMÉ

L'article suggère une approche évolutionniste du problème de la coordination économique. Au lieu de la notion néoclassique forte de coordination parfaite présentée par les points d'équilibre dans l'espace Prix-Quantité-Qualité (PQQ), on développe la notion d'un corridor dans l'espace PQQ-Temps. Ce corridor s'établit spontanément sous la pression des forces internes et externes qui contrôlent la divergence. A l'intérieur du corridor, des mouvements individuels relativement erratiques sont possibles dans l'espace PQQ, mais, à cause des forces de sélection, des changements systématiques apparaissent si les frontières sont dépassées. Quelques caractéristiques de cette approche alternative sont mises en évidence sur un modèle simple et sont comparées aux caractéristiques des phénomènes d'auto-organisation dans les sciences de la nature.

REFERENCES

Burdett, K., Judd, K.L. (1983), «Equilibrium Price Dispersion», *Econometrica*, Vol. 51, 955-969.

Chan, Y.-S., Leland, H. (1982), «Prices and Qualities in Markets with Costly Information», *Review of Economic Studies*, Vol. XLIX, 499-516.

Debreu, G. (1959), *Theory of Value*, New Haven: Yale Univ. Press.

Edgeworth, F.Y. (1881), *Mathematical Psychics*, London: Kegan Paul.

Faber, M., Proops, J.L.R. (1985), «Interdisciplinary Research Between Economists and Physical Scientists: Retrospect and Prospect», *Kyklos*, Vol. 38, 599-616.

Fisher, F.M. (1983), *Disequilibrium Foundations of Equilibrium Economics*, Cambridge: Cambridge Univ. Press.

Friedman, M. (1953), «The Methodology of Positive Economics», in M. Friedman, *Essays in Positive Economics*, Chicago: Univ. of Chicago Press, 3-43.

Georgescu-Roegen, N. (1971), *The Entropy Law and the Economic Process*, Cambridge, Mass.: Harvard Univ. Press.

Haken, H. (1978), *Synergetics*, 2nd edit., Berlin-Heidelberg-New York: Springer.

Hayek, F.A. (1967), «The Results of Human Action but not of Human Design», in F.A. Hayek, *Studies in Philosophy, Politics and Economics*, London: Routledge & Paul, 96-105.

Hey, J.D. (1979), *Uncertainty in Microeconomics*, Oxford: Robertson.

Kirzner, I.M. (1976), «Equilibrium versus Market Process», in E.G. Dolan (ed.), *The Foundations of Modern Austrian Economics*, Kansas City: Sheed & Ward, 115-125.

Lachmann, L.M. (1976), «On the Central Concept of Austrian Economics: Market Process», in E.G. Dolan (ed.). *The Foundations of Modern Austrian Economics*, Kansas City: Sheed & Ward.

Marshall, A. (1938), *Principles of Economics*, 8th ed., London: McMillan.

Mensch, G.O. (1985), «Threats and Opportunities in Technological Innovation», discussion paper presented to the Havard Business School 75th Anniversary Colloquim on Productivity and Technology.

Negishi, T. (1962), «The Stability of A Competitive Economy: A Survey Article», *Econometrica*, Vol. 30, 635-669.

Nelson, R.R., Winter, S.G. (1982), *An Evolutionary Theory of Economic Change*, Cambridge, Mass.: Harvard Univ. Press.

Polanyi, K., Arensberg, C.M., Pearson, H.W. (eds.) (1957), *Trade and Market in the Early Empires*, Glencoe, Ill.: The Free Press.

Schumpeter, J. (1912), *Theorie der wirtschaftlichen Entwicklung*, Leipzig: Duncker & Humblot.

Walras, L. (1926), *Eléments d'Economie Politique Pure*, édition définitive, Lausanne-Paris.

Weidlich, W.., Haag, G. (1983), *Concepts and Models of a Quantitative Sociology*, Berlin-Heidelberg-New York: Springer.

Witt, U. (1980), *Marktprozesse — Neoklassische vs. evolutorische Theorie der Preis- und Mengendynamik*, Königstein/Ts.: Atheneum.

— (1986), *Individualistische Grundlagen der evolutorischen Ökonomik*, Tübingen: Mohr.

— Perske, J. (1982), *SMS — A Program Package for Simulation and Gaming of Stochastic Market Processes and Learning Behavior*, Lecture Notes in Economics and Mathematical Systems, Vol. 202, Berlin-Heidelberg-New York: Springer.

Part VI
Cultural Evolution and
Spontaneous Order

[19]

Journal of Economic Behavior and Organization 1 (1980) 97–121. © North-Holland

SOCIOBIOLOGY, CULTURE AND ECONOMIC THEORY*

Robert BOYD and Peter J. RICHERSON

University of California, Davis, CA 95616, USA

Received December 1979, final version received March 1980

'To study metaphysics, as they have always been studied appears to me to be like puzzling at astronomy without mechanics.'

Charles Darwin, *N notebook*, p. 5, 3 Oct. 1838.

'Origin of man now proved. — Metaphysics must florish. — He who understand baboon would do more toward metaphysics than Locke.'

Charles Darwin, *M notebook*, p. 84, 16 Aug. 1838.

1. Introduction

The summer and fall of 1838 were a period of intense effort in the life of Charles Darwin, culminating late in the year with the first formulation of the theory of evolution by inherited variation and selective retention. His recently transcribed [Gruber and Barrett (1974)] *M* and *N notebooks* on 'Man, Mind and Materialism' show that Darwin believed at the outset that a valid theory of evolution would have profound consequences for the study of human behavior. Darwin's logic was simple and compelling. Humans are descended from apes. The differences between men and their primate ancestors are due to natural selection. Therefore human nature is not a question for philosophical speculation but rather scientific inquiry; an understanding of natural selection coupled with knowledge of the environment in which humans evolved will yield a science of man.

Darwin's sanguine prediction notwithstanding, evolutionary biology has made very little real contribution to the social sciences, largely because biologists failed to develop an adequate theory of the evolution of the social behavior of any animal, human or otherwise.[1] In the past two decades,

---

*A version of this paper was presented at the meeting of the Western Economic Association, June 1979. The authors would like to thank Richard Day, Victor Goldberg, Jack Hirshleifer and Scott Moreland for their helpful comments on earlier drafts. As always thanks to Dolores DuMont for her patience.

[1]Perhaps the most telling early case of the failure of Darwin's ideas to persuade other observers about the human case is Wallace's (1905) exception of humans from the operation of natural selection. The rejection of Darwinian perspectives by the mainstream of twentieth century social sciences is an historical process of some complexity. Some elements include the

however, evolutionary ecology has rapidly developed to the point where such a theory is now available. It is this theory and the supporting evidence that are the subject of E.O. Wilson's synthetic review, *Sociobiology*. Inevitably, sociobiological theory has been applied to human behavior and, perhaps also inevitably, the response of most social scientists to these efforts has been extremely critical.[2] In contrast, some economists, particularly those who conceive of economics as a general theory of human behavior, have been

---

fact that natural selection was ill appreciated until the mid-century synthesis [Gruber and Barrett (1974)], that Social Darwinism was not very Darwinian [Leeds (1974)], and that in experimental psychology evolutionary hypotheses were, until quite recently, regarded as unscientific [Garcia, McGowan and Green (1972)]. For whatever reasons, it is clear that the biological and social scientific views of humans have produced a set of contradictory and paradoxical positions that we know as the nature-nurture problem. The most influential modern attempt to reconcile Darwinian evolutionary theory ('nature') with the position of the social sciences and humanities that our species possesses unique properties because we are cultural ('nurture') was that of Dobzhansky (1962). Rather sensibly, Dobzhansky argued that both genes and culture interact in humans in a unified evolutionary process. But it is quite clear that his treatment of the mechanics of the unified process was a recipe for diplomatically ignoring critical problems rather than resolving them. Within the space of a single page of *Mankind Evolving*, Dobzhansky (p. 20) first asserts that 'The interrelations between the biological and cultural components of human evolution may be brought out most clearly if we consider that they seem to serve the same basic function — adaptation to and control of man's environment'. Assuming the usual neo-Darwinian definition of adaptation as fitness enhancement, this statement sounds like simple biological determinism — nature paramount. However, after briefly recounting the biological basis of the capacity for culture and the adaptive advantages of culture he writes '...in producing the genetic basis of culture, biological evolution has transcended itself — it has produced the superorganic'. If Darwin could have written the first quote, certainly Wallace (and most contemporary social scientists) would approve of the second. Then, as if to put a fine point on the paradox, Dobzhansky goes on to say that the 'superorganic has not annulled the organic'. Dobzhansky's opinions thus gave an authoritative justification to the common practice of both human biologists and social scientists during the middle half of the century — confident pursuit of research questions without much interaction with each other except in the context of disputes framed by the 'nature-nurture' dichotomy.

[2]The modern version of the nature-nurture controversy began with the semi-popular applications of ethological ideas to humans by Lorenz (1966), the occasional interest displayed by social scientists in this body of information [e.g., Tiger and Fox (1971)] and similar books and papers. The greatly increased sophistication of the theory on the evolutionary biology of animal social organization reviewed in E.O. Wilson's treatise *Sociobiology* (1975) and the synthetic writings of Alexander (1974) has led both to a considerable literature interpreting various human behaviors as strategies for optimizing genetic fitness [e.g., Hamilton (1975), Hartung (1976), Irons (1979), Alexander (1977), Greene (1978), Trivers (1974), Van den Berghe and Barash (1977), Van den Berghe (1975)] and to a highly ideological objection based on the rationale that so interpreting human behavior implies that significant genetic differences must exist within and between human groups and hence that sociobiological models can buttress ideologies of race discrimination and class domination [e.g., Allen et al. (1975), Allen et al. (1976), Sahlins (1976b)]. Clearly any ideological message could be read from sociobiology partly because of the problem of the Naturalistic Fallacy [Moore (1903)] as Petersen and Somit (1978) show. For our purposes here, one might have hoped that the challenge of sociobiological theories would have produced a detailed, positive statement of a 'nurture' position to contrast with the relatively clear statement of the sociobiologists. However, to our knowledge, no adequate one exists. See Richerson's (1976) critique of Sahlin's more technical book *Culture and Practical Reason* (1976a) in this connection. Gould's (1976) analysis of the problem is essentially the same as Dobzhansky's.

very receptive. Hirshleifer (1977) has gone so far as to propose that the other social sciences be divided by the neighboring academic powers of sociobiology and economics. We are, in many ways, sympathetic to this proposal. Ultimately, the social sciences must rest on a theory of human nature that has its roots in evolutionary biology, and we believe that such a theory will share the deductive theoretical approach common to both sociobiology and economics.

On the other hand, we believe that conventional sociobiological theory contains a serious lacuna when applied to humans: it takes no explicit account of the fact that a substantial portion of human behavior is acquired culturally. Recently, several investigators, including ourselves, with rather diverse backgrounds have been attempting to amend sociobiological theory to include cultural transmission of behavior — we call the result dual inheritance theory. Our own central conclusion is that even if one makes strongly Darwinian assumptions about the origin of the human capacity for culture, the theorems of sociobiology do not necessarily apply to human behavior. In effect, dual inheritance theory presents economists with a warning and a promise. The warning: dual inheritance models show that the predictions of a too conservatively neo-Darwinian sociobiology theory may not be robust when applied to the human case. Be careful before you make it your own. The promise: dual inheritance models may be useful in attacking some outstanding problems in economic theory.

We will begin by reviewing the features of conventional sociobiological theory that make it attractive to economists. Then we will briefly outline the dual inheritance approach. Finally, we will illustrate both the warning and the promise by applying this approach to a problem drawn from economic theory — the evolutionary theory of the firm.

2. Sociobiology and economic man

Evolutionary ecologists who seek to explain the observed behavior of some species or population, typically begin by assuming that the behavior is the equilibrium result of natural selection. They then apply what might be called the 'fundamental theorem' of evolutionary ecology which holds that the equilibrium result of natural selection is animals who behave in such a way as to maximize a quantity called individual inclusive fitness. The concept of fitness is generally applicable to the evolution of any trait, behavioral or otherwise; it increases with the number of offspring and the probability that those offspring reach adulthood and successfully mate. The adjectives 'individual' and 'inclusive' are of special importance for the study of the evolution of social behavior. A fundamental aspect of social traits is that the fitness of any given individual depends not only on its own behavior but also on the behavioral traits of other individuals in the population with which it interacts socially. The fitness of such traits is said to be frequency dependent, and when this is the case, the traits that maximize the average fitness of the population may be different than the traits that maximize the fitness of the individual. For example, the average fitness of a population of predators might be maximized if their behavior resulted in maintaining the stock of their prey at the point of maximum sustained yield, but selection will favor individuals who harvest at a higher rate. Thus it is sometimes argued that the result of natural selection is predators who overexploit their prey. Numerous other examples should occur to the economist reader as the analogy with the problem of the voluntary provision of public goods is both clear and correct. The main point is that, in general, the natural selection process behaves 'as if' it optimizes fitness at the level of the individual. The major exception to this generalization is when the interacting individuals are genetic kin. In this case selection can be shown to weigh a marginal change in the fitness of a relative, caused by a modification of one's own behavior, compared to one's own fitness by a factor called the coefficient of relationship, r. In the usual case with monogamous matings r is $1/2$ for sibs, $1/4$ aunts and uncles and grandparents, $1/8$ for cousins and so on. Thus the more closely related the social group, the more that selection will favor group beneficial traits (e.g., the provision of costly public goods).

When an attempt is made to apply the body of theory that derives from this general approach to the explanation of human behavior a problem immediately arises: How does one account for the rather extreme behavioral diversity of the human species both between and within cultural groups? There are two possible explanations. Different behaviors may result from genetic differences between individuals or from the interaction of a general genetic program with the particular ecological and social environment in which an individual finds itself. For non-human organisms it is apparent that both these sources of behavioral diversity are important, but the great majority of human sociobiologists believe that the latter mechanism is of overwhelming importance in humans. This view is supported by empirical evidence that the genetic differences between human groups are relatively trivial.

Thus sociobiology makes several general statements about human nature. These can be translated into the terminology of economics as follows:

(1) Individuals should, for the most part, behave so as to maximize some (utility) function by their consumption of various resources (goods). In the past, at least, this utility function should have been closely related to the number and quality of one's offspring, but given the rapid change in modern technological societies, this need no longer be precisely true.

(2) The main exception to statement (1) is that individual utility functions should contain as arguments the consumption of relatives. The consumption of near relatives should be more important than distant ones.

(3) More complex patterns of social behavior amongst unrelated individuals result from the interaction of selfish individuals. There are no tendencies towards solidarity, cooperation or altruism other than those that are in accord with the interests of the actors.

(4) Behavioral differences between individuals are most likely not due to genetic differences between individuals but rather to the response of the same genetic program to different environments. In more familiar terms — human behavior results from *choice* based on a utility function whose general properties are similar to all people in all times.

Simply put, sociobiology predicts that natural selection should have produced *Homo economicus*.[3] This is a very powerful argument on which to base incursions by economists into the other social sciences. A theory of molecular biology that required atoms to have different properties than those predicted by chemistry would be untenable. Similarly, if sociobiology is accepted as an adequate theory of the evolution of human behavior, non-economic paradigms of human social behavior, such as functionalism in sociology or substantive economics in anthropology, become suspect, and economists should feel encouraged in their attempts to apply the economic paradigm to 'non-economic' behavior.

It is perhaps not surprising that it is precisely these conclusions of sociobiological theory that social scientists in fields outside economics find most objectionable. The usual objection to human sociobiology is that our behavior is culturally determined and thus results that assume genetic determination of behavior are not applicable. A common reply amongst sociobiologists is that since the capacity for culture *arose* by the process of natural selection, therefore the behaviors that result *must be adaptive*.[4] There has been surprisingly little theoretical attention given to this problem.[5] Our

---

[3]The importance of statement (4) to economic theory has been pointed out by Stigler and Becker (1977). Sociobiological theory is largely silent on how perfectly organisms ought to optimize in the presence of costly or imperfect information. [For an exception see Arnold (1978).] Thus satisficing and similar models are also consistent with a sociobiological interpretation of human behavior.

[4]Although he is critical of sociobiology, even as it applies to non-cultural animals, Durham (1976, 1977, 1978) provides the plainest statement of this argument.

[5]Campbell (1965) is the first modern author to argue that the Darwinian mechanism of natural selection is so general that is must apply to cultural as well as the genetic inheritance and that a theory of human evolution therefore should begin by taking seriously the similarities of genetic and cultural inheritance. This idea is perhaps implicit in Darwin's (1871) ideas of human evolution. Darwin never rejected the possibility of inherited effects of use and disuse and in *The Descent of Man* frequently discussed the idea of 'inherited habit' as being important in the ineritance of the 'intellectual and moral facilities'. It seems likely to us that Darwin was reluctant to abandon the Lamarckian notion of inheritance of acquired variation because of the obvious need for such an effect to account for what we now distinguish as cultural influences on the behavior of humans. Not wanting to consider humans radically distinct in this regard [see Galef (1976) for a modern discussion of the social transmission of acquired behavior in non-human animals], and lacking any useful understanding of mechanisms of inheritance, Darwin

goal is to amend neo-Darwinian theory to include the possibility of cultural transmission of behavior and then determine what, if any, changes are required in its conclusions.

3. A sketch of dual inheritance theory

We begin by defining culture quite broadly as the transmission of the determinants of behavior from individual to individual, and thus from generation to generation, by social learning, imitation or some other similar process. From our point of view, the essence of culture is that it constitutes a second, supplementary system of inheritance. The consequences of having a second (cultural) system of inheritance are best understood by contrasting the evolutionary process of a population of organisms with cultural transmission of phenotype with that of another population whose evolution involves only genetic transmission. Fig. 1 gives a schematic representation of the evolution of two such populations.[6] For simplicity, we assume that these organisms have discrete generations and perfectly synchronized life histories with discrete, non-overlapping stages. A generation is defined to start at a point during the life cycle after development but before reproduction. At this time each population can be characterized by a distribution of phenotypes,[7] which we will label ϕ_t. In order to reproduce, individual organisms must survive until the appropriate time to perhaps do such things as obtain territories, establish a position in a dominance hierarchy, win mating contests, attract mates and so on. The net effect of all these ecological

---

simply avoided any distinction between what we now call genes and culture. Of course, if pangenesis had turned out to be a correct theory of inheritance, the modern radical distinction based on underlying mechanics might not have been required. Campbell's point is that our better understanding of inheritance mechanisms and the clear distinction between genes and culture does not invalidate Darwin's broad claims about efficacy of natural selection. Quite the contrary, selection may be the *only* fundamental mechanism for generating the ordered structures of biotic and cultural phenomena. See also extensions and elaborations of Campbell's argument and an account of the intellectual history of the idea [Campbell (1975)]. For more recent work in this area see Durham (1976, 1977, 1978), Ruyle (1973), Cloak (1975), Ruyle, Cloak, Slobodkin and Durham (1977), Pulliam and Dunford (1980), Barkow (1977), Richerson and Boyd (1978), Boyd and Richerson (1980). The rigorous, theoretical examination of cultural inheritance using the mathematical approach of population genetics has been initiated in a very important series of papers by Cavalli-Sforza and Feldman (see note 10). This literature should be distinguished from a much larger one in which the resemblances between cultural and genetic inheritance are noted but in which either the differences are held to make culture so radically different from genes as to make the issue not worth detailed examination [this is the conventional treatment in basic Anthropology texts, e.g., Harris (1971)] or in which the issue is not so systematically explored [e.g., Bajema (1972), Dawkins (1976), Geertz (1966), Gerard, Kluckhohn and Rapoport (1956), Harris (1960), Lorenz (1977)].

[6]This figure is adapted from Lewontin (1974) and a similarly amended one presented by Cavalli-Sforza and Feldman in their class on cultural evolution, Stanford, California, 1978.

[7]Phenotype refers to the actual, observable behavior, morphology and physiology of an organism. The genotype is the genetic code or message carried by an organism.

processes will be that some phenotypes will be more successful than others and the distribution of reproductivity effective phenotypes in the population after these events, which we will label ϕ_t^g, will, in general, be different from the initial distribution of phenotypes, ϕ_t. The complex of processes that transform ϕ_t into ϕ_t^g is the differential survival and reproduction portion of the process of natural selection. Recombination of gametes then leads to a distribution of genotypes, G_{t+1}, that will lead to individuals in a population of offspring (the inherited variation part of natural selection).

a.

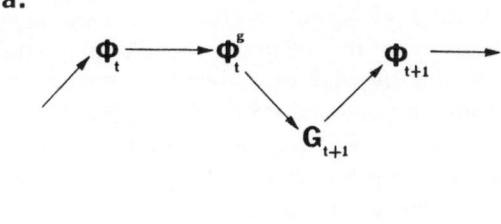

b.

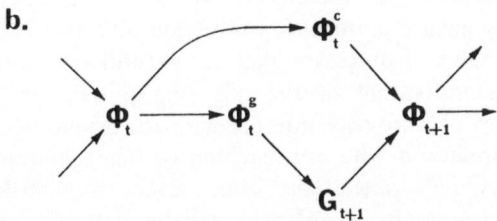

Fig. 1. Part a represents ordinary genetic evolution. ϕ_t is the distribution of phenotypes in the population prior to selection and ϕ_t^g is the distribution after selection of individuals who participate in reproduction. Mating creates a distribution of zygotes with the distribution of genotypes G_{t+1}. The interaction of genotypes and environment yields a new distribution of phenotypes, ϕ_{t+1}. Part b represents the evolution of a culture bearing organism. ϕ_t, ϕ_t^g and G_{t+1} have the same meaning as above. ϕ_t^c is the distribution of phenotypes participating in cultural transmission. ϕ_{t+1} results in the interaction of G_{t+1}, ϕ_t^c and the environment.

In the non-cultural population (fig. 1a) the distribution of genotypes will be transformed by the processes of ontogeny into a new population of mature individuals to begin the next generation. The essence of neo-Darwinian theory is that if the selection processes that transform ϕ_t into ϕ_t^g favor certain kinds of phenotypes, say some optimal size or diet, and if any part of the phenotypic variation is inherited, then ϕ_{t+1} will have a higher frequency of these favored individuals than ϕ_t. After some number of generations, an equilibrium will be reached in which the forces of selection increasing the frequency of the optimal phenotype will be balanced by the random forces of mutation and non-inherited environmental phenotypic variability. In reality, the details of the population dynamics of the organism and of genetic transmission may greatly complicate this simple picture, but most evolutionary ecologists dealing with complex behavioral traits subject to polygenic control assume that at equilibrium the mean individual in the population approximate the selectively optimal phenotype.[8]

In a cultural population the evolutionary problems are, in some respects, analogous to, although in other respects rather different from, a purely genetic population. At least some individuals in the parent population must survive until the appropriate time for cultural transmission. The extent to which they are imitated by, or have an opportunity to teach, individuals in the offspring population may also depend on more than surviving beyond genetic reproduction. It will be necessary to stay in proximity to at least some individuals in the offspring population, which in turn may entail obligations to the offspring or its relatives. Relative success in cultural transmission may also depend on attaining a particular social position, for example, teacher, priest, or big man. The net effect of all these processes is that the distribution of reproductively effective phenotypes with respect to culture, ϕ_t^c, will, in general, be different from both ϕ_t and ϕ_t^g. That is, selective processes will cause some phenotypes to be more likely to teach or be imitated than others, but phenotypes which ensure genetic reproduction will not necessarily ensure cultural reproduction and visa-versa. We will call this analogous complex of processes 'cultural natural selection'. At this point, for any particular individual in the offspring population, the genetically controlled processes of ontogeny interact with the phenotypes of individuals in the parental population who are teaching or being imitated to determine the offspring individual's phenotype. Thus, given the distribution of geno-types, G_{t+1}, that results from ordinary genetic natural selection, and the distribution of phenotypes, ϕ_t^c, that results from cultural and genetic natural selection *and* the rules of cultural transmission, we could, at least in theory, predict the distribution of phenotypes that would begin the next generation, ϕ_{t+1}.

This process, which we have termed dual inheritance, is more complicated than ordinary genetic transmission. However, a rough but simple characterization of the equilibrium result, analogous to the neo-Darwinian principle of fitness maximization that applies to genetic inheritance, is relatively straightforward. First, we will suppose that the rules of cultural transmission are *fixed* and deduce equilibrium phenotype. Then we will consider how natural selection might affect the rules of cultural transmission.

We have defined cultural transmission as the inheritance of determinants of phenotype through learning or imitation. This definition carries with it the implication that, holding everything else constant, if the frequency of some phenotype in the population of cultural transmitters is increased, the frequency of that phenotype in the offspring population will be increased.

---

[8]For discussions of the pitfalls involved in optimization arguments, see Stearns (1977), Maynard-Smith (1978) and Oster and Wilson (1978, ch. 8).

Or, put another way, like creates like. The processes we have labeled cultural natural selection are one class of forces which will change the frequencies of various phenotypes in ϕ_i^c. Thus, if cultural natural selection favors some phenotype, say some optimal amount of parental care, then all other things held constant, we would expect that phenotype to increase each generation. To take a hypothetical example, suppose that children inherit their social behavior by imitating their fathers and mothers. In this case, one might suppose that those fathers who provide substantial amounts of parental care, and by doing so maintain frequent contact with their offspring, are more likely to be imitated than those fathers who largely absent themselves after conception and leave socialization mostly to mothers. If all the other forces determining phenotypes were held constant, one might expect that the frequency of paternal care would increase. A simple calculation will show that this is the case for any trait that is copied disproportionately from mothers when fathers are neglectful. In the case of parental care, if mothers who were raised by devoted fathers have some tendency to raise devoted sons, even when her husband is neglectful, male parental care will increase to fixation. So long as fathers must be actively present to transmit their behavior, the neglectful phenotype will suffer in cultural transmission. Practically speaking, a mother raised to value devoted fathers may not only pass the trait to sons directly but also substitute other devoted males as role models when husbands are absent, including her own father and brothers. Since not all fathers are actually devoted, the effect must be complicated by other factors as in the case of genetic inheritance.

The abstract notion that culture is a system of inheritance, thus producing important analogies between culture and genes, does not strike everyone as immediately commonsensical. After all, we all have the experience of rejecting some of our parent's beliefs and with the feeling that we play a more active role in acquiring our cultural repertoire than we do in acquiring our genotype. However, the argument does not depend on culture being exactly like genes nor upon denying individuals an active role in acquiring culture. It does require that enough culture be acquired by simply copying of others' behavior so that a reasonably strong statistical correlation exists between the culture individuals possess and the culture of their 'parents', where cultural 'parents' include not only an individual's biological parents, but also other people whose behavior is available to be observed and imitated. Two general lines of evidence suggest that the like-begets-like effect is present in culture. One is the mechanism of cultural acquisition. Rosenthal and Zimmerman (1978) review an extensive series of experimental studies of children's acquisition of their culture repertoire, showing how efficiently and automatically children induce rules from behavior modelled for them by adults and stably incorporate such rules into their behavior. Even unusual and out-of-normal-sequence rules are copied in experimental settings, showing that the development of a cultural repertoire is not closely controlled by natural ontogeny. These studies underpin the common idea of psychologists that basic and enduring personality traits are determined, in part at least, by cultural acquisitions in childhood. No doubt older juveniles and adults play a more active role when imitating other adults, but even here the evidence from studies of dialect change [Labov (1972)] suggests an important role for an unconscious copying process. The other line of evidence is the observed high parent-offspring correlation for many cultural traits. In the case of cultural traits acquired by young children, culture behaves so much like genes that the heritable variance each causes is almost impossible to separate. The controversy over the genetic versus cultural determination of I.Q. is a prominent example. Only the most careful studies of inter-racial adoptions [Scarr and Weinberg (1977)] have shown directly how large is the cultural component of I.Q. Less rigorously, a large number of observations of parent-offspring correlations for such things as political party affiliations, religious preferences, drinking and smoking habits, and the like indicate the relative effectiveness and stability of cultural transmission. The effectiveness and stability of the adult-acquired repertoire is less well studied and admittedly more problematical, but an effective, partly unconscious socialization process seems to impose widespread similarities of behavior among adults with extensive exposure to one another. For example, at professional meetings, one can observe many marked differences between and similarities within simple observable traits of ecologists, anthropologists and economists (to draw upon our own observations). Dress among ecologists tends to be carelessly informal, among anthropologists academic-tweedy in the older generation but aggressively work-shirt informal in the younger generation, and among economists even business suits are observed. More generally, the fact that different cultures show considerable continuity in time and space is indirect evidence that cultural inheritance is an important effect.

Our point in emphasizing the idea that culture is an inheritance system is not that this fact immediately allows broad generalizations about behavior, but that it directs theoretical attention to the evolutionary forces that control the content of culture. As Campbell (1975) has cogently argued, natural selection is certainly one force that must be considered, since it will act on any system of heritable variation. But even a preliminary analysis suggests other evolutionary forces are important. In fact there are three other general classes of directional forces that may affect the evolutionary dynamic of such an organism. First, ordinary genetic natural selection acting in parallel to cultural natural selection may be increasing the frequency of quite different phenotypes. To return to our hypothetical example, suppose that in some particular ecological circumstances that minimizing paternal care is the behavioral phenotype favored by genetic natural selection.[9] Thus the two

---

[9]Polygyny is in the fact mating structure in a large majority of mammalian species.

selective processes will be competitive — selection on genes increasing the frequency of rakes and cultural natural selection increasing the frequency of devoted fathers.

Secondly, there is the possibility that, unlike genetic transmission, the cultural transmission process itself may not be neutral with respect to the behavior being transmitted. That is, individuals in the offspring population may be genetically predisposed to more readily imitate or know some traits rather than others. We have labeled this phenomenon 'biased transmission'. For example, even though devoted fathers may be much better situated to enculturate their offspring, the offspring may much more readily learn to be rakes from an occasional odd contact with such an individual, all the while tending to acquire many other behavioral traits from their fathers. Unlike the case of genetic transmission, the offspring phenotype can interact with the parental phenotype in the process of transmission to bias what is acquired from other individuals. This effect occurs because cultural transmission occurs sequentially, after genetic transmission and typically after the transmission of other cultural traits. In the particular example we have been considering, it may be easy to acquire rakish cultural traits because of genetically coded sexual pleasure.

Third, cultural inheritance is Lamarckian. The generation of cultural variation is not entirely dependent on chance mutation. Trial-and-error learning and strategic calculation may produce variants that increase felt satisfactions of the original learners, and these may be spread to children and colleagues without the imitators paying the cost of learning errors.

The equilibrium phenotype resulting from the repeated action of these several directional forces will depend on the details of the genetic and cultural life histories of the organism and particularly on the details of the rules of transmission. One crucial task in the development of a mature theory of the evolution of culture-bearing organism will be the building of a family of detailed dynamic models, akin to those used in population genetics, that allow the determination of the properties of this equilibrium. A significant beginning in this direction has been made by Feldman and Cavalli-Sforza[10]

[10]By explicit, dynamic models, we mean ones which predict trajectory of the distribution of phenotypes and genotypes in a population given some set of cultural transmission rules and cultural and genetic selective environments. The construction of such models is crucial because the evolutionary properties of such systems can be surprisingly different from those associated with ordinary genetic transmission. By far the most complete and sophisticated treatment of these questions may be found in a series of papers by Cavalli-Sforza and Feldman. In Cavalli-Sforza and Feldman (1973a, b) and Feldman and Cavalli-Sforza (1975), models of blending inheritance with more than two cultural parents in finite populations are examined. Subsequently in Cavalli-Sforza and Feldman (1976, 1978) and Feldman and Cavalli-Sforza (1977), they consider complex genetic and cultural transmission of a single metrical trait by two parents selected from an infinite population subject to a single selection criteria. Finally, in Feldman and Cavalli-Sforza (1976), they consider a very general model of bi-parental complex transmission of a two valued cultural trait and a genetic modifier trait, again subject to a single selection criteria. This last model is especially interesting because it considers the properties of a

in a very important series of papers but much work remains to be done in this area. However, to make our point here, we do not require a detailed characterization of the equilibrium, rather, it is only necessary that *under some rules of transmission* that the equilibrium phenotype can differ substantially from that which would be predicted by ordinary neo-Darwinian theory. And this much is clear from the argument given above. If cultural selection is strong enough, genetic selection, biases, and Lamarckian effects weak enough, and the rules of transmission allow a cultural inheritance to exert a strong influence on phenotype, the phenotype that characterizes the mean individual in the population will be shifted away from the phenotype favored by ordinary genetic selection towards that favored by cultural selection.

The question thus becomes, given that some rules of cultural transmission allow such a thing to happen, can one imagine any circumstances in which ordinary natural selections would result in a system of cultural transmission with such rules? In other words, is it conceivable that having a cultural system of inheritance, with rules ensuring that phenotype cannot be governed by genetic considerations alone, can be a genetic advantage?

At least initially, the organic structures, which we will call culture capacity, that allow cultural transmission will also determine the extent to which the cultural system has a different life cycle from genes, such as the ability to acquire culture from age mates or teachers in addition to biological parents. To explain the origin of any particular form of cultural transmission, one must be able to show why individuals with that kind of culture capacity have a genetic selective advantage over culture capacities leading to other forms of cultural transmission or no culture capacity at all. As illustrated in the hypothetical example of devoted fathers vs. rakes, the equilibrium value of culturally transmitted traits will generally be different from the trait value that is optimal with respect to genetic natural selection. Since the organic adaptations that constitute culture capacity are themselves genetically transmitted, one would expect that culture capacities which cause the dual inheritance process to diverge from ordinary genetic inheritance to be selected against and culture capacities which constrain the dual inheritance so that it results in phenotypes near the genetic optimum to be selected for.

Thus, culture capacities with strongly divergent life histories could only arise if there is some additional genetic benefit directly associated with having an inheritance system with a different life history. Essentially, the fact

---

cultural transmission system whose rules are quite different from genetic transmission. See May (1977) for a commentary on some of these models. Boyd and Richerson (manuscript) analyse the interaction of multi-parent, non-linear cultural transmission of a two valued trait and a single selection criteria in spatially disaggregated populations. Much work remains to be done in this area. For example, there is no explicit dynamic analysis of the very important case of a dual inheritance system with two selection criteria or one in which the two systems have different generation times, nor of the asymmetries made possible by more than one cultural trait or many other phenomena that are likely to have interesting and perhaps even crucial evolutionary properties.

that the equilibrium value of culturally transmitted traits can diverge from the genetic optimum imposes a cost on having cultural transmission. A particular form of culture capacity will be selected for only if there are some over-balancing benefits. Or put anthropomorphically, culture has to offer genes something they cannot do for themselves as a price of some liberty to respond independently to evolutionary forces.

Much of our current research is directed at this problem. We postulate simple asymmetric systems of cultural transmission, e.g., transmission by more than two 'cultural' parents or 'horizontal' transmission between individuals of a single generation, and investigate their evolutionary properties, with an eye to conditions under which they might be genetically advantageous. While this work is far from complete, we have already discovered several examples of asymmetric cultural rules of transmission that can be of genetic benefit. While this work is too involved to describe here, generally speaking, asymmetric cultural transmission systems often allow an organism to better adapt to spatially or temporally varying environments. For example, multiple parent cultural transmission systems may allow local populations to more accurately adapt to local environmental conditions.

Given that asymmetric systems exist which can increase the genetic fitness of their bearers in spite of the fact that many culturally transmitted traits will not appear to maximize genetic fitness, conventional sociobiological theory may not predict the resulting phenotypes.

Contrary to this reasoning, some sociobiologists [Irons (1979), Alexander (1979), Durham (1978)] have asserted that the forces of biased transmission and the Lamarckian incorporation of acquired traits, are *a priori*, sufficient to insure that culturally acquired traits maximize genetic fitness. While this view is not necessarily incorrect, we find it extremely implausible for several reasons: It is an empirical fact that much of human cultural transmission is strongly asymmetrical in terms of the identity and number of cultural parents and the timing of transmission, and there appears to be little important genetic variation in the determinants of behavior between human groups. There is little reason to believe that biases and learning criteria are sufficiently detailed to specify the behavior in the vast variety of cultural environments that characterize the human species. Moreover, if one accepts the theoretical argument that the advantage of cultural transmission of behavior is a more flexible and faster system of adaptation, it is hard to conceive of a mechanism by which culture can be subjected to detailed genetic control without sacrificing its speed and flexibility.

4. Cultural transmission and the evolutionary theory of the firm

To this point we have argued that sociobiology predicts that natural selection should have resulted in economic man, and that if sociobiology is regarded as an adequate theory of human origins, then this coincidence provides a strong *a priori* case for extending economic analysis to non-economic aspects of human social behavior. By the same token, if we are correct and the inclusion of cultural transmission can radically alter the predictions that one might make based on man's evolutionary origins, then one should be cautious about the assumption of economic man even within the economic sphere, since the explicit inclusion of cultural transmission in models of human behavior may create rather different kinds of behavior.

In the remainder of this paper we will illustrate some of the effects of cultural transmission the context of an example taken from economic theory, the evolutionary theory of the firm. The purpose of this example is twofold: First we will show how asymmetric cultural transmission can lead to behavior not predicted by sociobiological theory, and second illustrate how models of cultural transmission can be applied to economic problems. In these models we will assume that the individuals are genetically identical and that behavior results from the interaction of cultural change and individual strategizing. Given the slow rate of genetic change and the lack of genetic differentiation among modern human groups, this assumption will be typical of applications of cultural transmission models to contemporary human behavior. Consideration of the simultaneous evolution of both the genetic and cultural systems is necessary only when one is concerned with the origins of the human capacity for culture.

In sociobiology it is predicted and in economics it is assumed that individuals seek to maximize their own utility. When individuals interact in a group, they pursue group goals only to the extent that they coincide with individual ones. This assumption conflicts with the apparently purposive behavior of many groups, of which the economic firm is a prominent example. As many critics of microeconomic theory have pointed out, the notion that firms behave as unitary profit maximizers seems to be inconsistent with the fundamental assumption that individuals are rational utility maximizers. Surely, it is argued, the interest of individuals and the interest of the firm cannot be perfectly coincident. The literature dealing with various aspects of this problem is extensive.

We will focus on one particular analysis of this problem — namely the evolutionary theory of the firm explored by Alchian (1950), Enke (1951), Friedman (1953), Winter (1966, 1971, 1975) and Nelson and Winter (1974) and others. This literature is reviewed by Hirshleifer (1977). We have chosen this example for pedagogical reasons; it is a problem where economists have attempted to resolve the conflict between individual optimization and group performance using an explicitly evolutionary approach. We hope that this example will allow a clear illustration of the potentially important effects of cultural inheritance in a familiar context. We do not suppose that the models we will present precisely describe socialization or decision making in real corporations.

The basic notion of the evolutionary theory of the firm is simple. Suppose that by some unspecified mechanisms, managers in a particular firm arrive at some mechanism for making decisions about, say, output and price. Winter (1975) calls this the firm's 'routine'. It is further assumed that by chance various firms arrive at different routines. Economic competition will favor those firms whose routines yield higher profits. If this process is allowed to continue in an unchanging environment, only those firms whose routines lead to profit maximizing behavior will ultimately survive bankruptcy. Thus, natural selection will result in profit maximizing behavior regardless of the motives of managers, and economic theorists, at least when considering long-run equilibrium, are justified in assuming that firms act 'as if' their managers had the unitary goal of maximizing profits.

This defense of profit maximizing firms has been attacked on several grounds [especially by Winter (1966, 1975)]. Most of these criticisms center about the efficacy of natural selection in changing environments, i.e., natural selection cannot lead to firms whose behavior tracks a changing environment in an optimal way.[11] In contrast, most authors seem to agree that in a *constant* environment, the natural selection argument in effect rescues the profit maximizing firm. We believe, to the contrary, that even in this special case, the assumption that managers are rational utility maximizers is inconsistent with natural selection resulting in profit maximization or, in fact, with natural selection acting on characteristics of a firms at all.

For natural selection to be effective, the behavior of firms must have some continuity in time. Firms that are characterized by a particular routine during period t must have some strong tendency to exhibit the same routine in period $t+1$. If decision rules are freely *chosen* by ideally rational managers, there is no reason that any single firm should exhibit such continuity. Given an environment and the utility function of the manager (or managers), behavior should be determined. There may be differences between firms due to the fact that their managers have different utility functions or different expectations about the future, but given that there is executive turnover, it does not seem to us that rational choice can lead to the necessary continuity in the firm's routine.[12] For example, in period t, firm A

[11]Winter (1966) provides an extensive catalogue of reasons why in a temporally varying environment natural selection might not lead to profit maximization. In general, evolutionary problems involving such environments are much more difficult than equilibrium problems since the dynamics are of importance [e.g., Gillespie (1978)]. The dynamic properties of biological evolution are often very sensitive to the details of the underlying genetic mechanism, which for most traits is unknown.

[12]There are several factors other than cultural transmission that might lead to some continuity in the behavior of firms over time. Presumably different economic environments would often evoke different responses from rational managers. Thus if different firms face different environments that are autocorrelated in time, there might be sustained differences in the behavior of firms. One example of this phenomenon would be capital inputs that survive more than one 'generation'. This might be particularly important for firms with natural resource endowments.

might be managed by an ageing executive whose utility function places a high value on the 'quiet life', while in period $t+1$, they might be replaced by ambitious younger men who place a high value on their reputation for generating corporate growth. In firm B the reverse might be true. In evolutionary biology such variation is termed 'non-heritable'; selection acting on non-heritable variance cannot lead to directional, cumulative change.

An amendment of some sort is required so that managers in firm A 'traditionally' do things one way and in firm B, another. The one we suggest is that tradition is maintained in a firm by a sort of enculturation process — new employees learn from old employees how things are done at firm A. While several authors [Winter (1966), Leibenstein (1976)] mention corporate traditions in passing, their importance for the natural selection argument has not been clarified. In what follows, we apply one of our models of cultural transmission to the maintenance of such traditions. We will show that selection amongst firms yields profit maximization when traditions are transmitted according to some rules but not others. But the dilemma for economic theory remains; the rules that yield profit maximization by the firm are exactly those that cause managers to act contrary to their own preferences.

First, suppose that the industry is composed of a large number of firms, each with n managers. Each manager can be characterized by one of two possible behaviors, E (for earnest) and S (for easy-going). Every manager has a utility function that causes him to prefer S to E. However, the profitability of a given firm increases monotonically with the number of earnest managers it contains. The profit maximizing firm is characterized by n earnest managers. The probability that a firm goes out of business is inversely proportional to its profitability. This model is meant to provide a very simple caricature of the problem of the firm wherein the interests of managers and the firm diverge, and imperfect information or the costs of policing managerial behavior allow managers at least some latitude to act in their own individual interest. That is, there undoubtedly are important economic forces rewarding earnest managers and punishing easy-going ones, especially reciprocal agreements among managers and between managers and stockholders. But the cost of monitoring and policing these agreements will allow individuals at least some room to pursue their own interests at the expense of the firm's. We suppose an easy-going (S) manager takes advantage of this situation while an earnest (E) manager does not.

The model is roughly consistent with several recent institutional analyses of the firm. For example, Alchian and Demsetz (1972) argue that each manager has some opportunity for undetected slacking and prefers to do so. However, the firm as a whole would be better off if everyone worked to their utmost. Leibenstein (1976) presents data that suggests that the inefficiency due to such slacking can be substantial. Broadly similar views are presented by Hirschman (1970) and Williamson (1975).

If one supposes that each manager chooses his behavior rationally, with perfect knowledge, then the outcome is that every manager will choose S and there will be no variation between firms to select upon. If imperfect information causes managers to erroneously choose E with some probability, sampling error will cause binomial variation in the number of efficient managers, and therefore the profitability of firms. But there will be no correlation between the profitability of a firm from one generation of managers to the next. Simple choice does not lead to heritable traditions within firms.

To create the possibility of traditions, we assume that each firm also contains n management trainees who will become managers upon the retirement of existing managers. Management trainees in firm i permanently adopt behavior E with probability P_E. We assume

$$P_E(q_{i,t}) = q_{i,t} + \beta(q_{i,t}), \tag{1}$$

where $q_{i,t}$ is the proportion of managers[13] in firm i who exhibit earnest (E) behavior, during period t (a period consists of the tenure of one cohort of managers). $\beta(q_{i,t})$ is a non-positive function with the general form shown in fig. 2a.[14] Eq. (1) can be interpreted as follows: Trainees choose their behavior from among the behaviors that they are exposed to. Thus if a firm is composed of n earnest managers, all trainees will be earnest, i.e., there is no independent invention of behavior. The first, linear term indicates that the trainee's choice of whether to be earnest is influenced by the proportion of earnest managers in the firm. The second term, $\beta(q_{i,t})$, represents the influence of the trainee's own interests on his choice of behavior. Increasing the absolute value of $\beta(\cdot)$ increases the relative importance of the trainee's interests and decreases the importance of tradition. Thus in fig. 2b, tradition dominates and in fig. 2c trainee interest dominates the probability that a given trainee will choose to be earnest.

In terms of the more general model of the previous section, the managerial trait is transmitted via biased cultural transmission, with the extent of the bias represented by the importance of the $\beta(\cdot)$ term. As such, we would expect the bias to be in favor of the trait that the individual would prefer; a preference some might argue is ultimately rooted in the genes. Note that we make the assumption that there are no genetic differences in the tendency of managers or trainees to be either earnest or easy-going. Working against the ego-oriented force of biased transmission is cultural natural selection in the

---

[13]Eq. (1) implies that each manager is of equal importance in the socialization process. The results of this paper can be easily generalized to the case where different managers have different linear weightings.

[14]To be more precise, β is a non-positive unimodal function for $0 \leq q_{i,t} \leq 1$ such that $\beta(0) = \beta(1) = 0$. Moreover $|\beta(q_{i,t})| \leq q_{i,t}$ for each $q_{i,t}$.

form of the higher rates of bankruptcies in firms with a higher proportion of
easy going managers.

While this model of choice is certainly not a standard one in economics,
we believe that it is intuitively reasonable. Trainees are unlikely to have
perfect knowledge of the costs and benefits of the different ways they might
behave in their future positions. They must infer this information from

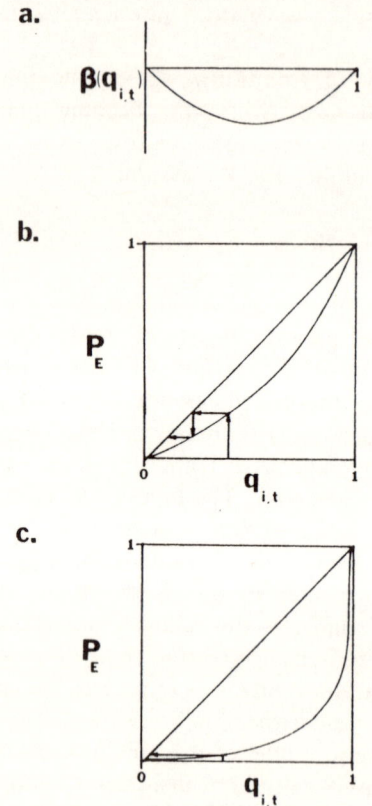

Fig. 2. Part a shows the assumed form of the function $\beta(\cdot)$. Parts b and c show the form of P_E
as a function of $q_{i,t}$. In Part c, the trainees more strongly prefer trait S. The arrows show the
time path of $q_{i,t}$ assuming no other forces acted to determine managerial behavior.

observing existing managers. If, as was supposed, the benefits are due to
undetected slacking, they may be difficult to perceive. Thus trainees might
reasonably use the proportion of managers exhibiting a trait as a measure of
its desireability.

Eq. (1) will also result if one supposes that each trainee associates closely
enough with a small number of managers, their 'mentors', so that they have
a good idea of the costs and benefits of different sorts of managerial behavior

and that they choose from among their mentor's behavior rationally. For example, suppose each trainee has two mentors. If both of them are either earnest or easy going, then the trainee chooses that behavior. If one mentor is earnest and the other easy going, then the trainee always chooses S. If one supposes that trainees associate with mentors at random then

$$P_E = q_{i,t} - \tfrac{1}{2} q_{i,t}(1 - q_{i,t}), \tag{2}$$

which has the same form as (1).

Now suppose that some small fraction, m, of trainees change firms (at random) after adopting their behaviors.[15] Then, assuming firms are large, the proportion of efficient managers in firm i, if it avoids bankruptcy is

$$q_{i,t+1} = P_E(q_{i,t})(1 - m) + m\bar{q}_t, \tag{3}$$

where $\bar{q}$ is the average proportion of efficient managers in the industry. New firms which enter the industry to replace bankrupt ones are assumed to draw their managers from the existing pool, i.e., $q_{i,t+1} = \bar{q}$.

Given the bankruptcy rate as a function of $q_{i,t}$, one can determine the equilibrium of the set of coupled recursions implied by (3). It turns out that these equations are precisely the same as those for a process known as 'classical' group selection in evolutionary theory and thus have been analysed in some detail [e.g., Eshel (1972), Levin and Kilmer (1974), Wade (1978)]. The conclusion of this work is that generally the equilibrium is an industry in which all managers are easy-going. For selection on firms to maintain even a mixture of E and S types requires that n be quite small ($\simeq 10$), m to be quite small (on the order of one individual per firm per period) and the rate of bankruptcy to be high.[16] The reason for this result is intuitive: in each firm, S increases each period because of the tendency of individuals to choose that behavior. This tendency is counteracted by the selection against firms containing large numbers of S individuals. However, this second process is likely to be much weaker since (1) the turnover of managers is likely to occur with much higher frequency than the bankruptcy of firms and (2) the variance between firms upon which selection must act is constantly being eroded by the exchange of individuals (or ideas) between firms and the tendency for individuals to choose S.

[15]It is not necessary to assume that there is an actual exchange of individuals between groups; only that there is some process that leads to some exchange of behaviors between firms. One might suppose that an occasional trainee adopts a behavior observed at conventions or the like.

[16]The relative strength of the inter-firm selection will also depend on the model of entry of new firms that one assumes. If one supposes that the individual managers of entering firms are selected at random from the whole population of managers, then inter-firm selection is very weak. If on the other hand, the management of entering firms is taken en masse from a single existing one, then inter-firm selection will be stronger. This latter case has not been as well analysed as the former. For a discussion in a biological context, see Wade (1978).

The economic natural selection model can be revived if one is willing to assume a slightly more elaborate rule for cultural transmission. We now suppose that the probability that a trainee in firm i adopts behavior E, P_E is

$$P_E = q_{i,t} + \beta(q_{i,t}) + \delta(q_{i,t}), \tag{4}$$

where $\delta(q_{i,t})$ has the form shown in fig. 3a.[17] This form of $\delta(\cdot)$ was chosen to represent the idea that trainees have some tendency to adopt the behavior that characterizes the majority of the managers in their firm. We have termed this process conformist transmission. In effect we are adding another behavioral postulate. Trainees use the porportion of managers exhibiting a behavior as an indication of its desirability in the particular way specified, i.e., if 60% of the managers are earnest, in the absence of any other information, each trainee has a more than 60% chance of becoming earnest. If conformist transmission is roughly comparable in effect to the tendency to choose S, then $P_E(q_{i,t})$ has the form shown in fig. 3b. Thus, in the absence of any other forces, the equilibrium of the firm depends on its initial state. If it starts with a large enough proportion of E individuals, conformist transmission will overbalance the effects of individual preference and the equilibrium will be a firm composed solely of earnest individuals. If the initial value of $q_{i,t}$ is lower, then the result is a firm composed solely of easy-going managers.

A recursion for $q_{i,t}$ can be written down by making the same assumptions as before. It turns out that when there is conformist transmission (as shown in fig. 3b), the result of the entire process is completely reversed. Under a wide variety of conditions, one can show that selection acting on firms yields an equilibrium in which all firms are composed only of E individuals, i.e., profit maximizing firms.[18] Intuitively, the reason that inter-firm selection is stronger in this case is that the conformist transmission preserves the variation between firms against variability destroying forces of rational choice and exchange of managers (or ideas) between firms. When $\delta(q_{i,t}) \equiv 0$, bankruptcies must occur frequently enough to maintain enough variation between firms for inter-firm selection to act upon. If $\delta(q_{i,t})$ is sufficiently large, some firms will be maintained indefinitely with a high proportion of earnest managers. Since these firms have a higher survival rate, they will eventually predominate in the industry.

---

[17]More precisely, in the range $[0,1]$ δ is a bimodal function such that $\delta(0) = \delta(1/2) = \delta(1) = 0$ and for $0 < q_{i,t} < 1/2$, $\delta(q_{i,t}) < 0$ and for $1/2 < q_{i,t} < 1$, $\delta(q_{i,t}) > 0$. It is also necessary that $|\delta(q_{i,t})| < \min(q_{i,t}, 1 - q_{i,t})$.

[18]The conditions under which this result is obtained are quite broad. There is no restriction on the number of managers per firm or the relative strengths of selection between firms and the preference for the behavior S. The only requirement is that the conformist transmission effect be strong enough to maintain some firms with a large number of E individuals against the diluting effect of exchange of managers.

R. Boyd and P.J. Richerson, Sociobiology, culture and economic theory   117

a.

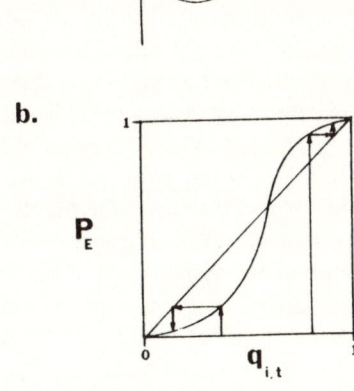

b.

Figs. 3. Part a shows the assumed form of $\delta(\cdot)$. Part b shows the form of P_E as a function of $q_{i,t}$ assuming the action of both individual choice and conformist transmission.

5. Reprise

We hope to convince the reader of three basic points:

(1) Conventional sociobiology predicts that evolution should have produced *Homo economicus* and therefore that human social organization should be explicable in terms of the interactions of selfish rational individuals.
(2) Dual inheritance theory shows that evolution can result in humans whose culturally transmitted behavior is quite different from that predicted by sociobiology or posited by economists. This theory is a simple mechanistic amendment to Darwinian theory and requires no special properties for humans other than a capacity for a cultural system of inheritance.
(3) Cultural inheritance models will be useful to economists precisely because they allow a mechanistic explanation of human behaviors that are troubling or paradoxical under the assumption of self-interested rationality.

The example of economic selection amongst firms was chosen to illustrate these points. Sociobiology and economics both predict that humans should act to maximize their own individual welfare. If groups of individuals, of which the firm is one example, interact ecologically or economically, the collective interest of the group may not be coincident with that of the individual. This problem is, of course, a subject of a large body of theory in economics. The general prediction of both economics and sociobiology is that such systems will not result in behavior at the group optimum. Nonetheless, many such groups, and again firms are an example, *do* appear to behave so as to maximize group goals.

We argue that selection amongst firms staffed by rational selfish maximizers cannot extricate us from this dilemma. To make selection work, we must adopt a new psychological postulate; namely, individuals do not choose their behavior with perfect knowledge from the set of all possible behaviors. Rather, they choose from among the behaviors of other individuals within the firm, and in making this choice, some process causes there to be a positive correlation between the proportion of individuals in a firm who exhibit some behavior and the probability that naive individuals choose that behavior. While this model of human behavior is not standard in economics, common experience lends it plausibility. It seems almost undeniable that we are influenced in our choice of what to do or who to be by what we observe in the people around us.

The central point we wish to make is that this process of cultural transmission of behavior can lead to behavior that is qualitatively different than that predicted by the usual paradigms of economics and sociobiology. In our example, conformist cultural transmission created and maintained variation in the aggregated behavior of individuals in different firms. Firms with a greater proportion of earnest employees had a higher survival rate. Eventually only efficient firms comprised of earnest individuals survived. More generally, systems of cultural transmission can cause persistent, heritable variation in behavior between individuals or groups of individuals. The existence of such variation allows economic (or social) selective processes to operate. If the behaviors preferred by rational individuals differ from the behaviors favored by this cultural selection, the predictions of dual inheritance theory and economic theory (or sociobiological theory) diverge. Put another way, if an individual's choice of behavior is partly determined by the behavior of those around him, then to predict individual behavior, one must know the behavioral composition of the entire population. To predict that composition, one must consider the economic and social processes that affect the population. Dual inheritance models are attempts to construct rudimentary mathematical descriptions of this phenomenon.

There are many other aspects of human behavior which are, at best, only partially explained by the neo-Darwinian or the rationalist paradigm. Behavior under the uncertainty (i.e., probabilities unknown), ritualistic or symbolic behavior and behavior in conflict or game theoretic situations are perhaps the most prominent examples. A unified science of humans must provide an explanation of such phenomena. We believe that even though a simple combination of the *results* of sociobiology and economics will be insufficient to resolve these outstanding puzzles, the *methods* they share indicate the most promising approach for theory. Explicit models of cultural inheritance are a useful starting point for such theorizing.

References

Alchian, A., 1950, Uncertainty, evolution and economic theory, Journal of Political Economy 58, 211-222.

Alchian, A. and H. Demsetz, 1972, Production, information costs and economic organization, Amer. Econ. Rev. 62, 777-795.

Alexander, R.D., 1974, The evolution of social behavior, Ann. Rev. Ecol. Syst. 5, 325-383.

Alexander, R.D., 1977, Natural selection and the analysis of human sociality, in: C.E. Goulden, ed., The changing scene in the natural sciences, 1776-1976, Academy of Natural Sciences, Special Publ. 12 (Philadelphia).

Alexander, R.D., 1979, Evolution and culture, in: N.A. Chagnon and W. Irons, eds., Evolutionary biology and human social behavior: An anthropological perspective (Duxbury Press, North Scituate, MA) 59-79.

Allen, E. et al., 1975, Against sociobiology, The New York Review of Books, Nov. 13, 182, 184-186.

Allen, E. et al., 1976, Sociobiology — another biological determinism, Bioscience 26, 182-186.

Arnold, S.J., 1978, The evolution of a special class of modifiable behaviors in relationship to environmental pattern, Amer. Natur. 112, 415-427.

Bajema, C.J., 1972, Transmission of information about the environment in the human species: A cybernetic view of genetic and cultural evolution, Social Biology 19, 224-226.

Barkow, J., 1977, Culture and sociobiology, Amer. Anthrop. 80, 5-20.

Boyd, R. and P.J. Richerson, 1980, Culture, biology, and the evolution of variation between human groups, in: M. Collins et al., eds., Biology, culture and human evolution (American Association for the Advancement of Science, Washington, DC).

Boyd, R. and P.J. Richerson, manuscript, Multiple parents and non-linear cultural inheritance.

Campbell, D.T., 1965, Variation and selective retention in socio-cultural evolution, in: H.R. Barringer, et al., eds., Social change in developing areas: A reinterpretation of evolutionary theory (Schenkman, Cambridge), 19-49.

Campbell, D.T., 1975, On the conflicts between biological and social evolution and between psychology and moral tradition, Amer. Psychol. 30, 1103-1126.

Cavalli-Sforza, L.L. and M.W. Feldman, 1973a, Models for cultural inheritance I, Group mean and within group variation, Theor. Pop. Biol. 4, 42-55.

Cavalli-Sforza, L.L. and M.W. Feldman, 1973b, Cultural versus biological inheritance: Phenotypic transmission from parents to children (a theory of the effect of parental phenotypes on children's phenotypes), Amer. J. Hum. Genet. 25, 218-637.

Cavalli-Sforza, L.L. and M.W. Feldman, 1976, Evolution of continuous variation: Direct approach through joint distribution of genotypes and phenotypes, Proc. Nat. Acad. Sci. 73, 1689-1692.

Cavalli-Sforza, L.L. and M.W. Feldman, 1978, The evolution of continuous variation, III, Joint transmission of genotype, phenotype and environment, Genetics 90, 391-425.

Cloak, F.T., 1975, Is a cultural ethology possible? Human Ecology 3, 161-182.

Darwin, C., 1871, Descent of man and selection in relation to sex (Murray, London).

Dawkins, R., 1976, The selfish gene (Oxford University Press, New York).

Dobzhansky, T., 1962, Mankind evolving (Columbia University Press, New York).

Durham, W.H., 1976, The adaptive significance of cultural behavior, Human Ecology 4, 89-121.

Durham, W.H., 1977, Adaptive significance of cultural behavior: Comments and a reply, Human Ecology 5, 59-67.

Durham, W.H., 1978, Toward a coevolutionary view of human biology and culture, in: A. Caplan, ed., The sociobiology debate (Harper and Row, New York) 428-448.

Enke, S., 1951, On maximizing profits: A distinction between Chamberlin and Robinson, Amer. Econ. Rev. 41, 566-578.

Eshel, I., 1972, On the neighborhood effect and the evolution of altruistic traits, Theo. Pop. Biol. 3, 258-277.

Feldman, M.W. and L.L. Cavalli-Sforza, 1975, Models for cultural inheritance, A general linear model, Human Biol. 2, 215–226.

Feldman, M.W. and L.L. Cavalli-Sforza, 1976, Cultural and biological evolutionary processes, selection for a trait under complex transmission, Theor. Pop. Biol. 9, 238–259.

Feldman, M.W. and L.L. Cavalli-Sforza, 1977, The evolution of continuous variation, II, Complex transmission and assortative mating, Theor. Pop. Biol. 11, 161–181.

Friedman, M., 1953, Essays in Positive Economics (University of Chicago Press, Chicago, IL).

Galef, B.G.J., 1976, Social transmission of acquired behavior: A discussion of tradition and social learning in vertebrates, Advances in the Study of Behavior 6, 77–100.

Garcia, J., B.K. McGowan and K.F. Green, 1972, Biological constraints on conditioning, in: A.H. Black and W.F. Porkasy, eds., Classical conditioning II: Current theory and research (Appleton-Century-Crofts, New York) 3–27.

Geertz, C., 1966, Religion as a cultural system, in: M. Benton, ed., Anthropological Approaches to the Study of Religion (Travistock, London) 1–46.

Gerard, R.W., C. Kluckhohn and A Rapoport, 1956, Biological and cultural evolution: Some analogies and explorations, Behav. Sci. 1, 6–34.

Gillespie, J., 1978, A general model to account for enzyme variation in natural populations, V. SAS-CFF model, Theor. Pop. Biol. 14, 1–45.

Gould, S.J., 1976, Biological potential vs. biological determinism, in: A.L. Caplan, ed., The sociobiology debate (Harper and Row, New York) 343–351.

Greene, P.S., 1978, Promiscuity, paternity and culture, Amer. Ethnologist 5, 151–159.

Gruber, H.E. and P.H. Barrett, 1974, Darwin on man (Dutton, New York).

Hamilton, W.D., 1975, Innate social aptitudes of man: An approach from evolutionary genetics, in: R. Fox, ed., Biosocial anthropology (Halstead, London) 133–155.

Harris, M., 1960, Adaptation in biological and cultural science, Trans. N.Y. Acad. Sci. 23, 59–65.

Harris, M., 1971, Culture, man and nature (Crowell, New York).

Hartung, J., 1976, On natural selection and the inheritance of wealth, Current Anthropology 17, 607–622.

Hirschman, A.O., 1970, Exit, voice and loyalty (Harvard University Press, Cambridge, MA).

Hirshleifer, J., 1977, Economics from a biological point of view, J. Law and Economics 20, 1–52.

Irons, W.E., 1979, Cultural and biological success, in: N.A. Chagnon and W.E. Irons, eds., Evolutionary biology and human social behavior: An anthropological perspective (Duxbury, North Scituate, MA) 257–272.

Labov, W., 1972, Sociolinguistic patterns (University of Pennsylvania Press, Philadelphia, PA).

Leeds, A., 1974, Darwinism and 'Darwinian' evolutionism in the study of society and culture, in: T.F. Glick, ed., The comparative reception of Darwinism (University of Texas Press, Austin, TX) 437–485.

Leibenstein, H., 1976, Beyond economic man (Harvard University Press, Cambridge, MA).

Levin, B.R. and W.L. Kilmer, 1974, Interdemic selection and the evolution of altruism, Evolution 28, 527–545.

Lewontin, R.L., 1974, The genetic basis of evolutionary change (Columbia University Press, New York).

Lorenz, K., 1966, On aggression (Harcourt, Brace and World, New York).

Lorenz, K., 1977, Behind the mirror (Harcourt, Brace, Jovanovich, New York).

May, R.M., 1977, Population genetics and cultural inheritance, Nature 268, 11–13.

Maynard Smith, J., 1978, Optimization theory in evolution, Ann. Rev. Ecol. Syst. 9, 31–57.

Moore, G.E., 1903, Principia ethica (Cambridge University Press, Cambridge, MA).

Nelson, R. and S.G. Winter, 1974, Neoclassical vs. evolutionary models of economic growth: Critique and prospectus, Econ. J. 84, 886–905.

Oster, G.F. and E.O. Wilson, 1978, Caste and ecology in the social insects, Princeton Monographs in Population Biology, no. 12 (Princeton University Press, Princeton, NJ).

Peterson, S.A. and A. Somit, 1978, Sociobiology and politics, in: A. Caplan, ed., The sociobiology debate (Harper and Row, New York) 449–461.

Pulliam, H.R. and C. Dunford, 1980, Programmed to learn: An essay on the evolution of culture (Columbia University Press, New York).

Richerson, P. J., 1976, Review of M. Sahlins culture and practical reason, Human Ecology 6, 117–121.

Richerson, P.J. and R. Boyd, 1978, A dual inheritance model of the human evolutionary process I: Basic postulates and a simple model, J. Social Biol. Struct. 1, 127–154.

Rosenthal, T.L. and B.J. Zimmerman, 1978, Social learning and cognition (Academic Press, New York).

Ruyle, E.E., 1973, Genetic and cultural pools: Some suggestions for a unified theory of biocultural evolution, Human Ecology 1, 201–215.

Ruyle, E.E., F.T. Cloak, L.B. Slobodkin and W.H. Durham, 1977, The adaptive significance of cultural behavior: Comments and reply, Human Ecology 5, 49–67.

Sahlins, M., 1976a, Culture and practical reason (University Chicago Press, Chicago, IL).

Sahlins, M., 1976b, The use and abuse of biology: An anthropological critique of sociobiology (University of Michigan Press, Ann Arbor, MI).

Scarr, S. and P.A. Weinberg, 1977, Intellectual similarities within families of both adopted and biological children, Intelligence 1, 170–191.

Stearns, S., 1977, The evolution of life history strategies, a critique of the theory and review of the data, Ann. Rev. Ecol. Syst. 8, 145–171.

Stigler, G. and G. Becker, 1977, De gustibus non est disputandum, Amer. Econ. Rev. 67, 76–90.

Tiger, L. and R. Fox, 1971, The imperial animal (Holt, Rinehart and Winston, New York).

Trivers, R.L., 1974, Parent offspring conflict, Amer. Zoologist 19, 249–269.

Van den Berghe, P.L., 1975, Man in society: A biosocial view (Elsevier, New York).

Van den Berghe, P.L. and D.P. Barash, 1977, Inclusive fitness and human family structure, Amer. Anthrop. 54, 8–17.

Wade, M., 1978, A critical review of the models of group selection, Quart. Rev. Biol. 53, 101–114.

Wallace, A.D., 1905, Man's place in the universe (McClure Phillips, New York).

Williamson, O.E., 1975, Markets and hierarchies (The Free Press, New York).

Wilson, E.O., 1975, Sociobiology (Harvard University Press, Cambridge, MA).

Winter, S.G., 1966, Economic natural selection and the theory of the firm, Yale Economic Essays 4, 225–272.

Winter, S.G., 1971, Satisficing, selection and the innovating remnant, Quart. J. Econ. 85, 237–261.

Winter, S.G., 1975, Optimization and evolution in the theory of the firm, in: R. Day and T. Groves, eds., Adaptive economic models (Academic Press, New York) 73–118.

[20]

Excerpt from *Studies in Philosophy, Politics and Economics*, 66–81.

CHAPTER FOUR

Notes on the Evolution of Systems of Rules of Conduct

(The Interplay between Rules of Individual Conduct and the Social Order of Actions)

I

The purpose of these notes is to clarify the conceptual tools with which we describe facts, not to present new facts. More particularly, their aim is to make clear the important distinction between the systems of rules of conduct which govern the behaviour of the individual members of a group (or of the elements of any order) on the one hand and, on the other hand, the order or pattern of actions which results from this for the group as a whole.[1] It does not matter for this purpose whether the individual members which make up the group are animals or men,[2] nor whether the rules of conduct are innate (transmitted genetically) or learnt (transmitted culturally). We know that cultural transmission by learning occurs at least among some of the higher animals, and there can be no doubt that men also obey some rules of conduct which are innate. The two sorts of rules will therefore often interact. Throughout it

---

[1] We shall use '(social) order' and '(social) pattern' interchangeably to describe the structure of the actions of all the members of a group, but shall avoid the more common term 'social organization', because 'organization' has an intentionalist (anthropomorphic) connotation and is therefore better reserved for orders which are the product of design. Similarly we shall occasionally use the pairs of concepts 'order and its elements' and 'groups and individuals' interchangeably, although the former is of course the more general term of which the relation between group and individual is a particular instance.

[2] Or even whether they are living organisms or perhaps some sort of reduplicating mechanical structures. Cf. L. S. Penrose, 'Self-Reproducing Machines', *Scientific American*, June 1959.

Notes on the Evolution of Systems of Rules of Conduct

should be clearly understood that the term 'rule' is used for a statement by which a regularity of the conduct of individuals can be described, irrespective of whether such a rule is 'known' to the individuals in any other sense than that they normally act in accordance with it. We shall not consider here the interesting question of how such rules can be transmitted culturally long before the individuals are capable of stating them in words and therefore of explicitly teaching them, or how they learn abstract rules 'by analogy' from concrete instances.

That the systems of rules of individual conduct and the order of actions which results from the individuals acting in accordance with them are not the same thing should be obvious as soon as it is stated, although the two are in fact frequently confused. (Lawyers are particularly prone to do so by using the term 'order of law' for both.) Not every system of rules of individual conduct will produce an overall order of the actions of a group of individuals; and whether a given system of rules of individual conduct will produce an order of actions, and what kind of order, will depend on the circumstances in which the individuals act. The classical instance in which the very regularity of the behaviour of the elements produces 'perfect disorder' is the second law of thermodynamics, the entropy principle. It is evident that in a group of living beings many possible rules of individual conduct would also produce only disorder or make the existence of the group as such impossible. A society of animals or men is always a number of individuals observing such common rules of conduct as, in the circumstances in which they live, will produce an order of actions.

For the understanding of animal and human societies the distinction is particularly important because the genetic (and in a great measure also the cultural) *transmission* of rules of conduct takes place *from individual to individual*, while what may be called the natural *selection* of rules will operate on the basis of the greater or lesser efficiency of the resulting *order of the group*.[3] For the purposes of this discussion we shall define the different kinds of elements of which groups consist by the rules of conduct which they obey, and regard the appearance of a transmittable 'mutation' of these rules of individual conduct as the equivalent of the appearance of new elements, or as a progressive change in the character of all the elements of the group.

---

[3] Cf. Alexander Carr-Saunders, *The Population Problem*, London, 1922, p. 223: 'Those groups practising the most advantageous customs will have an advantage in the constant struggle with adjacent groups.'

Philosophy

II

The necessity of distinguishing between the order of actions of the group and the rules of conduct of the individuals may be further supported by the following considerations:

1. A particular order of actions can be observed and described without knowledge of the rules of conduct of the individuals which bring it about: and it is at least conceivable that the same overall order of actions may be produced by different sets of rules of individual conduct.

2. The same set of rules of individual conduct may in some circumstances bring about a certain order of actions, but not do so in different external circumstances.

3. It is the resulting overall order of actions but not the regularity of the actions of the separate individuals as such which is important for the preservation of the group; and a certain kind of overall order may in the same manner contribute to the survival of the members of the group whatever the particular rules of individual conduct which bring it about.

4. The evolutionary selection of different rules of individual conduct operates through the viability of the order it will produce, and any given rules of individual conduct may prove beneficial as part of one set of such rules, or in one set of external circumstances, and harmful as part of another set of rules or in another set of external circumstances.

5. Although the overall order of actions arises in appropriate circumstances as the joint product of the actions of many individuals who are governed by certain rules, the production of the overall order is of course not the conscious aim of individual action since the individual will not have any knowledge of the overall order, so that it will not be an awareness of what is needed to preserve or restore the overall order at a particular moment but an abstract rule which will guide the actions of the individual.

6. The concrete individual action will always be the joint effect of internal impulses, such as hunger, the particular external events acting upon the individual (including the actions of other members of the group), and the rules applicable to the situation thus determined. The rules upon which different individual members of a group will at any moment act may therefore be different either because the drives or external circumstances acting upon them make different rules applicable, or because different rules apply to different individuals according to age, sex, status, or some particular state in which each individual finds itself at the moment.

7. It is important always to remember that a rule of conduct will never

Notes on the Evolution of Systems of Rules of Conduct

by itself be a sufficient cause of action but that the impulse for actions of a certain kind will always come either from a particular external stimulus or from an internal drive (and usually from a combination of both), and that the rules of conduct will always act only as a restraint on actions induced by other causes.

8. The orderliness of the system of actions will in general show itself in the fact that actions of the different individuals will be so co-ordinated, or mutually adjusted to each other, that the result of their actions will remove the initial stimulus or make inoperative the drive which has been the cause of activity.

9. The difference between the orderliness of the whole and the regularity of the actions of any of its individual parts is also shown by the fact that a whole may be orderly without the action of any particular individual element showing any regularity. This might be the case, for instance, if the order of the whole were brought about by an authority commanding all particular actions and choosing the individuals who have to perform any one action at a given moment at random, say by drawing lots. There might in such a group well exist a recognizable order in the sense that certain roles were always filled by somebody; but no rules guiding the actions of any one individual (other than perhaps the commanding authority) could be formulated. The actions taken there by any one individual would not be derived by means of a rule from any of its properties or any of the circumstances acting on it (other than the commands of the organizer).

III

The most easily observed instances in which the rules of individual conduct produce an overall order are those where this order consists in a spatial pattern such as will occur in the marching, defence, or hunting of a group of animals or men. The arrow formation of migrating wild geese, the defensive ring of the buffaloes, or the manner in which lionesses drive the prey towards the male for the kill, are simple instances in which presumably it is not an awareness of the overall pattern by the individual but some rules of how to respond to the immediate environment which co-ordinate the actions of the several individuals.

More instructive are the abstract and more complex orders based on a division of labour which we find in such insect societies as those of bees, ants, and termites. There is perhaps less temptation in these instances to ascribe the changes in the activities of the individual either to a central command or to an 'insight' on the part of the individual into what at the

Philosophy

particular moment is needed by the whole. There can be little doubt that the successive activities which a worker bee performs at the different stages of its career, at intervals varying in length according to the requirements of the situation[4] (and apparently even reverting to stages already passed when the 'needs' of the hive require it), could be explained by comparatively simple rules of individual conduct, if we only knew them. Similarly the elaborate structures which termites build, the genetics of which A. E. Emerson has so revealingly described,[5] must ultimately be accounted for by innate rules of conduct of the individuals of which we are largely ignorant.

When we are concerned with primitive human societies, on the other hand, it is often easier to ascertain the rules of individual conduct than to trace from them the resulting overall and often highly abstract order. The individuals will often themselves be able to tell us what they regard as appropriate action in different circumstances, though they may be able to do this only for particular instances but not to articulate the rules in accordance with which they act;[6] but the 'functions' which these rules serve we shall be able to discover only after we have reconstructed the overall order which is produced by actions in accordance with them. The individual may have no idea what this overall order is that results from his observing such rules as those concerning kinship and inter-marriage, or the succession to property, or which function this overall order serves. Yet all the individuals of the species which exist will behave in that manner because groups of individuals which have thus behaved have displaced those which did not do so.[7]

IV

The overall order of actions in a group is in two respects more than the totality of regularities observable in the actions of the individuals and cannot be wholly reduced to them. It is so not only in the trivial sense in which a whole is more than the mere *sum* of its parts but presupposes also that these elements are related to each other in a particular manner.[8] It is

[4] See K. von Frisch, *The Dancing Bees*, New York, 1955.

[5] A. E. Emerson, 'Termite Nests—A Study of Phylogeny of Behavior', *Ecological Monographs*, VIII, 1938.

[6] Cf. Edward Sapir, *The Selected Writings*, ed. D. G. Mandelbaum, University of California Press, 1949, p. 548 *et seq.*

[7] Ample further illustrations of the kind of orders briefly sketched in this section will be found in V. C. Wynne-Edwards, *Animal Dispersion in Relation to Social Behaviour*, Edinburgh, 1962; Anne Roe and G. G. Simpson, *Behavior and Evolution*, Yale University Press, 1958; and Robert Ardrey, *The Territorial Imperative*, New York, 1966.

[8] Cf. K. R. Popper, *The Poverty of Historicism*, London, 1957, section 7, and Ernest Nagel, *The Structure of Science*, New York, 1961, pp. 380–97.

Notes on the Evolution of Systems of Rules of Conduct

more also because the existence of those relations which are essential for the existence of the whole cannot be accounted for wholly by the inter-action of the parts but only by their interaction with an outside world both of the individual parts and the whole. If there exist recurrent and persistent structures of a certain type (i.e., showing a certain order), this is due to the elements responding to external influences which they are likely to encounter in a manner which brings about the preservation or restoration of this order; and on this, in turn, may be dependent the chances of the individuals to preserve themselves.

From any given set of rules of conduct of the elements will arise a steady structure (showing 'homeostatic' control) only in an environment in which there prevails a certain probability of encountering the sort of circumstances to which the rules of conduct are adapted. A change of environment may require, if the whole is to persist, a change in the order of the group and therefore in the rules of conduct of the individuals; and a spontaneous change of the rules of individual conduct and of the resulting order may enable the group to persist in circumstances which, without such change, would have led to its destruction.

These considerations are mainly intended to bring out that systems of rules of conduct will develop as wholes, or that the selection process of evolution will operate on the order as a whole; and that, whether a new rule will, in combination with all the other rules of the group, and in the particular environment in which it exists, increase or decrease the efficiency of the group as a whole, will depend on the order to which such individual conduct leads. One consequence of this is that a new rule of individual conduct which in one position may prove detrimental, may in another prove to be beneficial. Another is that changes in one rule may make beneficial other changes, both of a behavioural or somatic character, which before were harmful. It is thus likely that even culturally transmitted patterns of individual behaviour (or the resulting patterns of action of the group) may contribute to determine the selection among genetic changes of a behavioural or somatic kind.[9]

It is evident that this interplay of the rules of conduct of the in-dividuals with the actions of other individuals and the external circum-stances in producing an overall order may be a highly complex affair. The whole task of social theory consists in little else but an effort to reconstruct the overall orders which are thus formed, and the reason why that special apparatus of conceptual construction is needed which social theory represents is the complexity of this task. It will also be clear that such a distinct theory of social structures can provide only an explanation

[9] Cf. Sir Alister Hardy, *The Living Stream*, London 1966, especially lecture II.

Philosophy

of certain general and highly abstract features of the different types of structures (or only of the 'qualitative aspects'), because these abstract features will be all that all the structures of a certain type will have in common, and therefore all that will be predictable or provide useful guidance for action.

Of theories of this type economic theory, the theory of the market order of free human societies, is so far the only one which has been systematically developed over a long period and, together with linguistics, perhaps one of a very few which, because of the peculiar complexity of their subject, require such elaboration. Yet, though the whole of economic theory (and, I believe, of linguistic theory) may be interpreted as nothing else but an endeavour to reconstruct from regularities of the individual actions the character of the resulting order, it can hardly be said that economists are fully aware that this is what they are doing. The nature of the different kinds of rules of individual conduct (some voluntarily and even unconsciously observed and some enforced), which the formation of the overall order presupposes, is frequently left obscure.[10] The important question of which of these rules of individual action can be deliberately and profitably altered, and which are likely to evolve gradually with or without such deliberate collective decisions as legislation involves, is rarely systematically considered.

V

Although the existence and preservation of the order of actions of a group can be accounted for only from the rules of conduct which the individuals obey, these rules of individual conduct have developed because the individuals have been living in groups whose structures have gradually changed. In other words, the properties of the individuals which are significant for the existence and preservation of the group, and through this also for the existence and preservation of the individuals themselves, have been shaped by the selection of those from the individuals living in groups which at each stage of the evolution of the group tended to act according to such rules as made the group more efficient.

Thus for the explanation of the functioning of the social order at any one time the rules of individual conduct must be assumed to be given. Yet these rules have been selected and formed by the effects they have

[10] As is shown by the unprofitable discussions about the degree of 'rationality' which economic theory is alleged to assume. What is said above, incidentally, also implies that social theory is, strictly speaking, not a science of behaviour and that to regard it as part of 'behavioural science' is at least misleading.

Notes on the Evolution of Systems of Rules of Conduct

on the social order; and in so far as psychology does not wish to content itself with describing the rules which individuals actually obey, but undertakes to explain why they observe these rules, at least a great part of it will have to become evolutionary social psychology. Or, to put this differently, though social theory constructs social orders from the rules of conduct assumed to be given at any one time, these rules of conduct have themselves developed as part of a larger whole, and at each stage of this development the then prevailing overall order determined what effect any one change in the rules of individual conduct had.

Though we cannot here further pursue the question of the relation of psychology to social theory, it will contribute to the main purpose of these notes if we add a few remarks on the difference between an order which is brought about by the direction of a central organ such as the brain, and the formation of an order determined by the regularity of the actions towards each other of the elements of a structure. Michael Polanyi has usefully described this distinction as that between a monocentric and a polycentric order.[11] The first point which it is in this connection important to note is that the brain of an organism which acts as the directing centre for that organism is itself in turn a polycentric order, that is, that its actions are determined by the relation and mutual adjustment to each other of the elements of which it consists.

As we are all tempted to assume that wherever we find an order it must be directed by a central organ, which, if we applied this to the brain, evidently would lead to an infinite regress, it will be useful briefly to consider the advantage derived from the fact that one such polycentric order is set aside in a part of the whole and governs the action of the rest. This advantage consists in the possibility of trying out beforehand on a model the various alternative complexes of actions and selecting from them the most promising before action is taken by the whole organism. There is no reason why any one of these complex patterns of actions should not be determined by the direct interaction of the parts without this pattern being first formed in another centre, and then directed by it. The unique attribute of the brain is that it can produce a representative model on which the alternative actions and their consequences can be tried out beforehand. The structure which the brain directs may have a repertoire of possible patterns of actions quite as big as the one the brain can pre-form; but if it actually had to take that action before it was tried out on a model, it might discover its harmful effects only when it was too late and it might be destroyed as a result. If, on the other hand, such action is

11 M. Polanyi, *The Logic of Liberty*, London, 1951, especially Chapters 8 and 9.

Philosophy

first tried out on a model in a separate part of the whole set aside for the purpose, not the actual effect but a representation of the effect to be expected will act as a signal that the particular action is not to be taken.

There is, therefore, no reason why a polycentric order in which each element is guided only by rules and receives no orders from a centre should not be capable of bringing about as complex and apparently as 'purposive' an adaptation to circumstances as could be produced in a system where a part is set aside to preform such an order on an analogue or model before it is put into execution by the larger structure. In so far as the self-organizing forces of a structure as a whole lead at once to the right kind of action (or to tentative actions which can be retraced before too much harm is done), such a single-stage order need not be inferior to a hierarchic one in which the whole merely carries out what has first been tried out in a part. Such a non-hierarchic order dispenses with the necessity of first communicating all the information on which its several elements act to a common centre and conceivably may make the use of more information possible than could be transmitted to, and digested by, a centre.

Such spontaneous orders as those of societies, although they will often produce results similar to those which could be produced by a brain, are thus organized on principles different from those which govern the relations between a brain and the organism which it directs. Although the brain may be organized on principles similar to those on which a society is organized, society is not a brain and must not be represented as a sort of super-brain, because in it the acting parts and those between which the relations determining the structure are established are the same, and the ordering task is not deputized to any part in which a model is preformed.

VI

The existence of such ordered structures as galaxies, solar systems, organisms, and social orders in a multiplicity of instances showing certain common features and observing as wholes regularities which cannot be wholly reduced to the regularities of the parts, because they also depend on the interaction of the whole with the environment which placed and keeps the part in the order necessary for the specific behaviour of the whole, creates certain difficulties for a theory of scientific method which regards as its aim the discovery of 'universal laws of nature'. Though it is reasonable to believe that structures of the kind will in a

[74]

Notes on the Evolution of Systems of Rules of Conduct

definable environment always behave as they do, the existence of such structures may in fact depend not only on that environment, but also on the existence in the past of many other environments, indeed on a definite sequence of such environments which have succeeded in that order only once in the history of the universe. The theoretical disciplines which are concerned with the structures of such complexes have thus an object the very existence of which is due to circumstances (and a process of evolution determined by them) which, though in principle repeatable, may in fact have been unique and never occur again. In consequence, the laws which govern the behaviour of these complexes, though 'in principle universally valid' (whatever that means), apply in fact only to structures to be found in a particular space-time sector of that universe.

Just as apparently the existence of life on earth is due to events which could have happened only in the peculiar conditions prevailing during an early phase of its history, so the existence of our kind of society, and even of human beings thinking as we do, may be due to phases in the evolution of our species without which neither the present order nor the existing kinds of individual minds could have arisen, and from the legacy of which we can never wholly free ourselves. We can judge and modify all our views and beliefs only within a framework of opinions and values which, though they will gradually change, are for us a given result of that evolution.

Yet the problem of the formation of such structures is still a theoretical and not a historical problem, because it is concerned with those factors in a sequence of events which are in principle repeatable, though in fact they may have occurred only once. We may call the answer 'conjectural history' (and much of modern social theory derives indeed from what the eighteenth-century thinkers called conjectural history), if we remain aware that the aim of such 'conjectural history' is not to account for all particular attributes which a unique event possesses, but only for those which under conditions which may be repeated can be produced again in the same combination. Conjectural history in this sense is the reconstruction of a hypothetical kind of process which may never have been observed but which, if it had taken place, would have produced phenomena of the kind we observe. The assumption that such a process has taken place may be tested by seeking for yet unobserved consequences which follow from it, and by asking whether all regular structures of the kind in question which we find can be accounted for by that assumption.

As was clearly recognized by Carl Menger, in the sphere of complex phenomena *'this genetic element is inseparable from the idea of theoretical*

[75]

Philosophy

sciences'.[12] Or, to put it differently, the existence of the structures with which the theory of complex phenomena is concerned can be made intelligible only by what the physicists would call a cosmology, that is, a theory of their evolution.[13] The problem of how galaxies or solar systems are formed and what is their resulting structure is much more like the problems which the social sciences have to face than the problems of mechanics; and for the understanding of the methodological problems of the social sciences a study of the procedures of geology or biology is therefore much more instructive than that of physics. In all these fields the structures or steady states which they study, the kind of objects with which they are concerned, though they may within a particular space-time region occur in millions or billions of instances, can be fully accounted for only by considering also circumstances which are not properties of the structures themselves but particular facts of the environment in which they have developed and exist.

VII

Societies differ from simpler complex structures by the fact that their elements are themselves complex structures whose chance to persist depends on (or at least is improved by) their being part of the more comprehensive structure. We have to deal here with integration on at least two different levels,[14] with on the one hand the more comprehensive order assisting the preservation of ordered structures on the lower level, and, on the other, the kind of order which on the lower level determines the regularities of individual conduct assisting the prospect of the survival of the individual only through its effect on the overall order of the society. This means that the individual with a particular structure and behaviour owes its existence in this form to a society of a particular structure, because only within such a society has it been advantageous to develop some of its peculiar characteristics, while the order of society

[12] Carl Menger, *Untersuchungen über die Methode der Socialwissenschaften und der Politischen Ökonomie insbesondere*, Leipzig, 1883, p. 88, English translation by F. J. Nock, ed. by Louis Schneider under the title *Problems of Economics and Sociology*, Urbana, Ill., 1963, p. 94. Italics in the original.

[13] I assume it need not be stressed here that a theory of evolution does not imply 'laws of evolution' in the sense of necessary sequences of particular forms or stages, a mistake often made by the same people who interpret the genetical as a historical problem. A theory of genetics describes a mechanism capable of producing an infinite variety of particular results.

[14] Cf. R. Redfield (ed.), *Levels of Integration in Biological and Social Systems (Biological Symposia*, ed. J. Catell, Vol. VIII) Lancaster, Penn., 1941. 'Integration', in this context, means of course simply the formation of an order or the incorporation in an already existing order.

Notes on the Evolution of Systems of Rules of Conduct

in turn is a result of these regularities of conduct which the individuals have developed in society.

This implies a sort of inversion of the relation between cause and effect in the sense that the structures possessing a kind of order will exist because the elements do what is necessary to secure the persistence of that order. The 'final cause' or 'purpose', i.e., the adaptation of the parts to the requirements of the whole, becomes a necessary part of the explanation of why structures of the kind exist: we are bound to explain the fact that the elements behave in a certain way by the circumstance that this sort of conduct is most likely to preserve the whole—on the preservation of which depends the preservation of the individuals, which would therefore not exist if they did not behave in this manner. A 'teleological' explanation is thus entirely in order so long as it does not imply design by a maker but merely the recognition that the kind of structure would not have perpetuated itself if it did not act in a manner likely to produce certain effects,[15] and that it has evolved through those prevailing at each stage who did.

The reason why we are reluctant to describe such actions as purposive is that the order which will form as the result of these actions is of course in no sense 'part of the purpose' or of the motive of the acting individuals. The immediate cause, the impulse which drives them to act, will be something affecting them only; and it is merely because in doing so they are restrained by rules that an overall order results, while this consequence of observing these rules is wholly beyond their knowledge or intentions. In Adam Smith's classical phrase, man 'is led to promote an end which is no part of his intentions',[16] just as the animal defending its territory has no idea that it thereby contributes to regulate the numbers of its species.[17] It was indeed what I have elsewhere called the twin ideas of evolution and spontaneous order,[18] the great contributions of Bernard Mandeville and David Hume, of Adam Ferguson and Adam Smith, which have opened the way for an understanding, both in biological and social theory, of that interaction between the regularity of the conduct of the elements and the regularity of the resulting structure. What they

[15] Cf. David Hume, *Dialogues Concerning Natural Religion* (1779), in *A Treatise of Human Nature*, ed. T. H. Green and T. H. Grose, new ed., London, 1890, Vol. II, pp. 428–9: 'I would fain know how an animal could subsist unless its parts were so adjusted? ... No form ... can subsist unless it possesses those powers and organs, requisite for its subsistence: some new order of œconomy must be tried, and so on, without intermission, till at last some order which can support and maintain itself, is fallen upon.'

[16] Adam Smith, *Wealth of Nations*, ed. Cannan, I, p. 421.

[17] See V. C. Wynne-Edwards, *op. cit.*

[18] See my lecture, 'Dr. Bernard Mandeville', *Proceedings of the British Academy*, LII, 1966.

Philosophy

did not make clear, and what even in the subsequent development of social theory has not been brought out with sufficient clarity, is that it is always some regularity in the behaviour of the elements which produces, in interaction with the environment, what may be a wholly different regularity of the actions of the whole.

Earlier groping efforts towards such an understanding which have left their traces on modern jurisprudence ran in terms of the adequacy of the rules of individual conduct to the *natura rei*, the nature of the thing. By this was meant just that overall order which would be affected by a change in any one of the rules of individual conduct—with the consequence that the effects of such a change in any one rule can be assessed only out of an understanding of all the factors determining the overall order. The true element in this is that the normative rules often serve to adapt an action to an order which exists as a fact. That there always exists such an order beyond the regularities of the actions of any one individual, an order at which the particular rules 'aim' and into which any one new rule has to be fitted, is the insight which only a theory of the formation of that overall order can adequately give.

VIII

A few observations may be added in conclusion on certain peculiarities of social orders which rest on learnt (culturally transmitted) rules in addition to the innate (genetically transmitted) ones. Such rules will presumably be less strictly observed and it will need some continuous outside pressure to secure that individuals will continue to observe them. This will in part be effected if behaviour according to the rules serves as a sort of mark of recognition of membership of the group. If deviant behaviour results in non-acceptance by the other members of the group, and observance of the rules is a condition of successful co-operation with them, an effective pressure for the preservation of an established set of rules will be maintained. Expulsion from the group is probably the earliest and most effective sanction or 'punishment' which secures conformity, first by mere actual elimination from the group of the individuals who do not conform while later, in higher stages of intellectual development, the fear of expulsion may act as a deterrent.

Such systems of learnt rules will probably nevertheless be more flexible than a system of innate rules and a few more remarks on the process by which they may change will be in place. This process will be closely connected with that by which individuals learn by imitation how to observe abstract rules; a process of which we know very little.

[78]

Notes on the Evolution of Systems of Rules of Conduct

One factor influencing it will be the order of dominance of the individuals within the group. There will be, on the one end of the scale, a greater margin of tolerance for the young who are still in the process of learning and who are accepted as members of the group, not because they have already learnt all the rules peculiar to the group, but because as natural offspring they are attached to particular adult members of the group. On the other end of the scale there will be dominant old individuals who are firmly set in their ways and not likely to change their habits, but whose position is such that if they do acquire new practices they are more likely to be imitated than to be expelled from the group. The order of rank is thus undoubtedly an important factor in determining what alterations will be tolerated or will spread, though not necessarily in the sense that it will always be the high-ranking who initiate change.[19]

A point which deserves more consideration than it usually receives, however, is that the preference for acting according to established rules, and the fear of the consequences if one deviates from them, is probably much older and more basic than the ascription of these rules to the will of a personal, human or super-natural, agent, or to the fear of punishment that may be inflicted by such an agent. The partial awareness of a regularity of the world, of the difference between a known and predictable and an unknown and unpredictable part of the events in the environment, must create a preference for the kinds of actions whose consequences are predictable and a fear of the kinds of actions whose consequences are unpredictable. Though in an animistically interpreted world this fear is likely to become a fear of retribution by the agent whose will is disregarded, such a fear of the unknown or unusual action must operate much earlier to keep the individual to the tried ways. The knowledge of some regularities of the environment will create a preference for those kinds of conduct which produce a confident expectation of certain consequences, and an aversion to doing something unfamiliar and fear when it has been done. This establishes a sort of connection between the knowledge that rules exist in the objective world and a disinclination to deviate from the rules commonly followed in action, and therefore also between the belief that events follow rules and the feeling that one 'ought' to observe rules in one's conduct.

Our knowledge of fact (and especially of that complex order of society

---

[19] It would seem, e.g., that among monkeys new food habits are acquired more readily by the young and may then spread to the older members of the group: see the observations by J. Itani reported by S. Kawamura, 'The Process of Sub-cultural Propagation among Japanese Macaques', in Charles H. Southwick (ed.), *Primate Social Behavior*, Princeton, 1963, p. 85.

Philosophy

within which we move as much as within the order of nature) tells us mainly what will be the consequences of some of our actions in some circumstances. While this will help us to decide what to do if we want to obtain a particular result, or are driven by a particular impulse, it needs to be supplemented in a largely unknown world by some principle which inhibits actions to which our internal drives might lead us but which are inappropriate to the circumstances. The rules of fact which one knows can be relied upon only so long as one plays the game oneself according to the rules, i.e., keeps within the kind of actions the consequences of which are tolerably predictable. Norms are thus an adaptation to a factual regularity on which we depend but which we know only partially and on which we can count only if we observe those norms. If I know that if I do not observe the rules of my group, not only will I not be accepted and in consequence not be able to do most of the things I want to do and must do to preserve my life, but also that, if I do not observe these rules, I may release the most terrifying events and enter a world in which I can no longer orient myself, such rules will be as much a necessary guidance to successful action as rules that tell me how the objects in my environment will behave. The factual belief that such and such is the only way in which a certain result can be brought about, and the normative belief that this is the only way in which it ought to be pursued, are thus closely associated. The individual will feel that it exposes itself to dangers by transgressing the rules even if there is nobody there to punish it, and the fear of this will keep even the animal to the customary way. But once such rules are deliberately taught, and taught in an animistic language, they come almost inevitably to be associated with the will of the teacher or the punishment or the supernatural sanctions threatened by him.

Man does not so much choose between alternative actions according to their known consequences as prefer those the consequences of which are predictable over those the consequences of which are unknown. What he most fears, and what puts him in a state of terror when it has happened, is to lose his bearings and no longer to know what to do. Though we all tend to associate conscience with the fear of blame or punishment by another will, the state of mind which it represents is psychologically little different from the alarm experienced by somebody who, while manipulating a powerful and complicated machinery, has inadvertently pulled the wrong levers and thereby produced wholly unexpected movements. The resulting feeling that something dreadful is going to happen because one has infringed rules of conduct is but one form of the panic produced when one realizes that one has entered an unknown world. A

Notes on the Evolution of Systems of Rules of Conduct

bad conscience is the fear of the dangers to which one has thus exposed oneself by having left the known path and entered such an unknown world. The world is fairly predictable only so long as one adheres to the established procedures, but it becomes frightening when one deviates from them.

In order to live successfully and to achieve one's aims within a world which is only very partially understood, it is therefore quite as important to obey certain inhibiting rules which prevent one from exposing oneself to danger as to understand the rules on which this world operates. Taboos or negative rules acting through the paralysing action of fear will, as a kind of knowledge of what *not* to do, constitute just as significant information about the environment as any positive knowledge of the attributes of the objects of this environment. While the latter enables us to predict the consequences of particular actions, the former just warns us not to take certain kinds of action. At least so long as the normative rules consist of prohibitions, as most of them probably did before they were interpreted as commands of another will, the 'Thou shalt not' kind of rule may after all not be so very different from the rules giving us information about what is.[20]

---

[20] The possibility contemplated here is not that all normative rules can be interpreted as descriptive or explanatory rules, but that the latter may be meaningful only within a framework of a system of normative rules.

[21]

Economics and Philosophy, 2, 1986, 75–100. Printed in the United States of America.

SPONTANEOUS MARKET ORDER AND SOCIAL RULES

A Critical Examination of F. A. Hayek's Theory of Cultural Evolution

VIKTOR VANBERG
Department of Economics
George Mason University

I. Introduction

Discoverers of "market failures" as well as advocates of the general efficiency of a "true, unhampered market" sometimes seem to disregard the fundamental fact that there is no such thing as a "market as such." What we call a market is always a system of social interaction characterized by a specific *institutional framework*, that is, by a *set of rules* defining certain restrictions on the behavior of the market participants, whether these rules are *informal*, enforced by private sanctions, or *formal*, enforced by a particular agency, the "protective state," in J. M. Buchanan's (1975) terminology.

"Market failure" arguments sometimes tend to ignore that the rules upon which a market is based may well be *variable* and that an adjustment in these rules may often be a better way to deal with alleged shortcomings than to replace market forces by a political mechanism. Arguments using the notion of a "true, unhampered market," on the other hand, sometimes either sound as if markets operate in an institutional vacuum, or seem to presuppose that an "unhampered" market is, by definition, one that is based on "proper" or "appropri-

I am indebted to James M. Buchanan for helpful comments. Thanks are also due to the editors of this journal and an anonymous referee for useful suggestions.

ate" rules—begging the question of what rules actually characterize a "true, unhampered market."

Once it is recognized that the operation of a market can be meaningfully discussed only with reference to a specified institutional framework, economic analysis necessarily must pay attention to the issue of how the character of and changes in the framework of rules and institutions affect the working properties of a market as well as to the issue of how the emergence of and changes in systems of rules and institutions can be explained. Much of what is called "Constitutional Economics" (McKenzie, 1984) or "New Institutional Economics" (Furubotn and Richter, 1984) is just on these issues.

This paper takes a closer look at a theoretical conception that has been stressed by F.A. Hayek but, with variations, is to be found in other approaches to an "economic analysis of institutions" as well: the notion of the development of rules as an evolutionary process, or, as Hayek calls it, the notion of cultural evolution. Section II discusses Hayek's arguments on the relation between the character of a spontaneous social order and two kinds of rules governing people's behavior: genetic rules and cultural rules. Section III examines the general notion of the evolution of cultural rules. In Section IV two different specifications of the process of evolution are distinguished that can be found in Hayek's writings: an individualistic, invisible-hand notion of cultural evolution and the notion of cultural group selection. Section V discusses the notion of group selection, and section VI analyzes the scope and limits of an invisible hand theory of cultural evolution. Some conclusions are drawn in Section VII.

II. SPONTANEOUS SOCIAL ORDER AND TWO KINDS OF RULES

Hayek's theory of social or cultural evolution is closely related to his conception of the market as a *spontaneous order,* and for an examination of the former it is appropriate to start from the latter.

The idea of the spontaneous formation of a social order, an idea he considers the cornerstone of social theory (1964, pp. 4f.), is the central theme of Hayek's writings. As Hayek (1973, pp. 36f.) points out, the spontaneous order of the market is only one instance—albeit paradigmatic—of the general principle of spontaneous order, examples of which are to be found in the physical as well as in the biological or in the social sphere. The peculiar feature that all spontaneous orders have in common is that they emerge out of the interaction of a multiplicity of *elements* which, in their responses to their particular environment, are governed by certain general *rules* (1964, pp. 6f.). It is the character of these rules that is crucial for the character of the overall order or pattern that will emerge out of the interaction of the elements (1973, pp. 43f.). More specifically: The character of these rules will determine certain general features of the overall pattern, while the particular content of the resulting order will always be dependent on the specific circumstances to which the elements respond (1973, p. 40).

In case of spontaneous *social* orders, of which the order of the market is the most systematically analyzed instance (1967, p. 72), the elements are human individuals and a specific feature of social theory results, as Hayek (1967, p. 66; 1973, p. 155) notes, from the fact that social orders are based on "two kinds of rules": first, the *innate, genetically inherited* universal rules of human behavior, which have been shaped in the process of the biological evolution of the human species, and second, the *learned, culturally transmitted* rules of human conduct. Since, compared to the process of man's genetic evolution, the history of human civilization – encompassing the potential subjects of social theoretical analysis – is an extremely short period only, it seems reasonable that, for the purposes of social theory, the innate behavioral rules can be assumed to be essentially uniform over time and space. That, in this sense, "human nature" can be assumed to be homogeneous is, in fact, the implicit premise underlying those approaches to social theory which – as economics – explicitly start from a general model of man. The cultural rules, on the other hand, appear to be exceptionally variable and, hence, it is the variability of these rules that accounts for the diversity of social orders revealed by historical records and cross-cultural observations.

To state that human behavior is governed by certain rules is to say that individuals in their conduct exhibit certain patterns or regularities that can be described in terms of rules – whether or not the individuals are aware of these regularities and whether or not they have ever been explicitly stated as rules (Hayek, 1967, pp. 66f.). The behavioral regularities we describe as *genetic rules* are due to certain constraints or characteristics in their biological endowment, which all human individuals share as members of the human species. In stating that individuals are governed by cultural rules we refer to regularities of conduct individuals exhibit because certain conditions or constraints prevail in their social environment, conditions which may be more or less specific to particular social communities.[1] In their verbally articulated form, cultural rules

---

1. There may be cultural rules that reflect peculiar features of one specific social community only, and there may be others that are almost "universal" in reflecting certain intrinsic features of human social life in general. Though it is common to state that "rules constrain behavior," it should be obvious that not *rules* as such, i.e. as normative or positive statements describing regularities of behavior, impose constraints on individuals' behavior. Rather, it is only certain *social facts* that can exert an influence on people's behavioral choices, e.g. the fact that other people will react negatively in

typically take the form of normative, prescriptive statements, according to which individuals in a social community, if confronting a situation of type Y, *have to* or *should* show a behavior of type Z. Whether, and to what extent individuals in a social community actually exhibit behavioral regularities that correspond to such normative rules will depend on the extent to which conditions actually prevail in their respective social environment that make them act accordingly, given their genetic endowment.

By stressing the relevance of the cultural rules, Hayek explicitly recognized that there is no spontaneous market order "as such" that can be assumed generally to be "efficient" or "beneficial," independent of the rules and institutions governing the behavior of the market participants. There is, to be sure, a general feature all spontaneous market orders share independently of the particular set of rules they are based upon, a general feature that Hayek has stressed as the essential source of the potential efficiency of market arrangements compared to centralized, deliberately planned arrangements: by allowing the individual participants – within the confines set by certain general rules – to respond to the particular circumstances of time and place, a spontaneous order utilizes much more knowledge than can possibly be made accessible to any central agent or agency imposing a deliberately planned order.[2] But, though accounting for its potential efficiency, its special capacity to utilize dispersed knowledge cannot guarantee that a spontaneous market order *in all instances* will be "beneficial," independently of the kind of rules upon which it is based. As Hayek (1978, pp. 124f., 135) explicitly stresses, the classical "invisible hand" conception as well as his own notion of the spontaneous order of the market recognize that a "beneficial" working of the market mechanism requires that the market participants are governed in their behavior by "appropriate" rules, and he suggests that this issue is not granted the attention it deserves (1967, p. 12; 1948, pp. 101f.).

The notion that "appropriate" rules are required to give the spontaneous order of the market a "beneficial" character raises, of course, the question of what is meant by a "beneficial" order and what is meant by "appropriate" rules. To Hayek, as a classical liberal, a social order is beneficial if, and to the extent that, it serves the interests of the individuals involved. Apart from specifying certain general criteria rules must meet in order to allow for the formation of a spontaneous

---

case of rule-violating behavior, or the *fact* that certain persons explicitly articulate a rule, etc. Thus, it is not "the rule," as such, that can explain behavioral regularities, but the social facts or constraints that induce individuals to act in accordance to the rule. This issue is discussed more fully in Vanberg, 1984, pp. 123ff.

2. Hayek has elaborated this argument, notably in his essay "The Use of Knowledge in Society," 1948, pp. 77–91.

social order,[3] Hayek does not provide an independent definition of what "appropriate" rules are, beyond the notion that they contribute to a *beneficial social order*.[4] Instead, he draws our attention to the processes of generation and change of cultural rules and to the question of what characteristics of those processes can be expected to further or to inhibit the emergence of rules that allow for a beneficial order. Hayek's theory of cultural evolution is a contribution to this issue.

III. THE NOTION OF THE EVOLUTION OF RULES

With respect to rule-generating and rule-changing processes a basic distinction can be made between, first, *political processes*, i.e. those cases in which rules are deliberately chosen for, and implemented in, a social community by some agent or agency, whether this is a dictator, a conqueror, a democratically elected assembly, or whatever, and, second, *spontaneous processes*, i.e. those cases in which rules emerge as an unintended social outcome of the interaction of individuals separately pursuing their own ends.[5]

The distinction between "deliberate design" and "spontaneous growth" of rules and institutions plays a central role in Hayek's writings. Criticizing "a conception which assumes that all social institutions are, and ought to be the product of deliberate design" (1973, p. 5), he advocates a view stressing that the rules and institutions contributing to a beneficial social order are "largely due to a process de-

3. For the purposes of the present discussion it can be ignored that Hayek's definition of a "beneficial social order" or a "good society" as "one in which the chances of anyone selected at random are likely to be as great as possible" (Hayek, 1976, p. 132), is not totally unambiguous. It is open to a Benthamite-*utilitarian* interpretation, an interpretation Hayek (1976, pp. 22f.) explicitly criticizes. And it is open to a Rawls-Buchanan-*contractarian* interpretation. The first, utilitarian interpretation is suggested, for instance by a statement like: ". . . the aim in altering or developing them [the rules of just conduct – VV] should be to improve as much as possible the chances of anyone selected at random" (Hayek, 1976, pp. 129f.). The second, contractarian interpretation is suggested by Hayek's (*ibid.*, p. 132) statement: ". . . we should regard as the most desirable order of society one which we would choose if we knew that our initial position in it would be decided purely by chance (such as the fact of our being born into a particular family)."

4. The present discussion will disregard the issue that in talking of the "appropriateness" of rules it may be necessary to specify the *relevant group* for which the resulting order is to be judged beneficial.

5. This distinction is not necessarily mutually exclusive, but allows for "intermediate" cases, combining elements of both kinds of processes. The basic distinction made here is analogous to Carl Menger's (1963, pp. 139ff.) distinction between social structures of "pragmatic origin" ("a product of agreement or of positive legislation") and those of "organic origin" ("unintended results of efforts serving individual interests").

scribed at first as 'growth' and later as 'evolution' " (*ibid.*, p. 9). According to Hayek, this "evolutionary view" holds "that the present order of society has largely arisen, not by design, but by the prevalence of the more effective institutions in a process of competition" (1979, pp. 154f.), that man is "governed by rules which have by a process of selection evolved in the society in which he lives" (1976, p. 11) rules which "have been selected in a process of evolution" (ibid., p. 21). In what follows a closer look shall be taken at Hayek's arguments on the *nature* of the process of cultural evolution.

More clearly than is done in some of the recent contributions to an evolutionary approach in economics, Hayek stresses the essential difference between the *genetic evolution* of man's universal behavioral traits and the *social evolution* of cultural rules of conduct. While noting that the "basic conception of evolution" is the same in both fields (1973, p. 23), Hayek mentions as a crucial difference between genetic and cultural evolution that the latter is "relying on the transmission of acquired properties" and, therefore, is a much faster process than genetic evolution (1979, p. 156). As for the common basic conception of evolution, Hayek repeatedly has pointed out that originally – and counter to a prevailing view – the notion of an evolutionary process was not "imported" from biology into social theory, but that "the idea of cultural evolution is undoubtedly older than the biological concept of evolution" (1979, p. 154). The pre-Darwinian notion of socio-cultural evolution, to which he refers, is the social theory of the Scottish moral philosophers of the eighteenth century, whom Hayek celebrates as discoverers of "the twin ideas of evolution and spontaneous order" (1967, p. 77).

The central feature of the social theory of the Scottish moral philosophers is its *methodological individualism*, the guiding principle that aggregate social phenomena can be and should be explained in terms of individual actions, their interrelations, and their – largely unintended – combined effects (Vanberg, 1975, pp. 5–29). This methodological approach is behind Adam Smith's notion of the "invisible hand" as it is behind Adam Ferguson's conception of social institutions as "the result of human action but not of human design" (Hayek, 1967, pp. 96 ff.). And it is this individualistic perspective that seems to have had an impact on the shift in perspective that is essential to Darwinian evolutionary theory: from the species as the theoretical unit to the individual organism as the central unit of analysis (Schweber, 1977, pp. 233, 277ff.). Just as the Scottish moral philosophers explained phenomena at the social, aggregate level as the systematic outcome of processes at the level of individuals, it was Darwin's contribution to show how processes at the level of individual organisms systematically bring about certain, apparently "useful" features at the aggregate, species-level.

In talking of the "twin conceptions of evolution and spontaneous order" Hayek apparently is making the claim that his theory of cultural evolution is based on the same explanatory logic as the individualistic theory of the spontaneous order of the market. Taking up Adam Smith's cue this type of explanation has been called "invisible-hand explanation."[6] Providing an invisible-hand explanation of the rules themselves upon which a spontaneous social order is based, would mean to show how the behavioral regularities, which a theory of spontaneous order assumes as given, can be explained as an unintended, but systematic outcome of a process of interaction among individuals who are separately pursuing their own ends.

Accordingly, a theory of cultural evolution, that qualifies as a "twin conception" of the notion of spontaneous social order, would have to specify – as invisible-hand explanations in general – a process or mechanism of aggregation "which takes as 'input' the dispersed actions of the participating individuals and produces as 'output' the overall social pattern" (Ullmann-Margalit, 1978, p. 270) to be explained, i.e. the behavioral regularities in question. More specifically, such a theory of cultural evolution would have to specify that the process by which rules spontaneously emerge and change is an *evolutionary* process, i.e., characterized by certain features that can be considered peculiar to an "evolutionary" process.

IV. CULTURAL EVOLUTION: "INVISIBLE HAND EXPLANATION" VS. "GROUP SELECTION"

According to what seems to be the core idea of the notion of evolution in biology, to interpret the emergence of rules as an evolutionary process supposes that it is determined by the interaction of two processes (Hayek 1967, p. 32):

1. a *process of variation* in which continuously new transmittable variants, i.e., ways of behavior, are generated, and
2. a *process of selection* in which out of all variants (ways of behavior) generated, those become systematically selected that are actually transmitted, i.e. that become *behavioral regularities* in social communities.

6. Cf. Nozick, 1974, p. 19; Elster, 1979, p. 30. E. Ullmann-Margalit in a excellent essay on "Invisible-Hand Explanations" (1978, p. 267) has characterized this type of explanation as follows: "It typically replaces an easily forthcoming and initially plausible explanation according to which the explanandum phenomenon is the product of intentional design with a rival account according to which it is brought about through a process involving the separate actions of many individuals who are supposed to be minding their own business unaware of, and a fortiori not intending to produce, the ultimate overall outcome."

An individualistic, invisible-hand conception of cultural evolution would have to specify these two processes in terms of separate individual choices, analogous to the theory of the spontaneous order of the market and its notion of a competitive process in which individual choices continuously generate new variants, goods and services, and determine which among competing products will prevail in the market.

Looking through Hayek's writings, one will, in fact, find various arguments that clearly seem to imply such an individualistic, invisible-hand interpretation of the idea of cultural evolution. For instance, Hayek (1979, p. 161) stresses the role of those individuals who by deviating from traditional rules and by experimenting with new practices act as innovators and generate "new variants" which may become new behavioral regularities in a social community if, in competition with traditional as well as alternative new ways of behavior, they prevail in the sense of being imitated by more and more individuals in the group (1979, p. 167). Such an argument obviously contains the idea of a *process of* variation by individual innovations and a *process of* selection by individual imitation.

When Hayek (1967, p. 71) refers to cultural evolution as a process by which adaptations to changing circumstances and solutions to new problems, faced by a group, are brought about, it is obvious that, according to an individualistic, invisible-hand notion, only the individual actors are the ones who perceive "problems" and who respond to changing circumstances by choosing those practices which they expect to serve their interests. It cannot be simply postulated that from a process of variation, based on *individual* innovations, and a process of selection, based on *individual* imitation, rules will emerge that benefit the group. Rather, one would have to show *why* and *under what conditions* the process of individual innovation and individual imitation can be expected to generate socially beneficial rules – just as the theory of spontaneous social order does not simply *postulate* that all spontaneously generated social outcomes are necessarily beneficial, but *explains* why this can be expected, given certain "appropriate" conditions. And Hayek (1973, p.22) clearly suggests that he has such an individualistic explanation of the evolution of "useful" rules in mind when he call special attention to Carl Menger as the one who, a hundred years after Adam Smith, restated and elaborated the Scottish approach to a theory of cultural evolution. As Hayek stresses, Carl Menger has systematically addressed the question of "how it is possible that institutions which serve the common welfare and are most important for its advancement can arise without a common will aiming at their creation" (1979a, pp. 146f.), institutions that are "preserved by, and depend for their functioning on, the actions of people who are not guided by the desire to keep them in existence" (ibid., p. 149).

A closer examination of Hayek's writings on this topic reveals that, in actual fact, he neither systematically elaborates nor consistently pursues such an individualistic, evolutionary approach to the question of why it is that rules can be expected spontaneously to emerge that increase the "efficiency of the group as a whole" (Hayek 1967, p. 71) and that provide solutions to "problems of society" (Hayek, 1980, p. 28). Rather there is a tacit shift in Hayek's argument from the notion that behavioral regularities emerge and prevail because they benefit the individual practicing them, to the quite different notions that rules come to be observed because they are advantageous to the group.[7]

To refer to group advantage rather than to individual benefits and to argue that "rules of conduct . . . have evolved because the groups who practiced them were more successful" (Hayek 1973, p. 18), is of course, quite different from providing an "invisible-hand explanation." It rather sounds like the *functionalist* type of argument, according to which its contribution to the "maintenance" of a social system explains the existence of a social pattern or institution, a type of argument that for some time has been popular in sociology and social anthropology.[8] And Hayek's explanation of social rules in terms of "group advantage" is subject to the same objection that has been raised against functionalism: in order to provide an explanation at all, a functionalist argument would have to specify a *process* by which the fact that a social pattern (rule, institution) is advantageous to a group or social system can with reason be assumed systematically to contribute to the existence and persistence of the pattern (rule, institution) in question.[9]

There seem essentially to be two ways the beneficial effects a rule has for the group in which it is practiced can be assumed, as such, to account for the rule's existence:

1. One can either assume that there is a "feedback," based on the perception of its beneficial effects, i.e. based on the fact that individuals recognize the beneficial consequences which certain regularities of

---

7. Cf. e.g. Hayek, 1979, where it is argued that new rules emerged "because the groups which acted on them prospered more than others" (p. 161), and that "rules are adopted . . . because those groups who practice them are successful" (p. 204). Cf. also Hayek, 1973, pp. 17ff.

8. Hayek, in fact, sometimes uses arguments that sound quite similar to functionalist arguments in sociology. So, for instance, he talks of "the adaptation of the parts to requirements of the whole" (1967, p. 77) and states that "we are bound to explain the fact that the elements behave in a certain way by the circumstance that this sort of conduct is most likely to preserve the whole" (*ibid.*). Or he argues that "the term 'function' . . . is an almost indispensable term for the discussion of those self-maintaining structures which we find alike in biological organisms and in spontaneous social orders" (1973, p. 28).

9. That functionalism is subject to these objections seems to be the prevailing view, at least, though arguments to the contrary are to be found too. Cf. Cohen, 1978, pp. 249ff.

conduct have for a group and take actions – individually or collectively – to implement and to enforce the rule;

2. Or, one has to assume that a distinct feedback-mechanism operates at the group- or aggregate level, a feedback mechanism that is "autonomous" in the sense of not being simply dependent on intentional action aimed at achieving the beneficial effects, whether individual, separate or collective, organized action.

Both notions of feedback-mechanisms are, for different reasons, necessarily in conflict with the invisible-hand notion of the theory of spontaneous social order: while being based on the same strict individualistic footing as an invisible-hand approach (explaining social patterns as an aggregate outcome of individual human action) the first notion would stress the significance of *deliberate design* rather than *unintended emergence*. It would focus on *political processes* by which rules are chosen, changed and enforced and *not* the invisible-hand process by which rules emerge out of the interaction of individuals which are separately pursuing their own ends. Such kinds of feedback-mechanisms surely operate in social reality, but the thrust of Hayek's writing is to remind us of the limits of these processes (1979, p. 159; 1960, p. 110), and he certainly would not want to suggest that political processes (of what kind?) can be expected systematically to select those rules that "serve the common welfare."

The second notion, which may be appropriately characterized as "collectivist functionalism," is also fundamentally incompatible with an individualistic, invisible-hand approach. Like the latter it stresses the idea of "useful" social patterns being *not* a result of deliberate design but rather an *unintended outcome* of a social process. It explicitly rejects, however, the idea that this social process can be explained (at least "in principle")[10] in terms of *individual actions*, maintaining, instead, that the feedback process in question is operating at the aggregate, collective level as such and cannot be theoretically reconstructed as a systematic outcome of processes operating at the level of individual interaction.

Apparently, and strangely enough, Hayek appeals to such a *collectivist, functionalist* notion (1967, pp. 70f., 74) when he stresses that, in cultural evolution, a process of *"group selection"* is of "greatest importance" (1979, p. 202), a selection process which Hayek obviously considers to be different from the process of variation and selection by *individual choices*, described above. According to this notion of *group*

10. As Hayek has stressed, social theory – like all theories of "complex phenomena" – can only be expected to provide "pattern predictions" or "explanations in principle" of the formation of social structures, since the specific manifestation of any particular social order will depend on all the specific circumstances the individual actors are facing. The social theorist can neither know these specific circumstances in their entirety, nor take into account all their specific effects; cf. notably Hayek's essay on "The Theory of Complex Phenomena," in 1967, pp. 22ff.

selection, cultural rules are "the result of a process of winnowing or sifting, directed by the differential advantages gained by groups from practices adopted for some unknown and perhaps purely accidental reasons" (1979, p. 155). That is, group selection is regarded as a process that establishes a *direct link* between the social beneficial *effects* of cultural rules and their emergence and persistence, a process in which "rules of conduct . . . have evolved *because* the groups who practiced them were more successful and displaced others."[11]

That Hayek's appeal to a process of cultural evolution operating at the group-level as such stands in contrast to his explicit methodological individualism (1979a, pp. 61ff.) and to what is otherwise the main thrust of his work, has been repeatedly pointed out (Steele, 1984; Gray, 1984, pp. 52, 55; Ullmann-Margalit, 1978, pp. 282ff.). Yet although it represents a major flaw in Hayek's reasoning, this inconsistency in itself does not provide a sufficient argument against the notion of group selection.[12] Rather it has to be judged on its own grounds, that is, based on the question whether it is apt to contribute to our understanding of the process of cultural evolution or not.

V. GROUP SELECTION AND THE FREE RIDER PROBLEM

When Hayek made the notion of group selection a key concept in his theory of cultural evolution he obviously was influenced by the discus-

11. Hayek, 1973, p. 18 (emphasis added). Cf. also *ibid.*, p. 9, and 1979, p. 159. Hayek has increasingly stressed the notion of "group selection" in his more recent writings (cf. e.g. Hayek, 1984), parallel to an individualistic, invisible-hand interpretation of the process of cultural evolution. The group selection notion appears, however, in his earlier writings, too (cf. e.g. his "Notes on the Evolution of Systems of Rules of Conduct" in Hayek, 1967, pp. 66ff.).

12. It should be noted that Hayek, in some places, seems to characterize the process of group selection in a way that would allow for a consistent, individualistic interpretation. Thus, he argues, for instance, that groups practicing more "appropriate" or "successful" rules will expand "by the attraction of outsiders" (Hayek, 1979, p. 159), or that more successful orders will tend to prevail by being imitated by "outsiders." For such processes of *between-group migration* and *between-group imitation* to be taken into account, it is not necessary, however, to appeal to a special theory of *group selection* that would have to be added to the *individualistic* conception of cultural evolution described above. Imitation by outsiders can either mean that rules spread by an invisible-hand process of separate individual imitation, or, that they spread because of deliberate, collective choices by "outside groups" to adopt what is perceived as a "successful" rule. Reference to individual between-group migration leaves open the question of how the emergence and persistence of the system of rules in the "successful group" is to be explained (as the outcome of an invisible-hand process, the result of some political process – or something else?) and it would face the objection that, because of considerable natural and artificially erected barriers to migration, individual migration can hardly be expected to be an effective mechanism that will systematically tend to select "beneficial" rules.

sion on "group selection" in biology, and notably by V.C. Wynne-Edwards' (1962) treatise on the subject (Hayek, 1967, p. 70; 1973, p. 164; 1979, p. 202). In biology, the issue that gave rise to the notion of group selection is the question of how the evolution of those patterns of animal behavior can be explained that apparently are advantageous to the species or the group rather than to the individual exhibiting the respective behavior. The existence of such group-advantageous patterns of behavior seems to pose a problem to the classical, "individualistic" Darwinian approach that explains the evolution of features of a species in terms of the genetic reproductive advantage to the individual organisms which happen to acquire these features. A discussion of this issue should distinguish between two kinds of cases.

First, those cases in which individuals are exhibiting a pattern of behavior that is advantageous to the group in which they live, but at the same time can be shown to be advantageous to the individuals themselves. These cases, obviously, allow for a Darwinian explanation, since the fact that the behavioral pattern in question benefits the individual, provides a sufficient argument for its being selected.

The crucial issue arises obviously with the second kind of cases in which individuals are exhibiting patterns of behavior that, while benefiting the group, appear to be disadvantageous, self-sacrificing on the part of the individuals themselves. Because the explanation of those patterns seems to pose an insurmountable problem to an individualistic Darwinian approach, some authors appealed to the notion of group selection, i.e., the idea of a process of selection operating at the level of groups rather than of individual organisms. Since its appearance, however, the notion of group selection has been vehemently disputed in biology, the main objection being that since, after all, genetic inheritance is a matter of individual reproduction, a theory of group selection runs into a basic paradox, that D.T. Campbell (1980, p. 73) states as follows: "Any socially useful self-sacrificial behavior benefits both the 'altruists' and the nonaltruists in the group, the *net* benefit being greater to the nonaltruists because the gains to the altruists are reduced by the self-sacrificial risk costs they bear." That is, within the group the "free riders" will be better off than those who exhibit the self-sacrificing behavior, and, accordingly, self-sacrificing behavioral patterns can be expected to evolve and persist only if and to the extent that the intergroup advantage from self-sacrificing behavior outweighs the intragroup disadvantage. It seems to be dominant opinion among biologists that the conditions needed for this rarely exist in nature (Clutton-Brock and Harvey, 1978, p. 6; Maynard-Smith, 1980, p. 23). And, accordingly, the research strategy they typically seem to favor is, in the case of apparently group-advantageous behavioral patterns, to look for benefits that, it may be in a somewhat indirect and less obvious way, accrue to the individual organism exhibiting the respective behavior (Trivers, 1985, pp., 67ff.), if reference is not made to the notion of "kin selection" (to be strictly distinguished from "group selection"), in order to explain, on a genetic basis, the evolution of "group beneficial behavior among sufficiently related individuals" (Wilson, 1980, pp. 55ff.; Maynard-Smith, 1978, pp. 22ff.).

A direct parallel can be drawn from the use of the notion of group selection in biology to Hayek's appeal to the concept, which apparently reflects his doubt that an individualistic evolutionary conception cannot adequately account for the evolution of certain cultural rules which appear to be advantageous to the group, without rendering direct benefits to the individual practicing them. Here, again, for the clarity of discussion two kinds of cases should be distinguished. First, those cases in which a socially beneficial behavioral regularity can be shown directly to benefit the individual practicing it. These cases, obviously, do not cause any essential problem for an individualistic, invisible hand approach. Once it can be shown that a certain type of behavior is advantageous to the individual exhibiting it, its explanation in terms of individual benefits seems to be the least onerous (Kummer, 1980, p. 34).

Here, too, the crucial issue arises with the second kind of cases, i.e. with those behavioral patterns that apparently are advantageous to the group in which they are practiced, but appear to be disadvantageous on the part of the individuals exhibiting them. It is obviously with respect to these cases that Hayek considers recourse to the notion of group selection to be necessary. Being aware of the debate in biology, he has conceded in more recent writings (1979, p. 202; 1984, p. 318) that group selection "in biological evolution seems to play only a minor role" yet he maintains "that cultural evolution operates chiefly through group selection." The same basic argument, however, that has cast a doubt upon the notion of group selection in biology, seems equally to undermine the notion of cultural group selection. Since, after all, it is the individuals who are to adopt and to practice the behavioral regularities which are supposed to be selected, the same type of paradox arises: though individuals who live in groups in which "appropriate" rules are practiced are better off compared to individuals that live in groups with "less appropriate" rules, within the groups those bearing the costs of socially beneficial but self-sacrificing behavior would be relatively *worse off* than those who *free* ride, who enjoy the group-advantage without sharing the costs of its production. Hence, despite the between-group advantage from practicing "appropriate" rules, there would be a within-group disadvantage for those who actually practice them compared to those who free ride. It is true that in cultural evolution the free-rider problem can be overcome because of men's capability deliberately to change the constraints under which they are acting so as to make adherence to socially beneficial practices individually advantageous.[13] But incorporating these mechanisms into a theory of cultural evolution would mean to assign a significant role to organized, political processes and would not seem to leave much room for some autonomous process of group selection operating beyond the level of man's choice.

A theory of the emergence and persistence of cultural rules has to cope with the problem that group advantage as such simply cannot explain why the individuals within the group will actually exhibit such group-beneficial behavioral regularities, given the incentive to free-ride. Whatever the between-group advantages may be, group-beneficial behavioral regularities cannot be expected to spread and to be maintained, unless conditions prevail within the group that make it advantageous to the individuals themselves to act accordingly. What a theory explaining the emergence of such group-beneficial behavioral regularities would have to show is how these conditions are actually brought about. It would have to show either how they emerge spontaneously in the process of interaction among individuals separately pursuing their own ends, or, how they are brought about as a result of organized, collective action. That is, rather than to resort to the vague notion of group selection, one would have to engage in a systematic theoretical analysis of the two kinds of processes distinguished above: the process of spontaneous generation and change of rules, on which an individualistic, invisible-hand notion of cultural evolution properly focuses, and the process of deliberate changes in and enforcement of rules by organized, collective choices.

Raising the above objections against the notion of cultural group selection is by no means equivalent to saying that the chances of a behavioral pattern's persisting is not affected by its beneficial or detri-

13. When in discussions on the issue of group selection it is argued (cf., e.g., Hirshleifer, 1982, p. 30) that, at the level of *Homo sapiens*, there might be reasons allowing for a social evolution of group-beneficial behavioral regularities, reference is typically made to two arguments: it is either stressed that man's special capability of "long-term learning" provides the prerequisite for the mechanism of *reciprocal reinforcement* to generate socially beneficial behavioral patterns (this is, actually, the central theoretical argument in an individualistic evolutionist conception), or it is stressed that men are capable of restructuring the social conditions under which they are acting through deliberately coordinated, organized action, to generate the conditions required to make them act in accordance with socially beneficial rules. Cf. e.g. Markl, p. 168: "Reciprocal altruism . . . requires long-term learning/memory on the part of the recipient of the altruistic act. Thus it may be restricted to higher animals . . . Rousseau's notion of the *Social Contract*, in which cheating is prevented by collective action, may be a force for social evolution in humans." Cf. also Kummer, 1980, p. 45: "Human morality can increase the benefits of social life beyond the level which noncultural mechanisms of behavior can produce. One example is cooperative sanction."

mental consequences for the group in which it is practiced. Feedbacks from the social effects of rules to their persistence certainly exist. The argument rather is that because of the highly complex nature of these feedbacks – being mediated by such diverse variables as individual migration, economic prosperity, political structure, military strength, etc. – the general notion that social systems with "more successful" systems of rules will eventually win out, seems to be too vague to allow for sufficiently interesting conclusions about the systematic operation of a group selection process, at least as we move beyond the prehistoric stage, when men lived in small hunter and gatherer bands (Hayek, 1979, p. 160), and begin to deal with cultural variety and change in modern societies.[14]

VI. THE SCOPE AND LIMITS OF AN INDIVIDUALISTIC-EVOLUTIONIST CONCEPTION

When Carl Menger (1963, pp. 129–59) elaborated the distinction between what he called the "pragmatic" and the "organic" interpretation of social phenomena, i.e., their interpretation as "the results of a common will directed toward their establishment (agreement, positive legislation, etc.)" versus their interpretation as the unintended "result of human efforts aimed at attaining essentially individual goals" (ibid., p. 133), he took pains to make clear that if the notion of the "organic

14. In his latest writings, notably in his forthcoming book *The Fatal Conceit*, Hayek seems more and more to suggest an interpretation of the notion of group selection which is not based on the claim that individuals practice certain rules *because* they are beneficial to the group (a claim the above criticism of the group selection notion focuses on). Rather the argument is that those groups in which, *for whatever reason*, individuals are made to follow socially beneficial rules will be superior to groups with less beneficial rules, and that – via the superiority of the group – cultural evolution will select for appropriate rules. According to this interpretation, it could be acknowledged that certain rules cannot be expected to emerge and to be enforced spontaneously, but require some "organized apparatus" for their enforcement, while at the same time the claim could still be made that – independent of how groups manage to acquire and to enforce these rules – a group selection process will favor the more advantageous systems of rules. The idea of such a politically mediated process of cultural selection is left extremely vague in Hayek's writings and it raises a bundle of issues. As D.R. Steele (1984) has rightly criticized, it is unclear for what period of human history Hayek considers this interpretation to be appropriate. And it is unclear what normative and positive significance Hayek wants to assign, for instance, to the criterion of "multiplication and expansion in numbers," which he seems to consider a relevant indicator for "group success." The idea of a process of cultural evolution that operates beyond the level of individual selection of practices and organized enforcement of rules may, perhaps, be appropriate for a view measuring cultural development in terms of millenia, but it has very little significance for the issue of what is an appropriate attitude towards the systems of rules in which men find themselves placed.

origin" of social institutions is to be more than an empty phrase, it is necessary to specify the nature of the process by which institutions emerge independently of a "common will directéd at their establishment" (ibid., pp. 224, 230, 149). The same caveat applies, of course, to the notion of cultural evolution which Hayek stresses in his own restatement of the social-theory perspective he adopts from Menger and the Scottish moral philosophers. Of the two conceptions of "cultural evolution" analyzed above only the individualistic, invisible-hand notion actually allows for a systematic theoretical specification, and only this notion qualifies as a "twin conception" of the notion of spontaneous social order. It is the scope and limits of such an individualistic evolutionist conception that will be discussed in this section.

Hayek is well aware of the fact that, de facto, only a part of the rules upon which the spontaneous order of a market is based will be the outcome of an "evolutionary process" in the above sense (1979, pp. 159f.), and that, hence, an evolutionist interpretation cannot be considered equally suitable for all culturally transmitted rules. It will, necessarily, be the less appropriate, the more we turn from the rules of customs and morals or conventions to those rules which are subject to legislation, i.e., to deliberate collective choice (Hayek, 1960, p. 63). And Hayek (1973, p. 45) even explicitly acknowledges that the rules of law which are deliberately chosen and altered by legislation are of special interest since they "become the chief instrument whereby we can affect the resulting order."

That there are, in this sense, de facto limits to the explanatory appropriateness of an evolutionist conception is obvious and is not the issue of interest here. Attention shall be focused here, rather, on the systematic limits to the potential scope of an evolutionist invisible-hand approach, in the sense that—while there are certain types of rules which can, at least "in principle," be expected to emerge from an invisible-hand process, though, de facto, they may be an outcome of deliberate choice—there are other rules for which it cannot be plausibly assumed that they *could* "in principle" emerge from a spontaneous, invisible-hand process.

As Hayek (1976, p. 21) states, social rules typically provide solutions to "recurring problem situations" in social interaction. And a fruitful approach to the issue at stake is to refer to specific types of stylized problem situations that can be described in terms of game theory matrices, and to analyze whether an invisible-hand process can plausibly be assumed "in principle" to generate a behavioral regularity providing a solution to the problem in question.[15] A variety of stylized

15. This approach is characteristic of E. Ullmann-Margalit's book on *The Emergence of Norms* (1977) as well as of A. Schotter's contribution to *The Economic Theory of Social*

problem situations have been specified and analyzed in game theory, but for the purposes of this paper, it is sufficient to confine discussion to the two types that seem to be of major relevance for social theoretical analysis: coordination problems and PD problems.[16]

A typical example of a coordination type recurring problem situation is traffic on a road. Drivers approaching each other, going in opposite directions, somehow have to coordinate their actions to get by each other without collision. A rule (e.g., always to drive at the right/ left side of the road) that would provide a general solution to this recurring coordination problem is clearly preferable to all participants, compared to arranging for a new solution in any particular case. The question of interest here is whether such a rule or behavioral regularity, which obviously is "socially beneficial," can *in principle*, be explained as the outcome of an invisible hand process. In general terms, coordination problems have the following characteristics (Ullmann-Margalit, 1977, pp. 77ff.): they consist of situations involving two or more persons, each one facing a choice between two or more alternative courses of action, the outcomes of which are dependent on the choice(s) made by the other actor(s) involved. Specifically, there are at least two combinations of choices which all parties prefer to all other possible combinations. For the simplified "two actors, two alternatives" case this type of problem situation can be illustrated by the following matrix (with actor A facing the alternatives a_1, b_1, and actor B facing the alternatives b_1, b_2; the figures in the matrix representing the hypothetical payoffs):[17]

Institutions (1981). The basic argument of Ullmann-Margalit's analysis (1977, p. 9) is "that certain types of norms are solutions to problems posed by certain interaction situations. These problems inhere in the structure—in the game-theoretical sense of structure—of the situations concerned, pertaining to some or all of the interacting participants." Schotter (1981, p. 17) states as "the major point" of his book, "that economic and social institutions emerge in society in response to a set of recurrent societal problems."

16. J. Hirshleifer (1982) also discusses the issue of an "evolutionary approach" in a game-theory framework (*ibid.*, pp. 13ff.), and he, as well as E. Ullmann-Margalit (1977) and A. Schotter (1981), include additional types of problem situations in their analysis. But in all cases, coordination problems and PD-problems are the ones that are of major systematic relevance.

17. What is essential to coordination problems is that among all possib'e combinations there is a subset of at least two combinations which all parties involved prefer to the rest. With respect to this subset they may either be *indifferent* to which particular combination is realized, or they may *not* be indifferent (as in the matrix used here). And their preferences within the subset may either harmonize (as in the matrix used here), or they may be in conflict—as long as their *common interest* in realizing one of the combinations in the subset *dominates* their conflicting interests in which one should be realized.

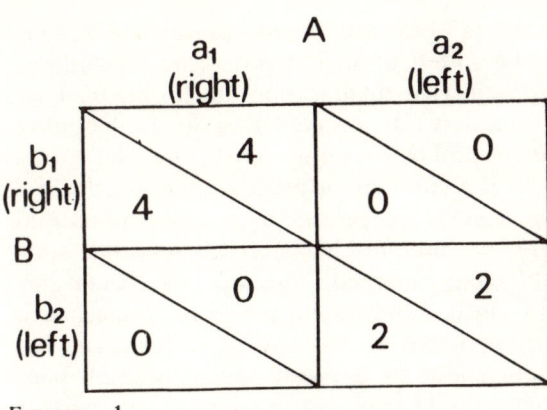

FIGURE 1

If A and B exhibit a behavioral regularity (e.g. always to drive on the right/left side of the road) that makes them end up with the combinations a_1, b_1 or a_2, b_2, a problem-solving rule would be established. Such a rule could, of course, be established by explicit, deliberate agreement. The issue we have to address here, however, is whether and how such a problem-solving behavioral regularity can be expected to emerge by an invisible-hand process. With respect to coordination problems it is typically possible to provide, in principle, a theoretical reconstruction of a process by which, out of a situation without any rules, gradually, and without any deliberate agreement, rules emerge as a social result only of separate individual actions, pursuing individual interests. The essential "ingredients" to such invisible-hand explanations are the following assumptions. First, in the original situation individual choices among the alternative courses of actions are, roughly, distributed at random, since there are no systematic preferences within the population for specific alternatives. Second, by chance a specific alternative becomes more often practiced (or is perceived as being more often practiced) than others. This makes it slightly more advantageous to choose this alternative rather than others. Third, the more often a particular alternative is chosen relative to others, the stronger the incentives to practice it and the greater the disadvantages of choosing some alternative course of action. Accordingly, a cumulative process can be expected to operate that eventually leads to a particular strategy being generally practiced. Fourth, once a particular strategy is "established" in this sense as a behavioral regularity, there are (under normal, typical conditions) no incentives for the individual to deviate from the rule. That is, rules providing solutions to coordination problems cannot only be expected, in principle, to emerge spontaneously, they also tend to be self-policing or self-enforcing.

Coordination rules, or, as they are called, *conventions* (Lewis, 1969), seem especially to be suited to an individualistic, evolutionist explanation, but there are still two qualifications to be made. First, there is nothing in the spontaneous process that guarantees that, among potential alternative problem-solving rules, the "best" one will necessarily emerge. By the cumulative process mentioned above a behavioral regularity may come to prevail in a social community that serves the interests of the individuals concerned less than some alternative rule that *could* have emerged, but did not (Hirshleifer, 1982, p. 37). And, second, once a coordination rule is established in a group, it cannot be assumed that a shift to a more beneficial rule can, in general, be brought about by a spontaneous, invisible-hand process. Even if individuals should consider other practices more attractive than those that are *conventional* in their respective group, it might be too disadvantageous for them unilaterally to deviate from established conventions and to initiate a spontaneous change in rules – for the very same reasons that account for the self-enforcing character of these rules. Certainly, the costs of experimenting with new practices and, accordingly, the chances for a spontaneous, gradual shift to alternative rules vary over different kinds of conventions (e.g. rules of etiquette vs rules of the road). But, still, due to the same social conditions that spontaneously enforce a particular convention, it may very well be that a shift to a more beneficial rule cannot, in principle, be expected to be brought about by an invisible-hand process, but only by deliberate, concerted action: by an organized simultaneous switch of all individuals concerned from one practice to another (e.g. from driving on the left side to driving on the right side of the road).

PD-problems, a typical illustration of which is the story of two prisoners from which the name "prisoners' dilemma" (PD) is derived, can generally be described in terms of the following characteristics (Ullmann-Margalit, 1977, pp. 18ff.): they comprise situations involving two or more persons, each of whom faces a choice between two alternative courses of action, x or not-x (to cheat or not to cheat; to defect or to cooperate), the outcomes of which will be dependent on the choice(s) made by the other actor(s), in such a way that

1. both (or all) participants are worse off (than they could be) if they both (or all) choose x;
2. both (or all) *benefit*, are better off, if they both (or all) choose not-x;
3. the most attractive combination for the individual is to choose x while the other players choose not-x;
4. the most disadvantageous combination for the individual is to choose not-x while the other players choose x.

94 VIKTOR VANBERG

For the simplified "two actors" case this type of problem situation can be illustrated by the following matrix[18]:

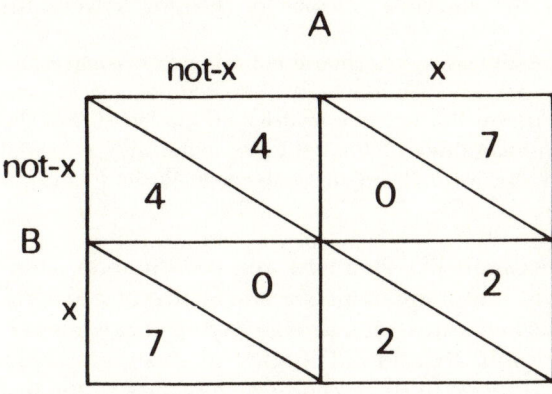

FIGURE 2

Problem situations of this type create a *dilemma* for the actors involved, because by attempting to get into the most attractive position and/or to protect themselves against ending up in the most disadvantageous position, they will both end up with the combination (x, x), rather than with the more attractive combination (not-x, not-x), which they *could* realize. Hence, it would be in A's and B's common interest if they both followed the rule, in recurring situations of this type always to choose not-x. And the issue that is of interest here is whether and how such a problem-solving behavioral regularity can, in principle, be expected to emerge by an invisible-hand process.

There are obviously characteristic differences in the typical incentive-structure of recurring coordination problems and recurring PD-problems and because of these differences the above arguments on the spontaneous emergence of conventions cannot be simply transferred to PD-situations.

1. In the original situation there will be no *random* distribution among the alternative strategies. There is, rather, a strong incentive for the participating individuals *not* to choose the cooperative strategy (not-x) at all.

18. The matrix represents a simplified case in various respects. As R. Axelrod (1984, p. 17) rightfully points out: "1. The payoffs of the players need not be comparable at all. . . . 2. The payoffs certainly do not have to be symmetric. . . . The only thing that has to be assumed is that, for each player, the four payoffs are ordered as required for by the definition of the Prisoner's Dilemma. 3. The payoffs of a player do not have to be measured on an absolute scale. They need only be measured relative to each other. 4. Cooperation need not be considered desirable from the point of view of the rest of the world."

2. If a growing number of participants should choose the cooperative
    strategy, this, *per se*, would not imply that there is an incentive for the
    individual actor to choose this strategy too. Rather it increases the
    chances to realize the attractive situation of choosing x while the
    others choose not-x.
3. If a behavioral regularity always to choose not-x should become estab-
    lished in a group, it cannot be assumed to be self-policing or self-
    enforcing. It does (normally) not pay to drive on the left side of the
    road while all the others drive on the right side. But it may very well
    pay to be the only one who cheats or steals while all the others are
    honest.

That these differences between PD-situations and coordination situations exist does not imply that a spontaneous emergence of problem-
solving behavioral regularities can never be expected in recurring PD-
situations. But it does imply that for PD-norms to emerge, certain
additional incentives – additional to the incentives embodied in the immediate situation – have to be generated spontaneously, incentives by
which the original incentive structure is changed so that the individual
can no longer expect to be best off by defecting (choosing x) while the
others cooperate (choose not-x), and can be sufficiently sure that by
cooperating (choosing not-x) he will not end up in the worst situation
of being the only honest player in a world of cheaters. Throughout the
tradition of individualistic social theory a specific social mechanism has
been stressed that, indeed, can be expected spontaneously to generate
such additional incentives, namely, the mechanism of *reciprocity*, of
reciprocal reinforcement by mutually exchanging rewards and punishment in social interaction. Where individuals are in an ongoing, continuous interaction with others, they have to take into account the
future consequences of their present choices.[19] Immediate gains from
non-cooperation may well be overcompensated by the future losses
from unfavorable responses one elicits. That the mechanism of reciprocity is a major source of cooperation among individuals with divergent interests was a central theme of the social-theory paradigm articulated by David Hume, Adam Smith, and other Scottish moral
philosophers of the 18th century. And it is a theoretical notion that,
while remaining a central element in the individualistic tradition of
social theory, has been repeatedly reemphasized (Vanberg, 1975,
pp. 15ff., 55ff.), more recently, and with interesting new insights in
R. Axelrod's (1984) treatise on *The Evolution of Cooperation*.

Yet, though in principle allowing for an invisible-hand explanation

19. The impact of expected future consequences on present choices has been modelled
    in game-theory contributions on recurrent PD problems. A result of particular inter-
    est is that of a cooperative solution to infinite-horizon supergames (cf. Friedman,
    1977; Taylor, 1976; Schotter, 1981).

of the emergence of PD-norms, the mechanism of reciprocity cannot be expected to generate sufficient incentives for cooperative behavior generally, but under certain restrictive conditions only. In general, the chance that the interacting parties may meet again and the chance that a defector can be identified as such have to be large enough that sufficient expected gains and losses from future interaction are at stake to make cooperation (not-x) the preferable choice. These chances typically decrease, however, (other things being equal) with increasing numbers of individuals involved in the relevant setting and with a decreasing length of the time-horizon with which individuals engage in particular groups (e.g. because of increasing social mobility). In social settings – e.g. in large groups of highly mobile individuals – in which the mechanism of reciprocity cannot be expected spontaneously to generate sufficient informal private sanctions to discourage defection, *organized enforcement* will be required in order to make cooperative behavioral regularities viable, whether such organized enforcement is based on some deliberate social contract entered into by the relevant group, or whether it is imposed by some sufficiently powerful (internal or external) party.[20]

Implicitly, Hayek refers to the crucial distinction between PD-type and coordination-type rules when he argues that there are rules which all individuals "will follow spontaneously," while there are others "which they have to be made to obey," because, though all would benefit from general adherence to these rules "it would be in the interest of each to disregard them" (1973, p. 45). He explicitly emphasizes that a spontaneous market order cannot be considered in general to be completely self-regulating, but that in "order to enforce the rules required for the formation of this spontaneous order, an order of the other kind, an organization, is also required" (Hayek, 1964, p. 8), the organization we call government (1973, p. 47). However, these aspects are merely added to, rather than systematically integrated with Hayek's theory of cultural evolution. Their systematic incorporation would require Hayek's theory to be much more specific about the nature, scope, and limits of *evolutionary* principles and their relation to or interaction with the forces of organized, political choice in cultural change.

VII. CONCLUSION

The problem I started from is the crucial relation between the character of the spontaneous order of a market and the character of the rules upon which it is based. Spontaneous market processes cannot be ex-

---

20. The "social-contract"-solution to this problem is discussed in detail in Buchanan, 1975 and 1977.

pected simply to generate beneficial outcomes independent of the rules governing the behavior of the market participants. This raises the issue of what rules can be considered "appropriate" in the sense of allowing for a beneficial working of the market mechanism.

Hayek has to be credited for having addressed this issue more explicitly and more systematically than most "free market economists." He is obviously skeptical about attempts to define, in general terms and once and for all, what "appropriate" rules are, because he realizes that changing social and other conditions may require changing answers to the question. Consequently, he shifts attention to the process by which rules are generated and changed, stressing the idea of an evolutionary process and suggesting – often more implicitly than explicitly – that *cultural evolution* can be expected systematically to select for appropriate rules.

The conclusion from the above examination of Hayek's arguments is that a systematic analysis of the idea of cultural evolution does not provide any reason to assume that there is some general spontaneous process at work on which we could rely for the generation of appropriate rules. The notion of cultural group selection is theoretically vague, inconsistent with the basic thrust of Hayek's individualistic approach, and faulty judged on its own grounds. The individualistic, invisible-hand notion of cultural evolution is a consistent element in Hayek's system of thought and it is a valid conception of considerable theoretical content. But the range of its explanatory applicability and the normative inferences it allows for are clearly limited, not only because, as a matter of fact, many rules upon which spontaneous market orders are based are implemented and enforced by some organized apparatus, but also because, for systematic reasons, certain kinds of rules cannot be expected to emerge from and to be enforced by a spontaneous process, except under certain restrictive conditions. This means, when addressing the issue of what "appropriate" rules for a spontaneous market order are, that there is no justification for appealing to the simple answer that, if only let alone, spontaneous forces would automatically generate "appropriate" rules.[21] There is no such simple solution to the issue. Rather one has to face the more difficult task of analyzing the specific characteristics of alternative rules, their working properties, the ways they have been brought about and are enforced by separate, individual or collective, organized action, and the various

21. Though Hayek has repeatedly stressed that spontaneous evolution does not necessarily result in socially beneficial outcomes, his writings are not completely free from arguments suggesting such a view. Cf. e.g. Hayek, 1979, p. 163: "The basic tools of civilization – language, morals, law, and money – are all the result of spontaneous growth and not of design, and of the last two organized power has got hold and thoroughly corrupted them."

VIKTOR VANBERG

means available to the people concerned to express their own evaluation of these rules and the outcomes they produce. That is, one has to engage in institutional or constitutional economics, analyzing how alternative rules affect, and are affected by, private choices as well as public choices.

It may be appropriate to conclude by quoting a comment of Carl Menger, made about one century ago, on a related issue. With respect to a theoretically unsubstantiated, general belief in the "higher wisdom" of unintentionally created common law Menger (1963, pp. 233f.) stated:[22]

> This assertion is, however, erroneous in every conceivable respect. For common law has also proved harmful to the common good often enough, and on the contrary, legislation has just as often changed common law in a way benefiting the common good . . . The theory of the "higher wisdom" of common law thus not only contradicts experience but is at the same time rooted in a vague feeling, in a misunderstanding. It is an exaggeration carried to the point of distortion, of the true statement that positive legislation has upon occasion not comprehended the unintended wisdom in common law, and, in trying to change the latter in the sense of the common good, has not infrequently produced the opposite result . . . If the rules and institutions of common law not infrequently prove to be highly suitable in respect to the common good, it was the task of science to make us understand this advantage . . . But never, and this is the essential point in the matter under review, may science dispense with testing for their suitability those institutions which have come about "organically" . . . No era may renounce this "calling."

REFERENCES

Axelrod, Robert. 1984. *The Evolution of Cooperation*. New York: Basic Books.
Buchanan, James M. 1975. *The Limits of Liberty – Between Anarchy and Leviathan*. Chicago/London: The University of Chicago Press.
———. 1977. *Freedom in Constitutional Contract*. College Station: Texas A&M University Press.
Campbell, D.T. 1980. "Social Morality Norms as Evidence of Conflict Between Biological Human Nature and Social System Requirements." In *Morality as a Biological Phenomenon*, edited by G.S. Stent pp. 67–82. Berkeley/New York/London: University of California Press, rev. ed., 1980.
Clutton-Brock, T.H., and P.H. Harvey (editors). 1978. *Readings in Sociobiology*. Reading, Eng., and San Francisco: W.H. Freeman.
Cohen, G. A. 1978. *Karl Marx's Theory of History – A Defense*. Princeton, N.J.: Princeton University Press.

22. The issue of common law vs. legislation, on which Menger comments, is only related to but not identical with the issue of evolution vs. design of rules as discussed in this paper, since the process by which common law develops, based on decisions made by judges, is obviously different from an invisible-hand process in the sense specified above.

Elster, John. 1979. *Ulysses and the Sirens. Studies in Rationality and Irrationality*. Cambridge: Cambridge University Press.

Friedman, James W. 1977. *Oligopoly and the Theory of Games*. Amsterdam: North Holland.

Furubotn, E.G., and Richter, R. (editors). 1984. "The New Institutional Economics – a Symposium." *Zeitschrift für die gesamte Staatswissenschaft*, 140, 1: 1–6.

Gould, Stephen J. 1983. "Evolutionary Flexibility and Human Consciousness." Paper prepared for Liberty Fund/Civitas Symposium "Evolution und Freiheit," Munich, May 8–11, 1983.

Gray, John. 1984. *Hayek on Liberty*. New York: Basil Blackwell.

Hayek, Friedrich A. 1948. *Individualism and Economic Order*. Chicago: University of Chicago Press.

———. 1964. "Kinds of Order in Society." *New Individualist Review* 3: 3–12.

———. 1967. *Studies in Philosophy, Politics and Economics*. Chicago: University of Chicago Press.

———. 1973. *Law, Legislation and Liberty, Vol. 1: Rules and Order*. London: Routledge & Kegan Paul.

———. 1976. *Law, Legislation and Liberty, Vol. 2: The Mirage of Social Justice*. London: Routledge & Kegan Paul.

———. 1978. *New Studies in Philosophy, Politics, Economics and the History of Ideas*. Chicago: University of Chicago Press.

———. 1979. *Law, Legislation and Liberty, Vol. 3: The Political Order of a Free People*. London: Routledge & Kegan Paul.

———. 1979a. *The Counter-Revolution of Science*. Glencoe, Ill.: Free Press, 1952; 2nd ed., Indianapolis: Liberty Press.

———. 1984. The Origins and Effects of Our Morals: A Problem for Science. In *The Essence of Hayek*, edited by Ch. Nishiyama and K.R. Leube, Stanford, Cal.: Hoover Institution Press, pp. 318–30.

———. *The Fatal Conceit*. Forthcoming.

Hirshleifer, Jack. 1982. "Evolutionary Models in Economics and Law: Cooperation vs. Conflict Strategies." In *Evolutionary Models in Economics and Law, Vol. 4*, edited by P.H. Rubin and R.O. Zerbe, Jr., Greenwich, Conn. and London: JAI Press, pp. 1–60.

Hume, David. 1967. *A Treatise of Human Nature*. Oxford: Clarendon Press.

Kummer, H. 1980. "Analogs of Morality Among Nonhuman Primates." In *Morality as a Biological Phenomenon*, edited by G.S. Stent, Berkeley, Los Angeles, London: University of California Press, pp. 31–47.

Lewis, David. 1969. *Convention: A Philosophical Study*. Cambridge, Mass.: Harvard University Press.

Markl, Hubert (editor). 1980. *Evolution of Social Behavior: Hypotheses and Empirical Tests*. Weinheim/Deerfield Beach, Florida/Basel: VCH, Pubs.

Maynard-Smith, J. 1978. "Group Selection." In *Readings in Sociobiology*, edited by T.H. Clutton-Brock and P.H. Harvey, Reading, Eng., and San Francisco: W.H. Freeman, pp. 20–30.

———. 1980. "The Concepts of Sociobiology." In *Morality as a Biological Phenomenon*, edited by G.S. Stent, Berkeley, Los Angeles, London: University of California Press, pp. 21–30.

McKenzie, Richard B. (editor). 1984. *Constitutional Economics: Containing the Economic Powers of Government*. Lexington, Mass.: D.C. Heath.

Menger, Carl (editor). 1963. *Problems of Economics and Sociology*. With an introduction by Louis Schneider. Urbana: University of Illinois Press.

Nishiyama, Chiaki and Kurt R. Leube (editors). 1984. *The Essence of Hayek*. Stanford, Cal.: Hoover Institution Press.

Nozick, Robert. 1974. *Anarchy, State, and Utopia*. New York: Basic Books.

Rubin, Paul H., and Richard O. Zerbe, Jr. (editors). 1982. *Evolutionary Models in Economics and Law, Research in Law and Economics, Vol. 4*. Greenwich, Conn. and London: JAI Press, Inc.

Schweber, S.S. 1977. "The Origin of the *Origin* Revisited." *Journal of the History of Biology* 10: 229–316.

Schotter, Andrew. 1981. *The Economic Theory of Social Institutions*. Cambridge: Cambridge University Press.

Steele, David Ramsay. 1984. "Hayek's Theory of Cultural Group Selection." Paper presented at the Midwestern Libertarian Scholars' Conference, Chicago, April 13–14.

Stent, Gunther S. (editor). 1978. *Morality as a Biological Phenomenon: The Presuppositions of Sociobiological Research*. Berkeley, Los Angeles, London (revised ed., 1980): University of California Press.

Taylor, Michael. 1976. *Anarchy and Cooperation*. London: Wiley.

Trivers, Robert. 1985. *Social Evolution*. Menlo Park, Cal.: Benjamin/Cummings.

Ullmann-Margalit, Edna. 1978. "Invisible Hand Explanations." *Synthese* 39: 263–91.

———. 1977. *The Emergence of Norms*. Oxford: Clarendon Press.

Vanberg, Viktor 1975. *Die zwei Soziologien – Individualismus und Kollektivismus in der Sozialtheorie*. Tübingen: J.C.B. Mohr (Paul Siebeck).

———. 1984. " 'Unsichtbare-Hand Erklärung' und soziale Normen." In *Normgeleitetes Verhalten in den Sozialwissenschaften, Schriften des Vereins fuer Socialpolitik, N.F. Vol. 141*, edited by H. Todt, Berlin: Duncker & Humblot, pp. 115–46.

Watkins, J.W.N. 1978. *Freiheit und Entscheidung*. Tübingen: J.C.B. Mohr (Paul Siebeck).

Wilson, Edward O. 1980. *Sociobiology, the Abridged Edition*. Cambridge, Mass. and London: Harvard University Press.

Wynne-Edwards, V.C. 1962. *Animal Dispersion in Relation to Social Behavior*. Edinburgh: Oliver and Boyd.

[22]

Journal of Economic Perspectives— Volume 3, Number 4— Fall 1989— Pages 85–97

Spontaneous Order

Robert Sugden

In a fishing village on the Yorkshire coast there used to be an unwritten rule about the gathering of driftwood after a storm. Whoever was first onto a stretch of the shore after high tide was allowed to take whatever he wished, without interference from later arrivals, and to gather it into piles above the high-tide line. Provided he placed two stones on the top of each pile, the wood was regarded as his property, for him to carry away when he chose. If, however, a pile had not been removed after two more high tides, this ownership right lapsed (Walmsley, 1932, pp. 70–71). The writer who describes this "first-on" rule does not tell us how it came into existence. Probably its origins had been long forgotten. Nor does he tell us why people obeyed it: only that they did. But we can be sure that the inhabitants of a fishing village would not have appealed to law courts or police to enforce a custom about driftwood. Somehow this rule was self-enforcing. The first-on rule is an example of what Friedrich Hayek (1960, 1979) calls "spontaneous order."

An economist would notice the efficiency properties of a rule that quickly establishes ownership rights over unowned but valuable objects. The principle that the first person on the shore is given a free hand to collect what he wants allows the gathering of driftwood to be carried out in a way that is economical of labor as compared with a system in which everyone scrambles to get to the best wood first. And the principle of the marked piles does away with the need to guard the wood before it is taken home. But if a rule has never consciously been chosen, can its efficiency be an explanation of its existence? To think so would be to ignore the lesson of the Prisoner's Dilemma: even if everyone is better off when everyone follows the rule than when no one follows it, following that rule is not necessarily rational for any individual.

■ *Robert Sugden is Professor of Economics, School of Economic and Social Studies, University of East Anglia, Norwich, England.*

So how are we to explain the existence of this rule? And why this particular rule for assigning property rights, rather than any other? The first-on rule is only one of many rules, or as I shall say, conventions, that could fix property rights in driftwood. Why not allocate each person a day for collecting wood? Or why not use a lottery? Either of these alternatives might have been more efficient than the first-on rule. By using a kind of race (the race to be first on the shore) to assign property rights, the first-on rule encourages everyone to expend effort in an attempt to win; this competitive expenditure of effort in the race is a deadweight loss. Are some sorts of convention —even if inefficient—more likely to emerge or more able to survive than others?

My concern is to try to explain how rules regulating human action can evolve without conscious human design, and can maintain themselves without there being any formal machinery for enforcing them. I want to be able to say something about the kinds of rules that are likely to evolve and survive. And I want to find how these rules link with rationality and with morality.

Why, it might be asked, should economists concern themselves with such questions? One answer is that the market itself is in important respects a spontaneous order. Many of the institutions of a market economy are conventions that no one has designed, but that have simply evolved. Think of the arrangements by which buyers and sellers make contact. How does it come to be common knowledge that advertisements for a particular kind of job will be placed in one newspaper rather than another, and that it is the task of the buyer of labor, not the seller, to advertise? What makes one part of a city the business district? What makes some stock markets more important than others? Although markets may work more smoothly when property rights are defined by formal laws and enforced by the state, they can come into existence and persist without any such external support. Think of how markets in foreign currency, gambling, prostitution, alcohol and narcotics can continue despite the attempts of governments to suppress them. Such markets can continue only because the participants recognise *de facto* property rights that the state does not. This raises the possibility that the institution of property itself may ultimately be a form of spontaneous order.

An analysis of spontaneous order may also throw light on some theoretical problems about rationality. Game theorists typically assume that their games are played by ideally rational individuals who have full knowledge of each other's preferences and attitudes to risk. Many game theorists have regarded it as self-evident that, in such a situation, there must be a uniquely rational strategy for each player, which can be identified by deductive reasoning (for example, Harsanyi and Selten, 1988). If this is true, then individuals who follow conventions cannot be fully rational. (The essential feature of a convention is that it is one of several possible solutions to a game.) Conversely, if it can be rational to follow a convention, the claim that every game has a uniquely rational solution must be false.

Finally, the idea of spontaneous order may have implications for how we approach normative questions. Economists tend to think of moral judgments as judgments about the overall welfare of society, made from some neutral standpoint. They are attracted to moral theories like classical utilitarianism, or John Rawls's (1972) theory of justice, which allow social welfare functions to be constructed according to simple sets of rational principles. Hayek (1960, 1979) offers an entirely different perspective. For Hayek, the idea that we can, as it were, stand outside our society and rationally appraise its institutions is a dangerous illusion. The institutions and the moral beliefs of a free society, he argues, are the unplanned consequences of a process of evolution. The conventions which create order in a free society are supported by moral beliefs: people believe that they ought to keep to these conventions. But there is no independent principle of justice that provides a rational basis for these beliefs. The belief that one ought to follow a convention is the product of the same process of evolution as the convention itself. Thus the study of spontaneous order may help to explain why we have some of the moral beliefs that we do have, without in any way being able to show that we *ought* to have them. It is to this enterprise that this paper, and the book (Sugden, 1986) on which it is based, belongs.

Conventions

The game of Chicken provides a simple model of how rules of property might come into existence. Imagine two individuals disputing about which of them should take something they both want (perhaps driftwood). Each has a choice between two (pure) strategies, an aggressive one and a conciliatory one. Mixing avian metaphors, I shall use the language of theoretical biology and call these strategies "Hawk" and "Dove." The intuitive idea is that to play Hawk is to hold out for all the good at the risk of deadlock or conflict. To play Dove is to seek compromise but to be ready to back down at the slightest sign of determination by one's opponent. If one player chooses Hawk while the other chooses Dove, the former scores 1 (which may be thought of as the utility of the good) and the latter 0. If both choose Dove, each scores 0.5: we may imagine that they agree to divide the good equally. If both choose Hawk, each scores -1. (Nothing depends on my having chosen this particular number; all that matters is that each player's score in a Hawk-Hawk encounter is negative.) The crucial assumption here is that if you knew your opponent was sure to be aggressive, it would pay you to be conciliatory.

Each player has a range of options in this game. A player might adopt the "pure" strategy of playing Hawk with certainty, or of playing Dove with certainty. Or he might adopt a "mixed" strategy, playing Hawk with some probability p and Dove with probability $1 - p$. The game is said to be in (Nash) equilibrium if the strategy chosen by each player is a best reply to his opponent's strategy.

I wish to argue that the only *stable* equilibria (a term to be defined more completely later) are ones in which the two players behave differently. But this can make sense only if the players are distinguished in *some* way; if they were literally identical, they would be unable to reason to different conclusions. I shall therefore introduce an explicit mechanism for labelling the players. Suppose that each player, before making a move, receives a signal, which may take the value A or B. For each player the prior probability of each value is 0.5. The signals are perfectly and negatively correlated, such that if one player receives the signal A, that player can be sure the opponent has received the signal B, and vice versa. Thus these signals label the players as "*A*" and "*B*" and this labelling is common knowledge. (For example, if we treat it as a matter of chance who reaches the shore first after a storm, *A* might be the first on the shore and *B* the second.) Notice, however, that the signals provide no information about the structure of the game: they merely provide a point of reference for the players.[1]

This version of Chicken has three Nash equilibria. One is a mixed-strategy equilibrium in which each player plays Hawk with probability 1/3 irrespective of the signal received. The other two are pure-strategy equilibria. In one, the player who is *A* plays Hawk while his opponent plays Dove. In the other, *B* plays Hawk and *A* plays Dove. For the moment, I shall concentrate on these pure-strategy equilibria, which I shall call conventions. (I shall define "convention" formally later, and explain why the mixed-strategy equilibrium is unstable.)

The rule that whichever player has received (say) the *A*-signal should take the disputed good seems arbitrary: although it is self-sustaining—each player will choose to follow this rule provided he expects his opponent to follow it—just the same is true of the opposite rule. Indeed it is arbitrary that the players should use this particular signal to coordinate their behavior: any signal that gave one label to one player and a different label to the other would serve equally well. Any such convention may be understood as a *de facto* rule of property. The rule assigns the good to whichever of the two players has been identified by a particular signal. Each player receives the signal and each knows the convention (and knows that the other knows it, and so on). Given the behavior of the other, each player benefits by following the convention. In this sense the rule is self-enforcing.

Rationality and Experience

Is it rational to follow conventions? There is a tradition in game theory, traceable to John von Neumann and Oskar Morgenstern (1947, especially pp. 146–148), of analyzing games as unrepeated interactions between players who are fully rational, who know each other's utility functions, and whose rationality is common knowledge. On this view, the ultimate objective of game theory is to show that rational analysis uniquely prescribes a particular strategy for each player in a game. It is as if each player sits in a room by himself, knowing nothing about the other player except his utility function and that he is rational, and knowing nothing about how the game may have been played by other people. Each player must decide what to do, applying unlimited powers of rationality to this severely restricted information and to nothing else. The guiding idea—which is assumed rather than proved—is that a fully rational individual, given this information, must be able to reach a determinate conclusion; and that any two rational individuals, reasoning from the same data, must reach the

[1]The idea that the players of a game may be able to make their choice of strategies contingent on some jointly-observed random event corresponds with Robert Aumann's (1987) concept of coordinated equilibrium.

same conclusion (see, for example, Aumann, 1987). If this program could be carried out, we should have a theory of behavior that was based on axioms of rationality and on nothing more. For rational players, conventions would be redundant.

One of the major achievements of Thomas Schelling (who was featured in the Spring 1989 issue of this journal) has been to show that games like Chicken cannot be "solved" in this way. The ideally rational but completely inexperienced players of classical game theory would find they had insufficient data to determine what they should do. In contrast, ordinary people with limited rationality but some degree of experience and imagination might have no difficulty in coordinating their behavior. On this view, the program of classical game theory is a blind alley: it requires us to throw away the information that players need if they are to work out what it is rational for them to do.

The problem is that rational analysis, as understood in classical game theory, has a circular character. Certainly we can be sure that *if there were* a uniquely rational strategy for each player in any game, these strategies would be in Nash equilibrium with one another. (If one player has a uniquely rational strategy, the other, being rational, will be able to work out what it is; thus each must choose a strategy that is a best reply to the one he knows his opponent will play.) But this does *not* imply that if a game has a unique Nash equilibrium, that equilibrium is uniquely rational. To prove this latter proposition, we need the additional assumption that every game has a uniquely rational solution, and this is precisely what is in question. And in any case, games like Chicken have more than one Nash equilibrium.

To see the circular nature of reasoning about rationality, suppose we begin with the hypothesis that "*A* plays Hawk, *B* plays Dove" is uniquely prescribed by rationality. Then whichever player is *A* can deduce that the opponent, being rational, will play Dove. And so, since Hawk is the unique best reply to Dove, "*A* plays Hawk" *is* uniquely prescribed by rational analysis. Similarly, whichever player is *B* can deduce that his opponent will play Hawk, to which the unique best reply is Dove. So the original hypothesis is self-fulfilling: if both players believed it to be true, each would behave in a way that would make it true for the other. But, of course, exactly the same can be said about the hypothesis that rational analysis uniquely prescribes "*A* plays Dove, *B* plays Hawk."[2] There seems to be no way in which rational analysis could discriminate between two such self-fulfilling hypotheses. The implication seems to be that a convention such as "*A* plays Hawk, *B* plays Dove" is *consistent with*, but not *prescribed by*, rationality. When people follow such a convention, they are guided by something more than the axioms of rational choice, as economists normally understand them.

What, then, is this missing ingredient? Schelling (1960, pp. 54–58) finds it in the concept of *prominence* (sometimes called "salience" or the idea of a "focal point"). A famous "coordination game" of Schelling's illustrates the idea. You are paired off with

---

[2]The same argument cannot be applied to the mixed-strategy equilibrium. The supposition that it is *uniquely* rational for each player to play Hawk with probability 1/3 is self-contradictory: if you know your opponent will play this particular mixed strategy, any reply is as good as any other.

a partner, whom you are trying to meet. He is trying to meet you too. You cannot communicate with one another. You are each told to choose one place in New York City to go in the hope of meeting the other. Where should you go? The problem is to think of the place that your partner would be most likely to choose, given that he is trying to think of the place you would be most likely to choose, and given that he knows you are trying to think.... As Schelling shows, people are often remarkably good at solving this sort of problem. That is, they can converge on the same answers: the only test of a good answer is that it agrees with other people's. (For example: more than half of Schelling's respondents, who were all from New Haven, Connecticut, presumably in the late 1950s, knew to go to Grand Central Station.) Some ways of coordinating behavior seem to strike people as more obvious than others: this is the property of prominence.

If people can coordinate their behavior without communicating with one another, they must be drawing—consciously or unconsciously—on some fund of ideas that they have in common. The most important source of such ideas, I suggest, is common experience. Suppose I am driving down a narrow lane somewhere in England, and meet another car coming the other way. There is just room for two cars to pass. To which side of the road should I steer? I would steer left, expecting the other driver to do the same. But what are the grounds for this expectation? The game, we may assume, is entirely symmetrical; there is no advantage to our both steering left rather than right. If this were a genuinely unrepeated game, and if all I had to go on was the knowledge that my opponent was rational, I would be at a loss to know what to do. Because I have played the game before, I can draw on my experience of English driving, which tells me that drivers almost always steer left in situations like this.

A rational-choice theorist might still ask why this experience is relevant. If my opponent and I are both rational, why isn't our behavior determined by the payoffs of the particular game we are playing? Why should it matter to us what other people have done in the past? The answer, surely, is that there is no uniquely rational solution to our problem. If we are to coordinate our behavior, as we both wish to do, we must rely on some shared notion of prominence. Our common experience of English driving provides the clue we need. Steering left is prominent because it is common knowledge that this is what people generally do: we have each observed this, we can each assume the other has observed it, and so on. What classical game theory is requiring is that rational individuals should ignore as irrelevant the information that comes to them because they are human beings with common experiences—the very information they need to use in order to coordinate their behavior. This is surely far too narrow a view of rationality.

Evolutionary Stability

Conventions, I have argued, cannot be understood if we use the starting point of classical game theory—perfectly rational individuals in unrepeated interactions. It may be more useful to put less stress on rationality and to think of conventions as the product of evolutionary processes. A fruitful way to begin is to look at how game theory has been used to explain evolutionary processes in biology. Here the central concept is that of *evolutionary stability*, developed by John Maynard Smith and his collaborators (Maynard Smith and Price, 1973; Maynard Smith and Parker, 1976; Maynard Smith, 1982) to explain how animals of a given species behave when they come into conflict with one another. In these theories, interactions between animals are modelled as games, in which the payoffs are measured in terms of biological fitness. If we substitute utility for fitness and learning for natural selection, this approach can be adapted to explain human behavior.

Imagine a large population from which pairs of individuals are repeatedly drawn at random to play a particular two-person game. (I use a two-person game for convenience: the generalization is obvious.) If, as in my version of Chicken, there is some signal which assigns labels to the players, then a strategy must specify what is to be done given every possible value of the signal. For example, one strategy in Chicken is "If *A*, play Hawk; if *B*, play Dove." Players do not know, or do not remember, the identities of their opponents; a strategy is successful, then, to the extent that it performs well against opponents in general. There is no assumption that players are rational enough to work out optimal strategies by deductive reasoning; instead it is assumed that through a process of trial and error and imitation, they gravitate towards successful strategies. (This is the human analogue of mutation and natural selection.) An *evolutionarily stable strategy* (or ESS) is a pattern of behavior such that, if it is generally followed in the population, any small number of people who deviate from it will do less well than the others. This, then, is a state of rest in the evolutionary process. I shall define a convention as any ESS in a game that has two or more ESS's. The idea here is that a convention is one of two or more rules of behavior, any one of which, once established, would be self-enforcing.

To test whether a strategy is evolutionarily stable, we must consider not only whether any individual can gain by deviating unilaterally, but also whether any small group of individuals would gain if they happened to deviate in the same way at the same time. The significance of this test can be seen by looking again at Chicken. Recall that this game has three Nash equilibria. These can be described by the following three strategies: (i) If *A*, play Hawk; if *B*, play Dove, (ii) If *A*, play Dove; if *B*, play Hawk, and (iii) Whether you are *A* or *B*, play Hawk with probability 1/3. Clearly, any strategy that does not correspond with a Nash equilibrium cannot be evolutionarily stable. (If a given strategy is not a Nash equilibrium, then in a situation in which the strategy is generally followed, some individuals can gain by deviating unilaterally.) But not all Nash equilibria are evolutionarily stable.

Each of the strategies (i) and (ii) is the *unique* best reply to itself. (That is, these strategies correspond with "strong" or "strict" Nash equilibria.) This is a sufficient condition for evolutionary stability. To say that a given strategy is the unique best reply to itself is to say that, against opponents who play that strategy, individuals who deviate from the strategy do less well than those who do not deviate. Thus in a situation in which almost everyone follows the strategy (that is, in which the proportion of deviants is vanishingly small), deviants must do less well than non-deviants. But while strategies (i) and (ii) are evolutionarily stable, strategy (iii) is not. To see why not, suppose almost everyone follows this strategy, but a few individuals simultaneously hit on the idea of playing strategy (i). Against an opponent who plays Hawk with probability 1/3, *every* strategy, pure or mixed, gives the same expected utility (that is, 1/3). So to the extent that his opponents play strategy (iii), an individual loses nothing by playing (i) rather than (iii). But on the rare occasions when (i)-playing deviants meet, they will be able to coordinate with one another. Thus the deviants will do slightly better overall than the rest of the population, and so there will be a tendency for the deviant strategy to be repeated and imitated. But the more frequently the deviant strategy is played, the greater is the incentive to play it. Thus strategy (iii) is not evolutionarily stable: as Maynard Smith and Parker (1976) show, the only ESS's in Chicken are those that exploit asymmetries.

How far does the idea of an ESS differ from equilibrium conditions used in conventional game theory? As I have shown, evolutionary stability is a stronger requirement than (or, in the language of game theory, a "refinement" of) Nash equilibrium. There are some similarities between an ESS and Reinhard Selten's (1975) concept of a *trembling-hand equilibrium*, which is also a refinement of Nash equilibrium. Roughly, Selten supposes that there is some probability, vanishingly small but not zero, that each strategy that is available to any player will be played by mistake: this is the tremble. Then each player's equilibrium strategy must be a best reply to the opponent's, after making allowance for the possibility that the opponent will tremble. Deviant play in the evolutionary approach might be regarded as a kind of tremble, since *in the first instance* it is not governed by any rational calculus, but is essentially random.

However, there is an important difference between the two ways of thinking about nonrational behavior. In Selten's theory, the frequency of each type of tremble is taken as given—as the product of some unexplained psychological mechanism. To test whether a particular state of affairs is an equilibrium, we ask whether rational players are optimizing, given their knowledge of the frequency of trembles. The results of this kind of analysis can depend critically on the assumptions that are made about trembles; but it is not at all clear what constitutes a satisfactory hypothesis here. Since trembles are irrational, they resist explanation in terms of the concepts of classical game theory. This issue is pursued in Binmore (1987). In the evolutionary approach, in contrast, the crucial mechanism is not the responses of rational players to the possibility of nonrational play, but the tendency for deviant play, if successful, to be repeated and imitated. Deviant play, then, is more like experiment than error. Although the initial appearance of any deviant strategy is unexplained (analogously with the role of mutation in biological theories), the extent to which it is then played depends on its degree of success. In this sense, deviant play is explained within the theory.

Which Convention?

In games like Chicken, evolutionary processes will produce conventions that exploit asymmetries between the players. But *which* asymmetries? The evolutionary approach can also be used to throw light on the question of which conventions are most likely to evolve and survive.

One implication of evolutionary theory is that conventions can be evolutionarily stable even if they are not Pareto-efficient. This can be seen if we introduce some asymmetry into the payoffs of Chicken. Suppose the utility of the good is 1.1 for the *A*-player and 0.9 for the *B*-player; if both players play Dove, *A* gets 0.55 and *B* gets 0.45. Otherwise the game is exactly as before. As in the original version, there are two ESSs: "If *A*, play Hawk; if *B*, play Dove" and "If *A*, play Dove; if *B*, play Hawk." Recall that in any game, each player is equally likely to be labelled as *A* or *B*. Viewed from the start of the game—before the labelling signal is received—the convention under which *A* plays Hawk gives each player an expected utility of 0.55 (i.e. a fifty-fifty chance of 1.1 or zero), while the convention under which *B* plays Hawk gives each an expected utility of 0.45. Thus the second convention is Pareto-inferior to the first. Nevertheless, once established, the inefficient convention is self-perpetuating: no individual or small group can gain by deviating from it.

If conventions were the result of deliberate collective choice, we might expect that inefficient conventions would not be chosen. But conventions are not chosen; they evolve. If we are to explain why one convention is found rather than another, it is not very useful to start from a comparison between a world in which everyone follows one convention and a world in which everyone follows the other: either of these worlds, once achieved, would be self-perpetuating. Instead we must consider the process by which conventions evolve. More particularly, we must look at how they *start* to evolve. Once a convention has started to evolve—once significantly more people are following it than are following any other convention—a self-reinforcing process is in motion. The conventions that establish themselves will be the ones that can take root (biological metaphors are almost unavoidable) most quickly in a convention-free world.

A convention can start to evolve as soon as some people believe that other people are following it. But what gives rise to this initial belief? One possibility is that the same forces are at work as enable people to coordinate their actions without communication in unrepeated games. Some forms of coordination are more prominent than others, and people have a prior expectation of finding the most prominent ones. But, I have argued, prominence is largely a matter of common experience. The implication is that conventions may spread by analogy from one context to another. If it is a matter of common knowledge that a particular convention is followed in one situation, then that convention acquires prominence for other, analogous situations. For example: on my journey to work there is a narrow bridge, not wide enough for two vehicles to pass. If two drivers approach from opposite directions, which of them should give way? Coming on this problem for the first time, my prior expectation was when the drivers came into view of one another, whoever was closer to the bridge would be given the right of way. This expectation—which proved correct—was based on an analogy with the "first come, first served" principle.

If conventions can spread by analogy, then the conventions that are best able to spread are those that are most susceptible to analogy. Thus we should expect to find family relationships among conventions, and not just a chaos of arbitrary and unrelated rules. One such family relationship, I suggest, is the idea of favoring first possessors and first arrivals. This lies behind both the "first-on" rule in the driftwood example and the "closer driver" rule in the example of the bridge. It also lies behind the "first come, first served" principle of queuing and the "last in, first out" rule for determining which workers should be laid off first in a recession. The same idea is of enormous importance in international affairs. Think of how the positions reached by the American and Soviet armies at the end of the Second World War determined the political map of Europe, each power tacitly respecting the other's claim to the areas its armies had reached first.

Of course, it would be surprising if everyone had exactly the same expectations about which convention would evolve in any given context. Even if everyone is looking for analogies with similar problems, the concepts of similarity and analogy are subjective: different people may draw different analogies. However, in looking for analogies, people are playing another coordination game: each is trying to pick, not the analogy that most appeals to him, but the same analogy as everyone else. Thus we should expect some common principles for drawing analogies to evolve.

Even so, several different conventions might start to evolve simultaneously, each corresponding with a different set of expectations. But over time there will be a tendency for people to gravitate towards whichever convention is most successful; the other conventions (to use another biological metaphor) will die out. So we need to consider what makes for success at this early stage. The most obvious factor is simply popularity: other things equal, the more people follow a convention, the more it pays people to follow it. This takes us back to prominence again.

Another factor is versatility. A convention is versatile if someone who follows it can expect to do reasonably well against opponents following any of the other conventions that might be beginning to evolve at the same time. In the vital early stages of evolution, this may be more important than doing well against opponents like oneself.[3]

These explanations of how conventions start to evolve share a common feature: they do not necessarily favor rules that are Pareto-efficient. An inefficient convention may be more prominent than an efficient one. (For example, rules favoring first arrivals seem to have prominence, even though they can lead to wasteful races.) Because of the tendency for conventions to spread by analogy, we should not necessarily expect them to be well-adapted (in an economic efficiency sense) to the particular problems of coordination that they resolve. Similarly, versatility is a matter of the payoffs from following a convention *before* it becomes firmly established; once the convention is established, its versatility is redundant. Evolution will tend to favor versatile but inefficient conventions relative to ones that are less versatile but more efficient.

---

[3] Robert Axelrod (1981, 1984) argues that "tit-for-tat" (that is, cooperate in the first round and then repeat your opponent's last move) is a particularly versatile strategy in a repeated Prisoner's Dilemma game, and sees this as one of the main reasons for its success in his famous tournaments.

Conventions and Norms

Rules of behavior, I have been arguing, can evolve spontaneously. Up to now I have meant by a "rule" nothing more than an established pattern of behavior. But now I shall argue that such patterns can become rules in a stronger sense. People can come to believe that they *ought* to act in ways that maintain these patterns: conventions can become norms. This will not be a moral argument. I have nothing to say about what moral beliefs people ought to hold. My concern is to explain the beliefs they *do* hold.

How conventions can become norms was first explained by David Hume (1740, Bk. 3, part 2, sec. 1-3). My analysis of the evolution of conventions is in many ways similar to—and inspired by—Hume's account of the origin of principles of justice. Hume argues that rules of property are conventions that evolve spontaneously; if we are to explain why these rules take the particular forms they do, we must look to "the imagination" rather than to "reason and public interest." Hume's idea of the importance of imagination is remarkably similar to Schelling's concept of prominence. But having argued that principles of justice (and in particular, rules of property) evolve out of the repeated interactions of individuals pursuing their separate interests, Hume goes on to argue that we "annex the idea of virtue to justice."

The mechanism that can transform conventions into norms is the human desire for the approval of others. Although this desire is rarely considered by modern economists, introspection surely tells us that it is at least as fundamental as the desire for most consumption goods. That we desire approval should not be surprising: we are, after all, social animals, biologically fitted to live in groups.

For most of us, being the focus of another person's ill-will, resentment or anger is a source of unease—something we prefer to avoid. This is a psychological externality: one person's *state of mind*, as interpreted by another person, can affect that other person's happiness or utility. This is not to be confused with punishment, which is an *act* by which one person harms another. Most people have the ability to inflict some harm on most others—for example, by physical violence or by theft. But this works both ways. Because you have the ability to harm me, you can choose to punish me when I breach a rule; but you must take account of my ability to retaliate. So if we are roughly equal in the ability to inflict harm on each other, your punishing me is likely to be costly for you as well as for me. If we are to explain acts of punishment, then, we have to explain why those who punish incur these costs. In contrast, your feeling ill-will towards me is not an act of choice on your part; it is merely a psychological state. For your ill-will to cause me unease, it is not even necessary that you should choose to express it: it is sufficient that I can infer your state of mind.[4]

To see the significance of all this, consider any convention that assigns *de facto* property rights in a valuable resource. Suppose the convention is well-established.

---

[4]Skeptical readers may try the following experiment. Have a meal at an expensive restaurant and leave without giving a tip. Do you feel uneasy as you do so, even if the waiter is perfectly polite?

Then each person has a well-grounded expectation—an expectation grounded in induction from experience—that other people will follow the convention. Given this expectation, each person finds it in his interest to follow the convention. And given that a person is following the convention himself, he not only *expects* the people with whom he interacts to demand no more than the convention allows them, he also *wants* them to behave in this way. Think of the first-on rule for collecting wood. Suppose you are on the shore before me, but I start collecting wood. You had expected me to let you have the pick of the wood. My action is harming you by frustrating an expectation that you had good reason to hold. Further, you have reason to suspect that I know that this is what I am doing: I presumably know the convention as well as you do. My action will surely provoke anger and resentment from you. To explain these reactions, we do not need to appeal to any prior moral beliefs: that I am frustrating your expectations is sufficient explanation. And even if you do not express your feelings, I will be able to deduce what they are from my knowledge that I am frustrating your expectations.

In addition, anyone who is favored by the convention on at least some occasions is likely to regard any breach of the convention as an indirect threat to himself. Thus someone who demands more than the convention allows him will tend to arouse the resentment, not only of those who are directly harmed by this demand, but also of third parties. Suppose someone sees me taking the wood that, according to the first-on rule, is yours. He relies on this rule to protect his claims when he is first on the shore. So the existence of people like me is a threat to him. He will thus be inclined to sympathize with, and in some degree to share, your resentment against me.

Why, it might be asked, does the third party not see my breach of the convention as setting a precedent that he could profitably follow when he is the second person on the shore? Why does he sympathize with you rather than with me? Because the convention is well-established. Occasional breaches of the convention by mavericks like me will not cause it to collapse. Given that almost everyone follows the convention, my action can only harm other people.

This argument does not depend on any assumption that everyone benefits from the existence of the convention, or that the convention increases the overall welfare of society.[5] All that matters for the argument is that breaches of the convention are harmful *to all those people who follow it*. Admittedly, this would not be true of a convention which *always* favored the members of one group of people over another (men over women, for example), since then the disfavored group would have no reason to disapprove of breaches of the convention. But it could be true of a convention whose overall effect was to benefit one group at the expense of another. The point is this: the standpoint from which behavior is judged is a state of affairs in

---

[5]Much of the argument in this section has followed David Lewis (1969, especially p. 99). Lewis, however, restricts the application of this argument to "coordination problems"—games in which the players' main concern is to coordinate their behavior in some way, and in which they are indifferent (or almost indifferent) between alternative conventions. Thus, unlike me, he stops short of arguing that conventions that favor some people at the expense of others can become norms.

which the convention is generally followed. The convention, we might say, is being judged from inside, not outside.

Conclusion

Order in human affairs, I have argued, can arise spontaneously, in the form of conventions. These are patterns of behavior that are self-perpetuating—that can replicate themselves. In particular, rules of property—the essential preconditions for markets to work—can evolve in this way. These rules are not the result of any process of collective choice. Nor do they result from the kind of abstract rational analysis employed in classical game theory, in which individuals are modelled as having unlimited powers of deductive reasoning but no imagination and no common human experience. In this sense, at least, conventions are not the product of our reason.

Nor are these patterns of behavior necessarily efficient. They have evolved because they are more successful at replicating themselves than other patterns: if they can be said to have any purpose or function, it is simply replication. They do not serve any overarching social purpose; thus they cannot, in general, be justified in terms of any system of morality that sees society as having an overall objective or welfare function. The conventions that we follow may, however, have moral force for us. But if they do, that is because our moral beliefs are the products of the same process of evolution.

References

Aumann, R. J., "Correlated Equilibrium as an Expression of Bayesian Rationality," *Econometrica*, 1987, *55*, 1–18.

Axelrod, R., "The Emergence of Cooperation Among Egoists," *American Political Science Review*, 1981, *75*, 941–973.

Axelrod, R., *The Evolution of Cooperation*. New York: Basic Books, 1984.

Binmore, K., "Modeling Rational Players," *Economics and Philosophy*, 1987, *3*, 179–214.

Harsanyi, J. C., and R. Selten, *A General Theory of Equilibrium Selection in Games*. Cambridge: MIT Press, 1988.

Hayek, F., *The Constitution of Liberty*. London: Routledge and Kegan Paul, 1960.

Hayek, F., *Law, Legislation and Liberty*. London: Routledge and Kegan Paul, 1979. (In three volumes: Vol. 1 published 1973, Vol. 2 published 1976, Vol. 3 published 1979.)

Hume, D. (1740), *A Treatise of Human Nature*. 2nd Edition, Selby-Bigge, L.A., ed. Oxford: Clarendon Press, 1978.

Lewis, D., *Convention: A Philosophical Study*. Cambridge: Harvard University Press, 1969.

Maynard Smith, J., *Evolution and the Theory of Games*. Cambridge: Cambridge University Press, 1982.

Maynard Smith, J., and G. Parker, "The Logic of Asymmetric Contests," *Animal Behavior*, 1976, *24*, 159–175.

Maynard Smith, J., and G. Price, "The Logic of Animal Conflict," *Nature*, 1973, *246*, 15–18.

Neumann, J. von, and O. Morgenstern, *Theory of Games and Economic Behavior*, 2nd Edition. Princeton: Princeton University Press, 1947.

Rawls, J., *A Theory of Justice*. Oxford: Oxford University Press, 1972.

Schelling, T., *The Strategy of Conflict*. Cambridge: Harvard University Press, 1960.

Selten, R., "Reexamination of the Perfectness Concept for Equilibrium Points in Extensive Games," *International Journal of Game Theory*, 1975, *4*, 25–55.

Sugden, R., *The Economics of Rights, Co-operation and Welfare*. Oxford: Basil Blackwell, 1986.

Walmsley, L., *Three Fevers*. London: Collins, 1932.

Part VII
Economic Growth and Development in the Long Run

[23]

Excerpt from *Evolutionary Economics*, 23–47.

CHAPTER *1*

The Basic Evolutionary Model

The Evolution of Evolutionary Thought

In 1898 Thorstein Veblen published his famous paper entitled "Why Is Economics Not an Evolutionary Science?"[1] The answer I think at that time was clear, although Veblen did not give it. In 1898 there was not very much evolutionary science, and even what there was, unfortunately, Veblen did not understand very well. What he was really looking for was a kind of celestial mechanics of society, a set of stable parameters uniting events of successive time periods. This kind of theory has indeed developed in the last few decades, particularly in the form of the application of difference equations and econometric dynamic models to the study of economic life, but this is not really what is meant by evolution. My own definition of evolution is that it consists of ongoing ecological interaction, of populations of species of all kinds which affect each other, under conditions of constantly changing parameters. These species and populations consist not only of biological species like robins and horses, but of physical species like water molecules or oxygen molecules, and social species like gas stations and automobiles. Ecological interaction, particularly as it is spread out in space as well as in time, is extremely complex, though simple models of it which assume, for instance, that each species has an equilibrium population which is a function of the size of all the other populations, have some usefulness.

Since 1898 we have developed a good deal more evolutionary science, especially in the biological sciences, than we had then. In 1898, for instance, genetics was in its infancy; Mendel had barely been rediscovered, ecology as an organized discipline had still to come into existence, molecular biology lay well in the future, and the study of the development of individual organisms from their fertilized eggs or other origins was still very primitive. Since then substantial advances have been made in all these fields and it may be, therefore, that the time has come to take another look at economics, to see in the first place if it has anything to contribute to evolutionary science, and in the second place to see if evolutionary science has anything to contribute to it.

Economics as Studying the Provision, Exchange, and Transfer of Goods

Economics centers on the study of how society is organized through the provision, exchange, and transfer of commodities or economic goods. The definition of economic goods, like all important categories, is a little vague, but certainly clear enough to be useful, even though there may be some doubtful cases. Economic goods are an important subset of the total set of social species. There are three major categories of social species: things—that is, human artifacts, such as typewriters or automobiles; organizations, like families, national states, or corporations; and persons, insofar as the characteristics of persons are produced by interaction and communication with other persons and by the learning processes within the body of the person. Every human being is in part a biological artifact resulting from the information in the original fertilized egg, and in part a social artifact insofar as learned images, knowledge, and behavior, such as language, skills, and so on, are acquired in the course of life.

Economic goods consist mainly of human artifacts, "things"—shoes and ships and sealing wax and cabbages—though they also include the services of people as labor which is sold for wages, or even kings who are ransomed. They also include organizations, as, for instance, when a firm is bought or sold. In some societies they include people as slaves.

Production as Getting from the Genotype to the Phenotype

Individual "phenotypes," members of both biological and social species, including economic goods, come into being as a result of processes of production. Any individual member of any species, biological or social, at a moment of time, must be thought of as a cross section of its "life," a kind of four-dimensional "worm" in the space-time continuum, with a beginning at conception or production-plan and an end in death or destruction.

All processes of production, whether biological, social, or economic, originate in some kind of information structure or "know-how." In the biological individual this is the genetic information as it exists in its origin in the fertilized egg or divided cell. In social systems the genetic material consists of knowledge in the heads of persons, or in the blueprints, plans, libraries, or computers of organizations, including one-person organizations in the form of the single craftsman. If the product or phenotype is to be realized, this know-how or genetic information must be able to direct energy for three purposes: first, to maintain temperatures at which processes can be carried out, whether this is the blood temperature of the body or the heat of the kiln or the furnace; second, to do work in the form of transporting and transforming selected materials into the improbable structures of the phenotype; and third, to transmit information either as coded energy (nerve impulses, sound waves, telephones) or as coded materials (enzymes, hormones, documents, letters). These must also be the right materials, in the right quantities, capable of being transformed into the structure of the phenotype.

Biological and Social Species

Thus, the process by which a fertilized egg becomes a chicken is not essentially different from the process by which knowledge in the minds of automobile company members is transformed into an automobile. An automobile indeed is just as much an ecological species as a horse or a chicken; it is just as natural, just as much a product of the general process of evolution. There are major differences, however, between social and economic artifacts and biological artifacts or phenotypes. One difference is that whereas the biosphere never got beyond two sexes, with one or two possible exceptions, social artifacts are multiparental in the sense that the genetic information which underlies them is drawn from large numbers of different social species. Thus, a stallion and a mare can produce another horse in a bisexual union. An automobile, however, is produced as the result of the interaction of hundreds of different social species—mining equipment, lake steamers, steel mills, trucks, assembly lines, factories, and so on, on the material side; large numbers of organizations—different firms, social structures, and so on; and a great variety of different types of persons—miners, seamen, truck drivers, assembly line workers, executives, lawyers, policemen, and so on. They all come together, however, in an organized process which eventually produces the automobile in the womb of the factory, out of which it is born.

Another important difference between social and biological artifacts is that in the biological artifact the genetic instructions are carried in the artifact itself, at least in part. Thus, in organisms that have asexual repro- duction, like the amoeba, the genetic instructions are contained in the cell itself, and when the cell divides the instructions are replicated and a complete set is found in each of the halves of the original cell. In sexual reproduction, all the genetic instructions are contained within each sex, with the exception that the male has a small deficiency, but the fertilized egg contains roughly half the genetic instructions of each parent. In the case of social artifacts, however, the genetic instructions are contained in other artifacts. Thus, the instructions for making an automobile are not contained within the automobile itself, but are contained in blueprints, computers, and so on of the automobile company. This is what makes the multiparental character of social artifacts possible, and it also contributes to the great rapidity of evolution in social artifacts, because the artifacts which contain the genetic instructions have become specialized and hence are particularly subject to change. In the horse there is not a new model every year—it takes a very long time to make one—unlike the automobile. A machine which contained the instructions and a program for making a replica of itself (like the "Türing Machine") is conceivable, but none have been made yet.

Another major difference between social and biological species is that biological species continue to grow after birth, although their eventual decay and death is written into the genetic instructions, whereas social species like automobiles begin to decay as soon as they are born and do not actually grow after they have been moved from the factory, although they do decay and eventually die by being scrapped. There are some possible exceptions to this rule—houses receive additions; even automobiles get reconstructed—and, of course, there is a large social apparatus for repair, which somewhat parallels the repair processes of simple organism biological organizations, by which cuts are healed, brain damage repaired; and even in some cases new heads, tails, or limbs may be grown to replace those lost. All repair involves the reapplication of genetic knowledge to the reconstruction of damaged artifacts.

The "Factors of Production" as Know-How, Energy, Materials, Not Land, Labor, and Capital

Looking at economics from an evolutionary point of view, one sees clearly that the traditional three "factors of production"—land, labor, and capital—are extremely unsatisfactory categories from the point of view of production. Alfred Marshall tried to solve this problem, without much success, by introducing a fourth factor, which he called organization. In this, as in many other ways, he was seeking for an evolutionary approach which he never quite mastered, again perhaps because of the primitive state of evolutionary science in the late nineteenth century.[2] It is much more accurate to identify the factors of production as know-how (that is, genetic information structure), energy, and materials, for, as we have seen, all processes of production involve the direction of energy by some know-how structure toward the selection, transportation, and transformation of materials into the product.

Each of the three traditional factors of production are varying combinations of know-how, energy, and materials. Labor, for instance, consists partly in the know-how in the nervous system of the laborer, both in the brain and in the lower nervous system of the muscles; partly in the energy of human muscles, powered ultimately by "burning" (oxidizing) food; partly in the materials which constitute the laborer. Capital consists of human artifacts, mainly though not exclusively material ones in the form of machines, buildings, and so on. These may contain know-how in themselves, as in automatic machinery. They may simply maintain temperatures at which human activity can be carried on, like buildings, furnaces, and thermostats. They may involve means of transporting materials or people, or of selecting and arranging parts into a complete object, like an automobile assembly line. They may involve the utilization of human knowledge or biological know-how, as in the development of domesticated animals and crops, and so on, in a very large variety of combinations of know-how, energy, and materials. Land, likewise, may involve mere space within which the activity of human beings and machines, or processes of shelter and heat maintenance, can be carried on. Or it may mean the capacity of the soil to provide materials and the sun to provide energy for the growing of crops.

Land, Labor, and Capital as Factors of Distribution, Not of Production

It is clear that land, labor, and capital are extremely heterogeneous aggregates from the point of view of the theory of production. In this respect they have all the scientific validity of the medieval elements of earth, air, fire, and water. They do, however, have significance as factors of distribution, simply because in an aggregate form they participate in the system of exchange and the distribution of income. A wage, for instance, is a price for the use of a certain amount of the services of a human being, so the concept of labor here makes sense. Similarly, the concept of rent per acre has significance in the exchange system. The concept of a rate of interest or a rate of profit has different dimensions from these, but also has some significance from the point of view of distribution of income. The idea of a production function of land, labor, and capital, however, is almost pure alchemy and has misled economists into many a vain search for empirical verification. Thus, attempts to relate the growth in the real product of society under processes of economic development to increases in land, labor, and capital must universally come up with a severe deficiency which has to be explained by a vague concept called "technology," which is something of a surrogate for "know-how." Increase in know-how continually changes the production functions—that is, changes the amount of product per unit of labor of some kind, or of capital of some kind, or of land of some kind. The whole concept of the traditional production function in which product is written as a function of the amount of inputs of land, labor, and capital is virtually useless except over very short periods.

Economic development is primarily a process in the increase of human know-how. This is strongly related, of course, to the increase in know-what, particularly as manifested in science. Materials and energy are limiting factors which may prevent the transformation of know-how into the product which the know-how knows how to make. The increase in know-how, however, has continually pushed back the boundaries at which these limiting factors come into play; for instance, in the discovery of fossil fuels, especially oil and natural gas, and in the discovery of new materials, like aluminum, titanium, and so on. This does not preclude the possibility that production may exhaust existing stocks of materials and energy. Historically, indeed, it has frequently done so; for instance, through soil exhaustion or erosion, or through the destruction of forests and exhaustion of mines. There is legitimate alarm at present as to whether the continued expansion of the human race and its products will not produce a crisis both of materials and of energy sharply limiting any further growth and leading to a decline within the next 100 or 200 years. This all depends, however, as it has done many times in the past, on the extent to which an increase in know-how can push back the limits of materials and energy, by finding new sources and new forms.

Space and Time as Limiting Factors

We perhaps should add two more factors of production—space and time—to the three previously mentioned, for all processes of production require these, and they also may be limiting factors. A population may be so crowded in space that it cannot produce enough of its own offspring. Space indeed operates as a limiting factor in two ways—having too much of it or too little. If processes are spread over too much space, the costs of transportation become a limiting factor. If there is too little space, crowding prevents the proper operation of the processes involved. Time, likewise, can be a limiting factor, because all processes take time and cannot be hurried beyond a certain point. Why they take time is an interesting question, to which there may be a number of answers. Sometimes this is a time pattern of chemical processes which is important, as in the maturing of wines. Sometimes it is the velocity of transportation, either of information or of materials, which is the limiting factor. Sometimes it is the time taken to remove obstacles, such as legal proceedings, licensing, and so on; or the removal of physical obstacles to the transportation of materials or energy. Increase in know-how can reduce these times. This would qualify as a "capital saving improvement" in terms of the old factors. An increase in know-how can also economize space in some circumstances. The development of the steel-frame building, for instance, permitted the building of skyscrapers, expanded the cities in the vertical dimension, and economized land. An increase in know-how which increases the yield of crops per acre likewise economizes space. Improvements in transportation have the same effect as a reduction in the limitation of space. The space limitation has an effect on the number of species and on the amount of interaction in social species; for instance, the amount of trade is increased with reduction in the cost of transportation. This means also that specialization may increase and productivity may increase in a very complicated positive feedback. This was recognized by Adam Smith in his famous Book I, Chapter 3, of *The Wealth of Nations.*

"Coevolution" of Cooperative or Symbiotic Species

The positive feedback processes in all patterns of evolution may be of great importance; this is "coevolution"—the opportunities for one species which are opened up by a change in another. The great expansion of the human race and of its artifacts in the last 10,000 years and the spectacular expansion of the last 200 years are a result essentially of a positive feedback process of this kind, whereby the human race becomes cooperative with its own artifacts and the artifacts are cooperative with the increase in knowledge and know-how, and therefore push back the limitations of the limiting factors. This is a process of great complexity which is hard to spell out in detail. It is found in biological evolution (symbiotic species, like the algae and fungus in lichen), and is of great importance in societal evolution at many levels.

Selection as Ecological Interaction

The basic concepts of mutation and selection apply to societal and economic evolution just as they do to biological evolution. In both cases selection is essentially the process of ecological interaction. The population of any species, whether of horses or of automobiles, grows if the additions to it exceed the subtractions. In the case of a biological population, the additions consist of births and the subtractions, deaths; or, if we are considering a subset of a population within a given area, additions consist of births plus inmigrations and subtractions consist of deaths plus outmigrations. The population (stock) of commodities likewise in any given area increases by production (births) and imports (inmigration) and decreases by consumption (deaths) and exports (outmigration).

Neglecting migration for the moment, the birth rate and the death rate of any population can be regarded as a function of its own size and the size of all relevant populations in its environment. If its environment is taken for the moment as fixed, the birth rate and the death rate can be treated as functions of the size of the population of the species in question. If a population increases in a given environment, the birth rate may increase somewhat at first because of higher population density; as population density increases, however, the birth rate may eventually decline because of the stresses of overcrowding. The relation between population and the death rate is likely to be more dramatic: As population increases, the death rate will eventually rise because of over-crowding, food shortages, increased predation, and so on, until at some equilibrium population the death rate and the birth rate are equal. This equilibrium population is the "niche" of the species. Usually this will be a stable equilibrium. If the population is below the equilibrium level, the birth rate will exceed the death rate and the population will rise; if it is above the equilibrium level, the death rate will exceed the birth rate and the population will fall. The introduction of migration increases the complexity of the system somewhat. A species, for instance, may have an excess of births over deaths and still be in equilibrium in a given area if this is counterbalanced by an excess of outmigration.

Ecological Equilibrium

An ecological equilibrium is a situation in which the population of each of the interacting species occupies a niche—that is, is neither rising nor falling. If we suppose that the equilibrium population for each species is a function of the actual population of all the others, this gives us *n* equations with *n* unknowns. These equations may have a real solution and, if they do, we have an equilibrium ecosystem in which each population is at the level of equilibrium which is consistent with the equilibrium level of all others. If there is any species for which the equilibrium population is not positive, the species will constantly decline; its death rate will be above its birth rate until it becomes extinct and the population is zero. This will then change the niches of all the other related species in the system. The processes of ecological dynamics, of course, are extremely complex. Especially in systems with rather small numbers of species, we can easily get fluctuations in populations, for instance, of predators and prey; and, if the amplitude of these is large enough, a population may become extinct through dynamic processes even though it could theroretically coexist in the niche with the others.

Mutation

Mutation in its most general form is the process by which the parameters of the system of ecological interaction change. In a simple model we can suppose that what changes is the parameters of the equations of ecological equilibrium, but the world is a dynamic system and equilibrium is very rarely attained, so that what is really significant is change in the parameters which affect the relationship between the total system and the birth and death rates of any given population. There are several forms of these mutational changes. In the biosphere, for in- stance, they may take the form of climatic changes, erosion or deposition of soils, the filling up of lakes, and so on. They also take the form of genetic mutations. These go on all the time. Usually they are adverse to the individual and the individuals possessing these mutations die out without this much affecting the species. Occasionally, however, they are favorable and there is a change in the gene pool of the species.

Successful mutation ordinarily may be expected to increase the niche of the species—that is, to permit it to have a larger stable population in a given environment. It is not inconceivable, however, that a mutation which is favorable to the survival of the changed (mutated) individuals of the species relative to the unchanged ones, may be adverse to the total species and result in a diminution of the niche. The niche of one species cannot change without changing the niches of all the others in the ecosystem. If it rises, some may change favorably, those, for instance, which are cooperative with the first species. Some may be affected unfavorably, those which are competitive with the first species. If the unfavorable change is sufficient, a species may become extinct. This is essentially how selection operates.

In the biosphere, in spite of Darwin's unfortunate metaphor about the struggle for existence, struggle in the sense of organized fighting, or even goal-oriented activity, plays very little role in the selection process. Selection essentially is a process of ecological interaction which takes place along many different lines—predation, symbiosis, competition for a common food supply, and so on. The situation is greatly complicated by the fact that the terrain on which biological interaction takes place is very heterogeneous. The interaction of species does not take place equally at all points in it. Heterogeneity often provides "shelters" for species within which they can survive, where they might not be able to survive out in the larger ecosystem. This is important in general evolutionary theory because the existence of these heterogeneities and shelters increases the variety of the total gene pool, which may affect the ultimate history of the evolutionary process. When conditions become more favorable outside the shelter, a sheltered species may emerge and occupy a larger habitat.

Ecosystems of Social Species

Looking now at social species, and especially the species of economic commodities, we see much the same principles at work, with, however, some additional complexities. The stock of any commodity is its population; production, as we have seen, corresponds to births and consumption to deaths. There is a little semantic problem here in that the term consumption has frequently been used in economics to mean simply household purchases, as if the commodity disappeared into a tomb once it entered the doors of the household. It is more realistic to regard consumption as the destruction of a commodity; in this case it becomes exactly parallel to death in the case of a biological species. Again, production and consumption are likely to be functions of the stock of the commodity—that is, of the population of the species. In the case of economic goods, however, this relationship is mediated mainly through the system of relative prices.

There is no exact counterpart to a price structure in the biosphere, though each species does have certain rates of exchange of materials and energy with its environment, and, if the situation is to be a true equilibrium, there must be "recycling" as we find in things like the nitrogen cycle and the carbon cycle. The symbiosis of plants and animals, for instance, on which the complexity of the biosphere so much depends, is in part a result of the fact that animals take in oxygen and give out carbon dioxide, while plants, in sunlight at least, take in carbon dioxide and give out oxygen. There is something here like a balance of trade and indeed the disturbance of this may have had some evolutionary consequences, as, for instance, in the carboniferous era when presumably plant life was so vigorous that it captured a great deal of the CO_2 from the atmosphere, changed its composition and probably its temperature, and hence created a change in the ecological equilibrium, which may have destroyed the whole carboniferous ecosystem. Similar things can easily happen in an economy, for instance, that is dependent on exhaustible resources—like our present economy!

Specialization, Exchange, and Relative Prices

Economic systems are characterized by the specialization of persons in the production of different commodities. Material artifacts and organizations are also specialized in this way, so that we have groups of persons, organizations, and artifacts specialized, for instance, in the production of wheat or steel. Commodities then are exchanged for each other, the exchange being enormously facilitated by the existence of money as a medium of exchange, as a store of value, and as a liquid asset. The wheat producer sells the wheat that is produced for money. This is distributed among all those who contributed to the production of the wheat and with the money these persons can buy clothing, furniture, automobiles, and so on, which are produced by other groups. A very important characteristic of such a system is the relative price structure; the price of each commodity, for instance, can be expressed in terms of a monetary unit such as a dollar, and this list immediately enables us to calculate the rate at which any one commodity can be exchanged for any other. If wheat is $4 a bushel, and an automobile costs $4000, then 1000 bushels of wheat can be exchanged for one automobile.

The relative price structure is an extremely important factor in determining the structure of the distribution of real income among the persons participating in the economy, because the relative price structure determines each person's terms of trade—that is, how much he gets per unit of what he gives in exchange. A rise in the price of any one commodity such as wheat, for instance, will redistribute real income toward wheat producers and away from the producers of all the things that wheat producers buy. Corresponding to any relative price structure, therefore, there is a structure of the distribution of real income.

An Equilibrium Price Structure

Economists postulate the existence of an equilibrium price structure such that the corresponding distribution of real income will not induce anyone to change their occupations to produce less of one commodity and more of another. This corresponds very closely to the idea of ecological equilibrium. The connecting link here is that the relative price structure under given conditions of demand is a function of the relative stocks of the different commodities. A rise, for instance, in the relative stock of wheat is likely to cause a decline in its market price, and a fall in the stock, an increase in the price. Exchange always involves the redistribution of existing stocks among owners and in any given distribution of demand for these stocks there will be some set of relative prices at which on balance people are willing to hold what is there to be held. If the relative price set is different from this equilibrium set, some prices will be perceived as "too high"; there will be on balance an excess offered for sale over what is purchased, and these prices will fall. Other prices will be perceived as "too low," there will be an excess of offers to purchase over offers for sale, and these prices will rise. The situation is complicated in practice by the fact that the demand for holding stocks of various commodities depends on the expectation of the change in their prices, so that we get speculative changes which may not correspond to the long-run equilibrium.

The structure of demand is of great importance in explaining the survival of commodities and the size of the "niche" (equilibrium stock) of each. This is something for which there is no exact counterpart in the biosphere, where there are really no decisions about exchange. Demand, as we have seen above, may depend in part on speculative expectations about future price changes. These average out in the long run and ultimately, apart from these disturbances, the structure of demand is a function of human tastes and preferences. These in turn are in large part learned and depend on the learning processes of a culture and may even depend in part on the price structure itself. There is, for instance, what might be called the "diamonds" phenomenon by which a certain item becomes demanded *because* it has a high price and is therefore a symbol of affluence and conspicuous consumption. In spite of these exceptions, however, there is a rather fundamentally basic structure of human demands, which varies considerably from culture to culture but nevertheless exhibits strong common patterns, in spite of vagaries of vanity and fashion. A commodity for which the demand is not large enough to generate production of it, under a price structure which will return adequate income to its producers, will not survive. Even if it exists, its production will decline below its consumption and the stocks will shrink until it becomes virtually extinct or fossilized, like sedan chairs or primitive hand-cranked computers.

Social and Economic Mutation

Mutations in the economic system and in the social system may be on the supply or the demand side. On the supply side they generally consist of invention and innovation; that is, the development of new social genetic structures involving new ideas, new forms of know-how, and, if mutations are favorable, new products and new social species occupying newly created niches. These new products, as they are produced, interact with the old species and may drive some of them to extinction, though they may also expand the niches of some old commodities which are cooperative with the innovation and may even create new niches which are at present empty, waiting for mutations to come. The discovery of oil in 1859 and the production of cheap gasoline (originally as an unwanted by-product of kerosene!) opened up an enormous niche for the automobile which was gradually filled by invention and innovation. This in turn opened up niches for gas stations, garages, repair shops, and so on; also for tax offices, policemen, courts, highways, cement production, shopping centers, and a great variety of new artifacts. Here again, the heterogeneity of the social environment may preserve shelters for commodities; for instance, the Amish horses and buggies which have become almost extinct in the rest of society. The preservation of these shelters may be important for the perpetuation of the complexity of the human knowledge structure and the long-run history of societal evolution. One sees the same phenomenon with ideas, forms of organizations, types of persons, and other human artifacts.

Mutations in Demand

Mutations also take place in the structure of demand. This may happen because of fashion. There is a certain itch for change in the human race. We get tired of the "same old thing," even if it performs its function satisfactorily. We often see change almost for its own sake. Almost every society has fashion leaders and the changes in their demands—for instance, for clothing, foods, styles of architecture, or even politics—may have a profound effect on the demands of millions of people who look to them as guides. This phenomenon is even more striking in the socialist countries, where the fashions of a very small group of people at the top, in the Politburo or some equivalent organization, may change the demands of millions of people who look to them for guidance. Change in demand can also take place as a result of increased know-how; for instance, when it was discovered that the drug thalidomide had catastrophic effects on the development of infants in the womb, the demand for it completely disappeared. A constant learning process goes on in the operations of buying and selling. We learn often by experience what are the commodities we like or do not like; those that disappoint us we tend not to purchase again, and our demand for them shrinks.

Profit and Interest

A phenomenon in economic systems for which it is hard to find a counterpart in biological systems is that of the rate of profit or the rate of interest. The case of the rate of profit represents essentially a rate of growth of the gross relative value of some stock of commodities organized into a process of production. Thus, an automobile company owns factories, machines, assembly lines, raw materials, land, and stocks of finished automobiles. All these are listed in its balance sheets on the asset side, together with its stock of money and interest-bearing securities. On the liability side we have its debts, its obligations, and its net worth, which is the total value of its assets minus the value of its contractual liabilities. In the course of a year, let us say, automobiles are produced; as they are produced, money is paid out for wages, raw materials, salaries, and other purchases. Plants and machinery are depreciated, their value diminished because of their aging and wear and tear, all of which diminishes net worth. When an automobile is produced it is usually valued at cost until it is sold. Only if it is sold at more than its cost does its production increase the net worth of the business. If a business is successful, the value of sales of its products will exceed what has been sacrificed in net worth and costs, so there will be a net addition to net worth. This is profit. The rate of profit is the rate at which the net worth grows as profits are earned and before they are distributed.

Interest Contracts

Similarly, a rate of interest is the rate of gross growth of the value of a stock of debts or financial instruments, such as bonds or promissory notes. Thus, if the rate of interest is 6 percent per annum, an undisturbed debt (like a savings account) will grow at this rate continually.

Interest is always established by some kind of original contract between the borrower and the lender. The terms of the contract spell out how much will be paid in the first instance by the lender to the borrower and what sums the borrower will repay at specified times in the future. Some of these contracts may be very short term, perhaps only a few days, or months; some like mortgages may go for 20 or even 30 years. For many of these contracts, there is a market in which the contract can be bought and sold, so that the owner of such a contract may not be the original lender, who often sells the contract to somebody else, who may then resell it, and so on. The price at which an interest contract is sold determines the future rate of interest on it for the purchaser, and the rate of interest which the past contract has actually carried for the seller. If A lends B $1000, paid immediately, and B writes a contract to give A $200 on the anniversary of the original contract for each of seven years, and $57 on the eighth year, the rate of interest on this contract, as we see in Table 1, is 10 percent per annum, reckoned annually. If the contract were sold at its 10 percent per annum capital value (line 2, Table 1) at any time (say, for $536 in year four), the seller and the purchaser would both be getting 10 percent on their investment. If it is sold for more than the 10 percent per annum capital value, the seller who made the original loan will be getting more than 10 percent on his investment, and the buyer will be getting less than 10 percent. In general, the higher the price of a given expectation of payments, the less the rate of interest on it. If there is an active market in these contracts, the future rate of interest on them is determined by the price which they fetch in the market. It rises or falls as this price falls or rises.

Several different forms of interest contracts go by somewhat different names: *notes* are rather brief contracts often with a single repayment; *bonds* are contracts which extend for a considerable period of time, often with a constant amount paid every year, sometimes with a larger amount at the end of the contract; *mortgages* are made usually on the

Table 1

Year	0	1	2	3	4	5	6	7	8
Capital	1000	900	790	669	536	390	229	52	0
10% Interest		100	90	79	67	54	39	23	5
Payment		200	200	200	200	200	200	200	57
Repayment of Capital		100	110	121	133	146	161	177	52

security of real estate and tend usually to involve payment of a fixed sum each year until the capital value of the debt falls to zero. The principles involved, however, are the same in all types of interest contracts.

Stocks as Contracts

Stocks are somewhat different. They represent a contract to pay to the owner of the security not fixed amounts at given dates in the future, but variable amounts depending on the profits of the organization. The price of stocks may vary, therefore, not only because the rate of interest itself varies, but also because expectations of the payments made on the stock, or the price of the stock itself, in the future may change, as the prospects of the business improve or decline. Expectations may also affect the price of bonds and interest contracts, where there is uncertainty about whether the contracted payments will actually be made.

Tendencies to Equalizing Profit or Interest Rates

In societies in which there is freedom of ownership and of exchange in securities of various kinds, there is a strong tendency for rates of profit and of interest in different groups and complexes to approach equality, subject to a compensation for nonmonetary factors such as uncertainty, respectability, liquidity, convenience, and so on, which are also relevant to decisions to hold property in one form rather than in another. If all these nonmonetary advantages and disadvantages of various forms of property were equal in all occupations, then if the rate of profit or interest were different for different combinations, there would be a general attempt to buy into those combinations with a high rate and to sell out of those with a low rate. This would raise the price of the combinations with high rates of profit or interest and so lower the rate, and would raise the price of combinations with low rates of profit or interest and so raise the rate, until all the rates came to equality. In fact, of course, the existence of nonmonetary advantages and disadvantages means that forms of property with high nonmonetary advantages will have low monetary advantages—that is, low monetary rates of return, and vice versa. The same phenomenon may be observed in labor markets, where occupations with high monetary advantages or low investment costs tend to have a low money wage compared with occupations with high nonmonetary disadvantages or high investment costs. Again, it is hard to think of a counterpart for this phenomenon in the biological field.

Centrally Planned Chickens Versus Free-Market Ecosystems

Another phenomenon of interest in the economy is the existence of two major "ideal types" of economic systems, neither of which exists in a pure form, but where there is a distinct clustering to one end of the spectrum or the other. One of these types is the centrally planned economy as we find it in the communist countries, in which private property is severely restricted and most productive capital is owned by the state. In this case the survival of a commodity or an occupation or even of types of persons depends on the decisions of the state, operating through the central planning agency, and the social genetic structure (know-how) of the society is concentrated very heavily in a small group of people of great power in the planning office or in the central political organization. At the other end of the scale, we have market-type economies in which private property and free exchange are permitted over large areas of the society, and in which, therefore, the survival of a commodity depends on its ability to satisfy the demand sufficient to ensure a price which will return compensation in real terms to its producers sufficient to persuade them to stay in the occupation and not transfer to some other one.

The centrally planned economy has some parallel to the single biological organism. A chicken is a centrally planned economy derived from the plan in its original fertilized egg. The plan is carried out because of the ability of the genetic structure to direct energy, as we have seen, toward the selection, transportation, and transformation of materials into the form of the phenotype. A market-type economy by contrast is much more like an ecosystem, in which all the various commodities and social products of all kinds interact with each other ecologically and survive if they can find a niche in the total system. Strictly, of course, survival always consists of finding a niche. In the case of the centrally planned economy, however, the niche is very largely determined by the planners, not by the demands of the bulk of the people in the society. This is not to say, of course, that even a centrally planned economy is incapable of organizing itself to respond to the demands of its people, but this response itself depends on the will of the planners, not on the will of the people as individuals, unless the political structure permits the people to replace unacceptable planners.

The Budget as a Plan and the Measure of Failure

All organizations, from the smallest to the largest, involve some degree of central planning, the capitalist corporation just as much as a socialist state. The major instrument of planning is the budget. It is essentially a plan for the allocation of expenditure of money for the purchase of specific kinds of labor and goods. This is the basic genetic structure of the period of the plan—that is, of the budget. The budget, of course, assumes certain know-how and production functions and assumes that doing certain things will produce certain products. And there may, of course, be contingency plans in the budgets if things do not work out as expected. The size of the budget is very strongly related to the money income or inflow of the organization. In the case of the socialist state, this is from sales, from state subsidies ultimately derived from taxes, or from the profits of the state enterprises—that is, the excess of the value of the product over the outlays required to make them. In the case of the capitalist firm or corporation the inflow of money is largely a function of the sales of the product.

The question as to what constitutes a failure is interesting. In the case of the socialist organization, this is the perception of failure to conform to the plan on the part of the planners themselves, who may, of course, be deceived by the people who are supposed to carry out the plan. In the case of the capitalist enterprise failure is measured primarily in the inability to make profits, although this too sometimes is temporarily hidden from the owners by the obfuscation of accounts. Other indicators besides profits also come in, such as public esteem, proneness to government regulation, and so on. Almost all capitalist firms could increase their profits by the sacrifice of a certain sense of prestige and security.

The difference between the chicken and the organization is that the plan of the chicken carries it through growth, into maturity, and eventually to death, whereas the plans of organizations are rarely that long term, and usually run only for a limited period of time after which the plan is revised, often on an annual basis. Socialist countries are rather fond of five-year plans. They are very rarely carried out in full and almost always have to be revised as time goes on. It is a very rare organization that plans at its inception for its own extinction. A few foundations have done this, and the death of an organization, though it not infrequently happens through bankruptcy in the case of the firm, or conquest in the case of the state, is almost always unplanned and comes as an unpleasant surprise.

Dialectics Versus Ecology

The role of dialectical processes in biological and societal evolution is a question of great interest though of considerable difficulty. Dialectical processes can be defined as those which involve struggle, fighting, and conflict among organized systems. This implies some degree of consciousness, in the sense that it represents a form of interaction of large organized systems in which the perception of each system by the other is an important element in the total process. In biological systems dialectical processes as thus defined are of very little importance. What we have, as we have seen, is ecological interaction, most of which is highly unconscious. Almost the only dialectical processes which occur are those involved in the fighting of males and females in sexual selection, and even this frequently leads to extinction rather than to survival of a species. The predator-prey relationship might be interpreted in some sense as a dialectical relationship. Thus, the evolutionary development of protective coloration, speed, elusiveness, and so on, suggests that predator-prey relationships do modify the character and behavior of the species involved. These, however, I would regard as not true dialectical processes simply because for the species the concept of "winning" or "losing" is virtually meaningless. A predator which exterminates its prey will itself become extinct, and the stability of the predator-prey relationship depends on a subtle balance of the skills of the predator and the skills of the prey. Actually the predator-prey relationship is apt to be a very stable one, more stable than mutual cooperation or mutual competition.[3]

In social systems dialectical processes are more significant, and organized conscious struggle has occasionally had important effects on societal evolution. We could ask the question in the form perhaps: How often did it really matter who won a fight? As history is usually written from the point of view of one of the participants in fighting, historians tend to overestimate the significance of these processes. Actually, if we look at the overall evolution of society in knowledge, technology, and culture, we find that these dialectical processes are much less significant than appears at first sight. The ecological processes of invention, discovery, and diffusion explain much more than evolution of human artifacts, or the growth of human populations of different kinds and the great ongoing processes by which the human race moved from the first eolith to the space lab, than do the ups and downs of wars, conquests, revolutions, the rise and fall of empires, political parties, even of religions and classes.

One is tempted to argue that on the whole dialectical processes are the waves and storms on the great streams and tides of human history rather than the streams and tides themselves. Nevertheless, one cannot deny the possibility that at particular times and places it has mattered who won a fight, particularly in what might be called "watershed situations," in which going from one side to the other of an evolutionary watershed may make a great difference in the ultimate result. The overall estimation of the significance of these dialectical processes, however, would involve a very detailed study of the actual historical processes of human evolution and even this would probably not resolve the question. The if's and and's of history are very hard to determine, especially in view of the strong random elements in the processes of human historical development.

Evolution as Lacking Predictive Power

One of the difficulties of evolutionary theory, both in biology and in social systems, is that it does not have very much predictive power. This is inherent in the nature of the process itself and is not simply a remediable defect of human knowledge. Prediction of the future is possible only in systems that have stable parameters like celestial mechanics. The only reason why prediction is so successful in celestial mechanics is that the evolution of the solar system has virtually ground to a halt in what is essentially a dynamic equilibrium with stable parameters. Evolutionary systems, however, by their very nature have unstable parameters. They are disequilibrium systems and in such systems our power of prediction, though not zero, is very limited because of the unpredictability of the parameters themselves. If, of course, it were possible to predict the change in the parameters, then there would be other parameters which were unchanged, but the search for ultimately stable parameters in evolutionary systems is futile, for they probably do not exist.

We do not really know whether the universe is a determinant system or whether it has real randomness in it. This is a question that the human mind can probably never resolve. What is significant for us is that it has epistemological randomness—that is, uncertainty—that beyond a certain point is irreducible. We see this even in physics in the Heisenberg principle—that we cannot "ask" an electron where it is without changing its position. Social systems have Heisenberg principles all over the place, for we cannot predict the future without changing it. Predictions themselves are part of the parameters of the system. What power of prediction we have in evolutionary systems depends on the probability that at least some parameters will not change. The further we look into the future, however, the more the parameters will change and ordinarily the greater the uncertainty.

Convergent Evolution

There is one possible exception to this rule in the case of what might be called "convergent evolution," and there is some evidence for this. We would like to think, for instance, that all evolutionary processes have a high probability of producing intelligence if they go on long enough. On the other hand, as one reflects on the extraordinarily narrow physical limits within which evolution has proceeded on the earth, one realizes that the kind of evolutionary processes which would produce something like the human race may be very rare indeed and always have some probability of being interrupted and stopped. If the earth had been a little bigger or a little smaller, or a little further from the sun, or a little closer to it, or perhaps even if it had not had a moon, or if it had not had the particular combination of elements which it does, then it would have been as sterile of evolution as Venus or Mars. Nevertheless, it is hard not to feel, even though this feeling is something of a leap of faith, that given the kind of physical limits which the earth has had, then the evolution of something like the human race was certainly highly probable.

The "Time's Arrow" of Evolution

We do seem to perceive a "time's arrow" in evolution, certainly toward complexity and control systems, more hesitantly toward awareness, consciousness, and something hard to put a name on that perhaps we dare call intelligence. This may happen because, as we have seen, it is know-how that is the essential element of the processes of production. Energy and materials are limiting factors, but not creative or formative factors. They can limit the realization of know-how and they are necessary to carry and encode the information which is involved in know-how, but evolution fundamentally is a process in genetic material, whether of biological genes or of social know-how, and the phenotypes are just the carriers. Samuel Butler said that "a hen is only an egg's way of making another egg."[4] Biologically, human beings are only gene transmitters. Sociologically, they are more than that because they are self-generators of know-how and value structures. Nevertheless, from the point of view of societal evolution in the large the individual human being is again significant mainly as a knowledge transmitter, however much fun the person may have on the way. If knowledge—that is, the social genetic structure—is not transmitted from one generation to the next, the phenotypes, the artifacts which this knowledge produces, will disappear in a single lifetime. As we become conscious of processes, of course, we change them. The development of the human race, with its capacity for immensely complex images of the world, for images of the future, and for consciousness itself, represents a profound gear change in the whole evolutionary process, as profound indeed as the change which took place with the development of DNA and the beginning of life itself.

One puzzling and rather frightening thing about evolution, whether biological or societal, is that it seems to accelerate in some sense as measured by the intelligence, the complexity, or the amount of know-how which characterizes the state of the system at any one time. Whether this acceleration is an inherent property of the system we do not really know. I do not know of a theoretical model which really produces it, except the one that know-how increases the capacity to know more. Perhaps we can express this by saying that evolution itself evolves, that it is not a single process, but that the process itself constantly changes, and that this leads to acceleration.

Evolutionary Potential

One of the trickiest and yet most important concepts in evolutionary theory is the concept of evolutionary potential. There are some mutations, such as the formation of life itself, for instance, which have in themselves the potential of all that follows. Mutations like the development of sex or the vertebrate skeleton or the central nervous system or the human race itself obviously in hindsight had enormous potential. Evolutionary potential is difficult to define, or to identify, and we do not understand the processes which lead to its generation. We see exactly the same phenomenon in social systems. There are times and places in history in which great evolutionary potential is created—for instance, in the origins of the great religions, the great empires, the great states, the great movements of mankind like science, and so on. We see these potentials, however, only by hindsight. Certainly nobody at the time ever recognizes them. What is even harder to recognize is the potentials that were frustrated, that did not materialize. It is much harder to study and to understand what did not happen than what did. Yet the difficulty is that we cannot really understand what did happen unless we understand *why* what did not happen did not happen. All this suggests not only that evolution is a pattern which does not endow us with great predictive power but that it is a pattern where even our understanding of the past is very limited and will probably always remain so. Nevertheless, it is all we have, for this is what the world is like, and we must make the best of it.

Economic Development as the Evolution of Commodities

Societal development is a process by which the human race realizes the evolutionary potential for producing artifacts that is inherent in its biologically produced brains. This is the process that goes from the first *Homo* and *Mulier sapiens* with their primitive concepts and artifacts, to Einstein and space shuttles. Economic development is a subset of this process through time and space, now confined to the surface of the earth. It concentrates particularly on the evolution of *commodities*—that is, valued artifacts that at least potentially have the capacity for entering into exchange and transfer. We shall explore this in the next chapter.

Notes

1. Thorstein Veblen, "Why Is Economics Not an Evolutionary Science?" *Quarterly Journal of Economics* XIII (1898): 373.
2. Alfred Marshall, *Principles of Economics* (London: Macmillan, 1st ed., 1890).
3. See Kenneth E. Boulding, *Ecodynamics* (Beverly Hills: Sage Publications, 1978), p. 78.
4. Samuel Butler, *Life and Habit.*

[24]

TECHNOLOGICAL FORECASTING AND SOCIAL CHANGE 18, 267–282 (1980)

Society as a Learning System: Discovery, Invention, and Innovation Cycles Revisited

CESARE MARCHETTI

ABSTRACT

The very simple heuristic suggestion that society as a whole and its numerous subsets operate like learning systems, basically governed by Volterra–Lotka equations, has been extremely valuable in organizing a most variegated collection of statistical sets of time series, ranging from the structure of energy markets to the efficiency of machinery and the expansion of empires. In this paper an attempt is made to treat invention and entrepreneurship, generally perceived as the most "free" of human activities but actually subject to iron rules. Invention and innovation during the last 250 years appear in precisely structured waves that lend themselves to robust prediction. The present wave will reach its maximum momentum around 1990. Furthermore, the introduction, maximum market penetrations, and prices of new primary energies show a very strong link to these innovation waves. This stresses once more that economic features may be the expression of deeper "physical" phenomena related to the basic working of society and thus become predictable up to a point through a very abstract and noneconomic analysis.

This work has been done in the frame of IIASA's Energy Systems Program and can be considered as an outgrowth of and complement to the research on the evolution of energy systems described in IIASA Research Reports 79–12, 79–13, and 77–22. There it was found that a new primary energy coming into the market must be observed for 10 or 20 years if one is to extract the basic features necessary to predict its long-term market behavior. Specifically, it was concluded that the dates at which new primary energies come into play cannot be predicted. In this paper innovations are considered not one by one but as an abstract set, whose behavior is analyzed. In this frame possible birth dates for new energy sources can be identified, thus enhancing the quality of very long-term forecasting in the energy field. Also, prices appear predictable, at least in their gross features.

Introduction

The success of logistic market penetration analysis in describing the long-term behavior of energy markets and submarkets [1] stimulated an effort in theoretical research in order to reduce the empirically efficient logistic relationship to more basic and already accepted scientific axioms. A remarkable effort was made by Peterka [2], who was able to demonstrate that under constant productivity differentials competing industries win and lose the market following logistic paths.

Fleck [3] considers market penetration as a diffusion process in which the buyer is a scattering element in a Markov chain. From the properties of this microelement Fleck reconstructs the macroscopic behavior. This is an interesting reduction, although the properties of the microelement cannot yet be established a priori, and consequently the parameters of the logistic equation cannot be calculated before the penetration process starts. Fleck still limits his consideration to man as an economic animal.

CESARE MARCHETTI is associated with the International Institute for Applied System Analysis (IIASA), Laxenburg, Austria. This paper was invited for presentation at a meeting on Marketing and Product Innovation Facing Social and Technological Change organized by the Italian Association for Marketing Studies (AISM) in Turin, 18–19 April, 1980.

I would like to go one step further toward abstraction and simplicity and assume that *society is a learning system*, that learning is basically a random search with filters, and that random searches are characterized by logistic functions [4, 5]. The most natural way to proceed is through examples of increasing complexity. Abstraction is then possible and some deductions can be drawn.

The first and most important link in all human chains and feedback loops is man. It can be interesting to see him at work, for example, as a child trying to appropriate and get command of an intricate structure like that of a language. As a monitor of progress I chose the growth of the child's vocabulary. The result is given in Figure 1, where the curve is fit to a function of the form $\log(F/1-F)=at+b$ and F is a measure of the number of words the child can command: the fraction of a vocabulary for current use of about 2500 words.

My second example concerns a group of people interconnected by informational links, much as scholarly journals, and working on a common task, say pounding molecules to pieces in order to separate the unbreakable components, the stable atoms. That game drove the chemists crazy in the period 1750–1850, roughly, when about 50

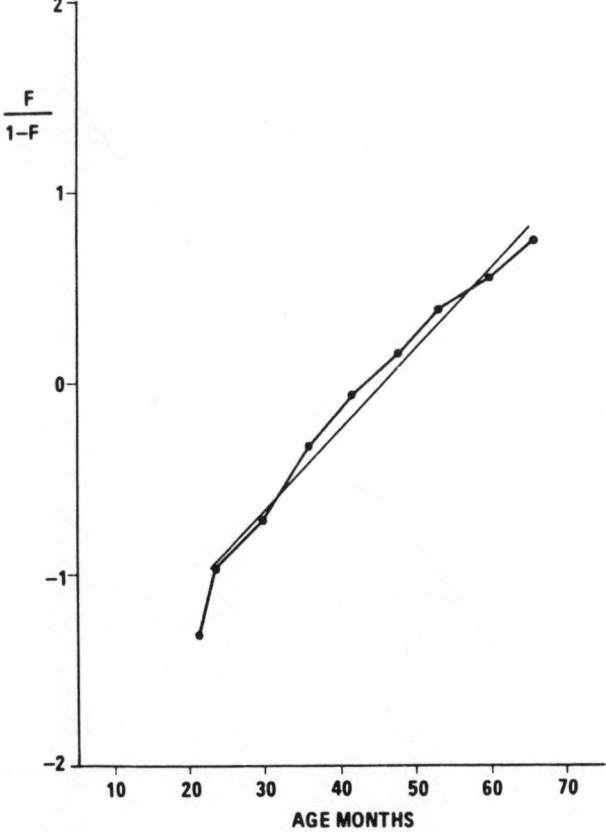

Fig. 1. Evolution of the vocabulary of a child. The final set of words used in current language is about 2500 words. $F(t)$ is the fraction of that set under control at time t. *Source:* Whiston [6].

stable elements were discovered. In Figure 2 the glorious progress is reported. The child and the learned guild seem to behave the same way, or at least the same functional relationship takes care of the two cases.

The third example bears some similarity to the second, except that the objects to be reached do not have a physical existence in the sense of words or chemical elements but belong to conceptual sets, like the set of ideas in the Platonic scheme. In Figure 3 the evolutionary trends of three technologies, embodied in machines of evolving performance, are reported. In a sense inventors, wandering in the world of all possible machines, picked those that looked best, ready to throw them away for the better ones as they appear, like Alice in Wonderland with her flowers. Here only one parameter, but a very important and subtle one, was taken as an indicator of performance: thermodynamic efficiency. This efficiency ϵ is plotted as ratio of $\epsilon/1\text{-}\epsilon$, efficiency over inefficiency, and the data are fitted with a logistic equation.

Inventors are not organized in a guild, and their stimulus and financing come from a wide variety of sources. They are, however, interconnected by a literature and through

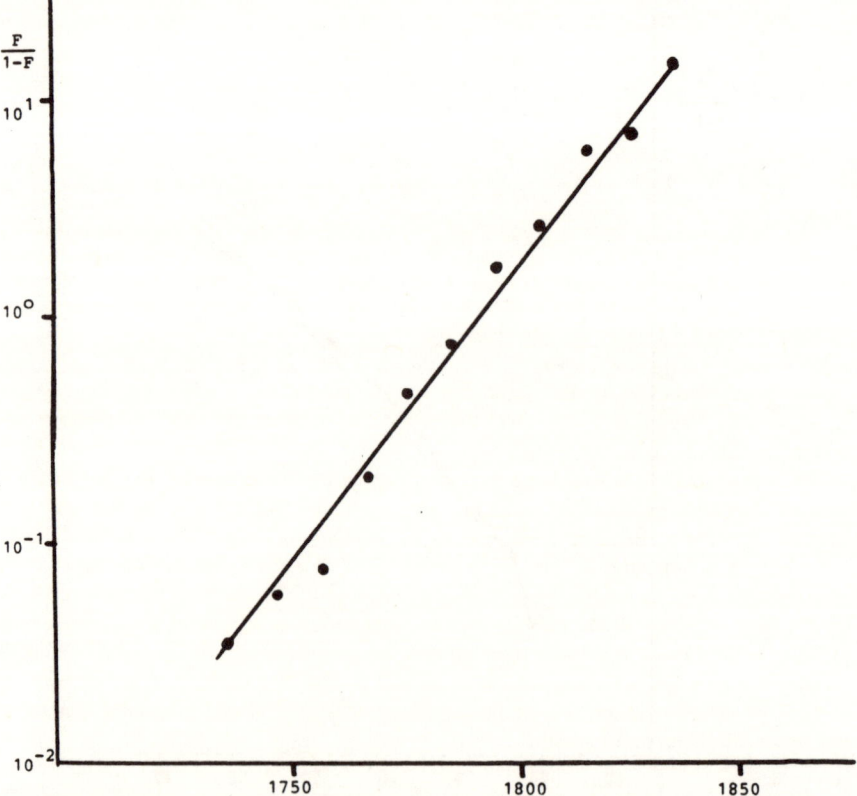

Fig. 2. The set of about 50 stable chemical elements that were discovered in the period under scrutiny can be defined as the elements accessible with current chemical technology. This defines the task and the means. $F(t)$ is the fraction of this set already discovered at time t. *Source: The World Almanic* [7].

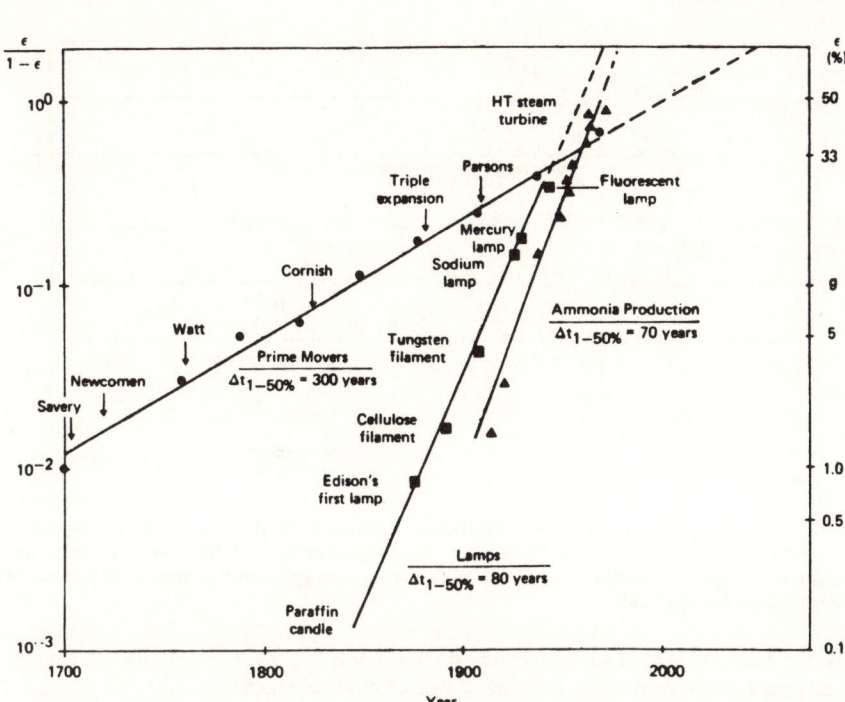

Fig. 3. The evolution of efficiency here given by reporting the efficiency of the best commercial machine at a given time. This efficiency is referred to the maximum possible thermodynamically. Consequently steam engines efficiency refers not to Carnot but to free energy in the fuel. The time constant Δt represents the slope given as the time to go from 10^{-2} to 10^{0} (1% to 50% efficiency). This figure, reporting efficiency/inefficiency, I christened "the Yang–Ying plot." *Source:* Marchetti [8].

inspection of competing products, and they seem to behave like a single structure, operating toward its purpose and insensitive to historical trivialities, like wars, pestilences, and economic crises.

The fourth example is of large industries capillarily interconnected to many strata of society—technical, economic, financial, and political—and drawing stimuli and constraints from them. Because the elements are industries, I again took thermodynamic efficiency as an indicator. As the statistical data show (Figure 4), the evolutionary pattern is exactly the same as before. Here, however, because of the visibility of the objects and their strong coupling, a war may be felt, perhaps bombing or a shortage of new equipment, as in the case of the British steel industry. It is remarkable, however, that some kind of internal clock keeps ticking, and finally the time lost is recovered in a well adjusted dash. This elastic reabsorption of perturbations is a general and surprising feature of practically all the systems studied.

The last example of the series (Figure 5) involves humanity as a whole and its behavior with respect to a very important item, the use of primary energy sources during the last century or so [1]. As can be seen, the fit of the statistical data and to the logistic curve is very snug over this very long period of time. Humanity, too, seems to behave like an interconnected system learning toward an objective at an extremely stable rate. Inciden-

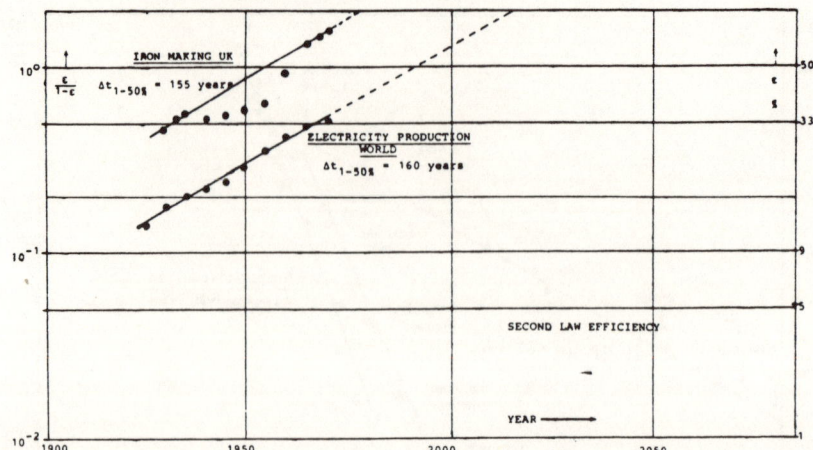

Fig. 4. Historical trends in efficiency, plotted much as Figure 3. The efficiency for electricity production is defined as the electrical energy/fuel energy. The assumption for fossil fuels that free energy and enthalpy of combustion coincide is adequate. With nuclear energy the definition should perhaps be revised. *Source:* **Marchetti [8].**

tally, the concepts of prices and resources do not appear necessary to describe the system. Prices appear contextual to the working of deeper physical mechanisms.

Armed with the working hypothesis that all sorts of societal subsets may operate in this way, I revisited a stimulating collection of data [10, 11] referring to waves of innovation in world industry during the last couple of hundred years (Figure 6).

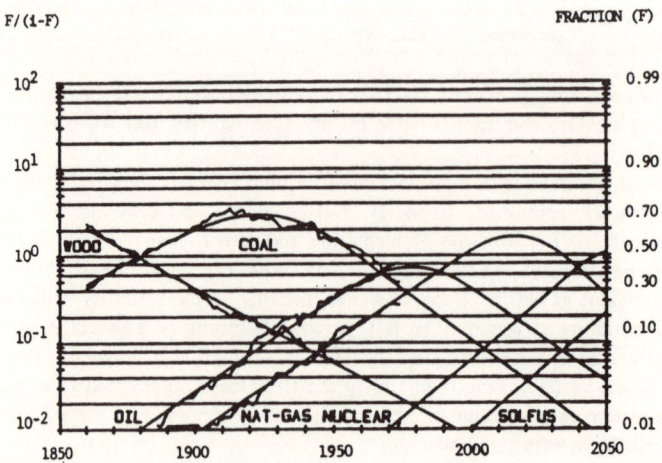

Fig. 5. World fractional energy substitution. *F* **is here the fraction of the market, defined in energy units (e.g., tons coal equivalent) taken by each primary energy at any time. The wriggling lines represent statistical data. Nuclear fuel has not yet much penetrated, and consequently the slope is hypothetical. Solar and fusion energy (SOLFUS) are hypothetical for both slope and initiation point.** *Source:* **Marchetti [1, 9].**

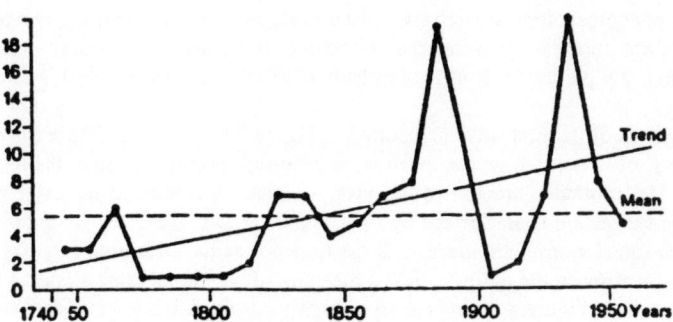

Fig. 6. Frequency of basic innovations, 1740–1960. The numbers of basic innovations reported here are given in 10 years bunches. Basic innovation is what gives rise to a brand new industry. *Source:* **Mensch [10].**

Contrary to current perception, innovations do not trickle from science to technology to industry, with a lag that keeps decreasing in time. Historical analysis shows that they come in season, like cherries. Some time later the cherry tree is reduced to a mere bunch of branches, ready to sprout, blossom, and produce for the next round.

For the analysis of the first wave (Figure 7 and Table 2), the data are taken from Mensch [10], who also quotes other sets assembled by other authors, claiming they do not differ substantially. The inventions and innovations belonging to this set are listed in Table 1. *Innovation*—or basic innovation, if we go to finer distinctions—*is defined as something that starts a new industry*. The grammophone, to give an example, is a (basic) innovation. Improvements in the process of manufacturing or in the quality of the products, which in the current language are also called innovations, are not considered here. *Inventions refer to the discoveries that are at the base of the innovations*. The two sets have been matched in the sense that inventions that did not develop into innovations are not listed.

TABLE 1
Invention and Innovation Cycles

Innovations center point	1828	1880	1937	(1992)	
Inventions center point	1775	1833	1905	(1968)	
Midpoint of the cycle	1802	1857	1921	(1980)	
Δ*t* between invention and innovation centers		52y	47y	33y	(24y)
Innovation time constant		47y	33y	23y	(16y)
Invention time constant		120y	85y	55y	(38y)
Δ*t* between innovation centers		53y	57y	(55y)	
Δ*t* between invention centers		58y	72y	(63y)	
Δ*t* between midpoints		55y	63y	(59y)	
Saturation of market penetration for primary energies	~1800	~1860	1921	1980	
	Wood	Hay	Coal	Oil	
	(U.S.)	for	(World)	(World)	
		Animal			
		Power			
		(U.S.)			

As my phenomenological analysis will be made in relative terms, the completeness of the sets is not important provided the selection of the cases is reasonably random. On the other hand, my prejudices could not influence the choice of data, which was made by Mensch.

The analysis of the first wave is reported in Figure 7 and Table 2. There the cumulative number F of inventions and innovations is reported, normalized over the total set in the wave. The ordinates are the usual ones, to make the logistic behavior optically evident. The curves are characterized by their middle points, the dates when 50% of the inventions or innovations were made, and the time constants, measured in years elapsed between two decades in the ordinate. It is a meaningful way to measure slope. A piece of one of the curves of Figure 5 about primary energies substitution is superposed, following a suggestion by Graham and Senge [11] that innovation cycles and primary energy cycles may be interconnected.

Because of the number of elements in a set is quite limited, the fitting curves should be cut off below $F=5\%$ and above $F=95\%$ or so. The graphs, however, are often prolonged to $F=1\%$ in order to show some interesting links to the energy cycles. The middle point between the central dates is also of significance in this connection. I will also use it to characterize the wave: 1802 thus locates the first wave.

Mensch made the interesting observation that the two sets are basically similar, that is, ordered. In other words, inventions go into innovations following the rule "first come, first served." Consequently, one can predict the date of the innovation if the invention can

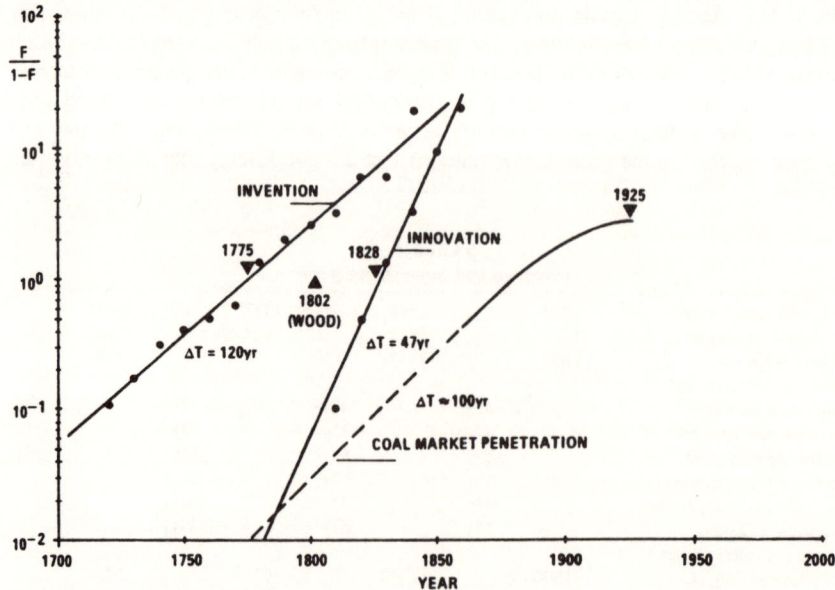

Fig. 7. The 1802 wave. F is here the fraction of total set of basic innovations implemented up to time t. This set is made of 21 items listed in Table 2 and further explained for the case of the locomotive. The set of corresponding inventions is displayed in the same way $F(t)$ being the fraction of them discovered up to time t. ΔT denotes the time from $F = 0.10$ to $F = 0.90$, (i.e., from 10% to 90% of the whole set.)

TABLE 2
The 1802 Cycle

	Innovation	Invention
Power generator	1849	1820
Electromedical stimulator	1846	1831
Deep sea cable	1866	1847
Electricity production	1800	1708
Insulated conductors	1820	1744
Arc lights	1844	1810
Pedal bicycle	1839	1818
Rolled rails	1835	1773
Rolled wires	1820	1773
Puddling furnace	1824	1783
Blast furnace with coke	1796	1713
Crucible steel	1811	1740
Locomotives	1824	1769
Telegraph	1833	1793
Lead chamber process	1819	1740
Pharmaceutical industries	1827	1771
Quinine industries	1820	1790
Hard rubber	1852	1832
Portland cement	1824	1756
Potassium chloride	1831	1777
Photography	1838	1727

How invention and innovation dates are chosen:
The case of locomotives.

1769	Watt: Low pressure machine
1770	Cugnot: Steam gun vehicle
1790	Read: Steam road vehicle
1800	Watts: Patent on steam engines expires
1801	Trevithick starts work on locomotives
1804	Evans: Road locomotive
1811	Blenkinskop: First toothed gear locomotive
1813	Hadley: Locomotive on rails
1814	Stephenson starts work
1824	Stephenson builds first locomotive plant
1825	Stephenson opens Stockton-Darlington line

Source: Mensch [10].

be located. The time between the two keeps decreasing along the wave; it will start as large again in the next one, as we shall see. The current idea of a secular reduction of the delay from invention to innovation is certainly false, although more subtle accelerations actually occur.

The 1857 cycle is reported in Figure 8 and Table 3. Topologically it is identical to the previous one. All the time constants are different, however, and shorter: 85 years for inventions and 33 years for innovations, instead of 120 and 47 years, respectively, showing a certain level of acceleration.

The 1920 cycle is reported in Figure 9 and Table 4 with nothing special to report except, again, the excellent fit of the data to the logistic interpolation and a further shortening of the time constants, to 55 years for inventions and only 23 years for innovation. The distance between the centers, too, is reduced—to 32 years, strangely reminiscent of the 33 years of the innovation time constant of the 1857 wave. Incidentally, the

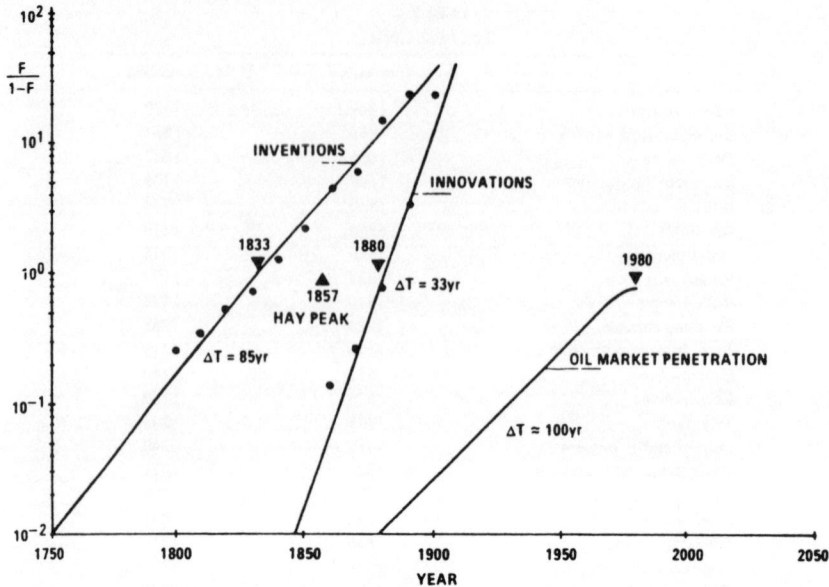

Fig. 8. The 1857 wave, dealt with as the previous one. The set includes 40 items listed in Table 3.

distance between the centers of this wave is 47 years, which perfectly coincides with the 47 years time constant of the 1802 innovation wave.

These can certainly be coincidences, if improbable, but regularities raise suspicion of clockwork sitting behind the face, and suspicion stimulates curiosity. I therefore put together, in Table 1, the various figures connected to the three waves to see if more suspicious regularities would appear.

They do, in fact. One is that the distance between waves is about 55 years, measured at center points of innovations. This has been observed by Mensch and by Senge, and has been correlated to the Kondratiev cycle, by Mensch as a driving force of the cycle and by Senge as an effect of it.

The time constants of the innovation waves become shorter and they have the constant geometric ratio of roughly 1.42 or $\sqrt{2}$. In the century or so covering the three dashes, the speed has increased by a factor of 2.

Furthermore, the introduction of new primary energy sources seems to be somehow in tune with the innovation waves, crossing them around the 10^{-2} level, and the saturation point for coal in 1923 coincides with the midpoint of the 1921 cycle. I then looked for a saturation point corresponding to the 1880 cycle, and with some difficulty collecting data I found one around 1860 for presteam mechanical power, that is, draw-animals, whose primary source of energy is hay. It sounds a little queer today, but at that time in the United States 80% of all mechanical power (including sailing ships) was located in draw-animals. 1802 should be the peak or at least a sharp bend for wood fuel, but I have not been able to prove it.

Using all these bits and pieces I tried to reconstruct the characteristics of the next wave. It is certainly better than reading tea leaves, and the fact that various things interlock with a smooth click may be the expression of sound mechanics.

TABLE 3
The 1857 Cycle

	Innovation	Invention
Thomas steel	1878	1855
Safety matches	1866	1805
Aniline dyes	1860	1771
Cooking fat	1882	1811
Indigo synthesis	1897	1880
Sodium carbonate	1861	1791
Aluminum	1887	1827
Refrigeration	1895	1873
Rayon	1890	1857
Gas heating	1875	1780
Oxyacetylene welding	1892	1862
Dynamite	1867	1844
Chemical fertilizer	1885	1840
Preservatives	1873	1839
Electrolysis	1887	1789
Antitoxin	1894	1877
Chloroform	1884	1831
Iodoform (antiseptic)	1880	1822
Veronal (barbiturate)	1882	1862
Aspirin	1898	1853
Phenazone (synthetic painkiller)	1883	1828
Baking powder	1856	1764
Plaster cast	1852	1750
Mass production of sulphuric acid	1875	1819
Synthetic alkaloid (cocaine)	1885	1844
Synthetic alkaloid (chinoline)	1880	1834
High-grade steel	1856	1771
Electrodynamic measurement	1846	1745
Lead battery	1859	1780
Double armature dynamo	1867	1820
Commutator	1869	1833
Cylinder armatured motor	1872	1785
Arc lamp	1873	1802
Incandescent light bulb	1879	1800
Electric locomotive	1879	1841
Electric heating	1882	1859
Cable construction	1882	1820
Telephone	1881	1854
Steam turbine	1884	1842
Water turbine	1880	1824
Transformer	1885	1831
Resistance welding	1886	1841
Arc welding	1898	1849
Induction smelting	1891	1860
Meters	1888	1844
Electric railroad	1895	1879
Long-distance telephoning	1910	1893
High tension insulation	1910	1897
Gasoline motor	1886	1860

Source: Mensch [10].

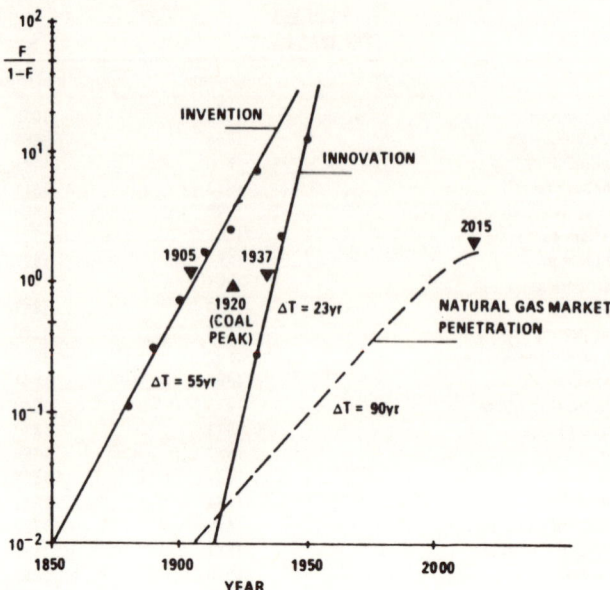

Fig. 9. The 1920 wave, also dealt with as in Figure 7. The set includes 51 items listed in Table 4.

The exercise, already given in parenthesis in Table 1, is presented graphically in Figure 10. The 55-year cycle gives 1993 as centerpoint for the innovation wave. The time constant of 16 years comes from that of the previous cycle, 23 years, divided by 1.42. The centerpoint distance is equal to the time constant of the previous cycle, or 23 years, bringing the centerpoint of inventions to 1969–1970. The time constant of inventions is derived from the previous one, 55 years divided by 1.42, which gives 38 years. *The midpoint is 1980, which neatly corresponds to the maximum of oil penetration*, as shown in Figure 5. Also, the intersection of 1% of the nuclear energy line and the innovation line matches previous coincidences.

The real starting point of the new wave will be 1984, a date that Orwell made famous in a not very different context, perhaps prophetically. That should also be the end of the recession inside which willy-nilly we are muddling, and in a powerful 16-year dash the world economy should ride the wave again.

As the inventions curve shows, 80% of the inventions that will go into the next rush are already made in 1980. We don't really know yet where they are, and everybody can have his guesses. Obvious ones are linked to information management and manipulation, including genetic engineering and the new very sophisticated chemistry, even base chemistry, that can come from that. Less obvious ones are linked to the management of new energy sources, in this special case nuclear energy. As the electrical systems will become saturated with nuclear energy in various countries, precisely at the beginning of the 1990s, technologies to go from nuclear energy to chemicals and synthetic fuels will have a real chance to enter the industrial web. Around that date, too, air traffic will need

TABLE 4
The 1921 Cycle

	Invention	Innovation
Nylon, perlon	1927	1938
Penicillin	1922	1941
Polyethylene	1933	1953
Power steering	1900	1930
Radar	1887	1934
Radio	1887	1922
Rockets	1903	1935
Silicones	1904	1946
Streptomycin	1921	1944
Sulzer loom	1928	1945
Synthetic detergents	1886	1928
Gyrocompass	1827	1909
Synthetic light polarizer	1857	1932
Television	1907	1936
"Terylene" polyester fiber	1941	1955
No-knock gasoline	1912	1935
Titanium	1885	1937
Transistor	1940	1950
Tungsten carbide	1900	1926
Xerography	1934	1950
Zipper	1891	1923
Automatic drive	1904	1939
Hydraulic clutch	1904	1937
Rollpoint pen	1888	1938
Catalytic cracking of petroleum	1915	1935
Watertight cellophane	1900	1926
Cinerama	1937	1953
Continuous steelcasting	1927	1948
Continuous hot strip rolling	1892	1923
Cotton picker (Campbell)	1920	1942
Cotton picker (Rust)	1924	1941
Wrinkle-free fabrics	1906	1932
Diesel locomotive	1895	1934
Fluorescent lighting	1852	1934
Helicopter	1904	1936
Insulin	1889	1922
Jet engine	1928	1941
Kodachrome	1910	1935
Magnetic tape recording	1898	1937
Plexiglas	1877	1935
Neoprene	1906	1932

Source: Mensch [4].

performance almost beyond the potential of present technology [12], and a breakthrough is in sight with planes redesigned around the use of liquid hydrogen as a fuel, for example, with cryohypersustentation and hypersonic flight [13]. Cars fueled with H2 may go into the same niche around the synthetics from nuclear.

In the field of food and agriculture, many innovations are hovering around in search of a sponsor [14]. For some this may be their last chance. The next round is half a century away!

The question of how many innovations will pop up in this cycle can also be answered

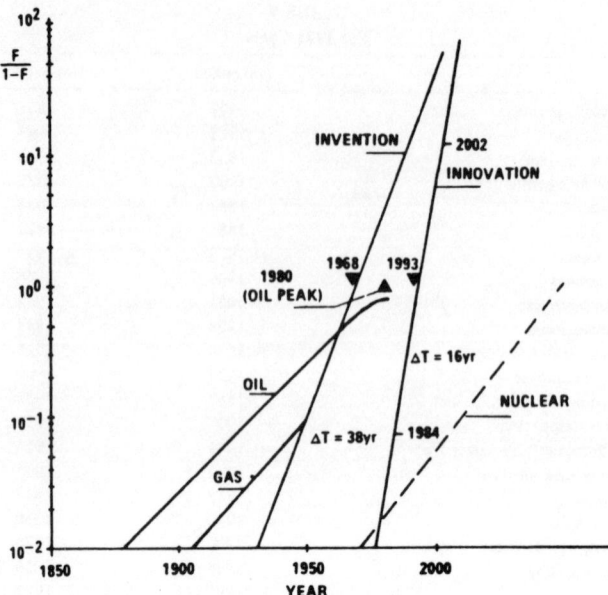

Fig. 10. Using the regularities of the previous three waves, the forthcoming one, the 1980 wave, has been constructed. Although the process has already started, the crucial years appear to be between 1984 and 2000, when 80% of the basic innovations will have been introduced. What the innovations are, and how many, is however unknown.

up to a point. The phenomenological equation says that 10% will be on line in 1984, so the only thing we have to do is to go out and count them now: The wave will have ten times as many. My personal projection is for the launching of about 100 new industries before the end of the century.

These and other considerations make *our* round appear very plausible, and so I kept playing the game in a scenario spirit, building the next waves, too. The result of the exercise is reported in the lower part of Figure 11. Posterity may have fun in cross-checking it.

What comes out again makes much sense. The next round of primary energies is required around 2025, which is a safer date than the year 2000 of Figure 5, a date we chose under the pressure of solar and fusion enthusiasts. Back of the envelope calculations show that a sensible and successful course for fusion will give just around 1% of the market in 2025, but then the peak of natural gas is going to move forward to around 2040, which is precisely what the coincidence with the center of the fifth cycle is asking for. On the other hand, the business as usual rate of penetration for nuclear (100 years time constant) would be confirmed and its saturation in the year 2090, at around 60% of the market, would match beautifully the sixth cycle.

I took the poetic license of calling the new primary energy associated with that cycle μ-sion, with the argument that scientists tampering with more and more elementary particles, will presumably find a way to squeeze energy out of them. Also possible is solar power beamed from Venus.

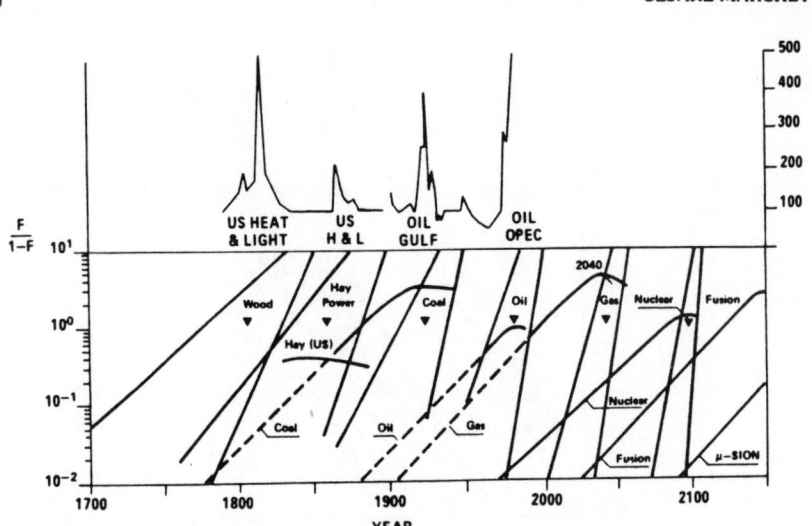

Fig. 11. Invention and innovation waves, the secular set: The first three waves of the series are historical. We live in the fourth. The following two are indicated to show the interlocking of the various components. In the upper part of the figure the indexed prices for energy are reported to show the precise match between energy price flaring and wave centers. By analogy one should expect a rapid fall of the real price for oil in the next few years. *Sources:* For the U.S. cost index, U.S. Department of Commerce [15]. For the Gulf and OPEC oil cost index, Beijdorff and Lukas [16].

The description of the structure of the energy market in Figure 5 is in physical terms, and the very simple set of logistic equations behind it permits precision forecasting and backcasting over at least 50 years. This means that prices that move around all the time cannot be considered voluntaristic causes, as economists tend to think, but only contextual indicators, as I find it almost inevitable to think. Assuming that prices are effects and the physical structures are causes, I looked for some secular correlations. The indexed price for energy is shown in the upper part of Figure 11. The remarkable fact here is that the *prices* for energy "flared" in coincidence with the midpoints of the cycles— three times in the past and now, at the presumed midpoint of the 1980 cycle. This coincidence helps support the method of forecasting I used, the click of another piece falling into place. It also opens the way to the far-reaching speculation that *in real terms the price of energy in general and of oil in particular will fall sharply during the next few years*.

At this point the canonical questions come in: What are the mechanisms of such regularities, and what determines the length of the period between innovation cycles?

Concerning the first question, I would say that man and societal feedback loops have been the same for many centuries, contrary to our feeling of fast change, and that the concept of a learning society is the heuristic path to a microscopic description in the spirit of the statistical mechanics that came to buttress macroscopic thermodynamics in the physical sciences. It took a century, however, for this very intricate branch of science to come to maturity.

To a physicist's eye, present-day econometric models still look much like toddling

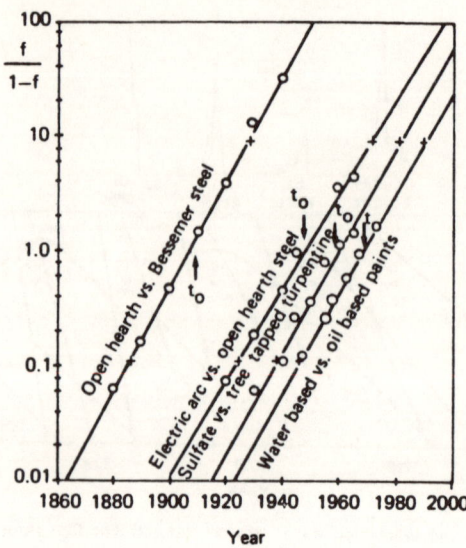

Fig. 12. Market penetration of four processes or machines in the United States. The time constant is about 50 years for all four cases. Here the process is one way and there are no cycles involved. My presumption is that the rate of these penetration processes is the primary clock of economy. This rate may be closely linked to human behavior and may be the deep reason for the stability of the cycles' length.

and stuttering. What I think most dangerous and misleading is their blind devotion to monetary concepts. All my analysis of economic systems tends to show that monetary variables are the manifestation of a deeper stratum of phenomena, where the real mechanisms lie. The description of the evolution of the energy market in Figure 5 does not require the concept of money at all and beats any econometric model in precision, simplicity, and capacity to forecast.

Concerning the second question, I lean much toward the interpretation that the behavior of the final consumer is the "central clock" of the system. The time constants for market penetration among numerous consumers and for capital products as well [17] (Figure 12) tend to cluster around 50 years. It is a current observation that when a product nears saturation of the market the corresponding industry enters into trouble. Volterra equations for interacting populations show oscillatory behavior [4], while industry probably exhausts its potential for incremental and managerial innovation, thus reducing its capacity to cope with change.

If many industries happen to be born together, they will enter into the embalming stage together, and this will liberate capital for new enterprises. Such a Schumpeterian view gives good hints concerning the self-amplifying mechanism of the waves. The reason why innovation, and even more invention, fit the straightjacket of precise functional relationships remains a deep mystery, however. Societal mechanisms seem capable of switching genius on and off.

The above considerations are not really meant to explain in scientific terms but only to wind up for the next run of analysis.

Conclusions

During the last 300 years basic inventions and innovations appear in waves, of precise configuration and frequency, that are substantially isomorphic with a "contraction" of the time scale by roughly a factor of 2 every century. The introduction of new primary energies, their phasing out of the market and their prices appear to be rigidly linked to these cycles, adding another dimension to forecasting in the field of energy systems.

The concept of a *learning society*, with its implications on the ecological Volterra equations, represents a very powerful tool in organizing social behavior and hints to the possibility of a unified theory for genetic evolution, ecology, sociology, and economics.

References

1. Marchetti C., and Nakicenovic, N., The Dynamics of Energy Systems and the Logistic Substitution Model, RR-79-13, International Institute for Applied Systems Analysis, Laxenburg, Austria, December 1979.
2. Peterka, V., Macrodynamics of Technological Change: Market Penetration by New Technologies, RR-77-22, International Institute for Applied Systems Analysis, Laxenburg, Austria, November 1977.
3. Fleck, F., Regelmäßigkeiten bei Marktdurchdringungsprozessen als Folge des individuellen Nachfrageverhaltens. Dissertation, Fakult+t für Wirtschaftswissenschaften der Universität Fridericiana Karlsruhe (Technische Hochschule), Karlsruhe, West Germany, 1980.
4. Goel, N. S., Maitra, S. C. and Montroll, E. W., On the Volterra nonlinear Models of Interacting Populations. *Rev. Mod. Phys.* 43, 231 (1971).
5. Bush, R. R. and Mosteller, F., 2Stochastic Models for Learning, Wiley, New York, 1955.
6. Whiston, T. G., Life is Logarithmic, in *Advances in Cybernetics and Systems* (J. Rose, ed.), Gordon and Breach, London, 1974.
7. *The World Almanac*, Doubleday, 1971.
8. Marchetti, C., Energy Systems—The Broader Context, *Technol. Forecast. Soc. Change* 14, 191–203 (1979).
9. Marchetti, C., Primary Energy Substitution Models, Technol. Forecast. Soc. Change 10, 350 (1977).
10. Mensch, G., *Das technologische Patt*, Umschau Verlag, Frankfurt/Main, 1975; for details on how the data have been selected, the German edition is preferable to the English edition, *Stalemate in Technology*, Ballinger, Cambridge, Mass., 1979. These books are also recommended for a good bibliography on research on the innovation process.
11. Graham, A. K., and Senge, P. M., A Long-Wave Hypothesis on Innovation, workshop on National Innovation Policy and Firm Strategy, December 1979, International Institute for Applied Systems Analysis, Laxenburg, Austria; also *Technol. Forecast. Soc. Change* 17, 283–311 (1980).
12. Marchetti, C., *The Evolution of the Energy Systems and the Aircraft Industry*, Proceedings of the Symposium on Hydrogen in Air Transportation, 11–14 September 1979, DFVLR Deutsche Forschungs- und Versuchsanstalt für Luft- und Raumfahrt e. V. Stuttgart, F.R.G.
13. Brewer, G. D., *Characteristics of Liquid Hydrogen Fueled Aircraft*, Proceedings of the Symposium Hydrogen in Air Transportation, 11–14 September 1979, DFVLR Deutsche Forschungs- und Versuchsanstalt für Luft- und Raumfahrt e. V., Stuttgart, F.R.G.
14. Marchetti, C., On Energy and Agriculture: From Hunting–Gathering to Landless Farming, RR-79-10, International Institute for Applied Systems Analysis, Laxenburg, Austria, December 1979.
15. *Historical Statistics of the United States*, U.S. Department of Commerce, Washington, D.C., 1975.
16. Beijdorff, A. F., and Lukas, J. H., *Energy Price: Pervasive Carrier of Information*, Group Planning Shell Internation Petroleum Company, Shell Centre, London.
17. Fisher, J. C., and Pry, R. H., A Simple Substitution Model of Technological Change, 70-C-215, General Electric Company, Research and Development Center, Schenectady, N. Y., Technical Information Series, 1970; see also *Technol. Forecast. Soc. Change* 3, 75–88 (1971).

Received 4 December 1980

[25]

Excerpt from *Economic Complexity: Chaos, Sunspots, Bubbles, and Nonlinearity*, 253–89.

CHAPTER 11

Economic growth in the very long run: on the multiple-phase interaction of population, technology, and social infrastructure

Richard H. Day and Jean-Luc Walter

Our ultimate goal is to form laws of cultural dynamics.
— *Paul Martin*

The archaeological data suggest that we must...break
away from the assumption that human cultures are
inherently stable.... — *Mark Nathan Cohen*

Abstract: Economic growth in the very long run is described by a mutiple-phase, dynamic process with potentially complex dynamics during transitions between regimes. Technology is assumed to rest on a managerial–administrative infrastructure that influences natality, productivity, and mortality. A population adopts a temporarily efficient techno-infrastructure and determines the population of its heirs. Growth can occur within a regime by the reorganization of population into new groups, but this process cannot continue forever because of externalities. A way out exists in the adoption of a new regime. Economic and social evolution is possible, but the probability of escape from an old regime need not be unity. Fluctuations can occur with or without reswitching, and under certain conditions a population can be trapped in a complex pattern of growth, fluctuation, reswitching, and collapse. It is shown that realistic scenarios can be generated by the model. The chapter concludes with a formal analysis of the possible events and the construction of probabilities that describe the chance that phases will switch and that various kinds of qualitative histories can unfold.

The theory of economic growth that flourished after midcentury was motivated, at least in part, by the exponential trend in aggregate output exhibited by the industrialized countries during the preceding century or

The present study was initially stimulated by discussions at Harvard in 1976 with J. Sablov concerning the Classic Mayan Collapse. Sablov later organized an advanced seminar of the

254   **Richard H. Day and Jean-Luc Walter**

two. Indeed, Tinbergen referred to his contribution as "a theory of the trend," and Solow's seminal work reflected the same stylized fact. That stylized fact, however, is only a relatively short-run movement from the perspective of archaeologists for whom a generation or even a century is a short period, and who think in terms of millennia when contemplating changes in human culture. Although the details become increasingly obscure in the more remote reaches of time, scientists in this field have established a reasonably clear picture of human socioeconomic development in its broadest terms. That development has taken us from the epoch of hunting and food collecting to horticultural settlements and complex, nonliterate societies, then to the historical epoch of urban civilization, household agriculture, and trading empires, and very recently to the industrialized economy. Some pundits believe we are already in the midst of a transition to a new epoch of postindustrialization.

At some places and times the transition between epochs seems to have been smooth; at others, crises seem to have occurred with "jumping" and "reswitching" prior to successful adoption of a new regime. Moreover, examples exist in which a rapid collapse and reversion to a preceding regime seems to have occurred. Population fluctuations within a particular way of life appear in the archaeological and historical records, and in some well-known cases of relatively isolated cultures, the socioeconomic process seems to have been stuck in a more or less stationary or fluctuating state for very long periods of time.

The present contribution provides a model of this complex picture of socioeconomic evolution. Economic growth is described by a multiple-phase, dynamic process. The effective use of a technology (or set of technologies) is assumed to rest on an associated social system that incorporates managerial–administrative practice and measures for public health,

Footnote *(cont.)*
Center for American Studies in Santa Fe in the fall of 1978 involving archaeologists M. Aldenderfer, L. Cordell, G. Low, C. Renfrew, and E. Zubrow, a mathematician K. Cooke, a philosopher J. Bell, and the first author, an economist. A book resulted with essays by the participants: Sablov (1980). Further inspiration was provided by successive interdisciplinary conferences sponsored by Ilya Prigogine's Institute in Theoretical and Applied Thermodynamics in March 1982 and March 1984, and by a continuing interdisciplinary seminar led by A. Iberall (physics) and including A. Moore and D. White (anthropology), L. Goldberg (biology), R. Baum and D. Wilkerson (political science), P. Wohlmuth (law), and the first author (economics). All of the computations and diagrams for this study were prepared by Weihong Huang. Section 4 of this chapter has benefited from discussions with Guilio Pianigiani. Although the first author's original notes on the subject were set down more than a decade ago, and these served as the basis for a lecture on the subject at the University of Paris in the spring of 1985, it was during a month of research at Gunnar Eliasson's Industrial Institute for Economic and Social Research in October 1986 that he finally began to put these ideas into a form suitable for publication.

welfare, and defense. Natality, productivity, and mortality are all assumed to depend on this social system. A *regime* consists of more or less independent *groups,* each organized within a technology–social system pair that we call a techno-infrastructure. A population adopts a temporarily efficient techno-infrastructure and determines the population of its heirs. Although expansion within a group is limited by internal diseconomies of group size, growth can occur in a regime by the reorganization of population into new groups. This process cannot continue forever because of external diseconomies associated with the total population. A way out exists in the adoption of a new technology and its associated infrastructure. The probability of escape from an old regime need not be unity, however. Fluctuations can occur with or without reswitching. Under certain conditions a population can be trapped in a complex pattern of growth, fluctuation, collapse, reversion to an old regime, and renewed growth.

Although the picture that emerges is very different in some ways from the models of growth that have dominated economic thinking until now, it is built up from classical ingredients: the interaction of population, productivity, and reproductive behavior. But there are crucial new elements that, when added to the classical assumptions, lead away from stationary states or steady, balanced growth.

The present introduction to this theory is divided into four parts:

1 a background survey of the major epochs and the hypotheses of social infrastructure, productivity, and demoeconomic behavior on which the analysis rests;
2 the statement of a formal model that expresses these hypotheses;
3 an illustration of the kinds of histories that can be generated by the model and an explanation of how a variety of scenarios that seem like "real world" developments can occur; and
4 an introduction to the mathematical analysis of processes of this kind.

1   Background

a   *The epochs*

Some 50 millennia ago, when modern people replaced their Neanderthal predecessors, the change was associated with an improvement in social organization and technology. According to Butzer (1977), the new bands were probably twice the size of the earlier groups. Their hunting–gathering technology involved an expanded ensemble of specialized stone implements of consummately skilled manufacture for various tasks of killing game, processing food, and fabricating clothing and habitations. This great advance was apparently made possible by an improved brain, as well as by vocal organs that yielded a distinct advantage in communication and hence in social interaction. The new linguistic capacity may also have been intimately related to a superior creative capacity that made possible the striking improvement in technology and the adaptation to virtually every nook and cranny of the globe, a process that came to an end some 10,000 years ago when the world (both old and new) was essentially filled with representatives of the hunting and gathering culture.

Binford (1968) and, in an especially comprehensive treatise, Cohen (1977) demonstrate that during the closing of the global frontier, three roughly coincident developments occurred: the disappearance of the megafaunal species, the appearance of villages, and the domestication of plants and animals. The subsequent agricultural and herding societies, based on horticulture and animal husbandry, marked the beginning of a transition to a new epoch that spread throughout a very large part of the world. The new culture displayed considerably more variety of technology and social style, and it supported a denser population. As this new culture spread, and it seems to have done so quite steadily, human numbers exhibited a worldwide surge. "Earlier" peoples were displaced, settled themselves, or fused into larger, more productive groups than before. Hunting cultures gradually retreated into remote areas relatively unsuited for agricultural activity.

About 3,000–5,000 years ago urban–agricultural societies began to organize into centrally controlled, bureaucratically administered city states that used writing and accounting to monitor and control economic transactions. Sagan (1985) suggests that these early civilizations were preceded by intermediate, complex societies that possessed roads, schools, police, standing armies, and bureaucracies but not written languages, prominent examples of which persisted in Africa and Polynesia until the European commercial expansion. In any event, the emergence about 1,500 B.C. of empires based on widespread trading networks made possible a great increase in specialization and a pronounced expansion again in productivity. Another surge in population followed. Social, cultural, and scientific progress of various kinds occurred throughout this age, leading, after the Renaissance, to a breakthrough to a new commercial age when nation states and trading empires spread their civilizations throughout much of the world. Then came the industrial revolution, based on power technology and large-scale capital. It led to still another surge in productivity and population and, compared to previous rates of increase, a truly explosive one, due in large measure to the decrease in mortality rates that accompanied this regime.

This in barest outline is the grand dynamics of *Homo sapiens sapiens*. The actual number of epochs used in describing it is somewhat arbitrary.[1] More importantly, in the major epochs that mark these vast rearrangements of human activity and numbers, various goods, techniques, rules of behavior, and institutional forms were invented, innovated, diffused, and abandoned in overlapping waves of activity and organization, a process that has accelerated with growing amplitude and shortening period. Economic evolution is, thus, much richer and more varied than this brief sketch portrays. What is crucial to the present analysis, however, is the practical existence of distinct socioeconomic epochs.[2]

b   *The techno-infrastructure*

The key to understanding the significance of epochs for the theory of economic growth is the explicit recognition that each one is based on a distinct managerial–administrative infrastructure. Butzer already emphasized the point that it was more efficient organization that enabled humans to specialize in the harvest of dominant species (mammoth, horse, etc.) and to adopt quasipermanent settlements, religion, and specialization in the production of weapons and other implements.

When agriculture emerged, higher levels of organization and more complex societies evolved with it. People assembled into villages; classes and political organizations emerged. The increasingly intensive systems of cultivation required them. A literate elite, large-scale public architecture, a standing military, and a permanent bureaucracy characterized civilized urban centers based on irrigated agriculture, all stemming from the need to organize local production and long-distance trade. When the modern industrial economy began to emerge, its growing armies of white- and blue-collar workers depended on their abilities to function appropriately within vast systems of transportation, education, police, justice, and public health. These systems require huge forces of workers and administrators.[3]

---

[1] A splendid, boldly synthetic survey of this vast process that vividly portrays its dynamic character will be found in Barraclough (1984). See also Sherratt (1980) for another helpful overview for the nonspecialist.

[2] Deevey, for example, bases his survey on seven major epochs whereas, at the other extreme, Easterlin (1983) uses three gross epochs, those of hunting and food collecting, settled agriculture, and modern growth. The present theory can actually accommodate as many or as few distinct regimes as is meaningful or that are convenient for the purpose at hand. See Day and Cigno (1978) and Day (1987) for very general expositions.

[3] Barraclough (1984, p. 52). See also Sagan (1985, pp. xvi–xxiii) on complex societies in this context.

Evidently, a salient feature of socioeconomic life in all the great epochs is the division of effort between *managerial and organizational infrastructure* and *work*. The former produces the social cohesion, coordination, and knowledge on which the productivity of labor is based. Given that effort, the work force can effectively process materials and fabricate goods. A technology defines the possibilities for specialization and cooperation. Its effective implementation depends on the existence of the infrastructure and its managerial "know-how," a prerequisite that Boserup (1981) calls the administrative technology.

In the simplest social groups, this infrastructure may be created by many or even all individuals part of the time. Even in paleolithic hunting bands, individuals played distinct, specialized roles of social and religious leadership. Although the term *infrastructure* may exaggerate these functions in such simple societies, the presence of such a division of labor is obviously crucial to cohesiveness in the very large, nonliterate, complex societies and in the huge agglomerations of early civilization and of our own industrial age. It is clear on the basis of these observations that for society to switch from one epoch to another, it is essential for it to possess a large enough population to support the new technology by providing an appropriate infrastructure. The infrastructure requirements constitute a threshold of population that must be surpassed before a transition is possible.

In addition to this lower threshold, there is an upper bound on population beyond which the effective operation of technology with a given infrastructure cannot be maintained. This is because an excessive population cannot be coordinated: The planning, organization, and control of public goods and services cannot be effectively managed. Technology and infrastructure are, therefore, characterized by both lower and upper thresholds that define its *domain of viability*. This combination of production and administrative technology, with its division of effort between work and management (where these terms are broadly conceived) and with its population range of viability, we shall call a *techno-infrastructure*.

In addition to the internal diseconomy caused by expanding group size, due to problems of information, communication, and coordination in a group possessing a fixed infrastructure, there exists also an *external diseconomy*, also determined by the technology, that derives from aggregate population size. It is induced by the absorbing capacity of the environment. The earth's absorbing capacity for peoples possessing a given techno-infrastructure can be stated in terms of the space available, which depends on the technology and which can be expressed in terms of the average population density. The supply of nonhuman resources is diminished when human densities become too large: The productivity of agriculture is reduced due to the scarcity of land, water, and other resources, and the waste-absorbing capacity of the environment is gradually exhausted.

The externality factor is a characteristic of the techno-infrastructure in that the absorbing capacity of the earth depends on the implied way of life. For example, hunting–gathering societies are limited by the available game and natural produce; horticultural societies by the supply of arable land and water; and industrial society by the supplies of water, oxygen, and the waste-absorbing capacity of the environment. A change in regime may overcome a constraint. Once the process of fission and diffusion of groups in a culture has run its course, a change in regime is the only avenue for further development. It is the only avenue, that is, given the absence of technological innovation and diffusion that is "neutral" to the techno-infrastructure in the sense of being compatible with the social system. This latter type of technological change, of course, plays an important role and occurs more or less continually. Its effect, however, is to accelerate growth in a regime, which, as shall become evident, hastens the process of switching among alternative regimes. Consequently, little is lost if in this study we abstract from neutral technological change *to focus on the process of epochal development in the sense defined here.*

c   *Population*

Population size evidently plays an essential role in determining which techno-infrastructures are viable. A sufficient population size is necessary for any productive activity; and after a technology has been adapted, productivity is influenced by growth in numbers. Eventually, this productivity must decline because of internal and external diseconomies. Any idea of well-being must depend on productivity, and this initial formalization of the theory will follow Cohen in using average product as the key variable. If average product is adequate, population can expand. If it is not, the attendant adversity will motivate a reorganization of society in a search for a means to insure survival and to improve welfare. This process of switching is the heart of the matter, but the relation of population to welfare is its crucial antecedent.

Within the limits of survivability, the "demand for children" can be expressed like a demand for any other costly good, but the correlation of net population growth rates with welfare need not be thought of in literally rational terms. When welfare is low enough, no children will survive. When some threshold of material well-being is surpassed, some children will survive; and this surviving number will increase with rising well-being until the choices of individuals, social customs, or biological constraints introduce sufficient pressure to place an upper bound on further expansion.

The connection between productivity and population growth rates was the essence of the classical theory of development, and it has been incorporated in toto by modern anthropological–economic growth theorists such as Cohen and Boserup. Obviously, the connection is subtle and variable, but for purposes of analyzing economic development in the very long run, it would be inadmissible to omit it. For purposes of developing a formal model, the connection must be made precise; this will be done using the standard form, long incorporated by Nelson (1956), Solow (1956), Haavelmo (1956), or more recently by Day (1983) or Day, Kim, and Macunovich (in press).

What we have then is the interaction of population, productivity, welfare, and population growth rates that forms the basis of the classical theory of economic growth. What has been added to the classical theory is the concept of the techno-infrastructure and the explicit incorporation of internal and external diseconomies associated with excessive population within a given technology and administrative framework.

d   *Fission, fusion, and the switch in regime*

The key hypothesis originated by Binford, developed in Boserup and buttressed in a comprehensive survey of the evidence by Cohen, is that population growth brings about a need to switch to progressively more intensive techniques to avoid an excessive decline in well-being and that, in order to switch, an appropriate infrastructure is required. According to this theory, population growth is necessary to bring about major reorganizations of society and is sufficient to create the economic pressures that motivate social transformations.

This process of socioeconomic evolution can be most easily identified at the transition between the hunting and food-collecting epoch and the succeeding epoch of settled agriculture. Under favorable conditions, a hunting and food-collecting band grows. As it does, it draws on a greater and greater area whose scope eventually taxes the energies of the group. Productivity and, hence, welfare begin to fall. At some point the band may split to form two groups or in a more gradual way may "shed" some of its members, who will fuse with others who have separated from other bands to form a new productive entity. The new groups move apart, each occupying about the same space as the original bands and each following essentially the same life as before. In this way (in a process originally described by Birdsell, 1958), an originally small, insignificant population spreads itself throughout all those areas where hunting and food collecting are possible.

The process is slow or fast depending on the yield of the environment, the quality and specialization of implements, and the effectiveness of co-operation in the hunt. Also crucial are the mores of reproduction, conditions of hygiene, and external environmental factors that determine mortality in the group. The process can take place at a very high rate, as shown in recent simulation studies by Martin (1987).

New groups that emerge could choose a new technology, but this may not be possible until there is a large enough population for groups to be fused; or it may be that the old technology makes possible a superior well-being just by splitting the groups, each adopting the same infrastructure-technology pair as before. But once the world becomes "full" – that is, once the external diseconomies of total population using a given techno-infrastructure become prominent enough – well-being cannot be maintained by further group formation. It can be accomplished (given the previously mentioned caveat about neutral technological change) only by a jump to a new techno-infrastructure.

The process of fission that characterized the expansion throughout the epoch of the hunting–gathering band did not disappear at the end of the age. It is still an important phenomenon. Fusion became increasingly important at the beginning of the next regime as formerly disparate groups were conquered and assimilated, or combined among themselves to form new civilizations to oppose the others. Nonetheless, during the spread of civilization, great empires that had once been formed often broke up into smaller geographical units within which growth eventually resumed. The Roman Empire, for example, divided into a considerable number of smaller states. Although population declined in some places, particularly in Rome, population growth in Europe quickly resumed. Similar breakups and reunifications occurred in China. Although fusion and fission in advanced societies is usually, if not universally, accompanied by war, it seems likely that the underlying economic forces causing these changes include those of population growth, productivity, and the efficacy of administrative technology in a manner described in general and somewhat abstract terms set forth here.

e   *Alternative scenarios of economic development*

The transition to a new techno-infrastructure rests both on its sufficient productivity and on its "reachability." In the absence of a reachable regime, the expansion of population could converge to an equilibrium or, more likely, to a fluctuation in numbers as originally argued by Malthus and in the archaeological literature by Zubrow (1971), who provides evidence of such dynamics in the data on prehistoric agriculture in what is now the southwestern United States. In either case, economic evolution would come to a halt, awaiting the discovery of new techniques and the requisite social forms.

A more extreme result of long-run growth in the absence of a reachable regime is the overshoot of an equilibrium and the collapse of the culture, with an attendant reversion to a preceding, "less advanced" techno-infrastructure. Such a collapse, for which there are several notable examples in the archaeological record (e.g., ancient Egypt and Teotihuacan), could be followed by a new expansion and evolution, but it could also be followed by still another collapse. See Renfrew (1980) and Sablov (1980).

Finally, it may be that a regime is reachable, but because of the previous development history an expansion within a regime is followed by fluctuations with switching and reswitching that delay an eventual permanent transition to a new epoch. Such a scenario seems to mimic events that have been played out at one place or another in former times. Sagan (1985, p. 235), for example, observes that prior to contact with Western culture some societies appear to have spent hundreds of years alternating between band organizations and primitive, kinship societies.

Broadly speaking, however, the general trend of growth has involved a progression from one regime to another, each marked by the increasing size and complexity of its managerial infrastructure and each requiring a striking advance in administrative as well as production technology.

2 A formal model

The grand dynamics of our story can be portrayed by a formal model that illuminates the underlying interaction of population, productivity, welfare, and social organization. The first step is to reconsider the aggregate production function; the second is to summarize the salient features of natality and mortality; and the third step is to combine these classical but now modified ingredients to obtain a more general theory of growth that applies, not just to a single epoch, but to change within epochs and the switching from one techno-infrastructure to another.

a *Production in a group*

For simplicity, consider a communal group made of heterosexual pairs and their children. Each pair supplies one adult equivalent of effort to society, either as part of the work force or as part of the infrastructure; the other adult equivalent of effort is used in household production, child

Economic growth in the very long run   263

rearing, or leisure. The group possesses a technology that rests on a managerial and administrative infrastructure whose presence is necessary for effective production. Given this infrastructure, effective work can be undertaken with the available technology. With this setup, two distinct inputs must be distinguished: administrative or managerial effort M and labor L. If the group size is x (measured in numbers of adult pairs), then $x = M + L$.

According to the theory under consideration, the planning, coordination, and control of economic activity becomes increasingly difficult as group population grows. For simplicity, it can be assumed that for any regime there is some maximum number compatible with any effective socioeconomic order. Let this number be N and call it the *upper viability threshold*. The term $S = N - x$ represents the *social space* or *social slack* within which the group functions. If S is relatively large, a group can increase its population for some time with little depressing effect on productivity. When S is relatively small, there is little room for expansion, and increases in group size begin to lower productivity. If $S \leq 0$, the group cannot function.

Suppose now that the *intragroup production function* can be represented by the product of three factors involving separately the managerial input M, the labor input L, and the social space S; that is, let $f(M, L, S) = g(M)h(L)k(S)$, where $g(\cdot)$, $h(\cdot)$, and $k(\cdot)$ are strictly increasing concave functions on $\mathfrak{R}^+$ with $g(M) = h(L) = k(S) = 0$ for $M, L, S \leq 0$. Suppose also that M is fixed so that it is a parameter for a given group. Then, the production function for the group can be reexpressed as

$$Y = f(x; M, N) := \begin{cases} g(M)h(x-M)k(N-x), & M \leq x \leq N, \\ 0, & x \leq M \text{ or } x \geq N. \end{cases} \tag{1}$$

The separate factors in the production function all have positive marginal productivity. When the constraints implied by the lower and upper thresholds M and N are taken into account, however, group effort as a whole has increasing and then diminishing average productivity and, after a maximum output is reached, declining absolute productivity. The interval (M, N) is the group's *viability domain* given its fixed techno-infrastructure.[4] Group size must exceed M but not N.

---

[4] If effort allocated to management were freely substitutable for work, then we could derive aggregate production as a function of group size alone by using an efficient combination of the two inputs. Thus, we could define $f(x; M, N) := \max_{M, L}\{g(M)h(L)k(S) \mid M+L \leq x, S = N - x\}$. Indeed, any number of separate types of effort could be subsumed in this way. Suppose, however, that there is a residuum of effort that is not substitutable within a given regime. Such a socially nonfungible type of effort is what we associate with the variable M.

264   **Richard H. Day and Jean-Luc Walter**

b   *Fission, fusion, and the social production function*

Given a fixed techno-infrastructure, a population could expand beyond the feasibility domain for a single group by fission, the splitting of a group, or by shedding and fusion, the formation of a new group from individuals splitting off from existing groups.

Let x be the total population organized into n groups of average size x/n. For n groups, production is

$$nf\left(\frac{x}{n}\right) = Kh\left(\max\left\{0, \frac{x}{n} - M\right\}\right) \cdot k\left(\max\left\{0, N - \frac{x}{n}\right\}\right), \quad K = g(M).$$

Clearly, $nf(x/n) > 0$ on the open interval $V_n := (nM, nN)$. According to the theory, the processes of fission and shedding and fusion occur so as to maintain temporarily efficient production. Consequently, social production is $\max_{n \in \mathfrak{N}} \{nf(x/n)\}$, where $\mathfrak{N}$ is the set of positive integers. Thus, the production function as a whole is the efficiency frontier of a scalloped sequence of overlapping component functions, each member of which is an integer multiple of its predecessor: n times the range of viability and n times the maximum attainable output. It presumes that, as population expands, groups split or shed and fuse so as to maintain overall population productivity at as high a level as possible.

Eventually, the absorbing capacity of the environment must be exceeded, and this absorbing capacity cannot be expanded by forming new groups. Denote this externality factor by the term $p(x; \bar{x})$, a decreasing function on $[0, \bar{x}]$ with $p(0, \bar{x}) = 1$ and $p(x, \bar{x}) = 0$, all $x \geq \bar{x}$. Incorporating this externality, the *social production function* is

$$Y = F(x) := \max_{n \in \mathfrak{N}} \left\{nf\left(\frac{x}{n}\right)\right\} p(x; \bar{x}). \tag{2}$$

Evidently, population is bounded above by $\bar{x}$. Define $\bar{n} := \max_n \{nM \leq \bar{x}\}$. Then $\bar{n}$ is the maximum number of groups compatible with $\bar{x}$ and the requirements of the techno-infrastructure.[5]

Figure 1 shows an example in which $\bar{n} = 3$. The dotted lines show the successive production functions for 1, 2, and 3 groups when the externality factor does not play a role. The solid lines show how these are modified

---

[5] Evidently, $nf(x/n) \geq 0$ for all $x \in V_n$, $n \leq \bar{n}$, and on $V_{\bar{n}} \cap (0, \bar{x})$. Note that the effect of the externality is to compress the production function "downward and backward." Thus, $V_n = (\bar{n}M, \min\{\bar{n}N, \bar{x}\})$ and $F(x) \leq \max_n \{nf(x)\}$. Note that $V_n \cap V_{n+1}$ may be empty. Thus, suppose $N \leq 2M$; then $V_1 \cap V_2 = \emptyset$. In general, if $nN \geq (n+1)M$ then $V_m \cap V_{m+1} = \emptyset$, $m = 1, \ldots, n$. From this it does *not* follow that $V_n \cap V_{n+1} = \emptyset$ for all n. But suppose $nN \geq (n+1)M$; then $V_n \cap V_{n+1} \neq \emptyset$. If $N \geq 2M$ then it follows by induction that $V_n \cap V_{n+1} \neq \emptyset$ for all n.

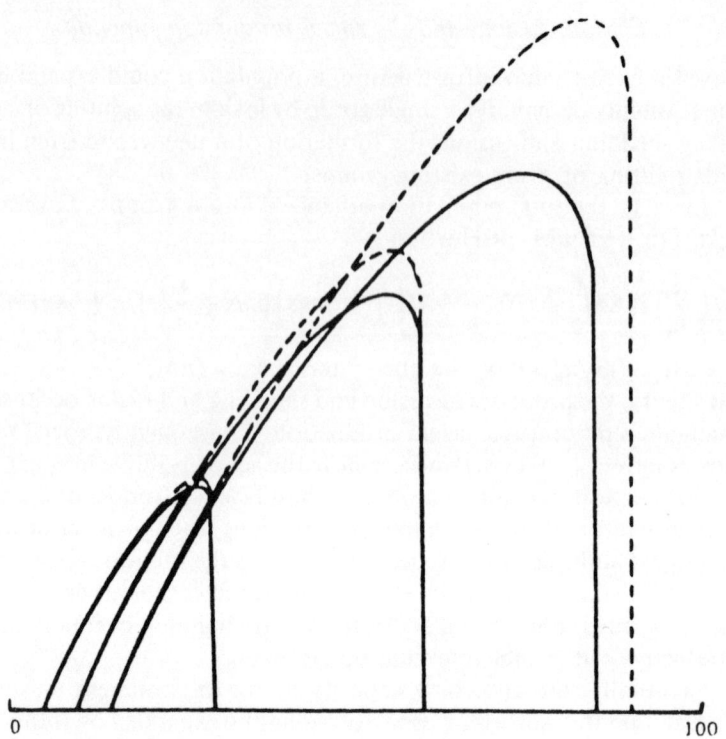

Figure 1. The social production function. Equation (1′) was used for 1, 2, and 3 groups. The parameters are $\beta = 0.9$, $\lambda = 0.1$, $\delta = 0.1$, $M = 5$, $N = 30$, $\bar{x} = 0.85$.

by the externality factor. The social production function is the envelope of the solid lines.

Average productivity, which plays a key role in the theory, is

$$y = \frac{Y}{x} = F(x). \tag{3}$$

Given a social production function like that shown in Figure 1, the graph of average productivity in a regime would be like that shown in Figure 2.

c   *The aggregate social production function and average family welfare*

Suppose now that we have a collection of alternative regimes waiting to be discovered or created in some kind of morphogenesis that occurs when

266   **Richard H. Day and Jean-Luc Walter**

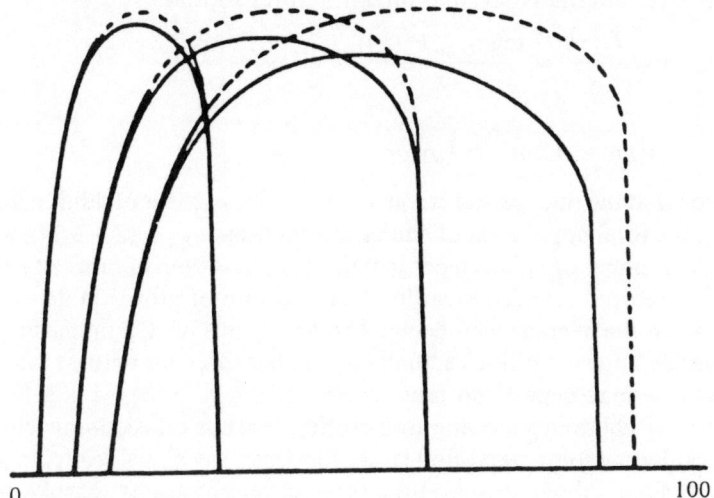

0   100

Figure 2. Average productivity. Using the social production function of Figure 1.

productivity falls, each represented by a technology and by its characteristic threshold parameters. A population can now choose between expansion within a regime by fission and diffusion *or* by a switch in regime.

Let us denote the sequence of alternative technologies by

$$\mathfrak{J} = \{1, 2, 3, \ldots\} \subset \mathfrak{N}.$$

Assuming that society uses an efficient technology, the *aggregate production function* is

$$G(x) = \max_{i \in \mathfrak{J}} \{F^i(x)\}, \tag{4}$$

where each F^i is defined by (2) and each component group production function f^i is defined by (1). The aggregate production function is the efficiency frontier of a scalloped sequence of overlapping, scalloped social production functions, each member of which is made up from the basic production function for a single group for a given regime. The aggregate technology $\{[x, G(x)]; x \in \mathfrak{R}^+\}$ is, of course, nonconvex.[6]

The efficiency criterion underlying the aggregate production function implies that the average aggregate product is maximized temporarily and

---

[6] The set $V^i := \bigcup_{n \in \mathfrak{N}} V_n^i \cap (0, \bar{x})$, where $V_n^i := (nM^i, nN^i)$, is the feasibility domain for each technology $i \in \tau$; the set $V^* := \bigcup_{i \in \tau} V^i$ is the *aggregate feasibility domain* for G defined on $\mathfrak{J}$. The set $\mathfrak{R}^+ \setminus V^* := V^0$ is the *null domain* given the menu $\mathfrak{J}$.

locally over alternative techno-infrastructures so that

$$y = \frac{G(x)}{x} = \frac{\max_{i \in 3}\{F^i(x)\}}{x} = \max_{i \in 3}\left\{\frac{F^i(x)}{x}\right\}. \tag{5}$$

d   *Demoeconomic behavior*

Assume that the time period is a generation. The number of adult pairs being x_t, the total population of adults and children is $P_t = (2 + b_t)x_t$, where b_t is the number of children per female. The maximum number of surviving children per female (Ricardo's "natural rate of growth") depends in general on the average well-being. The actual surviving number may be, and under some conditions actually is, smaller than this natural rate. The actual rate may depend on preferences and social mores. Likewise, the number of children surviving to maturity depends on economic circumstances. Below some starvation level of income, say c_i, naturally, survival is impossible. Above this level the survival rate increases sharply. It approaches unity and possibly dips somewhat at very high income levels.[7]

For the sake of the theory, the net result of these considerations is the specification of a *demoeconomic function* that defines the average number of adult females that emerge in a given period per female existing in the preceding period. Formally, we suppose that $\pi(\cdot)$ is a function of average well-being that is fixed for a given infrastructure but may change when a transition occurs. Thus we index $\pi_i(y)$, $i \in 3$. We shall assume that $\pi_i(y)$ is quasiconcave for $y \geq c_i \geq 0$ with $\pi_i(y) = 0$, $0 \leq y \leq c_i$, $i \in 3$. The parameter c_i will be called the *net birth income threshold* for the ith regime. Let $\lambda_i := \sup_{y \geq 0} \pi_i(y)$. Then λ_i is the maximum net rate of population growth in regime i.

e   *Phase structures and regimes*

Given the assumptions made so far, the number of households that emerge in time period $t + 1$ from the population of period t, when the latter is organized into groups with the ith techno-infrastructure, is $x_{t+1} = \pi_i(y_t)x_t$. Recalling that the average well-being is assumed to be the average product $y = G(x)/x$, then

$$x_{t+1} = \theta_i(x_t) := \pi_i\left[\frac{F^i(x_t)}{x_t}\right]x_t \tag{6}$$

when the population is organized in the ith techno-infrastructure. The map $\theta_i(\cdot)$ is called the ith *phase structure*.

---

[7] All of this can be encompassed within a standard economic decision-making framework as is outlined in Day, Kim, and Macunovich (in press), which reviews the empirical background.

268   **Richard H. Day and Jean-Luc Walter**

It could be that for some n, i there exist feasible $x \in (nM^i, nN^i)$ such that $\theta_i(x) = 0$ because $F^i(x)/x < c_i$. If in the course of development from an initial population x_0 such a population is generated, then it is the last because $x = 0$ is a fixpoint for any phase structure (6). This motivates the following:

Definition 1: Regimes and the viability domain.   *The set* $\mathcal{Q}^* := \{x \mid \theta_i(x) > 0 \text{ for some } i\}$ *is called the* viability domain. *Define*

$$I(x) := \min\{\arg\max_{i \in \mathfrak{I}}\{F^i(x)\}\} \quad \text{for all } x \in \mathcal{Q}^* \tag{6a}$$

and

$$I(x) := 0 \quad \text{for all } x \in \mathcal{Q}_0 := \mathcal{R} \setminus \mathcal{Q}^*. \tag{6b}$$

Now let

$$\mathcal{Q}_i := \{x \mid I(x) = i\}, \tag{7}$$

the set of populations for which the ith phase structure governs development. We shall call it the ith regime. *Thus, when $x \in \mathcal{Q}_i$, the ith phase structure determines the succeeding population. The set $\mathcal{Q}_0$ is called the* null *regime. For any $x \in \mathcal{Q}_0$, the succeeding population is zero, so we define $\theta_0(x) := 0$ for all $x \in \mathcal{Q}_0$.*

Obviously, $\mathcal{Q}^* := \bigcup_{i \in \mathfrak{I}} \{x \mid F^i(x)/x > c_i\}$.

f   *The multiple-phase dynamic process*

The grand dynamics of demoeconomic development – involving the interaction of population, productivity, technology, and social infrastructure – can now be represented as the *multiple-phase dynamic process,*

$$x_{t+1} = \theta(x_t) := \theta_{I(x_t)}(x_t) = \theta_i(x_t), \quad x_t \in \mathcal{Q}_i. \tag{8}$$

Nothing guarantees that every phase zone is nonempty. An empty phase zone for a given regime means that it is dominated by other uniformly more productive regimes. Moreover, not all techno-infrastructures may be reachable from an initial population. But some history of phases unfolds for any initial population. The *phase progression $I(x_t)$, $t = 0, 1, \ldots$,* represents this history. *It describes economic development as an epochal evolution.*

For change to occur within a given regime, there must be a number n of groups, into which the population is divided, that are compatible with the population viability thresholds M_i and N_i. If regime $\mathcal{Q}_i$ governs growth during period t, then there exists a number of groups, say $n(t)$, such that $n(t)M^i \leq x_t \leq n(t)N^i$.

Begin with an initial population of adult pairs x_0 in some base period. Suppose $I(x_t) = 1$ for $t = 0, \ldots, s_1$ but that the regimes switch and $I(x_t) = i_2$ when $t = s_1 + 1$. The first epoch lasted for s_1 generations. Suppose that $I(x_t) = i_2$ for $t = s_1 + 1, \ldots, s_2$ but not for $t = s_2 + 1$. Then again the regime switches, let us say to i_3. The second epoch lasted $(s_2 - s_1)$ generations. The third regime is i_3 with duration $s_3 - s_1 - s_2$, and so on. In each epoch the number of groups $n_i(t)$ changes when fission or shedding and fusion occurs, so the number of groups in the ith regime forms a sequence n_{ij}, $j = 1, \ldots, g_i$, where n_{i1} is the initial number of groups formed at the switch to regime i. This process can continue so long as there are productive techno-infrastructures to be adopted when a population becomes sufficiently large.

3   "Real world" histories

The model specified above is probably the minimal variation on the classical–neoclassical growth theory that incorporates the new theory of socio-economic growth in the very long run. Some examples will illustrate how the theory can "explain" some of the more complex patterns of development found in the archaeological–anthropological–economic historical literature.

a   *Specific functional forms*

First, we must adopt specific functional forms for the components of the theory. Consider the group production function for techno-infrastructure i:

$$y = f^i(x) = K_i(x - M_i)^{\beta_i}(N_i - x)^{\gamma_i}, \quad M_i < x < N_i. \tag{1'}$$

Let the externality factor $p(x; \bar{x}_i) := (1 - x/\bar{x}_i)^{\delta_i}$ for $x \in [0, \bar{x}_i]$.[8] The social production function for a given techno-infrastructure can be shown to be

$$y = F^i(x) = K_i \max_{n \in \mathfrak{N}} \left\{ n^{1 - \beta_i - \gamma_i}(x - nM_i)^{\beta_i}(nN_i - x)^{\gamma_i} \left(1 - \frac{x}{\bar{x}_i}\right)^{\delta_i} \right\}. \tag{2'}$$

Next, suppose the demoeconomic function is

$$\pi_i(y) := \max\{0, \min\{\alpha_i(y - c_i), \lambda_i\}\},$$

which gives a positive linear function with positive slope α_i on the interval $[c_i, \lambda_i/\alpha_i - c_i]$.

---

[8] The externality factor could be written in terms of population density. Let d be the maximum possible average density and S the total space available for a given regime. Then $\bar{x} = Sd$.

270   **Richard H. Day and Jean-Luc Walter**

From these, the ith phase equations must be

$$x_{t+1} = \theta_i(x_t) = \max\{0, \min\{\alpha_i[F^i(x_t) - c_i x_t], \lambda_i x_t\}\}.^9 \qquad (5')$$

The production function (1′) is concave on its feasibility domain

$$v^i = (M^i, N^i)$$

when $0 < \beta_i, \gamma_i < 1$. When fission occurs, this function is "stretched," but because of the externality, it may become quasiconcave near $\bar{x}_i$. The function $F^i(\cdot)$ is certainly piecewise quasiconcave and piecewise monotonic. Because $\alpha_i c_i x$ is linear, the term $\alpha_i F^i(x_t) - \alpha_i c_i x_t$ retains essentially the same profile as $F^i(\cdot)$.

Given all this, the ith regime is

$$\mathcal{Q}_i = \left\{x; \frac{F^i(x)}{x} > c_i\right\}, \quad i \in \mathfrak{I}, \qquad \mathcal{Q}_0 := \left\{x; \frac{F^i(x)}{x} \le c_i\right\}.$$

The multiple-phase dynamic process is given by

$$x_{t+1} = \begin{cases} \theta_i(x_t) = \min\{\alpha_i[F^i(x_t) - c_i x_t], \lambda_i x_t\}, & x_t \in \mathcal{Q}_i, \\ 0, & x_t \in \mathcal{Q}_0. \end{cases} \qquad (8')$$

b   *Complex dynamics at the transition*

One of the most striking possibilities in this multiple-phase process is one in which fluctuations occur between the regimes, with switching and reswitching occurring at irregular intervals, and then a permanent switch followed by growth within a succeeding regime. *Development in the long*

---

[9] Note that each phase structure has three potential "subregimes" with corresponding "subphase structures." These are

$$\theta^i(x_t) = \theta^{i0}(x_t) := 0 \quad \text{when } F^i(x_t)/x_t \le c^i, \qquad (7a)$$

$$\theta^i(x_t) = \theta^{i1}(x_t) := \alpha^i F^i(x_t) - \alpha^i c_i x_t \quad \text{when } G^i(x_t)/x_t \le c_i + \lambda^i/d^i, \qquad (7b)$$

$$\theta^i(x_t) = \theta^{i2}(x_t) := \lambda^i x_t \quad \text{when } F^i(x_t)/x_t \ge c^i + \lambda^i/\alpha^i. \qquad (7c)$$

Of course, when $x_t \notin (M^i n, N^i n)$ for some n, then subregime i_0 holds. Suppose there exists an A such that $F^i(x)/x \ge \lambda^i/\alpha^i + c$; then there is a set made up of a finite union of intervals on which $F^i(x)/x \ge \lambda^i/\alpha^i + y^i$, where each interval corresponds to a particular value of n, the efficient number of groups. In this case there must be values of A where subphase i_1 holds.

The switching among subphases within a regime is governed by the average product. When it is below the threshold c, people cannot or will not raise children. Above c_i but below $\lambda_i/\alpha_i + c_i$, the preference for children is manifest but may be less than or greater than the number required for a growing population. When the average product is above $c_i + \lambda_i/\alpha_i$, population growth is exponential, the rate of growth being determined by the adult mortality rate and the minimum of the maximum possible number of children and the maximum desired number of children, λ_i.

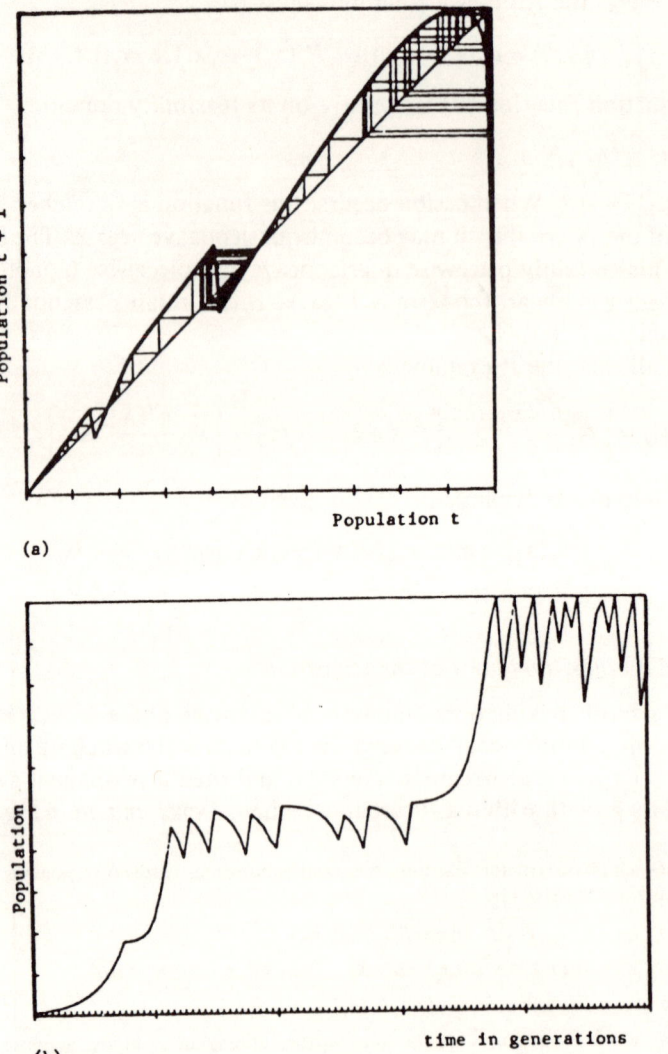

Figure 3.   Complex dynamics with reswitching. (a) Phase diagram and (b) implied history.

run is portrayed as a sequence of growth trends interspersed with fluctuations. Smooth transitions can also occur, with monotonic growth continuing at some transitions but fluctuations and crises at others.

In Figure 3a, a phase diagram for equation (8′) using specific parameter values is displayed. In Figure 3b a trajectory beginning from a very

272   **Richard H. Day and Jean-Luc Walter**

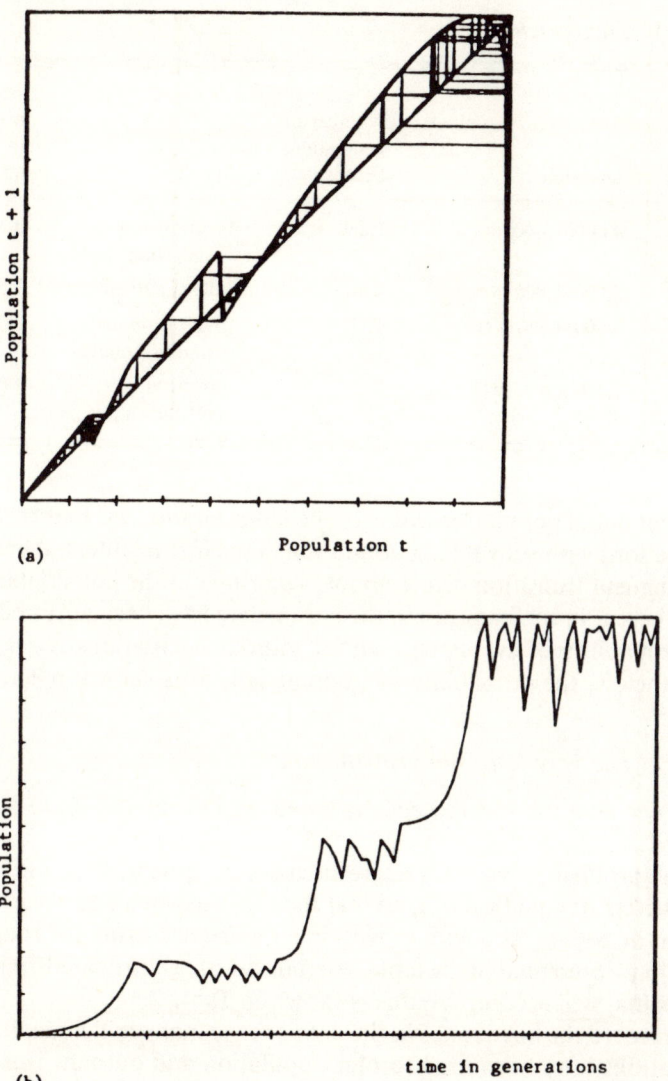

Figure 4.   Complex dynamics with reswitching. (a) Phase diagram and
(b) implied history.

small population is shown. After a period of growth, a smooth transition
to a second regime occurs. This is followed by growth, then fluctuations
with reswitching – a prolonged period of crises, if you will – followed by
a successful jump, further growth, and then fluctuations again. Figure 4
presents another phase diagram and trajectory starting from a slightly

Table 1. *The epochs*

Regime	Duration	Number of generations before 1975	Epoch	Beginning population (number of households)
1	40,000–8,000 B.C.	1,680	Hunting and collecting	$0.325K^2$
2	8,000–3,000 B.C.	400	Village agriculture	$1.5K^2$
3	3,000–1,750 B.C.	200	Civilization and trading empires	$25K^2$
4	1,750 A.D.–1,975 A.D.	9	Industrial revolution	$250K^2$

different initial population *but with the same parameters*. In this example, fluctuations with reswitching occur even in the first regime, but eventually a permanent transition comes about. To bring out the potential instabilities inherent in such a process, the parameters have been adjusted so that the probability of switching regimes without fluctuations is very small. Nonetheless, the probability of jumping is 1, as is shown in Theorem 1.

c   *The very long run growth trend*

Consider now the stylized epochs based on Deevey (1960), as shown in Table 1.

Our problem, given this aggregated set of epochs, is to estimate the parameters of equation (8'), so that the regime switchings occur more or less in the order – and with growth in a regime occurring for roughly the duration – presented in the table. A crude set of "guestimated" parameter values that will accomplish this is shown in Table 2.[10]

To record the huge range in the data over so many millennia, log transformations have been used to plot population and output. This has the effect of giving the early epochs, which lasted a long time, a weight comparable to the more recent epochs, which grew at accelerating rates for much shorter durations.

Figure 5a shows the aggregate production function. Figure 5b illustrates the implied average product. Because of the logarithmic scale we

---

[10] An attempt to estimate parameters using econometric methods would be interesting, perhaps even worthwhile, but not justified for our illustrative purposes and given the data at hand. Crude estimates will be sufficient for illustrative purposes and will give us a good idea if further research along this line is warranted.

274   **Richard H. Day and Jean-Luc Walter**

Table 2. *Parameter values*

Regime	M	N	$\geq$	K	β	γ	δ	λ
1	5	30	$104K$	7	0.9	0.1	0.1	1.001196
2	40	100	$2.2K^2$	20	0.6	0.1	0.1	1.012167
3	$50K$	$2K^2$	$180K^2$	5	0.6	0.1	0.1	0.014128
4	$5K^2$	$500K^2$	$1.3K^3$	800	0.6	0.1	0.1	1.222845

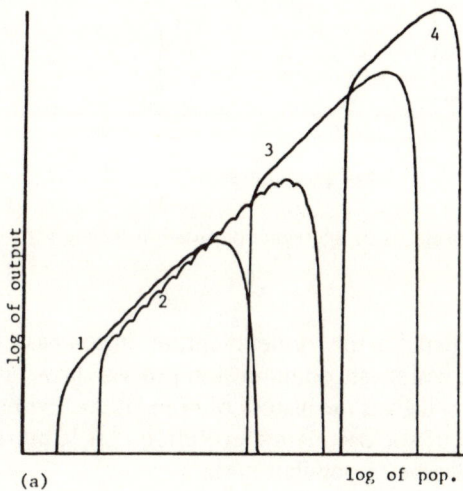

(a)

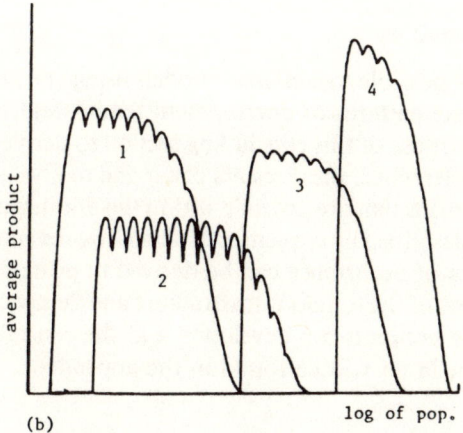

(b)

Figure 5.   The aggregate production function and average product with four regimes. (a) Aggregate production and (b) average product. See Table 1.

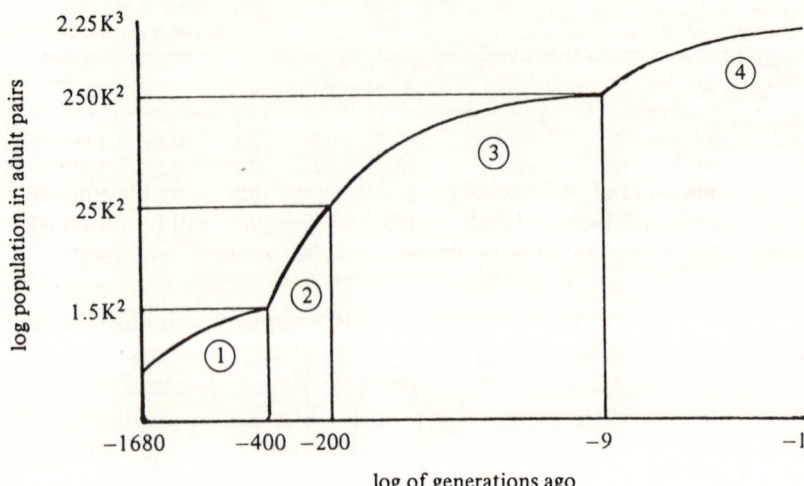

Figure 6.   The progress of aggregate population through the four major epochs.

cannot see much of the detail in the former diagram. In contrast, the scalloped profile due to the fission–shedding–fusion process shows up boldly in the latter chart. Figure 6 gives the history of population. Evidently, the model presents a story of socioeconomic evolution that is more or less like that described by Deevey's population data.

4   Mathematical analysis

We have shown that it is possible to construct models using specific functional forms that generate patterns of development reminiscent of those in the record. It is the purpose of this concluding section to derive precise "general" conditions under which these results occur and to give a formal characterization of scenarios that are possible within this framework. For this purpose, history is described by sequences of qualitative events whose conditional probabilities of occurrence can be derived in principle from the underlying parameters of the techno-infrastructure and demoeconomic behavior. The necessary concepts are developed and the central results presented. Proofs of the latter will be found in the appendix.

a   *Trajectories and orbits*

A *trajectory* of (8), with initial condition $x_0 = x$, is a sequence $\tau(x) :=$ $(x_n)_{n=0}^{\infty}$ such that x_{n+1}, x_n satisfy (8) for all n. If $\theta^n(x)$ is the nth iterated

276   **Richard H. Day and Jean-Luc Walter**

map generated from θ, then $\tau(x) = [\theta^n(x)]_{n=0}^{\infty}$. A trajectory is a model-generated history or scenario, and in what follows will be referred to synonymously as such.

b   *Viability*

To keep the number of evolutionary possibilities within reasonable bounds and to simplify the analysis, some regularity conditions will be adopted.

First, assume that the number of distinct infrastructures is finite [i.e., that $\mathfrak{J} = \{1, \ldots, r < \infty\}$]. Next, to insure that $\mathfrak{Q}^*$ is a connected set, assume that the infrastructure M_i is less than one-half the upper feasibility bound on group size; that is, assume that $M_i < \frac{1}{2}N_i$ for all $i \in \mathfrak{J}$. Also assume that $M_i < M_{i+1} < \bar{x}_i < \bar{x}_{i+1}$, so that neighboring feasibility domains overlap and are well ordered. If it is also assumed that $\max_x \theta(x) \leq \bar{x}_r$, then it is easily seen that $\theta(\cdot)$ is continuous and maps into $[0, \bar{x}_r]$, but it need not be that $\theta(\mathfrak{Q}^*) \subset \mathfrak{Q}^*$. Indeed, if M_1 or c_1 is positive, then $\theta(x) = 0$ for any $i \in \mathfrak{J}$ and any x such that $G^i(x)/x < c_i$. Such x will exist sufficiently close to M_1 and $\bar{x}_r$ and perhaps at other populations as well. Hence,

$$\mathfrak{Q}_0 \cap (0, \bar{x}_r) \neq \emptyset,$$

and evolution comes to an end for any trajectory that enters $\mathfrak{Q}_0$. Such a possibility is worth thinking about because extinction is such a common occurrence in the biological world of which we are a part. Nonetheless, the insights of the present theory are of considerable interest in the absence of such catastrophes, so we shall assume M_1 and c_1 are zero. Then, $\theta(0) = 0 = \theta(\bar{x}_r)$; and, given the previous assumptions, $\theta(x) > 0$ for all $x \in (0, \bar{x}_r)$. Thus, $\mathfrak{Q}^* = (0, \bar{x}_r)$ and $\theta(\mathfrak{Q}^*) \subset \mathfrak{Q}^*$; once the system "starts up," it can continue.[11]

c   *Peaks and tails*

It is evident from the preceding sections that local minima can occur for the map $\theta(\cdot)$ at population levels for which the number of groups in the

[11] Using a function-stretching argument analogous to that exploited in Day (1982), one can now easily derive conditions on the underlying group production functions in $\mathfrak{J}$ for the existence of a "chaos" point $x \in \mathcal{V}^*$ such that $\theta^3(x) < x < \theta(x)$. The implication is that under these conditions, which essentially mean that some technologies are productive enough, there exists an uncountable scrambled set C such that $\omega(C) = C$, where $\omega(C)$ is the limit set for all trajectories originating in C and such that $\tau(x)$ is chaotic in the sense of Li and Yorke (1975) for all $x \in C$.

Moreover, if a point $z \in \mathcal{V}^*$, and if there exists an odd integer n such that $\theta^n(z) < z < \theta(z)$ or such that $\theta^n(z) > z > \theta(z)$, then similarly – according to Li, Misiurewicz, Pianigiani, and Yorke (1982), known as LMPY – a scrambled set exists. Points that satisfy this LMPY condition are easy to find in the sample trajectories shown in Figure 6.

population changes within a given regime, or at populations for which a regime switch occurs (and the preexisting groups are fused to form a smaller, or decomposed to form a larger, number of groups). These local minima, or *tails,* are turning points at which the slope of $\theta(\cdot)$ changes from negative to positive. Between these tails are local maxima, or *peaks,* that are associated with the maximum population possible for a given number of groups within a given regime. For our present purposes the two kinds of switch points, one due to a change in the number of groups and one due to a switch in regime, need not be distinguished.

Let $\beta_0 = 0$, $\beta_1 < \beta_2 < \cdots < \beta_s = \bar{x}_r$, be the $s+1$ local minimizers and let α_i, $i = 1, \ldots, s$, be the local maximizers of θ. Of course, $\beta_{i-1} < \alpha_i < \beta_i$, $i = 1, \ldots, s$. By definition, the peak $\theta(\alpha_i)$ is the maximum emerging population that can occur from established populations in the neighborhood of α_i. Likewise, the tail $\theta(\beta_i)$ is the minimum population that can emerge in the neighborhood of β_i. Note that because of the splitting of socioeconomic groups, s will not be smaller than r.

Now let Z be an interval and let $\theta_Z(\cdot)$ be the restriction of $\theta(\cdot)$ to this interval. It will be assumed that for all $x \in [\beta_{i-1}, \alpha_i]$, θ is strictly increasing and $\theta(x) > x$. It will further be assumed that θ is concave and strictly decreasing on $[\alpha_i, \beta_i]$, $i = 1, \ldots, s$. Thus, θ is not constant in the neighborhood of a peak. These assumptions mean only that θ_i is concave on the relevant parts of its domain. They rule out feasible regimes in which only a contraction can occur. Although models that violate these assumptions would be of considerable interest for describing some kinds of history, to exclude them reduces the number of cases to be explored, which (as shall soon be seen) is still quite large. The instability or local expansiveness of the map θ plays a crucial role in the present theory. Specifically, we shall make use of

Condition E: $\theta'(x) < -1$ for all $x \in (\alpha_i, \beta_i)$.

This condition rules out convergence to a stationary state almost surely. When it prevails, we can get very strong results.

d   *Events*

Now consider the set of trajectories $S := \{\tau(x) \mid x \in (0, \alpha_1)\}$. Our objective is to give a characterization for all trajectories in S. To proceed, we decompose $[0, \bar{x}_r]$ into intervals according to the following definition.

Definition 2: Event thresholds and event zones.   *Set* $\gamma_1 = \beta_0 = 0$, $\gamma_{s+1} = \beta_s = \bar{x}_r$. *For* $i = 2, \ldots, s$, *define* $\gamma_i \in [\beta_{i-1}, \alpha_i]$ *by*

$$\gamma_i = \theta(\gamma_i) \quad \text{if } \theta(\beta_i) \le \beta_i,$$
$$\gamma_i = \beta_i \quad \text{if } \theta(\beta_i) > \beta_i.$$

The interval $Z_i := [\gamma_i, \gamma_{i+1}]$, $i = 1, \ldots, s$, *will be called the ith* event zone *and the parameter γ_i the ith* event threshold.

The types of trajectories that occur can now be characterized in terms of these event zones. For this purpose, the following definitions will be used.

Definition 3: Events.   *An event S_i is a subset of $S := \{\tau(x) \mid x \in [0, \alpha_1]\}$ defined with reference to the ith zone. The* null event N_i *contains trajectories that never reach the ith zone; the* reaching event Γ_i *contains all trajectories that surpass the ith event threshold. The* touching event Γ_i^* *contains all reaching trajectories whose first element past the ith threshold belongs to the ith event zone. The* skipping event J_i^k *contains trajectories that skip the ith event zone the first time they enter a higher zone (i.e., $J_i^k = \Gamma_i \backslash \Gamma_i^*$); the* growth event J_i^g *contains trajectories that grow monotonically in Z_i after initially surpassing the ith event threshold and then jump to a higher zone; they may return to Z_i or to some lower event zone after this first escape; the* fluctuation and jumping, *or* local chaos event J_i^{lc}, *contains trajectories that oscillate a finite number of periods and jump to a higher zone after first entering Z_i; the* sticking event T_i^s *contains trajectories that do not escape Z_i; the* reversion event T_i^r *contains trajectories that touch Z_i, revert to an earlier event zone, and never exceed γ_{i+1}. The* jumping event $J_i := J_i^g \cup J^{lc} \cup J_i^k$ *contains all trajectories that skip Z_i or that enter Z_i and then jump to a higher zone Z_j, $j > i$. The* trapping event $T_i := T_i^s \cup T_i^r$ *contains all trajectories that enter Z_i but never reach a higher zone.*

Figure 7 shows a map $\theta(\cdot)$ that satisfies the assumptions made so far. Generally speaking, any trajectories that enter the sets G_i grow, those that enter the sets F_i fluctuate, and those that enter the sets E_i escape to a higher zone.

Consider an initial condition $x_0 \in Z_1$. Note that $Z_1 = (0, \beta_1) = \alpha_1$. Growth in G_1 and a smooth transition to the second regime occurs unless $\theta^s(x_0) = \beta_1$ for some s. Because there are only a countable number of points mapping into β_1, almost all trajectories beginning in $(0, \alpha_1)$ must enter the escape interval E_1. Thus, we can see that the monotonic growth and jump event J_1^g occurs almost surely for x chosen at random in $(0, \alpha_1)$.

In regime 2, growth continues. If the trajectory enters the escape interval E_2, a jump to regime 3 occurs. If, instead, the trajectory enters the interval F_2, then fluctuations emerge. Note that a switch in regime occurs if x_t enters the subinterval (β_2, γ_3), but population declines and regime 2 is re-adopted. As one can see, there is a small interval in F_2 that leads to E_2

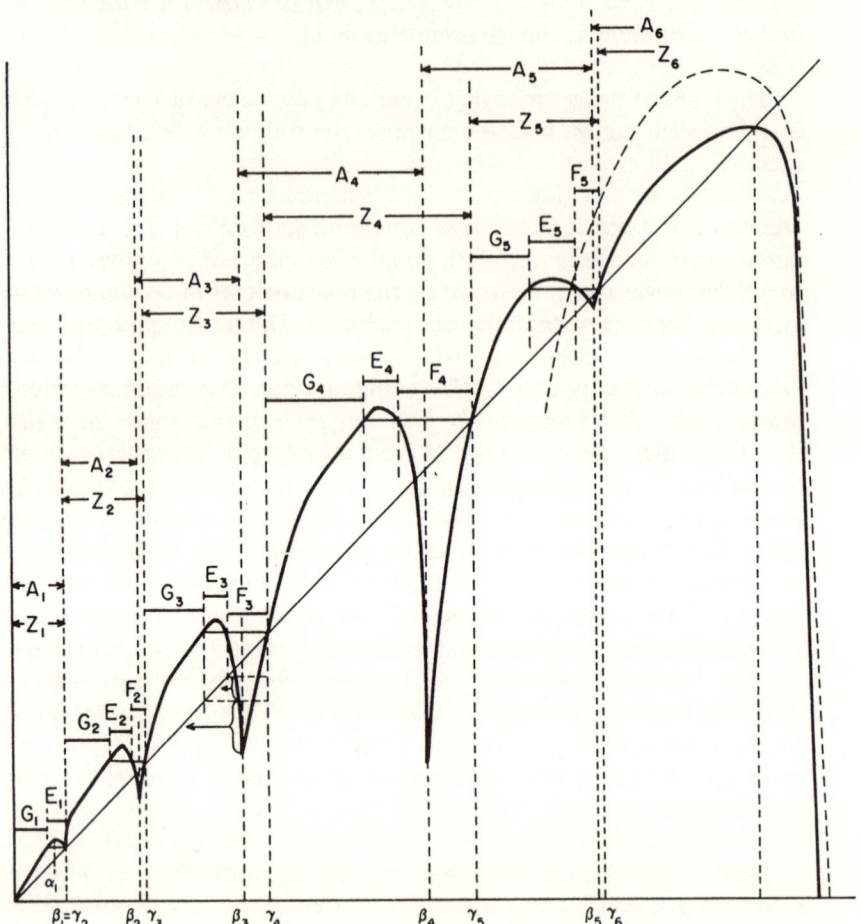

Figure 7.   Multiple-phase dynamics. There are six or seven regimes, each exhibiting a different canonical type of transition possibility.

and a successful jump to regime 3. What is the probability of escape when the trajectory enters F_2? Evidently, it is positive. Is it one? That question is answered in the affirmative below when Condition E prevails.

Suppose, then, that the trajectory passes γ_3 and into event zone Z_3. Evidently, if the interval E_3 is entered, we have J_3^8. A jump to regime 4 with further growth would occur. If the interval F_3 were entered, fluctuations with reswitching could occur. Note that there are intervals in F_3 from which trajectories will enter E_3 or G_3. In the former case, escape to the next regime occurs. In the latter case, growth within regime 3 resumes, followed by all the possibilities already noted. Must a jump to regime 4 occur, or could "history" be trapped in regime 3? It is shown below that if Condition E prevails, a jump must occur. If that condition does not hold, then a trapping event could occur with positive probability.

Suppose an escape to regime 4 does occur. As in the previous case, if x_t enters E_4, a transition occurs. But if it enters F_4, fluctuations emerge again with the possibility of switching and reswitching. The trajectory may enter E_4 and escape, emerging into regime 5 and a continuation of growth in G_5. Or it may revert to G_4. If so, growth resumes, and the story is repeated with the possibility of a successful jump or a crisis with fluctuations and reswitching. But there are also small intervals in F_4 that will lead to a reversion to regime 3. If this happens, then all the qualitative histories already described can unfold. Given this possibility of switching, reswitching, and reversion, does the probability of escape equal 1? Or can society be trapped with positive probability into an endless pattern of growth and complex fluctuations among regimes 3, 4, and 5? If Condition E does not hold, then the latter is possible. If it does, growth will resume almost surely.

If a successful jump is made to regime 5 then growth does resume, and (as shown in the diagram) a smooth transition to regime 6 is possible. In contrast, however, if the interval F_5 is entered, the economy is trapped. Inside these interval cycles, chaotic fluctuations or convergence can occur but not escape. Thus, there is a positive probability that a trajectory beginning in the interval $(0, \alpha_1)$ will be trapped in F_5. If Condition E prevails then fluctuations would continue. Otherwise, trajectories would converge to a classical stationary state with positive probability.

If the transition to regime 6 does occur, then population converges to a stationary state. Suppose that the socioeconomic menu is augmented by phase structure 7. Then growth would resume, fluctuations would re-emerge, and a reversion to some earlier techno-infrastructure would take place.

e   *Peaks, tails, and types of transitions*

Whether or not jumps, traps, reversions, and so on occur depends essentially on the local peaks and tails of the θ_{Z_i} (the restriction of θ to the ith event zone). To give this observation precise meaning, we specify the following definition.

Definition 4.

   (i)   *Let* $\theta(\alpha_i) \in Z_{j_i}$. *Then* $h_i : j_i - i$ *will be called the size of the* ith peak.

(ii)   *The size of the i*th *tail is*

$t_i = 0$ *if* $\theta(\beta_i) \geq \gamma_{i+1}$,

$t_i = 2 + k$ *if* $\gamma_{i-k} \leq \theta(\beta_i) < \gamma_{i-k+1}$, $k = 1, \ldots$.

If $\theta(\beta_i) < \beta_i$ *and* $h_i \geq 1$, *then* γ_{i+1} *has two preimages in* Z_{i1}, *say* $\phi_i < \psi_i$. *Then,*

$t_i = 1$ *if* $\psi_i \leq \theta(\beta_i) < \beta_i$,

$t_i = 2$ *if* $\gamma_i \leq \theta(\beta_i) < \psi_i$.

(iii)   *The interval* $E_i := (\phi_i, \psi_i)$ *will be called the i*th *escape zone.*
(iv)   *The interval* $F_i := (\psi_i, \gamma_{i+1})$ *will be called the i*th fluctuation zone.

The size of the ith peak determines the highest regime reachable from trajectories entering Z_i. The size of the ith tail determines the lowest regime reachable from trajectories entering Z_i. Figure 8 illustrates the types of transitions from one event zone to another and shows how these are determined by the peaks and tails. Three distinct types are shown. In Figure 8a, the probability of escape from Z_i is zero: in part i convergence to a stationary state occurs; in part ii, fluctuations within a fixed regime take place; and in part iii, endless (possibly chaotic) fluctuations occur with re-switching (in the number of groups and/or techno-infrastructures). When such sticking events occur, further development in the sense of transitions to regimes with larger managerial infrastructures and higher productivity cannot occur.

In Figure 8b, there is a positive probability for the monotonic growth and jumping event J_i^g but also a positive probability of the sticking event T_i^s, in which endless chaotic fluctuations are possible.

In Figure 8c, transition types occur in which the probability of jumping from event zone Z_i is unity, but locally chaotic fluctuation with re-switching may occur between an initial period of growth and the jump to a higher regime, or the reversion to a lower regime can occur.

f   *Qualitative history*

We can now think of history as a sequence of qualitative events. To determine the probability of given event sequences, we need to derive a conditional probability measure on the event zone Z_i. To do this, let p be a probability measure on $[0, \alpha_1]$ that is absolutely continuous with respect to Lebesgue measure μ, so that the density of any point $x \in [0, \alpha_1]$ can be represented by a continuous function, say $\delta(\cdot)$, and the probability of "choosing" any $x \in [a, b] \subset [0, \alpha_1]$ is $\int_a^b \delta(x) \, dx$. The density $\delta(\cdot)$ can be used to represent a prior degree of reasonable belief (Jeffries probability) that population in the initial regime occurred within a certain interval.

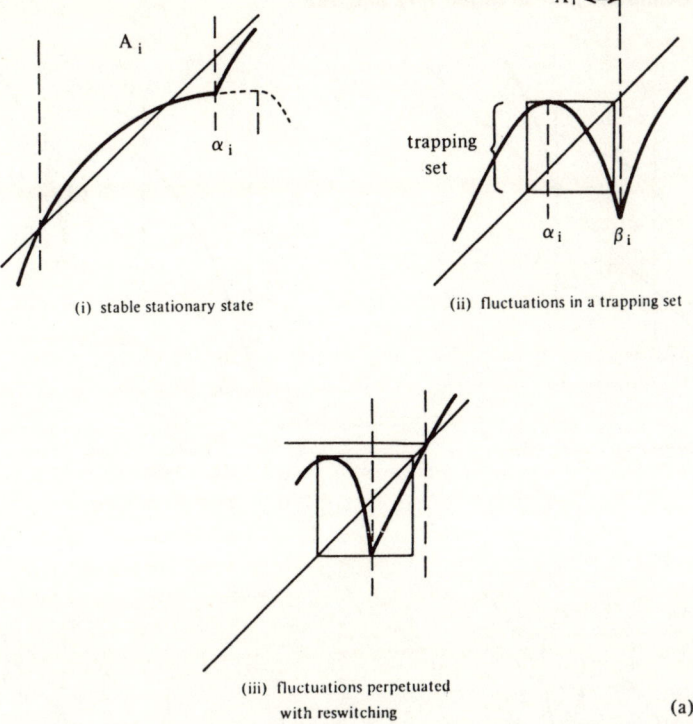

(i) stable stationary state

(ii) fluctuations in a trapping set

(iii) fluctuations perpetuated
with reswitching

(a)

Figure 8. Transitions. (a) Type 1: probability of escape $= 0$ (sticking events). (b) Type 2: probability of escape and probability of sticking are positive. (c) Type 3: probability of escape is 1.

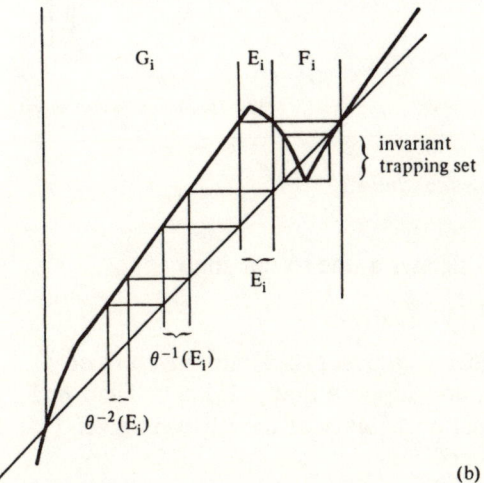

(b)

Figure 8. Transitions *(continued)*.

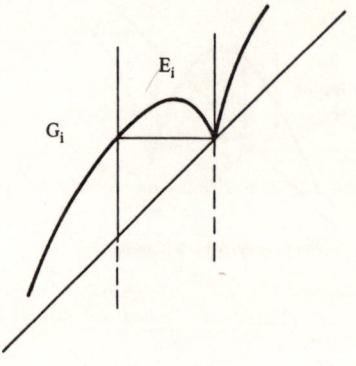

growth and jump almost surely

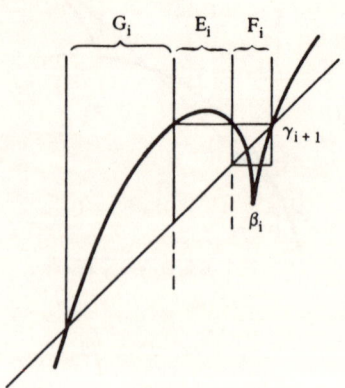

growth or fluctuations and
jump almost surely

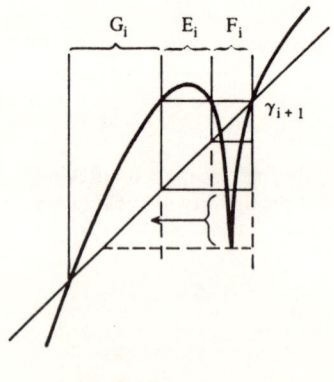

growth or fluctuations and jump

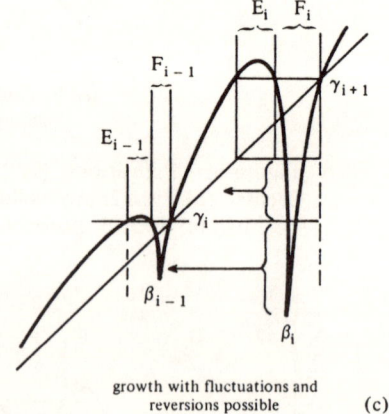

growth with fluctuations and
reversions possible (c)

Figure 8.   Transitions *(continued)*.

Because the trajectory $\tau(x)$ defines a one-to-one map

$$\tau : [0, \alpha_1] \to S := \{[\theta_n(x)]_{n=0}^{\infty}\},$$

the measure p can be considered to be a probability measure on S.

Let S_i be an event in Γ_i, and suppose that $p(\Gamma_i) > 0$. Then $p_i(S_i) := p(S_i)/p(\Gamma_i)$ is the conditional probability of the ith event given that the ith reaching event has occurred.

Using this concept, qualitative history can be given a rigorous treatment within the framework of our theory. Indeed, we have the following theorem whose proof, given in the appendix, characterizes the chance that given trajectories exhibit specific characteristics. We recall that *events* can be associated either with the fission of groups or with the switch in techno-infrastructures.

Theorem 1.

(i) *If* $\Gamma_i^* \neq \emptyset$, $h_i = 0$, *and* $t_i = 1$, *then the* ith *sticking event* T_i^s *has conditional probability one; that is,* $p_i(T_i^s) = 1$.

(ii) *If* $\Gamma_i^* \neq \emptyset$, $h_i \geq 1$, *and* $t_i = 0$, *then the* ith *growth event* J_i^g *has conditional probability one; that is,* $p_i(J_i^g) = 1$.

(iii) *If* $\Gamma_i \neq \emptyset$ *and there exists* $j < i$ *such that* $j + h_j > i$, *then the* ith *skipping event* J_i^k *has conditional positive probability; that is,* $p_i(J_i^k) > 0$.

(iv) *If* $\Gamma_i^* \neq \emptyset$, $h_i \geq 1$, *and* $t_i = 1$, *then the* ith *growth event* J_i^g *and the* ith *sticking event* T_i^s *have positive probability; that is,* $p_i(J_i^g) > 0$, $p_i(T_i^s) > 0$, *and* $p_i(J_i^g) + p_i(T_i^s) = 1$.

(v) *If* $\Gamma_i^* \neq \emptyset$, $h_i \geq 1$, *and* $t_i = 2$ *or* 3, *then the* ith *growth event* J_i^g *and the* ith *local chaos event* J_i^{lc} *have positive probability. Moreover, if Condition E is satisfied, then the probability of jumping is unity; that is,* $p(J_i) = p(J_i^g) + p(J_i^{lc}) = 1$. *If this condition is not satisfied, then the probability of sticking in* Z_i *is nonnegative; that is,* $p(T_i^s) \geq 0$ *and* $p(J_i^g) + p(J_i^{lc}) + p(T^s) = 1$.

(vi) *If* $i \geq 2$, $\Gamma_i^* \neq \emptyset$, $h_i = 0$, *and* $t_i < 3$, *then the* ith *trapping and reversion event* T_i^r *has positive probability. If in addition Condition E is satisfied, then* $p_i(T_i^r) = 1$.

(vii) *If* $i \geq 2$, $\Gamma_i^* \neq \emptyset$, $h_i \geq 1$, *and* $t_i < 2$, *then the* ith *growth event* J_i^g *and the* ith *reversion event have positive probability. If in addition Condition E is satisfied, then* $p(J_i^g) + p(T_i^r) = 1$.

Consider now sequences of events $S_1, \ldots, S_q$ that constitute a qualitative history in terms of the event zones $Z_1, \ldots, Z_q$. Suppose, for example, that $p(T_1) > 0$. Then $p(N_i) > 0$, $i = 2, \ldots, q$. History could be trapped in the first event zone with positive probability, experiencing endless fluctuations, perhaps with reswitching between phase structures θ_1 and θ_2 in the interval (ψ_1, γ_2).

Suppose, by way of contrast, that $h_j \geq 1$, with $j = 1, \ldots, \tau - 1$. Then we have $p[\theta(x) \in \bigcap_{j=1}^{r-1} J_j] > 0$. If, in addition, $t_j \neq 1$ with $j = 1, \ldots, r - 1$, then $p[\tau(x) \in \bigcap_{j=1}^{r-1} J_j] = 1$. If, however, $t_j = 1$ for some $1 \leq j < r$, then evolution would have a positive probability of being trapped in a set bounded by the $j + 1$ event threshold γ_{j+1}.

In this way we can give an exact meaning to the probability of occurrence of any qualitative history. If we are dealing with an unstable system, trajectories that do not get trapped evolve. Those that are trapped fluctuate, and those that are trapped and have large tails revert almost surely. These facts are stated formally in the last two theorems, which are simple corollaries of Theorem 1.

Theorem 2: Evolving trajectories.

(i) *Suppose that $\Gamma_i \neq \emptyset$, $h_i \geq 1$, and that Condition E prevails for all Z_j, $j = 1, ..., i$.*

(ii) *Let $G_i := \{\tau(x) \in \Gamma_i \mid there\ exists\ no\ t\ such\ that\ \theta'(x) \in [\psi_j, \gamma_{j+1}]$ with $t_j = 1$, $0 \leq j \leq i\}$.*

(iii) *Suppose that for all Z_j, $j = 1, ..., i$, Condition E prevails.*

Then, for all $\tau(x) \in G_i$, there exists n such that $\theta^n(x) > \gamma_{i+1}$.

Recall that the interval $[\psi_j, \gamma_{j+1}]$ traps all trajectories that enter if $t_j = 1$. The theorem states that almost all trajectories that are not trapped will evolve if the humps are big enough ($h_i \geq 1$) and the map is expansive in the zone of fluctuation.

On the other hand, if the hump is small ($h_i = 0$) and the tail large, almost all trajectories will revert to a zone of lesser index:

Theorem 3: Reverting trajectories. *Suppose that $p(\Gamma_i^*) > 0$, $h_i = 0$, $t_i > 2$, and Condition E_i prevails. Then for any $\tau(x) \in \Gamma_i^*$, $p_i(T_i^r) = 1$.*

5 Summary

1 Evolution in this theory is driven by an unstable, deterministic (intrinsic) process, not by a random shock (extrinsic) process.

2 Nonetheless, the probabilities of various possible historical scenarios can be derived in terms of sequences of qualitative events.

3 If the socioeconomic menu is finite, then evolution in terms of continued progression to higher regimes eventually comes to an end.

4 If the map $\theta(\cdot)$ is unstable and closed, then history must involve endless fluctuations, eventually sticking with a given regime or cycling in a nonperiodic fashion through an endless reversion sequence of regimes.

5 If, by way of contrast, there were one last reachable regime with a stable stationary state, world history could converge after possibly many periods of local chaos to a classical equilibrium.

It is easy to see that the probability of trapping events is increased if *ceteris paribus* successive infrastructures are "large." They must occur if

286   **Richard H. Day and Jean-Luc Walter**

at least one peak is "small" ($h_i = 0$). But a given hump h_i can be increased by *decreasing* the successive infrastructure M_{i+1} while maintaining productivity [increase $g(M_{i+1})$]. *Thus, the key to continued evolution is the identification of new socioeconomic infrastructures that overcome the internal and external diseconomies of population.*

An improvement in production within a given techno-infrastructural regime is also a possible way, one that we have not incorporated in the present analysis so as to highlight a new point of view. But it should be clear that improvements in technological productivity alone that leave unchanged the techno-infrastructural thresholds M_i and N_i can only accelerate progress through the several epochs. The moral of the theory would seem to be that it is the creative human faculty focused on the design for group living that is the ultimate resource in a finite world.

Appendix

Proof of Theorem 1:   (i) In this case $\theta(Z_i) \subset Z_i$, so all trajectories that enter Z_i remain there. Because the stationary state in Z_i is unstable, fluctuations persist. These may converge to cycles or they may be chaotic.

(ii) Here $\theta(\beta_i) \geq \beta_i = \gamma_{i+1}$. In this case γ_i and possibly β_i (if $\theta(\beta_i) = \beta_i$) are fix points, but by assumption they are repellant. By concavity $\theta(x) > x$ for all $x \in (\gamma_i, \beta_i)$; so except for the countable sequence $\theta^{-'}(\beta_i)t = 1, \ldots$ (if β_i is a fix point), for all x there must exist an n such that $\theta^n(x) > \beta_i = \gamma_{i+1}$.

(iii) $\Gamma_i \neq \phi$ implies there exists j ($1 \leq j < i$), with $j + h_j > i$ such that $p(J_h) > 1$ for all $1 \leq h \leq j$. Consequently, $\Gamma_j^* \neq \emptyset$ and $p(J_j) = \prod_{h=1}^{j} p(J_h) > 1$. Let E_j be the escape interval in j. It is nondegenerate because $h_j > i - j$. By continuity and concavity of $\theta(\cdot)$ there exists a nondegenerate interval $E_j^{h_j} \subset E_j$ such that $\theta(x) \in Z_{j+h_j}$ for all $x \in E_j^{h_j}$. Let

$$E_j^* := \{\tau(x) \in \Gamma^* - j \,|\, x_{n_j}(x) \in E_j^{h_j}\}.$$

Then $p_j(E_j^{h_j}) = p(E_j^*)/p(\Gamma_j^*) > 0$ but $p(J_i^k) \geq p_j(E_j^{h_j})$.

(iv) Here $\theta(\beta_i) < \beta_i$, and γ_{i+1} (the event threshold for event $i+1$) has two preimages $\phi < \psi$. Let $\gamma = \gamma_{i+1}$. We shall call the open interval $E := (\phi, \psi)$ the *jump interval* and the set $F := (\psi, \gamma)$ the *fluctuation interval*. Any trajectories that enter E jump to a higher zone [i.e., for any $x_n \in E$, $x_{n+1} = \theta(s_n) > \gamma$]. The set $\gamma^{-n}(E)$, therefore, gives the set of points that jump into a higher zone after $n+1$ periods, and the open set

$$J := \bigcup_{n \in \mathfrak{N}} \theta^{-n}(E)$$

gives the set of all initial conditions that eventually jump.

The map θ_{Z_i} is an increasing C_1 diffeomorphism, so its inverse image $g := \theta_{Z_i}^{-1}$ is likewise an increasing diffeomorphism from $[\gamma_i, \gamma]$ to $[\gamma_i, \phi]$.

Economic growth in the very long run   287

For all $x \in (\gamma_i, \phi)$, $\theta(x) > x$, so $g(x) < x$. Let $(\phi^n)_{n \in \mathfrak{N}}$ be two sequences defined by $\phi^{n+1} = g(\phi^n)$ and $\psi^{n+1} = g(\psi^n)$, respectively. Because $g(x) < x$ for all $x \in (0, \phi)$,

$$\phi^{n+1} < \psi^{n+1} < \phi^n < \psi^n$$

for all $n \in \mathfrak{N}$. Because 0 is the only fixpoint on $[\gamma_i, \phi]$, we have

$$\lim_n \phi^n = \lim_n \psi^n = 0.$$

Because ϕ has only a single inverse image on $(0, \psi)$,

$$\theta^{-1}(E) = \quad (g(\phi), g(\psi)) \quad = (\phi^1, \psi^1)$$
$$\theta^{-2}(E) = \quad (g(\phi^1), g(\psi^1)) \quad = (\phi^2, \psi^2)$$
$$\vdots$$
$$\theta^{-i}(E) = (g(\theta^{i-1}), g(\psi^{i-1})) = (\phi^i, \psi^i),$$

so

$$J_i^g = \left\{ \tau(x) \in S \,\middle|\, x \in \bigcup_{i=1}^\infty (\theta^i, \psi^i) = J \subset\subset Z_i \right\} \quad \text{and} \quad p(J_i^g) = \sum_{i=1}^\infty p(\phi^i, \psi^i) < 1.$$

Obviously, $\theta(F) \subset F$. Moreover, by an argument similar to the preceding, let $T_1^\delta = \{\tau(x) \in S \,|\, x \in \bigcup_{i=1}^\infty \theta^{-1}(F)\}$, where $\theta^{-1}(F) = (\theta^{-1}(\psi), \theta^{-1}(\gamma))$. Because $\theta_{[\gamma_i, d_i]}$ is monotonically increasing, any trajectory in S must enter either E or F. Consequently, $p(J_i^g) + p(T_i^\delta) = 1$.

(v) By the same argument as that used in case (iii), the probability of the growth event is positive. Hence, $p(J_i) > 0$. Now consider the fluctuating set $F = [\phi, \psi]$, where ϕ, ψ are the preimages of γ_{i+1}. Because $t_i = 2$, $\phi_i < \theta(\beta_i) < \psi_i$. Hence, there exists a set $E_j^1 \subset F$ such that $\theta(x) \in E_j$ for all $x \in D_j^1$. Hence, all trajectories that enter $\bigcup_t \theta^{-t}(E_j^1)$ escape. But by an argument similar to that used in case (iii), this is a measurable set and so $p(J^{lc}) > 0$.

If $\theta'(x) < -1$ for all $x \in [\psi, \gamma_{i+1}]$ then it is expansive, and from Pianigiani (1981) we conclude that all trajectories escape F [i.e., $p(J_i) = 1$]. An obvious extension of the argument can be used where $t = 3$.

(vi) Obviously, $p(\Gamma_{i+1}) = 0$. Since $t_i < 3$ there exist sets $E_1, \ldots, D_{t_i - 3}$ such that $\theta(x) \in Z_{i-j}$ for all $x \in E_j$, $j = 1, \ldots, t_i - 3$. But by our familiar techniques we can show that, for almost all $x \in \Gamma_i^*$, $n > n_i(x)$ such that $\theta^n(x) \in E_j$ for some $j = 1, \ldots, t_i - 3$, so almost all histories revert.

(vii) The result is obtained by combining the arguments for cases (v) and (vi).   ∎

REFERENCES

Adams, R. (1956), "Some hypotheses on the development of early civilization," *American Antiquity*, 21, 227–32.

288 **Richard H. Day and Jean-Luc Walter**

(1978), "Strategies of maximization, stability and resilience in Mesopotamian society, settlement and agriculture," in *Proceedings of the American Philosophical Society,* 122, 329–35.

Barraclough, G., ed. (1984), *The Times Atlas of World History,* rev. ed., Maplewood, N.J.: Hammond, Inc.

Binford, L. (1968), "Post Pleistocene adaptations," in *New Perspectives in Archeology,* ed. by M. Leane, Chicago: Aldine Publishers, Ch. 21.

Birdsell, J. (1957), "Some population problems involving Pleistocene man," in *Cold Spring Harbor Symposia on Quantitative Biology,* 22, 47–69.

(1958), "On population structure in generalized hunting and collecting populations," *Evolution,* 12, 189–205.

Boserup, E. (1975), *The Condition of Agricultural Growth,* Chicago: Aldine Publishers.

(1981), *Population and Technological Change,* Chicago: The University of Chicago Press.

Butzer, K. (1977), "Environment, culture, and human evolution," *American Scientist,* 65, 572–84.

Cohen, M. (1977), *The Food Crisis in Prehistory,* New Haven: Yale University Press.

Day, R. (1981), "Dynamic systems and epochal change," in *Simulations in Archeology,* ed. by J. Sablov, Albuquerque: University of New Mexico Press.

(1982), "Instability in the transition from manorialism," *Explorations in Entrepreneurial History,* 19, 321–38.

(1983), "The emergence of chaos from classical economic growth," *Quarterly Journal of Economics,* 210–13, May.

(1987), "The general theory of disequilibrium economics and economic evolution," in *Economic Evolution and Structural Adjustment,* ed. by D. Batten, J. Casti, B. Johansson, Berlin: Springer-Verlag.

Day, R., and Cigno, A. (1978), *Modelling Economic Change: The Recursive Programming Approach,* Amsterdam: North-Holland.

Day, R., Kim, K.-H., and Macunovich, D. (in press), "Demoeconomic dynamics: A classical analysis," *Journal of Population Economics,* forthcoming.

Deevey, E. (1960), "The human population," *Scientific American,* 203, 194–204 (September).

Easterlin, R. (1983), "The epoch of modern economic growth," lecture presented at the Caltech/Weingart Social Science History Association Conference, March 26, 1983.

Eberts, R. W. (1986), "Estimating the contribution of urban public infrastructure to regional growth," Federal Reserve Bank of Cleveland, W.P. 8610.

Eliasson, G., et al. (1986), *Kunskap Information och Tjä nstar.* Stockholm: IUI, Ch. 4, p. 98.

Flannery, K. (1965), "The ecology of early food production in Mesopotamia," *Science,* 147, 1247–55.

Goodwin, R. (1978), "Wicksell and the Malthusian catastrophe," *The Scandinavian Journal of Economics,* 80, 190–8.

Haavelmo, T. (1956), *A Study in the Theory of Economic Evolution,* Amsterdam: North-Holland.

Hansen, N. (1965), "Unbalanced growth and regional development," *Western Economic Journal,* 4, 3–14.

Helms, J. (1985), "The effects of state and local taxes on economic growth," *Review of Economics and Statistics,* 7, 574–82.

Hole, F., and Heizer, R. (1973), *An Introduction to Prehistoric Archeology,* New York: Holt, Rinehart and Winston, p. 448.

Iberall, I. (1972), *Toward a General Science of Viable Systems,* New York: McGraw-Hill.

Iberall, I., and Soodak, H. (1978), "Physical basis for complex systems – Some propositions relating levels of organization," *Collective Phenomena,* 3, 9–24.

Iberall, I., and Wilkenson, D. (1984), "Human sociogeophysics – Phase I: Explaining the macroscopic patterns of man on earth," *Geo Journal,* 8.2, 171–9; "Human sociogeophysics – Phase II: The diffusion of human ethnicity by remixing," ibid., 9.4, 387–91; "Human sociogeophysics – Phase II (continued): Criticality in the diffusion of ethnicity produces civil society," ibid., 11.2, 152–8.

Jacobs, J. (1970), *The Economy of Cities,* New York: Vintage Books.

Lee, R. (1972), "Population growth," in *Population Growth: Anthropological Implications,* ed. by B. Spooner, Cambridge: The MIT Press.

Li, T., and Yorke, J. (1975), "Period three implies chaos," *American Mathematical Monthly,* 82, 985.

Li, T., Misiurewicz, M., Pianigiani, G., and Yorke, J. (1982), "Odd chaos," *Physics Letters,* 87A, 271–3.

Looney, R., and Federikkson, P. (1981), "The regional impact of infrastructure investment in Mexico," *Regional Studies,* 15, 285–96.

Martin, P. S. (1971), "The revolution in archeology," *Science,* 36, 1–8.

    (1987), "Clovisia the beautiful," *Natural History,* 96, 10–13.

Mera, K. (1975), *Income Distribution and Regional Development,* Tokyo: University of Tokyo Press.

MIT (1970), *Man's Impact on the Global Environment,* Cambridge: The MIT Press.

Nelson, R. (1956), "A theory of the low-level equilibrium trap in underdeveloped countries," *American Economic Review,* 46, 894–908.

Pianigiani, G. (1981), "Conditionally invariant measures and exponential decay," *Journal of Mathematical Analysis and Application,* 82, 75–88.

Renfrew, C. (1980), "The simulator as demiurge," in *Simulations in Archeology,* ed. by J. Sablov, Albuquerque: University of New Mexico Press.

Sablov, J., ed. (1980), *Simulations in Archeology,* Albuquerque: University of New Mexico Press.

Sagan, E. (1985), *At the Dawn of Tyranny,* New York: Alfred A. Knopf.

Sherratt, A., ed. (1980), *The Cambridge Encyclopedia of Archeology,* New York: Cambridge University Press.

Smith, V. (1975), "The primitive hunter culture, Pleistocene extinction and the rise of agriculture," *Journal of Political Economy,* 83, 727–55.

Solow, R. (1956), "A contribution to the theory of economic growth," *Quarterly Journal of Economics,* 57, 65–94.

Zubrow, E. (1971), "Carrying capacity and dynamic equilibrium in the prehistoric Southwest," *American Antiquity,* 36, 127–38.

Name Index

The International Library of Critical Writings in Economics

The Economics of Technical Change
Edwin Mansfield

Economics and Discrimination
William A. Darity, Jr

Financial Intermediaries
M.K. Lewis

The Rhetoric of Economics
Donald McCloskey

Ethics and Economics
Amitai Etzioni

Migration
Oded Stark

The Economics of Ageing
John Creedy

The Economics of Privatization and Deregulation
Elizabeth E. Bailey and Janet Rothenberg Pack

Markets and Socialism
Alec Nove and Ian Thatcher

Gender and Economics
Jane Humphries